Historical Dictionaries of Asia, Oceania, and the Middle East

Edited by Jon Woronoff

Asia

1. *Vietnam*, by William J. Duiker. 1989. *Out of print. See No. 57.*
2. *Bangladesh*, 2nd ed., by Craig Baxter and Syedur Rahman. 1996. *Out of print. See No. 48.*
3. *Pakistan*, by Shahid Javed Burki. 1991. *Out of print. See No. 61.*
4. *Jordan*, by Peter Gubser. 1991.
5. *Afghanistan*, by Ludwig W. Adamec. 1991. *Out of print. See No. 47.*
6. *Laos*, by Martin Stuart-Fox and Mary Kooyman. 1992. *Out of print. See No. 67.*
7. *Singapore*, by K. Mulliner and Lian The-Mulliner. 1991.
8. *Israel*, by Bernard Reich. 1992. *Out of print. See No. 68.*
9. *Indonesia*, by Robert Cribb. 1992. *Out of print. See No. 51.*
10. *Hong Kong and Macau*, by Elfed Vaughan Roberts, Sum Ngai Ling, and Peter Bradshaw. 1992.
11. *Korea*, by Andrew C. Nahm. 1993. *Out of print. See No. 52.*
12. *Taiwan*, by John F. Copper. 1993. *Out of print. See No. 64.*
13. *Malaysia*, by Amarjit Kaur. 1993. *Out of print. See No. 36.*
14. *Saudi Arabia*, by J. E. Peterson. 1993. *Out of print. See No. 45.*
15. *Myanmar*, by Jan Becka. 1995. *Out of print. See No. 59.*
16. *Iran*, by John H. Lorentz. 1995. *Out of print. See No. 62.*
17. *Yemen*, by Robert D. Burrowes. 1995. *Out of print. See No. 72*
18. *Thailand*, by May Kyi Win and Harold Smith. 1995. *Out of print. See No. 55.*
19. *Mongolia*, by Alan J. K. Sanders. 1996. *Out of print. See No. 42.*
20. *India*, by Surjit Mansingh. 1996. *Out of print. See No. 58.*
21. *Gulf Arab States*, by Malcolm C. Peck. 1996. *Out of print. See No. 66.*
22. *Syria*, by David Commins. 1996. *Out of print. See No. 50.*
23. *Palestine*, by Nafez Y. Nazzal and Laila A. Nazzal. 1997.
24. *Philippines*, by Artemio R. Guillermo and May Kyi Win. 1997. *Out of print. See No. 54.*

Oceania

1. *Australia*, by James C. Docherty. 1992. *Out of print. See No. 65.*
2. *Polynesia*, by Robert D. Craig. 1993. *Out of print. See No. 39.*

Historical Dictionary of Tajikistan

Second Edition

Kamoludin Abdullaev
Shahram Akbarzadeh

*Historical Dictionaries of Asia, Oceania,
and the Middle East, No. 73*

The Scarecrow Press, Inc.
Lanham • Toronto • Plymouth, UK
2010

Published by Scarecrow Press, Inc.
A wholly owned subsidary of The Rowman & Littlefield Publishing Group, Inc.
4501 Forbes Boulevard, Suite 200, Lanham, Maryland 20706
http://www.scarecrowpress.com

Estover Road, Plymouth PL6 7PY, United Kingdom

British Library Cataloguing in Publication Information Available

Library of Congress Cataloging-in-Publication Data

Abdullaev, Kamoludin, 1950–
    Historical dictionary of Tajikistan / Kamoludin Abdullaev, Shahram
Akbarzadeh. — 2nd ed.
        p. cm. — (Historical dictionaries of Asia, Oceania, and the Middle East ;
no. 73)
    Includes bibliographical references.
    ISBN 978-0-8108-6061-2 (cloth : alk. paper) — ISBN 978-0-8108-7379-7
(ebook)
    1. Tajikistan—History—Dictionaries. I. Akbarzadeh, Shahram. II. Title.
DK922.14.A23 2010
958.6003—dc22   2009040005

♾ ™ The paper used in this publication meets the minimum requirements of
American National Standard for Information Sciences—Permanence of Paper
for Printed Library Materials, ANSI/NISO Z39.48-1992.

Printed in the United States of America

Contents

Editor's Foreword

The new Central Asian republics seem geographically nice and neat, each named after a major ethnic group and occupying the region associated with it. But closer consideration reveals that these republics are artificial in nature, the result of both arbitrary decisions by Russians and British engaged in the "Great Game" and then Stalin's even more ruthless interventions. This appears most starkly in Tajikistan, the weakest and poorest of the group. It is not solely the land of the Tajiks: although they are the majority, Uzbeks constitute almost one sixth of the population, and more Tajiks live outside the republic than inside. The country's historical roots were obliterated when the great centers of learning were allocated to other countries and Islam was suppressed. Decades of planning, from Moscow mainly, did little to create a unified or rational economy. For 70 years of Soviet rule, Tajikistan was abjectly dependent, so not surprisingly the suddenly independent republic encountered many political, economic, and social difficulties and became enmeshed in a nasty and prolonged civil war. Now that peace has returned, the country is tentatively sorting things out and making progress—but the way ahead will probably never be easy.

Nonetheless, Tajikistan is an independent state, a member of the United Nations and many other organizations, and an integral part of the international community. The fact that it is still poorly known is no excuse for not finding out more. But where to go? A good place to start is this *Historical Dictionary of Tajikistan*, now going into its second edition, extensively updated and substantially expanded. Its list of acronyms and abbreviations is clearly important, since so much of the literature is filled with these. The chronology, reaching far back in time, traces the history of the region and country to the present day. The introduction presents the new state and its predecessors, shows their successes and failures, and hints at future progression. The dictionary contains hundreds of entries on significant people, places, events, institutions, and ethnic groups, as well as various political, economic, social, and cultural features. Readers who want to learn more should turn to the bibliography, which, while still meager and largely in languages other than English, shows that more is being written than ever before, and much of the new material is worthy of attention.

Writing a historical dictionary of an underresearched country is not an easy task, but it has been well acquitted by Kamoludin Abdullaev, building on the first edition he wrote with Shahram Akbarzadeh. Dr. Abdullaev knows the country unusually well, having grown up there and studied at the Tajik State University. He began his professional career at the Institute of History of the Tajik Academy of Sciences and later the Institute of History of the Communist Party, which was transformed in 1990 into the Institute of Political Research, where he was appointed department head. Since the collapse of the Soviet Union, he has been with the Tajik State University, while also working as project officer at the Aga Khan Humanities Project for Central Asia. During some 40 years, Dr. Abdullaev has studied and taught about Central Asia—especially Tajikistan—both at home and in the United States. He has authored or co-authored 8 books and published over 50 articles. This historical dictionary, directed at the broader public, is certainly a welcome addition to the series on Asia, Oceania, and the Middle East and a good place to get started.

Jon Woronoff
Series Editor

Preface

When my colleague and co-author Shahram Akbarzadeh and I were writing the first edition of this book, information on independent Tajikistan was scarce. Tajikistan was recovering from its brutal civil war of 1992–1997; major international NGOs operating in the country were involved in the urgent tasks of practical reconciliation, while the government of independent Tajikistan was in the process of establishing its basic institutions and services. For this reason, the balance of information in the first edition leaned in favor of setting out the overall historical framework of pre- and post-Soviet Tajikistan as well as the major facts related to the civil war and reconciliation.

Since the first edition was published in 2002, the situation in and around Tajikistan has changed a great deal. The peace settlement was concluded, and the country, with the help of the international community, launched large-scale development projects and reforms. Fresh faces and political parties have appeared, and important events have occurred in Tajikistan. Many places on the map and even personalities, including the president of the country, have changed their names in the years since. It is natural that dictionaries like this one should be updated.

In this second edition of the *Historical Dictionary of Tajikistan*, we included more articles on places and subjects and updated most entries from the previous publication. However, a need to renew information was not the only reason for the publication of this book. Almost two decades have passed since Tajikistan became independent. The Western expert community, scholars, and politicians have come to understand that Central Asia is not a conglomeration of homogenous "stans" that should be lumped together and understood through some familiar analytical framework or hackneyed cliché such as the "Great Game," "Soviet policies," "oil and gas," "Islam," or "war on terror." Such a narrow vision, common to superficial journalistic accounts, has been proven invalid not just for an understanding of the region in general, but even for an individual country.

The *Historical Dictionary of Tajikistan* focuses not only on many of the above-mentioned topics that are indeed worthy of attention, but also on the country's culture and society in a broad sense. Entries encompass information about various subject areas and personalities, including political leaders, poets, artists, writers, musicians, singers, important events and places, political parties, literature, arts, and sports. We have also expanded the component related to foreign policy, the economy, and finance.

The last 10 years have seen a massive information inflow into Tajikistan from sources around the world. Many articles, books, and Internet sites have emerged that touch on significant aspects of Tajikistan's history. The updated bibliography includes major Web sites where students of Tajikistan can obtain useful facts and verifiable contextual information.

This book could not have been written without the help of my friend and colleague Dr. Shahram Akbarzadeh of the University of Melbourne, who made a major contribution in the first edition. Although he was not able to join me in writing the second edition, his important contribution to the development of a Tajik historical dictionary remains clear.

I would also like to thank one of my best students from the Ohio State University, Matt Luby, who helped with the editing of the major articles in this book. The gifted Tajik journalist Bahrom Mannonov, who knew almost everything about modern Tajiks and Tajikistan, is owed my thanks for his expert advice and friendly support during the preparation of this book. Regrettably, my beloved friend Bahromkhon-ako passed away in January 2009 when this book was almost complete.

Of course, I must take personal responsibility for everything written in this book.

Reader's Notes

More than 70 years of Soviet rule over Tajikistan resulted in the Russianization of names. Moreover, spelling of some terms was borrowed from the Turkic, mostly Uzbek vocabulary, dominant in Central Asia. In the absence of alternative sources, the Russianized and to a lesser extent Turkicized versions of Tajik names and geographical sites were generally accepted as the convention by many Western scholars. But often such spellings were inadequate or confusing: for example, *Parkhar, Kafirnigan,* instead of *Farkhor, Kofarnihon.* After gaining independence in 1991, the Tajiks strove to restore the original spellings.

With the minor exception of widely known place names, throughout this text we have tried to use the names as they sound in the modern Tajik language. For example, *Samarqand* for the Tajiks (and the Uzbeks) is more accurate than *Samarkand.* The same is true for *Qurghonteppa* and *Qarategin* versus *Kurgan-tyube* and *Karategin. Qyshloq* is more accurate than *Kishlak.* In most cases, personal names are spelled in the way that the bearers prefer to be known: for example, *Akhmedov and Mamadshoh Ilolov,* rather than the more correct *Ahmadov and Muhammadshoh Hilolov.*

To reflect the transition to a more nationally aware labeling, we have used the new Tajik terms for administrative divisions, *nohiya* and *veloyat,* rather than the old Russian words *rayon* and *oblast,* although both versions continue to be widely used and recognized.

The spelling in this volume best reflects the sounds in the Tajik language and is based on how the Tajiks prefer to identify themselves.

Cross-references in each dictionary entry are printed in boldface type.

Acronyms and Abbreviations

AKDN	Aga Khan Development Network
AKEF	Aga Khan Education Fund
AKF	Aga Khan Foundation
APJ	Adolatkhoh Party of Justice
APT	Agrarian Party of Tajikistan (Hizbi Agrarii Tojikiston)
BEC	Bukharan Executive Committee
BPSR	Bukharan People's Soviet Republic
BSSR	Bukharan Socialist Soviet Republic
CACO	Central Asian Cooperation Organization
CC	Central Committee
CEC	Central Executive Committee
CICA	Confidence-Building Measures in Asia
CIS	Commonwealth of Independent States
CNR	Commission for National Reconciliation
CNUT	Congress of National Unity of Tajikistan (Kongresi Yagonagii Mellii Tojikiston)
CP	Communist Party (Hizbi Kommunist)
CPB	Communist Party of Bukhara
CPSU	Communist Party of the Soviet Union (Hizbi Kommunisti Ittihodi Shuravi)
CPT	Communist Party of Tajikistan (Hizbi Kommunisti Tojikiston)
CSTO	Collective Security Treaty Organization
DPT	Democratic Party of Tajikistan (Hizbi Demokrati Tojikiston)
DPTA	Democratic Party of Tajikistan Almaty Platform
DPTT	Democratic Party of Tajikistan Tehran Platform
ECO	Economic Cooperation Organization
Eurasec	Eurasian Economic Community
GDP	Gross domestic product
HuT	Hizb-ut-Tahrir

ICPPT	Ittihod: Civil-Patriotic Party of Tajikistan
IDB	Islamic Development Bank
IMF	International Monetary Fund
IMU	Islamic Movement of Uzbekistan
IRPT	Islamic Renaissance Party of Tajikistan (Hizbi Nahzati Islomi Tojikiston)
KGB	Komitet Gosydarstvennoi Bezopasnosti (State Security Committee)
KMS	Kollektivniye Mirotvorcheskie Sily v Respublike Tadzhikistan (Collective Peacekeeping Force in the Republic of Tajikistan)
KOMSOMOL	Kommunisticheskiy Soiyz Molodezhi (Communist Youth League)
MBAV	Mountainous Badakhshon Autonomous Veloyat
MIRT	Movement for Islamic Revival in Tajikistan (Harakati Nahzati Islomi Tojikiston)
MNURT	Movement for National Unity and Revival in Tajikistan (Harakati Vahdati Melli va Ehyoi Tojikiston)
NRC	Nohiyas under Republican Control (Nohiyahoi Tobei Jumhuri)
OIC	Organization of the Islamic Conference
OSCE	Organization for Security and Cooperation in Europe
PDPT	People's Democratic Party of Tajikistan (Hizbi Khalqi-Demokratii Tojikiston)
PNMT	Party of the National Movement of Tajikistan
PPERT	Party of Political and Economic Regeneration of Tajikistan (Hizbi Ehyoi Siyosi va Iqtisodii Tojikiston)
PPU	Party of People's Unity (Hizbi Yagonagii Khalqi)
RSFSR	Russian Soviet Federated Socialist Republic
SDPT	Social-Democratic Party of Tajikistan (Hizbi Social-Demokratii Tojikiston)
SPT	Socialist Party of Tajikistan (Hizbo Socialisti Tojikiston)
Tajik ASSR	Tajik Autonomous Soviet Socialist Republic
Tajik SSR	Tajik Soviet Socialist Republic
TCP	Turkistan Communist Party
TASSR	Tajik Autonomous Soviet Socialist Republic

UN	United Nations
UNDP	United Nations Development Program
UNHCR	United Nations High Commissioner for Refugees
UNMOT	United Nations Mission of Observers in Tajikistan
UNTOP	United Nations Tajikistan Office of Peace Building
USSR	Union of Soviet Socialist Republics
UTO	United Tajik Opposition

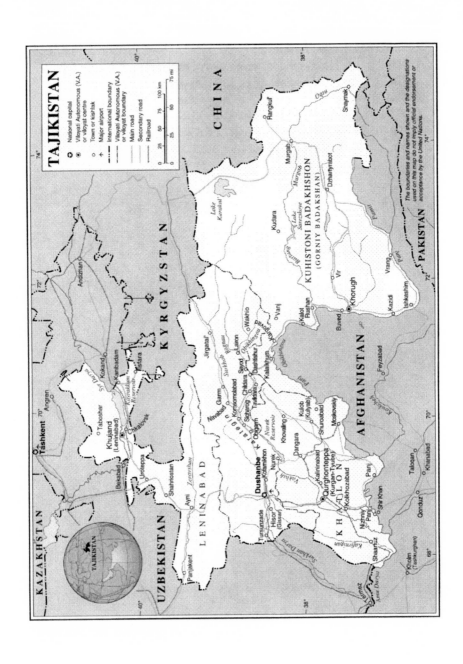

Chronology

2000 BCE   First irrigation system in Central Asia.

500 BCE   Sogd, Bactria, and Khorazm polities established. Avesta written.

500–300 BCE   Achaemenid rule over Central Asia.

519 BCE   First accounts of Saks, Baktrians, and Khorzmians in Bekhi Sutun inscriptions.

329–327 BCE   Spitamen's rebellion against Alexander the Great in Sogd and Bactria.

300–200 BCE   Kushan rule over Central Asia.

200–100 BCE   Greco-Bactrian rule over Central Asia.

1–200 CE   Rise and fall of the Kushan empire.

710–711   Arab warlord Qutaiba invades Samarqand and Bukhara.

720–722   Anti-Arab rebellion of Sogdians under Divashtich.

722   Khujand falls to Arab forces.

749–1258   Abbasids rule.

766–780   Anti-Arab uprisings led by Mukanna in Movarounnahr.

821–873   Tahirid rule in Central Asia.

849   Ismail Somoni, founder of the Samanids, born.

858   Rudaki, poet and founder of classical Farsi-Tajik literature, born in Panj Rud village (Panjakent).

873–903   Saffarid rule in Central Asia.

875–999   Samanid period.

934   Abulqasem Firdawsi, poet and author of Shohnoma, born in Tus, Khurasan.

980   Abuali ibn Sino (Avicenna) born in Afshana, near Bukhara.

997–1186   Ghaznevid dynasty.

1026–1027   Rise of the Qarakhanids.

11th c.   Seljukid rule in Central Asia.

1219–1221   Mongol invasion of Central Asia.

1220   Defense of Khujand by Timurmalik forces.

1370–1405   Reign of Timur.

1405–1506   Timurids rule in Iran and Central Asia.

1501–1732   Safavids rule in Iran.

16th c.   Shaybanid rule in Central Asia.

1601   Ashtarkhanid rule in Bukhara.

1747   Manthyt rule in Bukhara.

1866   Russian annexation of Khujand and Uroteppa.

1867   Creation of Russian Turkistan (Turkistan gubernatorial).

1868   Bukharan emirate becomes protectorate of Russian empire.

1872   Conclusion of Anglo-Russian Convention; Amu Darya River recognized as northern border of a neutral Afghanistan.

1876   Kokand khanate absorbed into Turkistan gubernatorial.

1895   Pamir demarcation and formal resolution of Anglo-Russian border dispute in Central Asia.

1910   Growth of Bukharan Jadidism and formation of *Tarbiyai Atfol* (children's education).

1912   First Tajik newspaper, *Bukhoroi Sharif*.

1916   Popular uprising against tsarism in Khujand.

1917   February: Revolution in Russia; first political Muslim associations: *Shuroi Islomia* and *Jamiyati Ulamo.* **April:** Clashes over political reforms in Bukhara. **November:** Soviet power established in northern Tajikistan.

1918   February: Overthrow of Kokand autonomy and rise of Basmachi movement in northern Tajikistan. **September:** Formation of Bukharan Communist Party.

1919   First Soviet Tajik newspaper, *Shulai Inqilob*, in Samarqand.

1920   January: Formation of Young Bukharans party. **September:** fall of Bukharan emirate and flight of Emir Said Alim Khan to eastern Bukhara; Bukharan People's Soviet Republic established.

1921   March: Dushanbe captured by Red Army detachments; last Bukharan emir leaves Central Asia for Afghanistan; spread of Basmachi movement to eastern Bukhara.

1922   Defeat of Basmachi forces in southern Tajikistan; death of Enver Pasha in Baljuvon.

1921–1926   First wave of emigration: 250,000 Tajiks and Uzbeks flee to Afghanistan to escape civil war.

1924   August: Launch of *Ovozi Tojik*, Uzbekistan's republican newspaper in Tajiki. **September:** National delimitation of Central Asia. **October:** Tajik Autonomous Soviet Socialist Republic formed as part of Uzbek Soviet Socialist Republic.

1925   January: Mountainous Badakhshon Autonomous Province formed as part of Tajik Autonomous Soviet Socialist Republic. **March:** Launch of first Tajik Soviet newspaper, *Bedori-i Tojik.*

1925–1926   Red Army campaign against remaining Basmachi forces in Tajikistan.

1926   Opening of first pedagogical college in Dushanbe.

1926–1928   Switch from Arabic to Latin script.

1927–1931   First wave of Stalinist purges.

1929   Completion of Termez-Dushanbe railroad. **October:** Inclusion of Khujand province in Tajikistan and formation of Tajik Soviet

Socialist Republic. Opening of first professional Tajik theater in Dushanbe, named after Lahuti.

1929–1932   Second wave of emigration: tens of thousands of Tajiks and Uzbeks flee to Afghanistan to escape forcible collectivization and religious persecution. Defeat of Basmachi remnants in Tajikistan.

1929–1934   Cultivation of Vakhsh valley and forcible resettlement of peasant communities; formation of first kolkhoz farms in Tajikistan.

1931   Opening of first higher education institute in Tajikistan.

1932   Launch of Tajik base for Academy of Sciences of the Soviet Union.

1934   Screening of first Tajik movie, *Emigrant*, by Kamil Yarmatov.

1937   Tajikistan becomes leading thin-fiber cotton producer in Soviet Union.

1937–1938   Second wave of Stalinist purges.

1939–1945   More than 200,000 Tajikistanis involved in World War II.

1940   Conversion of Tajik alphabet from Latin to Cyrillic.

1947   Publication of Bobojon Ghafurov's *Outline of the History of the Tajik People*.

1948   Opening of Tajik State University.

1949   **10 July:** Earthquake in Hoit (Gharm) destroys 150 villages; 29,000 casualties.

1951   Formation of Academy of Sciences of Tajikistan.

1960   Opening of Tajikistan's television station in Dushanbe.

1972   Publication of Bobojon Ghafurov's *The Tajiks*.

1979   Norak hydropower station reaches projected capacity.

1981   Record Tajikistan cotton harvest: over 1 million tons.

1990   **February:** Civil disturbances in Dushanbe. **August:** Democratic Party of Tajikistan (DPT) formed.

1991 **August:** President of Tajik SSR, Qahor Mahkamov, resigns. **September:** Tajikistan's declaration of independence; 14-day rally in Dushanbe and demolition of statue of Lenin; suspension of Communist Party of Tajikistan. **September–October:** Curfew in Dushanbe. **November:** Rahmon Nabiev defeats Davlatnazar Khudonazarov in first direct presidential elections. **December:** Commonwealth of Independent States (CIS) formed.

1992 **March:** Opening of U.S. embassy in Dushanbe. **March–May:** Opposition rallies in Dushanbe; formation of Government of National Reconciliation. **April:** Extraordinary Session of Soviet of Mountainous Badakhshon Autonomous *Veloyat* adopts declaration to transform province into Pamiri-Badakhshoni Autonomous Republic within Tajikistan. **May–December:** Military clashes in Dushanbe and veloyats of Kulob and Qurghonteppa cost 50,000 lives and cause $7 billion in damages. **September:** Forcible resignation of President Nabiev. **November:** 16th session of Supreme Soviet abolishes position of presidency and elects Emomali Rahmon (Rakhmonov) as parliamentary chair and head of state. **December:** 60,000 Tajiks flee to Afghanistan to escape civil war.

1993 **January:** Ban imposed on opposition parties and movements. **February:** Armed clashes in Romit and Gharm. **May:** Signing of Agreement on Friendship, Cooperation, and Mutual Assistance between Russian Federation and Republic of Tajikistan. The first 300 refugees return from Afghanistan. **June:** First session of parliament since beginning of civil war. Formation of United Tajik Opposition (UTO); UTO fighters penetrate Tajik territory from Afghanistan and kill 24 Russian frontier guards. **August:** Heavy fighting in Tavildara; preliminary preparations for peace talks between opposition and government.

1994 **March:** First round of Inter-Tajik Peace Talks held in Moscow under auspices of United Nations and Russia. **September:** DPT splits into Almaty and Tehran platforms. **November:** Constitution of Tajikistan adopted in referendum; office of presidency reestablished; Emomali Rakhmonov elected president. **December:** UN Mission of Observers in Tajikistan (UNMOT) opens office in Dushanbe.

1995 **February:** Elections for Majlisi Oli (parliament). **June:** Extensive e-mail connections established. **August:** President Rakhmonov and

UTO leader Said Abdullo Nuri meet in Dushanbe and sign Protocol on Main Principles of Peace and National Accord in Tajikistan.

1996 January: Tajikistan's Mufti Sharifzoda Fathullonon and his family members assassinated in Hisor on first day of holy month of Ramadan. **February:** Colonel Mahmud Khudoiberdyev and former mayor of Tursunzade mutiny in Qurghonteppa and Hisor. **March:** 30 associations, parties, movements, and religious communities sign agreement with President Rakhmonov on National Accord and establish Societal Council. **May:** Academicians Iskhaki and Gulamov killed in Dushanbe; civil unrest in Khujand. **July:** Academician Asimi killed.

1997 April: Attempt on President Rakhmonov's life in Khujand. **June:** Signing of General Agreement of Establishment of Peace and National Accord in Moscow. **August:** Committee of National Reconciliation (CNR) starts to work in Dushanbe. **September:** CNR chair, Said Abdullo Nuri, meets with President Rakhmonov in Dushanbe; repatriation of refugees from Afghanistan begins.

1998 January: Under amnesty law, Tajikistan's prosecutor general drops cases against UTO leaders. **March:** Tajikistan joins Central Asian Economic Alliance. Population of Tajikistan reaches 6 million. **July:** Four UNMOT personnel brutally murdered in Gharm. Colonel Mahmud Khudoiberdyev leads military incursion into Tajikistan's territory (Leninobod) from Uzbekistan. **November:** New tax code adopted.

1999 January: New 35-kilometer motor road connecting Kulob and Qalai Khumb opens. **April:** Signing of Agreement on Statute and Condition of Presence of Russian Military Base in Tajikistan's Territory. **May:** Construction resumes on Anzob tunnel. **August:** UTO declares end of military opposition and formation of political opposition; Islamic Movement of Uzbekistan crosses from Tajikistan to southern Batken regions of Kyrgyzstan. **September:** Celebration of 1,100th anniversary of Samanids. **November:** Presidential elections; Emomali Rakhmonov wins second term in office. **December:** Agreement on stationing Russian troops in Tajikistan ratified by Majlisi Oli.

2000 Repatriation of refugees to Tajikistan officially complete. **February:** Census held. **March:** Assassination attempt on mayor of Dushanbe, Ubaidulloev; elections to Majlisi Namoyandagon and Majlisi Melli; the CNR ends its work. **April:** UNMOT closes its office;

President Lukashenko of Belorussia visits Tajikistan. **June:** Heads of CIS approve Russian military base to replace Collective Peacekeeping Forces in Tajikistan. **September:** Taliban approach Tajik borders. **October:** Bombings in Sonmin missionary center in Dushanbe: 7 dead, 50 wounded. Assassination attempt on M. Iskandarov, chair of Democratic Party of Tajikistan.

2001 February: Russian Duma (parliament) ratifies Agreement on Statute and Condition of Presence of Russian Military Base in Tajikistan's Territory. **April:** Habibulo Sanginov, deputy minister of interior, assassinated in Dushanbe; Ahmad Shah Massoud, leader of Northern Alliance in Afghanistan, visits Dushanbe after trip to Europe. **21 September:** President Rakhmonov declares Tajikistan's support for U.S. fight against terrorism. **8 October:** Tajik government confirms stationing of U.S. forces in Tajikistan. **22 October:** Dushanbe hosts meeting of presidents of Tajikistan, Russia, and Afghanistan to discuss post-Taliban political arrangement in Afghanistan. **30 October:** Tommy Franks, head of U.S. Central Command, visits Tajikistan; **3 November:** Donald Rumsfeld, U.S. secretary of defense, meets President Rakhmonov in Dushanbe to discuss use of Kulob air base.

2002 January: Government forces kill warlord Saidmukhtor Yorov and three bodyguards in shoot-out near Dushanbe. **February:** Trial begins of Homidov Abdujalil, former head of Sughd province, charged with planning attempted murder of two political figures. **April:** Tajik police arrest Khudonazar Asoev in Soghd veloyat for heading cell of banned Islamist party Hizb-ut-Tahrir. **May:** 82 members of Tajikistan's former armed Islamic opposition go on trial for murder and terrorism. India presents Tajikistan with two military transport helicopters. Tajik authorities agree to transfer to China 1,000 square kilometers of disputed territory in Greater Pamir. **June:** Delimitation of Tajik-Uzbek border starts. **July:** Joint Tajik-French training sessions for military rescuers start at Fakhrabad air strip. **August:** 10 Muslim clerics in Isfara district banned from service for activities incompatible with their status. Air link between Teheran and Dushanbe opens. U.S. government provides Tajikistan with $9 million interest-free credit to improve crackdown on drug-trafficking and $40 million to Health Ministry to build hospitals. **September:** India establishes first overseas military base (military hospital and airstrip) at Farkhor in Tajikistan. **October:** UN High Commissioner for Refugees (UNHCR) completes repatriation of

251 Tajik refugees from Pakistan. **November:** New Russian Embassy building in Dushanbe opens. **December:** President Rakhmonov arrives in United States on first official visit. Russian border guards officially transfer Tajik-Chinese frontier to Tajik control.

2003   February: 11 Islamic militants sentenced to death and dozens to lengthy jail sentences for murder and kidnapping during and after 1990s civil war. **April:** Russian President Vladimir Putin visits Tajikistan, announces plans to boost Russian military presence. **June:** Shamsiddin Shamsiddinov, deputy leader of opposition Islamic Renaissance Party of Tajikistan (IRPT), arrested and charged with murder. National referendum approves allowing President Rahmon to run for further terms. **July:** Parliament approves draft law abolishing death penalty for women and reducing number of crimes for which men can face punishment. Supreme Court sentences Shamsiddin Shamsiddinov to 16 years in jail.

2004   July: Parliament approves moratorium on death penalty. **October:** Russia formally opens military base and resumes control of space monitoring center Okno. **December:** Leader of opposition Democratic Party, Mahmadruzi Iskandarov, arrested in Moscow at request of Tajik prosecutor's office and his extradition sought for alleged involvement in terrorism, arms offenses, and corruption.

2005   January: Car bomb near government building in Dushanbe kills at least one person, and fire breaks out at Security Ministry. **February:** Ruling party wins overwhelming victory in parliamentary elections. International observers say polling failed to meet acceptable standards. **May:** Heavy rains and flooding damage hundreds of houses and destroy roads, crops, bridges, electricity pylons, and telegraph poles. Some 12,000 people affected, more than 10,000 evacuated. UNMOT terminated. **June:** Russian border guards complete withdrawal. **October:** Opposition leader Mahmadruzi Iskandarov sentenced in Dushanbe to 23 years in jail on terrorism and corruption charges.

2006   January: 20 people killed when avalanche engulfs apartment block in mountainous region northeast of Dushanbe. **August:** Gaffor Mirzoyev, former top military commander, sentenced to life imprisonment for terrorism and plotting to overthrow government. Said Abdullo Nuri, leader of IRPT, dies. **September:** Demining work is set to expand with two demining teams, newly trained by Swiss Foundation for Mine

Action (FSD), joining Tajik Mine Action Center. **November:** President Rakhmonov wins third term in election international observers say is neither free nor fair.

2007   January: Russia introduces national worker quotas and restrictions on activities migrants may perform. **March:** President Rakhmonov announces construction of Roghun station will be completed by international consortium, President Rakhmonov changes last name to Rahmon, dropping Russian spelling. **April:** 11 Tajik and Uzbek alleged members of Islamic Movement of Uzbekistan (IMU) sentenced to 19 years imprisonment. **June:** Bombing near Tajikistan's Supreme Court. At initiative of President Rahmon, government imposes limits on number of guests, meals, and cars at *tui* celebrations to stop Tajiks from bankrupting themselves. **July:** Earthquake in Rasht valley damages 1,200 houses. UNTOP terminated. **August:** U.S.-funded bridge over Amu Darya opens. **October:** Shanghai Cooperation Organization (SCO) signs agreement with Collective Security Treaty Organization (CSTO) to broaden cooperation on security, crime, and drug trafficking. **November:** Powerful explosion kills guard near presidential palace. In Russia, First Congress of peoples of Tajikistan convened.

2008   February: Tajikistan appeals for help from worst winter in 50 years and energy crisis. **March:** Majlisi Melli passes resolution redistricting six villages in Mountainous Badakhshon's Darvoz district into neighboring Tavildara district. Democratic, Social-Democratic, and Socialist parties propose national referendum on country's basic law to expand size and power of parliament and reduce power of presidency. **April:** International Monetary Fund (IMF) orders return of $47 million loan after it finds Tajikistan submitted false data. **July:** Russia agrees to write off $242 million in Tajikistan debt and take control of Okno space monitoring station. **August:** Tajikistan offers Russia exclusive use of airbase in Ayni. **December:** Tajik newspapers sharply criticize Russian Federation embassy note critical of media coverage of incidents involving migrant workers in Russia.

2009   January: Tajikistan agrees supplies can be transported via its territory to coalition forces in Afghanistan. Tajik border guards clash with Afghan drug dealers. Supreme Court outlaws Salafia religious movement. **February:** Military exercise conducted at Russian base in Tajikistan. Afghan drug traffickers killed in skirmish in Khatlon's

Shurobod district. **March:** Law on Freedom of Conscience and Religious Associations, gives priority to Islamic branch of Hanafiya; U.S. Commission on International Religious Freedom expresses concerns it may be highly restrictive. Tajik national killed by antipersonnel mine along Tajik-Uzbek border. **April:** Taghoinazar Salikhov, brother of ex-minister of internal affairs Mahmadnazar Salikhov, detained in Dushanbe on suspicion of killing and illegal possession of weapons. Majlisi Namoyandagon approves anti-crisis budget. Changes to law on national budget for 2009 require sharp reductions. **May:** Tajikistan appeals to UN and other international organizations for urgent assistance due to natural disasters. President Rahmon orders officials to remove photos or other depictions of them standing or sitting next to the president. Construction of Sangtuda-1 hydroelectric power plant suspended due to financing problems. Majlisi Namoyandagon confirms president's edict appointing Zarif Alizoda as ombudsman of Tajikistan. **June:** Former minister of internal affairs, Mahmadnazar Salikhov, commits suicide. 40 Salafis detained in police and security raid on mosque in Dushanbe. Tajik security forces conduct operation "Poppy 2009" in Tavildara and Rasht valley, possibly targeting civil war era commanders, including notorious Mullo Abdullo, reportedly hardened by years of fighting in Pakistan or Afghanistan. **July:** Former opposition commander and minister of emergency situations Mirzo Ziyoev killed in Tavildara.

Introduction

Tajikistan occupies the southeastern part of the region that 19th-century Russians and Europeans called Central Asia. In cultural and historical terms, Central Asia is the Turko-Iranian part of the Eurasian heartland. Its original population consisted of various Iranian peoples, whose gradual Turkization was interrupted by the formation in 1924 of the first state of Tajiks. Tajiks represent the oldest inhabitants of this region that stands out as one of the cradles of world civilization. Since the eighth century, Tajiks were a part of the Islamic world, but their culture combines Islamic characteristics with features of ancient Persian/Iranian, Greek, Buddhist, Zoroastrian, Turkic, and Russian civilizations. Moreover, it is important to consider the diversity and interactive plurality within each of these layers.

When the Tajik Autonomous Soviet Socialist Republic (TASSR) was established at the end of 1924, it became the first modern Tajik state. The TASSR brought most Tajiks living in the remote, mountainous parts of the former Bukharan emirate under Soviet control. In 1929, a Tajik-majority part of the Ferghana valley was transferred to Tajikistan. The Tajik ASSR eventually gained the status of a full Soviet Socialist Republic and remained one of the 15 republics of the Union of Soviet Socialist Republics (USSR) until 9 September 1991, when Tajikistan and other Soviet republics became independent.

The emergence of the independent Republic of Tajikistan (*Jumhurii Tojikiston*) was one of the most painful state-building attempts in post-Soviet history. From 1990, this country experienced a rise in political activism, freedom of speech, sharp political debates, collapse of state institutions, civic disorder, civil war, an internationally led peace process, return of exiled opposition and their militias, and redistribution of power. Serious problems notwithstanding, the country is continuing its gradual shift from the fragile, postwar recovery period toward a more

1

stable, peaceful, conventional, and transparent political order and an era of steady economic development.

LAND AND PEOPLE

Geography

The vast trans-river area of the Central Asian region of Movarounnahr ("beyond the river" in Arabic) is the historical residence of the Tajiks as well as Turkmen, Uzbek, Kyrgyz, Kazakh, and other smaller autochthonous groups. The ancient Greeks called the two rivers the Oxus and Jaxartes. The Persians named them the Syr Darya and the Amu Darya. For the most part, Tajikistan lies between these two great Eurasian rivers. The Republic of Tajikistan borders China (430 kilometers) to the east, Kyrgyzstan (870 kilometers) and Uzbekistan (1,161 kilometers) to the north and west, and Afghanistan (1,331 kilometers) to the south. The narrow, 15–65 kilometer-wide Vakhan (Wakhan) corridor in northeastern Afghanistan separates Tajikistan from Pakistan. Located between 36.4 and 41 degrees north latitude and 67.3 and 75.1 degrees east longitude, Tajikistan has no access to open seas. The state covers approximately 143,100 square kilometers.

Tajikistan is an alpine country; mountains occupy 93 percent of its territory. The altitude of more than half of the country is over 3,000 meters. Only 7 percent of Tajik territory allows for both irrigated and nonirrigated cultivation, and the shortage of agricultural lands is a perennial problem. Since Tajikistan lies in an active seismic belt, severe earthquakes are common.

The topography of Tajikistan can be divided roughly into four regions. The northern part of Tajikistan, where the current Sughd *veloyat* (province) is situated, is the river basin of the Zarafshon and Syr Darya and is characterized by semidesert plots of land graduating into foothills. The Ferghana valley, the most densely populated region in Central Asia, spreads across northern Tajikistan from Khujand in the west to Uzbekistan and Kyrgyzstan in the east. Northern Tajikistan borders on seven of the 12 veloyats of Uzbekistan (Qashqa Darya, Samarqand, Jizzakh, Syr Darya, Tashkent, Namangan, and Ferghana) and Batken oblasts of Kyrgyzstan. The eastern region, which is under the administrative control of the Mountainous Badakhshon Autonomous

Veloyat (MBAV), is the great alpine area known as the Pamir, or the Pamirs. This region can be divided into two parts: the Eastern Pamir, populated by Kyrgyz, and the Western Pamir, inhabited by Tajiks. The geopolitical position of the Pamirs is unique. It is a mountainous land that wedges into the very heart of Asia, dividing China's Xinjiang from Afghanistan, and Central Asia from India. The two highest mountain ranges of Central Asia, the Pamirs and the Tien-Shan, meet in this region. This most mountainous region is the geographically largest but least populous region of Tajikistan. Tajikistan's Pamirs hold the country's highest mountain—the peak of Ismail Somoni (7,495 meters)—and its biggest glacier—Fedchenko (77 kilometers in length, with ice more then 800 meters thick).

Mountainous Badakhshon borders with the Xinjiang Uighur Autonomous Region of China, the Osh oblast of Kyrgyzstan, and the Badakhshon province of Afghanistan. The Sughd province and the MBAV are connected to Tajikistan's capital city, Dushanbe, by mountain passes that are closed by snow for several months in the winter.

The landscape in central Tajikistan is less homogeneous than the northern and eastern regions. Central Tajikistan is a stretch of land leading from the alpine borders of Kyrgyzstan and the foothills of the Pamirs in the east to the fertile Hisor valley bordering Uzbekistan to the west. Central Tajikistan comprises 13 administrative districts, *nohiyas*, known as Nohiyas under Republican Control (NRCs). NRCs have no unified apparatus and are subordinated directly to the central government in Dushanbe. The fourth region is the southwest of Tajikistan under the administration of the Khatlon veloyat. This terrain is characterized by the plains of the Vakhsh and Panj river basins with their tributaries, although it is crisscrossed by relatively low mountain ranges. Khatlon borders on northern provinces of Afghanistan, including Balkh, Qunduz, Takhar, and Badakhshan, and on the Surkhan Darya province of Uzbekistan.

Like other Central Asian states, Tajikistan experiences dry periods and deficient condensation. The climate is continental, with a wide range of temperatures (between –20 to 0 degrees Celsius in January and from 0 to 30 degrees Celsius in July) depending on the altitude. The average precipitation rate gradually rises from the dry north and west to the foothills of the Tien-Shan and Pamir in the east. Rainfall can range between 150 to 2,000 millimeters yearly. Tajikistan has rich water resources, including snow, ice, and glaciers, and it is sheltered by a climate frontier that lies at an altitude of 3,500 meters in the west and rises up to 5,800 meters in the east. Half of the ice-covered space in Central Asia belongs to Tajikistan, where glaciers cover nearly 8,476 square kilometers. The republic is purported to have more than 1,000 glaciers, some more than 1.5 kilometers in length. More than 60 percent of all Central Asian water resources come from Tajikistan, making it the second largest source of water in the Commonwealth of Independent States (CIS) after only the Russian Federation. The country has about 1,300 lakes, covering a total area of 705 square kilometers, and rivers totaling 28,500 kilometers in length.

Tajikistan's mountain ranges are relatively young; they are rigid rather than contoured. By virtue of climate and human activity, they are fairly desolate and not densely forested. Tajikistan has sizable deposits of precious metals. These resources include gold and ore deposits in the Zarafshon valley. The Bolshoi Koni Mansur, in the north, has the second largest deposit of silver in the world. Other mineral deposits include antimony, lead, zinc, copper, bismuth, molybdenum, wolfram, strontium, iron, tin, coal, oil and gas, fluorspar, rock salt, and more. However, due to the isolation of the country, its undeveloped transportation infrastructure, and its mountainous terrain, only a small amount of these resources are now exploited.

There are as many as 40 species of fish in the rivers and lakes of Tajikistan. Hunting of some animals is allowed, but many species are protected. Tajikistan has three nature preserves and 14 special reserved zones. The most famous is the Beshai Palangon ("Tiger Bush") complex, founded in 1938. More recently, the Dashti Jum reservation was established to preserve the last population of the wild goat (*morkhur*). Mountains, woods, and rare animals are preserved in the Sari Khosor, Dashti Maidon, Chil Dukhtaron, and other reservations.

Tajikistan is potentially fairly rich in oil and gas, but proven reserves are modest. There are an estimated 12 million barrels of oil reserves, but daily production hardly reaches 3,500 barrels of crude oil. Tajik gas reserves, also modest, were estimated at 200 billion cubic feet in 2006. About 80 percent of all oil and gas reserves are concentrated in the southwestern part of Tajikistan. The remaining 20 percent of petroleum reserves are in the north of the country. However, virtually all oil and gas is imported from Uzbekistan and Turkmenistan. Most notably, 95 percent of Tajikistan's gas supplies must be imported. Due to the country's landscape and plentiful water resources, the major domestic energy resource is hydroelectric power. Tajikistan is second in the CIS for potential hydroelectric power resources. In theory, Tajikistan could generate more than 500 billion kilowatt hours of electricity per year, but it currently produces less than 3 percent of its potential.

The major environmental problems facing Tajikistan include scarce sanitation facilities, increasing levels of soil salinity, industrial pollution, excessive pesticides, and radioactive pollution. A Soviet-era uranium mining operation in northern Tajikistan left behind unreliably constructed repositories of radioactive waste. Aluminum processing in central Tajikistan increases industrial pollution in the Hisor valley, including its Uzbek part. Tajikistan (like Kyrgyzstan) is an upstream country of the major Central Asian rivers. Its use of the Syr Darya and Amu Darya's water for irrigation influences the quantity of water available downstream. Global warming also may negatively affect Tajikistan's ecosystem. Its abundant water reserves and glaciers have shrunk significantly since the mid-20th century. According to the 2007 Human Development Index (HDI), Tajikistan, with 0.1 percent of the world's population, has carbon dioxide emission levels below the averages for Central and Eastern Europe as well as the CIS.

People

Tajikistan means "land of Tajiks." Historically, the Tajiks of Central Asia and Afghanistan and the Persians of modern Iran come from related stock. Along with various other groups (mainly Turkic and Pushtun), Tajiks inhabit a vast territory between the mid-Syr Darya (the current Shymkent-Tashkent area) in the north to the southern slopes of the Afghan Hindu Kush (in the area of Ghazni) in the south, and from Bukhara and Herat (in Uzbekistan and Afghanistan, respectively) in the west to Xinjiang's Kashgar in the east. This zone is the heartland of the region's oldest population, the Farsi (Persian)-speaking population of Tajiks who follow Sunni Islam and the Hanafi School of law. Tajik *ulamo* (religious experts) point proudly to the fact that the founder of this school, Abu Hanifah (700–767), one of the great jurists of Islam, with the largest following among the Muslim community, came from Perso-Tajik stock. In 2008, President Emomali Rahmon announced that the year 2009 would be the Year of Imom-i Azam (Abu Hanifah) in Tajikistan.

Yet religion (Sunnism) and language are not definite markers for this ethnic group. Still today in the mountainous areas of Badakhshon, around 100,000 Pamiri Tajiks are followers of the Aga Khan's branch of Shia Islam. Also known as Ismailis, they speak Shughni, Rushoni, and other distinct east Iranian (not Persian) languages. A small group of highlanders known as Yaghnobis live in upper Zarafshon and speak the Neo-Sogdian language.

The Tajiks, or Tojik, are the only major Central Asian nationality that does not speak a Turkic tongue. The Tajik language (Tajiki) is a western Iranian language of the Indo-European family of languages, and it is very close to Farsi (spoken in Iran) and Dari (spoken in Afghanistan). After independence in 1991, the Tajik language was adopted as the official state language, while Russian is recognized as the language of international communication within Tajikistan. The Tajik culture is inextricably tied to "greater Iranian" culture.

The population of Tajikistan grew rapidly under Soviet rule. At the time of the first Soviet census in 1926, Tajikistan's population was 990,900. This rose to 1,568,800 by 1941. The 1970 census showed a population of 2,899,602. The rate of population growth, which averaged 3.1 percent per year in the 1970s, rose to 3.4 percent in the 1980s. According to the last Soviet census of 1989, Tajikistan's population was 5,092,603. This growth resulted from improved health, longer life expectancies, and Soviet migration policies.

Presumably, conditions in the country in the 1990s slowed the rapid population increases of the 1970s and 1980s. The major factor in the change was the civil war of 1992–1997 and its consequences, including 50,000 dead, extensive shifting of populations within Tajikistan, heavy emigration, a decreased birth rate, and a falling standard of living. The birth rate was estimated at 3.0 percent in 1992. Despite these factors, the population of independent Tajikistan has risen significantly. In January 1999, Tajikistan's population was 6,187,800. In July 2008, it reached 7,211,884; in January 2009, it was 7,510,000. The population of the country is concentrated at its lower elevations. Ninety percent of Tajikistanis live in valleys, often in densely concentrated major urban centers: Dushanbe, Khujand, Qurghonteppa, and Kulob. The average population density in 1991 for the republic was 38.2 persons per square kilometer, but the figure varied greatly among the provinces. In Sughd, the density was 61.2; in Khatlon, 71.5; in NRC, including Dushanbe, 38.9; and in MBAV, whose borders encompass more than 40 percent of Tajikistan's territory, only 2.6.

Today Tajikistan is home to only 5.6 million Tajiks. More than 8 million Tajiks live in Afghanistan. According to Uzbek statistics, there are 1.35 million Tajiks in Uzbekistan; however, their real number is believed to be much higher.

Tajikistan is a multiethnic state, including 16 different ethnic groups of more than a thousand. The national composition of Tajikistan according to the last general census, held in 2000, was 79.9 percent Tajik, 15.3 percent Uzbek, 1.1 percent Russian, 0.3 percent Tatar, 1.0 percent Kyrgyz, 0.3 percent Turkmen, and 2.0 percent others (mostly local Turkic groups). Women make up 49.9 percent of the total population. Urbanization is in its infancy in Tajikistan. Some 73.5 percent of the population lives in rural areas where large families prevail (an average size of 6.1 members in 2000), although the number of large families has declined noticeably since 1960. People under 30 years of age constitute 70 percent of the population. The brutal civil war that started in 1992 led to a massive dislocation of people. Nearly 300,000 Russian residents of Tajikistan left the country during 1990–2000, thus reducing the Russian community in Tajikistan to 68,200 people. The emigration of non-Tajiks and Tajik refugees as well as the internal displacement of Tajiks seriously damaged state services in education, health, and the economy. After the collapse of the USSR, Tajikistan started to become progressively mono-ethnic. The share of Tajiks was 62.3 percent in 1989 but reached 79.9 percent in 2000.

Despite its severe decline in living standards, Tajikistan has the highest fertility rate among post-Soviet republics. Marriage is nearly universal, is often entered into early, and typically progresses quickly to childbearing. Childbirth out of wedlock is very rare in Tajikistan. The average life expectancy at birth for both sexes rose from 58.4 years in 1939 to 70.1 in 1987, then fell to 62.0 in 1993 and slightly rebounded to 64.61 years in 2007.

Sunni Muslims constitute 85 percent of Tajikistan's population, Shia Muslims are 5 percent, and other groups account for 10 percent. The Tajik Constitution of 1994 provides for religious freedom. Among non-Muslim religions, Russian Orthodoxy is the most widely practiced, although the Russian community shrank considerably in the early 1990s. Other Christian denominations include Roman Catholics (most of whom had Volga German ancestors), Seventh-Day Adventists, Baptists, and Armenian Apostolics. There are also small numbers of Jews and Bahais. The Bukharan Jews speak Bukhori, a distinct dialect of the Tajik language. The number of Jews and adherents of other non-Muslim religions decreased sharply in the 1990s because of the wave of emigration caused by the collapse of the Soviet Union.

HISTORY

Pre-Islamic Period (600 BCE–658 CE)

The territory of Tajikistan has been continuously inhabited since the early Stone Age. Bactria (Bokhtar), Sogdiana (Sughd), Merv, and Khwarezm were the principal areas of ancient Central Asia populated by the ancestors of the present-day Tajiks. Sogdiana was located partly in what is now the Sughd province of Tajikistan, while Bactria comprised northern Afghanistan and some areas of southern Tajikistan, including the capital city Dushanbe and Khatlon province. Bactria was probably the birthplace of Zoroastrianism during the Achaemenid period (550 BCE–329 BCE). Sogdiana and Bactria were provinces of the Persian empire until they were conquered by Alexander the Great. Bactrians and especially Sogdians, led by a local noble called Spitamen, put up fierce resistance to the invaders. Indeed, the Sogdians wounded Alexander near Kiropol (present-day Istravshan). To pacify them, Alexander married Roxana (Rukhshona), the daughter of a local ruler. Much of Tajikistan was part of the Greco-Bactrian kingdom in the third century BCE.

The Macedonian conquest opened up a period of intense commercial relations and cultural exchange between eastern Persia (where ancestors of modern Tajiks lived) and the Mediterranean world. But the eastern Scythians and Tokharians defeated the Hellenic Seleucids, and the Kushan empire was established in 30 CE. The Kushans created a powerful empire that competed with the Romans, Parthians, and Chinese Hans. The Kushan king Kanishka became famous for exporting Buddhism from Central Asia to China. Meanwhile, in Iran, the Sassanid empire replaced the Parthian empire, while the weakened Kushans were conquered by nomadic Chionites and the Hephthalites in 410 CE. The Hephthalites were defeated by the Turks in 565 CE, and the Eastern Turkic Kaganate was established in Central Asia.

Islamic Period (710–1218)

Prior to the Arab conquest at the beginning of the 8th century CE, the main religions practiced within the territory of modern Tajikistan were Zoroastrianism, Manicheanism, Buddhism, Hinduism, Nestorian Christianity, and Judaism. None of these religions enjoyed a dominant position. The Arabs invaded the dismembered Sogdian and Bactrian principalities and brought Islam with them during the period of the Umayyads (661–749 CE). Most of Movarounnahr was conquered by Ibn Qutaiba, a governor of Khurasan, between 710 and 715 CE. The people of Sogdiana and Bactria were converted to the religion of their conquerors, and the tongue of the Quran, Arabic, became the language of government and religious instruction. The second dynasty of the Islamic empire, under the Abbasids (749–1258), brought the Near East and Central Asia political and cultural unity, which allowed the ancestors of present-day Tajiks and Persians to fuse the heritage of Sassanid Iran with Arab-Islamic civilization. In the middle of the 9th century, the Samanid dynasty came to power in Khurasan and Movarounnahr.

The Samanids, the first purely Persian dynasty to return to power after the Arab conquest, encouraged the development of the modern Persian language, Dari, as well as trade and material culture. Under their rule, Bukhara and Samarqand were the focal points for the continuity of the old Persian civilization and the staging sites for the rebirth of the much celebrated Perso-Tajik literature. Not surprisingly, modern Tajiks consider Ismail Samani (Ismoili Somoni in Tajik) the founder of the first Tajik state. A monument in the center of Dushanbe was erected in 1999 to honor him.

At the very end of the 10th century, the Samanids were defeated as Turkic peoples penetrated the Abbasid empire. After the fall of the Samanids, political and military dominance in Central Asia passed to the Turk-Mongols. During the 10th to 13th centuries, a number of kingdoms succeeded one another in the Tajik-populated areas of Central Asia, including those of the Ghaznavids, Karakhanids, Ghurids, and Khwarezmshahs.

Tajiks under the Mongols, Timur, Timurids, and Uzbeks (1218–1800s)

In 1218, Genghiz Khan invaded the region, destroying the cities of Bukhara and Samarqand and looting and massacring people. At the end of the 14th century, Tajiks and Persians suffered further invasion by ruthless rulers of Turko-Mongolian stock. Timur, a member of the Turkicized Mongolian Barlas tribe who was nicknamed Timur-e Lang (in Dari) or Timur the Lame (which became Tamerlane in English), founded his empire in 1370. The last Timurid ruler was finally defeated by the Uzbek Muhammad Shaybani Khan in 1506. Samarqand and later Bukhara became the capitals of the Shaybanid state (1506–1598). From 1598–1740 followed the Astrakhanid (Janid) dynasty, whose members were again from the line of Genghiz Khan. In 1740, the Janid khanate was conquered by Nadir Shah, the ruler of Persia.

After the death of Nadir Shah in 1747, Muhammad Rahim Biy, the chief of the Manghyt tribe, strengthened his rule and was proclaimed leader of Bukhara in 1756. Because the Manghyts were not of Genghisid descent, they assumed the title of emir. The Emirate of Bukhara covered a territory of 180,000 square kilometers, and its predominantly Tajik-Uzbek-Turkmen population stood at approximately 2 million in the late 19th century. Demographically, Tajiks and Uzbeks made up approximately 80 percent of the population of the emirate. The territories of today's northern Tajikistan were also included in the Kokand (Khuqand) khanate, which emerged in the Ferghana valley in the mid-18th century and was ruled by the Uzbeks from the Ming tribe. Tajiks constituted the majority of the urban population of the Bukharan emirate and Kokand khanate, while the rural periphery was occupied by Tajik and Uzbek communities that lived next to each other. Some 15 percent of the population of these states lived as nomads and seminomads (Turkmen, Uzbek, Kyrgyz, and Kazakh tribes). About 10 percent of the population of the Bukharan emirate and Kokand khanate lived in urban settings. The remaining 75 percent lived in agricultural oases.

In the 19th century, a highly effective irrigation system was developed by Tajik and Uzbek rural communities in the Ferghana valley. Preserving and developing this system required the mutual cooperation of various ethnic groups for the common good. In the mid-19th century, the Tajiks of Khujand (current Sughd) used 60 percent of their fields for grain, 15 percent for fruits and vegetables, and 11.5 percent for cotton. Animal husbandry was rare among the plain-dwelling Tajiks but more common for populations in the mountainous Tajik regions (Darvoz, Badakhshon, and Qarategin), since they lacked irrigated lands. In Samarqand, Bukhara, Khujand, and other cities and towns, Tajiks engaged in urban professions and agriculture. According to Russian travelers in the early 1860s, Tajiks constituted about 70 percent of the city of Bukhara's total population of 75,000–90,000, with the majority of them engaged in trade and crafts.

Since the mid-13th century, the Tajiks were ruled by despotic regimes of Genghisid descent, which pursued ineffective and unpopular domestic and foreign policies. Under Turko-Mongol and Uzbek rule, the Tajiks, though deprived of political influence, were productive in agriculture, trade, arts, science, religion, the military, and administration. They preferred cooperation with the Turks to direct conflict, which is why the region of Central Asia has never seen ethnic wars.

The Great Game and Russian Colonization (1860s–1917)

By the 16th century, the region of Khurasan and Movarounnahr had lost its importance as a pivot of the world's politics, culture, and economy. The expansion of European powers into the heart of Asia gave Central Asia a new geostrategic importance. The area became a zone of rivalry between three empires: Russian, British, and to a much lesser extent Chinese. This political rivalry, often called the "Great Game," pitted against each other three powers that believed their arrival would bring improvement to stagnant and backward lands. The British arrived in Central Asia indirectly via their control of Afghanistan. Their sphere of influence ended around the Tajik-populated plains north of the Hindu Kush mountains in Afghanistan, close to the Amu Darya.

The Russians arrived in Central Asia directly by invasion. The Russian military conquest and colonization of Movarounnahr started in the fall of 1864. In May 1865, the Russians conquered Tashkent. Armed with modern weapons, the Russians had little difficulty conquering the Tajik-inhabited regions. In May 1866, General Romanovskiy defeated the Bukharans and captured Khujand and Nau; in October, General Abramov A.K. conquered Uroteppa (Istravshan). These were the first Tajik cities captured by the Russians. In January 1868, General Konstantin von Kaufman, governor of the newly established governor-generalate (*general-gubernatorstvo*) centered in Tashkent, signed a trade agreement with Khydayar Khan of Kokand, thus opening the khanate to Russian traders. Five months later, von Kaufman conquered Samarqand, a part of the Bukharan emirate. In some places like Tashkent, Uroteppa, and Jizzakh, the invaders met fierce resistance, while in others, local populations displeased by the cruel and unpopular policies of the emir took a neutral position; Samarqand, for example, was taken almost without firing a shot. After being badly defeated three times, Emir Muzafar sued for peace. On 23 June 1868, a peace accord was signed, which gave to Russia all the territories of the emirate that it had conquered, including Tajik-populated Samarqand, Khujand, and Uroteppa. The emir lost the right to conduct an independent foreign policy and was obliged to pay 500,000 rubles to compensate Russia for its military expenses. In August 1868, the city of Panjakent was taken by an expedition led by General Abramov, who over the next two years would also conquer the semi-independent mountainous Tajik principalities in upper Zarafshon, including Mastchoh, Yaghnob, and Falghar. Thus, from 1864 to 1868, Russian troops defeated the Kokand khanate and Bukharan emirate.

The conquest was relatively rapid and not very bloody. The defeated monarchs retained their formal status on their thrones, as Russia feared that its expansionist movement into Central Asia could cause an angry British reaction. In addition, Russia was not ready to contend with the stubborn peripheral principalities led by local *beks* and tribal confederations that tended to keep privileges of heavy autonomy and resisted any kind of government, local or foreign. At the end of the 1860s, the Tajiks and Uzbeks of the southeastern part of the Bukharan emirate rebelled against both their Russian conquerors and the emir's authority. Emir Muzafar asked for Russian assistance against the insurgents. Ultimately, the emir kept his emirate as a Russian protectorate and made up his losses by establishing control over the Tajik-dominated principalities of Hisor, Kulob, Baljuvon, Qarategin, and Darvoz in the second half of the 1870s. In the spring of 1875, another popular rebellion of Uzbeks, Tajiks, and Kyrgyz broke out in the Kokand khanate against Khudayar Khan, who later escaped to Tashkent to put himself under Russian protection. Khudayar's son Nasreddin assumed the throne on 26 June and declared a holy war (jihad) against the Russians.

On 22 August 1875, in a battle at Mahram (located between Khujand and Konibodom), a coalition of 10,000 Kokandis led by Abdurahman Oftobachi was defeated by von Kaufman's army. In this battle, almost 2,000 Muslims were killed, while the Russians, armed with modern weapons including light artillery, lost only five dead. After the Russians occupied Kokand on 29 August 1875, the governor general of Russian Turkistan, K. P. Von Kaufman, imposed upon the khan an agreement that put an end to the khanate's independence. The rebels continued their resistance, however, until they were defeated in November 1875. The last khan of Kokand, Pulat Khan (Nasreddin had surrendered to the Russians in early October), was executed by the Russians in January

1876. On 19 February 1876, the Kokand khanate was abolished and replaced by the province of Ferghana, ruled by the Russian military governor Colonel M. D. Skobelev.

The Pamirs were treated as a place of exceptional strategic importance in the Anglo-Russian rivalry in Central Asia. The British tried to keep the Russian advance from approaching Britain's Indian frontiers. With British support and encouragement, Emir Abdurahman, the ruler of the "buffer state" in Afghanistan, subjugated the borderlands of the Western Pamirs in 1883. Afghan rule in this part of the Pamirs lasted 10 years. In 1891–1892, two military expeditions led by Colonel M. Ionov were sent to the Pamirs. The Afghans were expelled and a fortress named the Pamirian Post (current Murghab of MBAV), housing a garrison of 250 Cossacks, was established as a token of Russian imperial power in the Pamirs. Negotiations for the division of Russian and British spheres of influence in the area were launched with the Russian-British Convention of 1872 and ended with the Demarcation of 1895. A joint Anglo-Russian commission settled the last dispute of the Great Game. After the settlement, Russia could not claim any territories south of the Amu Darya. The Western Pamirs, including Shughnan, Rushan, and Vakhan, formally became a part of the Bukharan emirate, while the deserted Eastern Pamirs (mostly the modern Murghab district) were regarded as a part of Russian Turkistan. In fact, however, Russian officers stationed in the Pamirian Post enjoyed the totality of power in the whole "Russian Pamir."

Thus, the main territories of Central Asia, including the northern part of Tajikistan and the main part of the Pamirs, joined the Russian empire. The governor-generalate of Turkistan that was formed in 1867 was renamed the Turkistanskii Krai in 1886. About 5,250,000 people inhabited this region at the end of the 19th century. Its territory was equal in size to the combined landmass of Germany, Austria-Hungary, Italy, and France, and it was home to a multinational population. Uzbeks, Turkmens, Kyrgyz, Tajiks, Kazakhs, Karakalpaks, Tajik-speaking Jews, Uzbek- and Tajik-speaking Arabs, Tajik-speaking Gypsies (called Luli or Jugis), and others resided in Central Asia, but no single group had an overwhelming numerical superiority.

The borders established at that time have been maintained until the present, although the states themselves have changed. The various Russian-British demarcations in 1895 created a Russian-Afghan frontier with a length of 2,330 kilometers. With the establishment of the Soviet

Union in 1924–1929, this boundary was transformed into segments of the Afghan-Turkmen (802 kilometers), Afghan-Uzbek (140 kilometers), and Afghan-Tajik (1,331 kilometers) borders. The Russian-Chinese boundary was created by the Peking Treaty of 1860, which demarcated a line between the Russian Pamirs and Chinese Xinjiang. With the fall of the Soviet Union, this line was recognized as the legal boundary between China and Tajikistan (430 kilometers).

British and Russian possessions in the Central Asian region never touched one another. Their closest encounter was along a narrow corridor of Afghan territory known as the Vakhan corridor, which is located at a great altitude (3,000 meters and higher) in the nearly inaccessible and sparsely settled part of the Eastern Pamirs populated by Kyrgyz and Tajiks. The British-Russian agreement of 1907 relieved the tensions and regulated the relations between the empires, thus laying the foundation for the creation of a political-military bloc between Russia, France, and Great Britain known as the Triple Entente.

Russian civil and military power in Central Asia was concentrated in the hands of military authorities in Tashkent, who alone were responsible for the entire region, including the Bukharan protectorate. Due to the remoteness of the area, the governor general of Turkistan, who was subordinate to the Russian minister of war, was entrusted with considerable power that included the execution of domestic and foreign policy, formulation of the budget, and setting tax rates, among others. The whole economy of Turkistan and Bukhara was directed to the external market, mainly to Russia. Cotton and wool were dispatched to the textile enterprises of Ivanovo-Voznesensk and other Russian cities. The most valuable Bukharan Astrakhan became fashionable and was highly valued on the European market. In 1913, Bukhara exported raw materials worth more than 45 million rubles to Russia. In exchange, Bukhara received Russian textiles, tea, metal wares, and other goods.

The Turkistanskii Krai was divided territorially, not ethnically. Tajiks lived more or less compactly in three oblasts (provinces) of Russian Turkistan: Ferghana, Samarqand, and Syr Darya. They occupied densely populated lands in the oases inhabited by their ancestors since ancient times, and so were protected from Russian rural colonization that started in the late 19th century. In the Bukharan emirate, where still more Tajiks lived, the Russians were present in an indirect way. The Russian representative (resident) had his office in Kagan or New Bukhara, which was a Russian settlement and railroad station near the city of Bukhara. Several Russian border and custom posts existed along the border with Afghanistan.

With the establishment of Russian rule, the absorption of disparate local identities into larger categories had started. However, for the Tajiks, this gradual incorporation of ungoverned subgroups into proto-national units, where ethnicity, language, and economics started to play growing roles, was hampered by geographical fragmentation and the dissimilarities of the Tajik proto-nation's constituent parts. A division and differentiation of the Tajiks along a north-south line became visible since the colonial era. The Tajiks of the northern districts, including Khujand, Samarqand, Konibodom, Uroteppa, and Panjakent joined the capitalist and more dynamic Russia, with its relatively developed infrastructure, railroad stations, industrial enterprises, oil extraction companies, hospitals, and modern schools. The southern Tajiks of Hisor, Kulob, Qarategin, and Darvoz remained in the Bukharan emirate, or more exactly, in its most isolated and least developed part, termed Eastern Bukhara by the Russians. Even more secluded from their northern and southern brethren were the Pamirian Tajiks of today's eastern Tajikistan. Control of some of their communities fell to the British in India and the Chinese in Xinjiang, while the majority of the Pamirian population was divided between those who lived on one side of the upper Amu Darya (Darya-i Panj) under Russian rule and their relatives on the opposite bank who lived in the Afghan state. Above these differences, Tajik groups had loose intranational ties, loyalties, and solidarities.

The establishment of a relationship of colonial dependence had a deep impact on the public consciousness. With the colonization and the danger of loss of Islamic sovereignty, the essential task for Central Asian society was to seek the path of regeneration. This search produced two responses to the European challenge: religious fundamentalism and reformism. When a protest movement began to arise, it took the shape of jihad, the holy war of Muslims against "infidels" who have proclaimed themselves masters of an Islamic state. These spontaneous anti-Russian revolts were led by religious leaders. In May–July 1898, Dukchi Ishan (also called Muhammad Ali), a Sufi leader from the town of Andijan with many followers among the Tajiks of Ferghana, called on the population to rise against the Russian colonizers and restore the khanate. The rebellion was put down bloodily, and Dukchi Ishan was hanged.

The Russians were mindful about the potency of Islam in traditional Tajik (and Uzbek) society and hence avoided breaking up the religious hierarchies or undermining Islamic institutions. All local affairs not of a political nature were delegated to traditional leaders: *beks*, *aqsaqals*, and others. Throughout the colonial period, local and Russian hierarchies coexisted in parallel with loose ties. Tajiks living in Russian Turkistan were not technically Russian subjects. As aliens, they were exempt from military service. Intermixing with the Russian population was feared by the Sunni Muslims of Central Asia, since it could force them to follow laws written by non-Muslims, violate Islamic principles, and bring non-Muslim intervention into religiously sanctioned affairs. Thus, when the Tsarist government issued an edict in 1916 that authorized the conscription of the indigenous peoples of Central Asia into the Russian army then in the midst of war in Europe, a popular uprising erupted in Khujand and soon spread all over Central Asia. During the cruel suppression of the uprising by tsarist forces, thousands of Tajiks were killed.

While jihadis accomplished the task of the physical defense of Islam, the activists of a movement known as the Jadidia were paying attention to internal reform. The most powerful source of reformism in Central Asia was the homegrown enlightenment of Ahmad Donish, a Tajik intellectual living in Bukhara at the end of the 19th century. Central Asian Jadidism began as a cultural enlightenment movement aimed at introducing *maktabi jadidi*, or "new-method schools." At these schools, religious sciences were taught alongside arithmetic, Farsi and Turkic, geography, and other secular disciplines. The Jadids supported secular education, a free press, theaters, libraries, and bookstores. In April 1917, backed by the representative of the Russian provisional government in Bukhara, the Jadids forced the emir to compromise and issue a manifesto of reforms. However, the Jadids' attempt at reform faced the government's resolute opposition and was cruelly suppressed by fundamentalist crowds. Lacking strong support within the emirate, the Bukharan Jadids hoped for help from revolutionary Russia, which had promised all peoples the right of self-determination. In March 1917, the Young Bukharan Party of revolutionary Bukharans, with its governing leadership consisting of Jadid leaders, was registered officially.

Tajikistan under the Soviet Rule

The tsarist regime in Russia fell in February 1917, and the first local political organizations in Russian Turkistan, known as Shuroi Islomiya and Jamiyati Ulamo, were formed in May–June. Their aim was to gather indigenous political forces and win self-determination for Central Asia democratically. These hopes were buried by the Bolshevik Revolution of 24 October in Petrograd. On 1 November 1917, this revolution arrived in Turkistan "by telegraph"; the revolutionary message arrived with no uprisings, mass rallies, and violence. By the spring of 1918, the Soviet regime, having met little resistance from the provisional government and passive attitudes from the local population, was established in the main regions of Central Asia, including the northern part of present-day Tajikistan.

The Shuroi Islomiya and Jamiyati Ulamo regarded the Petrograd revolutionaries positively at first. They were disillusioned, however, when the Third Regional Congress of the Soviets of Turkistan, meeting on 15 November 1917, organized a regional governing authority, the Soviet of People's Commissars of Turkistan, which excluded the indigenous population. The Jadid-dominated local political organizations subsequently led an attempt to oppose the Soviets, gathering in Kokand on 25 November to proclaim an alternative government for Turkistan known as the Kokand Autonomy. The Autonomy's political coalition was broad; it included Kazakh, Uzbek, Jewish, and Armenian nationalists, Russian bourgeoisie and colonial officials, and local *ulamo* (religious leaders). This government was not supported by either the local population or Russian settlers, both Red and White. On 21 February 1918, the Kokand Autonomy was brutally suppressed by the irregular pro-Bolshevik detachments called the Red Guard and ceased to exist. At the same time, in the Ferghana valley, local Muslim rebels who would come to be known as Basmachis began a jihad against the Bolsheviks and their supporters. The war against Basmachism in Ferghana lasted into the mid-1920s.

The Bukharan emirate had become independent after the collapse of the tsarist regime, but it had a slim chance of retaining this status after the Bolsheviks' victories against the White Russians and the Kokand Autonomy. As they planned the military seizure of Bukhara, the Bolsheviks suggested extending the scene of military actions and battles onto Afghan territory. Indeed, the military commissar of the Russian Soviet Federated Socialist Republic (RSFSR), Leon Trotsky, stated optimistically, "The way to Paris and London passes via the towns of Afghanistan, Punjab, and Bengal." On 29 August 1920, the regular Red Army, commanded by Mikhail Frunze, started firing on the city of Bukhara. The small, poorly armed, and untrained Bukharan army, despite its persistence in the face of great losses, could not offer serious resistance to the Red troops. On 2 September 1920, the emirate was overthrown. Soon the new organs of revolutionary power were formed. The Bukhara-wide Revolutionary Committee was headed by Abdulqadir Muhiddinov and the government by Faizullah Khojaev, both former Jadids. In October 1920, the Bukharan People's Soviet Republic (BPSR) was proclaimed.

The overthrown emir of Bukhara, Alim Khan, retreated to the eastern lands of Bukhara and there tried unsuccessfully to stop the Red forces using his own resources. Initially, he asked for support from the Afghan emir, Amanullah. However, the Afghan state interests gained the upper hand over a sense of religious unity. There was nothing for Alim Khan to do but to set his hopes on the help of the British. On 21 October 1920, from his Dushanbe residence, he appealed to his "brother" king, George V of Great Britain. The appeal of Alim Khan for assistance caused some discussions in Delhi and London. But soon the British officials put the entreaty for intervention at the back of the archive shelf. Failing to gain support from abroad, Alim Khan left for an Afghan exile.

By the second half of the 1920s, almost a quarter of a million *muhajirs* (émigrés) had left the territory of present-day Tajikistan and Uzbekistan following the emir who escaped to Afghanistan. One in four inhabitants of the Tajikistan of the day was a refugee. In spring 1921, in Hisor, Qurghonteppa, Kulob, Qarategin, and Darvoz, a popular uprising broke out against the Red Army and the government of Soviet Bukhara. This movement, termed Basmachestvo by Bolshevik agitators, soon became a formidable force. The population was called upon to support the *mujaheds* (holy warriors) in their struggle against infidels. The Basmachis had limited foreign support, mostly from some unofficial groups in Afghanistan. They had no positive political goal other than restoration of the emirate, viewing this "program" as the ultimate defense of Islam, since it would restore Islamic sovereignty and bring a "just order." Unsurprisingly, Bukharan Basmachis failed to merge with reformist Jadid intellectuals and create a genuine national liberation movement. In turn, the Soviets combined military pressure with propaganda while also offering a positive economic alternative to the people, a campaign which succeeded in isolating the Basmachis from the general population and potential foreign backers, presumed to be the Turks, British, and Afghans. The Bolsheviks created an official, state-sponsored Islam that also was instrumental in supporting their goals and fighting the Basmachis. The latent guerrilla war of the Basmachis in Tajikistan lasted until 1932.

Among the important steps in winning the hearts and minds of Tajiks were national delimitation, growing economic development, improving living standards, successes of secular education, and emancipation of women. In 1924–1926, the national delimitation of Central Asia put an end to the nations of Bukhara, Khiva, and Turkistan. These multinational states that commanded genuine political loyalty among Tajiks and other ethnic groups of the region were replaced by the ethno-national Soviet Socialist Republics of Uzbekistan and Turkmenistan, the Tajik Autonomous Soviet Socialist Republic, or Tajik ASSR (included in Uzbekistan), the Karakalpak Autonomous Oblast, and the Kyrgyz Autonomous Oblast. The major reason for national delimitation was to counter the potential threats of pan-Turkism and pan-Islamism. The delimitation dispelled the illusions of Turkic national communists who were eager to establish an independent "Turan Republic" uniting all Turks of the Soviet lands. Not only had the delimitation divided the various Turkic ethnic groups and placed them into separate republics, but it also resulted in the creation of Tajikistan, the only non-Turkic republic in the region. Furthermore, from the standpoint of virtually all the newborn Central Asian nations, the subdivision was carried out incorrectly. Particularly vexing for Tajiks, the ancient Tajik cities of Bukhara and Samarqand were not a part of the Tajik ASSR, while the Soviet republic of Tajikistan was left with mountainous terrain and none of the historic Tajik centers of learning, with the minor and belated exception of Khujand. Since then, the irredentist dispute over Samarqand and Bukhara has been a source of conflict between Tajikistan and Uzbekistan.

In 1924, Tajikistan had a population of about 1 million out of a total population of nearly 5 million in Uzbekistan as a whole. The first Tajik government, the Revolutionary Committee of the Tajik Autonomous Soviet Socialist Republic, was formed in November 1924. One month later, the nucleus of the Communist Party of Tajikistan was formed. The transfer of Khujand province (the current Sughd) from Uzbekistan to Tajikistan in 1929 enlarged Tajikistan enough for it to become a full republic of the Soviet Union in its own right. But as a result of the subdivision, Tajik populations were scattered across different Soviet republics. In addition, they were separated from their kindred peoples outside of the USSR. As citizens of Soviet Uzbekistan, thousands of Tajiks were pressured to favor their "Uzbek" identity. Most Tajik schools were closed, and Tajiks were deprived of leadership positions in Uzbekistan simply because of their ethnicity.

The delimitation was planned and implemented by Moscow, and the nations created were called formerly backward "children of October" that owed their progress to the Communist Party and the Russian people. The Bolsheviks established new borders and created ethnoterritorial enclaves in order to establish disputed areas and give Russia a permanent role as regional arbitrator. Together with this scheme, it was under Soviet rule that Tajiks, for the first time in their history, acquired the status of a titular nation deserving its own state. The Bolsheviks supported a secular, ethnic Soviet nationalism as the antithesis to Islamic nationalism, which is a religious and cultural phenomenon without reference to a state, language, or given territory.

With the creation of the Tajik Soviet Socialist Republic came the formation of institutions that, at least formally, were national. The first Tajik-language newspaper in Soviet Tajikistan, *Ovozi Tojik* ("The Tajik Voice"), began publication in 1926. During the 1930s and 1940s, national theaters, universities, libraries, research centers, and other cultural facilities were opened. Many Tajik intellectuals and nationalists, including former Jadids, believed the new regime brought progress to their people and joined the Communist Party. Having weakened the semi-universalistic Islamic worldview of Central Asian Muslims, the Soviets boosted the exclusivist, noncivic tradition of dividing people by nationality or ethnic and subethnic group. Not only did the national elites of the various Soviet republics compete for payments and subsidies from Moscow, but also the various subnational, regional Tajik elites competed for political domination and assets within the republic. In Tajikistan, this rivalry developed along the familiar north-south divide.

Since the late 1920s, the social and political development of Tajikistan was designed and conducted under the leadership of the Communist Party as a component of the unionwide plan of "construction of socialism in one country" that included industrialization, collectivization, and a cultural revolution. A powerful and repressive party apparatus was created to mobilize all available resources and manage the implementation of the plan. Since the early Soviet period, all policies in Tajikistan were based on judgments made by the Kremlin. The tradition of the central government's unconditional right to define and weigh political interests begun during Soviet rule has shaped the thinking of subsequent generations of Tajik leaders.

Industrialization policy was aimed at developing heavy industry as the basis of a strong military-industrial complex. In Tajikistan, the first industrial enterprises started to appear in the early 1910s, but large-scale industrial development occurred mostly following World War II. The construction of national industries was stalled mainly because of shortages of experts among local cadres. This problem was finally addressed through importing qualified professionals from Russia, which resulted in a prevalence of Russians in major urban centers (e.g., Dushanbe, Norak, Qurghonteppa). In fact, the diversification of employment opportunities led to a mass inflow of non-Tajiks and the marginalization of the newborn Tajik proletariat, suddenly unable to compete with the Russian-speaking newcomers. Despite the initial successes of industrialization, Tajikistan was to remain primarily an agricultural producer.

The collectivization of agriculture and the creation of state-owned *sovkhozes* and state-controlled *kolkhozes* that lasted from the late 1920s to 1940 did not achieve the stated political aim of fostering class conflict and introducing class consciousness to Tajik society. In fact, tens of thousands of farmers and educated people were declared "kulaks" (exploiters of poor peasants) and "mullahs" resistant to collectivization, and were thus deported to Uzbekistan, Kazakhstan, Russia, and the Caucasus. This policy was viewed by the frightened majority of Tajiks as unavoidable state-led violence rather than the "elimination of exploiters as a class," as the Soviets claimed. Instead of dividing Tajik villages along class lines, collectivization strengthened tribal, regional, and clan ties. People saw these identities as a counterbalance to and deliverance from the repressive state. The more practical reason behind collectivization was to increase irrigation and cotton production. Between 1934 and 1942, a modern irrigation system was constructed to support cotton production instead of food production in Tajikistan. The virgin Vakhsh valley was irrigated between the 1920s and the 1950s by various Tajik and Uzbek groups (both locals and those resettled from Qarategin, Pamir, and the Ferghana valley) with the goal of securing "the cotton independence of the USSR." With a rapidly growing, multi-ethnic population confined to a relatively small region, the Vakhsh valley lacked the potential to enlarge the population's arable land holdings. As a result, the valley became a place of unresolved and often bloody conflicts between Tajiks from various regions, Uzbeks (both local and migrant), and local Arabs and other smaller ethnicities.

The third and final component of the construction of socialism was a cultural revolution. It aimed to defeat the culturally homogenous, national, and religious unities of Central Asians and then to create a monolithic Soviet culture. At first glance, the Soviets' cultural revolution achieved visible results. The Soviets supported Tajik national opera, symphony orchestras, literature, modern painting, and sculpture, all of which attracted support from the Tajik public. To make socialist construction "indigenous," a new generation of working-class Tajiks was educated in Soviet schools and then became involved in the Communist Party apparatus, government administration, and other organs. The first Tajik government was chaired by Nusratullo Maqsum. Unlike the leaders of the Bukharan People's Soviet Republic (BPSR), who had come from rich Bukharan families, he was born to a poor Tajik family from Qarategin. Shirinsho Shotemur, the minister of finance and secretary of the Communist Party of Tajikistan in the second half of the 1920s, was a poor Pamiri Tajik. At the same time, the Soviets did everything possible to isolate and get rid of the prerevolutionary Jadid intellectuals, who were viewed by the Bolsheviks as professionally competent but politically unreliable. The former Jadid leaders and leaders of the Bukharan and Tajik republics, such as Faizulla Khojaev, Abduqadir Muhiddinov, Abdulrauf Fitrat, and many others, were executed during Joseph Stalin's purges in 1937–1938. Among the few Tajik Jadids who survived the repressions, the most famous was Sadriddin Ayni (1878–1954), a founder of Tajik Soviet literature and a classic writer of Uzbek Soviet literature, too.

Theoretically, nativization held a serious political risk for the Bolsheviks, as the first generations of the new Tajik leaders wanted to be more independent from the center, at least in the implementation of cultural policies. They tended to resist excessive centralization and "Soviet colonialism." This centrifugal tendency, characteristic of a number of leaders of the national republics of the USSR, was pointed out by Stalin in 1926; he called it "the national inclination" (*natsionalnyi uklon*). Since that time, accusations of national inclination, proved or unproved, became a common pretext for the "cleansing" of the Communist Party apparatus in Tajikistan. During the course of the Soviet period, the Kremlin undertook several such "purifications" of the high-ranking leadership of Tajikistan to sustain their favored atmosphere of uncertainty, distrust, and fear of reprisal. Among the first victims of Stalin's regime were Maqsum, Shotemur, Chinor Imomov, Ahmadbek Mavlanbekov, Abdulla Rahimbaev, and many other first-generation, locally born, and Soviet-educated Tajik leaders. They were charged with nationalism and executed in 1937–1938.

Another method for the separation of national cultures was linguistic manipulation for the purpose of national identification. From 1927 to 1940, the Soviets twice changed the alphabet in Central Asia. In 1927, Arabic script was replaced by Latin; in 1940, Cyrillic was introduced. Together with this process, virtually all mosques were demolished while religiously trained people were declared mullahs and persecuted by the atheistic Soviets. For about 13 years, Russian had risen as a *lingua franca* for all citizens of the USSR. State-proclaimed official bilingualism was asymmetric: the Tajiks learned Russian, but Russians generally did not learn Tajik. These policies were viewed as Russification by many Tajiks, who feared losing their genuine national identity. In general, industrialization, collectivization, and the USSR's cultural revolution did not achieve their stated aims. However, as a result of this "construction of socialism," by the end of the 1930s, a totalitarian system had been established across the USSR.

Soviet history is full of inconsistencies. Although modern Tajik literature was developed in the imposed Cyrillic script, the older Perso-Tajik literary heritage was carefully preserved and officially attributed to the newborn Tajik nation during Soviet times. The works of Rudaki, who was proclaimed a founder of Perso-Tajik literature, Saadi, and many other great writers were printed by the millions for use in the vast network of schools, colleges, and universities, helping to maintain Tajik as a primary language of instruction. Some books on history and literary criticism became bestsellers. This was particularly true of Ayni's *The Examples of Tajik Literature* (1926) and especially Bobojon Ghafurov's *The Tajiks: Archaic, Ancient, and Mediaeval History* (1972). These two most prominent Tajik thinkers of the Soviet period claimed the classical Persian historical and literary heritage for Tajiks. Since 1972, Ghafurov's book has been reissued in Russian, Tajik, and Farsi/Dari several times, with a circulation of hundreds of thousands of copies. Today, Tajiks do not take calls to return to the Arabic script seriously. At the same time, they criticize the Soviet leadership for limiting Persian influence from Iran and Afghanistan, and instead emphasizing the closeness of Tajiks to the Turkic peoples of Soviet Central Asia.

This dissatisfaction and frustration with Soviet nationality policy is partly responsible for the rise of anti-Uzbek sentiments and the state's recent desire to increase awareness of Tajikistan's "Aryan" heritage.

The Soviet system actually established the conditions for the emergence of nation-states. In the Soviet period, Tajiks started to recognize each other as belonging to the same Tajik nation. To ensure this development, the Soviets carefully shaped the system of mass education and made it a part of the new state apparatus. The results were impressive. The literacy rate in Tajikistan rocketed from 3.8 percent (averaged for both sexes) in 1926 to 81.1 percent by 1939 and 99.6 percent by 1970. In 1973, 645 books were published in Tajikistan, with a total print run of 4,820,000 copies. Talented Tajik youths were sent to the best universities and research centers of Moscow and Leningrad to study modern art and science. Once they returned, they could join one of the 59 research centers operating in Tajikistan by 1972. Objectively, Soviet Tajiks read more, ate better, and lived longer and healthier lives than their predecessors in Bukhara and Turkistan. From the 1930s until the 1970s, Tajikistan's gross domestic product (GDP) doubled every 10–15 years. In addition, spending on social programs stood at 20 percent of GDP in 1991 (in 2000, this figure dropped to 2.2 percent). Despite the emigration and casualties from the civil war in the 1920s and the repressions of 1937–1938, the number of Tajiks in Tajikistan grew from 738,100 in 1926 to 884, 000 in 1939 and to more than 3 million in 1989.

Created by Stalin as a "model republic of the Eastern countries at the gates of Hindustan," Tajikistan, despite its flawed borders and enormous cultural and human losses caused by cruel Soviet policies, served as a base for a newly created independent literary language, political and economic structure, and history. Tajiks attained a state, flag, anthem, and powerful national institutions. The positive consequences of Soviet modernization included: an increase in mass literacy, improved standards of health care and nutrition, the electrification of the entire republic, the creation of communication and transport networks, the expansion of mass media outlets, the diversification of employment opportunities and cultural facilities, the establishment of modern state institutions and a bureaucracy, the emancipation of women, urbanization, and secularization. The legacy of Soviet rule, however, is controversial for Tajiks and Tajikistan. The debate over its pluses and minuses will probably continue.

Collapse of the USSR

Mikhail Gorbachev's policies of *perestroika* and *glasnost* (1985–1991) coincided with the emergence in Tajikistan of religiously charged political movements that had started in 1979 with the impact of the Islamic revolution in Iran and the Soviet invasion of Afghanistan. Spurring the movements were Tajiks who listened to Iranian radio and young Tajik intellectuals who worked in Afghanistan, mostly as interpreters, during the Soviet-Afghan war of 1979–1989. By 1991, the chief official (*qazi*) of Tajikistan's Muslim Board, Hojji Akbar Turajonzoda, had become an influential political figure. Said Abdullo Nuri was another powerful religious leader in Tajikistan. Unlike Turajonzoda, who came from the family of a prestigious *ishan* (hereditary Sufi leader) and was a graduate from the *madrasa* (university) in Bukhara and the Islamic university in Amman, Jordan, Nuri was a home-educated mullah and college-trained technician, born to a family of poor Qaitegini Tajiks living in the Vakhsh valley. Turajonzoda and Nuri had a broad following, especially in central and southern Tajikistan.

The Islamic revival in Tajikistan resulted in the formation of the Hizbi Nahzati Islomi Tojikiston, or Islamic Renaissance Party of Tajikistan (IRPT), in October 1990. Initially, the IRPT commanded a relatively large following in Qarategin and among the resettled Qarateginis in the Vakhsh valley. This religious pressure group was mostly preoccupied with a particular Tajik political agenda and the promotion of national unity, rather than the establishment of a supranational Islamic state or the support of fellow Muslims in Uzbekistan, Afghanistan, and Iran. Official mullahs, representatives of modern political Islam, and leaders of "unofficial," "parallel," or "popular" Islam joined in criticizing the communist hard-liners. They called for political reform and official recognition of the importance of Islam in Tajikistani society. Tajik Islamists emphasized the primacy of electoral means, not the kind of street revolution that had occurred in Iran. Gradually, the IRPT expanded its membership nationwide, including northern Tajikistan, via its active involvement in mosques, whose attendance numbers had expanded enormously since 1989. In 1990, under the leadership of Turajonzoda, the Tirmizi Islamic University (in 2009 renamed Imomi Azam Islamic University), modeled after similar universities in the Near East, was established in Dushanbe. In 1991–1992, the Muslim communities of Tajikistan built 126 mosques and 2,870 prayer houses.

During the late Soviet period, Tajikistan, like other republics of the USSR, experienced unparalleled nationalist mobilization. The communist leadership could do nothing but let cultural revivalism and religious rebirth grow in Tajikistan. In 1989, the Tajik language was recognized as official, and a return to the "classic alphabet," which is what Tajiks call the Arabic alphabet, was proclaimed. The first democratic secular organization in Tajikistan was formed in September 1989 under the name Rastokhez. Rastokhez called for greater autonomy for Tajikistan, Tajik cultural revival, and pan-Persian solidarity with the Tajiks of Afghanistan and Uzbekistan as well as the Persians of Iran. The reputation of this nationalist movement was seriously damaged in February 1990, when public rallies protesting the relocation to and housing in Tajikistan of Armenian refugees left homeless by the war in Nagorno-Karabakh in January 1990 turned into anarchy and violence. The events of February 1990, which also constituted the first public rally of Tajiks since the revolution of 1917, left a bitter taste and resulted in mass emigration from Tajikistan. These events were the first sign of the approaching chaos and collapse of Soviet rule in Tajikistan. Though the involvement of Rastokhez in instigating the hostility was doubtful, the organization nevertheless was blamed for stimulating public unrest and violence directed against the local Russian population.

Tajik authorities, like leaders of other Soviet republics, demanded greater economic help and greater rights from Moscow. Discussion clubs and nationalist groups under governmental control were opened in Tajikistan and started to agitate for greater autonomy. The authorities naively hoped to use them as an institutional device to control the opposition. The government especially strongly supported protests against using Tajikistan as a highly chemically treated cotton field. Like others in Central Asia, the Tajik people demanded openness and democratic reforms but not complete autonomy or the demolition of the USSR. It was widely recognized, including by opposition leaders, that Tajikistan, the poorest and most isolated republic, was not ready for full independence. Despite their early efforts to manipulate the drive for reform in the country, Tajik authorities eventually gave up their positions one after the other, thus allowing dangerous erosion of state institutions. The opposition, composed of democrats and Islamists, failed to offer a feasible alternative (or alternatives) to the greatly discredited communist regime.

The main controversy revolved around the use of nationalism and Islamism as the antithesis to communism. Tajik ethno-nationalism was judged unacceptable by non-Tajiks, who accounted for nearly 35 percent of the population of 5.3 million. The Islamists' emphasis on religion was also rejected: a majority of the population did not support imposition of an Islamic order. Differences in political strategy were exacerbated by personal rivalries between major political leaders. Seeing no use in political discourse as a device for gaining mass support, most of them switched their attention to familiar or traditional institutions of power, mainly clannish extended families, neighborhoods, and regional interest groups.

On 8 December 1991, the three Slavic republics—Russia, Byelorussia, and Ukraine—dissolved the USSR and declared the Commonwealth of Independent States (CIS). Two weeks later, the heads of 11 Soviet republics, including the president of Tajikistan, signed the declaration of the CIS. As a result, over a century of Russian/Soviet rule came to an end in Tajikistan.

The Tajik War and Peace

Despite significant industrial development in the Soviet period, Tajikistan entered independence as a predominantly agricultural nation, with more than 50 percent of its labor force employed on farms. Both sectors of the Tajik economy had been heavily dependent on support from the RSFSR and the other republics of the Soviet Union. The other republics accounted for 80 percent of Tajikistan's exports and imports in 1990. Tajikistan's sociopolitical environment was no more promising than its economy. Moreover, although the Soviets had brought stability, education, and a better economic infrastructure to Tajikistan, Soviet policies had never achieved social integration among ethnic groups and subgroups. As a result, soon after the demise of Soviet rule, Tajikistan became, for the second time in its 20th-century history, a scene of civil war and one of the world's centers of religiously motivated political struggle, militancy, and mass cross-border migration.

The political argument between secular postcommunist elites and the Islamic opposition started in Tajikistan with a brutal conflict. When the first popular presidential elections were held in November 1991, Rahmon Nabiev (a Khujandi and Communist Party leader in 1982–1986) won a majority. The opposition, a coalition including the Democratic Party and IRPT, challenged the results and organized mass public demonstrations in Dushanbe. In March 1992, as the demonstrations continued, a counterforce including government supporters from Kulob and their patrons from Sughd province began to assemble. President Nabiev arranged for the distribution of weapons to his supporters from Kulob, Hisor, and Sughd, while the Qarategini-dominated Islamic opposition turned to their Afghan brethren for military aid.

Armed clashes between the two blocs erupted in early May when the opposition captured some government-held positions in the capital. To reduce tensions, a compromise agreement was made allowing Nabiev to remain president, but providing opposition representatives a place in the Government of National Reconciliation. However, Nabiev was forced to resign on 7 September 1992. On 23–24 October 1992, heavy battles between pro-Nabiev and opposition forces shook the capital, causing hundreds of civilian deaths. With the aid of the Russian military and Uzbekistan, pro-government forces routed the opposition, and in November 1992, at the 16th session of the Supreme Soviet of Tajikistan held in Khujand, Rahmon Nabiev resigned. A 40-year-old, regional-level communist leader, Emomali Rakhmonov (Rahmon since March 2007), was elected Supreme Soviet chair. This represented a shift in power from the old Khujandi elite to the Kulob regional bloc, from which Rahmon came. After opposition forces withdrew from Dushanbe, Rakhmonov took his post in the capital on 14 December 1992.

Both sides committed atrocities during the war. Until 1999, Khatlon, Qarategin (recently renamed the Rasht), Dushanbe, and Hisor were ravaged by violence, including the assassination of important individuals such as politicians and journalists, the destruction of ethnically distinct villages and neighborhoods, civilian massacres, summary executions, and the expulsion of the losers abroad. The war took on an interregional character: the Sitodi Melli (Popular Front), led by Kulobi militias backed by the traditional economic elite of Sughd, along with militias from the Uzbek-dominated region of Hisor and various other Uzbeks groups from Khatlon, were pitted against solely Tajik groups originating mainly from Qarategin and Mountainous Badakhshon, which united to form the Najoti Vatan (Rescuing the Motherland group), later renamed the United Tajik Opposition (UTO).

Tajikistan's neighbors and Russia, concerned about illegal drug trafficking and the ongoing transfer of armed opposition forces across the Tajik-Afghan border, mostly supported the secular regime of Rakhmonov and the Sitodi Melli. Russian border guards were deployed to protect the Afghan border and keep out infiltrators. The Russian Army's 201st Motorized Rifle Division remained in Tajikistan as part of a CIS peacekeeping force established in 1993. During the 1990s, Russia deployed around 25,000 different troops in Tajikistan. The violence was particularly bloody in 1993 in Qurghonteppa and its environs, the home of many Qarateginis (also known as Gharmis, since the city of Gharm is the biggest settlement and a historical center of the valley). Primarily because of the foreign support they received, the pro-Kulobi militias were able to defeat their adversaries from Qarategin and Badakhshon.

From late 1992 to 1996, more than 80,000 Tajiks, mostly resettled Gharmis living in southern Khatlon (including the Vakhsh valley), fled to Afghanistan, as had another generation of Tajiks 70 years before. Just as the Basmachis did in the 1920s, the Tajik opposition used northern Afghanistan as its center for conducting armed incursions into Tajikistan in the 1990s. Supported mostly by the fundamentalists of the Afghan north, the forces of the Tajik opposition posed a serious challenge to the Tajik government and the CIS units (mainly Russian, but also Kazakh and others) in Tajikistan by staging frequent raids across the border.

During the Tajik civil war, an alliance of Tajik and Uzbek Islamists began to emerge in the UTO-controlled part of mountainous central Tajikistan. The Islamic Movement of Uzbekistan (IMU), despite being persecuted and deprived of legal political statutes, managed to advocate the forceful overthrow of the Uzbek regime and was the leading opposition foe of the government in Tashkent. Most IMU activists, led by Jumaboi Namangani, left Uzbekistan's part of the Ferghana valley for Tajikistan, where they fought alongside the Tajik Islamists against the secular Tajik government in 1993–1996. In 1996, this Islamist alliance of the Tajiks and Uzbeks was undermined in favor of ethnic nationalism. The rise of the Pushtun-dominated Taliban in Afghanistan heralded an end of the Tajik civil war. The reluctance to support the Taliban led the Tajik opposition and the government to negotiations sponsored by the United Nations (UN). The capture of Kabul by the Taliban in September 1996 provided further incentive for the Tajik peace process. As a result, the religious coalition of Uzbek and Tajik Islamists split. The IRPT rejected the pro-Taliban course in favor of Tajik nationalism, while the IMU, being denied political participation in Uzbekistan and finding no place in reconciled Tajikistan, joined a regional geopolitical and terrorist network: the Taliban and bin Laden group.

The threat of the Talibanization of Afghanistan forced Russia, Iran, and the regional ex-Soviet neighbors to join efforts and bring stability to Tajikistan. Fortunately for Tajikistan, none of the external players was interested in keeping the Tajik war going. Frightened by the rise of the Taliban, the Russian government hastened to put pressure on the Tajik government, while Iran pushed Tajik Islamists to the bargaining table. In 1993–1999, prominent Tajik Islamists, including two top figures (Nuri and Turajonzoda), took refuge in Iran and therefore were sensitive to the opinions of the Iranian government. The Tajik-dominated Northern Alliance of Afghanistan was also interested in a stable and friendly Tajikistan. This most powerful political and military group of northern Afghanistan in the mid-1990s was in the midst of war against the Taliban and received military support from Russian bases in Tajikistan. Afghanistan's president at the time, Burhanuddin Rabbani (an ethnic Tajik), was one of the peace brokers for the Tajik reconciliation, and Tajik Islamists from both banks of the Amu Darya regarded as a national hero the military leader of the Northern Alliance, Ahmad Shah Massoud, who would be killed by Arab suicide bombers two days prior to the 11 September 2001 terrorist attacks on the United States.

Another important incentive for peace was that the opposing sides realized their conflict had gone too far toward bringing Tajikistan to the brink of national catastrophe. Seeing foreign jets bombing Tajik villages in Qarategin and ethnic Uzbek groups looting Tajik villagers, they felt that the involvement of Uzbekistan and Russia in Tajik internal affairs had reached its limits and that further outside intervention would cost Tajikistan its sovereignty. Finally, both warring factions represented parts of the Tajik south (Kulob and Qarategin) that were largely excluded from power in the Soviet era. The longer southern elites were in a brutal conflict with each other, the more they came to understand that the much-disliked northerners had lost their grip on centralized powers, and thus the moment for an agreement on power-sharing and international recognition of the south's new dominant position in Tajikistan had arrived.

Unlike the civil war of Central Asia in the 1920s, the tragedy of the Tajik civil war in the 1990s had commanded the world's attention. On 29 October 1992, at the invitation of Emomali Rakhmonov, the UN secretary-general sent a goodwill mission to Tajikistan. Three months later, a UN unit of officers was dispatched to Dushanbe to observe the situation on the ground. The secretary-general appointed a special envoy to Tajikistan on 26 April 1993. An internationally facilitated peace process under the aegis of the UN began in April 1994. Representatives from Afghanistan, Iran, Kazakhstan, Kyrgyzstan, Pakistan, Russia, Uzbekistan, Turkmenistan, the Organization for Security and Cooperation in Europe (OSCE), and the Organization of the Islamic Conference (OIC) all served as observers in the Tajik negotiations. During these talks, the opposition formed the unified, IRPT-dominated coalition called the United Tajik Opposition (UTO).

The UN special envoy chaired the first three of the eight rounds of the talks on Tajik national reconciliation, which resulted in a temporary cease-fire and the establishment of a joint commission for oversight of its implementation on 20 October 1994. On 16 December 1994, the UN Security Council established the United Nations Mission of Observers to Tajikistan (UNMOT). Meanwhile, on 6 November 1994, Rakhmonov was elected president with 58 percent of the vote, but international observers claimed the election was flawed by fraud and pressure. On the same day, the first new, post-Soviet constitution was approved by an absolute majority in a popular referendum. The UTO boycotted the election, and its forces continued their insurgency along the Tajik-Afghan border and in Qarategin and Tavildara, a frontier region between Qarategin and Badakhshon. Despite continued hostilities, talks between the government and the UTO continued. In order to find a lasting solution to the conflict, the UN secretary-general appointed Gerd Merrem as resident special representative and head of mission of the UNMOT in May 1996. The talks ended on 27 June 1997 in Moscow with the signing of the General Agreement on the Establishment of Peace and National Accord.

As a result of the brutal civil war, up to 50,000 people died and more than 650,000 people, a tenth of the country's population, were displaced. Up to 80,000 fled to Afghanistan. More than 35,000 homes were destroyed. The number of orphans reached 55,000, and 25,000 women became widows. The total war damage is estimated to be $7 billion.

The Commission for National Reconciliation (CNR), with equal representation from the government and the UTO, was created to implement the peace agreement signed in 1997. UTO leader and CNR chair Abdullo Nuri urged his major field commanders to put down their weapons. On 25 December 1998, he officially declared the return of all

UTO fighters to Tajikistan and the closing of all its bases outside Tajikistan. Eight months later, the opposition disbanded its military forces, thus opening the way for lifting the ban on the IRPT and other opposition groups, including the Democratic Party, Rastokhez, and the Lali Badakhshon movement. By 1999, the major UTO leaders and almost all Tajik refugees had returned to Tajikistan from northern Afghanistan and Iran.

Elections in 1999 and 2000 sealed the peace process and laid the foundations for a democratic Tajik state. In the November 1999 presidential elections, Rakhmonov won 96.91 percent of the vote, while his opponent from the IRPT got only 2.1 percent. Elections for the parliament's Chamber of Representatives were held in February 2000. The OSCE declined to monitor the presidential elections but did observe the 2000 parliamentary elections, together with the UNMOT, and concluded that though elections signaled an important benchmark in the implementation of the peace plan, they did not meet minimum standards. The parliament (Majlisi Oli) is composed of two chambers: the Chamber of Representatives (Majlisi Namoyandagon), with 63 deputies elected to five-year terms, and the 33-seat National Chamber (Majlisi Melli), which is partly elected (in April 2000) and partly appointed by the president. Three political parties were represented in the 2000–2005 parliament: the Communist Party, the Islamic Renaissance Party, and the People's Democratic Party.

By and large, Tajikistan's peace has been a success. The government and opposition cooperated successfully in facilitating the return of refugees and internationally displaced persons (IDPs), repressing extremist spoiler groups, organizing elections, and resisting the pressures of illegal Islamic movements like the IMU and Hizb-ut-Tahrir (HuT). The idea that guided the 1997 General Agreement was the principle of power sharing for a transitional period and then full integration under the unified state. The ultimate task was to turn opponents into partners in the difficult task of governing. The 30 percent quota granted to the UTO and the legalization of the IRPT provided the opposition with a place in government but did not lead to formation of a true coalition government. Many opposition members joined the party in power, the People's Democratic Party of Tajikistan (PDPT), while others, especially the formerly influential field commanders, were gradually marginalized or suspended their political activities.

The Tajik peace process shared a trait common to peace processes all over the world: a tendency toward collision between a "security first" peace approach and a more comprehensive, representative, and transparent peacemaking. In Tajikistan, the UN opted for a relatively narrow but realistic formula that focused on ending warfare. The UTO and the government both insisted on using this minimalist position to reach compromise. Because of this security first approach, the interests of some political forces (regions, parties, ethnic communities) that did not also resort to the use of weapons did not get a place at the table or seat in the transitional government. The most notable group among those excluded from the negotiations and power sharing was the northern elite of Sughd province. This approach was very successful in stopping the war, but it has not yet been as successful in establishing a more democratic system of governance.

From Rehabilitation to Sustainable Development

Throughout its history, Tajikistan has never been a failed state. Now, there is little or no public expression of anger or hatred among people of different regions. The nation-state and peace-building project appears to have overcome the desire for revenge. A resumption of war and a radicalization of political Islam are less likely than they were in the early 2000s. There are no terrorist organizations acting in or passing through Tajikistan.

President Rahmon's first priority has been to establish his authority over the country, including UTO-controlled Qarategin and Badakhshon. This campaign toward the consolidation of power has been welcomed by the majority of the population. Rahmon has also succeeded in freeing the central government from its dependency on warlords. The "field commanders" and their fighters (*boyeviks*) that compiled an appalling human rights record during the war were amnestied by the General Agreement in June 1997. In the aftermath of the civil war, they wanted to harness their demonstrable strength in an atmosphere of fragile national institutions. In the parliament (Majlisi Oli) of 1995–1999, there were approximately 20 former field commanders from the pro-governmental Sitodi Melli among the 181 deputies.

During the "privatization" campaign that followed the peace agreement, many of the "people's generals" and field commanders were granted state assets and profitable positions with formal and informal income, with the sole aim of convincing these potential spoilers that peace could be more profitable than war. A few of them, including former Kulabi military leaders like Generals Salim Yaqubov and Ghaffor Mirzoyev, were brought to justice for crimes committed after the proclamation of the general amnesty by the 1997 General Agreement. In 1999, a quick and effective campaign was undertaken to confiscate arms and prevent unauthorized persons from carrying weapons. The government also took care to restore national institutions by forming a national army, a police force, and a legal system and introducing the rule of law.

These measures bore results. In the Majlisi Oli of 2000–2005, there were virtually no warlords among the deputies. In general, these actions of the central powers were welcomed by most people and were regarded as bringing stability and encouraging the decline of warlordism in Tajikistan. Yet many former militia leaders, although disengaged from militant pursuits, continue to increase their personal wealth, some through the drug trade, tax evasion, barter deals, smuggling, and other criminal activities.

Not only warlords were sidelined from the political scene. Since 2001, important UTO members (mostly Islamists of Qarategini origin) have been purged from the government. President Rahmon sees strengthening his personal power base as a prerequisite for fighting real and imagined extremists within the country. During the international military campaign against the Taliban in Afghanistan in 2002, he launched his own "war on terror," accusing the IRPT of extremism. In 2002–2003, a number of former opposition activists were sentenced to imprisonment and death.

The secular opposition was also targeted by the government. Mahmadruzi Iskandarov, a chair of the DPT and former UTO member, was arrested in Russia in December 2004, held in custody, and in April 2005 forcibly repatriated. He was sentenced to 23 years in prison on terrorism and corruption charges in October 2005. In 2004–2005, President Rahmon accused international organizations and the independent media of attempting to undermine the integrity of Tajikistan. On 27 January 2005, the latest issue of the oppositional nongovernmental publication *Nerui Suhan* was banned.

Tajikistan is gradually recovering from its war wounds. The rehabilitation of former combatants is generally considered to have ended in 2000.

Former combatants obtained employment through a variety of programs financed by international organizations in the immediate postwar years. By 2001, funding for most of these programs had evaporated. In many communities, the former combatants have fully reintegrated into civilian life; almost 7,000 were disarmed. Yet the lack of jobs and skills continues to pose significant problems, and a large percentage of former fighters are working as migrant laborers in Russia. Almost all wartime refugees returned to Tajikistan. As per the UN High Commissioner for Refugees (UNHCR) decision, from 1 July 2006, the Tajiks who fled the civil war, including those currently living in neighboring Central Asian republics, are no longer considered refugees. At the same time, the UN Mine Action Center says 10,000 land mines and pieces of unexploded ordnance are scattered over 25 million square meters (10 square miles) of Tajikistan. Since 1992, there have been 300 confirmed deaths and an almost equal number of injuries recorded from mines in Tajikistan.

Rehabilitation and the successful consolidation of central authority have not been accompanied by adequately increased pluralism and public participation in the political decision-making process. Instead, a close leadership circle appears to increasingly monopolize its hold on power. Rahmon's substantial supremacy as president was further strengthened in a June 2003 constitutional referendum. Some 93 percent of those who voted approved a package of 56 amendments to the constitution, the most debatable of which allowed the president to serve two additional seven-year terms beyond the next presidential election in 2006. The Democratic Party of Tajikistan (DPT) boycotted the vote, while the IRPT and the Social-Democratic Party of Tajikistan (SDPT), having expressed their repudiation of the referendum, decided to abstain from open confrontation.

On the eve of the 2005 parliamentary elections, the government increased pressure on real and potential rivals, both individuals and political parties. Former Rahmon allies were jailed, including Ghaffor Mirzoyev, head of the Drug Control Agency, who was arrested in August 2004 on numerous criminal charges. The parliamentary elections in November 2005 ended in a trouble-free success for the presidential PDPT, which won 52 of 63 seats in Majlisi Namoyandagon. The Communist Party of Tajikistan won four seats, while the IRPT captured two seats. Observers from the OSCE concluded that despite some improvement over previous elections, the voting failed to meet many of the OSCE benchmarks for democratic elections.

The pressure amplified in the run-up to the November 2006 presidential election. Rivals of the acting leadership, including opposition parties, were sidelined by misuse of administrative resources, particularly by manipulations of the electoral process and registration procedures. Abdullo Nuri, the leader of the Tajik Islamists and at that time in extremely poor health, was the target of a lawsuit (he died on 9 August 2006). In April 2006, the DPT, which had been decapitated by the arrest of Iskandarov, split as a result of obvious government intervention. One wing was promptly registered by the government, and the unrecognized faction of the DPT boycotted the upcoming presidential elections. The IRPT declined to take part in the vote, pointing to defects in election laws. None of the four registered candidates opposing Rahmon in the presidential election had publicly criticized him. All of them were unknown to Tajikistanis. "No country in the world measures up to all the standards of the OSCE," was President Rahmon's retort to a group of journalists on 6 November 2006, the day he won a third term of office, capturing 76.4 percent of the vote. Taking into consideration the amendments made by the 2003 referendum, Rahmon can theoretically remain in office until 2020.

The absence of political pluralism and growing authoritarianism are not as important issues for Tajiks as labor migration, a central issue for the impoverished Tajik nation. Labor migration today provides Tajikistan with both problems and solutions. With the virtual collapse of the domestic economy and ensuing large-scale unemployment, large numbers of Tajikistanis are working abroad. The status of Tajik migrant laborers in Russia is, for the most part, unregulated. Most of them are required to have proper documentation, including work permits. In mid-January 2007, Russia introduced new legislation instituting national worker quotas and restrictions on the type of activities migrants may perform. The system leaves Tajik migrants more prone to human rights violations and abuses, such as racist skinhead attacks and the robbery of migrants' wages by police and mafia racketeers. Nevertheless, incomes generated by migrants have rescued both individual Tajik families and the national economy. In 2007, about $1.8 billion in remittances were channeled through the banking system. According to a World Bank report, Tajikistan (together with Moldova) took first position in the world for the share of remittances as a percentage of GDP in 2007. The report showed remittances to Tajikistan making up 36.2 percent of its GDP.

Sizable and irregular labor migration entails high social costs. With hundreds of thousands of Tajik men working in Russia, Tajik women and children have had to assume additional economic and family responsibilities. Women's and children's rights have been especially neglected. Domestic violence is pervasive but rarely recognized by the state and society. Drugs and people trafficking, especially of young women to the Middle East, is an issue of anxious concern. The threats to people's well-being and to the country's security and stability will grow if the "greed" factor coalesces with the rapidly expanding number of dissatisfied and aggrieved rural inhabitants and youth. Until now, the migration to Russia of up to 1 million workers out of a total labor force of approximately 3 million in Tajikistan provides a crucial safety valve to ensure that greediness and grievance do not explosively mix.

Like other post-Soviet states, Tajikistan has taken a new look at its history in order to define core symbols of the past that may serve as touchstones for Tajiks today. Since the end of the Soviet era, the figure of Ismail Somoni, a founder of the first Tajik state in the 9th–10th century, has been central for Tajik nationalist historians. In 1992, a statue of Lenin was demolished by a mob. It was replaced by a monument honoring Firdawsi, a 10th-century Persian poet, which in 1999 was succeeded by a massive complex dedicated to Ismail Somoni. The national currency and the country's highest mountain were named after Somoni in independent Tajikistan. In celebrating the dynasty of Samanids, President Rahmon wants Tajiks to think of his own regime as the first post-Samanid, genuine Tajik government. Also, the government declared 2006 the year of Aryan civilization. The state media have waged a campaign to promote the notion that the Tajiks are an Aryan nation. The government claims that its interpretation of Aryanism has nothing in common with Nazi German ideology. In the midst of the presidential campaign in early September 2006, Tajikistan celebrated simultaneously its 15th year of independence, the year of the Aryans, the 6th International Conference of the Tajiks of the World, and the 2,700th anniversary of the city of Kulob.

The Kulobi elite have ruled the country since November 1992. Officials from this region fill four of the most powerful ministries in addition to the general prosecutor's office, the Ministry of Education, the Ministry of Health, the National Bank, the office of president, the Council of Justice, the Committee on Radio and Television, the National University, the Medical University, the State Pedagogical University, and a plethora of other key positions. Mahmadsaid Ubaidulloev, who is the mayor of Dushanbe and chair of Majlisi Melli as well as Rahmon's top deputy, is from the Kulob region. For many, the celebrations in Kulob were a sign of the presidential clan's power and its domestic support.

Administrative divisions in Soviet Tajikistan acknowledged regionally based patronage networks that were not uncommon in other parts of the Soviet Union as well. Since 1992, the totality of political power and command of resources in Tajikistan belongs to a single ruling elite that prefers bargaining with local leaders to direct dialogue with embryonic civil society groups and political parties. The central powers are held by a de facto regional elite from Kulob that has captured the capital and tried to assert and legitimize its powers nationwide. Its rule is highly personalized, nontransparent, and beyond the reach of the state judiciary. This situation is ideal for sustained and systemic corruption.

Both the state and private media mostly campaign for Emomali Rahmon, calling him the only guarantor of peace and stability in Tajikistan. All positive developments in international relations and domestic politics are regarded as accomplishments of the president. Celebrations of national holidays and important events devolve into honoring President Rahmon as an enlightened ruler and the "fatherly steward of the nation." No one speaks openly against the president in Tajikistan. The only opposition newspaper, *Charoghi Ruz*, is published irregularly in exile. It charges Rahmon with corruption and nepotism, while criticizing him for violent politics built on the fear of renewed bloodshed.

Overall, President Rahmon's policies have been instrumental in creating a situation favorable to development. With the assistance of the international donor community, Tajik authorities are shifting the focus from short-term crisis management to the planning of prolonged strategic development. Economic growth reached 5.3 percent in 1998 and 10.6 percent in 2004, but it dropped to 8 percent in 2005 and then 7 percent in 2006. In 2007, Tajikistan's economic growth reached 7.8 percent, but due to the world economic crisis, growth slowed significantly over the course of 2008 (to 5.2 percent), well below the government's projections. The Tajik government intends to make Tajikistan a major exporter of hydropower in the region by finishing the delayed Soviet power projects and building new ones, including Roghun, Sangtuda-1, Sangtuda-2, and Dashtijum. Tajikistan may then reap the economic benefits of exporting surplus energy to Russia, the Central Asian states, Afghanistan, Pakistan, and China.

Despite the progress being made and a relatively stabilized macroeconomic framework, the Tajik economy remains extremely weak. Tajikistan is still one of the 20 poorest countries in the world. In 2007, 64 percent of citizens of Tajikistan lived below the poverty line. The 2007 Human Development Index (HDI) for Tajikistan is 0.673, ranking the country 122nd out of the 177 countries surveyed. According to the 2007 HDI, life expectancy at birth in Tajikistan stood at 66.3 years (114th place), the adult literacy rate was 99.5 percent (9th place), school enrollments stood at 70.8 percent (98th place), and GDP per capita was $1,356 (152nd place).

Tajikistan has adopted a foreign policy termed "multivectored." Alongside its strong relationship with the Russian Federation, Tajikistan supports stronger ties with neighbors like Iran, Afghanistan, and other countries sharing Tajikistan's language, history, and culture. The government has emphasized cooperation with China and India and increasing economic ties with the United States, Europe, and Japan. Russia remains its main strategic partner. On 16 October 2004, Russia and Tajikistan signed a bilateral agreement allowing Russia to maintain a military base in Dushanbe and continue its control of a former Soviet space monitoring center at Norak. In turn, Russia handed over control of the Tajik-Afghan border to Tajikistan; Russian troops abandoned their last border post on 12 July 2005. Keeping in mind the history of the border since the military expedition of Colonel Ionov to the Pamirs in 1891 and then the Anglo-Russian Demarcation four year later, this historic event presents a substantial shift in regional politics, with an impact that goes beyond just Russian-Tajik relations. With the help of the United States between 1999 and 2008, two out of a planned five bridges were constructed across the Amu Darya to connect Tajiks with Afghans, thus helping to bring coalition-controlled Afghanistan into the Central Asian orbit.

Tajikistan's relationship with Uzbekistan has always been uneasy. Both sides contest the demarcation of the shared border. After IMU terrorists invaded Uzbekistan from Tajikistan in 1999, the border was mined by Uzbekistan. The status of each state's ethnic counterparts in the other state has also been a point of tension. Other problems include the disputed use of water resources and obstructions regarding transport links and energy supplies regularly imposed on Tajikistan by Uzbekistan. Relations are cordial with Kazakhstan, Kyrgyzstan, and Turkmenistan as well as with Iran and Afghanistan.

Since the formation of the Tajik Autonomous Soviet Socialist Republic in 1924, the Tajik people have experienced dramatic and often contradictory events in their history. They were organized into a language-based community, only to be divided by arbitrarily drawn national borders. They were separated from the centers of Perso-Tajik culture. The Soviet regime promoted a Soviet national identity while concurrently allowing patronage networks to flourish and thus consolidate regional (subnational) affiliations. On the eve of the Soviet collapse, Tajik nationalism was officially discouraged; Tajik national assertiveness, which invariably carried Islamic connotations, was rejected. Post-Soviet statehood has been very costly for Tajiks. In the first years of the new millennium, Tajikistan broke out of its violent cycle of political insecurity and economic decline after ending a long civil conflict. Still, although human rights and political pluralism are not safeguarded, the county has made modest yet promising progress in recent years. And it remains clear that Tajikistan faces daunting challenges in the 21st century.

The Dictionary

– A –

ABBASIDS. The second dynasty of the Islamic empire after the Umayyad, the Abbasid dynasty lasted from 749 until the Mongol invasion in 1258. Under the Abbasids, the intelligence and sophistication of **Ajam** (non-Arabs) fused with **Arab**-Islamic civilization to reach a high point—especially in the eastern parts of the empire, which included the territory of present-day Tajikistan. The Abbasids did not actually control the empire; the **Samanids** ruled **Khurasan** and **Movarounnahr** as nominal vassals of the Abbasids.

ABDUJABBOR, TOHIR (1949–2009). A leader of the **Rastokhez** movement, Abdujabbor (Abdujabborov) was born in **Asht, Sughd veloyat**. He graduated from Tajik State University, with a degree in economics, in 1971. Between 1972 and 1990, he worked at the Institute of Economy, **Academy of Sciences of Tajikistan**. In the 1980s, he worked as a translator in **Iran** and **Afghanistan**. In 1989, he launched the Rastokhez civil movement and in the following year was elected to Tajikistan's **Supreme Soviet**. In 1990–1992, Abdujabbor worked with leaders of the **Islamic Renaissance Party of Tajikistan** and the **Democratic Party of Tajikistan** in the opposition bloc. From 1993 to 2006, he was in exile. He died in Dushanbe in 2009. *See also* CIVIL WAR.

ABDULLOEV, BAHODUR (1948–). A major general of state security, Abdulloev was born in **Bokhtar nohiya**. After graduating from the High School of the State Security Committee (Komitet Gosydarstvennoi Bezopasnosti, or KGB) of the Union of Soviet Socialist Republics (USSR) in 1972, he worked at various positions in Tajikistan's State Committee on National Security. From 1992 to 2002, he was deputy minister of Tajikistan's committee of national security. Abdulloev took part in all rounds of the **Inter-Tajik Peace Talks** from 1994 to 1997. In 1997–2000, he represented Tajikistan in the **Collective Security Treaty Organization** (Moscow). In 2002–2005, he was Tajik ambassador to China. From 2005 to 2008, he was an ambassador at large at Tajikistan's Ministry of Foreign Affairs.

ABDULLOEV, NAJMIDDIN (1917–1982). One of the leaders of the **Communist Party of Tajikistan**, Abdulloev was the only Soviet Tajik leader to head the republic's three **veloyats** and two **nohiyas.** Born in **Konibodom**, Abdulloev graduated from the Stalinabad (today Dushanbe) Pedagogical Institute in 1940 with a degree in chemistry. He was a lieutenant in the Soviet Army during **World War II.** In 1944, he began teaching chemistry in colleges and schools in the Tajik capital before being taken to the Central Committee of the Communist Party of Tajikistan in 1946. In 1947–1949, he worked first as secretary of Oktyabrskiy (**Bokhtar**), then in **Gharm** districts' committees of party. In 1952, he graduated from the First Secretaries of Committees courses of the Communist Party in Moscow. From 1949 to 1961, he headed the Communist Party organizations in **Gharm**, the **Mountainous Badakhshon Autonomous Veloyat**, and the Leninobod (**Sughd**) provinces. For a short period in 1955, he was Tajikistan's deputy minister of culture. From 1964 to 1978, he worked as deputy director general of the Tajikneft oil company.

ABDULLOJONOV, ABDUMALIK (1949–). Born in **Khujand**, Abdullojonov graduated from the Technological University, Odessa (Ukraine), in 1971 and from the Academy of People's Economy in 1986. In 1970–1980, he worked at grain mills in Kairakum and **Nau** (**Sughd**) at different posts up to manufacturing director. In 1980, he was appointed Tajikistan's deputy minister of **grain** supplies. In 1983–1986, he was the first deputy minister of grain products. In 1987–1992, he served as minister of grain products, which was reorganized to form the Ghalla (Grain) concern in 1992. In November 1992, Abdullojonov was appointed prime minister of Tajikistan but was replaced by **Jamshed Karimov** in January 1994. Abdullojonov was subsequently appointed Tajikistan's ambassador to the Russian Federation. He entered the presidential race and gained 40 percent of the vote in the November 1994 **elections**.

At the end of 1994, Tajikistan's procurator general brought charges of embezzlement against Abdullojonov, which disqualified him from entering any future elections. In January 1995, he resigned from his ambassadorial post in **Russia** but did not return to Tajikistan. At the end of 1994, Abdullojonov launched the **Party of People's Unity**; the party was banned at the end of 1998. Abdullojonov demanded to be included in the 1994–1997 **Inter-Tajik Peace Talks**, but to no avail. The Tajik government claims that he was one of the organizers of the **Mahmud Khudoiberdyev** raid on Leninobod veloyat in November 1998. As of 2009, Abdullojonov's whereabouts are unknown. *See also* CIVIL WAR.

ABDURAHIMOV, KHAIRIDDIN (1954–). A chair of the State Committee on National Security, Abdurahimov was born in the **Bokhtar nohiya, Qurghonteppa** veloyat, to a **Kulobi** family. He studied English at the Dushanbe State Pedagogical Institute, and after graduating in 1981, he was a teacher and then deputy director of the Bokhtar nohiya high school. In 1982, he was recruited for Tajikistan's KGB. Abdurahimov headed a department in the **Khatlon veloyat** branch of the Ministry of Security between 1993 and 1999. In November 1999, Colonel General Abdurahimov was appointed minister of security. In December 2006, the ministry became the State Committee on National Security.

ABDURAHMON JOMI NOHIYA. Known as Kuibyshev until 1997, then Khojamaston until 2007, when it was named after the poet **Abdurahmon Jomi**, this district is located in the basin of the **Vakhsh** and **Yovon**-Obiqiiq rivers in the **Qurghonteppa** region, **Khatlon** veloyat. It was established in 1930. With a territory of 1,393 square kilometers and a population of more than 100,000 (9,000 urban), **Tajiks** and **Uzbeks**, it has nine **jamoats**. The distance from the center of the district, Kuibyshevsk, to Qurghonteppa is 36 kilometers, to **Dushanbe** 86 kilometers, and to the nearest railway station in Vakhsh 12 kilometers. Average January and July temperatures are 9°C and 29°C respectively. The annual rainfall is 271 millimeters. Arable land amounts to 254,684 hectares. The main occupation is **agriculture**, including **cotton** production, livestock breeding, and vegetable gardening.

ABU HANIFAH. *See* HANAFIYA.

ACADEMICIAN. This is the highest academic rank of the **Academy of Sciences of Tajikistan**. Based on the Soviet system, academicians are selected by the Council of Academics from distinguished scholars, mostly **doctors of science** nominated by scientific institutions, public associations, universities, and eminent scholars. In 2007, there were 30 academicians in the Academy of Sciences of Tajikistan. *See also* AYNI, SADRIDDIN; CANDIDATE OF SCIENCES; UMAROV, SULTAN.

ACADEMY OF SCIENCES OF TAJIKISTAN. Modern academic research in Tajikistan was founded in the 1920s. In 1932, the Tajik branch of the Academy of Sciences of the Union of Soviet Socialist Republics (USSR)—the first scientific institution in Tajikistan—was established with the help of Russian scholars. It mainly focused on biological and geological research. In 1941, the Tajik base was transformed into the Tajik branch of the Academy of Sciences of the USSR, headed by **academician** E. N. Pavlovskiy. The Tajik branch included institutes of geology, botany, zoology and parasitology, history, and language and literature. It also coordinated research by the Astronomical Observatory and the **Vakhsh** Station for Soil Culture and Irrigation. Later in the 1940s, the Institute of Cattle Breeding and the Institute of Chemistry and Geophysics joined the Tajik branch and worked closely with the Academy of Sciences of the USSR. In 1951, the Academy of Sciences of the Tajik Soviet Socialist Republic was formed. The renowned Tajik writer and scholar **Sadriddin Ayni** was the first president of the Tajik Academy of Sciences. In 2007, the academy incorporated 17 research institutes, 3 science centers, and several departments with 3,000 specialists, including 880 **doctors of sciences** and 4,080 **candidates of sciences** in different academic fields.

Traditionally, a president of the academy was elected by an assembly of academicians. In 2007, President **Emomali Rahmon** took this responsibility upon himself. There were 30 academicians and 55 correspondent members in Tajikistan's academy that year, and the academy consisted of 22 institutes, including Physics and Techniques (1964), Mathematics (1973), Seismology and Seismologic Construction (1951), Geology (1941), Chemistry (1945), Botany (1951), Physiology and Biophysics of Plants (1964), Zoology and Parasitology (1951), Pamirian Biological Institute (1969), Gastroenterology (1965), Protection and Rational Using of Nature Resources (1969), History, Ethnography, and Archeology (1951), Philosophy (1951), Economics (1964), Tajik Language and Literature (1951), Oriental Studies (1970), Council for Investigation of Natural and Labor Resources (1951), Department of Manuscripts, and others. There are provincial branches (scientific centers) of the academy in **Pamir**, **Khatlon**, and **Sughd**. The academy runs its own publishing house, Donish, and prints two journals: *Doklady Akademii Nauk Tadzhikistana* (Academy of Sciences of Tajikistan's Reports) and *Akhboroti Akademiai Fanhoi Tojikiston: Izvestia Akademii Nauk Tadzhikistana* (Academy of Sciences of Tajikistan's Reports in Tajik and Russian respectively). There are series in the humanities (Oriental studies, history, and philology; economics and political science; biology and medical sciences; physics and mathematics; and philosophy and law). The academy also publishes *Problemy Gastroenterologii* (Problems of Gastroenterology).

In 2008, the academy's budget stood at $3.5 million, or 0.1 percent of the country's GDP. In addition, the International Science and Technology Center (ISTC) supported the academy's research projects on geophysical instrumentation, seismology and earthquake forecasting, alternate renewable energy sources such as solar energy, biotechnology, and lasers and plasma in medicine, worth $1.6 million.

The academy has 12 specialized councils on defense of dissertations. Unlike other former USSR republics, Tajikistan did not separate from the All-Union Attestation Commission after the collapse of the USSR in 1991. Tajik candidate and doctorate dissertations are certified by the All-Russian Attestation Commission.

Presidents of the Academy of Sciences of Tajikistan have been **Sadriddin Ayni** (1951–1954), **Sultan Umarov** (1957–1964), **Muhammad Asimov** (1965–1988), **Sabit Negmatulloev** (1988–1995), **Ulmas Mirsaidov** (June 1995–2005), and **Mamadshoh Ilolov** (2005–present).

ACHAEMENIDS. This Persian empire (6th–4th centuries BCE) stretched from Egypt and Ethiopia to **India**, and it included Central

Asian **Sogdiana, Bactria, Khurasan**, and Parthia. The Achaemenid period was of great cultural significance for Zoroastrianism, which originated in Bactria. A common state finance system, centralized administration, writing, and external trade were developed, and the Tajik cities of **Panjakent** and **Istravshan** were founded in this period. At the end of the 4th century BCE, **Alexander the Great** overran the Achaemenids.

ADAB. A system of courtesy or politeness, *adab* requires such behaviors as proper greetings on meeting or parting, joining in the carrying of a bier in a funeral procession, visiting the sick, assisting those in distress, and providing a guest with lodging and food. The system is reflected in the literary genre *adabiyot*. *See also* ETIQUETTE.

ADAT. In the Tajik **language**, *adat* (*odat*) means "tradition." The term refers to unwritten regional customs that have the force of social law alongside the civil code. *Adat* is rooted in pre-Islamic history and exists everywhere in the Islamic world. It serves as one of the important informal means of conflict resolution for cases involving land disputes, blood feuds, and even murder. The Soviets vainly tried to uproot *adat* practices. *See also* ISLAM.

ADIB. An *adib* is a writer, novelist, learned person, scholar, or educator.

ADMINISTRATIVE STRUCTURE. Tajikistan is organized in a descending hierarchy of provincial-level **veloyats** (*oblasts* in Russian) and administration of the capital city of **Dushanbe**; district-level **nohiyas** (*rayons* in Russian), including those of Dushanbe; community-level **shahraks** (townships, rural settlements), and **dehot** (villages). Tajikistan is presently divided into four administrative regions: a specially designated group of nohiyas and three veloyats. The **Nohiyas under Republican Control** (total 13) include the Kofarnihon area and the two valleys of Qarategin and **Hisor**. **Khujand** is the center of the **Sughd** veloyat (14 nohiyas), which includes mostly the **Zarafshon** and **Ferghana** valley. **Khorugh** is the center of the **Mountainous Badakhshon Autonomous Veloyat** (7 nohiyas).

Qurghonteppa is the center of the **Khatlon** veloyat (24 nohiyas) in the south. Each veloyat is divided into nohiyas and then cities and towns, which can also serve as the capital of the nohiya. Dushanbe city has 4 nohiyas.

In December 1994, the Law on Village Government was adopted by the **Majlisi Oli**, and a decentralizing reform program was launched. Village soviets have been replaced by **jamoats** (neighborhood self-governing groups) and **mahallas** (local communities). Each nohiya is subdivided into jamoats. A jamoat comprises varying numbers of **qyshloqs** (villages). The town or city in each nohiya has a local branch of the *hukumat* (government). In Tajikistan, there are 22 cities, 47 towns, 354 villages, and 3,570 settlements. Each veloyat, nohiya, and city has its hukumat. Consequently, there are three veloyat hukumats, 59 nohiya hukumats, 16 hukumats of veloyat and nohiya cities, and four Dushanbe city district hukumats. There are 401 jamoats in Tajikistan.

ADOLATKHOH PARTY OF JUSTICE (APJ). A small **political party** formed on 15 November 1995 in **Konibodom**, Leninobod veloyat, the APJ was registered on 6 March 1996. Its membership consisted of teachers, office workers, and builders. *Adolatkhoh* means "justice seeker" in **Tajik**. The APJ had its headquarters in Konibodom and operated several branches in **Dushanbe**, **Kulob**, **Isfara**, **Khujand**, and some other towns. The APJ was a signatory to the March 1996 **Agreement on National Accord**. The stated objective of the party was to "unite peoples and nations of the republic, and to create conditions for a democratic state." The party joined the Consultative Council in May 1999 and was chaired by **Abdurahmon Karimov**. It registered 22 candidates on the party list in the February 2000 parliamentary and local **elections** but received only 34,890 votes (1.35 percent of total votes), well below the 5 percent requirement for securing representation in the parliamentary assembly. In 2004, the APJ ceased to exist.

AFGHANISTAN. A neighboring country of Tajikistan, the Islamic Republic of Afghanistan shares a border on the south and southeast with **Pakistan**, on the west with **Iran**, on the north with **Uzbekistan**, Turkmenistan, Tajikistan, and **China**. The population of Afghanistan is about 32 million. The overwhelming majority are **Sunni** Muslims of the **Hanafi** rite, while Twelve-Imam Shiites make up about 15 percent of the population. In Badakhshon province, there are several tens of thousands of Tajik **Ismailis**. **Tajiks**, numbering approximately 7.5 million or about 25 percent of the population, are the second ethnic group, after the Pushtuns, both in terms of number and influence. Since 1747, when modern Afghanistan was established, the Pushtuns have ruled Afghanistan, except in 1929 and 1992–1996, when the country was headed by Tajiks (**Bachai Saqqao** and Burhanuddin Rabbani respectively).

The border between Afghanistan and Tajikistan, which stretches along the Panj-**Amu Darya** River, was drawn by Great Britain and **Russia**. In the 1920s, it saw almost unrestrained crossings of people, weapons, and **Basmachi** insurgents moving in both directions. From 1918 to 1932, almost 500,000 Tajiks and **Uzbeks** fled to Afghanistan to escape Soviet power. In the mid-1930s, the Soviets sealed the Tajik-Afghan border, stopping all kinds of contacts between kin communities on both sides of the Amu Darya. During the initial period of **World War II**, the situation on the Soviet-Afghan border was tense due to alleged attempts of the exiled Central Asian emigration to invade Tajikistan with the help of Nazi agents. On 5–6 November 1941, the Loya Jirgha (general assembly of Afghans) declared Afghanistan a neutral state; two years later, under Stalin's pressure, the government of Afghanistan dispatched from the country all German and Italian residents who did not have diplomatic status. Also, communities of Tajik and Uzbek exiles were deported from prefrontier regions to internal Afghan provinces in early 1943.

After World War II, the Soviet authorities used cultural similarities between Tajiks and Afghans to promote their own agenda. From the 1960s to the late 1980s, Moscow sent thousands of educated Soviet Tajiks to work in Afghanistan. Tajikistan was presented there as an example of the benefits of the communist system. Uzbekistan and Tajikistan served as a springboard for the Soviet invasion of Afghanistan in 1979, followed by a 10-year war.

Since the collapse of the USSR, inadequate border protection has made the Tajikistan-Afghanistan border very permeable. From 1992, an estimated 80,000 or more Tajikistanis—mostly opposition supporters—fled to northern Afghanistan. In 1993, the Tajik opposition established military bases there. Tajik Islamists received considerable support from their Afghan counterparts in the form of military training and supplies, and some Afghan units fought alongside the Tajik opposition against the Tajik government and Russian **frontier guards**. During Tajikistan's **civil war** (1992–1997), fighters of the **United Tajik Opposition** (UTO) established military bases and training camps in ethnically Tajik regions of northeastern Afghanistan. Military incursions northward were followed by large refugee flows south into Afghanistan when, in 1993, Tajik government forces emerged victorious in the civil war. Afghan leaders **Ahmad Shah Massoud** and President Burhanuddin Rabbani (ethnic Tajiks), interested in continuation of Russian military aid, had halted their support of Tajik Islamists in 1994. In 1994–2001, Tajikistan facilitated military assistance from Russia and Iran intended for some Tajik and Hazara (Persian-speaking predominantly Shiites of Mongol origin) groups fighting against the **Taliban**. The joint Tajik-Russian military base and airfield at **Kulob** served as the linchpin for the Tajik-dominated **Northern Alliance** forces in the Panjshir valley and northern Afghanistan.

The rise of the Pushtun-dominated Taliban in 1994 encouraged the Afghanistan and Iran-based Tajik opposition and Tajik government to enter negotiations during the civil war. The *mujahedin* government of Afghanistan led by Burhanuddin Rabbani encouraged mediation and supported the **Inter-Tajik Peace Talks**. The first rounds of the talks bore no results until in May 1995 the president of Afghanistan managed a meeting of President **Emomali Rahmon** (Rakhmonov) and his adversary **Said Abdullo Nuri** in Kabul. It was the first meeting of the two rivals. The Taliban's capture of Kabul in September 1996 provided further motivation for Tajik reconciliation. On 11 December 1996, Rahmon and Nuri met again under Rabbani's sponsorship in the Afghan village of **Khos Deh**, where they signed an important protocol on the cease-fire. This marked a turning point in the peace process. The Taliban's advance to the northern provinces in 1997 forced almost all Tajik exiles to leave Afghanistan for Tajikistan.

In the aftermath of the 11 September 2001 attacks on the World Trade Center and Pentagon in the **United States**, Tajikistan declared it would cooperate with the U.S.-led campaign to combat

terrorism. Tajikistan was primarily afraid that the Taliban could overrun the Northern Alliance and threaten its secular regime but was also concerned that thousands of refugees could pass the border and overwhelm Tajikistan.

Despite the ousting of the former Taliban government from power in Afghanistan in early 2002 and setting up of the Afghan government that established amicable relations with Tajikistan, Afghanistan continues to be a base of international terrorism, an area of civil conflict between the Taliban and the Afghan government, and the world's largest producer of opium. These negative factors produce cross-border effects that threaten Tajikistan's stability. The narcotics issue perpetuates the isolation of Afghanistan within the region, creating obstacles for closer cooperation with Tajikistan. Afghanistan remains the world's leading drug producer. As of 2009, 90 percent of the demand for Afghan heroin came from Europe and Russia. Overall drug production involves 2 million Afghans (10 percent of the population). Nearly all the money from the drug business goes to consuming and trafficking countries, not to Afghanistan. Cross-border raids into Tajikistan from Afghanistan have been commonplace, and violent clashes between drug smugglers and Tajik border guards remain common.

The actions of Tajik groups living on both sides of the border appeared largely rational, security-driven, and state-centered. None of the Afghan parties and forces, deeply involved in the struggle for power, were interested in attaining influence in Tajikistan and vice versa. The national sentiments that started to emerge between the Tajiks of Tajikistan and the Afghan Tajiks in the 1990s have not yet resulted in a unified cross-border nationalism.

Tajikistan and Afghanistan are members of the **Conference on Interaction and Confidence-Building Measures in Asia** (CICA) and the **Economic Cooperation Organization** (ECO). Unlike Pakistan, Iran, Mongolia, and **India**, Afghanistan does not intend to obtain membership or observer status in the **Shanghai Cooperation Organization** (SCO) dominated by Russia and China. Afghanistan and Tajikistan, which share a long border, are important agents in implementation of the U.S. **Greater Central Asia** strategy, aimed at promotion of cooperation in various spheres and creating a new region by uniting Central Asia with South Asia. With the help of the United States from 1999 to 2008, three out of five proposed bridges were constructed to connect Tajiks with Afghans and to bring Afghanistan into the Central Asian orbit. In May 2003, Tajikistan resumed supplies of electricity to the northern Afghanistan province of Qunduz; in 2006, the two countries signed a joint cooperative agreement in the power sector, which includes supply of electricity from Tajikistan during the spring and summer seasons, and within the limits of Tajikistan's capabilities during the autumn and winter seasons.

Tajikistan's cooperation with the government of Afghanistan has been on the increase. The two sides maintain an intensive political dialogue especially with regard to border protection, **drug trafficking**, trade, and technical cooperation. *See also* FOREIGN POLICY; TAJIKS OF AFGHANISTAN.

AFRASIAB. The ruins of Afrasiab mark the ancient hub of **Samarqand**. From the middle of the first millennium BCE up to the beginning of the 13th century, Afrasiab served as an important administrative, trade, and economic center for **Kushans**, **Sogdians**, and **Samanids**. Some researchers believe that the name comes from the mythical hero Afrasiab, a leader and warrior who fought against **Iran** and was described in *Shohnoma* by **Abulqasem Firdawsi**. Others claim that the name of the city is derived from the river Siab, on the banks of which Afrasiab is situated. Afrasiab was destroyed by Genghiz Khan in 1220. Samarqand's center later moved to the south of the Afrasiab ruins.

AGA KHAN IV (1936–). Prince Karim Aga Khan is the 49th hereditary imam (spiritual leader) of the Shia Imami (Nizari) **Ismaili** Muslims. He was born in Geneva, the elder son of Prince Aly Khan and Princess Joan Aly Khan (daughter of the third Baron Churston), and spent his early childhood in Nairobi, Kenya. He graduated from Harvard in 1959 with a B.A. in Islamic history and resides near Paris. He succeeded his grandfather Sir Sultan Mahomed Shah Aga Khan on 11 July 1957 at the age of 20. Aga Khan has adapted the complex system of administering the various Ismaili communities dispersed in Asia, Europe, Africa, and America. He has called on his adherents to become citizens of the countries in which they reside and to leave countries where they face discrimination and oppression.

In Tajikistan, Aga Khan is known not only among his followers, the Ismailis of **Badakhshon**, numbering nearly 150,000 people, but nationwide for his initiatives, which form part of an international network of institutions involved in fields that range from **education**, **health**, and rural development to architecture and the promotion of the private sector. *See also* AGA KHAN DEVELOPMENT NETWORK.

AGA KHAN DEVELOPMENT NETWORK (AKDN). This organization consists of a group of private development agencies established by **Aga Khan IV**, the hereditary imam of the **Ismaili** Muslims, to improve living conditions and opportunities in specific regions of the developing world. The constituent institutions of the AKDN include the Aga Khan Foundation (AKF), the Aga Khan University, the Aga Khan Fund for Economic Development, and the Aga Khan Trust for Culture, which includes the Aga Khan Program for Islamic Architecture at Harvard University and the Massachusetts Institute of Technology, the Aga Khan Award for Architecture, and the Historic Cities Support Program—all founded in the 1960s and 1970s. The network also includes the Aga Khan Health Services and the Aga Khan Education Services, providers of **health care**, schooling, and other educational services in South Asia and East Africa since the beginning of the 20th century.

In Tajikistan, the AKDN supported reconstruction and reconciliation processes and provided legal advice to the **Commission for National Reconciliation**. Since starting work in Tajikistan in 1992, the AKDN mobilized more than $110 million from its own resources. These funds have been raised from the Ismaili imamat, from the Ismaili community around the world, and from donor partners, including the government of Tajikistan.

Some of the main programs promoted by the AKDN are the Agricultural Reform Program of the AKF-sponsored Mountain Societies Development Support Program, the Aga Khan Education Service under the Aga Khan Education Fund (AKEF), and the Aga Khan Humanities Project for Central Asia, implemented by the Aga Khan Trust for Culture. The AKF has been working with the government of Tajikistan to complete the Pamir I power station in Badakhshon.

The AKDN has also supported the construction of several small hydroelectric power stations, and it has provided funds to repair bridges and roads in remote parts of the Badakhshon veloyat. The AKDN has facilitated the construction of the **Murghob-Kulma** motor road, linking Tajikistan with **China** and the **Karakoram Highway**, as well as providing support for the construction of roads linking **Kulob** with Qalai Khumb and Murghob with the Kulma Pass.

The AKDN has endowed a grant to the **United Nation**'s Drug Control Program (UNDCP) to undertake the mapping of poppy growing areas in Tajikistan, **Kyrgyzstan**, and Kazakhstan within the framework of the Memorandum of Understanding on Drug Control Measures between the UNDCP and the Republics of Tajikistan, Kyrgyzstan, **Uzbekistan**, Kazakhstan, and Turkmenistan. The AKDN became a signatory to this memorandum along with the **Russian Federation** in January 1998.

AGRARIAN PARTY OF TAJIKISTAN (APT). The Agrarian Party of Tajikistan (Hizbi Agrarii Tojikiston), initially chaired by Hikmatulloh Nasriddinov, was formed in July 1998 and registered in January 1999. Its membership consisted of agricultural workers who, according to the APT rules, "sincerely believe that the real revival of Tajikistan depends on the revival of Tajik villages." The highest organ of the party was its congress, which elected a political council and an executive committee. In April 1999, the Ministry of Justice suspended the APT's registration due to errors in the registration papers. The party was allowed to register in November 2005. Since 2005, the ATP chair has been Amir Karakulov. It has 1,300 members. The APT and its chair took part in the **presidential elections of 2006**. *See also* ELECTIONS; POLITICAL PARTIES.

AGREEMENT ON FRIENDSHIP, COOPERATION, AND MUTUAL ASSISTANCE BETWEEN THE RUSSIAN FEDERATION AND THE REPUBLIC OF TAJIKISTAN. Signed on 25 May 1993 in Moscow by Tajikistan's President **Emomali Rahmon** and President Boris Yeltsin of **Russia**, during Rahmon's first visit to Moscow, this agreement provides for political and military cooperation, coordination of military doctrines, the financing of military programs, orders of weapon and military technology, and testing. Tajikistan granted the Russian armed forces the right to use airfields in its territory. In case of security threats in **Central Asia,** both sides would consult and act in concert. In case of an act of military aggression, both sides pledged to commit the necessary military and other resources. Both sides promised not to take part in unions and blocs directed against any of the signatories. The agreement also provided for economic, trade, and scientific cooperation. The signatories granted each other the most favored status in interstate relations. This agreement allowed the conclusion of other supplementary military agreements, such as the Agreement on Cooperation in the Military Field between the Republic of Tajikistan and the Russian Federation (25 May 1993) and the Agreement on the Legal Status of the Frontier Guard Forces of the Russian Federation Engaged in the Republic of Tajikistan (25 May 1993). The five-year Agreement on Friendship will be renewed automatically, unless disputed by either of the signatories.

AGREEMENT ON NATIONAL ACCORD. This agreement was signed by 30 public associations, political movements and parties, national and religious organizations, and unions on 9 March 1996. The signatories declared their support for the government of President **Emomali Rahmon** in its negotiations in the **Inter-Tajik Peace Talks.** The signatories to the agreement formed the **Societal Council.** *See also* CIVIL WAR.

AGRICULTURE. Throughout their history, Tajiks have engaged in agriculture with a focus on labor-intensive crops. A dry and warm climate plus sophisticated irrigation systems have combined to make Tajik agriculture very productive. Traditionally Tajiks lived in village communities. Regular maintenance of the irrigation system demanded stability, readiness to compromise, and communal cooperation. Most of the arable land (up to 85 percent) was in the possession of secular and religious landowners, and many Tajik *dehqons* (farmers) knew little about private property and open market privileges even before the forceful **collectivization** and organization of large state-controlled farms in the 1930s. Agriculture still is a traditional occupation in independent Tajikistan, where most farmers are engaged in production of **cotton, grain,** fruits, and vegetables, and to a lesser extent in animal husbandry, including cattle, sheep, and goats.

Tajikistan has more than 827,000 hectares of arable land. In 1992, 46.8 percent of the population was engaged in agriculture. This grew to 67 percent in 2007. Although two-thirds of the population is engaged in agriculture, the real contribution of farmers to the national **economy** is modest. In 1998, agricultural production made up only 27 percent of the gross domestic product (GDP). This share decreased to 21.1 percent in 2007. Only 27 percent of the total land is used for agricultural purposes—6 percent as cropland and 23 percent as pasture. The reason for this lies not only in unprecedented labor outmigration but also in flawed and incomplete land **privatization** and the low capacity of national institutions.

From 1994, the distribution of "presidential land" began as a response to the devaluation of the Tajik ruble and the collapse of the state-run **kolkhoz** system. In 1994–1997, 75,000 hectares of *kolkhoz* (collective farm) lands were distributed to individual farmers. The farmers do not own the land but have hereditary rights, pay taxes, and supposedly are allowed to choose their crops. In practice, former leaders of kolkhozes maintain some power in agriculture. Even though many Soviet-era kolkhozes and **sovkhozes** (state farms) have been abolished, they still provide many rural families with a source of income. As a rule, individuals rent land from the kolkhoz, and the kolkhoz provides the inputs if the leaseholder agrees to produce a determined level of cash crop, mostly cotton.

Cotton is still the main crop in Tajikistan, and a cotton monopoly remains a great issue, inherited from Soviet times. Cotton is primarily grown in hot river valleys, particularly in the **Ferghana** valley in **Sughd** province; in the **Vakhsh**, Kyzylsu, and **Panj** valleys in **Khatlon**; and in Hisor valley. Cotton fiber is Tajikistan's leading agricultural export commodity, contributing 16 percent of total exports. Grain production has increased, but as it is predominantly grown on nonirrigated lands, the yield is low. Wheat and barley are cultivated mostly in the rain-fed plains of Khatlon and Sughd veloyats. Rice is grown in river valleys in Sughd and Khatlon veloyat. Other crops are potatoes, vegetables, melons, which are grown across the entire country, and **lemons** in the Vakhsh valley. The north of the country produces apricots, pears, plums, apples, cherries, pomegranates, figs, and nuts. Dried fruits are a traditional export for Tajikistan. *See also* COOPERATIVE FARMS; LABOR MIGRATION.

AIRLINES. Tajikistan has no direct access to the sea or advanced networks of **motor roads**. Therefore airlines are of paramount importance. Tajikistan has 40 airports (including 17 with paved runways). Over 80 percent of its international air traffic is with Russia, mostly due to migrant Tajik workers seeking seasonal employment. In 2005, 0.2 percent of Tajikistan's total passenger traffic (500,000 passengers) and more than 0.04 percent of freight traffic (3,700 tons) traveled on airlines.

The State Unitary Aviation Enterprise, Tojikiston, was founded in 1924 as part of the Aeroflot Regional Directorate. Since 1991, Tajik Air has been the national flag carrier. It is the only carrier performing international and domestic operations. In the domestic market, the carrier Samar Air also operates flights. In 2006, there were 646,000 international passengers. Tajik Air handles about 54 percent of the international market; 46 percent is served by 23 foreign carriers, of which 16 are Russian. Virtually no cargo traffic is transported by Tajik Air. In 2008, Tajik Air had regular flights to **Russia** (Moscow, Novosibirsk, Samara, St. Petersburg, and Ekaterinburg), Kazakhstan (Almaty), **Kyrgyzstan** (Bishkek), **China** (Urumchi), **Iran** (Tehran), United Arab Emirates (Sharjah), and Turkey (Istanbul). Within the country, Tajik Air connects Dushanbe with **Khujand**, **Khorugh**, and **Kulob** with regular flights. From 1992 to 2007, the management of the company changed four times. In October 2008, in accordance with World Bank requirements, the airline was split into five State Unitarian Enterprises, including International Airport Dushanbe, International Airport Khujand, International Airport Kulob, International Airport **Qurghonteppa**, and Tajik Air Navigation.

AJAM. In **Arab** tradition, *ajam* are non-Arabs. The term is mostly applied to Iranians and also refers to the kingdom and homeland of the Iranians. Ajam is also one of the components of **Shashmaqom**, Tajik classical **music** (e.g., Nawruzi Ajam, Bayoti Ajam).

AJINATEPPA. The remains of a **Buddhist** temple near **Qurghonteppa**, Ajinateppa is a rectangular building 100 by 50 meters and 6 meters in height. The main archeological find is a 12-meter-high sculpture of Buddha (Shakiamuni) made of clay. It is assumed that Ajinateppa was destroyed by **Arab** invaders in the 8th century. Excavations by Tajik archeologists were carried out between 1959 and 1973. The sculpture of Buddha was placed in the Historical Museum, **Dushanbe**. *See also* ARTS.

AKA (AKO). *Aka*, meaning "brother," is a polite form of reference used by a younger person to an older male person. It is also used with a person's first name (e.g., Kamol-ako). *See also* ETIQUETTE.

AKHMEDOV, YUSUF (1950–). A Tajik industrialist and politician, Akhmedov was born in **Konibodom** to a family of teachers. He graduated from the Tajik Agricultural Institute in 1972 and began work as an engineer with the Bodom joint stock company (known as the Avtozapchast factory before 1985, then as the brake equipment assembly plant of the Russian GAZ automobile factory until 1992). He rose to the positions of chief controller and chief engineer and in 1987 became director of the enterprise. Akhmedov left the **Communist Party of Tajikistan** in 1991 and was nominated as a presidential candidate in 1991. But he withdrew his candidacy in favor of **Rahmon Nabiev**, who won the race. In 1991, Akhmedov joined the **political party** of **Abdumalik Abdullojonov** but left in 1998. Akhmedov was a member of the **Supreme Soviet** in 1990–1995 and **Majlisi Oli** in 1995–2000. In 2000 and 2005, he was reelected to the **Majlisi Namoyandagon** and became chair of the standing committee on energy, industry, construction, and communications.

ALEXANDER THE GREAT (356–323 BCE). About 330–320 BCE, Alexander of Macedonia defeated the **Achaemenids**. His armies encountered fierce resistance from forces under the command of General **Spitamen** in **Bactria** and **Sogdiana**. Alexander was wounded in a battle near the Sogdian city of Kiropol, near present-day **Istravshan**. In order to gain the support of the local aristocracy, Alexander married Rukhshona (Roxana), the daughter of a Sogdian noble. According to Tajik legends, Alexander reached the upper stream of the **Zarafshon** River on his march to Sogdiana. The **Iskandarkul** (lake of Alexander) is named after him. During his reign, Alexander set up 8–10 Greco-Macedonian colonial cities (each called Alexandria) in Sogdiana and Bactria, where up to 20,000 infantry and 3,000 horsemen settled. The most famous of these cities was Alexandria-Eskhata, near present-day **Khujand**. After the fall of Alexander's empire in 306 BCE, Sogdiana and Bactria joined the Hellenic Selevkids for about 50 years.

ALI HAMADONI (1314–1384). Mir Said Ali bin Shihobuddin Muhammad Hamadoni was a medieval scholar and artist. A native of **Khurasan**, Hamadoni traveled to many Islamic centers and wrote nearly 70 books on **Sufism**, philosophy, and ethics. He died in **India** and was buried in **Kulob**. His mausoleum was renovated with the help of the **Iranian** government in 1994–1996. *See also* HAMADONI MAUSOLEUM.

ALICHUR. This is a mostly **Kyrgyz**-populated **jamoat** in the **Murghob** district in the Alichur valley on the **Khorugh**-Osh **motor road**. The Alichur jamoat comprises three **qyshloqs** (villages): Burunkul, Bashgunbez, and Alichur. The population in 2008 was 1,990.

ALICHUR RIVER. An upper stream of the Ghund River in the **Alichur valley**, the Alichur is 296 kilometers long. Its headwaters begin in the eastern edges of the southern Alichur glacier and feed Yashil Lake.

ALICHUR VALLEY. Located in the **Mountainous Badakhshon Autonomous Veloyat** in eastern **Pamir** about 4,000 meters above sea level, the Alichur valley stretches from the Naizatosh Pass to Yashil Lake. It is 90 kilometers long and 218 kilometers wide, with a population of about 2,000, mostly Pamirian **Kyrgyz**. Principal centers of the valley are Alichur and Oqchar villages of the **Murghob nohiya**. The **Khorugh**-Osh and Khorugh-**Kulma motor roads** pass through the valley. The main occupation is animal husbandry and cattle herding. A historical artifact of the 19th century, the Boshgunbaz mausoleum, is located at the center of the valley. Stone Age marks of hunters from the 9th–8th millennia BCE suggest a rich and ancient culture.

ALIEV, ABBAS (1899–1958). A professor and author of several works on the history of **Central Asia**, Aliev was one of the first **Bukharan** communists and an organizer of the **Bukharan People's Soviet Republic** and the **Tajik Soviet Socialist Republic**. He was Tajikistan's first education minister (*nazir*), serving from 1924 to 1927.

ALIMARDON, MURODALI (1960–). A deputy prime minister of Tajikistan, Alimardon was born in the **Hisor nohiya** and studied economics at the Tajik State University. After graduation in 1983, he joined the Cheptura branch of the Agrobank in Hisor. In 1991, he was appointed manager of the Hisor branch of Agrobank. At the end of 1993, Alimardon became president of the Sharq Agroprombank and in December 1996 was appointed chair of the **National Bank** of Tajikistan. In 2008, he became deputy prime minister of Tajikistan in charge of agriculture. In 2009, an audit indicated that from 1996 to 2008 Alimardon funneled around $856 million from the central bank to his Credit-Invest investment company. *See also* CORRUPTION.

ALIMOV, RASHID (1953–). Born in **Dushanbe** to a family of Khuandis, Alimov received a degree in history from the Tajik State University in 1975 and earned another from the Communist Party's Academy of Social Sciences. He started his career as deputy chair of the Tajik State University's joint trade union committee. In 1976–1990, he worked at different posts in the republican **Komsomol**: in 1976–1979 as head of the lecturers' group in the central committee; in 1979–1981 as instructor in the Agitation and Propaganda Department of the Frunze district committee of the **Communist Party of Tajikistan** (CPT) in Dushanbe; in 1981–1982 as instructor in the Agitation and Propaganda Department of the Dushanbe city committee of the CPT; in 1982–1986 as deputy head of the Agitation and Propaganda Department and first secretary of the republican Komsomol central committee. In 1988, he moved from the Komsomol to the CPT ruling bodies and was appointed first secretary of the Frunze district committee of the CPT. In 1989, he became second secretary of the Dushanbe city committee of the CPT. In 1990–1991, he was chair of the youth policy committee of the **Supreme Soviet.** In 1991–1992, he was a state adviser to the president of Tajikistan. Alimov was taken hostage by **Abdughafor Khudoidodov** (Mullo Abdughafor) between 31 August and 2 September 1992. In December 1992, he was appointed minister of foreign affairs and in December 1994 became Tajikistan's ambassador to the **United Nations**. He became Tajikistan's ambassador to **China** in October 2005.

ALOVKHONA. In mountainous Tajik villages, the *alovkhona* (house of fire) is situated next to and often attached to the local **mosque** and serves as a gathering place for men.

AMIR. An amir (emir) is a military commander, warlord, or chief of nomads. The term also was the title of the rulers of **Bukhara** in 1753–1920.

AMIRBEKOV, ATOBEK (1950–). Born in **Khorugh**, in the **Mountainous Badakhshon Autonomous Veloyat**, Amirbekov studied mathematics at the Dushanbe Pedagogical Institute and graduated in 1971. Between 1970 and 1975, he was a teacher at a high school in **Dushanbe** and then moved to the Dushanbe Pedagogical Institute as a lecturer and then deputy dean until 1992. In 1985, Amirbekov defended his **candidate** thesis on pedagogy in Kiev (Ukraine). In 1990, he organized the **La'li Badakhshon Association** and was forced to flee Tajikistan in the wake of Tajikistan's **civil war**. He joined the presidium of the **United Tajik Opposition** in 1995 and participated in three rounds of **Inter-Tajik Peace Talks** in Ashgabat, Tehran, and Moscow. Amirbekov was elected to the subcommission on military issues of the **Commission for National Reconciliation** in 1997. In 1999, he joined the **People's Democratic Party of Tajikistan** and in 2000 was elected to the **Majlisi Namoyandagon**.

AMLOK. *Amlok* is the term for land, real estate, or a possession, country, or state.

AMU DARYA. One of the longest rivers in **Central Asia**, the Amu Darya (Daryoi Amu in **Tajik**) was known to ancient Greeks as the Oxus River and to the Arabs as the Jayhun. The Amu Darya basin together with the Syr Darya basin covers the whole territory of Tajikistan and parts of its Central Asian neighbors. This area is known as one of the world's centers of civilization. The river rises in the high mountain area of the **Vakhan** corridor and Lake Zorkul as the Ab-e **Pamir** and the Ab-e Vakhan, which flow together to form the Panj River. This river joins with the Kukcha and Qunduz downstream (**Afghanistan**) and the **Vakhsh** (Tajikistan) to form the main

Amu Darya. Farther downstream, the Tashkorgan, Balkhab, Sar-e Pul, and Ab-e Qaysar (Afghanistan) are also tributaries to the Amu Darya. After forming Afghanistan's northern border with Tajikistan and **Uzbekistan** for about 1,100 kilometers, the Amu Darya flows north from Kerki to Turkmenabad (Turkmenistan) before tracing Tajikistan's border with Uzbekistan. Because of careless management, the Amu Darya disappears into the desert before reaching the Aral Sea.

The Amu Darya has a length of 2,540 kilometers and is heavily used for the irrigation of **cotton** and other crops. The river largely depends on the waters of its mountainous principal tributaries, the Vakhsh and the Panj. The larger part of these streams derives from melting snow and ice, increasing in spring and decreasing in winter. The river flow in Tajikistan, in comparison with its lower course, is more stable. In the aftermath of the Soviet collapse and the disappearance of central control, issues of water regulation and usage emerged as important points of contention between upstream and downstream states—Tajikistan and Kyrgyzstan versus Turkmenistan and Uzbekistan. *See also* WATER.

AMU DARYA TREASURES (TREASURE OF THE OXUS). This is a collection of **Iranian**, **Bactrian**, and **Sogdian** as well as Hellenic metalwork. It includes gold and silver coins, gems, figures, and other objects dated to the first millennium BCE. The treasures were found in **Qubodiyon** in 1877 by **Bukharan** merchants and were then taken to **India** for sale. The collection was later placed on display in the British Museum. In April 2007, the president of Tajikistan ordered experts to seek its return from Great Britain. *See also* ARTS.

ANZOB. A pass in the **Hisor** mountain range reaching an altitude of 3,372 meters above sea level, the Anzob is 90 kilometers north of Dushanbe. The Dushanbe-**Khujand** and Dushanbe-**Samarqand** roads pass through Anzob. This is the only way to link the south and the north without crossing national boundaries. The pass is open to traffic between June and November. In the final years of the Soviet regime, a tunnel through Anzob Pass was initiated, but construction was interrupted in its early stages. In 2006, the tunnel was completed. *See also* ISTIQLOL TUNNEL; MOTOR ROADS.

AQSAQAL (OQSAQOL). An *aqsaqal* (the Turkic word for *rish safed*, or "white beard" in **Tajik**) is a chief, elder, or administrator of a city or village. The term is also used for the head of a craft shop.

ARABS. One of the ethnic groups in Tajikistan, Arabs are descendants of Semitic Arabian nomadic tribes. They were **Sunni** Muslims who left their lands and settled in **Central Asia** in two waves, first during the Arab invasion in the 7th–8th centuries and then in the beginning of the 15th century, when **Timur** brought them to **Samarqand** after his victorious march to Damascus. Having settled in Central Asia, they were gradually assimilated into the sedentary culture of Central Asia and adopted the two main languages of the region: **Tajik** and **Uzbek**. In Tajikistan, Arabs mainly live in the southern **Khatlon veloyat** in **Shahritus**, **Qubodiyon**, Aivaj, and in the northern **Sughd veloyat** in **Khujand** and **Konibodom**. The Arabs of Tajikistan exhibit the region's cultural and ethnographical characteristics but have retained their ethnic self-awareness. This was evident in the beginning of the 1990s, when the Society of Arabs in Tajikistan was formed, which claims a membership of 20,000. Arabs also live in neighboring Turkmenistan and **Uzbekistan**, mostly in their southern areas, as well as in northern **Afghanistan**. Overpopulation and lack of arable land in southern regions of Tajikistan caused violent conflicts between Arabs and **Tajiks** at the end of 1991. During the 1992–1997 **civil war**, Tajikistani Arabs supported the pro-government **Sitodi Melli**.

ARBOB. An *arbob* is a village administrator, chieftain, or manager of communal works, especially for cleaning canals.

ARCHIVES. In June 1926, the archive of the revolutionary committee of the **Tajik Autonomous Soviet Socialist Republic** was established to collect and preserve documents of the first Tajik government. In March 1931, the government established a network of archive depositories all over the country. There are 12 state archives in Tajikistan, including the Central State Archive of Tajikistan with branches in all **nohiyas**, the Central Archive of Cinema and Photo Documents, three provincial archives, and the archive of the **Communist Party of Tajikistan**.

ARKHAR. A rare species of mountain sheep (*Ovis ammon poli*), the arkhar is big (up to 200 centimeters long and 125 centimeters high), with long legs and developed horns. A male's curved horns can reach 190 centimeters. Mature males weigh 110–120 kilograms, females 80–100 kilograms. This alpine animal can be found in **Pamir** at an altitude of 2,800–5,000 meters above sea level. More than 70,000 arkhars were registered in the area in 1969. Trophy hunting began in 1987. In the 1990s, the number of arkhars in eastern Pamir was estimated as 10,000–12,000.

ARMENIANS. Many Armenians arrived in **Central Asia** as refugees from Turkish persecution during World War I. In 1913, 15,500 Armenians lived in Central Asia. In 1917, they formed the Dashnaktsutun Nationalist Party in the **Ferghana** valley. The military wing of the party fought against the **Basmachi** in 1918–1919, but it was suppressed by the Red Army once Soviet power was consolidated in Central Asia. In the 1950s, another wave of Armenians migrated from Armenia to Tajikistan and other Central Asian republics. The Armenian community in Tajikistan in the Soviet period enjoyed access to social services and employment opportunities.

In January 1990, after Azeri-Armenian strife in Baku, Sumgait, and Nagorno-Karabakh, almost 3,000 Armenians sought shelter in **Dushanbe**. This new wave of refugees caused a backlash among Tajiks, leading to the **February 1990 events in Dushanbe**. The subsequent collapse of the **Soviet Union** and Tajikistan's **civil war** made the Armenian community uneasy about its future. In 1989, the Society of Armenians in Tajikistan named after Mesrop Mashtots was formed. It signed the **Agreement on National Accord** and joined the **Societal Council** in March 1996. The Armenian community in Tajikistan was 200 people (0.01 percent of the total population) in 1926, 5,700 (0.1 percent) in 1989, and 1,000 (0.05 percent) in 2000.

ARMY. General conscription in Tajikistan started in 1939. During **World War II**, more than 200,000 men from Tajikistan served in the Soviet Army. After the collapse of the Soviet Union, Soviet armed forces were divided into national militaries. According to the 1992 Treaty of Bishkek, all Soviet military equipment deployed within the boundaries of Soviet republics as of 31 August 1991 was declared the property of the host republics. However, the 201st division stationed in Tajikistan remained under Russian command. The government of Tajikistan tried to establish a national army in January 1993, but **civil war** interrupted that process. The **Russian Federation** provided crucial assistance in the formation of the Tajik national army. With its help, Tajikistan opened a military college with an annual enrollment of 150 cadets. More than 6,000 Tajiks were studying in military schools of the Russian Federation in 2000.

The core of Tajikistan's national armed forces was based on armed squads from **Sitodi Melli**, which brought the current regime to power in December 1992. However, the consolidation of the national army as a unitary force free of its bandit legacy was considered an urgent task. The civil war in Tajikistan, which had started in May 1992, led to the proliferation of armed self-defense bands. These groups, aligned with the two protagonists, often engaged in blood feuds and revenge killings. Following the signing of the **General Agreement on the Establishment of Peace and National Accord**, the rebel armed forces of the **United Tajik Opposition** (UTO) were incorporated into the Tajik national army. Some 2,000 troops from the UTO were absorbed into the army between 1997 and 1999. The conflict, however, has been a barrier to the establishment of a unified command system. During the 1990s, the loyalty of troops to President **Emomali Rahmon**, as commander in chief, remained suspect. Former army commander **Mahmud Khudoiberdyev** led three insurgencies against President Rahmon (January 1996, October 1997, and November 1998). The government accused **Uzbekistan** of sheltering Khudoiberdyev's forces and providing him with a hideout and a regrouping camp.

The president appoints the minister of defense, who is in charge of the army and formulating/implementing defense policies. The main commands are antiaircraft, air force, artillery, communication, infantry, and rear service. The Tajik Border Troops, previously under the Ministry of National Security, have their own directorate, separate from the national army since late 1993. The Tajik army possesses helicopters and aircraft; there is no separate air force. The army numbers 22,000 troops. Many conscript-age (18–27) young men seek migrant work outside Tajikistan to evade military service. Others bribe officials to obtain falsified certificates of service. In 2008, Tajikistan had difficulty finding 20,000 conscripts. Before the Soviet collapse

(1991), however, Tajikistan sent 120,000 men to the Soviet Army annually. Some claim state expenditure on the military amounts to 4 percent of annual GDP. In fact, however, the government spends up to one-third of total state revenue on maintenance of the military. The Tajik parliament and civil society do not have access to reports on military finance or administration.

Tajikistan is a member of the **Collective Security Treaty Organization** (15 May 1992). Its military doctrine is oriented toward Russia and the **Commonwealth of Independent States** (CIS). The CIS framework includes the Russian Federation, Belorussia, Tajikistan, Armenia, **Kyrgyzstan**, and Kazakhstan. Tajikistan is also establishing military cooperation with Germany, **China**, and **Iran**. Tajikistan's ministers of defense have included **Alexander Shishliannikov** (1993–1995) and **Sherali Khairulloev** (April 1995–present). Military expenditures are burdensome for Tajikistan, amounting to 3.9 percent of the GDP in 2008 (in 1998, 1.8 percent). *See also* COLLECTIVE PEACEKEEPING FORCE IN THE REPUBLIC OF TAJIKISTAN; RUSSIAN MILITARY BASE.

ARTS. Modern Tajiks associate their cultural heritage with a "historical Tajikistan" that is much broader than the "political Tajikistan" defined by the administrative borders drawn by the **Soviet Union** in 1924–1929. As the oldest indigenous people of **Central Asia**, they lay claim to the rich cultural legacy of their Iranian ancestors who populated a vast area, stretching from eastern Iran to western **China** and northern **India**. This approach emerged as a response to artificial borders that not only divided the peoples of Central Asia but also deprived Tajiks of their cultural centers—**Samarqand** and **Bukhara**. By associating themselves with "historical Tajikistan," modern Tajiks also oppose the old Russian/Soviet efforts to separate the Tajiks of Central Asia from Persian-speakers elsewhere.

Hellenic art became part of the culture of **Bactria** and **Sogdiana**. Sculptures, coins, gems, and other items were found at the site of the ancient town of Takhti Sangin (Throne of Stone) in **Qubodiyon nohiya**. Takhti Sangin and Ai Khanum (situated nearby on the Afghan side of the **Amu Darya**) had been inhabited by the ancestors of the **Tajiks** since the **Achaemenid** era (6th–4th centuries BCE). A collection of Bactrian, Sogdian, and Hellenic metalwork known as the **Amu Darya Treasures** was found in this area in 1877. Ancient Tajik visual art focusing on mythological and religious images can be seen in the monumental paintings and sculptures of **Panjakent, Afrasiab,** and Varakhsha (near **Bukhara**), in **Buddhist** wall paintings, and in sculptures of the **Kushan** period preserved in **Ajinateppa, Badakh- shon,** and **Tashkurgan.** When the **Arabs** invaded **Khurasan** and **Movarounnahr** in the 7th century, they found a local Iranian popu- lation competent in architecture, sculpture, book illustrating, wall painting, palace decoration, and other arts. In Panjakent, an extensive series of colorful, 7th-century wall paintings depicting the Persian epic *Shohnoma* were uncovered in the late 1950s. The *Shohnoma* influenced all art mediums, including pottery, crafts, painting, metal- work, carpet making, and graphic art.

Islamic doctrines on art treated figurative art as idolatrous. For that reason, the Arabs burned up and destroyed most paintings and banned the art of sculpture. With the arrival of **Islam**, the sophisti- cated Persian "high" culture fused with the more democratic spirit of the new religion. The charm of the Perso-Islamic cultural synthe- sis was so strong that it made the Turko-Mongol invaders fervent adherents to the cultural traditions of the subjugated local popula- tion. These conquerors made the Tajik-populated Samarqand and Bukhara the cultural centers of their empires. The most prominent Turko-Mongol ruler, **Timur**, spoke Persian as well as his native Turkic, and he is known for his patronage of Persian arts and letters. Timur laid out notable gardens around Samarqand and brought to his capital many skilled craft workers and artists from the captured cities of India, Persia, Syria, and Iraq. Chinese art had a high repu- tation in Central Asia following the Mongol invasions of the early 13th century. Rooted in the traditions of **Sassanid** court art, colorful miniatures of the **Timurid** period were inspired by the romantic spirit and beauty of Perso-Tajik poetry. Kamoliddin Behzod (1450–1535) was the greatest Persian miniature painter during the late Timurid and early **Safavid** periods. The Herat school of manuscript illustration is regarded as the apex of Perso-Tajik painting. Visual art in Persia and Central Asia followed the aniconic principles of Islam. Nonetheless, secular painting was employed widely by artists to decorate palaces and books.

The general decadence of the **Uzbek** dynasties ruling Central Asia in the 17th–20th centuries was accompanied by decadence in the arts. Tajik figurative (in fact, secular) painting had virtually perished, replaced by ornaments. Since the 19th century, the national traditions and creative talents of Tajiks flourished primarily in folk art, including metalwork, pottery, embroidery (*suzani*), wood carving, **kundal**, *gach kori* (architectural decoration), and other mediums associated mainly with the manufacture of household objects. The old names of Tajik **mahallas** (urban neighborhoods) reflect the importance of once popular crafts: Ohangaron (Blacksmiths), Pillakashon (Silk Weavers), Zargaron (Jewelers), Sangburron (Stonemasons), to name a few.

Under Soviet rule, the **mass media** and the arts were subject to political restrictions. Most Tajik folk arts lost their positions early in the Soviet period, as local products failed to compete with cheap, imported manufactured goods. As a result of the introduction of first the Latin and then the Cyrillic script, the closing of **mosques** and **madrasas**, and the elimination of **mullahs**, the art of handwriting employing Arabic script and known as Islamic calligraphy vanished. Tajik folk arts acquired some level of Soviet content to conform to political dictates.

In the first half of the 20th century, under the influence of Russian culture, Samarqand, Bukhara, **Khujand**, and then **Dushanbe** became, in turn, centers of modern Tajik art. In the late 1920s and early 1930s, Tajikistan became home for such talented Russian painters as E. G. Burtsev, M. G. Novik, P. I. Fal'bov, and A. N. Kamelin. In 1933 in Dushanbe, the Union of Artists, the School of Arts, and the Behzod Museum of Arts were opened. In the Soviet Union, the rigid doctrine of socialist realism was the only state-approved direction, and Tajik visual art, in general, lacked indigenous originality. The arts of Soviet Tajikistan were isolated from Islamic and Western culture. Once important and exciting arts, including Islamic calligraphy, were lost forever. Yet some Soviet artists managed to combine socialist realism with innovation. In the 1970s and 1980s, Tajik art became more diverse as a big group of artists familiar with modern styles of painting appeared. They tried to find their own way in art and did not want to imitate Russian artists. Among the Tajik painters of the Soviet school, Zuhur Habibulloev and Khushbakht Khushvaqtov were the most prominent.

In the 1990s, the **civil war** made many Tajikistani artists leave the country. After the marginalization of communist ideology, many other styles became known in Tajikistan and were absorbed into the arts. At the same time, some artists did not lose their connection with realism. Alexander Akilov and Rahim Safarov are among the most talented modern Tajik artists.

ASADULLOZODA, HASAN. *See* SADULLOEV, HASAN.

ASHRAFI, MUQADDAMA (1936–). Born in Tashkent to a Tajik family, Ashrafi is the daughter of Mukhtor Ashrafi, a famous composer in **Uzbekistan**. She graduated from the Tashkent Musical School in 1954 and in 1959 from the Moscow State University, where she studied art history. In 1959–1961, she worked at the Oriental Studies Department, Union of Soviet Socialist Republics (USSR) Academy of Sciences, Moscow. Between 1962 and 1968, she was a postgraduate student at the Institute of Oriental Studies, USSR Academy of Sciences. In 1969–1971, Ashrafi worked in the Department of Philosophy, **Academy of Sciences of Tajikistan** and in 1972 moved to the Institute of History at the academy. At the same time, she chaired the Department of Humanities at the Tajik Technological University. Ashrafi specializes in the **arts** and painting of medieval Central Asia. She is married to **Kamol Ayni**.

ASHT NOHIYA. Located in the **Sughd veloyat**, the Asht nohiya was formed in 1926. Asht is the most northern district of Tajikistan, situated on the slopes of the Kurama mountain range in the **Ferghana** valley. The center of the district is the **Shaidon** settlement. With a territory of 2,800 square kilometers and a population of about 811,000 people (**Tajiks** and **Uzbeks**), the district has six jamoats and two village centers. In this district, there are deposits of polimetals, fluorite, salt, and marble. Average January and July temperatures can reach –1°C and 27°C respectively; the average annual rainfall is 180 millimeters. There are 11,000 hectares of arable land. Local industries include a fruit conservation plant (Asht) and a salt plant (Qamishqurghan).

ASHUROV, ABDURAHIM (1949–). Born in **Varzob nohiya**, Ashurov graduated from the Tajik Polytechnic Institute with a degree in engineering and economics in 1971. From 1972 to 1997, he worked as an engineer at the institute, group head in the computing center at the Ministry of Automobile Transport of Tajikistan, department head of the Autotranssistema Industrial and Technical Association, deputy head and then head of the 13th Automobile Transport Unit of the Ministry of Transport, director general of the Association for Automobile Transport of the city of **Dushanbe**, and head of transport and road economy of Tajikistan. In 1997–2005, Ashurov worked as deputy and then first deputy to the minister of transport of Tajikistan. Since 2005, he has been minister of transport. In December 2006, this ministry was renamed the Ministry of Transport and Communications. *See also* GOVERNMENT.

ASIA-PLUS. The first independent media group in Tajikistan, Asia-Plus was launched in February 1996. The first issue of their information and analytical bulletin in English and Russian was brought out in April 1996. This media group publishes the weekly newspaper *Asia-Plus* in Russian (since January 2000) and the weekly bulletin *Asia-Plus* in Russian and English, which is available in print and online. In April 1997, the agency launched the daily supplement *Asia-Plus Blitz* in English and Russian. The Asia-Plus radio station started broadcasting in September 2002. The radio runs news bulletins in Tajik and Russian alternately on the hour, plays music, and is on the air in **Dushanbe** and its environs. In 2002, Asia-Plus launched a television studio producing news reports, documentary and educational films, and other programming. Since 2001, Asia-Plus has run a school of journalism. **Umed Babakhanov** is the director and founder of Asia-Plus. *See also* MANNONON, BAHROM; MASS MEDIA.

ASIMOV, MUHAMMAD (1920–1996). A Tajik politician and scholar also known as Muhammad Osimi, Asimov was an **academician** of the **Academy of Sciences of Tajikistan**, a corresponding member of the Academy of Sciences of the Union of Soviet Socialist Republics (USSR), and president of the Academy of Sciences of Tajikistan (1965–1988). Born in **Khujand**, Asimov studied at Rabfak (faculty for workers) in 1934–1937. He then moved to the Navoi State University in **Samarqand** and graduated in physics and mathematics in 1941. Asimov joined the Soviet Army after his graduation and participated in **World War II**. Between 1946 and 1952, he worked as a lecturer, then chair of physics and deputy director of the Leninobod (Khujand) State Pedagogical Institute. In 1952–1955, he studied at the Communist Party's Academy of Social Sciences in Moscow.

Between 1956 and 1962, Asimov was president of the Tajik Poly-technical Institute and in 1962 was appointed Tajikistan's minister of **education**. Between 1962 and 1965, he held various posts: chair of the control committee in the **Communist Party of Tajikistan** (CPT), secretary of the CPT, and deputy chair of Tajikistan's Soviet of Ministers. In 1965, Asimov was appointed president of the Tajikistan Academy of Sciences. His scholarly interests were the philosophy and history of sciences, history of philosophy, and Oriental studies. In the 1960s and 1970s, he was elected to the **Supreme Soviet** of the **Soviet Union** three times. Asimov founded the Paivand Society of Tajiks and Compatriots Abroad after the Soviet collapse. He was assassinated on 26 July 1996 in **Dushanbe**.

ASLONOV, QADRIDDIN (1947–1992). Born in the **Vakhsh valley** to a **Gharmi** family, Aslonov was secretary of the central committee of the **Communist Party of Tajikistan** (CPT), the first deputy of Tajikistan's Council of Ministers, and chair of the **Supreme Soviet** in 1990–1991. After the resignation of President **Qahor Mahkamov** on 31 August 1991, Aslonov became acting president. In September 1991, due to intense popular pressure, he was forced to resign from the CPT, ban the party, and permit the removal of Lenin's statue from a central square in **Dushanbe**. Aslonov was killed by **Sitodi Melli** militias in November 1992. *See also* CIVIL WAR.

ASROROV, MIRZOSHOHRUH (1953–). Born in **Ayni nohiya**, Asrorov received a degree in Oriental studies from the Tajik State University in 1975 and studied journalism at the Tashkent Institute of Political Sciences and Management, graduating in 1991. In 1975, he began working in **Afghanistan** as an interpreter and secretary of the **Komsomol** committee in a Soviet Army unit. In 1985, he became an executive official of Komsomol's central committee in Tajikistan. From 1986 to 1997, his positions included chief editor and then director of the Tajik State Radio, chief specialist of the managerial department of Tajikistan's Council of Ministers, chair of the committee on youth, head of the Ministry of Culture of Tajikistan. In 2003–2006, Asrorov headed the Department of Culture for the city of **Dushanbe**. He became Tajikistan's minister of culture in December 2006. *See also* GOVERNMENT.

ATOVULLOEV, DODOJON (1956–). Also known as Dodojoni Atovullo, Atovulloev is a dissident journalist and founder of the **Vatandor** movement. After receiving his journalism degree at the Moscow Humanities University, he worked as a reporter in **Dushanbe**. He founded the *Charogi Ruz* (Light of Day) newspaper in Tajikistan in 1991. The newspaper was closed in 1993, during the **civil war**, and Atovulloev left Tajikistan for Moscow, where he published *Charogi Ruz* in exile. In his publications, he criticized the policies of President **Emomali Rahmon** and proposed to oust him by mass actions of civil disobedience. In 2001, Atovulloev was detained in **Russia** at the request of the Tajik government. However, the Russian authorities refused to transfer him to Dushanbe and he was soon released. Since May 2006, Atovulloev has been living in Germany. Tajikistan's prosecutor general has instituted criminal proceedings against him. *See also* MASS MEDIA.

AVLOD. The extended family, known as the *avlod*, is a significant pillar of the social structure in Tajikistan and an institution of traditional authority. The avlod is a patriarchal extended family that can be developed into a clan based on patrilineage. Avlods encompass all living and deceased relatives and trace them (from the male side) to a common ancestor. In the modern age, the avlod system has considerably eroded, yet its influence can still be felt in Tajik society. According to a 1996 sociological survey, 68 percent of Tajiks consider themselves members of an avlod, and 25 percent of them trust only the head of their avlod.

AVZALOV, GHAIBULLO (1948–). Born in **Vose nohiya**, Kulob veloyat, Avzalov received a degree in veterinary science from the Tajik State Institute of Agriculture in 1969 and became chief veterinarian of a cooperative farm. In 1991, he graduated from the Tashkent Institute of Political Sciences and Management. A **candidate of sciences** in economics, he worked as head of the **Kulob** provincial department of agriculture, then as first secretary of Vose nohiya's committee of the Communist Party, director general of the Agricultural and Industrial Association in Kulob province, chair of the Safarzoda agricultural farm in Vose nohiya, deputy chair of Khatlon veloyat, director general of Tajikistan's Industrial Association of Forestry, and chair of Jilikul nohiya. Avzalov was a member of the Tajikistan **Supreme Soviet** in 1990–1995 and of the **Majlisi Namoyandagon** in 2002–2006. In February 2007, he was appointed chair of **Khatlon** veloyat.

AYNI NOHIYA. Known as Zahmatobod in 1930–1955, the Ayni nohiya, with a territory of 5,200 square kilometers, is located in the **Sughd veloyat** on the **Zarafshon River** and is named in honor of **Sadriddin Ayni**. The district was attached to the neighboring **Panjakent nohiya** in 1963 but was reformed again in 1965. It has an airport, and important highways that join **Dushanbe** with **Khujand** and with **Samarqand** run through Ayni. The district center is 177 kilometers from Khujand, 165 kilometers from Dushanbe, and 165 kilometers from Samarqand. Average July and January temperatures can reach 17°C and −1°C respectively. The average annual precipitation is 16–19 millimeters. The altitude of this mountainous region ranges from 950 meters (Urmetan) to 5,494 meters (Chimtarga) above sea level. One of the country's biggest and most beautiful lakes—**Iskandarkul**—lies in this nohiya. The **Yaghnob** historical area, populated by Yaghnobis who claim descent from the ancient **Sogdian** civilization, is located to the east of Ayni. Eight village centers (Ayni, Anzob, Dardar, Rarz, Urmetan, Fandarya, Shamtuch, and Zarafshon) are situated mainly in the Zarafshon and Fandarya valleys. The main occupation in this nohiya is **agriculture**, including tobacco, **grain**, and fruit production and livestock breeding. The republic's biggest coal mine, Fan-Yaghnob (1.8 billion ton capacity), and the gigantic **Anzob** Mountains Enriching Plant are located in Ayni.

AYNI, KAMOL (1928–). A Tajik scholar and **academician**, Ayni is the son of the writer **Sadriddin Ayni**. At the Leningrad State University, he focused on Oriental studies, graduating in 1949. Ayni worked in the Institute of (Tajik) Language and Literature at the **Academy of Sciences of Tajikistan** in 1953–1955, and he headed the Department of Manuscripts at the academy in 1956–1958. Between 1958 and 1990, he was a senior research fellow, then head of the Department of Iranian Studies and head of the Department of Manuscripts at the Institute of Oriental Studies. In 1991–1996, he headed the Department of Manuscripts at the Institute of Written Heritage of the Academy of Sciences. His research is primarily on Tajik classical **literature**. In 1996, Ayni succeeded **Muhammad**

Asimov as chair of the Paivand Society of Tajiks and Compatriots Abroad, but in 2002 he returned to the Institute of Oriental Studies. He is married to **Muqaddama Ashrafi**.

AYNI, SADRIDDIN (1878–1954). A famous Tajik writer and founder of the Soviet Tajik national **literature**, Ayni was born in the village of Gijduvan near **Bukhara**. As one of the leading reformist intellectuals of **Central Asia** in the **Jadidia** movement in the 1910s, he supported innovative liberal ideas against the conservative **Bukharan emirate**. Following the Bolshevist revolution, Ayni and other Jadidists in the early 1920s joined the Bolsheviks to overthrow the emir and revolutionize Central Asia. He was crucial in the establishment of Soviet-inspired literature in the region. In particular, he championed the formation and promulgation of a distinctive Tajik-Persian **language** and literature in the predominantly Turkic-speaking Central Asia. Ayni generated a precious treasury of poetry, fiction, journalism, historical writings, and lexicography. He was chair of the **Union of Writers of Tajikistan** (1933–1954) and the first president of the **Academy of Sciences of Tajikistan** (1951–1954). Today Ayni is regarded very highly in Tajikistan. In 1998, together with **Bobojon Ghafurov**, Ayni was awarded the newly established title National Hero of Tajikistan. *See also* AYNI, KAMOL.

AZIMOV, ABDURAHMON (1950–). Born in **Muminobod**, Kulob veloyat, Azimov studied in the Kulob Pedagogical Institute. Between 1973 and 1996, he worked in Tajikistan's state security. In 1993–1996, he headed the Provincial Department of the Ministry of Security in the **Khatlon** veloyat. He was elected to the **Majlisi Oli** in 1995 and served as Tajikistan's vice premier from August 1996 to the end of 1999. In 2000, he was elected to the **Majlisi Namoyandagon**. From January to November 2006, he chaired the State Committee on State Borders Protection. In 2007, Azimov was Tajikistan's vice premier. In January 2008, he was elected chair of the Standing Committee on Constitutional Order, Legislature, and Human Rights in the Majlisi Namoyandagon. Azimov is a member of the **People's Democratic Party of Tajikistan**.

AZIMOV, AMIRQUL (1948–). Born in **Ayni nohiya, Sughd veloyat**, Azimov studied law at the Tajik State University. After graduating in 1972, he worked as a detective, becoming chief detective of **Dushanbe** central nohiya's Procurator Office. In 1975–1979, he worked as a detective on especially important affairs in Tajikistan's Procurator Office. In 1979, he was recruited to the Communist Party's central committee. In 1987, he was appointed head of the Inquiry Department in Tajikistan's Procurator Office. From December 1992 to 1995, he was deputy minister of Internal Affairs. Azimov was appointed Tajikistan's procurator general in 1995 and chair of Tajikistan's Security Council in August 1996.

AZIMOV, YAHYO (1947–). A Tajik industrialist and politician, Azimov was born in **Khujand** and studied at the Tashkent Institute of Textile Industry. After his graduation in 1971, he worked at light industry enterprises in **Uroteppa**. Between 1975 and 1996, he worked at the Qairaqum rug plant as chief engineer, then as head of the Technical Department, director of rug production, director of the weaving factory, deputy chief engineer, and chief engineer. In 1992, he was elected president of the Kolinho stock company. Azimov served as Tajikistan's prime minister between February 1996 and December 1999. In 2000, he was appointed minister of economics and external economic relations. He lost this ministerial position in January 2001 when the Ministry of Economics and External Economical Relations and the state committee on contracts and trade were merged into a new Ministry of Economics and Trade. Since 2001, he has engaged in private business and entrepreneurship, keeping a low profile in Tajik politics.

– B –

BABAKHANOV, MANSUR (1931–). Born in **Konibodom**, Babakhanov received a degree in history from the Tajik State University in 1953. In 1958, he defended his **candidate** dissertation on the conception of capitalism in northern Tajikistan. For his **doctor of sciences** degree, his dissertation, defended in 1974, focused on relations between the Russian Bolsheviks and local toilers of **Turkistan** on the eve of the 1917 Russian Revolution. Babakhanov was dean of the history faculty in the Tajik State University from 1965 to 1974. During 1974–2000, he held various positions at the Tajik State University and Tajik-Russian Slavic University and since 2001 has been a professor at those institutions. Since 2007, he has been head of the Center for the Study of the Tajiks of the World, attached to the Tajik National University.

BABAKHANOV, UMED (1962–). A Tajik journalist and director of the **Asia-Plus** media group, Babakhanov was born in **Dushanbe** to the family of Tajik historian **Mansur Babakhanov**. He graduated from the Tajik State University in 1985, having focused on Oriental studies. He started his professional career as a journalist with the republican *Komsomolets Tadzhikistana* newspaper in 1987. In 1988–1991, he was a research fellow in the Institute of Political Studies in Dushanbe. Between 1991 and 1996, Babakhanov was a staff correspondent for the Moscow newspaper *Komsomolskaya Pravda* in Tajikistan. Between 1993 and 1999, he provided news and information on Tajikistan to the Moscow bureau of the Associated Press. Babakhanov launched Asia-Plus in February 1996. *See also* MASS MEDIA.

BACHAI SAQQAO (?–1929). An Afghani bandit, populist leader, and the only non-Pushtun (Tajik) emir of **Afghanistan**, Bachai Saqqao (literally "water carrier's son" in **Dari**) was the leader of the militant Islamist opposition to Emir Amanullah in 1928. Enthroned as the Afghan ruler Emir Habibulla II in January 1929, Bachai Saqqao openly sympathized with the Bukharan emigres in Afghanistan and the fugitive Emir **Said Alim Khan** in their attempts to restore the monarchy in **Bukhara**. In October 1929, he was overpowered and executed by British-supported Pushtun forces headed by Afghan Lord Nadir. *See also* TAJIKS OF AFGHANISTAN.

BACTRIA (BOKHTAR). An Ancient state in the 6th–2nd centuries BCE in **Amu Darya**'s middle stream, Bactria stretched from the **Hisor** mountain ranges in the north to the western Hindu Kush in the south, covering present-day northern **Afghanistan**, southwestern Tajikistan, and southeastern **Uzbekistan**. Bactria was the most ancient civilization in **Central Asia**. It seriously challenged the **Achaemenids** in the 6th century BCE and **Alexander the Great** in the 4th century BCE, but was nevertheless subdued and incorporated into the Achaemenid empire and later that of Alexander when he married

Rukhshona (Roxana), a local ruler's daughter, in order to obtain the support of the Bactrian elite. After the fall of Alexander's empire, Bactria was ruled successively by the Selevkids (est. 306 BCE), the Greco-Bactrians (est. 250 BCE), and the **Kushans** (second half of the 2nd century BCE).

Bactria is known not only as a cradle of Zoroastrianism but as a center of **Buddhism** in the region. The **Amu Darya Treasures** from Bactria are currently held at the British Museum. The Joint Archeological Expedition of the Union of Soviet Socialist Republics and Afghanistan in the 1960s discovered finds on Bactrian agriculture, trade, culture, and art in northern Afghanistan (Dilbarjin, Ai Khanum, Tilla Teppa, and others). The Bactrians were of Iranian stock and had a language close to other Iranian tongues. Together with the **Sogdians**, they were considered ancestors of the Tajiks. A district of Tajikistan, **Bokhtar nohiya**, is named after Bactria.

BADAKHSHON. A historical name for the western part of **Pamir**, Badakhshon covers northeastern **Afghanistan** (Badakhshon province) and eastern Tajikistan, where the upper stream of the **Amu Darya** flows through the **Mountainous Badakhshon Autonomous Veloyat**. The area was ruled by Hephthalites, Turks, **Arabs**, Afghans, Bukharans, and Russians. From the 13th century, a local dynasty ruled Badakhshon until the **Timurids** conquered it in the 15th century. Uzbek khans conquered this region and ruled it until 1822, when Murad Bek of Qunduz expelled the **Uzbeks** and established Afghan rule, which lasted until 1859. In the second half of the 19th century, Badakhshon grew in importance in the Anglo-Russian rivalry known as the Great Game. Negotiations resulted in the Anglo-Russian Convention of 1872 and the Demarcation of 1895. According to these agreements, **Russia** forfeited claims on territories to the south of the Amu Darya, and Great Britain passed direct control over small territories of southeastern Badakhshon, populated by **Vakhanis**, to Afghanistan. The mountainous area of Tajikistan was under Russian control after 1895. As a result of this colonial partition, Badakhshoni communities found themselves on opposite sides of the border. The establishment of the **Soviet Union** did not alter this division. Soviet power in Russian-controlled Badakhshon was established in 1918–1923. In 1925, the Mountainous Badakhshon Autonomous Veloyat was founded.

BALJUVON NOHIYA. The Baljuvon nohiya is named after a historical area in **Khatlon** veloyat, **Kulob** zone. In the 19th century, Baljuvon was part of the **Bukharan emirate**. Some 20,000 households with a total population of 60,000, mainly **Tajiks**, lived in Baljuvon in 1886. The advancing Red Army forced Jahongir, the last **bek** of Baljuvon, to flee to **Afghanistan** in 1921. In 2007, the nohiya included Sari Khosor, Kangurt, Jorub Kul, and Tutkavul village centers, with a population of 20,400, mainly Tajiks.

BALLET. See OPERA AND BALLET THEATER.

BALUCH (BALUJ, BALOJ). An ethnic group in Tajikistan of Iranian stock, the Baluch consists of **Sunni** Muslims. Several hundred Baluchis live in the southern districts of the **Khatlon** veloyat. The precise figure is unknown because they were registered as Tajiks in Soviet censuses. Baluchis speak **Tajik** but have distinctive clothing and housing structures.

BANKS. In 1994, under the guidance of the International Monetary Fund and the World Bank, reforms in Tajikistan's banking sector were launched. As of July 2007, there were nine banks and one branch of a foreign bank in Tajikistan (the Tijorat Bank Branch of **Iran** in Dushanbe), eight credit societies, one nonbanking financial institution, six micro credit deposit organizations, 23 micro lending organizations, and 38 micro lending funds. From 1 January 2005, the minimum capital for operating banks was set at $5 million and for credit societies $300,000. In 2001, Tajikistan and the International Monetary Fund agreed on a restructuring program for four of the country's largest banks: Orienbank, Tajiksodirotbank, Agroinvestbank, and Amonatbank. These banks controlled 85 percent of all assets in the banking sector but were ridden with bad debt—estimated to be about 95 percent of their overall portfolios. As of 2008, only Amonatbank remains fully state owned.

The banks in Tajikistan have not been rated by the major rating agencies, and approximately $1 billion is circulating in the Tajikistan economy outside the banking sector. The rate of consumer savings accounts remains low. During 2004–2008, the banking sector showed signs of improvement. After the government cancelled the 30 percent fee for bank transfers by physical entities in November 2001, Tajik migrant workers were more inclined to use official channels to send remittances from abroad to Tajikistan. In 2006, they sent home some $1.2 billion via Tajik commercial banks.

As of 1 May 2008, there were 12 commercial banks, including the Iranian Tijorat and Kazakh Kazcommetsbank, with a total deposit base of $689 million, and seven credit societies with total capital of $15 million. *See also* LABOR MIGRATION; NATIONAL BANK OF TAJIKISTAN.

BARLAS. An ethnic group in Tajikistan of Turkic stock, the Barlas are cattle breeders of the highlands and foothills in **Tursunzoda, Istravshan,** and **Panjakent.** Amir **Timur,** the founder of the **Timurids** (1382–1507), who is now venerated in **Uzbekistan** as a national hero, belonged to the Barlas Turks. Their precise number from 1926 to 1989 is unknown because the Barlas were registered as **Uzbeks** in Soviet censuses. An estimated 3,400 Barlas lived in Tajikistan in 2000. A greater number live in Uzbekistan, **Kyrgyzstan,** and **Afghanistan.**

BARQI TOJIK. A state joint stock holding company with a monopoly in electric power production and marketing in Tajikistan, Barqi Tojik was established in July 1992. It encompasses 23 enterprises, including the Norak, Baipaza, and Roghun hydroelectric stations, local electricity grids, and other entities. *See also* POWER GENERATION; TALCO.

BARTANG. The Bartang is a river in **Pamir,** a tributary of the Panj River, known as Aksu in its headwaters and as **Murghob** midway. With a total length of 654 kilometers, the Bartang runs through Pamir from east to west and enters the Panj River near Rushan.

BARTANGI. The Bartangi people constitute an ethnic group in the Bartang river basin, in the **Rushan nohiya** of the **Mountainous Badakhshon Autonomous Veloyat.** The total number of Bartangis is estimated at about 5,000. *See also* PAMIRIAN LANGUAGES.

BASMACHI. Fighters against Soviet rule in **Central Asia,** the Basmachi (Turkic for "robbers" or "bandits") appeared soon after the establishment of Soviet power in the **Ferghana** valley in 1918 and **Eastern Bukhara** at the end of 1920. The Basmachi movement reached its peak in the summer of 1922, when **Enver Pasha** raised 28,000 fighters all over Central Asia, especially in Tajikistan. In 1926, the Basmachi movement in Tajikistan suffered major defeats, forcing the Basmachi leader **Ibrahimbek** and remnants of his followers to flee to **Afghanistan**. Between 1926 and 1932, Basmachis carried out sporadic raids across the border into Soviet territories, mostly into Tajikistan. By the middle of the 1930s, the combination of Soviet military force, repressive measures against local supporters of the Basmachis, and improving economic conditions in Tajikistan undermined the Basmachis' ability to operate in Tajikistan. The border with Afghanistan was effectively sealed, preventing Basmachi penetration and putting an end to the resistance movement. Some sources report that Basmachis reemerged during **World War II** in mountainous regions of Tajikistan.

BEDORII TOJIK (TAJIK'S AWAKENING). The first Tajik Soviet newspaper, *Bedorii Tojik* was founded in March 1925 under the name *Idi Tojik* (Tajik's Feast) with a circulation of 1,000. From the second issue, the paper was renamed *Bedorii Tojik* and the circulation increased to 2,500. Between 1928 and January 1955, the paper was known as *Tojikistoni Surkh* (Red Tajikistan), and it was the organ of the central committee of the **Communist Party of Tajikistan**. Between 1955 and 1992, it was called *Tojikistoni Soveti* (Soviet Tajikistan). In 1991, *Tojikistoni Soveti* changed its name to *Junhuriyat* (Republic). *See also* MASS MEDIA.

BEK. A Turkic term, *bek* (ruler, master, sir) is a title for tribal leaders or feudal lords in the Near and Middle East. Relations between beks and central governments took a variety of forms. If the latter were strong, as in some periods of the **Bukharan emirate** or tsarist **Russia**, the beks could serve as municipal rulers on behalf of the central government and as semi-independent tribal chiefs. However, in periods of the central control's decline, the beks emerged as local sovereigns with almost unrestricted power within their domains. After the establishment of Soviet power and the elimination of the **Basmachi** movement, the beks disappeared as a sociopolitical phenomenon, but the term remains in use as an honorific title. *See also* IBRAHIMBEK.

BESHKENT. A valley in the **Shahritus nohiya, Khatlon** veloyat, Beshkent is a lowland area, 70 kilometers in length and 5 kilometers in width. It is dry, without any reliable source of water. Beshkent is the warmest valley in Tajikistan, with average temperatures in January and July of 3°C and 31°C respectively. The average annual precipitation is 140 millimeters.

BIOTUN (BIBI HOTUN). A religiously educated woman, a *biotun* is similar to a **mullah**. A biotun teaches religion to girls and performs religious rituals for and among women. *See also* FARANJI.

BOBO. The term *bobo* is used for a grandfather or old person.

BOBOEV (BOBOZODA), GHULOMJON (1957–). Born to a **Khujandi** family, Boboev received a degree in economics from the Tajik State University in 1979. He received his **candidate of sciences** degree in economics at the Almaty Institute of Economy, Academy of Sciences of Kazakhstan. In 1983–1989, Boboev was vice dean of the Department of Economics and Finance at the Tajik State University. In 1989–1990, he was a member of the state commission for economic reform of the government of Tajikistan. From 1990 to 1991, he was first deputy to the minister of finance. In 1991, Boboev was appointed head of the Department of Economics and Finances attached to the Cabinet of Ministers. Later he returned to the post of the deputy minister. In May 1996, President **Emomali Rahmon** appointed Boboev state adviser. From 2002–2006, he was minister for state incomes and collections. In December 2006, this ministry was renamed the Ministry of Economic Development and Trade, and Boboev was appointed the minister. He became Tajikistan's ambassador to Japan in October 2009. *See also* GOVERNMENT.

BOBOJON GHAFUROV NOHIYA. Located in the **Sughd veloyat**, this nohiya was formed in 1936 and until 1957 was known as the Leninobod nohiya. In 1957, the district was renamed **Khujand** nohiya. In June 1999, it was renamed in honor of **Bobojon Ghafurov**. The nohiya is 2,651 square kilometers with a population of about 260,000, mostly **Tajiks** and **Uzbeks**, but also **Kyrgyz, Russians**, Tatars, and others. There are 11 **jamoats** in this nohiya. The center is Ghafurov city, with a population of more than 14,000.

Average July and January temperatures can reach 28°C and –5°C respectively. The main occupation is **agriculture**, including **cotton** growing, gardening, and livestock breeding. The total arable land is 248,215 hectares.

BOBOKHONOV, BOBOJON (1945–). Tajikistan's prosecutor general, Bobokhonov was born in Kulob veloyat and in 1973 graduated from the Tajik State University, where he studied law. Between 1973 and 1978, he was a detective in the prosecutor's office of the **Vakhsh** nohiya, and in 1978–1979 he acted as prosecutor in the **Qurghonteppa** veloyat. In 1979–1985, Bobokhonov was deputy prosecutor of the Vakhsh nohiya, and in 1985–1990 was prosecutor of the Panj nohiya. In 1990–1993, Bobokhonov was senior assistant to the prosecutor of the Qurghonteppa veloyat, in 1993–1996 prosecutor of the **Khatlon** veloyat, and in 1996–1997 prosecutor of the Leninobod (**Sughd**) veloyat. Between 1997 and 2000, he acted as first deputy prosecutor general of Tajikistan. On 16 April 2000, he was appointed Tajikistan's prosecutor general.

BOKHTAR NOHIYA. Situated in the **Khatlon** veloyat, **Qurghonteppa** zone, in the **Vakhsh valley**, the Bokhtar nohiya was formed in 1980 and was known as the Communisti nohiya until 1992. The district is 633 square kilometers, with a population of 200,000 (20,000 urban dwellers), mainly **Tajiks** and **Uzbeks**, living in eight **jamoats** and 128 **qyshloqs**. The distance from the center of this nohiya, Somoni township (known as Oktyabrskiy until 1998), to **Dushanbe** is 113 kilometers, and to Qurghonteppa 16 kilometers. Average temperatures in January and July can reach –5°C and 30°C respectively; the average annual precipitation is 200–300 millimeters. The main occupation is **agriculture**, including **cotton** and grain production and livestock breeding. There are 24,771 hectares of arable land. *See also* BACTRIA.

BORBAD. A famous musician and singer, Borbad was a poet at the court of the **Sassanid** Shah Khosrov Parvez (590–628). In Perso-Tajik tradition, Borbad became synonymous with flawless singing. In 1990, Tajikistan celebrated the 1,400th anniversary of Borbad. The biggest concert hall in **Dushanbe** is named after him. *See also* MUSIC.

BUDDHISM. This **religion** first appeared in India around the 6th–5th centuries BCE. Archeological excavations in Darsha village in **Badakhshon** unearthed religious texts written in the Hindi script of Kharoshti (dating back to the 2nd–1st centuries BCE), testifying to the ancient presence of Buddhism in the territory that constitutes today's Tajikistan. Findings in **Ajinateppa** in the **Vakhsh valley** demonstrate that before the arrival of Islam in the 8th century, Buddhism together with Zoroastrianism and Manichaeism were widespread.

BUKHARA. The provincial center of the Bukharan province (from 1938) in **Uzbekistan**, Bukhara is home to a large **Tajik** community. Bukhara was established approximately 2,500 years ago. In the 9th–10th centuries, it was the seat of the **Samanid** dynasty, which embraced the whole territory of **Movarounnahr** and **Khurasan**. In ancient and early medieval times, Bukhara was a major trading hub on the Silk Road and a principal center of culture and the **arts**. Many famous Tajik poets and scholars, such as **Rudaki**, Daqiqi, Bal'ami, **Ibn Sino** (Avicenna), and Narshakhi, were connected with Bukhara, which had one of the richest libraries of the East, Savon-ul-Hikmat. Bukhara is internationally famous for its architectural heritage, which includes the Bukharan Ark (royal residence), the Kalon minaret, and the Ismail Somoni Mausoleum.

After the fall of the Samanids in 999, Bukhara came under the control of Turkic and Mongolian tribal dynasties such as the Karakhanids, Karakitais, Chingizids, and **Timurids**. In 1506, nomadic **Uzbek** tribes under the command of Shaybani Khan won control over Bukhara and established the Bukharan khanate. From the beginning of the 16th century to 1920, Bukhara was the seat of power for the Bukharan khanate and its successor, the **Bukharan emirate**, which was formed in 1754. Soviet power was established in this territory after the **Bukharan Revolution** in 1920, and the city became the capital of the newly established **Bukharan People's Soviet Republic**. In 1924, after the national delimitation of **Central Asia**, Bukhara entered the Soviet Socialist Republic of **Uzbekistan**. *See also* BUKHARAN SOVIET SOCIALIST REPUBLIC.

BUKHARAN EMIRATE. The biggest political entity in **Central Asia** in the 16th–20th centuries, the emirate was known as the Bukharan khanate between 1557 and 1753. The khanate was established in

1557 by the **Shaybanids** after the disintegration of the **Timurids**. The Bukharan khanate included vast territories from Persian **Khurasan** to Kashgar, and from the Aral Sea to the foothills of the Hindu Kush. Internal rivalries in the 17th century led to the replacement of the Shaybanids by the Ashtarkhanids, who remained locked in conflict with the neighboring Persian empire as well as with the tribal federations of Kazakhs to the north. Weakened by perpetual conflict and internal strife, the khanate suffered defeat at the hands of Nadir Shah of Persia in 1740 and lost large parts of its southern territories.

In 1753, the Manghyt, the last Uzbek dynasty, came to power in Bukhara. The Manghyts called themselves emirs to signify their devotion to Islam, giving the name emirate to their domain. During their reign, Bukhara fell into decay, lost Khiva and Kokand, and suffered a loss of real control over the eastern parts of the emirate (currently central and eastern Tajikistan). The emirate consisted of 25 provinces (veloyats) populated primarily by **Uzbeks**, **Tajiks**, and **Turkmens**. The power of the Bukharan emirate was further undermined by recurring wars with its Central Asian neighbors, the khanates of Kokand and Khiva, leaving the region open to Russian encroachments. In 1868, Emir Muzaffar's forces were defeated by the Russian imperial army and Bukhara was reduced to a Russian protectorate. At the beginning of September 1920, after the **Bukharan Revolution**, the emirate collapsed entirely and Emir **Said Alim Khan** escaped to Afghanistan. The **Bukharan People's Soviet Republic** was proclaimed in September 1920. *See also* BUKHARA.

BUKHARAN PEOPLE'S SOVIET REPUBLIC (BPSR). The Bukharan republic (1920–1924) was established in the wake of the **Jadidia** movement and the **Bukharan Revolution**. It covered a territory of 182,193 square kilometers with a population of more than 2 million: 50 percent **Uzbeks**, 31.8 percent **Tajiks**, and others including **Turkmens**, **Jews of Bukhara**, **Arabs**, and Iranians. The BPSR capital was the city of **Bukhara**, and the Tajik **language** was widely used in official affairs, business, and trade. The current republic of Tajikistan covers **Eastern Bukhara**, the BPSR's eastern regions: **Hisor**, **Khatlon**, Qarategin, and **Darvoz**.

The inaugural convention of the All-Bukharan Revolutionary Committee chaired by Muhiddinov Abduqadir in September 1920 officially proclaimed the creation of the BPSR. It also oversaw the creation of the government, the Soviet of People's Nazirs, chaired by **Faizullo Khojaev**, and the Supreme Revolutionary Tribunal. Another member of the Jadidia movement, Usman Khojaev, was appointed chair of the Bukharan **central executive committee** (CEC). The constitution of the BPSR was adopted in September 1921. The Communist Party of Bukhara (CPB) dominated the BPSR and facilitated the signing of bilateral agreements between **Russia** and the newborn Bukharan republic. Moscow's influence over Bukhara grew in 1922, when the CPB joined the Russian Communist Party (Bolshevik). BPSR rule was marred by continuous armed struggle against the **Basmachis**, especially in Eastern Bukhara, headed by **Said Alim Khan, Ibrahimbek**, and **Enver Pasha**. The responsibility for control over southern Tajikistan, which was in the throes of civil war in 1922–1924, rested with the All-Bukharan CEC's Extraordinary Dictatorial Commission on Eastern Bukhara Affairs (Chedeka). In September 1924, the BPSR gave way to the **Bukharan Soviet Socialist Republic**, and in October, as a result of the national delimitation of Central Asia, the Bukharan republic ceased to exist.

BUKHARAN REVOLUTION. The forcible overthrow of the **Bukharan emirate** and Emir **Said Alim Khan** by Soviet troops and Bukharan communists in the **Communist Party of Bukhara** on 31 August–2 September 1920, the Bukharan Revolution led to the establishment of the **Bukharan People's Soviet Republic**.

BUKHARAN SOVIET SOCIALIST REPUBLIC (BSSR). The **Bukharan People's Soviet Republic** adopted this new title on 19 September 1924, at the fifth All-Bukharan Congress of Soviets. The congress adopted a policy of launching a "socialist construction" program with help from "the advanced Russian proletariat" and transforming the feudal (emiri) regime. The BSSR's life was very short. In October 1924, the national delimitation of **Central Asia** led to the formation of the **Tajik Autonomous Soviet Socialist Republic** as part of the Uzbek Soviet Socialist Republic. *See also* BUKHARAN REVOLUTION.

BUKHOROI SHARIF. The first Tajik-language newspaper, *Bukhoroi Sharif* (Noble Bukhara) was published from 11 March 1912 to 2

January 1913 in Kogon, a suburb of **Bukhara**, under Russian subordination. *Bukhoroi Sharif* was published with the consent of tsarist officials in Kogon and the financial support of modernist Bukharan merchants. **Ayni**, Fitrat, and other **Jadids** cooperated with the newspaper, which propagated liberal and modernist views. A total of 153 issues were published before the paper was banned by the Bukharan government. To honor and commemorate the first issue, in 1998 the government of Tajikistan decreed the inauguration of Journalist Day on 11 March, replacing the Soviet Media Day, 5 May. *See also* MASS MEDIA.

BUZKASHI. A Tajik **sport** similar to polo and played on horseback, *buzkashi* (Tajik for "goat grabbing") is also popular in **Afghanistan**, **Uzbekistan**, **Kyrgyzstan**, Turkmenistan, and Kazakhstan. Among the Turkic people, the sport is known as *ko'k boru* and *ulaq tartysh*. Riders play individually and in teams. They have to grab a "goat," the wet carcass of a calf that weighs around 50 kilograms, then ride until they can manage to get clear of the other players, return to the starting point, and drop the carcass in a circle. Competition is usually ferocious, and riders have to protect themselves against other players' whips and boots. Buzkashi is played at **tuis**, **Nawruz** celebrations, and other national holidays, and can last for several days. The winning team or individuals receive valuable gifts (cattle, carpets, or in later years cars) or cash as a prize. Buzkashi has been played in Tajikistan for centuries.

–C –

CALENDARS. Tajikistan's official calendar since 1922 is the Gregorian, but religious institutions continue to use the Islamic Qamari (lunar) system. The Qamari and Shamsi (solar, secular, not adopted in Tajikistan) calendars date from the **hijrah** (hijra, hegira), the migration of the Prophet Muhammad and his followers from hostile Mecca to friendly Medina in 662. A Qamari year is 11 days shorter than the Georgian year. Consequently, the holy month of **Ramazon**, **Idi Qurbon**, and other religiously linked **national holidays** fall 11 days earlier each year, rotating around the seasons, completing a full cycle every 32–33 years.

CANDIDATE OF SCIENCES. Introduced in 1934, the candidate of sciences (*nomzadi fanho*) was the first academic degree in the **Soviet Union**, including Tajikistan. This degree was awarded by the Specialized Academic Council (at the most distinguished universities and academic institutions) to university graduates who passed their exams and publicly defended their candidate dissertations. It is equivalent to the doctor of philosophy degree in the **United States** and United Kingdom. *See also* ACADEMICIAN; ACADEMY OF SCIENCES OF TAJIKISTAN; DOCTOR OF SCIENCES; EDUCATION.

CENTRAL ASIA. In the heartland of the Eurasian subcontinent, Central Asia (*Sredniaya Aziya* in Russian) is the home of the **Tajiks**. The Central Asia designation was introduced to political and geographical terminology by Western and Russian explorers in the mid-19th century in the course of the Great Game, the competition for influence and control in the region. In cultural and historical terms, Central Asia is the western, Turko-Iranian part of Eurasia, whose indigenous population consisted of various Iranian peoples, most of whom have been Turkicized by now. The region stretches from the Caspian Sea in the west to the Altai Mountains (**Russia**) and Turfan oasis (**China**) in the east, and from the Kazakh steppes and southern Siberia in the north to the Hindu Kush range (**Afghanistan**) in the south. Central Asia is often identified with the five post-Soviet Central Asian republics plus eastern **Iran**, northern Afghanistan, and the Xinjiang province of China. *See also* KHURASAN; MOVAROUNNAHR.

CENTRAL ASIAN COOPERATION ORGANIZATION (CACO). A regional organization of the **Commonwealth of Independent States**, CACO was initially called the Central Asian Economic Union (CAEU), which was formally established on 30 April 1994 after the signing of the Agreement on the Formation of a Common Economic Space between Kazakhstan, **Kyrgyzstan**, and **Uzbekistan**. Tajikistan joined this agreement on 17 July 1998 and the Organization was then renamed the Central Asian Economic Cooperation (CAEC). On 28 February 2002, the CAEC was transformed into the Central Asian Cooperation Organization. Aside from some measures aimed at tax harmonization, including avoiding double taxation and the creation of the Interstate Bank of Cooperation and Development, the measures taken within the CAEC were relatively unsuccessful. On 28

May 2004, **Russia** joined CACO, and the center of gravity shifted. On 7 October 2005 at the CACO summit held in St. Petersburg, it was decided that CACO would merge with the **Eurasian Economic Community** (Eurasec).

CENTRAL ASIAN RAILWAY. The Central Asian Railway, a network of **railways** in **Uzbekistan**, Turkmenistan, Tajikistan, **Kyrgyzstan**, and Kazakhstan, made up part of the Soviet railway system. The total length of this railway is 6,200 kilometers. Its construction began in 1880 and continued up to 1914. In the west, by means of the Krasnovodsk-Baku ferry crossing, the railway connects with the Transcaucasus, and in the north it links with Kazakhstan railways (Chengeldy and Beineu stations). In the east, the network approaches the Chinese border, in the **Ferghana** valley. In 1991, the administration of this network was divided into national segments.

CENTRAL EXECUTIVE COMMITTEE (CEC). In 1918–1937, central executive committees (*tsentral'nyi ispolnitelnyi komitet* in Russian, and *kumitai ijroiyai markazi* in **Tajik**) were the supreme legislative, governing, and supervising bodies, elected by the **Congress of Soviets** and operating in the interval between congresses. The All-Bukharan CEC was formed in 1921, the **Tajik Autonomous Soviet Socialist Republic** CEC in 1924, and the **Tajik Soviet Socialist Republic** CEC in 1929. In 1938, the CEC was replaced by Tajikistan's **Supreme Soviet**. CECs were chaired in 1924–1933 by **Nusratullo Maqsum**, in 1933–1936 by **Shirinsho Shotemur**, in 1936–1937 by **Abdullo Rahimboyev**, and in 1937–1938 by **Minovar Shagadaev**. *See also* SOVIET OF PEOPLE'S DEPUTIES.

CHAGHATAIS. An ethnic group in Tajikistan and other parts of **Central Asia**, Chaghatais are of a Turko-Mongol stock with no tribal affiliation. Chaghatais consider themselves descendants of Chaghatai, Genghiz Khan's second son. They resisted later Turkic invaders in the 16th century. However, like other early Turkic groups, Chaghatais were assimilated, not only by **Uzbeks** but also by **Tajiks** in **Kulob**. In 1924, there were about 6,000 Chaghatais in southern Tajikistan. They constituted 3.5 percent of the total Uzbek population. Their current size is unknown because Chaghatais are no longer registered officially as a separate identity.

CHANG. A harplike, wing-shaped musical instrument, the chang is used in Tajik classical **music**. The chang has a wooden body and 42 three-chord steel strings. Sound is produced using two percussion sticks made of reed or bamboo.

CHINA. Tajikistan and the People's Republic of China share a 430-kilometer border in the eastern **Pamirs**. China, with a population of 1 billion and the third largest economy in the world, is Tajikistan's largest neighbor and a rapidly growing world power holding nuclear weapons. The **Tajiks** and Chinese have a long history of cooperation and mutually beneficial exchanges in trade, culture, and **religion**. Iranian peoples who lived in the territory of present-day Tajikistan were intermediaries on the Silk Road between China, the Middle East, South Asia, and Europe.

In 138 BCE, the first Chinese diplomatic mission, led by Chang Chien, was dispatched to the **Ferghana** valley. By the first century CE, the Han Chinese had developed business and diplomatic relations with **Sogdiana** and **Bactria**. The **Kushans** (2nd–4th centuries CE), who bordered with the Han in China, played an important role in the expansion of **Buddhism** by spreading the faith to the Sogdiana. Later, Sogdian merchants and missionaries brought this religion to China. Religious movements, particularly **Sufism**, played an equally important role in the preservation of **Islam** both in western China and **Movarounnahr**. Traders from the Tajik **Badakhshon**, **Bukhara**, and **Samarqand** brought the **Naqshbandiyah** order to Altishahr (six cities in the Tarim basin with a center in Kashghar) as early as the 14th century. From its base in Altishahr, the Naqshbandiyah spread further into China.

Actual Chinese control over its northwestern frontiers was established by the Qing dynasty (1644–1912), which gradually extended Chinese influence westward into the area that is now the Xinjiang-Uighur Autonomous Region, also known as Eastern (or Chinese) **Turkistan**. In the mid-18th century, Qianlong, the greatest of the Manchu emperors, brought Qing imperial rule there. This region, which today takes up about one-sixth of the territory of China, has been populated by various ethnic groups of Central Asian origin, including Tajiks. The decay of the Qing power resulted in the loss of Eastern Turkistan to local people who often allied with Muslim (**Uzbek-Kyrgyz**-Tajik) forces in the neighboring **Kokand khanate**.

According to a treaty signed in 1835, Kokand was allowed to open commercial agencies in the Altishahr and an embassy in Kashghar. Despite diplomatic exchanges and some privileges granted to the Tajik, Uzbek, and Kyrgyz traders, the conflict between the Muslims of the region and the Chinese authorities continued. It culminated in a Muslim incursion into Kashghar in 1865 by an allegedly Tajik adventurer, **Yakub Beg**. His rule was brutally oppressed by the Chinese in 1877 and the province was proclaimed Xinjiang (New Domain).

During the republican period (1912–1949), the province had been virtually independent from the weak central government, and the provincial authorities of Xinjiang were vulnerable to Russian/Soviet pressures. Soviet interventions and civil disturbances of the predominantly Muslim population that resulted in the establishment of the Turkic-Islamic Republic of Eastern Turkistan (1933–1934) and the East Turkistan Republic (1944–1949) were discontinued in 1949 when the Liberation Army of China entered Xinjiang and the People's Republic of China was declared. Six years later, the semi-independence of the province was abolished and the Xinjiang-Uighur Autonomous Region was formed. The high-altitude border between China and the **Tajik Soviet Socialist Republic** was securely sealed off, and the Pamirs turned into one of the world's most isolated and neglected regions.

The People's Republic of China was one of the first countries that recognized Tajikistan's independence and sovereignty. Its policy has followed the Five Principles of Peaceful Coexistence, which are premised on irreversible sovereignty and the expectation of reciprocal noninterference in internal affairs. Diplomatic relations between Tajikistan and China were established on 4 January 1992. During the **civil war** that afflicted Tajikistan in 1992–1997, China took a position of nonintervention and awaited the emergence of a stable regime in Tajikistan.

Unlike other (Turkic) Central Asian states, Tajikistan, as a Persian-speaking state, is immune from pan-Turkism; there is no ground to suggest that Tajikistan would support Uighur (Turkic) separatism in western China. Some 40,000 **Tajiks of China** living in the Xinjiang province express no irredentist or separatist feelings that might threaten the integrity of China. As of 2009, no Uighur groups living in Tajikistan were documented. Since the early 1990s, Tajikistan's internal market has become addicted to cheap Chinese goods, although no evidence of large-scale immigration of Chinese citizens to Tajikistan has been detected.

The only source of tension between China and Tajikistan was China's claim on the eastern part of the Tajik Pamirs. The dispute on the **China-Tajik border** was finally solved through a compromise in 2002. The settlement of the border dispute coincided with the international intervention in **Afghanistan** in October 2001 and the ensuing stabilization of both Afghanistan and Tajikistan. Beijing also realized that Islamic nationalism, not to mention pan-Turkism, posed no serious danger to China in Tajikistan. This allowed China to open the **Kulma** Pass on the border between the Xinjiang-Uighur Autonomous Region of China and Tajikistan in May 2004.

The Chinese stuck exclusively to market-oriented economic growth policies in Tajikistan while ignoring issues related to democracy, **human rights**, and political pluralism. Of special importance for Tajikistan is China's support of cross-border trade and building new transport connections. In addition to bringing security, these projects are likely to transform a natural resource-poor and landlocked Tajikistan into a transit country. China supports **power generation** projects in Tajikistan. In early 2007, China decided to invest $269 million in a 150 megawatt hydroelectric station on the **Zarafshon River**, but after the Uzbek authorities' energetic protests, this project was stalled. Tashkent argued that building dams on the Zarafshon will result in a deterioration of the irrigation system in four provinces of **Uzbekistan**.

Tajikistan is an active member of the China-led **Shanghai Cooperation Organization** (SCO). Within the SCO, Tajikistan and China have common interests in fighting **terrorism**, separatism, extremism, and **drug trafficking**. Chinese priorities in Tajikistan also include protecting access to Central Asian energy resources for the growing industry in Xinjiang province, securing infrastructure and transport corridors to the **Commonwealth of Independent States** and European markets, and resisting the growing influence of the United States in the region. *See also* FOREIGN INVESTMENT; FOREIGN POLICY; FOREIGN TRADE.

CHINA-TAJIK BORDER. Some 430 kilometers in length, this border separates the **Murghob nohiya** of the **Mountainous Badakhshon Autonomous Veloyat** (MBAV) from the Xinjiang-Uighur Autonomous Region of the People's Republic of **China**. This mountainous boundary runs along the **Sarikol** mountain range in eastern Tajikistan, reaching in **Pamir** the Afghan border at the Povalo-Shveikovskogo peak (5,543 meters above sea level). The **Kulma Pass** on this border is the main crossing point, connecting Tajikistan with the **Karakoram Highway**.

Until the end of the 19th century, the border between China and the territory of today's Tajikistan was designated only in general outline. In 1864, **Russia** and China signed the Protocol of Chuguchak, an important step in border settlement. The Pamirs, where the Chinese, Russian, and British empires intersected, was the focus of intense maneuvers. The Anglo-Russian agreement of 1873 (Granville-Gorchakov) delimited the border in Pamir by establishing a **Vakhan** corridor as a narrow Afghan buffer zone between British India and Russian **Central Asia**. However, the Russian and British foreign ministers did not draw the line eastward to meet the Chinese boundary. After **Yaqub Bek**'s ousting, the Chinese returned to take an active interest in Pamir and set up a fort in **Tashkurgan** in 1892. In 1894, after an exchange of diplomatic notes, the Chinese and Russians in practice partitioned the Pamirs along the Sarikol range. Between 1898 and 1901, in spite of China's protests, Russia had a temporary post at Sarikol.

Later, Communist China protested the major border agreements reached with tsarist Russia, claiming they were imposed on China after its defeat in the second Opium War (1856–1860) and that they stripped China of 1.5 million square kilometers of territory. According to China, tsarist Russia in 1892 occupied more than 20,000 square kilometers of "sacred Chinese territory" west of the Sarikol range.

Since the demise of the **Soviet Union**, China has attempted to solve border issues with Russia and other neighboring ex-Soviet states. Taking into account the troubled political situation in Tajikistan during the 1990s, China did not insist on a final settlement of the border problem, though Beijing openly questioned the accuracy of the Tajik-Chinese border. This dispute was addressed within a commission formed in 1992 by China, Russia, Tajikistan, Kazakhstan, and Kyrgyzstan. In 1992–1995, this commission failed to produce a border agreement. The border issue between China and its post-Soviet neighbors was largely solved within the Shanghai Five forum founded in 1996, later renamed the **Shanghai Cooperation Organization**

(SCO). An interim agreement, signed in April 1996, stipulated that no attacks would be launched across the border in either direction, and this agreement became the basis for a working relationship between the governments involved in the dispute.

In the border treaty signed with China in August 1999, Tajikistan retained sovereignty over a disputed area near the Karazak pass and ceded to China around 200 square kilometers of the area near the Markansu River (the northern part of the China-Tajik border). In a July 2000 border agreement involving China, Tajikistan, and Kyrgyzstan, the sides agreed to maintain the status quo before a final settlement is reached. In the summer of 2002, Tajikistan signed an agreement on border delimitation with China, solving a historical dispute, and relinquished some 992 square kilometers of disputed lands in the eastern Pamirs. The Tajik governmental position was that the territorial concession was insignificant compared with what the Chinese obtained from Russia, Kazakhstan, and Kyrgyzstan, and that this concession would improve the Tajik bid to reach the harbor of Karachi (Pakistan) via the Karakoram Highway in China. The demarcation of the border began in June 2006, and the China-Tajikistan border dispute now seems to have been resolved through the compromise between both sides. *See also* FOREIGN POLICY; TAJIKS OF CHINA.

CIVIL WAR (1992–1997). Armed clashes rocked post-Soviet Tajikistan in 1992 after months of rising tensions between the opposition and the ruling **Communist Party of Tajikistan** (CPT). In November 1991, CPT leader **Rahmon Nabiev** defeated the opposition candidate, **Davlatnazar Khudonazarov**, in the first direct presidential election. The results were challenged by the **Democratic Party of Tajikistan**, **Islamic Renaissance Party of Tajikistan**, **La'li Badakhshon**, and **Rastokhez**, who also had the backing of democrats in Moscow. On 6 March 1992, the mayor of **Dushanbe**, Maqsud Ikramov, was arrested on charges of corruption. But the opposition claimed this was a trumped-up charge against Ikramov, who had allowed the removal of Lenin's statue from the city center. Ikramov's arrest galvanized the opposition. Rallies were held in Dushanbe in support of Ikramov and demanding the disbanding of the Soviet-era elected **Supreme Soviet** and fresh elections to a new parliament. Support from democrats in Moscow and the fall of the pro-communist Najibullah government in

Afghanistan in April 1992 boosted the confidence of the Tajik opposition. On 17 April 1992, the Supreme Soviet of Tajikistan agreed to fresh parliamentary elections. **Safarali Kenjaev** resigned from his post as parliamentary chair but was immediately appointed head of Tajikistan's state security committee (KGB), now known as the state committee for national security.

Meanwhile, people from the valleys of Qarategin and **Vakhsh** and the **Kulob** and **Leninobod** veloyats were bused to Dushanbe by the opposing sides to show their popular strength. The capital city became the venue for two opposite rallies. The Democratic-Islamic bloc demonstrated in Shahidon square near the presidential palace, while a Kulobi-dominated pro-Nabiev rally gathered in Ozodi square near the Supreme Soviet building. On 2 May, Nabiev used his emergency powers to arm his Kulobi supporters and form a presidential guard, which later became the backbone of **Sitodi Melli**. Open street clashes began in May 1992, when the opposition captured the state television station and the presidential palace and attacked the office of the KGB.

In order to avoid an escalation of the violence, an attempt at reconciliation was made. The compromise deal stipulated Nabiev's continued presidency and the inclusion of opposition representatives in one-third of the government positions. The **Government of National Reconciliation** was formed on 11 May and was expected to stay in office until new presidential and parliamentary elections could be held. This compromise, however, did not ease tensions, which were increasingly taking on a regional coloring. Kulobis headed by Sangak Safarov, whose followers called him the "people's general," rejected the compromise and left Dushanbe for Kulob with their newly acquired guns.

In Kulob, the pro-Nabiev forces launched a campaign of terror against the opposition but met with fierce resistance from **Gharmi** residents of the Vakhsh valley. The civil war very soon acquired an interregional character. Islamists, the dominant force in Dushanbe and Kofarnihon (currently **Vahdat**), tried to place an embargo against Kulob and cut off food supplies. This was thwarted by goods supplied by air from Leninobod. The Leninobodi provincial leadership did not recognize the new government in Dushanbe and provided arms and supplies to Kulob in order to oust opposition leaders from office. The stated objective of the newly formed Sitodi Melli in Kulob was to restore the "legitimate government of President Nabiev" and break the blockade against the Kulob veloyat. As violence increased, ideological proclamations for the civil war were overshadowed by regional animosities.

The opposition was supported by Gharmis and Pamirs who united in the Najoti Vatan front. The civil war, which engulfed southern parts of Tajikistan, was most fiercely fought in the **Khatlon** veloyat. The most intense fighting took place in the second half of 1992 in the **Qurghonteppa** veloyat. In August 1992, nearly 100 armed opposition forces stormed the presidential palace and took 35 hostages, including some ministers. Nabiev, who was trying to escape to Leninobod, was arrested and forced to resign. **Akbarsho Iskandarov**, from **Badakhshon**, the chair of the Supreme Soviet, became the acting president of Tajikistan.

Russian troops in Tajikistan, the 201st Rifle Division, had tried to maintain neutrality, although providing limited assistance with weapons (including tanks and artillery) to anti-Islamist forces in Qurghonteppa. On 23–24 October 1992, Kenjaev, who had escaped to **Uzbekistan**, led a column of Uzbek and Tajik military groups from the Tajik-Uzbek border in Hisor toward the Tajik capital. After two days of heavy fighting and the loss of hundreds of lives, Kenjaev's advance was defeated. But pro-Nabiev forces in Qurghonteppa were scoring remarkable victories.

The opposition representatives in the coalition government openly rejected the Islamic model of government. But actions by some Islamists in the streets of Dushanbe, who harassed Russians and women wearing European clothing, caused concern. The government began to limit Russian-language radio and television programs, and it banned television programs from Uzbekistan. These were substituted by programs from Iran. As a result, popular support for the opposition began to dwindle. The Russian population, in particular, felt uneasy about the growth of Tajik nationalism. An exodus of the Russian population ensued. In the beginning of November, acting President Iskandarov tried unsuccessfully to persuade the Russian government to use the 201st Rifle Division as a peacekeeping force in Tajikistan.

On 10 November 1992, Iskandarov decided to convene a special session of the Supreme Soviet in **Khujand**. On 18 November, the 16th Session of the Supreme Soviet accepted by an overwhelming majority the resignation of Iskandarov. But Nabiev refused to be reinstated as president. The session elected **Emomali Rahmon,** from Kulob, as chair of the Supreme Soviet, and **Abdumalik Abdullojonov,** from Leninobod, as the new prime minister. On 6 December, forces loyal to the newly elected president moved toward Dushanbe via Hisor, backed by armed forces from Uzbekistan. The opposition was forced to retreat, and on 14 December Rahmon took office in Dushanbe.

Opposition forces, now formally joined in the **United Tajik Opposition** (UTO), were driven into exile. With their camps in northern Afghanistan, UTO forces conducted cross-border raids and engaged the forces of Sitodi Melli (now incorporated into Tajikistan's regular army). Peace talks to resolve the conflict started in March 1994 and continued until June 1997, resulting in the signing of the **General Agreement on the Establishment of Peace and National Accord.** This agreement formally ended the most violent period in Tajikistan's modern history. The civil war resulted in 50,000 casualties, more than 600,000 internally displaced people, and 502,000 refugees. *See also* RUSSIANS IN TAJIKISTAN; WOMEN'S ISSUES.

COAL. There are 15 industrial coal reserves in Tajikistan, but only two of them are being worked. The Shurab (**Isfara**) lignite field has 85 million tons of coal deposits. In 1998, Shurab produced only 6,000 tons of coal due to the dilapidated condition of equipment and shortage of specialists. The biggest deposit of coal is in the Fan-**Yaghnob** field in the **Zarafshon** river basin, with estimated reserves of 800 million tons, but production from this field only serves two adjacent nohiyas: **Ayni** and **Panjakent.** Deposits of coal in Tajikistan are reported to be around 5–6 billion tons, but extraction is low. Tajikistan's coal extraction amounted to 650,000 tons in 1985 and 98,000 in 2005.

COLLECTIVE PEACEKEEPING FORCE IN THE REPUBLIC OF TAJIKISTAN. The *Kollektivniye Mirotvorcheskie Sily v Respublike Tadzhikistan* (KMS) force was formed on 15 October 1993 in response to the Tajik government's request, endorsed at a summit of the **Commonwealth of Independent States** (CIS) on 24 September 1993. The KMS consisted of Russian Army units (201st Motorized Rifle Division) and small units from neighboring CIS states: Kazakhstan (500 troops, reduced to 300 in March 1999), **Kyrgyzstan** (500 troops, withdrawn in February 1999), and **Uzbekistan** (300 troops).

At that time, the KMS was the only disciplined and reliable force in Tajikistan. The stated objectives of the KMS were to secure the Tajik-Afghan border region, contribute to a peaceful resolution of the **civil war**, ensure safe delivery of humanitarian aid, and facilitate the repatriation of refugees from **Afghanistan**. The KMS also protected key strategic installations in Tajikistan. During its first five years, the KMS and the Russian frontier guards lost 30 officers and 100 soldiers in Tajikistan. The Protocol on Military Issues, signed in March 1997, gave KMS forces the important and delicate role of accompanying United Tajik Opposition (UTO) units from Afghanistan to the assembly areas under the supervision of the United Nations Mission of Observers in Tajikistan (UNMOT), which they conducted successfully. The KMS was dissolved in June 2000 at a summit of CIS foreign affairs ministers in Moscow. KMS commanders from October 1993 to June 2000 were General Lieutenant B. Piankov, General Colonel V. Patrikeev, General Lieutenant V. Zavarzin, General Lieutenant V. Bobryshev, General Lieutenant Diukov, General Lieutenant N. Pugachev, General Lieutenant V. Chilindin, and General Lieutenant A. Pimenov.

COLLECTIVE SECURITY TREATY ORGANIZATION (CSTO). Known in Russian as *Organizatsiya Dogovora o Kollektivnoi Bezopasnosti*, the Collective Security Treaty (CST) was signed on May 1992 by the post-Soviet states of Armenia, Kazakhstan, **Kyrgyzstan**, **Russia**, Tajikistan, and **Uzbekistan**. It was later joined by Azerbaijan (September 1993), Georgia (December 1993), and Belarus (December 1993). Azerbaijan and Georgia withdrew from the treaty in 1999. Uzbekistan withdrew in 1999.

The CST's participating states agreed to abstain from the use or threat of force. They were not entitled to join other military alliances or other groups of states. An aggression against one would be perceived as an aggression against the group. The CST was set to last for a five-year period unless extended. In October 2002, the six members of the CST signed a charter expanding it and renaming it the Collective Security Treaty Organization (CSTO). Nikolai Bordyuzha (Russia) was appointed secretary general of the new organization, which unites seven post-Soviet states. On 23 June 2006, Uzbekistan became a full-member of the CSTO.

At the Dushanbe summit of the **Commonwealth of Independent States** (CIS) in October 2007, the CSTO signed an agreement with the **Shanghai Cooperation Organization** (SCO) to broaden cooperation on issues such as security, crime, and **drug trafficking**. At that meeting, the CSTO members agreed to create a CSTO peacekeeping force that could deploy in its member states. In 2008, the Collective Rapid Reaction Forces were formed and have at their disposal 1,500 military personnel (3 battalions deployed in Kazakhstan, Kyrgyzstan, and Tajikistan), the battalion groups of the **Russian military base in Tajikistan**, and the air group of the Russian air base in Kant (Kyrgyzstan).

The CSTO employs a rotating presidency system, in which the country leading the CSTO alternates every year. *See also* ARMY; COLLECTIVE PEACEKEEPING FORCE IN THE REPUBLIC OF TAJIKISTAN; FOREIGN POLICY.

COLLECTIVIZATION. Soviet policies in the 1920s and 1930s included *collectivization*, in which private land holdings were appropriated and combined into large-scale collective farms, or **kolkhozes**. Collectivization led to extraordinary political, economic, and cultural upheavals. It was aimed at eliminating wealthy land holders and appeasing the poor and middle peasantry. Mass collectivization in Tajikistan began in 1929 and, in nearly a decade, 98 percent of the republic's arable land was collectivized.

The collectivization of **agriculture** and the creation of state-owned **sovkhozes** and state-controlled kolkhozes did not achieve the stated political aim of introducing class consciousness into Tajik society. There was almost no social antagonism among Tajiks, and the idea of elimination of the rich (*bays*, or *kulaks*) was doomed to failure. Possessions of those identified as "rich" were confiscated, and cattle were distributed among the poor, who were then formed into nuclei for collective farms. Tens of thousands of farmers and educated people were declared *kulaks* and deported to **Uzbekistan**, Kazakhstan, the **Russian Federation**, and the Caucasus. This policy was viewed by the frightened majority of Tajiks as unavoidable state-led violence rather than the "elimination of exploiters as a class."

Instead of dividing Tajik villages along class lines, the collectivization strengthened clan, tribal, and regional ties and loyalties. People saw them as a counterbalance to a repressive state.

Beyond ideology, the more practical reason for collectivization was to increase irrigation and **cotton** production. Collectivized agriculture in Tajikistan enjoyed substantial Soviet investment and the introduction of modern farming techniques. Between 1934 and 1942, the **Ferghana**, **Vakhsh**, and **Hisor** canals were constructed to support cotton versus food production. This was accompanied by the increased mechanization of agriculture and use of fertilizers, including phosphates and nitrogen. By **World War II**, Tajikistan had become the third largest producer of cotton in the Soviet Union (after Uzbekistan and Turkmenistan). The chronic food deficiency, particularly in meat and grain, was covered by supplies from the Russian Federation and other Soviet republics. The Soviet planned economy favored a regional division of labor, the introduction of cotton monoculture in Tajikistan, and subordination of local agriculture to the needs of a highly centralized, nonmarket system. The result for Tajikistan was ecological degradation, land erosion, and an excessively insecure and dependent economy. *See also* COOPERATIVE FARMS; PRIVATE FARMING; PRIVATIZATION.

COMMISSION FOR NATIONAL RECONCILIATION (CNR). Known as the *Komissiuni Musolihai Melli* in **Tajik**, the CNR was organized subsequent to the Moscow signing of the **General Agreement on the Establishment of Peace and National Accord** in June 1997. It consists of representatives of the government and the coalition bloc of the **United Tajik Opposition** (UTO). The commission is chaired by opposition leader **Said Abdullo Nuri**, and it operates with the help of four subcommissions. The CNR oversaw the exchange of prisoners from Tajikistan's **civil war** and the transfer of a limited number of armed opposition units to **Dushanbe**. In 1998, the UTO twice suspended its participation in the CNR due to the government's failure to meet its obligations under the General Agreement. In accordance with the General Agreement, after **elections** to the **Majlisi Namoyandagon**, the CNR ended its work on 26 March 2000.

Members of the CNR and its four subcommissions included **Abdulmajid Dostiev, Abdunabi Sattorov, Abdurahim Karimov, Atobek Amirbekov, Ibrahim Usmonov, Jumaboi Niyo-**

zov, **Habibullo Sanginov**, **Khalifabobo Khamidov**, **Muhammad Sharif Himmatzoda**, **Otakhon Latifi**, **Rahim Masov**, and **Shukurjon Zuhurov**.

COMMONWEALTH OF INDEPENDENT STATES (CIS). The CIS is a multilateral framework for cooperation in the economic and security spheres between 12 former republics of the Union of Soviet Socialist Republics (USSR). The CIS was formed by the presidents of **Russia**, Belorussia, and Ukraine in December 1991 after the dissolution of the USSR. Soon after its formation, Kazakhstan, **Uzbekistan**, Moldova, Georgia, Azerbaijan, Turkmenistan, Tajikistan, **Kyrgyzstan**, and Armenia joined the commonwealth. Three Baltic states—Estonia, Lithuania, and Latvia—did not join the CIS. In 2008, Georgia left the CIS. *See also* CENTRAL ASIAN COOPERATION ORGANIZATION; COLLECTIVE SECURITY TREATY ORGANIZATION; SOVIET UNION.

COMMUNIST PARTY OF BUKHARA (CPB). Organized by Russian Bolsheviks in 1918 in Tashkent, the CPB was primarily staffed by Russians and Tatars who were sent to Tashkent to further the Bolshevik cause. The CPB suffered a blow after the defeat of **Kolesov's March** in March 1918, but in 1920 the party regained respectability when the **Young Bukharans** joined it. The first congress of the CPB was held in September 1918, and an initiative group was organized to establish cells all over the **Bukharan emirate**. The second CPB congress was held in Tashkent in June 1919 and included 20 delegates. The congress elected a Tatar Bolshevik, Najib Khusainov, as chair of the central committee. The third congress took place in December 1919 (Tashkent), and the fourth on 16–19 August 1920, on the eve of the **Bukharan Revolution**. The fifth congress was held in February 1921, when Soviet control extended to most of Tajikistan. The sixth CPB congress in December 1921 resolved to join the Russian Communist Party (Bolshevik), and the official incorporation in February 1922 ended the short life of the Communist Party of Bukhara as an independent entity.

COMMUNIST PARTY OF TAJIKISTAN (CPT). The Communist Party of Tajikistan (*Hizbi Kommunisti Tojikiston*) was founded after the December 1924 national delimitation of **Central Asia**. The party organization in Tajikistan was managed by the Organizational Bureau of Uzbekistan's central committee in the **Tajik Autonomous Soviet Socialist Republic** (Tajik ASSR). With the transformation of the Tajik ASSR into the **Tajik Soviet Socialist Republic** in 1929, Tajikistan's Communist Party (Bolsheviks) was formed. The party was renamed the Communist Party of Tajikistan in 1952. The Tajikistan party organization was a member of the All-Soviet Communist Party (Bolsheviks) in 1924–1952 and the Communist Party of the Soviet Union (CPSU) in 1952–1991.

The party was led by Moscow-installed, mostly non-Tajik members until 1946. The party congress was the highest decision-making body and was convened by the party central committee at least once every five years. In interval periods between party congresses, the central committee (CC) was the leading organ of the CPT. A presidium of the CC was elected by the congress to consider critical political and organizational matters.

Following the collapse of the CPSU in August 1991, **Qahor Mahkamov**, the president of Tajikistan and the first secretary of the CPT, left the party and issued a decree on the termination of activities of political parties and social movements within state institutions. This action undermined the position of the CPT as the dominant political party in Tajikistan. The CPT was registered by the government in June 1991. On 4 September, the central committee declared the party's independence from the CPSU.

The 22nd Congress of the CPT on 21 September 1991 renamed the party the Socialist Party of Tajikistan. But on 2 October, the **Supreme Soviet** of Tajikistan suspended the party's activities. Following the election victory of **Emomali Rahmon** as head of state in December 1992, a special parliamentary commission overturned the earlier ban on the CPT. The party held the second half of its 22nd congress in January 1992 and restored its old name. The CPT was registered with the Ministry of Justice on 17 March 1992. Shodi Shabdolov was elected first secretary of the CPT and became its chair in June 1996.

The 23rd congress of the CPT was held in June 1996, to which representatives of Russian Communist parties and nine foreign communist and workers' parties were invited. The congress adopted a new party program and rules. The party declared the "restoration of the socialist way of development" as its goal, which it promised to pursue through "parliamentary and nonparliamentary methods." In the field of economics, the CPT aims "to strengthen the leading position of the state, collective and other forms of societal property." The CPT intends "to use values of Islam and other religious confessions to educate an ethically healthy society." The CPT cooperates with the restored **Komsomol** organization.

The CPT has two provincial committees in the **Mountainous Badakhshon Autonomous Veloyat** and the **Sughd veloyat**, as well as three regional committees in **Kulob, Qurghonteppa**, and **Gharm**, and 17 city and 42 nohiya committees. In 1999, the CPT had a membership over 70,000, with 4,240 party cells operating throughout Tajikistan. The most influential CPT members in the **government (2000)** were Prime Minister **Oqil Oqilov** and Minister of Labor and Employment **Rafiqa Musoeva**. The CPT publishes three occasional newspapers: *Nidoi Ranjbar* (Worker's Call) in Tajik, *Golos Tadzhikistana* (Voice of Tajikistan) in Russian, and *Tojikiston Ovozi* (Voice of Tajikistan) in Uzbek. On 6 March 1996, the CPT signed the Agreement on National Accord and joined the **Societal Council**. In 1995, the CPT joined the **Congress of National Unity of Tajikistan** but left that organization in 1998. In June 1997, the CPT joined the Movement for National Unity and Revival in Tajikistan. The CPT participated in all rounds of the **Inter-Tajik Peace Talks** and the Commission for National Reconciliation.

In elections to the **Majlisi Oli** and local majlises, the CPT nominated 20 candidates and received 533,000 votes (more than 20 percent of all votes). In the 2000 election to the **Majlisi Namoyandagon**, the CPT came second after the **People's Democratic Party of Tajikistan** with 13 elected deputies (including one deputy chair and three chairs of standing committees). The CPT is the only political party that maintains a parliamentary faction in the Majlisi Namoyandagon. In 2008, the party claimed 55,000 members in all nohiyas of the republic.

In independent Tajikistan, the president-run People's Democratic Party of Tajikistan (PDPT) is a ruling party, while the CPT and the **Islamic Renaissance Party of Tajikistan** (IRPT) are the two major political parties. The CPT won five seats in the parliament's lower chamber in 2000. In the 2005–2010 Majlisi Namoyandagon, the CPT occupied four of the 63 seats. *See also* ELECTIONS.

CONFERENCE ON INTERACTION AND CONFIDENCE-BUILDING MEASURES IN ASIA (CICA). An intergovernmental security forum in Asia, CICA was initiated by President Nursultan Nazarbaev of the Republic of Kazakhstan in October 1992 at the 62nd **United Nations** General Assembly. Its aim is to create a transcontinental "Conference on Security and Cooperation in Eurasia" as a multilateral mechanism for building confidence and stability in Asia. CICA currently has 18 members (**Afghanistan**, Azerbaijan, **China**, Egypt, **India**, Israel, **Iran**, **Kyrgyzstan**, Mongolia, **Pakistan**, Palestine, **Russia**, South Korea, Thailand, Tajikistan, Turkey, Kazakhstan, and **Uzbekistan**) and eight observers (Australia, Indonesia, Japan, Lebanon, Malaysia, Great Britain, the **United States**, and Vietnam). The UN and the **Organization for Security and Cooperation in Europe** have also been involved in an observer capacity. *See also* FOREIGN POLICY.

CONGRESS OF NATIONAL UNITY OF TAJIKISTAN (CNUT). Known in **Tajik** as the *Kongresi Yagonagii Mellii Tojikiston*, the CNUT is headed by **Saifiddin Turaev**. It was formed on 24 April 1995 (registered on 5 August 1995) at the initiative of the Scientific-Industrial Union, the **Istravshan** International Scientific-Manufacturing corporation, the **Communist Party of Tajikistan** (CPT), the Russian Community of Tajikistan, the Yaqut Industrial Enterprise, Tajikistan's National Association of Political Scientists, and the Society of the **Uzbeks** of Tajikistan. The CNUT attracted several other associations in the following years, but in 1998 it lost the support of the CPT, the National Association of Political Scientists, the Korean community, and the Trade Union Federation. The CNUT publishes the *Haft Ganj* and *Sorbon* newspapers, and its stated objective is the "unity of different segments and forces of Tajikistan in order to resolve the societal crisis." The CNUT nominated Saifiddin Turaev in the November 1999 presidential elections but failed to collect the required 145,000 signatures (5 percent of the total number of voters) for his registration. *See also* POLITICAL PARTIES.

CONGRESS OF SOVIETS. This was the highest state body in the **Tajik Autonomous Soviet Socialist Republic** (Tajik ASSR) and **Tajik Soviet Socialist Republic** (Tajik SSR) between 1926 and 1937. Six congresses were held in that period. The First Inaugural Congress of

Soviets, meeting in December 1926, formed the **central executive committee** (CEC) of the Tajik ASSR (legislative body) and the Soviet of People's Commissars (government). The second congress met in April 1929 and approved Tajikistan's first **constitution**. However, the third congress, in October 1929, transformed the Tajik ASSR into the Tajik SSR. At the fourth congress in spring 1931, the first constitution of the Tajik SSR was adopted. The fifth Congress of Soviets met in January 1935. In March 1937, the sixth and last Congress of Soviets approved a new constitution for the Tajik SSR. The Congress of Soviets was replaced by the **Supreme Soviet**.

CONSTITUTIONS OF TAJIKISTAN. Five state constitutions were adopted in Tajikistan between 1929 and 1999. The first constitution was adopted by the second **Congress of Soviets** of the **Tajik Autonomous Soviet Socialist Republic** (Tajik ASSR) in April 1929, subject to approval of the Congress of Soviets in **Uzbekistan**. But in November, before the constitution could be ratified, Tajikistan became a separate republic of the **Soviet Union**, the **Tajik Soviet Socialist Republic** (Tajik SSR).

In February 1931, the first constitution of the Tajik SSR was adopted by the fourth Congress of Soviets of the Tajik SSR. Modeled on the 1924 constitution of the Union of Soviet Socialist Republics (USSR), it proclaimed that "all power in the Tajik SSR belongs to the Soviets, by means of which the proletariat implements its dictatorship aimed at the oppression of class exploiters, the elimination of exploitation of man by man and the construction of communism." This constitution was the blueprint for "socialist construction."

In March 1937, the second constitution of the Tajik SSR was adopted by the sixth Congress of Soviets. It echoed the 1936 USSR constitution and declared the accomplishment of goals set in the previous constitution: the elimination of feudal and capitalist economic systems, private property, and human exploitation. The constitution proclaimed the establishment of a socialist **economy** in Tajikistan. According to this constitution, exploiting classes were eliminated, and power was held by workers and peasants. The immediate task of the state was to democratize the electoral system. The second constitution declared the "victory of socialism" in Tajikistan.

In 1978, the third constitution of the Tajik SSR was adopted by the **Supreme Soviet** of the Tajik SSR, modeled on the 1977 constitution of the USSR. It declared as complete Tajikistan's transition from a state of proletarian dictatorship to an "all-people socialist state, expressing the will and interests of workers, peasants, the intelligentsia, and different nationalities of the Republic." The sixth article stressed the leading role of the Communist Party of the Soviet Union (CPSU) in Soviet society. Each citizen of the Tajik SSR was at the same time a citizen of the USSR and as such enjoyed rights equal to those of other Soviet citizens economically, politically, socially, and culturally. Amendments to the third constitution were adopted by the Supreme Soviet in 1990. The perestroika period saw the abolition of the sixth article on the "leading role of the CPSU."

The first post-Soviet constitution of the Republic of Tajikistan was adopted on 6 November 1994. According to the first article, the republic of Tajikistan is a unitary and secular state. Legal principles defining the exercise of state power such as the rule of law, distribution of power, and protection of **human rights** and liberties are stipulated in the constitution, as are principles of political and economic diversity. Constitutional rule began with the November 1994 presidential and parliamentary **elections**.

The national referendum held in June 2003 obtained popular support for a package of some 55 constitutional amendments. Among these is an amendment of Article 65 of the Constitution, which previously limited the president to one seven-year term in office. This has now been extended to two terms.

COOPERATIVE FARMS. In the wake of the Soviet collapse, **kolkhozes** and **sovkhozes** were reorganized to form cooperative farms, or *khojagii dehqoni*. This form of organization dominates **agricultural** production in Tajikistan. In 1999, 810 cooperative farms owned over 80 percent of the country's arable lands and yielded 70 percent of the agricultural output. In 2007, there were 29,880 cooperative farms in Tajikistan. *See also* COTTON; PRIVATE FARMING; PRIVATIZATION.

CORRUPTION. On 10 December 1999, Tajikistan adopted a law "On the Fight against Corruption." Later the **United Nations** (UN) convention to fight corruption was signed, and a national strategy to fight corruption for the period 2008–2012 was adopted. In January 2007, by presidential decree, the Agency on State Financial Control and

Fight against Corruption was established in Tajikistan, which consolidated practically all anticorruption functions previously exercised by the State Tax Committee, the Office of the Prosecutor General, and other law enforcement bodies.

Nevertheless, Tajikistan has one of the highest levels of corruption. In 2008, the country was ranked 151 out of 180 countries on the Corruption Index of Transparency International. Corruption is at the core of Tajikistan's **economy**. Tajikistan is ranked 153 out of 178 world economies in the ease of doing business. Top state-owned companies, including **TALCO**, that are associated with the inner circle of President **Emomali Rahmon** monopolize business, evading control of the central government and local authorities. A 2006 UN-implemented survey by the Center for Strategic Research under the president of Tajikistan identified the courts, local administration, and law enforcement bodies as the most corrupt institutions. Corruption and cronyism are particularly widespread in the **cotton** and **nonferrous metallurgy** sectors (together making up 80 percent of Tajikistan's exports).

In 2008, the International Monetary Fund (IMF) demanded repayment of $47 million in loans amid charges that Tajik authorities doctored data on national reserves. In 2009, an international audit revealed another huge fraud in Tajikistan. From 1996 to 2008, according to an audit, a former chair of Tajikistan's **National Bank**, **Murodali Alimardon**, diverted more than $850 million to Credit Invest, a company run by himself and his family. These loans were issued to Credit Invest for the development of the cotton sector but were later used for unrelated business initiatives.

Much of the corruption in Tajikistan is due to low public-sector wages. **Drug trafficking** is another major source of corruption. An important feature of Tajik politics is localism (*mahalgaroi* in Tajik, *mestnichestvo* in Russian), defined as community solidarity or political loyalty, which is a strong impediment to fighting corruption. Most of the important governmental positions, including one in the anticorruption agency, are filled by individuals from the president's region (**Kulob** and **Danghara** particularly).

COTTON. Cotton growing in the territory that now constitutes Tajikistan predates **Islam**'s arrival in **Central Asia** around the 7th century. Cotton growing rose markedly after **Russia** colonized the area at the end of the 19th century. By 1913, cotton cultivated land reached 26,700 hectares—including 13,200 hectares in the **Khujand** area, 12,000 hectares in the **Vakhsh valley**, and 1,500 hectares in **Kulob**—with a gross harvest of 32,300 tons (average yield of 1,210 kilograms per hectare). Large-scale cotton production started after the establishment of Soviet rule and the implementation of land reforms (1925–1928) and the formation of state farms (1930s). In 1928, Tajikistan produced 38,600 tons of cotton; in 1938 (after the irrigation of the Vakhsh valley), 174,400 tons; in 1965, 609,500 tons; in 1975, 835,900 tons. In 1981, Tajikistan produced more than 1 million tons of cotton. Approximately 30 percent of the total harvest is thin-fiber cotton, known as Egyptian cotton (*Gossypium barbadense*).

The republic produced the highest cotton yield per hectare in the Union of Soviet Socialist Republics (USSR). In 1979, Tajikistan contributed 9.8 percent of the total USSR cotton production, while **Uzbekistan** produced 62.9 percent, Turkmenistan 13.3 percent, Azerbaijan 8.1 percent, Kazakhstan 3.6 percent, and Kyrgyzstan 2.3 percent. In 2006, cotton cultivated lands in Tajikistan amounted to 263,000 hectares, or 33 percent of the total arable land. In 2008, the harvest amounted to 349,220 tons. About 90 percent of the cotton fiber production is designed for export. The biggest importers of Tajikistan's cotton are Latvia (almost 48 percent), Russia (25 percent), **Iran** (14 percent), Switzerland (6 percent), and **China** (5 percent).

In independent Tajikistan, cotton provides employment to about 80 percent of the country's rural labor force, and cotton fiber is Tajikistan's second largest export, contributing almost 20 percent of total export revenues. Since 1992, Tajikistan has gradually **privatized** cotton farms by giving **collective** land tenure rights to individuals and families. Yet this strategy has not significantly increased individual farmers' authority, since former directors of collective farms that coalesced with state authorities maintain their power in cotton production. In theory, farmers can choose what to plant and whom to sell to, but in fact farmers are obliged to grow the amount of cotton the government "advises" them to produce and sell it to the state at low prices. Under pressure to fulfill state targets, local authorities make use of students and the local population, including the unpaid labor of schoolchildren, to harvest the largest amounts of raw cotton. As a result, most farmers owe the "futures companies" about $600 million. The government hopes to liquidate the debt with the help of international organizations. Starting in 2008, farmers were to be financed directly by **banks** without the intermediation of "futures companies." **Corruption** is particularly widespread in the cotton sector of the national **economy**. In 2007, cotton fiber exports reached $120 million, but cotton farmers are known as the poorest farmers in the country. *See also* ECONOMY; PRIVATE FARMING.

COUNCIL OF JUSTICE. A state organ under the president of Tajikistan, the Council of Justice coordinates legal reforms and increases the authority of courts. It includes the chairs of the Supreme Court and High Economic Court, the minister of justice, representatives of the standing committees of the parliament, and the chair of the Military Collegium. The Council of Justice was organized by presidential decree in December 1999 in keeping with amendments to the **constitution** of October 1999. It took over from the Ministry of Justice the right to appoint judges.

CURRENCY. Tajikistan experienced a monetary crisis after the collapse of the **Soviet Union** in 1991. It continued to use the Russian ruble while its neighbors switched to new independent currencies. Tajikistan faced a shortage of rubles and was forced to introduce its own currency, the Tajik ruble, in May 1995. That currency sank very quickly. On 30 October 2000, Tajikistan introduced a new currency, the somoni (SM). The somoni consists of 100 dirams. On the first day of its introduction, $1 equaled 2 somoni and 40 dirams. In March 2009, the exchange rate reached 3 somoni and 80 dirams. *See also* BANKS.

CUSTOMS UNION. This regional organization within the framework of the **Commonwealth of Independent States** (CIS) was formally established on 26 May 1996 after the signing of the Agreement between the Republic of Belorussia, Republic of Kazakhstan, **Kyrgyzstan**, and the **Russian Federation** on Integration in Economic and Humanitarian Spheres. Tajikistan joined this agreement in February 1999. The Customs Union (*Tamozhenny Soyuz*) was the most effective economic organization in the CIS in 1998. It covered 64.7 percent of the CIS population, 83.3 percent of its gross domestic products, 70.6 percent of its industrial output, 65.9 percent of its agricultural output, and 83.1 percent of the CIS trade turnover. At the October 2000 summit in Astana (Kazakhstan), member states adopted a plan to transform the Customs Union into the **Eurasian Economic Community**. *See also* COLLECTIVE SECURITY TREATY ORGANIZATION.

– **D** –

DANCE. Tajiks have ancient traditions of classic and folk dance that have been enriched by many cultures over the centuries. Tajik classical dance is connected to Islamic traditions. Conventionally, women danced for each other at women's gatherings and parties. There were also female dancers at court, as depicted in miniature paintings from the 14th–18th centuries. In public, dances sometimes were performed by a *bacha* (boy), who was often dressed as a woman. Tajik folk dances include dances performed at specific times and linked to particular occasions, such as the **Nawruz** holiday or funerals, as well as dances performed at any time for relaxation and entertainment (mostly at **tuis**).

A form of dance known as *raqs* is typically performed by a talented female dancer called a *raqossa*. Tajik *raqs* is distinguished by complex arm and hand movements, a mixture of spins and turns, and dynamic facial expressions. Musical accompaniment varies from purely rhythmic structures performed by a lone **doira** (tambourine) to classical *maqom* compositions played by an orchestra with singers of both sexes.

The surviving dance heritage of the Tajik people has expressed itself in three regional schools: **Pamiri**, **Khatloni**, and **Sughdi**, representing the Tajik east, south, and north respectively. The Pamiri folk dances are reminiscent of a Sufi whirling ritual called *zikr*, in which dancers travel in a circle with repetitive movements. The Khatloni (or **Kulobi**) dance performed by females dressed in special robes called *kurta chakan* is more simple, rooted in folklore and energetic. Dances from the predominantly urban Sughd are more lyrical and saturated with the spirit of classical and court traditions of the **Shashmaqom**.

As a rule, Tajik dance is performed solo. Female group dance has become popular since veiling was eliminated under the Soviets and Tajiks got acquainted with the modern **arts**. The Tajik School of Music and Ballet was formed in 1937, followed in 1940 by the Tajik

State Ensemble of Dance and Song. In that same year, Pamir ethnic and child dance groups were organized in **Khorugh**. The state dance ensembles Lola (Tulip) and Zebo (Beauty) became especially popular after **World War II**. The heads of these ensembles, the famed Tajik choreographers Ghaffor Valamatzoda and Zebo Aminzoda, created their own works through a fusion of classical and traditional dance with modern techniques of staging and choreography. Since independence, numerous amateur and professional ensembles have tried to preserve Tajik dance traditions.

Tajiks of all ages, any status, and both sexes love dance and dancing. No important event, official or private, is complete without dance. *See also* MUSIC; OPERA AND BALLET THEATER.

DANGHARA NOHIYA. Located in southern Tajikistan between the Qizilsu and **Vakhsh** rivers, the Danghara nohiya is the native home of President **Emomali Rahmon**. It was formed in 1932 and was known as the Aksu nohiya until 1936. Danghara was an administrative division of **Kulob** until 1993. In that year, after the merger of **Kulob** and **Qurghonteppa** into the **Khatlon** veloyat, Danghara became a part of Khatlon. The distance from the city of Danghara (25,835 population in 2008) to **Dushanbe** is 116 kilometers, and to Kulob 86 kilometers. The district is 2,000 square kilometers, with a population of more than 97,000, mainly Tajik. It has five jamoats. Average temperatures in January and June can reach 0°C and 28°C respectively, and the annual rainfall is about 500 millimeters. Arable lands amount to 30,381 hectares. The main occupation is **agriculture**, including **grain** and **cotton** production and livestock breeding. Poverty affects about 71 percent of the population.

DARBAND NOHIYA. *See* NUROBOD NOHIYA.

DARI. The classical Dari **language**, also known as classical **Farsi**, was widely used in the 9th–16th centuries in **Central Asia**, **India**, **Iran**, and **Afghanistan**. Dari (meaning "language of court") is the medium of the rich Farsi-**Tajik literature**. The Arabic script was adopted in the 9th–10th centuries, growing in prominence during the **Samanid** dynasty. In the second half of the 15th century, due to political and religious imperatives, three strands started to emerge from the Dari language: new Farsi currently used in Iran, Tajik, and

Afghan Farsi, or Dari Kabuli. Some lexical and grammatical differences have emerged between these languages as a result of their separate development.

DARVESH. A *darvesh* is a member of the **Sufi** order. The term is also used for a poor person, beggar, or tramp.

DARVOZ NOHIYA. The westernmost district in the **Mountainous Badakhshon Autonomous Veloyat**, Darvoz was an independent kingdom on the Panj River and was ruled by a *mir* (**amir**). Its capital was Qalai Khumb. In 1878, Darvoz became a part of the **Bukharan emirate**. From 1930, when the district was formed, till 1992, Darvoz was known as Qalai Khumb (Qalaikhum) district. The nohiya is 2,824 square kilometers, with a population of more than 24,800, consisting almost exclusively of **Sunni Tajiks** living in four **jamoats**. One of Darvoz's villages was populated by **Ismailis**. The distance from Qalai Khumb to **Dushanbe** is 286 kilometers, and to **Khorugh** 241 kilometers. Average temperatures in January and July can reach –5°C and 25°C respectively; annual precipitation is 500–900 millimeters. The main occupation is **agriculture**, including **grain** and corn production and livestock breeding. Darvoz is not a **cotton**-growing district. There are 2,308 hectares of arable land. A joint **gold**-mining venture, Darvoz, operates in this district.

DASTARKHON. The term *dastarkhon* is used to refer to a tablecloth and also to refreshments. *See also* ETIQUETTE.

DAVLAT. The term *davlat* refers to power, might, wealth, or property. It is also used to refer to government, governance, or the state.

DAVLATOV, DAVLATALI (1947–). The first deputy chair of President **Emomali Rahmon**'s ruling **People's Democratic Party of Tajikistan** (PDPT), Davlatov was born in the **Rudaki nohiya**. He received his training as an Orientalist at Tajik State University and was an interpreter for Soviet military advisers in Syria and Egypt in 1968–1973. Then he worked at the Institute of Oriental Studies of the **Academy of Sciences of Tajikistan**. He completed his thesis and in 1980 was awarded a degree from the Institute of Oriental Studies at the Union of Soviet Socialist Republics Academy of Sciences in

Moscow. In 1989, he was invited to work on the central committee of the **Communist Party of Tajikistan**. In 1993–1995, he was an adviser and press secretary of the president of Tajikistan. In November 1995, Davlatov became a state adviser on interethnic relations and public associations. In 1998, he took on the additional role of heading the Department for Public Relations, Culture, and Information. In 2004, he was appointed deputy chair of the PDPT.

DEH. A *deh* is a village, neighborhood, or rural settlement. The deh and **shahrak** are at the lowest (**jamoat**) tier of local government. *See also* ADMINISTRATIVE STRUCTURE.

DEHQON. A *dehqon* is a peasant or farmer. In earlier usage, the term referred to a feudal lord.

DEMOCRATIC PARTY OF TAJIKISTAN (DPT). The Democratic Party of Tajikistan (*Hizbi Demokrati Tojikiston* in **Tajik**) is the country's most influential secular opposition **political party**. The DPT was formed on 10 August 1990 in **Dushanbe** with **Shodmon Yusuf** as its chair and was registered by the Ministry of Justice on 21 June 1991. At this time, its membership stood at 3,500, drawn from all regions of the republic. In 1992, the DPT published a number of newspapers: *Adolat* in Dushanbe, *Oriyon* in **Khujand**, *Oinai Sikandar* in **Gharm**, and *Bomdod* in **Qurghonteppa**. They were all banned in 1993. During the 1991 **presidential elections**, the DPT together with the **Islamic Renaissance Party of Tajikistan** (IRPT), **Rastokhez**, and **La'li Badakhshon** endorsed the candidacy of **Davlatnazar Khudonazarov**. The DPT protested against irregularities in the election after Khudonazarov's defeat. Between March and May 1992, the DPT and its allies held a 52-day rally in Shahidon Square against the government of President **Rahmon Nabiev**. The DPT was embroiled in the ensuing Tajik **civil war**, which shook the country. In June 1993, the DPT and the IRPT formed the **United Tajik Opposition** (UTO) to coordinate their political and armed struggle against the government of **Emomali Rahmon**. The DPT was formally banned by Tajikistan's Supreme Court in June 1993.

Members of the party who had taken refuge in the **Commonwealth of Independent States** set up a coordinating center in Moscow and issued a public statement on the "resolution of military-political conflict in the Republic of Tajikistan." This document, which took a different approach from that of the UTO, foreshadowed a split in the DPT. Shodmon Yusuf endorsed this statement after initial hesitations and declared in October 1994 that the party was withdrawing from the UTO. Yusuf's position was challenged in December 1994 at a party congress in Almaty (Kazakhstan). The congress renewed its loyalty to the UTO and removed Yusuf as party chair. **Jumaboi Niyozov** was elected chair of the newly formed party, which called itself the **Democratic Party of Tajikistan Almaty Platform** (DPTA). The DPTA and the IRPT then constituted the core of the United Tajik Opposition and participated in the **Inter-Tajik Peace Talks** between 1994 and 1997.

Soon after this split, Shodmon Yusuf and his supporters, some of whom were based in Tehran at the time, drafted new party rules and formed the **Democratic Party of Tajikistan Tehran Platform** (DPTT). The DPTT did not participate in the UTO and Inter-Tajik Peace Talks. The DPTT demonstrated a willingness to work with the government and was legally registered in Tajikistan in July 1995. Following the signing in June 1997 of the **General Agreement on the Establishment of Peace and National Accord**, which allowed the return of all opposition parties to Tajikistan, leaders of the DPTT expressed a desire to reunite the DPT. In 1999, after Shodmon Yusuf was removed as chair of the DPTT, members of both wings of DPT reunited and elected **Mahmadruzi Iskandarov**, former UTO commander from **Tojikobod**, as chair. In December 1999, the Ministry of Justice lifted a ban on DPT activity.

In April 2004, Iskandarov was abducted in Moscow, where he had sought refuge to avoid politically motivated charges in Tajikistan. He later turned up in custody in Dushanbe and in October 2005 received a 23-year sentence on six charges, including **terrorism**, embezzlement, illegal possession of a weapon, and banditry. Despite the arrest and imprisonment of Iskandarov, the DPT in its congress in 2004 reelected him chair. The party received no seats in the legislative **elections** in February–March 2005. The party boycotted the **presidential election of 2006**.

In 2006, another split occurred within the DPT. In August 2006, the Vatan faction conducted a congress where Masud Sobirov was elected chair of the DPT. The decision was found legitimate by Tajikistan's Ministry of Justice, and the Tajik government officially registered Sobirov's DPT. The party's newspaper *Adolat* was shut down in early October 2006 following Sobirov's appeal filed with the Tajik government in which he asked the Ministry of Culture to deprive Iskandarov's bloc of the right to publish the newspaper. As of early 2009, two groups of Tajik democrats vied for the role of successor to the DPT. The party's stamp and the certificate belonged to an allegedly pro-government, yet inactive Masud Sobirov group. The supporters of Iskandarov, headed by his deputy Rahmatulloh Valiev, acted as an unregistered opposition party. They preserved the party cells all over the country and refused to join Sobirov's bloc.

DEMOCRATIC PARTY OF TAJIKISTAN ALMATY PLAT-FORM (DPTA). This party split from the **Democratic Party of Tajikistan** (DPT) in December 1994 at a congress in Almaty (Kazakhstan) and elected **Jumaboi Niyozov** as its chair. The DPTA was the second biggest force, after the **Islamic Renaissance Party of Tajikistan**, in the **United Tajik Opposition** (UTO). As a UTO member, the DPTA participated in the **Inter-Tajik Peace Talks** between 1994 and 1997. Two DPTA leaders, Jumaboi Niyozov and **Abdunabi Sattorov**, joined the newly formed **Commission for National Reconciliation** in 1997. In August 1999, Tajikistan's Supreme Court rescinded the ban on the DPT and in December 1999 it was registered as a legal **political party**. In September 1999, **Mahmadruzi Iskandarov** replaced Niyozov as chair of the party, and in October the DPTA pulled out of the UTO. In November 1999, the DPTA restarted publishing two newspapers: *Najot* in **Dushanbe** and *Oriyon* in **Khujand**. The DPTA joined with the **Democratic Party of Tajikistan Tehran Platform** (DPTT) to reunite the DPT toward the end of 1999.

DEMOCRATIC PARTY OF TAJIKISTAN TEHRAN PLAT-FORM (DPTT). Soon after the **Democratic Party of Tajikistan Almaty Platform** (DPTA) split from the **Democratic Party of Tajikistan** (DPT) in 1994, another faction within the party adopted new rules and reorganized as the DPT Tehran Platform. The founding session of the DPTT was held in Moscow, and **Shodmon Yusuf** was reaffirmed as chair. At this time, the party's prominent leaders were based in Tehran; these included Shodmon Yusuf, R. Musulmonqulov, Bozor Sobir, Azam Afzali, and M. Nuriddinov. In the newly adopted party rules, the DPTT defined itself as a "right-centrist" **political party**. The DPTT did not participate in the **United Tajik Opposition** (UTO). In March 1995, DPTT leaders met with representatives of President **Emomali Rahmon** in Moscow and expressed their willingness to work within the legal framework of the republic.

Following a presidential amnesty on DPTT leaders, the party held a conference in **Dushanbe** (22 May 1995) and was registered with the Ministry of Justice (22 July 1995). In March 1995, the DPTT signed a government-promoted Agreement on Societal Accord and became a member of the **Societal Council**. In 1998, the Center of Unity of the Democratic Party of Tajikistan was formed in Dushanbe to help reunite the two wings of the DPT. At the third congress of the DPTT in July 1999, Azam Afzali replaced Yusuf as party chair. Later that year, the DPTT joined with the DPTA to revive the DPT.

DEVON. A *devon* is a ministry, royal household, or court of law. The term is also used for a collection of articles or verses.

DOCTOR OF SCIENCES (DOKTORI FANHO). This is the second (after **candidate of sciences**) and final academic degree in Tajikistan and formerly the **Soviet Union**. It is granted by the Specialized Academic Council (at the most prestigious universities and academic institutions) to graduates (mostly candidates of science) who write and publicly defend their doctoral dissertation. *See also* ACADEMICIAN; ACADEMY OF SCIENCES.

DODKHUDOEV, NAZARSHOH (1915–2000). The chair of Tajikistan's government in 1956–1961, Dodkhudoev was born in **Rushan**, in the **Mountainous Badakhshon Autonomous Veloyat**. He graduated from the **Khorugh** Tekhnikum (college) in 1935 and the Institute of the Young Communist International under the Communist International (Moscow) in 1939. Dodkhudoev started his political career in **Komsomol** in 1934. In 1939–1940, he was the editor of the youth newspaper *Pioneer Tadzhikistana*. In 1940–1949, he worked in the People's Commissariat of Internal Affairs (NKVD). In 1949, he was appointed chair of the provincial executive committee of his native **Badakhshon** veloyat. In the following year, he became chair of the Presidium of the **Supreme Soviet** of Tajikistan. From 1956 to 1961, Dodkhudoev was chair of the Soviet of Ministers and minister of foreign affairs of the **Tajik Soviet Socialist Republic**. Dodkhudoev retired from his official duties in 1961. *See also* DODKHUDOEVA, LOLA.

DODKHUDOEVA, LOLA (1951–). A Tajik scholar and **candidate** of history, Dodkhudoeva was born in **Dushanbe** to the family of **Nazarshoh Dodkhudoev**. She graduated from the Leningrad State University in Arabic studies in 1973. In 1977, she started work as a researcher and then headed the Department in Medieval History in the Institute of History, Ethnography, and Archeology, **Academy of Sciences of Tajikistan**. In 1993–1994, Dodkhudoeva worked in Tajikistan's Ministry of Education and in 1996–1997 was deputy director of the Open Society Institute (Soros Foundation) in Tajikistan. In March 2000, Dodkhudoeva was appointed secretary general of the UNESCO national commission for Tajikistan. Her research is primarily focused on **Islam** in medieval **Central Asia**.

DOIRA. The *doira*, a tambourine, is the most widespread percussion musical instrument used to accompany popular and classical **music** in Tajikistan. Its name comes from a Tajik word for "circle." A doira is made from a leather membrane stretched across a wooden base to which jingles are attached. The diameter is about 50 centimeters and the depth is about 7 centimeters. *See also* NAI; SHASHMAQOM.

DOMULLOH. A *domulloh* is a schoolteacher or teacher in a **madrasa**.

DONISH, AHMAD (1826–1897). Known also as Ahmad Kalla and Ahmad Mahdum, Ahmad Donish was a Tajik writer, architect, scholar, artist, and pioneer of the **Jadidia** enlightenment movement in **Central Asia**. Donish's initial fame grew from his astrological studies in the service of Emir Nasrullah of **Bukhara**. He served as a diplomat on Bukharan missions to **Russia** in 1857, 1869–1870, and 1873–1874 during which he was to conduct diplomatic negotiations, but they also offered him an opportunity to become acquainted with liberal reformist ideas of the time. In 1885, he published his famous book *Navodir ul-Vaqoe* (Rare Stories), which sharply criticized the medieval character of Bukharan social life. Donish's views have been celebrated as critical for the growth of the nascent Jadidist movement in Central Asia. **Sadriddin Ayni**, a leading figure in the movement, paid homage to Donish and described himself as his disciple. *See also* LITERATURE.

DOSTIEV, ABDULMAJID (1946–). Born in the **Bokhtar nohiya** to a **Kulobi** family, Dostiev served in the Soviet Army in 1966–1968, and in 1968 he started working as a member of a **kolkhoz**. Dostiev studied entomology at the Tajik Institute of Agriculture, and upon graduation in 1974, he headed an agricultural brigade in the V. Lenin kolkhoz in the Bokhtar nohiya. In 1977, he became chief agronomist in the Department of Agriculture in the **Qurghonteppa** city executive committee. In 1977–1980, he was an instructor at the Organizational Department in the Qurghonteppa city committee of the **Communist Party of Tajikistan** (CPT). In 1980, he became secretary of the CPT committee in the Lenin kolkhoz and headed the Department of Agriculture in Qurghonteppa. In 1980–1987, he was head of the Organizational Department of the CPT in the Bokhtar nohiya. In 1987–1988, he headed the Bokhtar committee for people's control.

In 1992, Dostiev, together with **Emomali Rahmon**, joined the **Sitodi Melli** and became chair of the Bokhtar executive committee. At the November 1992 session of parliament, Dostiev was appointed first deputy of the **Supreme Soviet** of Tajikistan. In 1993, he created the People's Party of Tajikistan, which was renamed the **People's Democratic Party of Tajikistan** (PDPT) in June 1997. In March 1998, Emomali Rahmon replaced Dostiev as chair of the PDPT.

In 1995, Dostiev was elected to the **Majlisi Oli**. From February to March 1996, he chaired the **Khatlon** veloyat. From March 1996 to January 2000, he was the first deputy chair of the Majlisi Oli. In 1997, he was appointed deputy chair of the **Commission for National Reconciliation**. In 2000, Dostiev was elected to the **Majlisi Namoyandagon** and assumed the post of deputy parliamentary chair. In December 2006, he was appointed ambassador to the **Russian Federation**.

DRUG TRAFFICKING. Since the 1990s, Tajikistan has been one of the major transshipment zones for opiates and heroin from **Afghanistan** to **Russia** and Eastern Europe. For the drug mafia, Tajikistan provides an attractive target, due to the weakness of the state following the **civil war** (1992–1997) and the fact that it suffers from the lowest levels of human development in **Central Asia**. Trafficking until 1996 consisted primarily of opium. With the rise of the **Taliban** in Afghanistan, the first heroin seizures were made in Tajikistan in 1996. The withdrawal of Russian troops from the Tajik-Afghan border in 2002 further worsened the problem, since Tajik border guards were not sufficiently equipped, trained, or paid and were exposed to the risk of **corruption**. The main directions for smuggling drugs appear to be through the **Kulob** sector of the border and a route that passes through the mountainous areas of **Badakhshon**.

Border security on the Afghan side is weak, and many of the Afghan officers in charge of border control seemingly have strong links to the drug trade. The language and ethnic connections that span the Tajik-Afghan border provide communal support for trafficking networks. Further, most of the **Tajiks** of Tajikistan are fluent in Russian, which enables communication with Russia and Eastern Europe. According to a United Nations Development Program (UNDP) report, it is believed that up to 100 tons of heroin move through Tajikistan each year, equal to the annual heroin demand in Western Europe and North America combined. In Tajikistan, the annual income from the heroin trade amounts to between $500 million and $1 billion. This means that one-third of the country's GDP is linked to drug trafficking.

Tajikistan ranks third in drug seizures worldwide, after **Iran** and **Pakistan**. In 1999–2008, on the territory of Tajikistan, more than 60 tons of the opium group of drugs, including over 28 tons of heroin, were seized from illicit trafficking. In the first half of 2008, the share of Tajikistan's drug seizures of opium drugs in the CIS amounted to 43 percent and 66 percent in Central Asia.

The drugs that remain in Tajikistan tend to increase the level of crime, corruption, drug addiction, AIDS, and HIV infection. In Tajikistan, addiction affects up to 1 percent of the population (more than 70,000). Some 80 percent of those are heroin addicts. Widespread poverty and unemployment push more Tajiks into drug smuggling. Many of the traffickers arrested in Russia are Tajik nationals. In view of the internationally recognized gravity of the drug problem in the area, foreign states and international NGOs have offered support to Tajikistan. *See also* FOREIGN POLICY; TERRORISM.

DUSHANBE. Tajikistan's capital and its biggest city, Dushanbe is a major industrial and commercial center situated in the **Hisor** valley, where the **Varzob** and Kofarnihor rivers meet. The city's roots go back as far as the **Bactrian** period. Later, it was a site of an ancient town of **Kushans** and the site of Shishi Khon village and other medieval settlements. The first written record of Dushanbe dates to 1676, when the village was part of Balkh, occupying an important position at the crossroads of caravan routes connecting **Bukhara, Samarqand**, and **Ferghana** with Qarategin, **Badakhshon**, and **Afghanistan**. Dushanbe was a small **qyshloq** (village) when a military-political expedition of the Red Army and the government of the Bukharan People's Soviet Republic (Bukharan PSR) occupied the **Eastern Bukhara** in February 1921. The village was named after its weekly bazaar, held on Mondays: *dushanbe* means "Monday" in **Farsi**.

After Bolsheviks entered the area, Dushanbe became the principal town of Eastern Bukhara, and in 1925 it was made the capital of the **Tajik Autonomous Soviet Socialist Republic** (Tajik ASSR). Other small villages in the area, among them Shohmansur, Mavlono, and Sari Osiyo, became part of Dushanbe in the late 1920s. After the Tajik ASSR became the **Tajik Soviet Socialist Republic** (Tajik SSR) in 1929, the town was renamed Stalinabad. During the de-Stalinization period, the city was renamed Dushanbe in 1961.

Dushanbe experienced rapid growth and development after the construction of the Termez-Dushanbe **railway** in 1929, which connected the city with the Transcaspean railway. As the national capital, Dushanbe is the seat of Tajikistan's government and the **Majlisi Oli**. The capital city houses the **Academy of Sciences of Tajikistan**, 17 universities (50,100 students), 129 schools (13,500 pupils), 90 high schools (101,900 pupils), and 11 tekhnikums/colleges (19,400 students). Six professional theaters, eight museums, 30 public libraries, including the **Firdawsi State Library**, and other cultural institutions are situated in Dushanbe. There are 100 health care institutions with 3,500 doctors and 44,000 nurses and other personnel.

Dushanbe has housed the country's television center since 1960. The Tajik capital is a major center of transportation and communication in central and southern Tajikistan. The railway links Dushanbe with **Khujand**, after crossing into **Uzbekistan**. The main **motor roads** go to the north (341 kilometers to Khujand), to the east (527 kilometers to **Khorugh**), and to the south (91 kilometers to **Qurghonteppa** and 202 kilometers to **Kulob**). The capital's main artery, Rudaki (formerly Lenin) Street, links the southern and northern ends of the capital. The main administrative and cultural institutions, housed in European-style buildings, are situated along Rudaki Street. Dushanbe is headed by the *miri shahr* (city mayor) and is divided into four administrative districts (*nohiya*s): Ismoili Somoni, Sino, Firdawsi, and Shohmansur. The republic's only large civil aviation airport operates in Dushanbe, but there were no regular direct flights to Western Europe as of early 2009, although many to various cities of **Russia**.

Dushanbe is younger than Khujand, Kulob, **Gharm**, and other regional centers in Tajikistan. It is populated mainly by **Tajiks** from different regions, **Uzbeks**, and **Russians**. The headquarters of the Russian troops in Tajikistan are in Dushanbe.

The largest industries in Dushanbe include textiles, silk, oil, boots, milk, tobacco, leather, wine, bakery products, and knitted fabrics. Dushanbe is 750–930 meters above sea level and more than 1,250 square kilometers in area. Temperatures in January and July average 1°C and 28°C respectively.

Dushanbe's population in 1925 was 6,000; in 1994, 600,000. In 1990–1993, Dushanbe was rocked by fighting between armed bands belonging to the opposition and the government. In the 1990s, most of the Russian-speaking population left the capital, while hundreds of thousands of people, predominantly Tajik men from rural regions, moved to Dushanbe in search of employment. Most had no residency permit and were therefore not included in official data. In the early 2000s, the Ministry of State Security estimated Dushanbe's population to be around 1.2 million.

From Soviet times, Dushanbe had two major bazaars: Barakat (formerly Putovskiy) and Shomansur (known also as Zeleniy). Since the 1990s, other markets—Sahovat, Sultoni Kabir, Korvon, Rohi Abreshim, and Safariyon—opened in the environs of the city. There are also about 20 smaller bazaars operating in Dushanbe. The major **mosques** include Mavlono Yaqubi Charkhi, Shahmansur, and Sari Osiyo.

DUSTI BRIDGE. The Dusti is Tajikistan's biggest bridge across the Panj River between Sherkhon Bandar, **Afghanistan**, and Panji Poyon, Tajikistan. The bridge was officially opened on 26 August 2007. It is 673 meters long and can carry up to 1,000 vehicles per day. Built by the U.S. Army Corps of Engineers and the Italian firm

Rizzani de Eccher, it is the biggest infrastructure project funded by the U.S. government in Tajikistan, at a cost of $37.1 million. Norway also contributed nearly $900,000 for the construction of modern customs and border control facilities. Japan built a road from Panji Poyon to the town of Dusti in **Khatlon** veloyat to connect the bridge with Tajikistan's broader transport network. In Afghanistan, the Asian Development Bank rehabilitated a road link to the strategic Afghan Ring Road.

The bridge provides the region with the shortest distance between **Dushanbe** and Kabul. This should stimulate increased trade and economic development throughout **Greater Central Asia**. Afghanistan and Tajikistan agreed to create a free economic zone on both sides of the bridge and ease customs and visa regimes to promote trade. Unquestionably, the bridge is also of military importance for the United States, North Atlantic Treaty Organization, and their allies. *See also* FOREIGN INVESTMENT; FOREIGN POLICY; FOREIGN TRADE.

DUTAR. A *dutar* is a long-necked, two-stringed lute. Its name comes from the Tajik words for two strings, *du tar*. The strings are usually plucked. Modern dutars have silk or nylon strings. *See also* DOIRA; MUSIC; SHASHMAQOM.

– E –

EASTERN BUKHARA. In its official documents in the 19th century, **Russia** referred to the eastern part of the **Bukharan emirate** as Eastern Bukhara. The area included **Hisor, Khatlon**, Qarategin, and **Darvoz** in addition to Surkhan Darya province in **Uzbekistan**.

ECONOMIC COOPERATION ORGANIZATION (ECO). The ECO is an intergovernmental regional organization of non-**Arab** Muslim-majority countries in the region between Turkey and **Pakistan**. It succeeded the Regional Cooperation for Development which existed in 1964–1979. The ECO was established in 1985 by **Iran**, Turkey, and Pakistan for the purpose of promoting economic, technical, and cultural cooperation. On 28 November 1992, representatives of the new ECO member states **Afghanistan**, Azerbaijan, **Kyrgyz-**

stan, Kazakhstan, Tajikistan, Turkmenistan, and **Uzbekistan** signed a treaty in Islamabad (Pakistan). The common objective of the ECO is to establish a single market for goods and services, similar to the European Union. Since the mid-1990s, the ECO has embarked on several projects in Tajikistan in the fields of energy, trade, transportation, **agriculture**, and **drug** control. A major impediment for implementation of ECO projects is the poorly developed transport network between the member states. The ECO's mission overlaps with that of the **Conference on Interaction and Confidence-Building Measures in Asia** (CICA). **Dushanbe** hosted an ECO summit in September 2004. *See also* ECONOMY; FOREIGN POLICY.

ECONOMY. Traditionally, food production in **agriculture** and animal husbandry dominated the economy of the **Tajiks**. The period when northern Tajikistan (currently **Sughd veloyat**) was part of the Russian empire (1870–1914) featured the rapid development of **industry**, **railways**, **banking**, and regional trade markets. Then followed a decline caused by World War I, the fall of tsarism, revolution, and civil war.

Soviet Tajikistan's economy went through rapid changes in the late 1920s and 1930s. The economic reforms led to major transformations in the agricultural sector, giving priority to **cotton** production. Soviet planners also built large industrial complexes in Tajikistan to serve the needs of the vast Soviet economy. During **World War II**, many industrial enterprises were evacuated from the European part of the Union of Soviet Socialist Republics (USSR) to **Central Asia**. In Tajikistan, they included textile and silk plants, food-processing factories, and mechanical engineering and metal-processing enterprises.

After the war, Tajikistan accelerated the development of light industry and **power generation**. In the early 1960s, its economy was predominantly industrial. Industry accounted for 53.9 percent of the gross domestic product (GDP) in 1960, while agriculture amounted only to 21.5 percent. An ambitious project, the South Tajikistan Territorial Industrial Complex, included gigantic power stations on the **Vakhsh River** and **nonferrous metallurgy** enterprises. In agriculture, priority was given to capital-intensive projects such as irrigation tunnels, pumping stations, and large canals.

Despite this industrialization, when Tajikistan gained its independence in 1991, its economy was predominantly agricultural, with more than 50 percent of the labor force employed in agriculture. Both sectors of the economy were heavily dependent on input shipments from other parts of the **Soviet Union**. The USSR republics accounted for 80 percent of Tajik export and import flows in 1990. During the **civil war** (1992–1997), Tajikistan's fragile economy lost more than 60 percent of its GDP. The country also suffered widespread physical damage amounting to $7 billion and heavy human losses of up to 50,000 lives.

As of 2009, economic indicators remain below the benchmarks of 1991. Tajikistan's GDP suffered an 8.5 percent decline in 1991 and an even sharper 31 percent drop in 1992. The economic decline continued until 1997, when a modest growth of 1.7 percent was recorded, followed by 5.3 percent growth in 1998. Economic growth reached 10.6 percent in 2004 but dropped to 8 percent in 2005 and to 7 percent in 2006. Although GDP grew by 7.8 percent in 2007, it slowed sharply in 2008 as the country was hit by harsh winter conditions and related shortages in electricity supplies.

Agriculture produces about 22.7 percent of GDP. The industrial sector employs 8 percent of the labor force and contributes about 28.5 percent of GDP. Nearly half the workforce (43 percent) is employed in export-oriented cotton production, while Tajikistan depends on imported agricultural products. The cotton sector makes use of child labor and unpaid youth and women. Farmers are forced to grow cotton through a complex system of debts and obligations. Development of other agricultural products, such as pomegranates, apricots, melons, and grapes, has been slowed by the lack of a supportive industry and the poor transport network, which hampers export. The fastest-growing sector is the service industry, which accounts for 25 percent of the labor force and produces about 49 percent of GDP.

Tajikistan's economic situation remains weak due to the uneven implementation of structural reforms, poor governance, widespread unemployment, systemic **corruption**, and the **external debt** burden. The shadow economy in Tajikistan in 2005 was about 61 percent of the officially reported GDP figure. It included tax avoidance (33 percent), home production of food products for personal consumption (15 percent), and barter exchange (13 percent).

Tajikistan is one of the 20 poorest countries in the world. In 2007, 64 percent of Tajikistan citizens lived below the poverty line. **Labor migration** leads to shortages in the workforce in parts of the country. Migrants' remittances account for 30–50 percent of Tajikistan's GDP. According to the **National Bank** data, the average salary in 2007 was 156 somoni (about $45), the minimal pension was 20 somoni (close to $6), and the level of inflation was 12.4 percent. The planned budget for 2008 was $1.3 billion.

Tajikistan has the lowest per capita GDP among the former Soviet republics. It is the last among Central Asian states in the size of the private sector as a percentage of GDP (39.8 percent) and in the level of foreign direct investment (2 percent of GDP) that it attracts. *See also* FOREIGN INVESTMENT; FOREIGN TRADE.

EDUCATION. A modern education system was introduced in Tajikistan in the second half of the 1920s and incorporated into the Soviet education system. The first Tajik higher education institution was the State Pedagogical Institute opened in **Dushanbe** in 1931. Three years later, the Agrarian Institute was formed. The Tajik Medical Institute started its work in 1939, the Tajik State University was established in 1948, and the Tajik Polytechnic Institute opened its doors in 1956. Mass literacy in Tajikistan was achieved by the end of the 1930s. By the end of the 1980s, Tajikistan had established 20 higher education institutions. Under Soviet rule, access to education was recognized as a universal constitutional right for all citizens, guaranteed through an extensive system of free public schools.

During the **civil war** (1992–1997), many schools were destroyed and looted, and over 5,400 teachers left Tajikistan, creating a major deficit in the education system. The **Majlisi Oli** subsequently adopted various pieces of legislation on education policy and standards for secondary and higher vocational education. Tajikistan provides for "mandatory general education, accessible secondary and first-level professional schooling, and competitive subsequent education" for all citizens. The main priorities for higher education reform are set out in "Strategic Directions for Long-Term Reform of the Educational System in Tajikistan 2004–2015."

The education system in Tajikistan is divided into preschool, primary, secondary, and high school levels. Primary and secondary education in Tajikistan lasts 11 years, the first nine of which correspond to free and compulsory education. Education in Tajikistan is secular; religious organizations are barred from interfering in the state-run education system. Under Soviet rule, approximately 25 percent of the

budget was devoted to education. But economic collapse and budget-
ary deficits after 1991 seriously undermined the education system.
In 1996, expenditures on education accounted for 12 percent of the
national budget. Government spending began to increase in 2004.
The total government expenditure on education was 15.9 percent in
2005 and 19 percent in 2007.

Some 28 institutions of higher learning were operating in 2008,
with a total enrollment of about 146,000 students. The Tajik National
University (formerly Tajik State National University), with almost
17,000 students, is the biggest and most prestigious institution of
higher education in the county. Tajikistan also has the **Islamic University of Tajikistan**, funded by the central government since 2008.

In 2008, about 1.7 million pupils (approximately 24 percent of the
population) attended about 4,000 primary and secondary schools.
Primary enrollment reached 95 percent for girls and 99 percent for
boys. There is a gap in enrollment rates in compulsory education
between boys (90 percent) and girls (78 percent). In post-compul-
sory education, this gap increases noticeably. Widespread poverty,
labor migration, and unemployment resulted in the exclusion from
education of children from poor families. Even though child labor
was banned by the Labor Code in 1997, Tajik children are forced to
leave school to contribute to the family earnings. Many Tajikistanis
and international observers are skeptical of official claims of a 98
percent literacy level. The United Nations Development Program put
the average enrollment rate for all levels of education (ages 6–23) at
62 percent in 2002. Many children of both sexes fail to attend classes
due to economic needs in most of the regions.

Since Soviet times, the languages of instruction are **Tajik**, **Rus-
sian**, **Kyrgyz**, and **Uzbek**. *See also* ACADEMICIAN; ACADEMY
OF SCIENCES OF TAJIKISTAN; CANDIDATE OF SCIENCES;
DOCTOR OF SCIENCES.

ELECTIONS. Under the Soviet system, elections to the **Supreme
Soviet** as well as provincial or district soviets were held every five
years. These were carefully orchestrated affairs with only one Communist Party (CP) approved candidate per seat. In 1990, Tajikistan
experienced its first elections with somewhat relaxed control by the
Communist Party of Tajikistan. Some of the seats in the Supreme
Soviet were openly contested by representatives of the emerging

noncommunist political movements. In November 1991, the first direct presidential elections were held in Tajikistan, in which former CP boss **Rahmon Nabiev** defeated the opposition candidate, **Davlatnazar Khudonazarov**. In 1992, during the **civil war**, the presidential system was annulled by the Supreme Soviet, but later it was revived under the leadership of **Emomali Rahmon**, who won the direct presidential elections on 6 November 1994 against **Abdumalik Abdullojonov**.

Elections to the **Majlisi Oli**, the unicameral legislative assembly that replaced the Supreme Soviet, were held in February 1995. By this time, forces loyal to President Rahmon were still involved in fighting with the opposition forces, unified in the **United Tajik Opposition**, and no opposition candidate stood for election. The signing of the **General Agreement on the Establishment of Peace and National Accord** in June 1997 between the protagonists preceded preparations for the presidential elections in November 1999. However, the Electoral Council initially refused to register the opposition candidate, **Davlat Usmon**, and only allowed his registration a few days before the election. The incumbent president was reelected with an overwhelming majority. In December 1999, the adoption of the Law on Elections to Local Majlises of People's Deputies restructured the parliament into a bicameral assembly.

The first elections to the lower house, **Majlisi Namoyandagon**, were held on 27 February 2000, and to the upper house, **Majlisi Melli**, on 23 March 2000. It was the first multiparty election in the history of Tajikistan. Six **political parties** competed in the elections. The UTO representatives were included in the Central Commission on Elections and Referenda (CCER). The Majlisi Namoyandagon is composed of 63 deputies, directly elected by all eligible citizens in a secret ballot. The law introduces a mixed electoral system: 41 members are elected from single mandate constituencies and the remaining 22 on the basis of party lists. The results of the parliamentary elections in 2000 made the ruling **People's Democratic Party of Tajikistan** (PDPT) the biggest party in parliament (30 seats). The **Communist Party** won 13 seats, and the **Islamic Renaissance Party of Tajikistan** (IRPT) gained two. Eighteen deputies were elected as self-nominated candidates. The **Organization for Security and Cooperation in Europe** (OSCE) monitored these elections and concluded that they did not meet any minimum international standards.

In 2003, a referendum led to a change in the **constitution**, allowing Rahmon to stand for two more seven-year terms beginning in 2006. The final results of the February 2005 parliamentary elections showed that the ruling PDPT was the clear victor, winning 52 of 63 seats. The remaining seats were divided between the Communist Party (4 seats), the IRPT (2 seats), and five independent candidates, considered by most observers to be supporters of President Rahmon. Four opposition parties issued a joint statement after the elections accusing the authorities of irregularities. The parties stated that they did not recognize the elections in **Dushanbe** and demanded a reelection.

The presidential election in November 2006, despite the presence of five candidates, was characterized by an absence of real rivalry. The IRPT decided not to advance a candidate. All parties chose not to contest the election. According to the OSCE, the 2006 presidential election did not fully test democratic electoral practices. In the 2006 election, Rahmon won more than 79 percent of the votes. *See also* MAJLISI NAMOYANDAGON, 2000–2005 ELECTIONS; MAJLISI NAMOYANDAGON, 2005–2010 ELECTIONS; PRESIDENTIAL ELECTIONS OF 1999; PRESIDENTIAL ELECTIONS OF 2006; PRESIDENTS OF TAJIKISTAN.

EMBLEM. The state emblem of independent Tajikistan, adopted in September 1994, depicts a crown, a semicircle of seven stars above the crown, and a backdrop of the sun rising from behind snowcapped mountains. This image is flanked by wheat sheafs on the right and cotton branches on the left, joined together at the top by a three-colored ribbon. Below this is an open book on a stand. *See also* FLAG.

EMOM (IMOM). An *emom* is a Muslim leader or spiritual master who leads religious ceremonies and rituals in the **mosque**. *See also* ISLAM.

ENVER PASHA (1881–1922). The Turkish general Enver Pasha was a son-in-law of the Muslim caliph and one of the **Basmachi** leaders in Tajikistan. Enver and other leaders of the Young Turks government were criticized by most European powers for massacring Armenians, torturing Arabs, and murdering prisoners of war. In 1918, after Turkey was defeated in World War I, Enver with the assistance of German intelligence traveled to Soviet Russia to help the Bolsheviks against the Basmachis in **Central Asia**. But at the end of 1921, he surfaced in Tajikistan on the Basmachi side and soon succeeded in uniting disparate rebel bands to challenge Soviet power. He enjoyed the support of some high officials in the **Bukharan** government and Turkish officers serving in the Bukharan militia. The Soviet government responded with intensified military operations in southern Tajikistan and **Uzbekistan**. Consequently, Enver's "Muslim army" was dispersed, and on 4 August 1922, Enver was killed in battle in Obi Dara, **Baljuvon**. Enver's resting place and that of another local Basmachi, Davlatmandi, became a shrine (*mazor*) for the local population. In 1996, at the request of the Turkish government, Enver's remains were transferred to Turkey.

ETIQUETTE. The Tajik people pay great attention to good manners. According to *shariah*, the canonical law of **Islam**), it is recommended to greet a Muslim and it is obligatory to reply. The common greeting among **Tajiks** is *as salomu alaikum* and the expected reply is *walaikum as salom*. Juniors must greet seniors. Shaking hands is common among men, and it is a demonstration of respect to place the left hand over the heart. As a rule, men avoid crossing their arms with women. When greeting, Tajik women kiss on the cheeks, and a hug is common among male relatives and friends. As a rule, a man must never enter a home where there are only women.

Hospitality and respect are considered essential for successful communication in the culture. When sitting at a table for refreshments (**dastarkhon**), the elderly and guests are always given the place of honor. At large social congregations, men and women are often separated. Modern Tajiks do not eat pork and horse meat, but most consume alcoholic beverages. As a result of frequent exchanges with other nationalities, many Tajiks also speak the Russian and Uzbek **languages** and are tolerant of Russian and Western manners. *See also* ADAB; AKA.

EURASIAN ECONOMIC COMMUNITY (EURASEC). A **Russia**-dominated economic organization of former post-Soviet states, Eurasec (*Evraziiskoye Ekonomicheskoye Soobshestvo*, or *Evrazes*, in Russian) was formed in October 2000 and ratified in May 2001 by all five member states: Belarus, Kazakhstan, **Kyrgyzstan**, Russia, and Tajikistan. Eurasec grew out of the **Customs Union**. In October 2005, the members agreed that Eurasec should merge with the **Central Asian Cooperation Organization** (CACO). In August 2006, it was announced that a customs union would be formed by Russia, Belarus, and Kazakhstan by 2011 with other Eurasec members being able to join later. Russia's share in the Eurasec budget is 40 percent; Belarus, **Uzbekistan**, and Kazakhstan pay 15 percent each, and Kyrgyzstan and Tajikistan pay 7.5 percent each. Votes in the organization's Integration Committee equal a country's share in the budget. Armenia, Ukraine, and Moldova have observer status. Uzbekistan joined Eurasec in January 2006 but left in November 2008, calling the organization ineffective and useless.

Eurasec's main goal is to establish a customs union and unified economic space. Eurasec also envisages a closer rapprochement and unification of national legislations, carrying out actions increasing their economic potential, and harmonization of structural economic reforms.

EXTERNAL DEBT. Tajikistan is a heavily indebted country. During the **civil war**, the debt increased speedily, with the foreign debt to gross domestic product (GDP) ratio growing from zero in 1992 to 86 percent in 1997. The external debt grew at an annual rate of 39.4 percent, from $877 million as of April 2007 to $1.38 billion as of October 2008, thus constituting more than 29.1 percent of GDP. It rose to $1.69 billion by January 2009, or 38.8 percent of GDP. At that time, the average debt per person was $225. In 2008, the biggest bilateral creditors—**Russia** and **Uzbekistan**—accounted for about 50 percent of the total debt. After Russia forgave the bulk of the debt in exchange for ownership of the space tracking station **Okno** in July 2008, Tajikistan's two biggest bilateral creditors were **China** and Uzbekistan. As of January 2009, Tajikistan owed them $630 million and $43 million respectively. The largest contributors to an increase in net foreign debt are the International Monetary Fund (IMF), Asian Development Bank (ADB), and Islamic Development Bank (IDB): $812 million total in 2009. Regardless of several debt restructuring arrangements, Tajikistan has a low debt-servicing capacity. The situation further deteriorated in March 2008, when it became known that the **National Bank** of Tajikistan provided the IMF with incorrect information on the country's reserve funds in order to get government-guaranteed commercial credits to support the Credit Invest private company. *See also* CORRUPTION.

– F –

FALAK. The word *falak* (literally "cry to the sky") is used to refer to heaven or the cosmos but also to fate or destiny. Falak is also a distinct form of folk **music** widespread among the Tajiks of central and southern Tajikistan and **Badakhshon**. Falak sings of the ephemeral nature of life and a separation from loved ones because of inescapable fate. Traditionally, falak is played by amateurs at celebrations for weddings, circumcisions, and other occasions. According to a decree of President **Emomali Rahmon**, the state ensemble named Falak was formed in 2003, and 10 October was declared a Day of Falak. *See also* JURAEV, AKASHARIF; KHOSHIM, ODINA; SHASHMAQOM.

FARANJI (PARANJA). A foreigner or person of European (Frankish) origin may be called a *faranji*, but the term is also used for a cloak designed to cover the head, face, and body of Tajik females. The traditional Tajik faranji is a light robe made of silk or cotton with vestigial sleeves on the back and ornamented with embroidery, tassels, buttons, or other decoration. The faranji is paired with a veil made of heavy horsehair that is used to conceal the woman's face. Before the Soviet period, women and girls were required to wear a faranji over the top of the head upon leaving the household. This garment was popular among, and mandatory for, the females in the urban Tajik North (primarily the regions of **Ferghana**, **Bukhara**, and **Samarqand**); women in the mountainous regions of Tajikistan, including **Badakhshon**, were not familiar with the faranji and never covered their faces. The Soviets banned wearing of the faranji during the **hujum** campaign in the late 1920s. Many veils were burned in public, and by the end of the 1950s, the faranji had completely disappeared. *See also* HIJAB; WOMEN'S ISSUES.

FARSI. Called by Tajiks and Persians *Porsi-i dari*, Farsi is the **language** of the Persians and is the official language of **Iran**. Farsi belongs to the southwestern branch of the Iranian group of the Indo-European languages. Classical Farsi was formed in the 9th–10th centuries. It has common roots with **Tajik**. There was very little difference between Tajik, Farsi, and **Dari** until the 16th century. Farsi and Tajik are still close but use different scripts (Arabic for Farsi and Dari,

Cyrillic for Tajik). Since the second half of the 1980s, there has been a lively debate in the Tajik media about linguistic ties between Farsi, Tajik, and Dari and the necessity to return Tajik to Arabic script.

FATIR. A *fatir* is a puffed, bland loaf of bread baked in a **tanur** (oven).

FATTOEV, SAIMUROD (1958–). Born in **Kulob**, Fattoev graduated in 1981 from the Moscow State University, where he studied journalism, and started his career as a correspondent for the national newspaper *Tojikistoni Soveti*. Fattoev served as a military interpreter in **Afghanistan** in the mid-1980s. At the end of the 1980s, he worked as a consultant for the Central Committee of the **Communist Party of Tajikistan** (CPT). In 1991, he received a **candidate** degree in political science from the Institute of Political Science and Social Management in Minsk, Belarus. From 1994 to 2006, he headed the secretariat of Tajikistan's President **Emomali Rahmon**. In 2007, Fattoev became a state adviser to the president, responsible for social development and public relations.

FEBRUARY 1917 REVOLUTION. This revolution ended the tsarist regime in **Russia** and led to the establishment of a provisional government that vied for power with emerging Soviet organs. In April 1917, the **Turkistan** committee of the provisional government replaced Turkistan's tsarist governor general. The executive committee of the provisional government was formed in **Khujand**, and the All-Pamirian committee of the provisional government was formed in **Khorugh**. As in Russia proper, the fall of tsarism precipitated the rise of local soviets in Turkistan as well as among Russian residents of the **Bukharan emirate**. The February 1917 revolution also led to the emergence of the first Muslim political organizations: **Shuroi Islomia**, **Jamiyati Ulamo**, and **Young Bukharans**. In October 1917, the provisional government in Russia was overthrown by the Bolsheviks.

FEBRUARY 1990 EVENTS IN DUSHANBE. Mass demonstrations were held in **Dushanbe** following rumors that **Armenian** refugees from Azerbaijan would be settled in Dushanbe and given preferential assistance with housing. Street rallies, originally protesting the government, deteriorated into anarchy and resulted in the destruction of public buildings and private property on 13–17 February 1990. Russian residents of Dushanbe became the target of attacks by Tajik youth. Citizens of Dushanbe, both Russian and non-Russian, responded to the riots by forming self-defense units in residential areas. The military was deployed to contain the violence, but many people died and hundreds were wounded. **Rastokhez** and Islamic leaders formed mediating committees and organized peace rallies in an effort to end the rioting. The February 1990 events marked the beginning of the Russian mass exodus from Tajikistan. *See also* CIVIL WAR; RUSSIANS IN TAJIKISTAN.

FERGHANA. A historical and cultural center of **Central Asia** known since the 1st millennium BCE, Ferghana (Farghona in Tajik-Uzbek transcription) is situated in the **Syr Darya** river basin, surrounded by mountains. In Chinese chronicles, this valley was called Davan, famous for its horses. Ferghana remains an important **agricultural** producer. The three states of Tajikistan, **Kyrgyzstan**, and **Uzbekistan** border each other in the Ferghana valley. There is a Ferghana **veloyat** in Uzbekistan.

FIRDAWSI, ABULQASEM (940–1025). A poet of the classic period of Perso-Tajik **literature**, Firdawsi was born in Tus, **Khurasan**, and spent 35 years writing his masterpiece, the *Shohnoma* epic, to honor the **Samanid** rulers, who were supporters of **Iranian** culture after the **Arab** conquest of the 7th century. Firdawsi is revered in Tajikistan as a national poet.

FIRDAWSI STATE LIBRARY. Founded in 1931, the Firdawsi State Library (Kitobkhonai Davlatii Tojikiston ba nomi Firdawsi) in **Dushanbe** is Tajikistan's biggest library, with more than 4 million volumes. The library holds rare manuscripts of the 13th–18th centuries and is part of the Ministry of Culture and Information. It is named after the classical poet **Abulqasem Firdawsi**.

FIVE-YEAR PLAN FOR THE DEVELOPMENT OF THE PEOPLE'S ECONOMY. A program of socioeconomic planning in the Union of Soviet Socialist Republics (USSR) in 1929–1991, five-year plans were created by special planning committees, consisting of specialists in the **economy**. The plans were approved by the Communist

Party congresses. The five-year plans of the individual soviet republics were part of the USSR's five-year plans, subject to approval by CPT congresses. The collapse of the **Soviet Union** and the transition to a market economy ended the five-year plans.

FLAG. The national flag of Tajikistan was officially adopted by the **Majlisi Oli** in September 1994. It consists of a top color strip of red, a middle strip of white, and a bottom strip of green. The middle strip is one-and-a-half times the height of the color strips. In the middle of the white strip is a gold, stylized crown and a semicircle of seven stars. *See also* EMBLEM; STATE HYMN.

FOLBIN. A *folbin* is a shaman or fortune-teller. By a governmental decision of 13 December 2007, Tajikistan launched a crackdown on *folbini* (witchcraft and fortune-telling) as part of an antipoverty drive after earlier banning lavish weddings and expensive funerals. *See also* ETIQUETTE; ISLAM; TUI.

FOREIGN INVESTMENT. The adoption of the Law on Foreign Investments in the Republic of Tajikistan on 10 March 1992 opened the way for foreign direct investment. Since 1993, Tajikistan is a member of the International Association on Investment Guarantees as well as the International Center for the Settlement of Investment Disputes (Washington Convention). The Tajik government's economic development strategy for 2005–2015 has no discriminatory effects on foreign-owned investors. Foreign investors can purchase shares on the local stock exchange. If the share of a foreign investor is over 30 percent, it is exempt from profit tax for two years. The same benefit applies for foreign investors whose investments in a Tajikistani venture amount to $100,000–$500,000. If the share of a foreign partner in a joint venture ranges from $500,000 to $2 million, the grace period is three years. The grace period is five years if foreign investments amount to over $5 million. Foreign investors also can buy real estate; however, private land ownership is still prohibited.

The Tajikistan tax code that came into effect on 1 January 2005 complies with World Trade Organization (WTO) standards. The government enacted the Law on Free Trade Zones in 2004 and passed draft regulations to implement the law in 2005. WTO accession negotiations were launched in 2004 after preparatory work conducted by the Tajik government with assistance from the **United States** and other donors.

Despite this, Tajikistan attracts the lowest level of foreign direct investment among all the post-Soviet states of **Central Asia**. From 1997, when the **civil war** ended, to 2004, Tajikistan attracted only $224 million in foreign direct investments. The top three investors were Great Britain ($105.1 million), South Korea ($53.4 million), and Italy ($50 million).

According to the State Committee on Investment and State Property, on 1 January 2008 the nation's investment portfolio contained 53 programs with a total value of $1.369 billion. About $1 billion of this amount is foreign investment in the form of credit, and $160 million has been given to Tajikistan as a grant. Some $100 million is being spent from the state budget, and $40 million from other sources.

The inflows of foreign direct investment (FDI) are concentrated mostly in the aluminum, **power generation**, and transport infrastructure sectors. Of special strategic importance for Tajikistan is the construction of hydropower stations on the **Vakhsh River**, including Sangtuda-1 and Sangtuda-2. In January 2008, **Russia**'s state-controlled Unified Energy System (RAO YeES) launched Sangtuda-1. RAO YeES spent $500 million to build this station. As agreed, Russia retains a 75 percent share in Sangtuda-1, which will generate 2.7 billion kilowatt hours annually. The total value of Russia's FDI in the Tajik **economy** in 2006 reached $232 million.

Iran has been actively investing in the economy of Tajikistan, including the construction of Sangtuda-2 ($220 million), the **Istiqlol** and Shahriston tunnels, the power line from southern Tajikistan to Qunduz and Herat (**Afghanistan**) and further to Mashhad (Iran), the Chormaghzak tunnel (**Khatlon**), and some other projects.

The **Dusti Bridge** between Tajikistan and Afghanistan is a major U.S. project. In 2006, U.S. aid to Tajikistan totaled $32.7 million; in 2007, it increased to $50 million, redirecting the flow from the humanitarian sphere to development projects. The most striking change in Tajikistan since 2006 was the immense growth of Chinese involvement. Prior to this, at the end of May 2004, a **China-Tajik border** station was established in **Kulma**. In 2005, only $6 million of bilateral assistance was provided by China to Tajikistan, while in mid-2006, Beijing committed around $605 million to Tajikistan for a three-year period to improve **motor roads** and electrical supply systems. Another $400 million was committed in January 2007. In 2006, China started a $608 million renovation of Tajikistan's most important Dushanbe-Khujand-Chanak road, as well as construction of the Sharshar tunnel in the south and electricity transmission lines. Most of the transport related projects, including those connecting Afghanistan, Tajikistan, and **Kyrgyzstan**, are supported by investors from the United States, European Union, Russia, Japan, and Iran.

The largest investors in the Tajik economy are companies from Canada, the United States, Great Britain, Korea, Germany, Switzerland, Italy, Hungary, and Russia. Most prominent are the Nelson Gold Corporation (development and mining of gold and silver), Gulf International Minerals (gold mining), Credit Swiss First Boston (futures contracts for cotton), Kabool Textiles (textiles production), and Adjind International (textiles). Other successful joint ventures are Zerafshan, Darvaz, Aprelevka, Javoni, Rishta, Khujand Packaging, and Marmar. Tajikistan launched WTO accession negotiations in 2004. *See also* FOREIGN POLICY; FOREIGN TRADE.

FOREIGN POLICY. From the late 1940s, the Tajik Soviet Socialist Republic's (Tajik SSR) head of government also formally fulfilled the duties of minister of foreign affairs. In reality, the central government in Moscow had never given up its monopoly on external policy, and Tajikistan had no power to conduct its own diplomacy. When the republic became independent in 1991, its government lacked competent diplomats and foreign policy strategists capable of defining an agenda of national interests and priorities to be pursued in diplomacy.

In the first weeks after independence, Tajikistan was recognized by the international community at large. Over the course of 1992–1993, the country created its independent foreign policy agency and developed the diplomatic and commercial links that connected Tajikistan with the outside world. Tajikistan also became a member of the major international organizations. In 1995, Tajikistan opened its first embassy outside the former **Soviet Union**, in Turkey. The Ministry of Foreign Affairs is organized geographically, comprising four major departments: the CIS desk, the European and American desk, the Asian and African desk, and the international organizations desk.

Foreign policy in Tajikistan is defined by the president; its main goal has been to take advantage of the opportunities offered by independence. Tajikistan has opted for a "multivectored" foreign policy; it is pragmatic and free from both the cultural prejudices of the Soviet past and more recent value-based (liberal, Islamic, etc.) pressures. The country strives to secure **foreign investment** and promote regional security while ensuring its maximum autonomy in international affairs. Tajikistan has positive relationships with all the major powers firmly interested in this part of the world, including the **United States, China, Russia,** and **Iran.**

Three priorities have been defined as central by Tajikistan's diplomatic service. One is developing friendly relations and close cooperation with the Russian Federation and other **Commonwealth of Independent States** (CIS) countries, primarily neighboring **Uzbekistan, Kyrgyzstan,** Kazakhstan, and Turkmenistan. The second priority is supporting stronger ties with the nearby states of Iran, **Afghanistan, Pakistan,** and other countries sharing Tajikistan's **language,** history, and culture. The third priority is increasing economic ties and cooperation with the heavyweight powers of China, **India,** the United States, the European Union, and Japan.

The development of friendly relations, cooperation, and integration with the former Soviet states has always been a firm priority in the foreign policy of Tajikistan. The country joined the CIS, which was created in December 1991. At the Tashkent CIS summit in May 1992, the Collective Security Treaty was signed by the six former Soviet republics of Russia, Uzbekistan, Kyrgyzstan, Tajikistan, Kazakhstan, and Armenia. This organization was renamed the **Collective Security Treaty Organization** (CSTO) in October 2002.

The **civil war** that broke out in Tajikistan in 1992 fueled mostly exaggerated fears of Islamic fundamentalism among the CIS members. On 7 August 1993, the heads of Uzbekistan, Russia, Tajikistan, Kazakhstan, and Kyrgyzstan signed an agreement on cooperation in protecting the Tajik-Afghan border and decided to send a multinational peacekeeping force of as many as 5,000 troops to Tajikistan. However, Tajikistan's neighbors were reluctant to become involved in war-torn Tajikistan. Kazakhstan, Uzbekistan, and Kyrgyzstan disagreed over the nature and objectives of military cooperation between the Central Asian states.

Much to the regret of Tajik leaders, neither Russia nor the CIS in general was able to build even a rudimentary security architecture in the region. The disturbances of the civil war in 1992–1997 exacerbated the dependency of the inexperienced Tajik government on major external players, namely Russia, Iran, and Uzbekistan. Fortunately, the Russian and **Uzbek** governments that supported **Emomali Rahmon** and the Iranian authorities, who hosted the leaders of exiled Tajik opposition, joined in the effort to bring peace to Tajikistan.

Tajiks and Uzbeks are the closest neighbors; they have much more in common with each other in terms of race, history, and culture than the **Kyrgyz**, Kazakh, and **Turkmen** do with them. The relationship between Tajikistan and Uzbekistan is based in the Treaty on Good Neighborship and Friendly Cooperation, signed on 4 January 1993, and the agreement On Eternal Friendship signed during the official visit of President Islam Karimov of Uzbekistan to Tajikistan on 15 June 2000. Both countries are members of the CSTO, the **Eurasian Economic Community** (Eurasec), and the **Shanghai Cooperation Organization** (SCO). The cordiality rests on an unstable foundation, however. Tajikistan and Uzbekistan have perhaps Central Asia's most controversial relationship. In addition to issues related to the allocation of **water** resources and disputes on their border, both sides accuse each other of harboring terrorists and separatists. Uzbekistan controls major regional transport networks and uses economic blackmail regarding the security of natural gas supplies against Tajikistan. The mining of the shared border by Uzbekistan has further strained relations.

Tajikistan has friendly relations with Kazakhstan, Kyrgyzstan, and Turkmenistan. But between 1989 and 2004, there were water and land-related cross-border tensions at local levels between Tajiks and Kyrgyz in the **Ferghana** valley. Most of these conflicts have been settled at the local, nongovernmental level. Tajikistan is dependent on Uzbekistan and Kyrgyzstan road and rail links to access external markets. The borders between Tajikistan, Uzbekistan, and Kyrgyzstan continue to be the subject of ongoing discussions. However, Tajikistan and its neighbors have generally accepted the Soviet administrative borders and have not used the demarcation process as an occasion to reopen historical irredentist territorial claims.

Tajikistan joined the Central Asian Economic Union (created in April 1994 between Kazakhstan, Kyrgyzstan, and Uzbekistan) on 17 July 1998, and the organization was then renamed the Central Asian Economic Cooperation (CAEC). On 28 February 2002, the CAEC was transformed into the **Central Asian Cooperation Organization** (CACO). Within this regional intergovernmental organization, Central Asian neighbors have regulated custom duties, import tariffs, cross-border trade, and other issues. In October 2005, the CACO merged with Eurasec. The future of Eurasec is uncertain because of the power disparity among its members; the weaker members, including Tajikistan, may lose part of their national sovereignty to more powerful members like Russia, Kazakhstan, and Belarus.

Tajikistan is discovering Asia not as an object for political solidarity but as a potential investor and a partner in boosting regional security and the implementation of major economic projects. Since independence, Tajikistan's affairs have been closely intertwined with those of Afghanistan, its southern neighbor. In the aftermath of the terrorist attacks in the United States on 11 September 2001, Tajikistan officially declared its willingness to cooperate with the U.S.-led campaign to combat **terrorism** in Afghanistan. Tajikistan recognizes the government of Afghan President Hamid Karzai and refrains from informal contacts with Tajik warlords in Afghanistan. Almost no danger of cross-border nationalism exists along the Tajik-Afghan border. Nonetheless, Tajikistan hesitates to cooperate with its near-stateless, unstable, economically backward, and drug-producing southern neighbor, yet is excited to advertise its surpluses of electric power in Afghanistan and Pakistan and bolster Tajikistan's industry to meet the needs of the reconstruction in Afghanistan. However, it is going to take years to turn these plans into reality due to security concerns.

While international intervention in Afghanistan reduced the threat of Islamic insurgents crossing into Tajikistan, it has not affected the drug trade or low-level violence on the Tajik-Afghan border. Since early 2002, Tajikistan's cooperation with the Afghan government has been on the increase. In December 2002, the Kabul Declaration on Good Neighborly Relations was signed, by which Afghanistan and its neighbors reaffirmed their commitment to the bilateral relationships. Tajikistan and Afghanistan are members of the **Conference on Interaction and Confidence-Building Measures in Asia** (CICA) and the **Economic Cooperation Organization** (ECO). The two sides initiated an intensive political dialogue, especially with regard to border protection, **drug trafficking**, and trade and technical cooperation.

The Persians of Iran, Tajiks of Tajikistan, and a considerable Tajik minority in Afghanistan share strong cultural and linguistic ties. Iran was the first nation to establish an embassy in Dushanbe and a key facilitator of the 1997 agreement ending Tajikistan's civil war. Iran is one of four observers in the SCO. Authorities in Tehran try to cultivate closer ties with Afghanistan and Tajikistan, partly to ease international pressure over Iran's nuclear program. In the early 2000s, Iran funded major projects in Tajikistan, such as completion of the Sangtuda-2 hydroelectric power station and the **Istiqlol tunnel**. Relations between the two states are restricted, though, because of Tajikistan's secularism and Iran's position on the role of **Islam** in state affairs. Furthermore, the Tajiks are largely followers of **Sunnism** with a tiny Shia **Ismaili** minority, while Twelve-Imam **Shiism** has been Iran's official religion since the early 16th century. Normally, Sunni Islam does not lend itself to manipulation by the Shiite mullahs who carried out the Iranian revolution in 1979.

Tajikistan has an open door policy and is ready to cooperate with countries willing to invest in the country but also willing to respect Tajikistan's sovereignty and refrain from political pressure. Tajik leaders cite the example of Tajikistan's economic cooperation with China. Since the mid-1990s, Tajikistan has signed a series of bilateral treaties with its giant eastern neighbor. Both countries are members of the SCO. As of 2008, China has invested around $1 billion in the Tajik **economy**. President Rahmon described the relations between Tajikistan and the People's Republic of China as cordial. In contrast to Western organizations operating in Tajikistan (e.g., the Organization for Security and Cooperation in Europe, the European Union), the Russia- and China-dominated SCO has promoted joint initiatives for economic growth and security without rhetoric on **human rights** and democracy or placing other political conditions on member states. Growth in cross-border trade and new links in transportation and communications are of special importance to Tajikistan. The **Kulma** border station opened in May 2004 is a vital transit point for commercial trade to the Tajik economy. No irredentist feelings have been documented among the 41,000 **Tajiks of China** living in Xinjiang-Uighur Autonomous Region, which is adjacent to the Tajik **Badakhshon**. Tajikistan, like other SCO members, has never supported Uighur separatism, considering it a manifestation of international terrorism.

President Rahmon still sees Russia as an important strategic partner, but it is also apparent that he wants to tap into Western assistance. His government wants to promote a more sovereign and less
Russian-influenced image of Tajikistan internationally. Traditionally,
Western countries accepted Tajikistan as part of Russia's sphere of
influence. This status changed after 11 September 2001 as the United
States and its allies targeted Afghanistan in the war on terrorism.
Nevertheless, Russia runs several strategic resources in Tajikistan,
including the optic and electronic system **Okno**, a military base, and
an airbase in Ayni.

The United States and its allies needed the assistance of the states
of the region, including Tajikistan, in the form of bases, overflight
rights, supplies, and other considerations to conduct operations
against the **Taliban** regime in Afghanistan. Even more critically,
the 9/11 attacks made the United States and its allies see the danger
that Tajikistan—the weakest and poorest Central Asian state—could
become a base for international terrorist groups. In turn, Tajikistanis
have realized that the antiterrorism campaign has given their country
a real chance to rehabilitate the image of Tajikistan so that it is no
longer seen as a center of Islamic militancy and instability and thus
will attract substantial foreign investment.

Since the fall of 2001, Tajikistan's bilateral links have grown
significantly. In 2002, Great Britain, France, and Japan opened em-
bassies in Dushanbe. Tajikistan established permanent delegations in
Brussels, Berlin, and Washington in 2003. Under the framework of
the U.S.-initiated **Greater Central Asia** project, Dushanbe, despite
lacking energy resources for local consumption especially in winter,
trades its hydroelectric power to northern Afghanistan, supports the
construction of bridges across the **Amu Darya**, and promotes cross-
border cooperation with Afghan communities. On 26 August 2007,
the **Dusti Bridge** joining the two countries was officially opened. It
has been the largest infrastructure project funded by the United States
in Tajikistan. In addition, the French military, which has maintained
an airbase in the Tajik capital city since late 1992 for the purpose
of supporting humanitarian operations in Afghanistan, launched a
reconstruction of the runway of the Dushanbe airfield to make it
capable of bearing heavy airplanes. The United States has sought
political and economic influence in Tajikistan in order to prevent
the possible dominance of China or Russia, which have traditionally

excluded any American presence in Central Asia. By financing the construction of five bridges across the Amu Darya, the United States, Britain, and their partners intend to secure control over emerging Eurasian transport corridors and communication networks (Northern Europe-India, Western Europe-China-Japan), as well as various pipelines. The regional transport infrastructure financed by the United States and European Union is also capable of supporting military operations in this strategically important region. The Tajik-Afghan bridges may be used for military purposes by connecting American bases in Kyrgyzstan with Afghanistan via Tajik territory.

Some of these U.S.-backed strategic goals—particularly those pertaining to the country's breakthrough to the outside world and obtaining access to warm-water ports in the Indian Ocean and the international commodity market—coincide with the chief priorities of Tajikistan. However, achieving the overall U.S. strategy of long-lasting global leadership may bring problems to a weak Tajikistan. Tajiks feel ambivalent about Russia's role in the country's history, but that role has been too central for Russia to be moved out of its position of influence overnight.

Tajikistan maintains good relations with the European Union, which is, in addition to the United States, a major donor to development and security programs in Tajikistan. The EU signed a Partnership and Cooperation Agreement with Tajikistan in October 2004. In June 2007, the EU approved a new Central Asia strategy. Under the framework created by the EU, Tajikistan receives support for regional cooperation in trade, transportation, water, environmental concerns, social development, and statistics.

Tajikistan has recognized that it is dependent on regional integration to ensure its economic and political growth. Since its independence, it has cooperated closely with the **United Nations** and the OSCE. The country has secured membership in more than 50 major regional and broader organizations, including the Central Asia Regional Economic Cooperation Program (CAREC), World Health Organization (WHO), European Bank for Reconstruction and Development (EBRD), Organization of Islamic Conference (OIC), International Monetary Fund (IMF), International Bank for Reconstruction and Development (IBRD), International Labor Organization (ILO), International Postal Union, International Organization for Migration (IOM), Asian Development Bank (ADB), Islamic Development Bank (IDB), and NATO's Partnership for Peace program.

As of early 2009, Tajikistan has direct diplomatic relations with 110 states. The Tajik capital hosts 13 resident ambassadors. In addition, Moscow, Tashkent, Almaty, Ashgabat, Tehran, and Islamabad host 57 nonresident ambassadors to the Republic of Tajikistan. The Tajik government joined almost every international organization it could during the first 18 years of independence. However, membership in international organizations cannot bring better standards of living for citizens. Tajikistan's foreign policy reflects the fragility of the country's domestic situation. The official open door, multivectored foreign policy cannot be successful until Tajikistan defines its identity with some real meaning in relation to its religion, culture, language, history, and geography. Particularly amid its more powerful post-Soviet Turkic neighbors and the Islamic states of Afghanistan, Pakistan, and Iran, a non-Turkic and secular Tajikistan has to define a role for itself in the regional arena.

Recently, a struggle for leadership has broken out between countries of the region. In April 2007, President Nursultan Nazarbayev of Kazakhstan proposed the formation of a Central Asian Union. However, Uzbekistan, envious of Kazakhstan's current wealth, sees itself as the region's historic leader. President Karimov of Uzbekistan is the main opponent of a Kazakhstan-dominated Central Asian Union. At the same time, the Uzbek leadership does not get along with Tajikistan, Turkmenistan, and Kyrgyzstan. Surely, for impoverished Tajikistan, Kazakhstan's plan for a Russian-speaking, EU-modeled Central Asian Union is much more attractive than the proposal for the creation of a commonwealth of Turkic states made by Turkish prime minister Recep Tayyip Erdogan, since Nazarbayev's plan is not based on the shared culture, language, and history of Turkic nations. *See also* FOREIGN TRADE.

FOREIGN TRADE. During Soviet times, Tajikistan's links with the outside world were rudimentary and the central government in Moscow enjoyed a monopoly on external trade. Since 1991, the situation has changed and Tajikistan has been trading with various foreign countries. The turnover of foreign trade in 2007 reached $4.14 billion, of which $1.76 billion were from exports and $2.38 billion from imports. Imports were mainly from **Russia** (24 percent), **China** (19 percent), Kazakhstan (12 percent), **Uzbekistan** (11 percent), and Azerbaijan (8 percent). Export links mainly connected to Norway (8 percent), Russia (8 percent), Turkey (7.7 percent), Uzbekistan (5.9 percent), and the **United States** (4 percent). *See also* ECONOMY; FOREIGN INVESTMENT; FOREIGN POLICY.

FRONTIER GUARD OF THE RUSSIAN FEDERATION. Following the signing of the Agreement on Friendship, Cooperation, and Mutual Assistance between the **Russian Federation** and the Republic of Tajikistan, and the Agreement on Cooperation in the Military Field, the special Russian Frontier Guards for Tajikistan were formed on 19 October 1992. According to these agreements, Tajikistan delegated the protection of its Afghan and Chinese borders to the Russian Federation until it could secure its borders independently. This special frontier guard consisted of the Russian Frontier Guard Group, the Collective Peacekeeping Force in the Republic of Tajikistan, and the Frontier Guard Troops of Tajikistan. The group consisted of five detachments, one wing regiment, and one reserve of the commander in 1992, with about 17,000 troops. More than 80 percent of the military personnel were Tajik. Between 1992 and 1999, these frontier guards in Tajikistan detained 1,200 trespassers, prevented 7,000 attempts to violate the border, found 80 weapons caches, removed 800 gunnery units, and captured more than six tons of narcotics. Following the signing of the **General Agreement on the Establishment of Peace and National Accord** between the **United Tajik Opposition** (UTO) and the government that facilitated the incorporation of the UTO forces in Tajikistan's army, the frontier guard group in Tajikistan was reduced in size. From 2002 to October 2005, Russian frontier guards handed over the patrolling of Tajik borders to the **Frontier Guard Troops of Tajikistan** and left for Russia. *See also* ARMY; RUSSIAN MILITARY BASE IN TAJIKISTAN.

FRONTIER GUARD TROOPS OF TAJIKISTAN. In July 1994, the Tajikistan parliament transformed forces subordinate to the Department of Border Protection of the Ministry of Security to form the Frontier Guard Troops of the Republic of Tajikistan. In February 1997, a state committee on border protection was formed under the leadership of Saidanvar Kamolov. Frontier guard troops in Tajikistan consist of three brigades, a separate post in **Khujand**, and rear services. The troops are based in **nohiyas** of **Hamadoni** and **Panj**. In the **Shurobod nohiya** of the **Khatlon** veloyat, they shared the border post with the **frontier guard of the Russian Federation**. In 2005, the frontier guard of Tajikistan took full responsibility for patrolling Tajikistan's borders.

FUEL INDUSTRY. Tajikistan's exploitation of its oil and gas deposits is minimal: 2.6 percent of the total deposits, with a large potential for growth. Known coal deposits are located in Shuroob, Fan-Yaghnob, Maghion, Kshtut-Zaurin, Nazar-Ailoq, Ziddy, and Miyonadu. Ten deposits of oil and gas have been discovered in the south and the north. Tajikistan's gas is generally used in local **industries**, though it is also used domestically in the south. Four transit pipelines bring gas to Tajikistan. A northern pipeline provides transit of **Uzbek** gas from the **Ferghana** valley to Tajik territory. In 1997, the Tajik government adopted a program of energy security. In 1999, a limited gas extraction operation started in the Khoja Sartez gas deposit (estimated at 1.2 billion cubic meters of natural gas and 45,000 tons of gas condensate). The Rengan deposit (40–50 million cubic meters of natural gas) is in the process of cultivation. Both Khoja Sartez and Rengan are located in southern Tajikistan. The program, however, is of limited success because of the shortage of investment.

FUQARO. The term *fuqaro* is used to refer to the population, taxpayers, or the poor.

– G –

GAZ. A linear measure commonly used in **Central Asia** before the Russian conquest in the 19th century, the *gaz* varied from region to region, but the most common was equal to 95 centimeters.

GENERAL AGREEMENT ON THE ESTABLISHMENT OF PEACE AND NATIONAL ACCORD. This agreement ending the **civil war** that began in 1992 was signed on 27 June 1997 by President **Emomali Rahmon** and the leader of the **United Tajik Opposition** (UTO), **Said Abdullo Nuri**, as well as the UN special representative,

Gerd Merrem. The agreement was the culmination of the peace process known as the **Inter-Tajik Peace Talks**, which started in April 1994. The **Commission for National Reconciliation** (CNR), with equal representation from both the government and the UTO, was mandated to implement the terms of the General Agreement.

According to the General Agreement, the transition period could take 12–18 months and was designed to finally lead to new parliamentary **elections**. This agreement provided for the release of all prisoners of war and the release of all opposition prisoners under the amnesty law; reform of the government structure by including 30 percent of UTO representatives in all executive bodies (i.e., ministries, departments, local governments, administrations, judicial and law enforcement agencies); drafting **constitutional** amendments to be endorsed in a national referendum; drafting laws on **political parties**, public associations, **mass media**, and parliamentary elections to be adopted by the **Majlisi Oli**; lifting all restrictions and legal bans on political parties and movements affiliated with the UTO; freedom of the mass media; and forming a general Electoral Commission with 25 percent UTO representation for the holding of referenda and parliamentary elections. The implementation of these provisions took 32 months. On 27 February 2000, fresh parliamentary elections were held in Tajikistan, signaling the end of this transition period. On the national calendar, 27 June is now marked as the Peace Day Holiday.

GERMANS. Russian Germans arrived in Tajikistan mostly after **World War II**. In 1945–1946, the Soviet government gathered together those Russian Germans who had been evacuated to Germany from Ukraine by the German military during World War II and sent them to work under special settlement restrictions in the Urals, Siberia, and **Central Asia**. By 1950, the number of Russian German special settlers (*spetspereselensty*) in Tajikistan had reached 27,879. About 10 percent of the Russian Germans forcibly repatriated from the formerly German-occupied territories back to the Union of Soviet Socialist Republics (USSR) ended up in Tajikistan. Most of them were sent to **cotton kolkhozes** in **Vakhsh valley**. They lacked both material provisions and **human rights**. From 1954 to 1956, the Soviet government abolished the special settlement regime. In 1979, there were 38,853 Germans living in Tajikistan. From 1989 to 1999, practically all Russian Germans emigrated to Germany.

GHAFUROV, BOBOJON (1909–1977). A head of state and of the **Communist Party of Tajikistan** (CPT) from 1946–1956, Ghafurov was a Soviet Orientalist, **academician**, and founder of modern Tajik historiography. He was born in Isfisor, Leninobod **(Sughd)** veloyat, and studied at the high juridical school in **Samarqand** in 1928–1930. Ghafurov started work in the People's Commissariat of Justice in 1930. In 1935, he graduated from the All-Soviet Communist Institute of Journalism and became deputy editor and then editor of *Qizil Tojikiston*, an organ of the CPT in the Uzbek language. Then he devoted himself to party work, as instructor, head of the Publishing Department, deputy head of the Department of Propaganda and Agitation, and head of the central committee organization. In 1938, Ghafurov turned to research and joined the **candidate** course (*aspirantura*) of the Institute of the History of the Union of Soviet Socialist Republics (Moscow). After graduating from his research course, Ghafurov was appointed secretary for propaganda and agitation in the CPT (1941). In 1944–1946, he was the second secretary of the CPT, and in 1946 he was appointed first secretary of the party.

Ghafurov continued his research interests while in office. In 1947, he completed *Ta'rikhi Mukhtasari Khalqi Tojik* (Brief History of the Tajik People), the first complete manuscript on the history of the Tajiks by a Tajik. This manuscript was translated into Russian and published in Moscow. Ghafurov also compiled the first comprehensive collection of works on the Tajiks, *History of the Tajik People* (3 vols., 1963–1965), and he initiated the transcription of **Shashmaqom**, Tajik classical **music**. In 1972, he published his famous work *The Tajiks: Ancient and Medieval History* (2 vols.) in Russian. This work was translated into **Tajik** and **Farsi**. After 1977, it was amended and published under the revised title *The Tajiks: Ancient, Medieval, and Modern History*, extending the scope of the study up to 1917. From 1956 until his death in 1977, Ghafurov was director of the Institute of Oriental Studies at the Academy of Sciences of the Union of Soviet Socialist Republics. After independence in 1991, Bobojon Ghafurov and **Sadriddin Ayni** were proclaimed national heroes of Tajikistan.

GHARM. A mountainous area in the Surkhob river basin, Gharm covers **Nurobod**, **Rasht**, **Tojikobod**, **Tavildara**, and **Jirghatol** nohiyas, part of the **Nohiyas under Republican Control.**

GHARM NOHIYA. *See* RASHT NOHIYA.

GHAZNEVIDS (997–1186). A Central Asian ruling dynasty, the Ghaznevids were centered in Ghazna, northern **Afghanistan.** The dynasty was founded by Mahmud Ghaznevi, who captured **Khurasan** from the **Samanids** in 999 and threatened the latter dynasty from the south. Within 10 years, Ghaznevi captured almost all of **Movarounnahr**, inheriting Samanid territories. During his reign (998–1030), Mahmud Ghaznevi invaded **India** and Afghanistan under the banner of "holy war." At the end of the 12th century, the last Ghaznevid ruler (Khusrav Malik) was taken prisoner by the Gur, a new dynasty in Afghanistan.

GHIJJAK. A four-string, bowed musical instrument with a dome-shaped resonator, the *ghijjak* is reminiscent of the violin and Persian *kamancheh*, used by **Tajiks.** The surface is covered by a leather membrane. *See also* MUSIC.

GHONCHI NOHIYA. This district is adjacent to **Istravshan** (former Uroteppa) nohiya in the **Sughd veloyat**, bordering **Kyrgyzstan** in the east. The Ghonchi nohiya was formed in 1929, with a territory of 1,559 square kilometers. Its population in 2006 was about 120,000 (9,000 urban dwellers), **Tajiks** and **Uzbeks** living in seven **jamoats**. The distance from the Ghonchi administrative center to **Khujand** is 64 kilometers, and to **Dushanbe** 283 kilometers. Average temperatures in January and July can reach –5°C and 30°C respectively; the average annual precipitation is 200–300 millimeters. The main occupation is **agriculture**, including **cotton**, **grain**, and fruit production and livestock breeding. Arable lands amount to 121,884 hectares.

GHULOMOV, ASADULLO (1954–). Born in **Danghara nohiya**, Ghulomov graduated from the Tajik Polytechnic Institute in 1976 and the Academy of State Management in 2005. In 1976, he started his career as an engineer in various state transport companies. In 1995–2001, Ghulomov worked as first deputy director of the Tojiksokhtmon

State Construction Company. In 2001–2003, he was chair of the Frunze nohiya of **Dushanbe** city. From 2003 to 2006, Ghulomov was vice premier of the government. In December 2006, he was appointed first vice premier of Tajikistan. *See also* GOVERNMENT.

GOLD. There are an estimated 28 gold deposits in Tajikistan, with total reserves of 429.3 tons (some sources estimate reserves of up to 1,000 tons) and a gold output capacity of 9.5 tons. Tajik gold is of high quality but has no international certificate and is sold in the international market through intermediaries. Gold mining is conducted by the Tajikzoloto state company operating the Taror gold-mining mill in **Sughd**, the Tajik-British joint enterprise Zarafshon near **Panjakent** in Sughd (from 2004–2007), the Tajik-British joint enterprise Darvoz in **Khatlon**, and the Tajik-Canadian enterprise Aprelevka. The Tajik government reserves exclusive rights to extract gold in central and southern Tajikistan.

In July 2007, the copper and gold miner Zijin Mining Group purchased a subsidiary of Avocet Mining, whose main assets are gold mining and exploration rights in Tajikistan. Thus, Zijin Mining owns 75 percent of the Zeravshan Gold Corporation (ZGC). Since 2004, the annual extraction of Tajik gold is 2–3 tons. *See also* VOSTOKREDMET.

GORNO BADAKHSHAN. *See* MOUNTAINOUS BADAKHSHON AUTONOMOUS VELOYAT.

GOVERNMENT. In July 1991, the soviet of ministers of the **Tajik Soviet Socialist Republic** was reorganized as the cabinet of ministers. The chair of the soviet of ministers became known as the prime minister, and the deputy chair as the vice premier. Tajikistan was governed by nine governments between 1991 and 2009. In 1991–1992, President **Qahor Mahkamov** formed the last government of Soviet Tajikistan. It was headed by Prime Minister Izzatulloh Hayeev (from **Kulob**) and included **Jamshed Karimov** as first deputy prime minister and **Sadulloh Khairulloev** as one of the deputy prime ministers. (See the appendices for other members of this and subsequent governments.)

In the first openly contested presidential elections of post-Soviet Tajikistan, held in November 1991, **Rahmon Nabiev** received 59 percent of the votes, defeating the opposition candidate, **Davlatnazar Khudonazarov**, and becoming Tajikistan's first president. But Nabiev proved inept as a politician and unable to prevent Tajikistan's descent into **civil war**. In May 1992, an agreement among the opposing sides led to formation of the **Government of National Reconciliation**, which included a number of opposition figures. The prime minister and more than half the ministers in the 1991 government were replaced. The cabinet of ministers of the Government of National Reconciliation included Akbar Mirzoyev as prime minister, Jamshed Karimov as a first deputy prime minister, and Sadulloh Khairulloev and **Davlat Usmon** among the deputy prime ministers. In November 1992, the entire cabinet of ministers resigned at the 16th session of the **Supreme Soviet**, held in **Khujand**. **Emomali Rahmon** was appointed by the assembly to form a new cabinet. Rahmon's cabinet, formed in the following months, excluded opposition leaders and was heavily staffed by leaders from Kulob and **Sughd**. It included **Abdumalik Abdullojonov** as prime minister and **Mahmadsaid Ubaidulloev** as first vice premier.

In the third post-Soviet government (1994), Emomali Rahmon succeeded in removing the influential **Leninobodi** leader Abdumalik Abdullojonov from the cabinet of ministers. Leaders from Kulob dominated this government, which was formed by a presidential decree in December 1994. It included Jamshed Karimov as prime minister and Mahmadsaid Ubaidulloev as first vice premier.

In the 1996–1997 government, the position of Emomali Rahmon was significantly strengthened, and more loyal allies were brought into office. The government included **Yahyo Azimov** as prime minister, Yuriy Ponosov as first vice premier, and **Jamoliddin Mansurov** among the vice premiers.

The **General Agreement on the Establishment of Peace and National Accord** signed in June 1997 allocated a 30 percent quota of government positions to the **United Tajik Opposition** (UTO). Opposition leaders were included in the 1998–1999 cabinet of ministers. This government's term ended in December 1999 after the victory of Emomali Rahmon in the November 1999 presidential elections. The 1998–1999 government included Yahyo Azimov as prime minister, **Hoji Akbar Turajonzoda** (UTO) as first vice premier, and **Zakir Vazirov** (UTO) among the vice premiers.

A new cabinet was formed after the presidential elections of 1999 and excluded some members of the UTO. Women were included in the government in 2000. The prime minister was **Oqil Oqilov**.

The government of Tajikistan was reformed at the end of 2000 and the beginning of 2001 in response to advice from the International Monetary Fund and the World Bank, leading to a reduction in the number of ministries. In January 2001, the Ministry of Economics and External Economical Relations, headed by Yahyo Azimov, and the state committee on contracts and trade, headed by Hakim Saliev, were merged into a new Ministry of Economics and Trade, headed by H. Saliev. The Ministry of Labor and Employment, headed by **Rafiqa Musoeva**, was merged with the Ministry of Social Security, headed by Qimat Rustamova, to form the Ministry of Labor and Social Security, headed by Musoeva from Khujand. The State Statistics Agency was transformed into the state committee on statistics.

At the same time, the presidential office widened its authority. The Office of State Finance Control under the president of Tajikistan was formed in January 2001 by presidential decree. It assumed exclusive responsibility to control all finances, state property, and money flows (including foreign credits and humanitarian aid), tasks traditionally performed by the Ministry of Finance. Among other changes in the cabinet, **Khalifabobo Khamidov** replaced **Shavkat Ismoilov** as minister of justice, Abdurahim Rahmonov replaced **Bobokhon Mahmadov** as minister of culture, and Tursun Rahmatov replaced **Shodi Kabirov** as minister of agriculture.

These changes highlighted a number of issues. First, the presidential office increased its size and responsibilities, even duplicating the structure of the cabinet of ministries. Second, executive power shifted from the cabinet to the presidential office. Third, the judiciary was becoming more open to influence by the presidential office, as indicated in the scope of the **Council of Justice**. The president had exclusive control over the appointment of all high-ranking officials, including judges. According to the **constitution**, the parliament has some rights to influence presidential appointments in the cabinet, through official approval of presidential decrees, but it has no right to control the presidential office.

Moreover, most of the new appointees came from the presidential office. This included **Amirsho Miraliev** from Kulob, who served as adviser to the president in 1995–1999. He was removed from his position by the president but in 2000 was elected to the **Majlisi Namoyndagon**, and in 2001 he was appointed chair of the **Khatlon** veloyat. President Rahmon maintained Kulob's overrepresentation in the government. Four power ministries plus the general prosecutor and the Ministries of Culture, Information, Radio and TV, the national university, and other key positions are filled by officials from Kulob. The mayor of Dushanbe and chair of the **Majlisi Melli**, Mahmadsaid Ubaidulloev, the official number two person in Tajikistan, is also from Kulob.

The central government continued to assert its control over the country. By 2007, this process resulted in centralization of state power in the hands of the presidency, which other power structures and the general public have accepted with no confrontation. The national referendum held in June 2003 obtained popular support for a package of some 55 constitutional amendments. Among these was an amendment of Article 65 of the constitution, which previously limited presidents to one seven-year term in office. This has now been extended to two terms. After the **presidential elections of 2006**, the incumbent President Emomali Rahmon could theoretically remain in office until 2020. Most of the new 2006 governmental appointees came from the president's executive apparatus (e.g., **Abdujabbor Rahmonov**, Ranokhon Abdurahmanova, **Bakhtiyor Khudoyorov**). At the same time, the president continued distancing himself from once loyal lieutenants like **Abdulmajid Dostiev** and **Saidamir Zuhurov**.

During 2002–2008, many opposition members joined the ruling **People's Democratic Party of Tajikistan** (PDPT). Others, including former influential warlords, were gradually marginalized (e.g., **Mirzo Ziyoev**) or imprisoned (**Ghaffor Mirzoyev, Mahmadruzi Iskandarov**). Some former opponents of President Rahmon voluntarily suspended their political activities. The charismatic religious leader **Said Abdullo Nuri** died in August 2006, while the political influence of opposition leader **Rahmatulloh Zoirov** weakened mostly because of governmental pressure. By 2009, the vertical chain of command in Tajik government had been strengthened. The president as head of the central government appoints the heads of veloyat and nohiya governments (*hukumats*), while the latter nominate local **jamoat** chairs. By presidential decree, from November 2006 the government included Oqil Oqilov as prime minister and **Asadullo Ghulomov** as first vice premier.

Government in Tajikistan is based on a network of clan and patron-client relations. Virtually all powerful ministries (justice, foreign affairs, defense, finance, energy, education, health) and many other key governmental offices since the end of 1992 are headed by people from the one clan representing the president's home region (Kulob and **Danghara**). All ministries are headed by members of the PDPT. The **Islamic Renaissance Party of Tajikistan** (IRPT), the **Democratic Party of Tajikistan** (DPT), the **Communist Party of Tajikistan** (CPT), and other political parties have no representatives in the government, and there are few women in ministerial positions. This system contributed to the poor quality of public-sector administration and services, and it increases opportunities for **corruption**.

GOVERNMENT OF NATIONAL RECONCILIATION. Early in Tajikistan's **civil war**, an attempt at reconciliation was made. The compromise agreement stipulated that **Rahmon Nabiev** would continue as president, and opposition representatives would be included in one-third of the **government** positions. The Government of National Reconciliation formed on 11 May 1992 was expected to stay in office until new presidential and parliamentary elections could be held. However, violence continued. In November 1992, the entire cabinet of ministers resigned at the 16th session of the **Supreme Soviet**, held in **Khujand**. **Emomali Rahmon** was appointed by the assembly to form a new cabinet.

GRAIN. Since **Bactrian** times (4th century BCE), grain has been grown in Tajikistan, and grain farming is popularly regarded as a traditional occupation. Before the colonization by **Russia** in the 19th century and the subsequent spread of **cotton** cultivation, the two valleys of **Vakhsh** and **Hisor** supplied cereals to the entire **Bukharan emirate**. In Soviet times, grain was superseded by cotton as the most important **agricultural** product. The consequent decline in grain production meant insufficient grain supply to meet demands. In 1991, annual grain production stood at more than 304,000 tons. The collapse of the Soviet Union and the **civil war** in Tajikistan disrupted grain production. The government of Tajikistan is presently unable to meet the needs of the population. From 1996 to 2009, the country's grain output ranged between 548,000 and 960,000 tons, while Tajikistan's annual consumption was 1.5 million tons. Nearly one-third of all cereal consumed in the republic is imported, including food aid. About 90 percent of grain imports, mostly milling wheat, comes from Kazakhstan. In order to meet this challenge and provide food security throughout the republic, the government has allocated additional land to grain production, partly at the expense of cotton.

GREATER CENTRAL ASIA. In 2005, Frederick Starr of Johns Hopkins University's School of Advanced International Studies proposed that the United States lead in building a new Greater Central Asia region by combining post-Soviet **Central Asia** with South Asia via **Afghanistan**. The strategy calls for the transformation of the region, including Tajikistan, into a zone of protected sovereignties sharing practical market economies, secular and open systems of governance, respecting citizens rights, and maintaining positive relations with the United States.

In this framework, Tajikistan would export its hydroelectric power southward, support the construction of bridges connecting Tajikistan with Afghanistan, and allow trans-border trade with Afghan communities and companies. The Central Asia South Asia Regional Electricity Market (CASAREM) was set up by **Kyrgyzstan**, Tajikistan, **Pakistan**, and Afghanistan, and at a summit in Kabul in November 2007, an agreement was concluded on a $500 million electricity connection project between Central Asia and South Asia. The Asian Development Bank, Islamic Development Bank, and World Bank have been approached by CASAREM countries to consider financing this project.

However, most of the Tajik politicians and expert community at large are skeptical about the Greater Central Asia project, referring to the differences in cultural identification and limited cooperative experiences between Central Asians and the people of South Asia. The lack of trust between **India** and Pakistan, terrorist activities of militant **Taliban** groups, the booming drug business and warlordism in Afghanistan, a weak Afghan government and limited U.S. control over the situation in Afghanistan, and many other factors make implementation of large-scale, cross-border infrastructure projects almost impossible. The total electricity volume exported from the energy-thirsty Tajikistan to Afghanistan is limited. **Russia**, aware of the real aims of the Greater Central Asia strategy, indicates that it will refuse to accept the U.S. policy to remove Central Asian countries from Russia's sphere of influence. Tajikistan water reserves and energy reserves have been under firm Russian control. The Greater Central Asia strategy faces a plethora of practical problems in implementation. *See also* DRUG TRAFFICKING; DUSTI BRIDGE; FOREIGN INVESTMENT; FOREIGN POLICY; FOREIGN TRADE; POWER GENERATION.

GUL (GULOV), SHERALI (1950–). Born in Farkhor, Gul graduated from the Tajik Institute of Agriculture in 1974. Then he worked as an engineer of irrigation in his native **Kulob** province. In 1994, he was appointed chair of **Danghara nohiya** and worked at this position until 2001, when he became chair of the State Committee of State Property. Gul was appointed minister of energy and industry in December 2006.

GULAMOV, MINKHOJ (1929–1996). A Tajik scientist, doctor of psychotherapy, and **academician**, Gulamov was born in **Samarqand** and graduated from Samarqand's Medical Institute in 1952. He was a professor and deputy rector of the Tajik Medical University (appointed in 1970). Gulamov was killed along with **Iusuf Iskhaki** on 6 May 1996 in **Dushanbe**. His daughter Nigina Sharopova was a vice premier of Tajikistan in 2000–2002.

GULRUKHSOR (SAFIEVA GULRUKHSOR) (1947–). A Tajik poet, Gulrukhsor was born in the **Nurobod nohiya** and graduated from the Tajik State University in 1968. She then worked as a journalist for republican newspapers and journals. Gulrukhsor was a recipient of **Komsomol** awards and in 1989 was elected to the **Supreme Soviet** of the Union of Soviet Socialist Republics (USSR). In 1989–1991, she chaired the USSR fund for culture in Tajikistan. She continued to be involved in politics in 1990–1992 but later focused on literary work. *See also* LITERATURE.

GURUGHLI. A Tajik oral heroic epic, *Gurughli* describes the peasant utopia of a magic country called Chambul, ruled by a perfect sovereign named Gurughli (son of grave). It emerged chiefly among illiterate Tajik villagers and Uzbek herders in southern and central

Tajikistan and completed its formation by the 18th century. For centuries, *Gurughli* was passed from one generation to another by *gurughlikhons*, bards, who memorized the epic and recited it to the public. *Gurughli* was discovered by Russian travelers in **Eastern Bukhara** in 1870. The whole corpus was recorded from the 1930s to 1960s, and copies were preserved in the **Academy of Sciences of Tajikistan**. Many of the collected versions were published. *Gururugli* contains 100,000 poetic lines and consists of numerous *dastans* (poems). *See also* MUSIC.

GUSHTINGIRI. *Gushtingiri* is Tajik national wrestling. The wrestlers have to wear chapans (traditional coats) and fasten soft belts around their waists. In the late Soviet period, chapans were replaced by judo sport jackets and belts. Holds below the waist are prohibited. A *gushtingir* (wrestler) may hold the belt, sleeve, or collar of the opponent's chapan or jacket. Leg throws are allowed. A fight lasts 10 minutes, and the player who puts his opponent down first is eligible to receive a prize. The gushtingiri competition can be seen at **tuis,** **Nawruz** celebrations, and national sports competitions. Some Tajik athletes combine gushtingiri with classical wrestling, judo, and other related sports. *See also* SPORTS.

– H –

HABIBULLAEV (KHABIBILLAEV), ZUHUR (1932–). A Tajik painter born in **Dushanbe**, Habibullaev graduated from the Tajik College of Arts in 1952 and Leningrad Artistic-Industrial College in 1959. He was part of the first generation of Tajik artists, musicians, dancers, filmmakers, singers, and actors who returned to Tajikistan at the end of the 1950s after having received a modern education in **Russia**. Along with the classic music of **Ziyodullo Shahidi** and the films of **Boris Kimiagarov**, the paintings of Habibullaev created a unique artistic feeling in the Tajik art scene of the Soviet period. Habibullaev was awarded the title of People's Painter of Tajikistan in 1987. His landscape, still life, and portrait paintings are displayed in the Behzad State Museum of Arts. *See also* ARTS.

HAJI (HOJI). A person who has performed the **hajj** is given the honorable title *haji* or *hoji* (e.g., Hoji Akbar).

HAJJ. A religious duty of all Muslims is to go on pilgrimage to the holy city of Mecca, if possible. This duty is called the *hajj*. *See also* ISLAM.

HAKIMOV, ASKAR (1946–). A Tajik writer and chair of the **Tajikistan Union of Writers** (1991–2005), Hakimov was born in **Khujand**. He studied philology at the Tajik State University, graduating in 1967, and he graduated from the Moscow State University postgraduate course in 1972. In 1973–1974, Hakimov was a research fellow at the Institute of Language and Literature of the **Academy of Sciences of Tajikistan**. Between 1974 and 1991, he worked in various posts: senior editor of the state committee for radio and television, deputy chief editor of *Sadoi Sharq* magazine, secretary of the Union of Writers, and chief editor of the *Adabiyot va San'at* newspaper. He was appointed to the **Majlisi Melli** on 20 March 2000 by President **Emomali Rahmon**. At the first session on 17 April, Hakimov was appointed the parliament's deputy chair.

HAKIMOVA, SAADINISSO (SOFIA) (1924–). A Tajik scholar, gynecologist, and **academician**, Hakimova was born in **Konibodom, Sughd veloyat**, and graduated from the Tajik Medical Institute in 1943. She was subsequently appointed head of the **Qurghonteppa** veloyat Health Care Department. Between 1946 and 1950, she studied obstetrics and gynecology at the Academy of Medical Sciences (Moscow). She conducted her doctoral research at the First Moscow Medical Institute in 1951–1957. In 1958, Hakimova became chair of obstetrics and gynecology at the Tajik Medical Institute. She later founded and directed the Tajik Research Institute of Obstetrics, Gynecology, and Pediatrics. In 1993, in protest against the continuing **civil war**, Hakimova resigned her post and left Tajikistan. In 1999, she published the book *Zalozhniki Imperii* (Hostages of the Empire) about the extermination of Tajiks in the Soviet empire.

HAMADONI. *See* ALI HAMADONI.

HAMADONI MAUSOLEUM. Built in the 14th–17th centuries in **Kulob**, the Hamadoni Mausoleum is the burial place of the famous Persian-Tajik scholar and thinker Mir Said **Ali Hamadoni** (1314–1384) and his successors. The mausoleum has a portal cupola structure with an asymmetric plan. The building is made from burned brick on glue grout, and its cupolas are made with alabaster grout. The central hall is covered by twin domes. The mausoleum was renovated with the help of the Iranian government at the end of the 1990s. The structure attracts many pilgrims to the city of Kulob.

HAMADONI NOHIYA. This southern nohiya, known previously as Chubek and as Moskva, is situated in the **Kulob** region of the **Khatlon** veloyat. Hamadoni lies in the basin of the Surkhob and Panj rivers and borders **Afghanistan** to the south, **Shurobod** and **Vose** nohiyas to the north and northeast, and Farkhor to the west. It was formed in 1950, with a territory of 1,327 square kilometers. The population is over 123,800 (20,100 urban), mostly **Tajiks** living in seven **jamoats**. The center of the nohiya is Hamadoni **shahrak**. The distance from Hamadoni to **Dushanbe** is 182 kilometers, and to Kulob 33 kilometers. Average January and July temperatures are 1°C and 29°C respectively. The annual rainfall is 500–800 millimeters. It has 13,274 hectares of arable land. The main occupation is **agriculture**, including **cotton** and **grain** production and livestock breeding.

HANAFIYA. One of **Islam**'s four schools of law (**mazhabs**), the **Sunni** Hanafi school was the most popular, tolerant, and liberal theological orientation in Islam. The founder of this school was Abu Hanifah (699–767), also known as Imomi Azam (Great Imam). Abu Hanifah's school is known for placing a profound emphasis on *quiyas* (analogy, comparison), *ijma* (public consensus), and *ra'y* (private opinion) in the interpretation of Islamic canon law and principles. *Mazhab-i Hanafiya* (Hanafiya School) was refined by the intellectuals of **Samarqand**, **Bukhara**, and other urban centers of **Movarounnahr** and **Khurasan**. It promoted ideas of the equality of all Muslims, regardless of their ancestry, and advocated giving more rights to dynasties of local, non-Arab origin. During the 13th–14th centuries, Hanafiya spilled over into wider **Central Asia** and neighboring **India**, Iraq, Asia Minor, Syria, and lands of the Golden Horde.

In modern Tajikistan, Abu Hanifah is regarded as one of the best representatives of the Tajik people. Upon the initiative of President **Emomali Rahmon**, 2009 was declared the Year of Imomi Azam. Each Muslim is expected to adhere to only one of the mazhabs. Tajik **Salafis** and **Wahhabis** tend to consider themselves not attached to Hanafiya.

HASHAR. The term *hashar* refers to communal labor or cooperative work. It is a collective effort by volunteers to assist a person in need in the community. Residents of local communities or villages construct and repair bridges, build channels, or help one another with the construction and repair of residential houses. This tradition of unforced labor was used in Soviet times to build the Great **Ferghana** irrigation channel in the 1930s and the **Pamirian motor road** in the 1940s. In Soviet times, hashar was used to construct unregistered mosques. *See also* AVLOD; MAHALLA; MASH-VARAT; OSHI OSHTI.

HEALTH CARE. Independent Tajikistan inherited a Soviet health system. Its quality was rated below average for Soviet republics for most indicators of health conditions and care provided by physicians and nurses. In 1986, Tajikistan had 325 hospitals with a total of 50,115 beds, 697 outpatient clinics, 1,313 paramedic and midwife facilities, and 567 maternity and pediatric clinics and hospitals. In the late 1980s, the average number of hospital beds per 10,000 inhabitants in the USSR was 130, while Tajikistan's proportion was about 104 per 10,000. Health care expenditures accounted for up to 5.7 percent of the gross domestic product (GDP) in 1992. Most health care professionals in Tajikistan have been non-Tajiks, and many emigrated from the republic before, during, and after the **civil war** (1992–1997). Funding for the health sector collapsed in the mid-1990s as the **economy** worsened and since then has remained below 2 percent of GDP. Private health services are regulated by the 1997 law "On Public Health Protection" that allows medical professionals to engage in private medical practice.

In 1999, there were 3,552 medical institutions in Tajikistan (6 per 10,000 people). The number of doctors decreased from 14,504 in 1990 (about 27 per 10,000 people) to 12,456 (20 per 10,000 people) in 1996, and to 13,400 (about 19 per 10,000 people) in 2008. The number of women doctors dropped from 6,556 (about 46 percent of total number of doctors) in 1991 to 5,172 (38 percent) in 2007. Doctors were mainly concentrated in urban areas (e.g., 14 people per doctor in **Dushanbe** but 620 people per doctor in rural areas).

Despite immense international humanitarian health aid, health care in Tajikistan continues to be insufficient. Maternal and infant mortality rates are high (30 per 1,000 live births in 1998). The incidence of tuberculosis, malaria, typhoid, and cholera has continued to rise. The rates for illegal **drug** use, HIV infection, and sexually transmitted diseases have also risen. Most women suffer from anemia, associated with iron deficiencies from various causes. **Khatlon** veloyat was the area worst affected by contagious vector-borne diseases. The collapse of the economy produced a deterioration in the infrastructure and the water and sanitation systems, as well as insufficient resources, medication, modern medical equipment, and skilled local health personnel. The health system remains state owned and state run.

HIJAB. Since the mid-1990s, some Tajik women have started wearing the Muslim *hijab*, a plain, usually black scarf that covers a woman's hair and neck. The hijab is not indigenous to the region but imported from the Middle East and has nothing in common with the colorful Tajik **faranji.** In May 2007, Tajikistan's Ministry of Education ordered schools and universities to ban hijabs on campus. The council of religious scholars of Tajikistan in November 2008 issued a decree that calls the hijab a garment "alien to Tajik culture." *See also* HUJIM.

HIJRAH (HIJRA, HEGIRA). The *hijrah* was the Prophet Muhammad's migration in 622 from Mecca to Medina in order to escape persecution. This date represents the starting point of the Muslim **calendar**. The term is also used for the emigration of Muslims from **Central Asia** in 1918–1934. *See also* ISLAM.

HIMMATZODA, MUHAMMAD SHARIF (1953–). The first chair of the **Islamic Renaissance Party of Tajikistan** (IRPT) in 1990–1999, Himmatzoda has been a member of **Majlisi Namoyandagon** since 2000. He was born to a family of agricultural laborers of **Gharmi** origin and in the 1980s was one of the key figures of the Islamic underground movement in Tajikistan. In June 1992, he headed a force of 8,000 against **Rahmon Nabiev**'s forces during the **civil war**. At the end of 1992, forced to leave Tajikistan, Himmatzoda lived in exile in **Iran, Afghanistan**, and **Pakistan**. In 1993, he joined the **Movement for Islamic Revival in Tajikistan** (MIRT) and was appointed its deputy chair. Himmatzoda was involved in the **Inter-Tajik Peace Talks** and in 1997 was elected to the **Commission for National Reconciliation**. On the eve of the **presidential elections of 1999**, Himmatzoda was replaced by **Said Abdullo Nuri** as chair of the IRPT. In 2000 and 2005, Himmatzoda was elected to represent the IRPT in the Tajik parliament. In April 2009, Himmatzoda resigned from parliament to protest the country's new law on **religion**. *See also* ISLAM; POLITICAL PARTIES.

HISOR (HISAR). A *hisor* is a fortification, fortress, or fence.

HISOR NOHIYA. This district is within the **Nohiyas under Republican Control** (NURC). It was formed in 1932 in the western part of Tajikistan, in the Hisor valley. Hisor nohiya is 1,982 square kilometers, with a population of about 198,800, **Tajiks** and **Uzbeks**, living in 12 **jamoats**. The nohiya center is the city of Hisor (30,300 people), which was the center of **Eastern Bukhara** and the seat of local chiefs (**beks**) in the 16th–19th centuries. The historical Hisor fortress is located in this nohiya. Soviet power was established there at the beginning of 1921. The distance from Hisor to **Dushanbe** is 26 kilometers. Average temperatures in January and July can reach 0°C and 30°C respectively. Average annual precipitation is 600–700 millimeters. The main occupations are in **agriculture**, including **cotton, grain**, and fruit production, livestock breeding, and **industry**. Arable lands amount to 33,582 hectares.

HIZB-UT-TAHRIR AL ISLAMII (HuT). The international Islamic organization Hizb-ut-Tahrir al-Islamii (HuT) advocates the use of nonviolent means to create an Islamic caliphate based on sharia law. It operates mainly among **Tajiks** and **Uzbeks** in **Sughd veloyat** and, to a lesser extent, in regions around **Dushanbe** and southwestern **Khatlon**. The HuT is engaged almost exclusively in indoctrination and distributing leaflets. Tajikistan, **Uzbekistan**, and **Kyrgyzstan** consider the development of the HuT as a threat to their security and have opted for the strict repression of the group and its followers. The HuT is not involved in international **terrorism**, but the group's radical anti-Christian and anti-Semitic ideology is sympathetic to acts of violence against the West. The **Islamic Renaissance Party of Tajikistan** (IRPT) has not joined calls for the suppression of the HuT, yet it shares the government's view on the illegality of the party. It is alleged that the HuT views the IRPT as an infidel group, thus potentially laying the basis for the development of strong intra-Muslim political competition. *See also* ISLAM; SALAFIYA.

HOMIDOV, MASAID (1961–). Born in **Dushanbe**, Homidov graduated from the Polytechnic College and the Tajik Polytechnic Institute in 1994. From 1980 to 2000, he held various technical and managerial positions in state-owned companies. He became deputy minister of soil improvement and water industry in 2002. From May till December 2006, he was first deputy chair of the city of Dushanbe. President **Emomali Rahmon** appointed him minister of soil improvement and water recourses in December 2006.

HUJUM. The campaign launched in 1927 by communist parties in **Central Asia** against the veil (**faranji**) and for the incorporation of women in public life was called *hujum* (assault). This campaign was presented as a "struggle to liberate women from repression." In spite of resistance from the traditionalist clergy, in the first year of this campaign 14,495 women removed their faranji in northern Tajikistan and 600 others in Dushanbe. In addition, women were employed in light industries. Hujum was generally successful in removing the veil, although faranji continued to be used in rural lowlands of Tajikistan until the 1950s. *See also* HIJAB; WOMEN'S ISSUES.

HUKUMAT. The term *hukumat* refers to supremacy, executive power, government, and the administration of cities, **veloyats**, and **nohiyas**.

HUMAN RIGHTS. Tajikistan is a signatory to seven major **United Nations** (UN) international human rights pacts. As a member of the **Organization for Security and Cooperation in Europe** (OSCE), it is also bound to OSCE principles and commitments. By May 2009, the main governmental body handling human rights complaints was the Department of Constitutional Guarantees of Citizens Rights, created in 1997 within the office of President **Emomali Rahmon**. In 2002, the system of exit visas was abolished and the responsibility for overseeing the penitentiary system was transferred from the Ministry of Interior to the Ministry of Justice. The Tajik Criminal Code created basic guarantees against torture.

All residents of Tajikistan have the right to apply to the UN Committee on Human Rights with individual complaints in cases of violation of their civil or political rights by the state. By 2007, the UN Committee on Human Rights had considered more than 10 individual complaints of Tajik citizens. In 2002, nine high-ranking law enforcement officials in **Sughd veloyat** were arrested and sentenced by Tajikistan's Supreme Court for using torture. An institute of private attorneys authorized by the Ministry of Justice was established in Tajikistan. On 23 June 2007, President Rahmon signed a decree titled "Program of Judicial and Legal Reforms in Tajikistan." Its main goal is to strengthen judicial powers and increase the role of courts in the protection of rights, freedoms, and legal interests of citizens, the state, and organizations.

In 2007, at the initiative of the country's president, the preparation of a national institute on human rights (ombudsman) was launched. On 20 March 2008, the president signed the law under which the ombudsman is to be appointed by the president and confirmed by the parliament. In May 2009, the **Majlisi Namoyandagon** confirmed the appointment of Zarif Alizoda, formerly state adviser to the president for legal matters, as the ombudsman of Tajikistan.

Human rights problems in Tajikistan include restrictions on the right of citizens to change their government, restrictions on free speech, **mass media**, association, and **religion**, imprisonment of the political opposition (including journalists), human trafficking, child labor, due process violations, ill treatment in custody, and more. Tajikistan is an authoritarian state. The government exercises excessive control over nongovernmental organizations (NGOs), religious organizations, **political parties**, and the media. Political command over resources is within the hands of a restricted number of ruling elites, with President Rahmon at the top; these elites manage government bodies, legal institutions, and economic processes, all with the aim of serving their private interests. Since the end of the **civil war** in 1997, **Russia**, **China**, Western governments, international NGOs, and financial institutions have tended to strengthen the incumbent regime of Rahmon, and little political competition and freedom has been allowed in Tajikistan.

Numerous violations of human rights have been recorded in Tajikistan since the civil conflict ended in 1997. According to most political parties and international observers, the presidential and parliamentary **elections** to the Majlisi Namoyandagon in 1999–2000 and 2005–2006 proved to be undemocratic and breached Tajik law. Although the Tajik government maintains there are no political prisoners in the country, authorities arrested and questioned several members of the **Social-Democratic Party of Tajikistan** (SDPT), the **Islamic Renaissance Party of Tajikistan** (IRPT), and other rival factions from 2002 to 2008. The SDPT chair, **Rahmatulloh Zoirov**, was repeatedly questioned by the General Prosecutor's Office and accused of **Hizb-ut-Tahrir** membership. Zoirov later suffered from severe health problems and claimed to have been poisoned. In 2007, **Ghaffor Mirzoyev**, a former wartime field commander and chair of the Drug Control Agency, was sentenced to life imprisonment on charges including murder, illegal use of bodyguards, possession of arms, privatization of government property, and other illegal activities. **Mahmadruzi Iskandarov**, head of the **Democratic Party of Tajikistan**, was sentenced to 23 years in prison in 2005. Former interior minister **Yaqub Salimov** is serving a 15-year sentence for crimes against the state. Most observers believe that Mirzoyev, Iskandarov, and Salimov were indeed corrupt officials and criminals, but that their unanticipated arrests, closed trials, and harsh sentences were politically motivated and aimed at frightening the president's potential political rivals. The IRPT senior member Shamsiddin Shamsiddinov was arrested in 2003 and sentenced a year later for allegedly organizing a criminal group, crossing the border illegally, and polygamy. In April 2008, Shamsiddinov died of throat cancer in prison. In 2007, approximately 300 former fighters of the **United Tajik Opposition** (UTO) remained in prison.

In 2008, the country's 12 correctional institutions, including one colony for female convicts and six pretrial prisons, contained about 90,000 convicts. More than 1,000 were stricken with tuberculosis and 90 had HIV/AIDS. Tajikistan does not have the death penalty.

During 2004–2009, several ethnic **Uzbeks** were sentenced to long prison terms on charges of espionage after closed trials. More than 50 alleged members of the banned group Hizb-ut-Tahrir, including at least 20 women, were detained, and many were sentenced to long prison terms.

The 19 May 2007 law "On Public Associations" did not contribute to the improvement of the legal environment. By 1 January 2008, only about 2,000 of Tajikistan's 3,500 public associations passed reregistration in accordance with the law. The law provides for freedom of assembly, but a permit from the local executive committee is required to hold a public assembly or demonstration. In most cases, the government refuses to grant demonstration permits. In March 2008, some 300 demonstrators staged a public protest in **Khorugh**, the capital city of the **Mountainous Badakhshon Autonomous Veloyat**, to accuse local police of extortion and arbitrary enforcement of the law. The protesters also demanded the return of six villages in the **Darvoz nohiya** that had recently been transferred to the neighboring **Tavildara** by a decision of the Tajik parliament. The protesters argued that the Tajik **constitution** requires consent of the veloyat's legislature before any change to the administrative borders of the province can be made. Following this demonstration, the Khorugh branch of the SDPT intended to hold another demonstration, but their permit request was denied by provincial authorities.

Economic, social, and cultural rights of citizens are not fully protected in Tajikistan. The June 2007 law "On Traditions, Celebrations, and Ceremonies Regulation" violates the constitutional rights of citizens by restricting the number of guests at **tuis**, birthday parties, and funeral ceremonies. Celebration of some of the national traditions, such as *gahvorabandon* (40 days rocking a cradle) and the game **buzkashi**, was effectively outlawed. In 2007, the Department on Regulation of Traditions, Celebrations, and Ceremonies was created as a unit of the Executive Office of the President of Tajikistan. Local commissions working on a permanent basis under the local administration of **veloyats**, cities, **nohiyas**, and **jamoats** were also established to oversee implementation of the law. Representatives of some political parties in Tajikistan argue that the regulation of centuries-old traditions has no reason and is not the way to fight poverty.

Freedom of the media is constrained in Tajikistan. In 2004–2005, several journalists were jailed in high-profile cases. Mukhtor Boqizoda, chief editor of the popular independent newspaper *Nerui Sukhan*, was sentenced to two years' labor for the illegal use of electricity in 2005. Rajabi Mirzo, from the newspaper *Ruzi Nav*, was beaten by unknown assailants in 2004. *Nerui Sukhan* and *Ruzi Nav*, both known for criticizing government policy and the president, were closed by the government in 2005. In September 2008, the prosecutor's office started a criminal investigation against opposition journalist **Dodojon Atovulloev**, the leader of the opposition movement **Vatandor**. According to reports of international human rights organizations, Tajikistan's media are mainly controlled by the government and face many barriers, such as threats and pressure, difficulties with registration and obtaining licenses, and trouble using printing houses. In September 2007, the Communications Ministry ordered Internet service providers to block access to sites that "undermined the state's policies," including centrasia.ru, ferghana.ru, tajikistantimes.ru, charogiruz.ru, and arianastorm.com. One month later, the government reversed its decision after many complaints. In July 2007, the Tajik Criminal Code's subsections for criminal prosecution for slander and insult disseminated through traditional mass media and the Internet were amended. Tajik journalists believe that the recognition of the Internet as mass media contradicts the constitution of Tajikistan. Government agencies hold quarterly press conferences for journalists, but correspondents working with news agencies experience difficulties in getting useful information from governmental officials.

The administration of the city of **Dushanbe** started implementing a general plan for rebuilding the capital in 2007. In the course of implementation, cases on the forced eviction of citizens from their houses were processed in national courts. All such cases ended with court judgments in favor of state authorities.

The Tajik government's declared commitment to follow international standards in the field of freedom of religion is flawed. A law "On Freedom of Conscience and Religious Associations" was approved by the Majlisi Namoyandagon in March 2009, but critics argue that it makes religious organizations dependent on state bodies. In the preamble of this law, **Hanafiya** (the **Sunni** Hanafi school of law) is mentioned as "the official doctrine" of Tajikistan. This principle hinders the rights of adherents of other Muslim and non-Muslim religious beliefs, as well as those of atheist citizens of Tajikistan. On 11 October 2007, the government banned Jehovah's Witnesses. In February 2006, municipal authorities demolished a synagogue in Dushanbe.

The Tajik government does not follow the minimum standards for the prevention of human trafficking, although it has made significant efforts in this campaign. In 2006, law enforcement bodies initiated 45 criminal cases of human trafficking and 12 criminal cases of the trafficking of juveniles. In 2006, Tajik authorities assisted in the repatriation and rehabilitation of 92 victims of these crimes. About 100 Tajik citizens were returned from the United Arab Emirates, and 13 cases of girls being trafficked to foreign countries for sexual exploitation were identified over 10 months in 2007.

The rights of labor migrants remain unprotected. They have become objects of exploitation, dishonor, violence, and political machinations, both in Tajikistan and Russia. In Russia, Tajiks are often associated with illegal **drug trafficking**. From 2002 to 2009, campaigns and public demonstrations "to expel Tajiks from Russia" were conducted in Ekaterinburg and Moscow by Russian extremist public organizations. From January to October 2007, 377 labor migrants were deported to Tajikistan from Moscow. During 2003–2008, approximately 300–500 coffins with the bodies of Tajik labor migrants were delivered to Tajikistan from Russia annually. Most of those workers were murdered or died from illness.

The right to **education** is also restricted. According to UN data, Tajikistan's rate of attendance at educational institutions is less than 50 percent among senior pupils and less than 30 percent among children of preschool age. The rights of students are not respected. The Ministry of Education recommended a common uniform for school pupils and students of the universities. It is prohibited to wear expensive clothes at school, and university students are not permitted to drive cars. Girls are not allowed to wear the **hijab**. Beginning in 2009, not only students but also teachers are no longer allowed to bring mobile phones to school and university campuses. According to the law "On Education," it is prohibited to involve pupils and students in agricultural work. This law, however, is not enforced by local authorities, and many Tajik students are forced to "help" collect **cotton**, working all day long and taking their meals from home. Refusal to work may result in bad marks and even expulsion from school or university.

– I –

IBN SINO (980–1037). The Tajik medieval philosopher, scholar, doctor, and writer Abu-ali ibn Abdullah ibn Hasan ibn Ali, known as

Avicenna in the West and Ibn Sino in **Central Asia**, was born in Afshona village near **Bukhara**. After the fall of the **Samanids**, Ibn Sino escaped to Khorazm, then to Hamadan (**Iran**) and Isfahan. He died in Hamadan. He wrote numerous books on philosophy, science, medicine, and **literature**. One of his best-known works is *Al-Qanun fi tib* (Rules of Medicine), *Qanun* for short. It combined the achievements of Indian, Greek, Iranian, and **Arab** medicine. Ibn Sino wrote 20 books in Arabic and his native **Farsi**. The Tajik State Medical University is named in his honor.

IBRAHIMBEK (1889–1932). Ibrahimbek Chakobai Ughli was Tajikistan's **Basmachi** leader in 1921–1932. He was a descendant of the **Uzbek Laqai** tribe, a son of the tribal chief in the Ishon Khoja family. After Soviet forces invaded **Eastern Bukhara** in 1921, Ibrahimbek joined the Basmachis and established himself as the strongest warlord in southern Tajikistan, calling himself commander of Islamic forces. In 1922–1926, he combined all Basmachi forces in Tajikistan and, with some financial backing from the deposed Bukharan emir, **Said Alim Khan**, who had escaped to **Afghanistan**, fought the Red Army.

In June 1926, Ibrahimbek was forced to flee to Afghanistan. Between 1926 and 1929, he stayed in Kabul, on a pension from the Afghani government and Said Alim Khan, while his followers lived in northern Afghanistan. In 1929, Afghanistan was thrown into a political crisis when a populist emir, **Bachai Saqqao**, came to power. Bachai Saqqao sympathized with Ibrahimbek and the Basmachi movement. Consequently, Ibrahimbek moved to the north to mobilize the Bukharan émigrés in support of the new emir. In November 1929, Bachai Saqqao was overthrown and executed, and soon the new Afghan ruler, King Nadir Shah, moved to suppress Ibrahimbek's bands. In March 1931, after over a year of conflict in northern Afghanistan, Ibrahimbek with his tribal kin crossed the Soviet Tajikistan border. On 23 June 1931, he and his band were captured by local guards and Red Army detachments. The next day, they were sent to Tashkent to the Special Department of the Central Asian Military Okrug (Soviet Military Intelligence Service). His 15 companions in arms and relatives were shot on 10 August 1932; Ibrahimbek was executed on 31 August 1932.

IDI QURBON. The Muslim holiday Idi Qurbon (al-Adha in Arabic) is celebrated during the pilgrimage season. As part of the celebration, animals are killed for a feast. *See also* ISLAM; NATIONAL HOLIDAYS.

IDI RAMAZON. The Muslim holiday Idi Ramazon (al-Fitr in Arabic) is celebrated at the end of the holy month of Ramadan. *See also* IS-LAM; NATIONAL HOLIDAYS.

IKROMI, JALOL (1909–1993). A Tajik Soviet writer, Ikromi was born in **Bukhara** and received his primary education in prerevolutionary traditional schools. Following the **Bukharan Revolution**, he studied at the Bukharan Pedagogic School from 1922 to 1927. After a meeting with **Sadriddin Ayni** in 1927, Ikromi pursued a literary career. In 1930, he moved to Tajikistan and started work with *Rohbari Donish* magazine and later moved to the Tajik state publishing house. In 1942–1946, he headed the literary section of the Tajik drama theater named after **Abulqasem Lahuti**. In 1946, Ikromi returned to journalism and worked for *Sadoi Mardum* magazine. Like other pioneer Tajik writers in the modern era, Ikromi worked in different genres: drama, novel, and journalism. One of his best-known works is the historical trilogy *The Twelve Gates of Bukhara* devoted to the Bukharan Revolution. *See also* LITERATURE.

ILOLOV, MAMADSHOH (1948–). President of the **Academy of Science of Tajikistan**, an **academician**, and holder of a doctorate in mathematics, Ilolov was born in **Shughnon**, in the **Mountainous Badakhshon Autonomous Veloyat**, and studied mathematics at Voronezh State University (Russian Federation). Upon graduation in 1971, he joined the Tajik State University in a junior position and in 1973 became a lecturer in economic cybernetics. Between 1982 and 1989, Ilolov was an associate professor (*docent*) at the university. In 1990–1991, he headed the university's research department. In 1991, he joined the Ministry of Education as a departmental chair. Between 1992 and 1995, Ilolov was rector of Khorugh State University. He was elected to the **Majlisi Oli** in 1995 and chaired the committee on education, science, and youth policy. In 2000, he was elected to the **Majlisi Namoyandagon** and put in charge of the same committee. In February 2003, he was appointed minister of labor and social protection. In 2005, Ilolov became president of the Academy of Science and a member of the **Majlisi Melli**. Ilolov is a member of the **People's Democratic Party of Tajikistan**.

IMAM (IMOM). An *imam* is the leader or head of a **mosque**. *See also* ISLAM; MUFTI; OFFICIAL MUSLIM CLERGY.

IMOMI AZAM. *See* HANAFIYA.

IMOMOV, CHINOR (1898–1939). One of the first Tajik party and state leaders, Imomov was born in **Panjakent**. He graduated from a local Russian school in **Samarqand** in 1911. Imomov joined the Communist Party (CP) in 1918 and headed the revolutionary committee of Uroteppa. Between 1920 and 1924, he served on CP committees in Jizakh, Samarqand, and Tashkent. Imomov wrote for the first Soviet Tajik newspaper, *Ovozi Tojik* (Tajik Voice). With the formation of the **Tajik Autonomous Soviet Socialist Republic** (Tajik ASSR) in 1924, Imomov became secretary of the Organizational Bureau of the **Communist Party of Tajikistan** and secretary in charge of the Organizational Bureau of the Uzbekistan CP (Bolsheviks) in Tajikistan (1924–1928). In 1930, after two years of study at the Communist University in Leningrad, he was appointed Tajikistan's people's commissar (minister) of **education** (1931), and later people's commissar of **health** (1931–1933) and people's commissar of justice (1933–1934). In 1935, he was appointed secretary in charge of Tajikistan's **central executive committee** and in 1936–1937 headed Tajikistan's Soviet of People's Commissars (the government). In July 1937, Imomov was arrested on charges of counterrevolution, sentenced to death by the Military Collegium of the Union of Soviet Socialist Republics Supreme Court, and executed in the same year. In 1957, Imomov's reputation was rehabilitated.

INDIA. With an estimated population of more than 1.12 billion, India is the second most populous and third largest country in Asia, with the 12th largest **economy** and third largest military in the world. For independent Tajikistan, India is the closest democracy and a good neighbor. For India, Tajikistan is the closest **Central Asian** neighbor and partner. Diplomatic relations between the two states were established in 1992. India opened its embassy in **Dushanbe** in May 1994. Tajikistan opened its consulate in Delhi in 2003; it was upgraded to a full-fledged embassy in 2006.

India and Tajikistan have deep roots in history. The territory of present-day Tajikistan was part of ancient Persia and the **Kushan** realm, which had close cultural ties to India. The sophisticated Perso-Islamic synthesis that flourished in Moghul India in the 16th–19th centuries is preserved in modern Tajik culture, and this explains the **Tajiks'** close attachment to the Indian nation.

During the Soviet period, India and the Union of Soviet Socialist Republics (USSR) shared close relationships, especially in the military sphere. This guaranteed India easy access to all parts of the **Soviet Union**, including Tajikistan. After the collapse of the USSR, this trend continued, but to a lesser extent. India and Tajikistan were on the same side during the civil war in **Afghanistan** in the 1990s. In cooperation with **Russia**, they opposed the **Pakistan**-backed **Taliban** and helped the **Northern Alliance**. In the late 1990s, India set up a hospital at Farkhor, near Afghanistan's northern border, where wounded Afghans combating the Taliban were treated. Unlike Pakistan, India was not an observer at the **Inter-Tajik Peace Talks**.

In its relations with Tajikistan, the government of India has focused on important sectors such as pharmaceuticals, food processing, information technology, hydropower, and transportation. India also offered to rehabilitate the **Varzob**-1 hydropower plant in Tajikistan. In general, however, India was unable to exert its influence in Tajikistan to a degree equal to that of **China, Iran**, and even Pakistan. For the impoverished Tajikistan, the **foreign policy** priority has been procurement of foreign grants, advantaged credits, and other assistance projects. India, due to its weak economy when compared with China, and its physical isolation from Central Asia, cannot compete with Tajikistan's major regional neighbors.

More significant is military cooperation between the two countries. India, seeking a role as a global player, conducted its first overseas military exercise with Tajikistan in 2003. More importantly, in accordance with the 2002 bilateral defense agreement, India refurbished the Soviet-era military aerodrome in **Ayni**, 15 kilometers from **Dushanbe**, for around $1.77 million, completing the project in early 2007. It is anticipated that the base will be jointly maintained and commanded in rotation by India, Tajikistan, and Russia. India's plans in Tajikistan were put in question, however, when Russia disapproved of India's strategic drift toward the United States. In July 2007, reportedly at the request of Russia, the Tajik government moved away from allowing India a military base in Tajikistan. This sudden diplomatic reversal demonstrated the continuing vulnerability of Tajikistan's foreign policy to Russian pressure. *See also* FOREIGN INVESTMENT; FOREIGN TRADE; RUSSIAN MILITARY BASE IN TAJIKISTAN.

INDUSTRY. In the 1900s and 1910s, Russian capitalists built several industrial enterprises in territories that later constituted the northern part of Tajikistan. During the Soviet era, national industries appeared in the 1930s, when the first fruit and vegetable processing enterprises were constructed in Tajikistan's capital city, Stalinobod (**Dushanbe**). Large-scale industrial development began in the 1960s, when powerful electricity generating stations were built. In 1960, the share of industry in the gross domestic product (GDP) reached 53.9 percent. In 1990, nearly 100 industries were operating in Tajikistan. Industry was most developed in the north, in **Sughd** province.

Tajikistan's main industries declined sharply following the Soviet collapse in December 1991. The **civil war** (1992–1997) severely damaged the republic's industrial sector, and criminal bands maintained control over the Tajik aluminum plant known as **TALCO**, Tajikistan's chief industrial asset. After the **General Agreement on the Establishment of Peace and National Accord** was signed in June 1997, these bands were eliminated, and a gradual renewal of Tajikistan's industry began. In 1998, of 1,632 industrial enterprises, 1,171 were state owned (including 88 joint stock companies), and the rest were in the private sector. In 2007, the share of industry in Tajikistan's GDP was 15.4 percent.

Tajikistan's main industry is **nonferrous metallurgy. Power generation** and the **fuel industry** also contribute to the total industrial output. The production, transportation, and distribution of electricity is under the state-owned company **Barqi Tojik**. Other branches include mechanical engineering enterprises, chemical industry enterprises that produce mineral fertilizers, synthetic ammonia, sodium caustic, and lacquer paints. Tajikistan's light industry produces about 23 percent of total industrial output. This is primarily rough **cotton** cleaning. Tajikistan's cotton harvest is processed by the local cotton ginning industry, yet in Soviet times, only 20 percent of the total harvest was cleaned in the country. Foodstuff enterprises produce canned fruits and vegetables, dried fruits, cooking oil, soft drinks, mineral water, and liquors. Flour, **grain**, and mixed fodder enterprises make up about 5 percent of total industrial production. *See also* ECONOMY.

INTER-TAJIK PEACE TALKS. During Tajikistan's **civil war** (1992–1997), a series of talks took place between the government of President **Emomali Rahmon** and the **United Tajik Opposition** (UTO) under the aegis of the **United Nations** and with the endorsement of **Russia** and **Iran**. The talks started in April 1994 and ended in June 1997 with the signing in Moscow of the **General Agreement on the Establishment of Peace and National Accord**, putting an end to the Tajik civil war.

IRAN. The Islamic Republic of Iran, known as Persia until 1935, has a population of over 70 million. Iran stands out in the region of Central Eurasia as a unique Islamic republic that was formed in 1979 when a popular revolution overthrew the monarchy. **Shiite mullahs** then assumed political control. According to the 1979 constitution, the highest state authority is the supreme religious leader, the ayatollah.

Iranians and **Tajiks** share strong historical, cultural, and linguistic ties. Tajiks, like the Persians that constitute the majority of the population in Iran, are an Iranian people. Tajiks and Persians speak **Farsi**, which is also the official language of Iran. One important difference with the Farsi of Iran is that the **Tajik** language since 1940 has used a Cyrillic alphabet, and not many Tajiks can understand the modified Arabic script in which Iranian Farsi is written. Tajiks are predominantly **Sunni** Muslims, while Twelve-Imam **Shiism** has been the official religion of Iran since the early 16th century. Not surprisingly, Tajiks do not appear sympathetic to the religious zeal of Shia clerics of revolutionary Iran.

Iran was one of the first countries to recognize the newly independent Tajikistan in 1991 and the first nation to establish an embassy in **Dushanbe**. Because of the resurgence of Iranian culture within Tajikistan, Iran has encouraged cultural relations through visitor exchanges, joint conferences, and film festivals. Iran's leaders maintained amicable relations with Tajiks from opposing sides of the **civil**

war throughout the 1990s. Tehran never officially supported the Tajik Islamists' objective to create an Islamic state but directed their efforts toward a peaceful settlement of the civil war. However, Iran supported the emergence of the Tajik opposition in 1991–1992 and hosted Tajik opposition leaders from 1993 to 1998. In 1994–1997, Iran was a key sponsor of the **Inter-Tajik Peace Talks** and had the status of an official observer. Iran cooperated with **Russia** in negotiating a peace agreement between the Dushanbe government and the **United Tajik Opposition** (UTO). Iranian authorities hosted several rounds of the negotiations and two meetings between **Emomali Rahmon** and **Said Abdullo Nuri**. The direct participation of Iranian Foreign Minister Ali Akbar Velayati facilitated the signing of the Protocol on Refugees in January 1997.

In July 1995, Tajikistan opened an embassy in Tehran, one of its few outside the former **Soviet Union**. Both states were on the same side during the civil war in **Afghanistan** in the 1990s. In cooperation with Russia, they opposed the fiercely anti-Shiite and pro-Pushtun **Taliban** and helped the Tajik-dominated **Northern Alliance** and Hazara (Shia) groups.

As of 2009, Iran has a strong foothold in Tajikistan. Iran and Tajikistan are member states of the **Economic Cooperation Organization** (ECO) and **Confidence-Building Measures in Asia** (CICA), and Iran is an observer in the Russia- and China-dominated **Shanghai Cooperation Organization** (SCO) since June 2005. Tajikistan and Iran have signed a number of agreements reinforcing the economic ties between them. From 2002, Iranian companies have been actively investing in the **economy** of Tajikistan. Major projects include the hydroelectric power station Sangtuda-2, the **Istiqlol tunnel** and the Chormaghzak tunnel (**Khatlon**), and the power line from southern Tajikistan to Qunduz and Herat (Afghanistan) and further to Mashhad (Iran). During his visit to Tajikistan in July 2006, Iran's president, Mahmud Ahmadinejad, proposed establishing a Persian-language television network for Iranian, Tajik, and Afghan people. There are two Iranian book stores in **Dushanbe**, and regular air flights connect the two capital cities.

However, neither Tajikistan nor Iran sees the other as a strategic partner in **foreign policy**. Much of Iran's interest in Tajikistan concerns diplomacy and trade. Authorities in Tehran need Russian military hardware, and they try to cultivate closer ties with Tajikistan without targeting direct Russian interests. Tajikistan and the SCO membership offer Iran transit for the Chinese-Iranian trade route and access to the emerging Europe-Caucasus-Asia transport corridor. To boost its position regarding the United States and its rivals among powerful **Arab** neighbors to the south, Iran looks north—at the post-Soviet republics of **Central Asia**. But in addition to the U.S. economic embargo of Iran and similar restrictions internationally, Iran's nuclear program and support of radical Shia groups have created serious obstacles to establishing more amicable relations between Iran and Tajikistan. Another significant impediment for closer collaboration is that Tajikistan's government is secular while Iran's is Islamic.

IRFON. Formed in 1925 as the Tajikistan State Publishing House (Nashriyoti Davlatii Tojikiston, or Tadzhikgosizdat in Russian), Irfon specializes in publishing fiction as well as scientific, popular, agricultural, and translated **literature**.

ISFARA NOHIYA. Situated in the southeastern part of **Sughd veloyat**, on the northern slopes of the **Turkistan** mountain range, Isfara nohiya was formed in 1927. The district is 831.9 square kilometers, with a population of about 202,600, mainly **Tajiks** but also **Uzbeks**, **Kyrgyz**, and **Russians**. Isfara nohiya has nine **jamoats**, two villages, and one city. The administrative center is the city of Isfara. The distance from Isfara to **Khujand** is 107 kilometers, to **Dushanbe** 448 kilometers, and to the nearest railway station in **Konibodom** 37 kilometers. Average January and July temperatures can reach $-7°C$ and $25°C$ respectively. The annual rainfall is 200 millimeters. Isfara is widely known for its apricots, and there are deposits of brown **coal** (in Shurob) and oil (in Neftobod). This nohiya borders the Republic of **Kyrgyzstan** and was the scene of ethnic conflicts over **water** and land in the 1960s and the 1980s. *See also* VORUKH.

ISHAN. A highly respectful form of address for individual Sufi *shaykhs* (leaders), *ishan* was then extended to the organizations whose loyalty they commanded. This term is derived from the Persian third-person plural pronoun meaning "they" or "them." The ishan are treated by their **murids** (disciples) as living saints. Succession to the post of is-han normally passed from father to son, but the ishan could choose a favored disciple instead. Tajik *ishan-murid* groups supported various sides during the **civil war** in 1992–1997.

ISHKASHIM NOHIYA. This district is situated in the **Mountainous Badakhshon Autonomous Veloyat** on the southern slopes of the Ishkashim and Shahdara mountain range and part of the southern **Alichur**. It borders **Shughnon** and Roshtkala nohiyas to the north, **Murghob** to the east, and **Afghanistan** to the south. This mountainous region (altitudes range from 2,000 to 6,726 meters) was formed in 1932, with a territory of 3,700 square kilometers. The population is more than 26,000, mainly Ishkashimi and **Vakhani** Tajiks. It has six **jamoats**. The administrative center of the nohiya is the city of Ishkashim. The distance from Ishkashim to **Khorugh** is 104 kilometers and to **Dushanbe** 680 kilometers, making it one of the most remote regions in Tajikistan. Average January and July temperatures can reach –19°C and 31°C respectively. The annual rainfall is 100 millimeters. The mineral water source of Garmchashma is located in Ishkashim, and there are deposits of Badakhshoni rubies (la'l).

ISHKASHIMI. A Pamirian language, Ishkashimi is spoken mainly in northeastern **Afghanistan** and parts of Tajikistan (in Rin village, Ishkashim nohiya). Dialects of Ishkashimi (Zebaki and Sangliji) can be found in **Vakhan**. Ishkashimi is phonetically close to **Vakhani** and includes many **Tajik** loanwords. *See also* LANGUAGES.

ISKANDARKUL. This lake in the **Ayni nohiya** on the northern slopes of the **Hisor** mountain range is named for Alexander (Iskandar) of Macedonia—**Alexander the Great**. Formed from the Saratogh River, Iskandarkul lies 2,194 meters above sea level. It is 3.3 kilometers long, 2.9 kilometers wide, and 72 meters deep. The distance from Iskandarkul to **Dushanbe** is 134 kilometers, and to the Dushanbe-**Khujand** road 23 kilometers.

ISKANDAROV, AKBARSHO (1951–). Born in **Darvoz nohiya** in the **Mountainous Badakhshon Autonomous Veloyat** (MBAV), Iskandarov began working for the Qalai Khumb (currently Darvoz) district executive committee in 1970. In 1979, he graduated from the Tajik State University in economics (correspondence course). In 1982–1984, he worked at the Qalai Khumb district committee of the **Communist Party of Tajikistan** (CPT) and in 1984–1986 at the MBAV provincial committee of the CPT. In 1986, he graduated from the Tashkent Communist Party High School (correspondence course) and in 1986–1987 worked for the **Ishkashim** district executive committee. In 1987–1990, he was first secretary of the **Vanj nohiya** committee of the CPT. In 1990, he was appointed chair of the MBAV provincial executive committee and was elected to the **Supreme Soviet** of Tajikistan, where he was appointed deputy chair.

Heightened political tensions and gathering opposition to the ruling elite following the Soviet collapse led to the resignation of the parliamentary chair, **Safarali Kenjaev**, and the elevation of Iskandarov as acting chair in April 1992. This was the first time that a Badakhshoni held this post. Following the forced resignation of President **Rahmon Nabiev** in September, Iskandarov became Tajikistan's acting president. Unable to contain the rapidly deteriorating political crisis, and being accused of siding with opposition forces by the powerful Leninobod-**Kulob** camp in the **civil war**, Iskandarov submitted his resignation in November 1992.

Iskandarov served as Tajikistan's ambassador to Turkmenistan in 1993–2000. He was Tajikistan's ambassador to Kazakhstan from 2000 to 2007. From 2007, he has been ambassador at large of Tajikistan's Ministry of Foreign Affairs.

ISKANDAROV, MAHMADRUZI (1955–). Chair of the **Democratic Party of Tajikistan** (DPT), and one of the leading figures in the **United Tajik Opposition** (UTO), Iskandarov was born in **Tojikobod**, in the **Nohiyas under Republican Control**. He graduated from the Construction Tekhnikum (college) in **Dushanbe** and received a degree in economics from the Tajik State University (correspondence course) in 1982. From 1976 to 1992, he worked in the repair and rigger department of the Ministry of Health Care, making his way up to the post of department head. In 1991, Iskandarov joined the opposition movement in his native **Gharm** valley and headed a band of 500 fighters. He was one of the most moderate field commanders of the opposition during the **civil war**. Between 1993 and 1997, he was based in **Afghanistan**, but he returned to Dushanbe following the signing of the peace accord. In February 1999, Iskandarov was given the military rank of major general and was appointed chair of the committee on emergency situations. In

September 1999, he was appointed chair of the Tajikcomunservice state concern of Tajikistan. Under his leadership, the DPT left the UTO (October 1999) and was officially registered as a parliamentary **political party** (December 1999).

In November 2003, the prosecutor general of Tajikistan filed a case against Iskandarov, and in April 2004 he was kidnapped in Moscow and returned to Dushanbe. In October 2005, he received a 23-year sentence on charges including **terrorism**, embezzlement, illegal possession of a weapon, and banditry. Regardless of the arrest and imprisonment, the DPT in its 2004 congress reelected Iskandarov as its chair. *See also* DEMOCRATIC PARTY OF TAJIKISTAN ALMATY PLATFORM (DPTA).

ISKHAKI, IUSUF (1932–1996). A Tajik scholar, doctor of medicine, and **academician**, Iskhaki was born in **Khujand**. After graduating from the Tajik Medical Institute in 1954, he practiced medicine in Tajikistan in different capacities and became rector of the Tajik Medical Institute. He was assassinated in May 1996 by unknown **terrorists**.

ISLAM. This religion, revealed to the Prophet Muhammad in 610–632, is dominant in present-day Tajikistan. The conversion of the **Tajiks** to Islam was carried out by conquest and persuasion. Under the Umayyad dynasty (661–750), the **Arab** governor of the province of **Khurasan**, Qutayba ibn Muslim, subjugated the main parts of **Bactria**, **Sogdiana**, and **Ferghana** between 705 and 715. By 738, **Movarounnahr** and Khurasan were united as one province of the Arab Caliphate. Along with the Arab conquerors, Islamic missionaries and merchants of Persian and Arab origin also exposed the local population to Islam. As a result of these efforts, Islam pushed out all beliefs previously widespread in the region, including Zoroastrianism, Christianity, and **Buddhism**, and became not just another religion but the way of life for Tajiks.

Islam became the official religion of the **Samanid** state (875–999) centered in **Bukhara** and founded by a Perso-Tajik dynasty. During this era, the Tajik **language** became widespread. The great Perso-Tajik poets **Abuabdullo Rudaki** and **Abulqasem Firdawsi** wrote their epic poems, and a brilliant cohort of Central Asian scholars made valuable contributions to the world's intellectual history.

Islam's magnetism in Bukhara and **Samarqand** was so strong, it swallowed the nomad armies that invaded the region from the 10th century, the Seljuk Turks in the 10th–11th centuries, and Mongol invaders in the 13th–14th centuries, which enthusiastically embraced Islam. In addition to sponsoring the fine **arts**, Islamic architecture, **music**, and **literature**, the Turk, Mongol, and **Uzbek** dynasties that ruled Movarounnahr from the 11th century onward supported *ulamo* (scholars) and **madrasas** both directly and through **vaqf** foundations. Most of them were devoted disciples of charismatic Islamic figures.

Islam reached the rank of a world religion largely through the effort of **Sufi** brotherhoods, which proselytized extensively among various peoples of **Central Asia**, **India**, and **China**. Among the four most influential Sufi *tariqas* (orders), three were born in Central Asia. Sufi missionaries incorporated pre-Islamic popular practices into Islam in the region (e.g., shrine and tomb visitations, amulets). In general, Tajiks (and later, sedentary Uzbeks) adhere to Islam more thoroughly than their nomad neighbors. Tajik *ulamo* were teachers of Islam in Central Asia, and their tongue was the second language (after Arabic) in Islam. Learning **Farsi** was mandatory in Central Asian madrasas, and Sufi adepts practiced mostly in the language of the Tajiks.

Communities of **Shughnis and Rushanis, Ishkashimis, Bartangis, Vakhanis**, and other **Pamiris** are attached to **Shiite** Islamism. **Ismailia** first won adherents in **Badakhshon** in the early 10th century. Only 5 percent of Tajikistani Muslims are Ismailis. The dominant doctrine among Tajiks has been the **Hanafi** school of **Sunni** Islam. Unlike Shiite Persians, Sunni Hanafi Tajiks are unfamiliar with theocratic rule. They are used to life in a society where political power belongs to secular figures that enjoy the support of *ulamo*. *Ulamo* were trained in religious schools and served society as professional specialists in *sharia* (Islamic law). *Ulamo* and **mullahs** were responsible for keeping the equilibrium between rulers and ruled. Rulers needed Islam to make their power sacred, legitimate, and indispensable. For that reason, orthodox Islam in Central Asia has long been associated with established secular systems of government.

However, *ulamo* were not the exclusive guardians of religion for Tajiks. There was not an established religious hierarchy or national church responsible for the organization of religious affairs and mobilization of religious society among Tajiks. Religious authority was fragmented, divided between **official Muslim clergy**, state-appointed clerics, and unofficial (often uneducated, but very influential) leaders, including hereditary *pirs*, *ishans*, *shaikhs*, and other privileged persons who claimed to have a special, divine gift. The Hanafi school's emphasis on internal harmony and an understanding of true faith based in the heart (as compared to actions) allowed Tajik communities, including the isolated and mountainous ones, to preserve their customary life and pre-Islamic traditions, including Persian cultural heritage. Since the inception of Islam, Tajiks regard their various popular traditions as sacred and Islamic. Instead of an institution in the form of a church or mosque, more stable, long-lasting, emotionally charged, often kin-based and folk associations like the family, *avlod* (extended family), and neighborhood became central in this approach to religion, later called popular or people's Islam.

Religion took divergent courses in urban areas and rural territories. Sunni Islam of the Tajik urban centers, with its emphasis on centralized authority and the unquestionable superiority of Islamic law interpreted by erudite *ulamo*, contrasted with the sectarianism and rebelliousness of Sufi brotherhoods which flourished in the Central Asian periphery, including the Tajik **Eastern Bukhara**, an area not controlled fully by state authority until the late 19th century. The Sunni Islam of Central Asia was mostly occupied with the incorporation of Muslims rather than assimilation. This ethnocultural tolerance, in addition to the absence of a "church" as an officious institution, made Central Asian Islam equally attractive to Turks and Tajiks. Both a Bukhara-born, well-educated, Persian-speaking painter and a newly converted, illiterate, sectarian nomad of Dasht-i Qipchaq (Kazakh Steppe) were in harmony with themselves and the outside world as long as, in their eyes, the sovereignty of Islam was not harmed.

With the advent of colonization by **Russia** in the late 19th century, a social and intellectual movement began to appear as local Muslims' response to the challenge represented by the colonizers. The Islamic reformist movement, or **Jadidia**, was born in the urban centers of Muslim Russia. The jadids advocated cultural synthesis with non-Muslims and sharply criticized the corrupt and conservative *ulamo* and ignorant Sufis and *ishans*.

During the Soviet era, especially after the end of the 1920s, Islam and other religions were attacked directly by the communist authorities. **Mosques** and madrasas were destroyed, women's **faranji** veil was banned, and most of the religiously educated Tajiks were expelled, imprisoned, or executed. Under the banner of Islam, **Uzbek,** Tajik, **Kyrgyz,** and **Turkmen Basmachi** fought against the Soviets from 1918 to 1932. The authorities tried to weaken and even destroy the community-based people's Islam, particularly the connections between national and religious identities. As a result of Soviet policies, the link between the intellectual, bookish Islam and communities was broken. The introduction of mass secular **education** further isolated popular Islam. The Soviets also created an "official" Islam, regulated by officially appointed clergy. Founded during **World War II,** the Muslim Spiritual Board for Central Asia and Kazakhstan, headquartered in Tashkent and headed by **muftis** from an influential, pro-Communist Uzbek religious family, lasted until the 1990s, when it was replaced by national boards (muftiyats) in the various republics, including Tajikistan. Qazi-Kalon **Hoji Akbar Turajonzoda** was the official leader of Tajikistan's first independent religious agency (*qaziyat*).

Tajikistan is famous for becoming one of the centers of Islamic activism in the Soviet Union. In the late 1970s, an underground group of young Islamists emerged in the **Vakhsh valley.** In October 1990, they formed the core of the **Islamic Renaissance Party of Tajikistan** (IRPT). Tajik Islamists (or representatives of political Islam) are a modern phenomenon that has no precedent in Tajik history. They challenge, as they perceive it, both the corrupt and conformist "official" Islam and the passive, ignorant, and narrow-minded people's Islam. In contrast to those who support traditional Islam as something that reduces citizens to passive spectators, the Tajik Islamists believe that society should be Islamized only through social and political action. Unlike the Jadids, modern Tajik Islamists reject secularism and promote a return to the Quran and sharia law, which they believe do not need modernization. Most Islamists come from the urban youth and also the victimized communities of **Gharmis** resettled in the Vakhsh valley by the Soviets both before and after World War II. During Tajikistan's **civil war** (1992–1997), Tajik Islamists formed the backbone of the **United Tajik Opposition** (UTO). Led by the charismatic **Said Abdullo Nuri,** they believed Muslims had an obligation (*fard*) to revolt against communist rulers and kill "unbelievers."

After peace was concluded, in 1999 the IRPT was legally recognized and included in politics. Since that time, Islamism in Tajikistan has fused with nationalism. The political objectives of various (secular) political groups have merged with Islamic (religious) concerns. This tendency had emerged in the course of the civil war. In 1993–1994, the political movement of Ismaili Pamiris, **La'li Badakhshon**, joined the Sunni IRPT to form the UTO under the banner of a unified Tajik nationalism. During the first decade of its existence, the IRPT was involved in violent *jihad* (holy war) against "apostates and communists," but since 1999 it is a parliamentary party struggling to survive in secular Tajikistan and the modern world of participatory politics. Its activities are transparent, and the party's members avoid open conformity to Islamic standards, especially in politics. According to the international *jihadis* advocating war against the United States and the West, the IRPT "has relinquished the Islamic identity of the Tajikistani cause and has turned it into merely a dispute over power between the opposition and the government."

The legislative system of independent Tajikistan insists on a clear delineation between government and religion, and also between religion and political action. Despite the noticeable moderation of Tajik Islamism, many representatives of the government remain deeply suspicious of religious activity and the Islamic clergy. The State Committee on Religious Affairs was responsible for overseeing the work of clergy and religious institutions, but in December 2006 these functions were transferred to the Department of Religions at the Ministry of Culture. The pro-government, state-controlled Council of Learned Men (Shuroi Ulamo) systematically organizes affirmations of *imams* as chief managers of mosques. Also, the government regularly conducts the registration of existing and newly built mosques. The government officially supports the Hanafia sect and its founder Abu Hanifa, who is called Tajik, in order to minimize the influence of imported and non-Hanafi **Hizb-ut-Tahrir**, **Salafiya**, and **Wahhabism**. *See also* KHATMUL QURON; RELIGIONS; UNOFFICIAL MULLAHS.

ISLAMIC MOVEMENT OF UZBEKISTAN (IMU). The IMU is a fundamentalist militant movement that advocates the forceful overthrow of **Uzbekistan**'s government and the establishment of an Islamic state in **Central Asia**. The IMU has its roots in the pro-

Wahhabi Adolat (Justice) and Islam Lashkarlari (Fighters of Islam) groups formed in the late 1980s in the Uzbek part of the **Ferghana** valley (Namangon, Andijon, and Kokand). In 1991–1992, these groups took steps to forcibly introduce an Islamic state in the Ferghana valley. By 1993, they were cruelly repressed in Uzbekistan, and their activists, led by Tohir Yuldashev and **Jumaboi Namangani**, managed to withdraw to central Tajikistan (**Gharm** region). During the **civil war** in Tajikistan, Uzbek Islamists fought alongside the **United Tajik Opposition** (UTO) against the secular Tajik **government**. Also, between 1994 and 1998, Yuldashev and Namangani established relationships from their bases in Tajikistan with illegal drug dealers and extremist groups in **Pakistan** and **Afghanistan**, including al-Qaeda and the **Taliban**. They also received support from Pakistan's Inter-Services Intelligence and opened offices in Kabul, Mazar-i-Sharif (Afghanistan), and Peshawar (Pakistan).

The alliance of the UTO with Uzbek Islamic radicals proved to be short lived. A year after the Tajik peace accord was signed in 1997, **Said Abdullo Nuri**, the leader of Tajik Islamists, and former UTO commander Mirzo Ziyoev, under the pressure of the Tajik government, orchestrated the withdrawal of Namangani's group from Tajikistan. Their families were driven to the Uzbek border, while the fighters were given a "green corridor" by Russian and Tajik frontier guards to cross the Tajik-Afghan border.

In 1998, the IMU's creation was announced from Taliban-occupied Kabul. While in Afghanistan, the IMU joined the illegal trafficking and regional geopolitical **terrorist** networks of the Taliban and the Osama bin Laden group. The IMU also attracted many Tajik Islamic radicals left disaffected by the armistice in Tajikistan, which they viewed as a sellout. Operating out of their bases in Tajikistan and northern Afghanistan, the IMU launched a series of raids into **Kyrgyzstan** and Uzbekistan in 1999 and 2000. Perhaps most famously, in August 2000, the IMU kidnapped four American mountain climbers in the Kara-Su valley of Kyrgyzstan, holding them hostage until they escaped on 12 August. In response, the **United States** placed the IMU on its list of foreign terrorist organizations. In spring 2001, the IMU changed its name to the Islamic Movement of Turkistan.

An IMU group headed by Namangani was defeated in fall 2001 during the fighting in northern Afghanistan against the Taliban regime. However, the IMU remains a presence in Afghanistan, Pakistan, and

Tajikistan and is thought to still pose a threat to regional security. Many Tajik and Uzbek citizens accused of IMU membership have been arrested in the **Sughd veloyat**. It is believed that the IMU, now solely under the leadership of Tohir Yuldashev, is closely affiliated with al-Qaeda and has embraced Osama bin Laden's anti-American, anti-Western agenda.

Most Tajik Islamists see the IMU as an illegitimate Islamic force due to its rejection of Central Asian traditions, culture, and history and its dependence on foreign sources, including Wahhabism from Saudi Arabia and Deobandism from Pakistan.

ISLAMIC OPPOSITION. *See* CIVIL WAR; HIZB-UT-TAHRIR; ISLAMIC MOVEMENT OF UZBEKISTAN; ISLAMIC RENAISSANCE PARTY OF TAJIKISTAN; SALAFIYA; UNITED TAJIK OPPOSITION; UNOFFICIAL MULLAHS; WAHHABIYA.

ISLAMIC RENAISSANCE PARTY OF TAJIKISTAN (IRPT). The Islamic Renaissance Party of Tajikistan (Hizbi Nahzati Islomi Tojikiston in **Tajik**) grew from an underground youth organization that appeared in 1978 in **Qurghonteppa** and was led by **Said Abdullo Nuri**. The core of the organization were people resettled from **Gharm** in the **Vakhsh valley**, and other Gharmis still in their native region. In June 1990, **Davlat Usmon** and Said Ibrahim Gadoev took part in the founding congress of the All-Union Islamic Renaissance Party for the Muslims of the Soviet Union in Astrakhan (**Russia**). Following this congress, appeals to the **Supreme Soviet** in Tajikistan for an inaugural conference in the republic were rejected. The Supreme Soviet ruled that the new party "contradicted the constitution and laws of the Tajik SSR." The official clergy in Tajikistan, headed by the Qazi-kalon (Supreme Judge) **Hoji Akbar Turajonzoda**, confirmed the principle of the separation of church and state and advised against the political involvement of the clergy. Nevertheless, the IRPT held its inaugural conference on 6 October 1990 in a **mosque** in Chortut village (**Rudaki nohiya**) and declared itself the Tajik branch of the All-Union IRP. This violation of state laws resulted in fines for the organizers of the conference.

Soon after the collapse of the **Soviet Union** in September 1991, the IRPT formed a coalition bloc with other opposition parties: the secular movements of **Rastokhez**, **La'li Badakhshon**, and the **Democratic**

Party of Tajikistan (DPT). Following a series of public meetings, the Supreme Soviet was forced to rescind its earlier ban on the IRPT in October 1991. The first congress of the IRPT was officially held on 26 October 1991 with the participation of 657 delegates and 310 invited guests. **Muhammad Sharif Himmatzoda** was elected chair of the party, with **Davlat Usmon** and Said Ibrahim Gadoev as his two deputies. The congress approved the flag and emblem of the party. The IRPT was registered by the Ministry of Justice on 4 December 1991 and declared its independence from the All-Union IRP. At this point, the party membership was 20,000. **Islam** was declared the guiding principle of the party, while its immediate task, as stated by party leaders, was the establishment of a "legal and democratic state." The IRPT was the only Central Asian Islamic party to take part in general **elections**. In the November 1991 presidential elections, the opposition bloc, with the IRPT at its core, supported the candidacy of **Davlatnazar Khudonazarov**, who received nearly 31 percent of the votes against **Rahmon Nabiev**. The opposition claimed that support for its candidate was actually around 40 percent.

In the ensuing months, the opposition took its protest to the streets of **Dushanbe**. Opposition rallies in Shahidon Square, near the presidential palace, in the first half of 1992, and the defection of Qazikalon Turajonzoda to the opposition side forced the government to announce the formation of the **Government of National Reconciliation** in May 1992. This government was not recognized as legitimate in **Kulob** and **Sughd**, leading to armed clashes between opposition forces and forces loyal to the besieged President Nabiev in Kulob. The IRPT formed the Sitodi Najoti Vatan (Fatherland Liberation Front) to coordinate its armed struggle against the Kulobi forces of the Sitodi Milli (Popular Front). After the defeat of the opposition forces in November 1992, the IRPT's leaders escaped abroad. In 1993, the exiled IRPT in **Afghanistan** joined the **Movement for Islamic Revival in Tajikistan** (MIRT).

The IRPT constituted the backbone of the **United Tajik Opposition** (UTO), which presented a unified challenge to the **government** of Tajikistan. After four years of armed conflict, on 27 June 1997 a **General Agreement on the Establishment of Peace and National Accord** was signed under the aegis of the **United Nations** by IRPT leaders and the government of Tajikistan. The agreement stipulated the incorporation of opposition fighters in the ranks of the regular

army and the allocation of 30 percent of government posts (at central and regional levels) to the opposition.

The admission of the IRPT into the formal political arrangements was not easy. Only in November 1998 did the **Majlisi Oli** recommend the legalization of the party, leading to the August 1999 decision by the supreme court to reverse a 1993 ban on the IRPT, over two years after the signing of the agreement and too late for the party to effectively participate in the imminent presidential elections. The IRPT nominated Davlat Usmon for the November 1999 **presidential elections** but failed to collect the required 145,000 signatures (5 percent of the total number of voters) to register his candidacy. After repeated protests from the IRPT and under international pressure, Usmon's candidacy was registered on the eve of the elections. Usmon received 59,857 votes (2.1 percent of all votes). This episode caused internal strife in the ranks of the IRPT, which led to the departure of Turajonzoda from his party post of deputy head. The IRPT nonetheless remains the most powerful **political party**, with turbulent years ahead as it vies for political supremacy against the secular elite. In November 1999, Said Abdullo Nuri replaced Himmatzoda as chair of the IRPT. In 2006, after the death of Nuri, **Muhiddin Kabiri** was elected chair of the IRPT.

ISLAMIC UNIVERSITY OF TAJIKISTAN (IUT). The university began as the Islamic Institute of Tajikistan, which was officially inaugurated on 17 September 1990 as an educational department of Tajikistan's muftiyat (national board of muftis). Initially, at the initiative of **Hoji Akbar Turajonzoda**, it was designed to become the International Islamic University in Islamabad, a **Pakistan**-modeled modern Islamic institution. In 1990–1993, Turajonzoda secured financial assistance from Muslim countries for 150 instructors, who worked at the Islamic University of Tajikistan and in more than 10 **madrasas** of Tajikistan. In 1994, it had more than 1,000 students, half of them young women. In 1995, its number decreased to 40–45 students. In June 1997, the IUT was established as a private institution of higher education and became subject to greater pressure from political authorities. The university receives assistance from the Institute of Ismaili Studies in London.

Since 1997, the IUT curriculum contains religious and secular disciplines. There are three grades of training: *edodiya* (preparatory), two years; *mahad* (undergraduate), two years; and *fakultavi* (graduate), three years. The university runs its own high school for girls (*madrasai dukhtarona*) with 300 pupils in 2000, and a Quran readers' course (*madrasai al-qur'a*) with 200 students in 2000. The total annual enrollment was nearly 1,500 in 2000. The university has about 60 teachers and researchers, including religious teachers, associated with the Tajikistan **Academy of Sciences** and other universities. The university receives assistance from the Institute of Ismaili Studies in London. In 2000, the first group of IUT graduates (250) received their degrees.

In 2007, the central **government** took steps to bring the IUT under its control, subjecting teachers to a selection process, introducing secular disciplines, and placing its administration under the Ministry of Education. Since 2008, the university is funded by the central government. In February 2009, at the initiative of President **Emomali Rahmon**, the university was named after Imomi Azam. In 2008–2009, the university had more than 900 students, some 114 of them women. *See also* ISLAM.

ISLOMIDDINOV, MIRZOSHARIF (1949–). A Tajik politician and industrialist, Islomiddinov was born in **Isfara**, **Sughd veloyat**. After graduating from the Moscow Institute of Oil, Chemistry, and Gas Industry in 1971, he started work in the oil and gas extraction enterprise in Neftobod, Isfara nohiya. In 1980–1986, he headed the enterprise. In 1986–1991, he studied at the Communist Party High School and in 1988–1991 chaired the Isfara city executive committee. In 1991–1995, Islomiddinov was deputy chair of the city of Isfara. In 1995–1996, he was director general of Qairaqum Oil, a Tajik-American joint enterprise. In 1996–1999, Islomiddinov was deputy chair of the Sughd veloyat. From December 1999 to September 2003, he was vice premier of Tajikistan. From October 2003 to March 2005, he chaired the Isfara city **hukumat**. In 2005, he was elected to the **Majlisi Namoyandagon** and chaired the standing committee on energy production, industry, construction, and communication.

ISMAIL SAMANI PEAK. From 1931 to 1962, the Ismail Samani Peak, situated in northwest **Pamir**, was known as Stalin Peak, and from 1962 to 1998 as Communism Peak. This is the highest point of Tajikistan and the former **Soviet Union**. In 1928, a joint Soviet-German expedition calculated its height to be 7,495 meters. The peak was conquered for the first time by Soviet mountaineer E. Abalakov in 1933. In 1998, the peak acquired its present name to celebrate the **Samanid** dynasty.

ISMAILIS. The Shia Imami Ismaili Muslims, generally known as the Ismailis, belong to the **Shiite** branch of **Islam**. They are spread among more than 25 different countries, mainly in **Central Asia** (especially in Tajik and Afghan **Badakhshon**), Africa, the Middle East, and South Asia, as well as in Europe, North America, and Australia. Like other Shia Muslims, the Ismailis affirm that after the Prophet Muhammad's death, Hazrat Ali, his cousin and son-in-law, became the first **imam**—the spiritual leader—of the Muslim community, and that this spiritual leadership continues thereafter by hereditary succession through Ali and his wife Fatima, the Prophet's daughter. This sect began when the Shia Imam Ismail (son of Jafar al-Sadeq) died in 765. He was thought by his followers to be the final, Seventh Imam, who was to return on the day of judgment.

Spiritual devotion to the imam and adherence to the Shia Imami Ismaili *tariqah* (order) of Islam, according to the guidance of the current imam, have fostered in the Ismaili community ideals of self-sufficiency, unity, and a shared identity. Accounts of Badakhshonis' adoption of Ismaili teachings differ, but all agree that **Nasir Khusraw** (1004–1090) made a major contribution to the establishment of the Ismaili community in Badakhshon. Nasir Khusraw traveled in **Khurasan** and Badakhshon and spread Ismaili doctrine.

Under the direction and guidance of the **Aga Khan**, the Ismaili community in Tajikistan, as in other states, has established schools, hospitals, **health** centers, housing societies, and a variety of social, economic, **educational**, and cultural development institutions for the common good of all citizens, regardless of race or religion. *See also* AGA KHAN DEVELOPMENT NETWORK.

ISMOILOV, SHAVKAT (1951–). A Tajik lawyer and politician, Ismoilov was born in **Dushanbe**. He received a law degree from the Tajik State University in 1973 and accepted a teaching position at the university and later became dean of the Law Department. He was appointed minister of justice in 1993 and was replaced by **Khalifabobo Khamidov** in January 2001. In November 2001, he was elected to **Majlisi Namoyandagon**. *See also* GOVERNMENT.

ISTIQLOL TUNNEL. Nearly 5 kilometers long, the Istiqlol tunnel is situated in the **Hisor** mountain range at the **Anzob** Pass (90 kilometers north of **Dushanbe**) on the Dushanbe-Khujand **motor road**. The Istiqlol significantly improved transportation and communication between the country's central and northern regions all year round. This tunnel became known as Istiqlol ("independence" in **Farsi-Tajik**) in July 2006 during its official opening, inaugurated by President **Emomali Rahmon** and President of Iran Mahmud Ahmadinejad. Previously it had been called Anzob, then Ushtur, and its construction had been launched by the Soviet government in 1982. The construction was suspended in 1993 due to Tajikistan's **civil war** and lack of resources. In May 1999, the project resumed, and in 2003 Iran donated $10 million as a grant and provided the Tajik government with $21.5 million in credit. The construction, carried out jointly by Tajik companies and Iranian Sabir International, faced difficulties such as floods and required additional funding.

ISTRAVSHAN NOHIYA. Formed in 1936 and located in the **Sughd veloyat** on the northern slopes of the Turkistan mountain range, this nohiya was originally known as Uroteppa. The provincial majlis of Sughd renamed the nohiya and its central city Istravshan in July 2000.

Istravshan (or Ustrushana) is a historical province in Uroteppa and Shahristan lowlands. The 2,500th anniversary of the city was celebrated in Tajikistan in 2002. Istravshan was one of the most developed areas in the **Sogdian** period. In the 6th century, Istravshan was an independent kingdom, ruled by the Afshins from their seat of power in Bunjikat. It persistently resisted **Arab** incursions at the end of the 7th century. In 893, Istravshan was incorporated into the **Samanid** empire. On 2 October 1866, the Uroteppa fortress was captured by **Russia**. Soviet power was established there in November 1917.

Istravshan nohiya covers 1,830 square kilometers. The population of 185,000 is predominantly **Tajiks** and **Uzbeks**, living in the city of Istravshan (55,900) and 11 **jamoats**. The distance from the city of Istravshan to the Havas railway station is 45 kilometers, to **Khujand** 73 kilometers, and to **Dushanbe** 268 kilometers. Average temperatures in January and July can reach –2°C and 30°C respectively. The average annual precipitation is 200–800 millimeters. The main occupation in Istravshan nohiya is **agriculture**, including **cotton** and

grain production, gardening, and livestock breeding. Arable lands amount to 143,898 hectares.

ITTIHOD: CIVIL-PATRIOTIC PARTY OF TAJIKISTAN (ICPPT). Ittihod (which means "union" in **Tajik**) was a **political party** between 1994 and 1999. It was formed on 2 November 1994 and registered in April 1995 but was suspended by the Ministry of Justice in April 1999. At the time of registration, the ICPPT had 1,680 members. Its chair, **Bobokhon Mahmadov**, was Tajikistan's minister of culture and information. Its deputy chair, Said Ahmedov, was the governmental head of the state committee for religious affairs. Ittihod declared itself a parliamentary party with the objective of supporting "civil accord" and "struggle against political radicalism and separatism, rigorous fundamentalism, religious extremism, and clan, regional, and national discrimination." On the eve of parliamentary elections in 1999, Ittihod's registration was refused by the Ministry of Justice and the party suspended its activities.

IULDASHEV, KARIM (1940–2001). Born in Angren, in the Tashkent province of **Uzbekistan**, to a Tajik family, Iuldashev received a degree in Oriental studies from the Tajik State University in 1965. In 1966–1975, he worked as a translator in Soviet missions in **Arab** countries. Between 1975 and 1986, he worked in the Ministry of Foreign Affairs at different posts and then moved to the central committee of the **Communist Party of Tajikistan**. In 1991–1994, Iuldashev headed the International Department in the presidential apparatus and then the commission on international and economic affairs in the Council of Ministers. In September 1994, he was appointed state adviser on international affairs to President **Emomali Rahmon**. On 17 July 2001, he was assassinated in **Dushanbe**.

IUSUFI, KHAYRINISSO (1964–). Also known as Khairinisso Mavlonova, Iusufi was born in **Panjakent** in **Sughd veloyat**. She received a degree in veterinary science from the Tajik Institute of Agriculture in 1986, and a degree in philology from Khujand State University in 2003. In 2005, she graduated from the Academy of State Service in Moscow. Iusufi started her career in 1986 as chief veterinarian in a Panjakent veterinary station. From 1987 to 1996, she held command positions in the **Komsomol** district committee in Panjakent. From 1996–2004, Iusufi was deputy chair of the city of Panjakent and Sughd veloyat. During 2004–2008, she was Tajikistan's vice premier. On 28 January 2008, Iusufi was appointed chair of the Committee on Women and Family of the government of Tajikistan. *See also* GOVERNMENT.

– J –

JABBOR RASULOV NOHIYA. Based in **Sughd veloyat** and named in honor of **Jabbor Rasulov**, this **nohiya** was formed in 1935. It was known as Proletar until 1989. With a territory of 321.4 square kilometers and a population of 100,300 (17,000 urban dwellers), mostly **Tajiks** and **Uzbeks**, the nohiya has five **jamoats**. Proletarsk is the nohiya center. The nohiya is located in the western part of the **Ferghana valley** and borders **Uzbekistan** and **Kyrgyzstan**. Average January and July temperatures can reach –2°C and 30°C respectively; the average annual precipitation is 200–300 millimeters. The main occupation in this district is **agriculture**, including **cotton**, **grain**, fruit, and silkworm production and livestock breeding. Arable lands amount to 73,381 hectares. Proletarsk is connected by **motor road** to **Khujand** (20 kilometers) and **Dushanbe** (321 kilometers). Proletarsk is also connected to Dushanbe and Uzbekistan by **railway**.

JADIDIA. The reformist movement in **Central Asia** in the early 20th century was known as Jadidia, Jadid, or Jadidism (from the Arabic root of *jadid*, meaning "new"). Tatar Jadids were influential in bringing educational reformist ideas to Central Asia. Reformist ideas about **Islam** and **education** penetrated the region from modernist newspapers of Egypt, **India**, and Turkey. The Jadid movement in the **Bukharan emirate** was inspired by **Ahmad Donish**. The Bukharan Jadid movement passed through four phases.

Between 1910 and March 1917, Bukharan Jadidism emerged as a movement for cultural enlightenment, directed toward the introduction of the *usuli-Jadid* (new method) at schools: *maktabi jadid*. Among the first Jadids were the representatives of the influential merchant families of Bukhara—Mirzo Muhiddin (Abduqadir Muhiddinov's father), **Faizullo Khojaev**, Olimbek Jurabayev, and others.

Between March 1917 and March 1918, in the wake of the February revolution in Russia in 1917, Jadidism was politicized. In March 1917, the **Young Bukharan Party** was formed, led by Jadids Mirzo Abdulvohid Burkhanov (Munzim), Abdulrauf Fitrat, Usman Khojaev, Ato Khojaev, Faizullo Khojaev, and others. Jadids welcomed the overthrow of tsarism in **Russia** and demanded that the Russian provisional government admit them to the government of **Bukhara** to ensure the implementation of reforms. On 7 April 1917, Bukharan Emir **Said Alim Khan** issued a manifesto on reforms, but on 8 April, Jadids were beaten in the streets of Bukhara by supporters of the emir. This radicalized the Jadidist movement; Jadid leaders started to explore the idea of a forceful overthrow of the emir with outside help.

Between March 1918 and the end of 1921, Bukharan Jadids found in the Russian Bolsheviks a powerful ally against the Bukharan emir. But the failure of **Kolesov's March** forced Bukharan Jadidists to escape from Bukhara to Soviet Turkistan. Most of the Jadids joined the **Communist Party of Bukhara** and worked toward the 1920 **Bukharan Revolution** and the building of the **Bukharan People's Soviet Republic**. The consolidation of Soviet power in Central Asia dissipated the Jadids' illusion of independent statehood in Bukhara.

Between the end of 1921 and the late 1930s, Jadidism was effectively eradicated as an indigenous social movement. At the end of 1921, the Jadids were weakened by a split. A radical anti-Soviet faction, led by Usman Khojaev, Abulkhair Arifov, and others, came out in support of **Enver Pasha** and the **Basmachis**. Following the military defeat of the Basmachi movement in 1922, this group fled into exile. The other faction, led by Faizullo Khojaev and Abduqadir Muhiddinov, remained loyal to the Soviet regime. Many of the "Sovietized" Jadids worked as teachers, professors, writers, and journalists. In the late 1930s, they were eliminated during Stalin's purges. *See also* TARBIYAI ATFOL.

JALOLIDIN RUMI NOHIYA. Known as Tugalan until 1934, then Kolkhozobod until 2007, when it was named for the great Tajik poet, this **nohiya** is located in the **Vakhsh valley** of the **Qurghonteppa** region, **Khatlon** veloyat. It was formed in 1933 when irrigation of the Vakhsh valley began. The territory encompasses 1,142 square kilometers, with a population of more than 123,000

(17,400 urban). **Tajiks** constitute a majority; other ethnic groups include **Uzbeks** and **Turkmens**. The area has six **jamoats** and two villages; the district center is the village of Jalolidin Rumi. The distance from Jalolidin Rumi to Qurghonteppa is 32 kilometers, to **Dushanbe** 131 kilometers, and to the nearest **railway** station 4 kilometers. Average January and July temperatures are 0°C and 28°C respectively. The annual rainfall is 270 millimeters. The main occupation is **agriculture**, including **cotton** production and livestock breeding. *See also* RUMI, JALOLIDIN.

JAMIYATI ULAMO. Sometimes called *Shuroi Ulamo*, the Jamiyati Ulamo (Board of the Learned) was a Muslim political organization formed in June 1917 after a split from **Shuroi Islomia**. It was headed by the Kazakh **mullah** Shirali Lapin. The Jamiyat was conservative in its political orientation and opposed social reforms. It was often called Qadimist for its support of *Usuli Qadim* (the Old Method) in contrast to *Usuli Jadid* (the New Method). During elections to the Tashkent city council in August 1917, Jamiyati Ulamo and right-wing **Russian** groups attracted 60 percent of the votes. The Jamiyat rejected Soviet rule in Turkistan and supported the short-lived Kokand autonomy and the **Basmachi** movement. Jamiyati Ulamo ceased to exist in the first half of 1918. *See also* POLITICAL PARTIES.

JAMOATS. In 1994, village soviets were replaced with *jamoats*, neighborhood and local community groups forming an institution of self-government. In jamoats, decisions are adopted by open voting. Chairs are appointed by the head of the city or **nohiya**, who is appointed by the president. Jamoats enjoy a limited degree of independence for the administration of their territories. As of 2009, there were 401 jamoats in Tajikistan.

JEWS OF BUKHARA. Eastern Jews constitute an ethnic group in Tajikistan. This community first appeared in **Central Asia** in the 6th century BCE and settled in urban centers of **Khujand**, **Samarqand**, **Bukhara**, Kokand, Andijan, and Marghilan. They called themselves *Yahudi* or *b-nei Israel*. Tajiks used the terms *Juhud* and *Yahudi* for this group. The ancient language of the eastern Jews was Ivrit (Hebrew), but in medieval times it fell into disuse and was replaced by **Tajik**. Eastern Jews follow Judaism, although they were almost isolated from Judaic centers in the Near East and Europe. In the **Bukharan emirate**, where the Jewish community thrived, and in the **Kokand khanate**, Jews did not have the same rights as Muslims. They were banned from owning agricultural land and riding horses, for example, and were required to wear especially identifiable belts. Bukharan Jews nevertheless engaged in trade and commerce as well as **music** and the **arts**.

Islamized Bukharan Jews in Central Asia were known as *Chala*. Some *Chala mahalla* families may still be found in Khujand and other cities of Tajikistan. Jewish settlement in **Dushanbe** took place in the middle of the 19th century. It is estimated that over 20,000 Jews lived in Tajikistan in 1990. In addition to Bukharan Jews who numbered around 13,000 people, Tajikistan was home to 2,000 mountain Jews (known as Tats, originating from the Caucasus) and 7,000 European Jews (Ashkenazi). The first exodus (aliyah) of Jews from Central Asia took place in the 1890s. The second started in the 1970s. By the end of the 1980s, large numbers of the Jewish community migrated from Tajikistan to Israel, the **United States**, and other Western countries. By 1993, very few Bukharan Jews remained in Tajikistan, although a Jewish synagogue (built in early 1900s) remained in operation in Dushanbe. The Society of the Friends of the Jewish Culture, Khoverim, was formed in 1989 to promote Jewish culture and is a member of the **Societal Council** of Tajikistan.

The total number of Jews in Tajikistan (including Bukharan Jews) according to the official registry was 500 (0.1 percent of the total population) in 1926, 12,400 (0.6 percent) in 1959, 14,700 (0.3 percent) in 1989, and 600 (0.01 percent) in 1998. By 2009, the number of Bukharan Jews living in Tajikistan had decreased to several families. The Dushanbe synagogue was destroyed in June 2008 as part of an urban development plan. In March 2009, **Hasan Sadulloev**, an influential business leader, donated a house for a new synagogue in the center of Dushanbe. *See also* RELIGIONS.

JIHAD. The term *jihad*, which means "struggle," refers to a religious duty of Muslims to strengthen and spread **Islam**. Jihad may be conducted spiritually or physically. In **Central Asia**, jihad was declared against Soviet rule in order to defend existing social relations. **Basmachi** fighters were at the forefront of jihad against the establishment of Soviet rule in the 1920s. After the Soviet collapse, the **United Tajik Opposition** (UTO) sometimes used the term to justify its armed conflict with the **government** of President **Emomali Rahmon**. *See also* CIVIL WAR.

JILIKUL. Located in the **Khatlon** veloyat, **Qurghonteppa** zone, in the **Vakhsh** and **Panj** river basins, Jilikul **nohiya** borders **Afghanistan**. It was formed in 1930, disbanded in 1955, and reinstated in 1979. It has a territory of 1,225 square kilometers and a population of more than 84,700 (7,900 urban dwellers), **Tajiks** and **Uzbeks**, in five **jamoats**. The distance from Garavuti, Jilikul's center, to Qurghonteppa is 24 kilometers, and to **Dushanbe** 123 kilometers. Average temperatures in January and July can reach 0°C and 33°C respectively; the average annual precipitation is 200–300 millimeters. The main occupation is **agriculture**, including **cotton**, vegetable, and fruit production. Arable land amounts to 17,000 hectares.

JIRGHATOL. This mountainous **nohiya** is situated in the Surkhob river basin within the **Nohiyas under Republican Control** and borders the Osh province of **Kyrgyzstan** in the north. Jirghatol nohiya was formed in 1931 with a territory of 4,580 square kilometers. Its population is more than 55,700, **Kyrgyz** and **Tajiks**, in seven **jamoats**. Some Kyrgyzs escaped to Kyrgyzstan during the **civil war**. The distance from the city of Jirghatol, the administrative center, to **Dushanbe** is 284 kilometers. Average temperatures in January and July can reach –5°C and 20°C respectively; the average annual precipitation is 200–700 millimeters (in the valleys). The main occupation is **agriculture**, including cultivation of potatoes and other vegetables, tobacco production, and livestock breeding. Arable land amounts to 7,950 hectares.

JOMI, ABDURAHMON (1414–1492). A Tajik classical poet, Jomi was born in Jom, **Khurasan**, and lived in Herat (**Afghanistan**). He studied sciences, languages, theology, and poetry in **madrasas** of Herat and **Samarqand**. Jomi was devoted to the **Naqshbandiyah** order of Muslim mystics and headed this **Sufi** fraternity in Khurasan. He was the master of the famous **Uzbek** poet Alisher Navoi. Jomi left a tremendous literary heritage in 46 works. Europeans first learned of

Jomi in 1778 through the Latin translation of his Bahoriston poetry. In Tajikistan, four volumes of his selected works were published in 1964 in **Tajik** using the Cyrillic script. *See also* LITERATURE.

JUGI. *See* LULI.

JUNBESH. *See* PARTY OF THE NATIONAL MOVEMENT OF TAJIKISTAN.

JURAEV, AKASHARIF (1896–1966). A Tajik folk singer and composer, Juraev was born in **Darvoz** and lived in **Gharm** before he was invited to Stalinobod **(Dushanbe)** in 1935. He collected Tajik folk songs of the Gharm-Darvoz region and composed new songs. Juraev was awarded the title of Hofizi Khalqi (People's Singer). *See also* ARTS; FALAK; MUSIC.

– K –

KABIRI, MUHIDDIN (1966–). A Tajik politician and party leader, Kabiri graduated from the college of statistics in Ordzhonikidzeobad **(Vahdat)** and received a degree in Oriental studies from the Tajik State University. He also studied at the University of Sana (Yemen) and graduated from the Diplomatic Academy of the Ministry of Foreign Affairs of the Russian Federation (Moscow). Kabiri has a **candidate** degree in political science. He served as an expert during the **Inter-Tajik Peace Talks** and is a director of the Dialogue Center for Information and Analysis. From 1997, he was an assistant of **Said Abdullo Nuri**, the chair of the **Islamic Renaissance Party of Tajikistan** (IRPT). Nuri appointed Kabiri his deputy in 2000. In 2005, Kabiri was elected to the **Majlisi Namoyandagon** (by a party list). In 2006, after the death of Nuri, Kabiri was elected chair of the IRPT. *See also* POLITICAL PARTIES.

KABIROV, MIZROB (1958–). Born in **Kulob**, Kabirov started his professional life in 1975 as a court secretary and bailiff. After graduating from the Tajik State University with a degree in law in 1982, he worked in various capacities: state notary, deputy chair, and chair of the bar (attorney collegium) of the Republic of Tajikistan.

In May 1995, Kabirov was appointed state adviser on defense and legislature to President **Emomali Rahmon**. In December 1999, he was appointed chair of the **Council of Justice**. Since January 2003, he has been deputy chair of the Central Commission for Elections and Referenda.

KABIROV, SHODI (1945–). Born in Gharm nohiya, Kabirov graduated from the agricultural college in **Bokhtar** nohiya in 1970. Between 1970 and 1981, he worked as a teacher, deputy director, and director of a high school in **Vakhsh** nohiya. In 1981–1982, he was chair of the trade unions committee and in 1982–1986 secretary of the executive committee in Vakhsh nohiya. Between 1988 and 1992, Kabirov was director of the Nawruz **sovkhoz** in the same nohiya. After **Sitodi Melli** attacks on Vakhsh nohiya, he was forced to flee to **Russia** at the end of 1992. In 1997, Kabirov returned to Tajikistan and entered the **Commission for National Reconciliation** on the **United Tajik Opposition** team. He was appointed minister of **agriculture** (August 1998) in accordance with the 30 percent quota for opposition forces, negotiated in the **Inter-Tajik Peace Talks**. From September 2005, he has been deputy chair of **Khatlon** veloyat.

KADBONU. The term *kadbonu* refers to a woman who is a skillful, effective leader of her household. Kadbonu is also the name of Tajikistan's National Association of Business Women (NABW), a nongovernmental organization that originated in **Dushanbe** in 1992 and assisted women refugees during the **civil war** (1992–1997). Kadbonu was registered with the Ministry of Justice in 1999. It addresses **women's issues**, including women's rights, the development of women-run businesses, and other social and economic concerns.

KADKHUDO. The term *kadkhudo* refers to a master, manager, chieftain, or head of a family.

KALYM. *See* QALIN.

KARAKORAM HIGHWAY. The Karakoram Highway, 1,300 kilometers long, is the world's highest paved international road. It was built by **China** and **Pakistan** in 1966–1986. It is also referred to as National Highway 35, or N35. In China, it is also known as the

Friendship Highway. N35 connects China's Xinjiang with northern areas of Pakistan, crossing the Karakoram mountain range. The highway goes through what is known as the "collision zone," where China, Tajikistan, **Afghanistan**, Pakistan, and **India** come within 250 kilometers of each other. **Tashkurgan,** populated predominantly by **Tajiks,** sits on the Chinese end of the Karakoram Highway. *See also* KULMA PASS; TAJIKS OF CHINA.

KARIMOV, ABDURAHIM (1951–). Also known as Mullo Abdurahim, Karimov is a leader of the Islamic opposition movement in Tajikistan. He was born in **Khovaling** nohiya, **Kulob** veloyat, and finished his high school education in the same region. In 1991–1992, Karimov was Imam Khatib of the **Hamadoni mosque** in Kulob. In 1992, he joined the **Islamic Renaissance Party of Tajikistan.** In May 1992, he was forced to flee Kulob, fearing attacks from armed bands affiliated with the **Sitodi Melli.** With the escalation of the **civil war,** Karimov later escaped to **Afghanistan** with other Tajik refugees. On 2–5 October 1993, he was involved in an armed incursion into Tajikistan in the Moskva (Hamadoni) nohiya, **Khatlon** veloyat, and an attack on **Russia**'s 12th Frontier Guard post. In 1997, he returned to Tajikistan after he was appointed to the **Commission for National Reconciliation** by the **United Tajik Opposition.** In 1998, he was appointed head of Tajikistan's Custom Service in accordance with the 30 percent quota for opposition forces negotiated in the **Inter-Tajik Peace Talks,** but he was removed from that post in April 1999.

KARIMOV, ABDURAHMON (1942–). A Tajik teacher and politician, Karimov was born in **Konibodom, Sughd veloyat.** He received a degree in history from the Leninobod State University in 1967. In 1971, Karimov started work as a lecturer in political economy in the Tajik State University. Later he moved to Konibodom and in 1995 was elected chair of the **Adolatkhoh Party of Justice** (APJ) at the inaugural congress of that party. In 2004, after being refused registration, the APJ ceased its activities.

KARIMOV, JAMSHED (1940–). A Tajik politician and scholar, Karimov was born in **Dushanbe** to a family of academics. In 1962, he graduated from the Technological Institute of Light Industry

(Moscow). Karimov completed his postgraduate studies at the Central Institute of Economy and Mathematics of the Union of Soviet Socialist Republics Academy of Sciences. He obtained his doctorate in economics in 1976. In 1972, he was appointed deputy director and in 1978 director of the Institute of Economy and Economic-Mathematical Methods of Planning attached to the Center of Statistics of Tajikistan. In 1983–1989, he served as deputy chair of Tajikistan's state planning committee. In 1989, he moved to Communist Party work and was appointed first secretary of the Dushanbe city committee of the **Communist Party of Tajikistan** (CPT). Together with other high-ranking officials, Karimov was held hostage by **Abdughafor Khudoidodov** between 31 August and 2 September 1992.

After the government of President **Emomali Rahmon** came to power in December 1992, Karimov moved to diplomatic work. In 1992–1993, he was Tajikistan's plenipotentiary in the **Russian Federation**. He left the CPT in 1993. In 1993–1994, Karimov headed Tajikistan's interregional trade representation in Slovakia and the Czech Republic. In 1994, as the presidential adviser on social and economic policy, he represented Tajikistan on the economic commission of the Commonwealth of Independent States. In 1994–1995, Karimov was Tajikistan's prime minister. In 1996–1997, he became chief adviser to the president on international relations. From January 1997 to May 2002, Karimov was Tajikistan's ambassador to the People's Republic of **China**. Since 2003, he has been living in **Russia**.

KARNAI. A *karnai* is an ancient wind musical instrument made of copper. About two meters long, the karnai produces a very loud sound in a low register. It is traditionally played by men in ensemble with **surnai** and drums on various occasions, including **tuis, Nawruz,** and national celebrations. *See also* MUSIC.

KATIB. A *katib* is a secretary.

KENJAEV, SAFARALI (1942–1999). Born in the **Panjakent** nohiya, Kenjaev received a law degree from the Tajik State University in 1965 and started working in the Public Prosecutor's Office as a detective. He moved up the ladder as chief detective, head of the Detective Department, district prosecutor, Tajik transportation prosecutor, and deputy **Central Asian Railway** prosecutor. In 1990, Kenjaev was elected to the **Supreme Soviet** of Tajikistan and in 1991 was appointed chair of the control committee at the presidential office. In December 1991, Kenjaev was elected chair of the Supreme Soviet but was forced to resign in April 1992 to appease public demonstrators in **Dushanbe**. Shortly after that, however, he was appointed chair of Tajikistan's Committee on State Security by President **Rahmon Nabiev**.

During the Tajik **civil war**, Kenjaev was a leading figure in the Leninobod (**Khujand**), **Kulob**, and **Hisor** coalition, although asserting some independence from territorial groupings. Kenjaev headed the October 1992 raid on Dushanbe by armed bands of the **Sitodi Melli**. In 1993–1994, he was the city prosecutor of Qairaqum (**Sughd veloyat**). In 1994, he was reelected to the **Majlisi Oli**. In 1995, he was appointed chair of the parliamentary Committee on Law, Order, Legislation, and Human Rights. In 1996, he organized and headed the **Socialist Party of Tajikistan**. Kenjaev was assassinated in Dushanbe in March 1999.

KHAIRULLOEV, SADULLOH (1945–). Born in **Gharm**, Khairulloev studied at the Tajik Agricultural Institute. He chaired the Gharm nohiya executive committee between 1979 and 1985. He was then recruited for party work in the **Communist Party of Tajikistan**. In 1991, Khairulloev was appointed chair of the **Qurghonteppa veloyat** executive committee and in 1992 became vice premier of Tajikistan. In 1993–1994, he was the minister of environmental protection and in 1994–1995 was chair of the Gharm nohiya. In 1995, Khairulloev was appointed chair of the state committee for precious metals. He was elected to the **Majlisi Oli** in 1995 and chaired the Standing Committee for Land Resources and Land Tenure in 1998–2000. In February 2000, Khairulloev was elected to the **Majlisi Namoyandagon** from the Gharm electoral district. At the first parliamentary session on 27 March, he was elected (57 to 3) chair of the assembly.

KHAIRULLOEV, SHERALI (1945–). General Colonel Khairulloev was born in **Khovaling**, Kulob veloyat. He received a degree in economics from the Tajik State University in 1971 and then joined the Soviet Army. Stationed in Tashkent, Krasnoyarsk, Irkutsk, and Tuva, he served as assistant head of the Brigade Finance Department, head of the Finance Department, and head of the Battalion Foodstuff Services. After his release from the army in 1977, Khairulloev returned to Tajikistan. He was appointed deputy head of the Special Department in the Ministry of Internal Affairs and gradually worked his way up to the position of deputy minister. In April 1995, he became Tajikistan's minister of defense.

KHAMIDOV, KHALIFABOBO (1950–). A Tajik politician and lawyer, Khamidov was born in **Khujand**. He received a law degree from Moscow State University in 1973 and worked as a lecturer and later head of the Department of Law at the Tajik State University. In 1990, Khamidov joined the **Rastokhez** movement. In 1990–1992, he served as deputy minister of justice. In December 1994, he became an adviser to the president of Tajikistan on legal issues. Khamidov was a member of the **Commission for National Reconciliation** on the legal issues subcommission. In March 2000, he was elected to the **Majlisi Oli**, where he became chair of the parliamentary Commission on Control, Order of Business, and Logistics. Khamidov is a member of the **People's Democratic Party of Tajikistan**. He replaced **Shavkat Ismoilov** as minister of justice in January 2001. In December 2006, he was appointed head of the Department on Constitutional Guarantees of Civic Rights in the executive apparatus of the president of Tajikistan. *See also* GOVERNMENT.

KHAN (KHON). The title *khan* was used for feudal rulers and tribal chiefs and as an indicator of military rank.

KHANA (KHONA). A *khana* is a house, nest, place, inn, or store.

KHATLON. A southwestern province, Khatlon is the most populous and youngest province in Tajikistan. Khatlon was formed at the end of 1992 and consists of the former Kulob (1939–1955 and 1973–1992) and **Qurghonteppa** (1944–1947 and 1977–1992) veloyats. In the east, it borders the **Mountainous Badakhshon Autonomous Veloyat**, in the north the **Nohiyas under Republican Control**, in the west **Uzbekistan**, and in the south **Afghanistan**. Its territory is 24,600 square kilometers, and the population is more than 2 million (401,400 urban). Khatlon is the republic's most heterogeneous province in terms of ethnic, subregional, and family-based associations. These include **Kulobis**, **Gharmis** (Qarateginis), **Pamiris**, **Uzbeks**

(including **Laqais**), **Turkmens**, and local **Arabs**. This region was devastated during the **civil war**, especially in 1992–1993. A very large number of refugees and internally displaced people fled from Kulob and Qurghonteppa. The city of Qurghonteppa is the provincial center. The province is composed of 24 **nohiyas**, six cities, 18 towns, and 128 rural **jamoats**. The distance from Qurghonteppa to **Dushanbe** is 92 kilometers.

The republic's largest hydroelectric power station, **Norak**, is located in this province. Some 22.2 percent of Tajikistan's total industrial production comes from 101 **industrial** enterprises in the Khatlon veloyat. Khatlon is the largest **cotton**-growing region in Tajikistan. There are 107 preschool establishments with 9,823 children, 1,187 schools with 516,200 pupils, nine tekhnikums (colleges) with 3,794 students, and two universities with 7,592 students. Khatlon also houses three theaters, six museums, and 502 public libraries. In 1992, at the height of the civil war, Kulob veloyat was blockaded by opposition forces. In December 1992, Kulobis with the help of **Sughdis** wrested Dushanbe from the opposition. A majority of key politicians, including President **Emomali Rahmon**, are from Kulob. It is estimated that approximately 80 percent of all government assistance is allotted to Khatlon.

KHATMUL QURON. The *khatmul quron* is a religious ritual that involves a special prayer to mark the end (*khatm*) of the recitation of the Quran. In Tajikistan, the khatmul quron, or just khatm, is a collective reciting of the Quran at home, dedicated mostly to remembrance of the dead. Traditionally, the khatm involves adult male relatives, neighbors, elders, and community leaders. The recitation of the Quran by a **mullah** is generally followed by the serving of food, and reciters are paid. In addition, the family that arranges a khatm makes a donation to the local **mosque**. Under Soviet rule, the khatm was targeted as "a religious prejudice." The law "On Regulation of Traditions, Celebrations and Rituals," approved in June 2008, introduced a ban on lavish private ceremonies, including the khatmul quron. *See also* TUI.

KHAYYAM, OMAR (1040–1123). A Perso-Tajik poet, philosopher, and mathematician, Omar (Umar) Khayam was born in Nishopur

(**Iran**) and is famous for his free thinking and philosophical quatrains (*ruboiyat* in Persian). *See also* LITERATURE.

KHOJA. In **Central Asia**, *khoja* is a traditional local religious title. Khojas, sometimes also called *saids*, claim lineage from the Prophet Muhammad through his daughter Fatima and her husband Ali. Some khojas claim lineage from companions of Muhammad or holy men. Members of the clergy and the landholding aristocracy before Soviet rule usually adopted this title (e.g., **Faizullo Khojaev** and **Said Alim Khan**). But the title was not exclusive to the nobility; people of lower social status also claimed it. They consider themselves of noble birth and marry in the khoja community. Khojas do not have a distinct ethnic identity. Educated khojas were employed by the Soviet regime in the early 1920s, but they were targeted in political purges and antireligious campaigns in the 1930s. Khojas continue to enjoy respect among the **Tajiks**. *See also* ISLAM.

KHOJA ABDULAZIZ RASULOV (1852–1930). A Tajik singer, musician, and composer, Khoja Abdulaziz was born in **Samarqand**. He was a student of the famous **Bukharan Jewish** musician and singer Borukhi Kalhoti Samarqndi. Khoja Abdulaziz was a lyric tenor and a virtuoso in playing the **dutar**, **tanbur**, and other musical instruments. He had a great number of fans among the **Tajiks** and **Uzbeks** of Samarqand, **Bukhara**, **Ferghana**, and Tashkent. His "Ushoqi Samarqand" is a very popular song in Tajikistan and **Uzbekistan**. The **Shashmaqom** school of Khoja Abdulaziz influenced generations of modern Tajik and Uzbek musicians and composers, including **Ziyodullo Shahidi**. *See also* MUSIC.

KHOJAEV, FAIZULLO (1896–1938). Born in **Bukhara** to a rich Tajik merchant family, Khojaev joined the **Jadids** in 1913 and in 1916 helped form the party of **Young Bukharans**. After the October 1917 revolution in **Russia**, Khojaev joined the Bolsheviks. He was a leading figure in the **Bukharan Revolution** of 1920 and chaired the Soviet of People's Commissars of the **Bukharan People's Soviet Republic** between 1920 and 1924, actively fighting against the **Basmachi** movement in **Eastern Bukhara**. In 1925, he was appointed chair of the government of the Soviet Socialist Republic of

Uzbekistan. A victim of the Stalinist purges, Khojaev was arrested in 1937, charged with "nationalism and counterrevolutionary activity," and sentenced to death by the Military Collegium of the USSR Supreme Court. Khojaev was executed in 1938. His reputation was rehabilitated in 1957.

KHORUGH. The capital city of the **Mountainous Badakhshon Autonomous Veloyat** (MBAV), Khorugh is situated in the western part of **Pamir** on the Ghund River, 2,200 meters above sea level. Khorugh is one of the oldest settlements of the veloyat. The township of Khorugh became the administrative center of the newly proclaimed MBAV in 1925, and in 1932 it was registered as a city. Khorugh houses a theater, a state university (with 2,700 students), and a number of **industrial** enterprises. The population is more than 26,700 (12.7 percent of the total population of the MBAV), mostly **Ismaili Tajiks**. Average July and January temperatures are 22°C and −7°C respectively. The annual precipitation is 263 millimeters. During Soviet times, Khorugh was connected with **Dushanbe** by an old **motor road** via Qalai Khumb-**Darband**, which traverses the Khaburobod Pass and is only accessible in summer; the length of this road is 527 kilometers. A newer road of 610 kilometers connects Khorugh to **Kulob** and Dushanbe through Qalai Khumb and is open all year. Khorugh is also connected with the city of Osh in **Kyrgyzstan** through a road that is open only in summer, and a road through the **Kulma Pass** at the Chinese border. Khorugh is accessible by air.

KHOS DEH PROTOCOL. Signed in Khos Deh (northern **Afghanistan**) by President **Emomali Rahmon** and **Said Abdullo Nuri**, the leader of the **United Tajik Opposition**, on 11 December 1996, this protocol advanced the **Inter-Tajik Peace Talks** that helped end Tajikistan's **civil war**. Afghanistan's President Burhanuddin Rabbani and **Ahmad Shah Massoud**, who led the **Northern Alliance** against the **Taliban**, were also present at the Khos Deh meeting. The protocol paved the way for a cease-fire in the **Gharm** area and formation of the **Commission for National Reconciliation**.

KHOSHIM (KHOSHIMOV), ODINA (1938–1993). A Tajik folk singer and performer of **falak**, Khoshim was born in Dashtijum village, **Hamadoni nohiya**. He was trained as a musician and singer by his father, the famed Tajik singer Khoshim Qosimov. Khoshim was awarded the title of People's Singer of Tajikistan (Hofizi Khalqii Tojikiston) in 1963. He headed the People's Theater first in his native Hamadoni nohiya in 1965–1975 and then in **Kulob** in 1975–1979. As a performer of falak and the author of popular Tajik folk songs, he was also known in **Iran** and **Afghanistan**. *See also* MUSIC.

KHOVALING. A **nohiya** in the **Khatlon** veloyat, this district is situated in the northern part of the **Kulob** region in the Surkhob and Obi Mazor river basins, bordering the **Tavildara nohiya**. The Khovaling nohiya was formed in 1993 at the expense of the northern part of the **Vose nohiya**. Its population of more than 33,200 consists of **Tajiks** and **Uzbeks**. The town of Khovaling is the district center. The distance from Khovaling to Kulob is 80 kilometers, and to **Dushanbe** 270 kilometers. The main occupation is **agriculture**, including **grain**, vegetable, and fruit production and livestock breeding.

KHROMOV, ALBERT (1931–1993). A Tajik philologist and Iranist, Khromov was born in **Russia** and graduated from Moscow State University with a degree in Oriental studies in 1953. He moved to Tajikistan to take up a research post at the Institute of Language and Literature in the **Academy of Sciences of Tajikistan**. He started his research with the Mastchohi kuhi dialect of the **Tajik** language. In the 1970s, Khromov refocused on **Yaghnobi**. Toward the end of the 1970s, his interests included the **Sogdian** language. Khromov's publications included his historical linguistic research on the areas of Yaghnob and **Zarafshon** and the grammar of the Yaghnobi language. *See also* LANGUAGES.

KHUDOIBERDYEV, MAHMUD (1964–). A Tajik field commander and leader of a paramilitary gang, Khudoiberdyev was born in **Qurghonteppa** to a mixed Tajik-Uzbek family. Trained as a professional officer, Khudoiberdyev served in the Soviet army. On 10 October 1992, Lieutenant Khudoiberdyev, commander of the tank company of the 201st Russian Division located in **Kulob**, hijacked a tank and drove it to Kalininobod to help the Kulobis in Tajikistan's **civil war**. His intervention tilted the balance of power in favor of the Kulobis. After the government of President **Emomali Rahmon** came to power in 1993, Khudoiberdyev was appointed commander of the First Brigade of Rapid Reaction stationed in Qurghonteppa. Khudoiberdyev challenged the leadership of President Rahmon on three separate occasions (September 1995, January 1996, and summer 1997), demanding the removal of certain members of the **government** and the separation of Qurghonteppa veloyat from **Khatlon** veloyat. In August 1997, the presidential guard captured Qurghonteppa, and Khudoiberdyev was stripped of his military position in absentia. He reportedly escaped to **Afghanistan**. In November 1998, Khudoiberdyev resurfaced with an armed unit in **Sughd veloyat** but was soon pushed out of Tajikistan. Unofficial reports claim he retreated to **Uzbekistan**.

KHUDOIDODOV, ABDUGHAFOR (1954–1998). Born in **Gharm** to a religious family, Khudoidodov experienced dislocation early in his life. In the 1960s, his family was moved to the **Vakhsh valley** as part of an aggressive Soviet **cotton** cultivation campaign. In Vakhsh, Khudoidodov participated in unofficial religious activities. In 1986, he moved to **Dushanbe** and opened several illegal religious schools. Khudoidodov subsequently acquired the honorific title of Mullo Abdughafor and became one of the most influential Gharmi **ishans**. He took an active part in the May 1992 opposition rallies in Shahidon Square and led the capture of Tajik Television. Khudoidodov was also involved in the forced resignation of President **Rahmon Nabiev** in 1991. In September 1991, he commanded the takeover of the presidential palace. With the escalation of the **civil war**, Khudoidodov fled to **Afghanistan**. During an armed incursion into Tajikistan in 1997, he was captured and sentenced to death.

KHUDONAZAROV, DAVLATNAZAR (1944–). A Tajik politician and filmmaker, Khudonazarov was born in **Khorugh**, in the **Mountainous Badakhshon Autonomous Veloyat**, to a family of notable Soviet and Communist Party workers. He graduated from the All-Soviet Institute of Cinematography in 1966 and began working for the Tajikfilm studio as a cameraman and director. In 1986, he was elected chair of the Tajik Cinematographers Union. Between 1989 and 1991, he was a deputy in the **Supreme Soviet** of the Union of Soviet Socialist Republics (USSR). Khudonazarov was elected chair of the USSR Cinematographers Union in 1990 and was elected to the central committee of the Communist Party of the Soviet Union in

1991. Khudonazarov, having refused to join any **political party** in Tajikistan, was a candidate for Tajikistan's presidency in 1991. With the backing of various opposition parties, he received more than 30 percent of the vote, while **Rahmon Nabiev** received 56 percent. In October 1992, Khudonazarov was appointed senior adviser to the acting president of Tajikistan, **Akbarsho Iskandarov**. In November 1992, after **Emomali Rahmon** came to power, Khudonazarov escaped to **Russia**. In 1993, the government issued an arrest warrant for opposition leaders, including Khudonazarov, but closed the case in 1997. Khudonazarov has not returned to Tajikistan.

KHUDOYOROV, BAKHTIYOR (1956–). A Tajik politician and minister of justice, Khudoyorov was born in **Dushanbe**. He received a law degree from the Tajik State University in 1979. From 1979 to 1986, Khudoyorov held various positions in the procurator's office of the city of Dushanbe and the Republic of Tajikistan. From 1986 to 1992, he was a judge in the city of **Vahdat**. In 1992–2000, he was a deputy minister of justice for the Supreme Economic Court. In 2000, Khudoyorov became senior legal adviser to the president. In 2004–2006, he headed the department on constitutional guarantees of civic rights in the executive apparatus of the president of Tajikistan. Khudoyorov was appointed minister of justice in December 2006.

KHUJAND. The biggest city of northern Tajikistan, Khujand is the capital of **Sughd veloyat**. Khujand is one of the oldest cities of **Central Asia**. In 329, the city was captured by **Alexander the Great**. It was invaded by **Arabs** in the 7th century, Mongols in the 13th century, Timurids in the second half of the 15th century, and **Shaybanids** in the 16th century. Khujand was an important city on the famous Silk Road. In 1866, it was incorporated into **Russia**'s empire. Soviet power was established on 24 November 1917. Khujand was within the jurisdiction of **Uzbekistan** between 1924 and 1929, then transferred to Tajikistan. In 1936, the city and the province were renamed Leninobod, or "Lenin's creation." In February 1991, the newly independent Tajikistan renamed it Khujand.

The city is situated on the banks of the **Syr Darya**, in the western part of the **Ferghana** valley. The distance to **Dushanbe** is 341 kilometers. The population is more than 153,300, mainly **Tajiks** but also large communities of **Uzbeks** and **Russians**. Khujand is connected with the rest of the country by motor, rail, and airways. January and July temperatures can reach −1°C and 28°C respectively. The annual precipitation is 160 millimeters. Sheykh Muslihiddin's mausoleum (14th century) and remnants of the city citadel Urda (7th–8th centuries) are the most well-known historical sites. Local industries include textiles, silk, metallurgy, building materials production, and foodstuffs.

KHUJAND FORTRESS. Built in 3 BCE on the **Syr Darya**, this fortress used to protect the city of Khujand from nomads. It has the form of a high hill encircled by defensive walls and gates. Khujand fortress was destroyed in the 12th century but later restored.

KHURASAN. Now a northeastern province of **Iran**, with Mashad as the provincial center, Khurasan was in ancient and medieval times a vast area that included what is now northeastern Iran, northwestern **Afghanistan**, and parts of central and southern Turkmenistan. Khurasan and **Movarounnahr** are considered the historical homeland of the **Tajiks**. Khurasan has been known since the **Sassanid** period, dating back to the 3rd century. In the 7th century, Khurasan was brought under Muslim **Arab** rule. In the **Samanid** period, Khurasan and Movarounnahr were regarded as among the most developed parts of the Muslim world, where trade, science, and culture flourished. In the 1220s, Khurasan was sacked by Genghiz Khan's troops. In the 14th and 15th centuries, the province was brought under **Timurid** rule. In 1510–1763, Khurasan was incorporated into the Shia **Safavid** empire, and the province was formally separated from the **Sunni**-dominated Movarounnahr. Consequently, Tajiks and Persians since the 16th century, notwithstanding their common roots, have followed separate paths of development. *See also* CENTRAL ASIA; KHURASAN NOHIYA.

KHURASAN NOHIYA. This district formed in 1983 was known formerly as Ilyich (in honor of Vladimir Ilyich Lenin) and Ghozimalik (1992–2007). It is located in the **Khatlon** veloyat, **Qurghonteppa** zone, in the **Vakhsh valley**. Its territory is 890 square kilometers, with a population of more than 70,600, **Tajiks** and **Uzbeks**, living in five **jamoats**. The distance from Obikiik, the center, to **Dushanbe** is 38 kilometers. Average temperatures in January and July can reach

–5°C and 30°C respectively; the average annual precipitation is 200–700 millimeters. The main occupation is **agriculture**, including **cotton**, vegetables, and fruits. Arable land in this district covers 6,000 hectares.

KHUVAIDULLOEV, NURULLOH (1940–1992). A jurist and prosecutor general, Khuvaidulloev was born in **Asht nohiya, Sughd veloyat.** He received a law degree from the Tajik State University in 1962 and graduated from the Communist Party's Academy of Social Sciences in 1983. In 1962–1966, he served as a prosecutor in Tajikistan's general prosecutor's office. Between 1966 and 1970, he was a member of the Supreme Court of Tajikistan. In 1970–1974, Khuvaidulloev was chair of the Central District Court of **Dushanbe.** In 1974, he was appointed head of the Administrative-Juridical Department of the Soviet of Ministers in Tajikistan. In 1983, he was awarded a **candidate** degree in law. Khuvaidulloev was deputy head of the Administrative Department of the Central Committee of the **Communist Party of Tajikistan** in 1983–1986 and was subsequently appointed head of that department. In 1989, he was appointed head of the Legal Department of the CPT. Khuvaidulloev was elected to Tajikistan's **Supreme Soviet** in 1990. In March 1992, President **Rahmon Nabiev** appointed him prosecutor general. Khuvaidulloev was assassinated on 24 August 1992. *See also* CIVIL WAR.

KIMIAGAROV, BESION (BORIS) ARIEVICH (1920–1979). A Tajik filmmaker, Kimiagarov was born in **Samarqand** to a **Bukharan Jewish** family. He graduated from the State Institute of Cinematography (Moscow) in 1944. From 1944 to 1979, Kimiagarov made films that helped shape the Tajik national identity. These included a series on motifs of Firdawsi's *Shohnoma*.

KOFARNIHON. *See* VAHDAT.

KOKAND KHANATE. This khanate was a **Ferghana** valley fiefdom in the 18th–19th centuries, with the city of Kokand (Ququand, Huqand) as the seat of power. In 1710, Shohrukh bey, from the Turkic-Monghol Ming tribe, declared independence from the **Bukharan emirate** and established the Kokand khanate. During the reign of Madali Khan (1822–42), the khanate grew to incorporate the Tajik populated areas of **Khujand**, Qarategin, **Darvoz**, and **Kulob**, as well as Tashkent, Aq Masjit, Awliey Ata (Qizyl Orda and Jambul of Kazakhstan), and Pishpek (Bishkek). From its inception, Kokand was locked in conflict with **Bukhara** until it was captured by **Russia** in 1876. The khanate was dissolved and its territory was included in the Turkistan general gubernatorial of the Russian empire.

KOLESOV'S MARCH. On 1 March 1918, Kolesov, chair of Turkistan's Soviet government, led a military expedition to the **Bukharan emirate** in order to assist a planned insurgency by **Young Bukharans**. Kolesov's demand that the emir, **Said Alim Khan**, should recognize Soviet power was rejected by the emir, who had stalled Kolesov's expedition by prolonging negotiations while preparing for a counterattack. Kolesov's forces received a deadly blow and retreated from the emirate. On 25 March 1918, a peace agreement was signed between Soviet Turkistan and Bukhara representatives. Following Kolesov's defeat, Russian residents of Bukharan and Young Bukharans were publicly punished for their planned insurgency. *See also* COMMUNIST PARTY OF BUKHARA.

KOLKHOZ. *Kolkhoz* is the Russian acronym for *kollektivnoye khoziaistvo*, or collective farm. Kolkhozes were the main organization of **agricultural** production in the **Soviet Union**. Like all other republics of the Soviet Union in the 1930s, Tajikistan experienced forced **collectivization**. Kolkhoz members were known as collective farmers. *See also* COOPERATIVE FARMS; ECONOMY; SOVKHOZ.

KOMSOMOL. Established in 1918, Tajikistan's Communist Youth League (Kommunisticheskiy Soiyz Molodezhi Tadzhikistana), or Komsomol, was a republican branch of the all-Soviet Komsomol, working as an entry port to the **Communist Party of Tajikistan (CPT)**. Youths aged 14–28 joined the Komsomol following the approval of a local Komsomol committee. The Komsomol maintained cells at all schools, **army** institutions, and enterprises. As the youth arm of the CPT, it sought to advance goals set by the party. Following the banning of the CPT in 1991, the Komsomol was disbanded.

KONIBODOM NOHIYA. A district and city in the **Sughd veloyat** in the western part of the **Ferghana** valley, Konibodom (Kanibadam) was best known for almonds, from which its name City of Almonds is derived. Under its old name Kand, it dates back to the 9th century. In the 9th–10th centuries, it was part of the **Samanid** empire. In 1842, Konibodom witnessed a brutal skirmish between forces of Emir Nasrullah of **Bukhara** and Kokand Khan Madali, as a result of which thousands were killed. In 1875, in a battle at Mahram, one of Konibodom's suburbs, a coalition of 10,000 Kokandi **jihadis** led by Abdurahman Oftobachi were defeated by forces of the **Turkistan** governor, von Kaufman. In this battle, almost 2,000 **Tajiks**, **Uzbeks**, and **Kyrgyzs** were killed. When **Russia** captured Konibodom later that year, it had eight **madrasas** and 105 **maktabs**. The city of Konibodom was the home of the best calligraphers of the **Kokand khanate**.

As part of the Russian empire, Konibodom experienced rapid economic growth. In 1905, a Russian school was opened to train local Tajiks in Konibodom. The Russians opened a railway station, and the Central Asian Oil Company (Sredneaziatskoye Neftianoe Tovarischestvo), or SANTO, was set up in the nohiya. In 1917, SANTO was a colony populated by 1,010 Russian workers and engineers.

In 1918, Konibodom became part of the Ferghana oblast of the **Turkistan Soviet Republic**. During 1918–1925, Konibodom was in the center of the **Basmachi** movement. In 1924, after the national delimitation, the nohiya became part of the Kokand district of the Ferghana province of **Uzbekistan**. In April 1925, the Konibodomis succeeded in acquiring the status of a Tajik autonomous region within Uzbekistan. In 1929, Konibodom and other Tajik districts of the Ferghana valley joined the **Tajik Autonomous Soviet Republic**, facilitating the latter's upgrade into the **Tajik Soviet Socialist Republic**.

The nohiya is about 828 square kilometers, with a population of more than 157,500 (42,200 urban and 115,300 rural), **Tajiks** and **Uzbeks**, in six **jamoats**. Konibodom has 54 high schools and three colleges. The center of the nohiya is the city of Konibodom. The distance from Konibodom to **Khujand** is 80 kilometers, and to **Dushanbe** 420 kilometers. The average January and July temperatures are −2°C and 28°C respectively. The annual rainfall is 80 millimeters (in lowlands). Most of the labor force is employed in **agriculture**, including **cotton** and fruit production and livestock breeding.

KOREANS. A minority ethnic group in Tajikistan, Koreans arrived in the 1940s, following their mass resettlement from the Far East to

Uzbekistan and Kazakhstan (1937–1939). The Koreans enjoyed equal rights with other citizens in Tajikistan and stable positions in administration, science, **education**, medicine, and commerce. Koreans involved in **agriculture** mainly grow rice and onions. Koreans attend Russian schools, as the Korean language has nearly fallen into disuse, although Korean-language books and newspapers are accessible from **Uzbekistan** and **Russia**. In 1989, the Association of the Soviet Koreans in Tajikistan was formed. In the 1990s, Koreans began to migrate from Tajikistan to other states of the Commonwealth of Independent States. The number of Koreans in Tajikistan in 1959 was 2,400 (0.1 percent of the total population) and 13,400 (0.3 percent) in 1989.

KUHISTONI MASTCHOH (MOUNTAINOUS MASTCHOH). A remote mountainous **nohiya**, Kuhistoni Mastchoh is situated in the southeastern part of the **Sughd veloyat** on the **Zarafshon River**. It was formed at the beginning of 1996, after separation from the Mastchoh nohiya. It encompasses 52 villages, with a population of more than 15,800, almost exclusively **Tajik**. The distance from the center of the nohiya, Madrushkat village, to **Ayni** is 100 kilometers, to **Khujand** 277 kilometers, and to **Dushanbe** 264 kilometers. The main occupation is **agriculture**, including vegetable production and livestock breeding. Arable lands amount to 23,000 hectares.

KUIBYSHEV. *See* ABDURAHMON JOMI NOHIYA.

KULMA PASS. On the border between the Xinjiang-Uighur Autonomous Region of **China** and the **Mountainous Badakhshon Autonomous Veloyat** (MBAV) of Tajikistan, the Kulma mountain pass has an elevation of 4,362 meters. The pass was officially opened on 25 May 2004. It is the only maintained road between Tajikistan and China and is the location of the only official border crossing. The total cost of the project amounted to $14 million. The Islamic Development Bank provided a $9.7 million loan to the government of Tajikistan to finance the construction of the 32.6 kilometer road from **Murghob** to Kulma. The distance from Tajik **Khorugh** (a capital of the MBAV) to Kashghar in China is 700 kilometers.

Through this pass, Tajikistan became an integral part of a trans-Asian transport network that connects the country with **Pakistan** and **India** via the **Karakoram Highway**, which is the world's highest paved international road. The Murghob-Kulma road to China is the best way of connecting the people of MBAV with the rest of the world. Due to harsh conditions at the Kulma border crossing, the gateway is closed from November through April and at other times is open only about 15 days a month. Legal crossings in 2007 amounted to 1,611 trucks, 5,300 cars, and 22,700 tons of cargo over a seven-month period. The trade turnover between the two countries across the Kulma checkpoint in 2007 amounted to more than $6 million.

KULOB. A city in **Khatlon** veloyat, Kulob is situated in the Yakhsu river valley, 580 meters above sea level. Kulob was the center of Kulob veloyat between 1934 and 1994. Known since the 4th–6th centuries BCE, Kulob was part of the empire of **Alexander the Great** and later under the control of the **Samanids**, Mongols, **Timur**, and **Timurids**. In 1559, Kulob was incorporated into the **Bukharan emirate**. Soviet power was established in March 1921. The distance from Kulob to **Dushanbe** is 202 kilometers. Kulob's airport was recognized as international in 1997. The population is more than 86,900, mainly **Tajiks**.

KULOB NOHIYA. A district of the **Khatlon** veloyat, Kulob nohiya is situated in the Yakhsu river valley. It was formed in 1930 with a territory of 273 square kilometers. Its population is more than 73,800, mostly **Tajiks**, in four **jamoats**. The center of the district is the city of **Kulob**. The distance from Kulob to **Dushanbe** is 202 kilometers. Average January and July temperatures are 2°C and 30°C respectively. The annual precipitation is 500–600 millimeters. The main occupation is **agriculture**, including **cotton**, **grain**, and vegetable production and livestock breeding. Arable land amounts to 18,717 hectares.

KULOB VELOYAT. *See* KHATLON.

KUNDAL. An original wall-decorating technique, *kundal* has been used in **Central Asia** for over five centuries. A clay ornament, modeled on a plastered surface, is covered with a thin layer of **gold**. Then the gilding surface is painted blue or light blue, and the background of the relief is covered by pigments. As a result, a golden warp of the relief design twinkles, making the artwork lustrous. Kundal is used for interior decoration in Central Asian houses. *See also* ARTS.

KUSHANS (KUSHANAS). The Kushan empire emerged from the ruins of Greco-**Bactria** in the 2nd century. In the 3rd–4th centuries, the Kushans ruled over territories of present-day northern **India**, almost all of **Afghanistan**, southern **Central Asia**, and eastern **Turkistan**. To the east, the Kushans bordered with the Han in **China** and to the west with Parthia, thus constituting a link in the chain of four ancient centers of Eurasian civilizations that stretched from Britain to the Pacific. The Kushan civilization united three historical and cultural traditions: local Bactrian, Hellenic, and nomadic, all adapted to local cultural traditions of the people of Central and South Asia. In the 4th century, the Kushans were defeated by the **Sassanids**.

KYRGYZS. The Kyrgyz are a minority ethnic group in Tajikistan who live in **Jirghatol** and **Murghob**, two mountainous **nohiyas** in the central and eastern parts of the country, adjacent to **Kyrgyzstan**. The traditional Kyrgyz occupation is livestock breeding. They preserve their cultural heritage through Kyrgyz-language schools and media in Jirghatol and Murghob. Frontier disputes over water and land between Tajik **Vorukh** and Kyrgyz Batken caused violent clashes in the 1960s and 1980s. In 1989, the Society of Kyrgyzs of the Republic of Tajikistan was formed. Some Kyrgyzs of Tajikistan fled to the Kyrgyz Republic in the 1990s as a result of armed clashes during Tajikistan's **civil war**. The number of Kyrgyzs in Tajikistan in 1926 was 12,900 (1.3 percent of the total population), 28,000 (1.9 percent) in 1939, and 65,500 (1.07 percent) in 2000.

KYRGYZSTAN (KYRGYZ REPUBLIC). Northern Tajikistan shares a border with Kyrgyzstan extending for about 590 kilometers from eastern **Pamir** west to the environs of **Khujand** in the **Ferghana** valley. Kyrgyzstan was formed as the Kara-Kyrgyz Autonomous Oblast (province) within the **Russian Federation** on 14 October 1924. In 1925, this oblast became the Kyrgyz Autonomous Soviet Socialist Republic within the Russian Federation. On 5 December 1936, it was given the status of the Kyrgyz Soviet Socialist Republic. With a land area of 198,500 square kilometers, Kyrgyzstan is the second smallest country in **Central Asia**, after Tajikistan. Since 31 October 1991, Kyrgyzstan is an independent state. The population in 2007 was more than 5 million. The **Kyrgyz** make up 68 percent of the population, ethnic **Uzbeks** 14 percent, Russians 10 percent, and **Tajiks** 1.1 percent. Approximately 65,500 Kyrgyzs live in Tajikistan. Nearly all Kyrgyzs are **Sunni Hanafi** Muslims. The three southern Kyrgyz provinces—Osh, Jalal-Abad, and Batken—that border on Tajikistan and **Uzbekistan** are traditionally less urbanized and more religious than the northern provinces of Chui, Talas, and Ysyk Kol.

Tajiks and Kyrgyzs have related historical roots. Since antiquity, Central Asia has had a confluence of sedentary Iranian and nomadic Turkic cultures. Kyrgyzstan's history reaches back to the Eastern Turkic Kaganate in the 6th century. The Kyrgyz tribes were Islamized between the 12th and 19th centuries. Colonization by **Russia** in the 19th century and the Russian Revolution in 1917 brought Tajiks and Kyrgyzs into a single Russian/Soviet political system. Within this system, the Kyrgyzs experienced a significant rise in literacy.

Diplomatic relations between the independent Tajikistan and Kyrgyzstan were established on 14 January 1993. Both countries participate in the **Eurasian Economic Community** (Eurasec), **Shanghai Cooperation Organization** (SCO), **Commonwealth of Independent States** (CIS), **Conference on Interaction and Confidence-Building Measures in Asia** (CICA), **Economic Cooperation Organization** (ECO), and other organizations. Kyrgyzstan made a positive contribution in pacifying factions during Tajikistan's **civil war**. In October 1993, Kyrgyzstan sent a contingent of troops to Tajikistan as part of the **Collective Peacekeeping Force in the Republic of Tajikistan**. It also granted asylum to almost 60,000 Tajiks in 1992–1994 and sent medicine and other aid to its beleaguered neighbor. Kyrgyzstan was an observer at the **Inter-Tajik Peace Talks** and hosted an important meeting between **Emomali Rahmon** and **Said Abdullo Nuri** in May 1997.

Kyrgyzstan's embassy in **Dushanbe** opened in January 1997. The intergovernmental commission on the resolution of complex issues in bilateral relations was organized in 1996 to improve cooperation in the fields of hydroenergy, **mining**, transportation, **communication**, and other areas. Kyrgyzstan also provides Tajikistan with a transportation alternative to Uzbekistan. It connects Tajikistan's **Rasht valley** via a transport corridor with the outside world.

Tajiks and Kyrgyzs have settled various disputes on national, regional, and community levels, yet some problems remain. **Drug trafficking** is a major issue that strains Tajik-Kyrgyz relations. Narcotics from **Afghanistan** are smuggled to **Badakhshon** in Tajikistan and then to Kyrgyzstan. Another unresolved problem is the official demarcation of boundaries between the two states, which affects communities in the Ferghana valley and issues such as the lack of water, arable land, and jobs. *See also* FOREIGN POLICY; VORUKH.

– L –

LA'LI BADAKHSHON ASSOCIATION (LBA). This political movement, representing opposition figures from **Badakhshon**, was formed in **Dushanbe** on 4 March 1991 and was registered on 30 May 1991. The LBA was banned between June 1993 and August 1999 but continued to operate illegally. In 1999, the LBA had nearly 3,000 members (mainly members of the **Pamiri** intelligentsia). The LBA is a regional organization with the stated objective of **educational**, social, economic, and political development in Badakhshon. It publishes the *Bokhtar* newspaper. In the 1991 presidential elections, the LBA together with the **Democratic Party of Tajikistan** (DPT), the **Islamic Renaissance Party of Tajikistan** (IRPT), and **Rastokhez** supported the candidacy of **Davlatnazar Khudonazarov**. In the ensuing **civil war**, Pamiris were targeted for persecution by the **Sitodi Melli**. After 1993, the LBA joined the **United Tajik Opposition** (UTO), but its activities were limited to the territory of the **Mountainous Badakhshon Autonomous Veloyat**. The LBA took part in several rounds of the **Inter-Tajik Peace Talks** between 1994 and 1997. In June 1997, the LBA entered the **Commission for National Reconciliation**. In December 1999, the LBA left the UTO and from 2000 ceased to exist. The LBA was led by **Atobek Amirbekov**. *See also* POLITICAL PARTIES.

LABOR MIGRATION. Tajikistan's **civil war** in 1992–1997 created many internally displaced persons and refugees. Many returned home after the war, but since 2000, Tajikistan has been the largest emigrant labor supplier per capita in the world. About 700,000 Tajiks, or 10 percent of the total population, leave the country to work abroad.

Poverty, unemployment, lack of well-paid jobs, and high birthrates push many Tajiks to migrate. Almost 80 percent of labor migrants leave Tajikistan for **Russia**, attracted by its economic growth, relatively high wages, ease of migration, and availability of jobs. A small number of Tajiks also work in Kazakhstan, Ukraine, and Belarus. The Law on Refugees of August 2002 improved migration policies in Tajikistan, simplifying visa and passport requirements. Tajikistan is a member of the **Eurasian Economic Community** (Eurasec), and Tajik citizens do not need a visa to visit Russia for 90 days. However, transit visas are required to travel through **Uzbekistan**. Labor migrants are required to register with Russian authorities and obtain a work permit, but no less than 80 percent of temporary labor migrants purchase a fake registration or bribe local authorities. Although the majority of Tajiks are only interested in going abroad for short-term employment—from spring to fall—there are many long-term Tajik immigrants in Russia (mostly in Moscow and St. Petersburg). Most migrants to Russia are employed in poorly paid construction jobs, in trade and services, or in food preparation and **agriculture**.

Migrants' remittances have kept the Tajik **economy** afloat. The International Monetary Fund estimates that $1.8 billion of Tajikistan's $3.8 billion gross domestic product (GDP) was generated by migrant workers' remittances in 2007. According to the World Bank, Tajikistan (together with Moldova) took first position in the world for the share of remittances as a percentage of GDP in 2007. Most remittances are used for consumption, leading to increasing dependence on the part of families. Remittances are significantly responsible for poverty reduction in Tajikistan, but the country cannot rely on remittances to such a large extent. Moreover, work in Russia is not always safe. In January 2007, Russia introduced new legislation instituting national worker quotas and restrictions on the type of activities migrants may perform. The system leaves Tajik migrants more prone to **human rights** violations and abuse, such as racist attacks and theft of migrants' wages by corrupt police and mafia racketeers.

Considerable and unbalanced labor migration entails high social costs for Tajikistan. With hundreds of thousands of Tajik men working in Russia, Tajik women and children have had to assume additional economic and family responsibilities. Women's and children's rights have been especially neglected. Domestic violence is pervasive but rarely recognized by the state and society. In response to the world economic crisis, at the end of 2008 the Russian government ordered drastic cutbacks in the number of guest workers in the country. Decreasing remittances and the sudden influx of returning labor migrants could have disastrous economic, social, and political consequences for Tajikistan. *See also* WOMEN'S ISSUES.

LAHUTI, ABULQASEM (1887–1957). A Tajik-Iranian poet, and one of the founders of Tajik-Soviet **literature**, Lahuti (Lohuti) was born in Kirmanshah (**Iran**) and educated in Tehran. Involved in an unsuccessful revolutionary movement in Iran, Lahuti escaped to Baghdad, then Turkey, and in 1922 Soviet **Russia**. In 1924, he joined the Communist Party of the **Soviet Union**. In 1925, he settled in Tajikistan and was appointed deputy minister of **education**. Lahuti, together with **Sadriddin Ayni**, made significant contributions to the advancement of Tajik culture. Lahuti's writings constitute an important part of Tajikistan's cultural heritage. He wrote many verses and lyrics, still popular among Tajiks and used in educational curricula. Tajik theaters as well as many settlements and streets are named after Lahuti.

LALBEKOV, IZATULLOH (1945–). A Tajik banker, Lalbekov was born in **Khorugh, Mountainous Badakhshon Autonomous Veloyat**. He studied finance and credit at the Tajik State University, graduating in 1971. Later he studied at the Special Faculty of the Moscow Institute of Finance. He worked in various **banks** between 1965 and 1992. In 1992, he was appointed president of the Joint Stock Commercial Bank for Foreign Economic Activities (Tadzhikvnesheconom Bank). In June 1999, the bank was renamed TojikSodirotBonk (TSB). In July 2007, an extraordinary meeting of the bank's shareholders relieved Lalbekov of his post as president and elected Abduahad Ashurov as the new chair of TSB.

LAND MINES. Tajikistan has the largest land mine problem in **Central Asia**. Land mines were used by both sides throughout the **civil war** (1992–1997), and **Russian** troops stationed in the country in the 1990s laid minefields on the border with **Afghanistan**. In 1998, it was estimated there were as many as 200,000 land mines in Tajikistan. In addition, **Uzbekistan** began planting mines on part of its undemarcated border with Tajikistan and **Kyrgyzstan** in 1999 under the pretense of protecting Uzbek territory from Islamic militants.

Women and children account for many of the victims, as many men in rural areas migrate to Russia, leaving women to work the land. Demining work has been ongoing in mine fields in various parts of the country. The contamination along the border with Uzbekistan is especially challenging because both countries dispute the actual location of the border, and Tajikistan has not received records of land mine emplacement from Uzbek authorities. Some 325 mine deaths and 362 mine victims were reported in 1992–2008. The deadline set for total mine clearance in Tajikistan is 1 April 2010, but Tajikistan may not be able to meet that goal.

LANGUAGES. Tajik, Uzbek, Russian, Kyrgyz, Turkmen, Yaghnobi, and various **Pamirian languages** are currently spoken in Tajikistan. Since 1989, Tajik has been the state language. As of 2009, it is the country's lingua franca and the first language of 80 percent of the population.

From the 16th century, when **Central Asia** experienced the largest and last invasion of Turkophone Uzbeks, until the mid-1920s, the majority of Tajiks were bilingual, and Tajik-Uzbek bilingualism was the norm in Tajik-populated areas, mostly in lowland **Samarqand, Bukhara, Khujand, Kulob**, and **Hisor**. Over the course of the 20th century, knowledge of Russian spread rapidly, mostly in urban areas. From 1924, when the **Tajik Autonomous Soviet Socialist Republic** was formed, to 1991, Russian was the lingua franca among the various ethnic groups in Tajikistan. Most Tajiks in this period were bi- or trilingual: Tajik-Russian and Tajik-Russian-Uzbek. In the late Soviet period, Russian speakers constituted the majority of the population in **Dushanbe** and some other urban centers. The increasing popularity of Russian did not, however, preclude the attachment of the Tajiks to their native tongue. As a result, the Tajik language preserved its supremacy while Russian became the second language in Soviet Tajikistan.

Tajik-**Farsi** was declared the state language (*zaboni davlati*) on 22 July 1989, when the Language Act of the **Tajik Soviet Socialist Republic** was put in force. Russian was given the status of the language of communication between the nationalities, and the equality of all languages spoken within the borders of the country was proclaimed. In July 1994, Tajikistan's **Supreme Soviet** rejected a proposal to make Russian an official language alongside the state language of

Tajik-Farsi. Article 2 of the **constitution** adopted in November 1994 declares Tajik the state language. "Farsi" was dropped from the name of the official language in the constitution. Russian preserved its status as a language of communication between the nationalities. All nationalities and peoples living in the republic were entitled to use their mother tongues freely. Article 65 states that knowledge of the state language is obligatory for nomination to the post of president of Tajikistan.

Since the **civil war** and ensuing mass exodus of the non-Tajik, mostly Russian population, Tajikistan has progressed a great deal in promoting its titular language in administration, business, **education**, public use, and interpersonal communication. By the early 2000s, the use of Russian virtually disappeared in most parts of Tajikistan. Since 1992, all sessions of parliament and the cabinet of ministers have been conducted exclusively in the state language. Uzbeks, accounting for 15–17 percent of Tajikistan's population, have Uzbek as the language of instruction in their schools and **mass media**. Virtually all of them speak Tajik effortlessly and tend to associate themselves culturally and linguistically with Tajiks rather than Russian speakers. For most Kyrgyzs of **Jirghatol** and Turkmen of **Jilikul**, Tajik is also a second language. Kyrgyzs of the remote, high-elevation **Murghob nohiya** are the least integrated ethnic group and have a more limited knowledge of Tajik.

Russian cultural influence is in gradual decline in Tajikistan. De-russification and promotion of the Tajik language do not entail discrimination against minorities in Tajikistan; rather, these processes have more to do with demography than nationalism or geopolitics. In 2009, Russians constituted only 1 percent (some 70,000 people) of Tajikistan's total population. Since 2001, no ethnic Russians have occupied key governmental positions or been elected to the **Majlisi Oli**. It has been estimated that 12 percent of Tajikistani Russians are able to speak and write in Tajik freely. During the Soviet period, few Russian residents of Tajikistan were able to speak and write Tajik. In spite of the considerable drop in the Russian population and the subsequent decline of the Russian language since 1992, many Tajiks speak, read, and write in Russian. Russian-language schools and groups in universities are functioning all over the country, staffed mostly by ethnic Tajiks, Uzbeks, and Kyrgyzs. Russian television and radio outlets broadcast freely, and Russian-language papers printed both in Russia and locally are popular in Tajikistan. Many Tajiks realize that knowledge of Russian remains important for commercial and educational purposes, offering the best opportunities for aspiring business people, students, and labor-seekers in Russia.

Supporting the titular language is at the core of the cultural agenda of President **Emomali Rahmon**. Unlike other Central Asian presidents and the preceding leaders of Tajikistan, he experienced unbearable difficulties in speaking Russian and preferred therefore to make public presentations exclusively in his native Tajik. In October 1997, the state program "Development of the State Language and of Other Languages in Tajikistan" was launched as part of Tajikistan's language policy. The program laid out special arrangements aimed at the promotion of the Tajik language, including the organization of teaching courses, development of special educational programs, and introduction of Tajik into business, executive, and judicial documentation. The program also focused on preservation and development of other languages spoken in Tajikistan, including offering courses in those languages at educational institutions and protecting their use in television and radio broadcasts. As of 2009, the educational system continues to conduct classes in Tajik, Russian, Uzbek, and Kyrgyz languages, and all government officials are obliged to use written and oral Tajik in running their offices. A special state commission monitors and supports implementation of the program.

In the **Mountainous Badakhshon Autonomous Veloyat** (MBAV), the central government recognized to some extent the individual rights of the members of the Pamirian communities. According to a presidential decree of 1992, **Shughni** and **Rushani** are studied in some regions of **Badakhshon**, alongside the state language. By comparison, from 1935–1990, teaching and official communication in Shughni and Rushani were prohibited in MBAV. The Yaghnobi and **Yazghulami** are also taught in their respective communities in **Ayni nohiya** and Badakhshon. The Pamirian and Yaghnobi languages are considered by the government to be ancient Tajik languages, not languages of non-Tajik minorities. Some experts believe that the Pamirian languages, especially those other than Shughni and Rushani, are in danger of disappearance. However, no instances of rare and archaic language extinction have been recorded in Tajikistan since 1924.

Tajikistan is a multilingual state, but since independence, it has moved toward becoming a mononational state in which one language dominates. The Tajik government tries to boost the Tajik language by promoting indigenous cultural and linguistic traditions often rooted in folklore. **Islam** also serves as a tool to promote Tajik identity. The government endorses Abu Hanifa—the founder of **Hanafiya**, the most popular school of Sunni jurisprudence—as a prominent son of the Tajik nation who made the Tajik language important to Islam.

Despite the promotion of a distinct Tajik identity, Russia's presence is still strong in Tajikistan. Since 2000, Tajikistan has sent as many as 1.5 million labor migrants to Russia per annum. The majority are semiliterate, rural Tajiks who grew up during the civil war and do not speak Russian well. Largely out of political and economic reasons, Tajikistan avoids open confrontation with Russia's cultural influence and has allowed a modest revival in the use of the Russian language. At the same time, while reversing Russian influence and instead promoting the learning of English, Chinese, Turkish, French, and other foreign languages, Tajikistan is exploring opportunities to boost relations with regional Muslim and Asian neighbors and the wider world.

Recently there have been renewed calls to replace the Cyrillic alphabet with the Arabic one, which is called *khati niogon*, or "ancestors' script," by Tajiks. Debates about the issue were extremely sharp during perestroika at the end of the 1980s. They calmed down during the civil war and following reconciliation only to surface anew in the early 2000s. So far, President Rahmon has kept in reserve his right to issue the last word in this discussion. In the spring of 2009, the government was drafting a new law on state language that aimed to further widen use of Tajik.

LAQAIS. An **Uzbek**-language ethnic group in Tajikistan, the Laqais are descendants of seminomadic Turkified Mongols from the Kazakh steppes who migrated to **Movarounnahr** in the 16th century. The Laqai population fell drastically after the **Bukharan Revolution**, as most Laqais sided with the **Basmachi** and fought Soviet rule under the command of **Ibrahimbek**. Consequently, many Laqais were killed or exiled to **Afghanistan**. In 1924, about 25,000 Laqais were registered in Tajikistan, mostly in **Hisor** and **Baljuvon**. In the 1990s, the Laqais enjoyed a cultural revival and organized a cultural center in Tajikistan. The 2000 census recorded 51,000 Laqais in Tajikistan.

LATIFI, OTAKHON (1938–1998). A Tajik journalist and politician, Latifi was a leading figure in the Tajik opposition movement. He was born in **Panjakent, Sughd veloyat,** and studied journalism at the Leningrad State University. After graduating in 1961, he worked as a reporter for the *Komsomolets Tadzhikistana* newspaper and as a contributor to other media. In 1973, Latifi became Tajikistan's exclusive reporter for *Pravda,* the organ of the central committee of the Communist Party of the **Soviet Union.** In the 1980s, he became an advocate of perestroika in Tajikistan and left the Communist Party. In 1989–1991, he served as vice premier of the **government** of Tajikistan. Latifi was a founding member of **Rastokhez.** He spent over three years in exile (1993–1997), mostly in Moscow, and chaired the Coordinating Center for Tajikistan's Democratic Forces. He was also a leading figure in the **United Tajik Opposition.** After the signing of the **General Agreement on the Establishment of Peace and National Accord,** he returned to **Dushanbe** and was appointed to the **Commission for National Reconciliation.** He was assassinated in September 1998. *See also* MASS MEDIA.

LEMONS. Extensive lemon growing in trenches and sheltered constructions began in the 1950s in the **Vakhsh valley.** Tajikistan was the first producer of lemons in the **Soviet Union** in the 1970s, harvesting over 653 tons in 1978. In the 1990s, lemon production suffered as the Vakhsh valley was rocked by the **civil war.** *See also* AGRICULTURE.

LENIN NOHIYA. *See* RUDAKI NOHIYA.

LENIN PEAK. The second highest point (after the **Samanids** Peak) in Tajikistan and the former **Soviet Union,** Lenin Peak reaches 7,134 meters. Its highest point is on the Trans-Altai mountain range. The peak is situated on the border of Tajikistan and **Kyrgyzstan.** It was first explored and scaled in 1928 by a joint Soviet-German expedition. The peak was known as Chung Aidar until 1871 and as Kaufman in 1871–1928.

LENINOBOD. *See* KHUJAND.

LITERATURE. As a Persophone people, Tajiks are closely attached to what is known as Perso-Tajik literature and consider this world-class literary heritage a matter of national pride. The literary Persian-Tajik language was formulated in the 9th–10th centuries.

Abuabdullo Rudaki (858–c. 941), who was born in the village of Rudak near **Panjakent**, is considered in **Iran**, **Afghanistan**, and Tajikistan as the founder of Perso-Tajik classic literature. He used the Persian **language** in secular poetry and created a number of new literary genres. The golden age of Tajik literature began with Rudaki. He was followed by **Abulqasem Firdawsi** (940–1025), who created the celebrated heroic epic *Shohnoma*. Then came **Omar Khayyam** (1040–1123), who praised the power of reason and knowledge in his poems, and later Saadi (1184–1292), who provided readers with a rational picture of his time and raised his voice against tyranny in his *Bustan* and *Gulistan*. **Jalolidin Rumi** (1207–1273) and Hafiz (d. 1389) presented the best form of the ghazal to the world. The work of **Abdurahmon Jomi** (1414–1492) from Herat (**Afghanistan**) marks the close of the golden age of Perso-Tajik literature. This classic literature influenced the work of later writers, including Muhammad Iqbal (1877–1938), who wrote more often in Persian than in his native Urdu, Johann Wolfgang von Goethe (1749–1832), Alexander Pushkin (1799–1837), and many others.

The most important of the 19th-century Tajik writers was **Ahmad Donish**, known for his sharp critique of ignorant **mullahs** and corrupt aristocracy, depicted in his *Navodir ul-Vaqo'e* (Rarities of Events). In *Nomusi A'zam* (Great Dignity), he praised Russian culture, paving the way for the **Jadid** movement.

In the **Soviet** period, Persian books in Arabic script were not allowed into Tajikistan, and the only accepted literary style was socialist realism aimed at serving the "working class." The Tajik literary centers of **Bukhara** and **Samarqand** became part of **Uzbekistan**. Nevertheless, social change opened new horizons and made an enormous impact on the development of Tajik literature. **Sadriddin Ayni** (1878–1954) was the first author to launch modern Tajik literature. In his compendium of Tajik literature called *Namunahoi Adabiyoti Tojik* (The Examples of Tajik Literature), published in 1926, Ayni refers to Rudaki, Firdawsi, Hafiz, Saadi, and other poets of the golden age and emphasizes their belonging to the cultural heritage of the Tajiks. Ayni, a gifted novelist, established prose as a medium for expression in a society that used to love poetry alone. The most famous of Ayni's novels are *Dokhunda* (the first Tajik novel), *Bukhara, Memoirs* (four volumes) and *Slaves*. Ayni is also famed for his historical works on the last years of the **Bukharan emirate**, including *The Materials of the History of the Revolution of Bukhara, The Old-Style School, Death of a Usurer*, and others. **Abdulqasem Lahuti** (1887–1957) was a revolutionary Iranian poet who immigrated to the Soviet Union and eventually settled in Tajikistan.

The next generation of modern Tajik writers included **Jalol Ikromi**, Rahim Jalil, **Mirzo Tursunzoda**. Ayni, Lohuti, and Tursunzoda were major figures in Soviet Tajik literature. Thereafter, younger writers preserved and developed traditional forms and introduced Tajiks to drama and opera, infusing these previously alien genres with folk ideals and a communist message. In the later Soviet period, the poets **Sherali Loiq**, Bozor Sobir, and **Gulrukhsor Safieva** criticized the falsehoods of Soviet literature and raised their voices to protect Tajik culture and the Tajiks' unique national identity.

With the defeat of the **United Tajik Opposition** in the **civil war** in 1992–1997, the rebellious spirit of Tajik literature of the late Soviet period mostly vanished. Tajik writers try to preserve the precious heritage of classic Perso-Tajik literature and not capitulate on the major accomplishments of the Tajik Soviet period. *See also ADIB*; HAKIMOV, ASKAR; SHUKUROV, MUHAMMADJON; TAJIKISTAN UNION OF WRITERS.

LOIQ, SHERALI (1941–2000). A famed Tajik poet, Loiq was born in **Panjakent**. He graduated from the Dushanbe Pedagogical Institute in 1962 and started work in the republican **radio, television**, and local press. In the 1980s, he was secretary of **Tajikistan Union of Writers**. Loiq was chief editor of *Sadoi Mardum* (People's Voice) magazine and a prolific author. He used classical forms of poetry, while his chosen themes reflected his growing involvement in social issues. *See also LITERATURE*.

LULIS. An ethnic group in Tajikistan, the Lulis are known as the Gypsies of **Central Asia**. Their native language is **Tajik**, and they live in rural pockets. Lulis, sometimes called Jugis, often earn a living by fortune-telling and healing. They have resisted assimilation in Tajik and **Uzbek** cultures. Lulis have retained their own identity and do not marry outside their community. The total number of Lulis in Tajikistan is unknown, but estimates point to as many as 10,000.

– M –

MADRASA. A *madrasa* is an institution of higher education open to students of **Islam** after the **maktab**. Among the biggest madrasas in Tajikistan are Yaqybi Charkhi (**Dushanbe**), Mavlavi Regari (city of **Tursunzoda**), Khadicha, and Salman Forsi (**Isfara nohiya**).

MAHALLA. Urban neighborhoods are often known as *mahalla* or *guzar* in **Central Asia**. The mahalla is often run by local elders. All traditional ceremonies and feasts (e.g., **khatmul qurons, tuis**, funerals, **hashars**) are usually organized on the mahalla level under the leadership of local elders and members of the neighborhood or mahalla community. *See also* ETIQUETTE; MASHVARAT.

MAHKAMOV, QAHOR (1932–). A president of Tajikistan, Mahkamov was born in **Khujand** and graduated from the Institute of Mountain Mining in Leningrad in 1953. Mahkamov started work as an engineer in the Shurob coal mine (**Sughd**). Between 1961 and 1963, he served as chair of the Leninobod (Khujand) city **executive committee**. In 1963, he chaired the State Planning Commission (Gosplan) and then became deputy chair of the Council of Ministers in Tajikistan, a post he held until 1982. Between 1960 and 1992, Mahkamov was elected eight times to the **Supreme Soviet** of Tajikistan and once in 1978 to the Supreme Soviet of the **Soviet Union**. He chaired Tajikistan's Supreme Soviet between 1982 and 1986 and then became first secretary of the Central Committee of the **Communist Party of Tajikistan** (CPT). In March 1991, Mahkamov was elected president by Tajikistan's Supreme Soviet. Following the failure of the pro-communist coup in Moscow, Mahkamov was accused of supporting the coup plotters and was forced to resign his post in September 1991 by public pressure. As an ex-president, Mahkamov is a lifetime member of the **Majlisi Melli**. *See also* PRESIDENTS OF TAJIKISTAN.

MAHMADOV, BOBOKHON (1950–). Born in **Baljuvon, Kulob** veloyat, Mahmadov graduated from the Tajik Pedagogical Institute in
1972 with a degree in history. In 1972–1988, he worked in different
fields: **agriculture**, construction, and **mass media**. In 1988–1989,
he became the first deputy chair of Tajikistan's state committee for
publishing. In 1990, he was appointed minister of culture, press, and
information. In 1992, he organized and headed the Mehri Khatlon
cultural association. In 1994, Mahmadov was elected chair of **Ittihod: Civil-Patriotic Party of Tajikistan**. He served as minister of
culture in 1997–2001.

MAHMUDOV, SHAROF (1931–). A Tajik jurist and politician,
Mahmudov was born in **Konibodom** and in 1955 graduated from
the law school of the Tajik State University. He was a member of the
Leninobod (**Khujand**) provincial court in 1955–1962 and Tajikistan's
high court in 1962–1971. He was deputy minister of justice in 1971–
1978 and minister of justice in 1978–1990. In 1990, he was appointed
chair of the country's high court. Mahmudov retired in 1994.

MAJLIS. A *majlis* is a meeting, gathering, convention, or company.

MAJLISI MELLI (NATIONAL ASSEMBLY). The Majlisi Melli is
the upper chamber (senate) of the national parliament, the **Majlisi
Oli**. According to the constitutional laws on **elections** to the Majlisi
Oli and to local majlises of people's deputies, adopted in December
1999, the Majlisi Melli is elected for a five-year term and consists of
33 members, including five members from each of the three **veloyats**
and five members from the **Nohiyas under Republican Control**
and **Dushanbe**, all elected by local (veloyat, **nohiya**, and city) majlises. The remaining eight deputies are appointed by the president.
The Majlisi Melli's responsibilities include forming, changing, and
liquidating administrative and territorial units; electing and recalling
the chairs and their deputies of the constitutional, high, and economic courts (upon suggestion of the president); ratifying legislation
proposed by the **Majlisi Namoyandagon** (the lower chamber); con-
firming the appointments of and recalling the prosecutor general and
deputies. The Majlisi Melli meets at least twice a year.
    Joint sessions between the Majlisi Melli and the Majlisi Namoy-
andagon are held for the following occasions: the inauguration and

termination of the presidency; approving presidential decrees on the appointment of the prime minister and members of the government; presidential addresses; receiving visiting foreign leaders or diplomats; approving presidential decrees on introduction of martial and extraordinary laws. The first Majlisi Melli elections were held on 23 March 2000.

The first session of the Majlisi Melli convened on 17 April 2000 and elected **Mahmadsaid Ubaidulloev** as its chair. The chair's deputies, elected on the same day, were **Nazarbegim Muborakshoeva**, chair of Rushan nohiya, **Mountainous Badakhshon Autonomous Veloyat** (MBAV), and **Askar Hakimov**, chair of **Tajikistan Union of Writers**. The following members of the majlis were elected chairs of parliamentary standing committees: **Qosim Qosimov**, chair of **Sughd** veloyat (economics and communications); Davlatali Sharipov, chair of **Khatlon** veloyat (agrarian affairs, labor, and ecology); Salomiddin Sharofov, prosecutor general of Tajikistan (constitutional foundation of civil rights and law); **Ulmas Mirsaidov**, president of the **Academy of Sciences of Tajikistan** (social affairs, health care, science, culture, women, and youth politics in the society); **Alimamad Niyozmamadov**, chair of the MBAV (coordination of activities between the Majlisi Melli and the Majlisi Namoyandagon, executive power, public associations, media, and international relations).

MAJLISI NAMOYANDAGON (ASSEMBLY OF REPRESENTATIVES). The Majlisi Namoyandagon is the lower chamber of the **Majlisi Oli** (the national parliament). According to the constitutional laws on **elections** to the Majlisi Oli and on to the local majlises of people's deputies, adopted in December 1999, the Majlisi Namoyandagon is elected directly for a five-year term and consists of 63 deputies (65 percent as single district seats and 35 percent by party lists). The assembly is a permanent body sitting in session most of the year. Its responsibilities include forming the central commission on elections and referendums; initiating and presenting new legislation and projects to the **Majlisi Melli** (the upper chamber); accepting economic and social programs; accepting and conferring state credits; appointing referenda; forming courts; approving state symbols, state awards, and presidential decrees; and defining military and diplomatic ranks. The first elections to the Majlisi Namoyandagon were held on 27 February 2000. In 2000–2001, the **Communist Party of Tajikistan** formed a parliamentary faction. A second faction, People's Deputies, is supportive of the policies of President **Emomali Rahmon**.

On 27 March 2000, **Sadulloh Khairulloev** was elected chair of the Majlisi Namoyandagon. **Abdulmajid Dostiev**, member of the **People's Democratic Party of Tajikistan** (PDPT), Gulafzo Savriddinova (PDPT), and **Jamoliddin Mansurov, Communist Party of Tajikistan** (CPT) were elected deputy chairs. Chairs of nine standing committees were elected: Safar Safarov (CPT) (economics, budget, finance, and taxes); **Abdurahmon Azimov** (order, defense, and security); Zarif Aliev (constitutional legitimacy and legislature); **Yusuf Akhmedov** (energy, industry, construction, and communications); Shodibek Akhmedov (CPT) (agrarian policy and employment); Sanovbar Rahimova (PDPT) (social protection, family affairs, health, and environment); **Ibrahim Usmonov** (PDPT) (international affairs, public organizations, and information); Abdusattor Jabborov (PDPT) (statehood building and local governance); and **Mamadshoh Ilolov** (PDPT) (science, education, culture, and youth policy). At the first session of the assembly, two parliamentary commission chairs were also elected: **Amirsho Miraliev** (CPT) (ethics of deputies) and **Khalifabobo Khamidov** (PDPT) (control on order of business and logistics).

MAJLISI NAMOYANDAGON, 2000–2005 ELECTIONS. The first elections to the new assembly, the **Majlisi Namoyandagon**, were held on 27 February 2000. They were conducted on the basis of a mixed or half-proportional system in 41 electoral districts. Only six **political parties** fulfilled the registration requirements and presented their list of candidates. The **People's Democratic Party of Tajikistan** (PDPT) nominated 21 candidates, the **Communist Party of Tajikistan** (CPT) 20 candidates, the **Democratic Party of Tajikistan Almaty Platform** 19 candidates, the **Socialist Party of Tajikistan** (SPT) 18 candidates, the **Islamic Renaissance Party of Tajikistan** (IRPT) and the **Adolatkhoh Party of Justice** (APJ) 15 candidates each. The results were 41 deputies (65 percent) elected in single-mandate districts by majority vote in a two-round system, and 22 deputies (35 percent) elected by a proportional system of party lists.

According to the central electoral commission, more than 2.5 million people (92.2 percent of the total registered electorate) participated in the elections to the new parliament. In 13 electoral districts, voting was repeated on 12 March. Only three of the six political parties cleared the 5 percent barrier: the PDPT received 1.6 million votes (64.5 percent), the CPT 533,000 votes (20.6 percent), and the IRPT 193,000 votes (7.4 percent). The Democratic Party of Tajikistan Almaty Platform received only 90,000 votes (3.5 percent), Adolatkhoh 43,000 votes (1.3 percent), and the SPT 32,000 votes (1.2 percent) and were excluded from the parliament. According to observers from the **United Nations** and the **Organization for Security and Cooperation in Europe**, the electoral law in Tajikistan failed to meet international standards, especially in terms of the independence of electoral commissions and transparency of vote counting. The CPT and the IRPT also complained that their official representatives were sometimes not allowed in polling stations.

The PDPT is the largest party in the lower chamber, with 30 deputies (including two of the three deputy chairs and five of the nine standing committee chairs). The CPT is the second largest bloc, with 13 deputies (including one deputy chair and three standing committee chairs). The IRPT has only two deputies. Sixteen other deputies are not affiliated with any political party. Among the parties presented in the Majlisi Namoyandagon, only the CPT has formed a parliamentary faction.

Deputies elected to the lower chamber included 15 economists (23.8 percent); 15 cultural, educational, and medical professionals (23.8 percent); 10 teachers (15.8 percent); 10 engineers (15.8 percent); six jurists (9.5 percent); and five agrarian scientists (7.9 percent). There were nine women deputies (5.5 percent). All deputies were **Tajiks** or **Uzbeks** except for one **Russian**, Sergei Pavlenko, from the People's Democratic Party of Tajikistan.

MAJLISI NAMOYANDAGON, 2005–2010 ELECTIONS. The second **elections** since the end of the **civil war** in 1997 were held for the **Majlisi Namoyandagon** on 27 February 2005. A total of 227 candidates ran. More than 2.9 million voters (92.59 percent of the total registered electorate) participated. The participating **political parties** were the **Democratic Party of Tajikistan** (DPT), **Communist Party of Tajikistan** (CPT), **Islamic Renaissance Party of Ta-**

jikistan (IRPT), **Socialist Party of Tajikistan** (SPT), and **People's Democratic Party of Tajikistan** (PDPT). Those elected include 11 women, 11 lawyers, 12 engineers, seven economists, three agronomists and zootechnicians, 26 teachers, one physician, one journalist, one librarian, one specialist in international relations, and two veterinarians. Among this number, three are members of the **Academy of Sciences**, seven are **doctors of science**, and 11 are **candidates of science**. Of the 63 deputies elected in 2005, 46 are members of the PDPT, four are members of the CPT, two are members of the IRPT, and 11 have no party affiliation.

MAJLISI OLI. The Majlisi Oli is the supreme legislative and representative assembly in the Republic of Tajikistan. This was initially a unicameral assembly, elected for a period of five years. On 25 February 1995, the first **elections** to the Majlisi Oli were held. More than 2.4 million voters (91.7 percent of total registered voters) took part in these elections. A total of 181 deputies were elected to the Majlisi Oli.

The 181 members of the parliament were made up of 58 deputies (32 percent) from **Sughd**, 48 deputies (27 percent) from the **Kulob** region of **Khatlon** veloyat, 19 deputies (9 percent) from the **Qurghonteppa** region of Khatlon, 46 deputies (26 percent) from the **Nohiyas under Republican Control** and **Dushanbe**, and 10 deputies (6 percent) from **Badakhshon**. There were 164 Tajiks (90.5 percent), 14 **Uzbeks** (8 percent), two **Russians** (1 percent), and one **Kyrgyz** (0.5 percent). The overwhelming majority of deputies elected in February 1995 were state and local administrators and heads of state enterprises, government agencies, and the presidential office: 139 deputies (77 percent), including three chairs of the three veloyats and 66 chairs and deputy chairs of 33 nohiyas (from the total of 46). The second largest group was represented by the **army**, militia, and security forces: 19 deputies (10.5 percent), including nine **Sitodi Melli** field commanders incorporated into the national army. Business people were the third group: 16 deputies (9 percent), followed by two writers and journalists (1 percent), two doctors (1 percent), one engineer (0.5 percent), one professor (0.5 percent), and one international organization official (0.5 percent). In terms of the **political parties** represented, the **Communist Party of Tajikistan** commanded 60 deputies, the **People's Democratic**

Party of Tajikistan six deputies, the **Party of Political and Economic Regeneration of Tajikistan** two deputies, and Tajikistan's **Party of People's Unity** two deputies.

In 2000, in accordance with the **General Agreement on the Establishment of Peace and National Accord**, a bicameral parliament replaced the unicameral supreme assembly. To facilitate this transition, two constitutional laws were adopted on 10 December 1999: the Law on Elections to the Majlisi Oli of the Republic of Tajikistan and the Law on Elections to Local Majlises of People's Deputies. According to these, the Majlisi Oli now consists of two chambers: the **Majlisi Namoyandagon** (assembly of representatives, or lower chamber) and **Majlisi Melli** (national assembly, or senate).

MAKTAB. A *maktab* is a school or Islamic school.

MAN. A weight measure in medieval **Central Asia** that was used until the 1920s, the *man* varied from region to region and over time. In the 16th–18th centuries, 1 man in **Samarqand** and **Bukhara** was equal to 4,000 miskals, or 20 kilograms. At the beginning of the 20th century, 1 man was reportedly equal to 131 kilograms in Bukhara.

MANNONON, BAHROM (1947– 2009). A famous Tajik reporter, Mannonon was born in **Konibodom**, **Sughd veloyat**, to the family of a school teacher. He graduated from the Tajik State University with a degree in physics in 1970 and then served in the Soviet Army. In 1976–1980, he was a schoolteacher. In 1980–1991, he served as deputy director of the Technikum (college) of Technology in Konibodom. In 1991–1995, he was director of a school in Konibodom. In 1995, he was appointed adviser to the president of the Bodom stock company, a Tajikistan-based branch of the Gorkiy Automobile Production (GAZ) stock company, **Russia**. Since 2002, he has worked as senior correspondent and executive director of **Asia-Plus** information agency. *See also* MASS MEDIA.

MANSUROV, JAMOLIDDIN (1951–). Born in **Hisor**, Mansurov studied economics at the Tajik State University. After graduating in 1973, he worked as an economist in Hisor. He served in the military in 1977–1979 and then started Communist Party work. In 1984, he was appointed director of Druzhba **sovkhoz** in Hisor but returned to party work in 1986. Between 1989 and 1993, he headed the Hisor nohiya executive committee, and between 1993 and 1994 the **Dushanbe** executive committee. Mansurov was Tajikistan's vice premier from 1994 to 1999. In 2000, he was elected to the **Majlisi Namoyandagon** and was its deputy chair in 2000–2005. Mansurov is a member of the **Communist Party of Tajikistan**.

MAQSUM (LUTFULLOEV), NUSRATULLO (1881–1938). A party and state leader in Tajikistan, Maqsum fell victim to the Stalinist purges of the 1930s. Maqsum, also known as Nusratullo Lutfulloev, was born in **Gharm**. He started work in 1895 at an industrial enterprise in **Kokand** (currently in **Uzbekistan**) and was active in labor politics. He joined the Communist Party in 1921. In 1921–1923, Maqsum was the representative of the Bukharan executive committee (BEC) in **Eastern Bukhara** and was a member of the BEC extraordinary commission on Eastern Bukharan affairs. In 1923–1924, he was deputy chair of the Eastern Bukhara revolutionary soviet and chair of the Gharm **veloyat**'s executive committee. After the establishment of the **Tajik Autonomous Soviet Socialist Republic** in October 1924, he headed the first government of Tajikistan as chair of the revolutionary committee. In 1926–1929, he was chair of the Tajik ASSR **central executive committee** (CEC). After the formation of the **Tajik Soviet Socialist Republic** in 1929, he was chair of the Tajik SSR CEC. In 1933, he was removed from his post for alleged distortions of class lines and sent to study in Moscow. Maqsum was arrested in December 1937 and charged with counterrevolutionary activity; he was sentenced to death and executed in 1938. His reputation was rehabilitated in 1957 and he was reinstated to the Communist Party posthumously in 1964.

MASHVARAT. A traditional institution of authority, *mashvarat* (consultation) involves learned and respected people, including elders, who consult to solve urgent issues using resources from within the community. Usually officeholders and government officials are excluded from the mashvarat. *See also* MAHALLA.

MASOV, RAHIM (1939–). A Tajik historian and **academician**, Masov was born in **Vanj nohiya**, **Mountainous Badakhshon Autonomous Veloyat**, and received a degree in history from the Tajik

State University in 1961. He started work at the Institute of History, Archeology, and Ethnography of the **Academy of Sciences of Tajikistan** as a research fellow in 1961, later became head of the Department of the History of Soviet Society, and then director in 1989. Masov specialized in the historiography of Tajikistan during the Soviet period. In the 1990s, he published three books on the history of the 1924 national delimitation in **Central Asia**, which encouraged extreme nationalist, xenophobic, and racist tendencies in Tajikistan.

MASS MEDIA. The first newspaper in the **Tajik** language was *Bukhoroi Sharif* (Noble Bukhara), published in 1912–1913 by the **Jadids** of **Bukhara** with the support of Russian colonial authorities. The first Tajik-language journal, *Shu'lai Inqilob* (Fire of Revolution), was printed in April 1919 in **Samarqand**. In **Dushanbe** in December 1923, the Russian-language newspaper *Po Basmachu* (Against a Basmachi) was printed to serve the needs of the 13th Red Army Regiment stationed in **Eastern Bukhara**. This was the first paper ever published within the territory of what is now Tajikistan. The first Tajik-language Soviet newspaper, *Ovozi Tojik* (Tajik Voice), began in Samarqand in 1923. This paper was an organ of the Samarqand provincial committee of the Communist Party. After 1930, it became an organ of the central committee of the Communist Party of **Uzbekistan** under the name *Haqiqati Uzbekiston* (Truth of Uzbekistan).

In 1924, the **Tajik Autonomous Soviet Socialist Republic** was formed, while the first national newspaper in the Tajik language started publishing in 1925. This paper was run by the central committee of the **Communist Party of Tajikistan** under the names *Idi Tojik* (Feast of Tajik) and *Bedorii Tojik* (Tajik's Awakening) in 1925–1928, *Tojikistoni Surkh* (Red Tajikistan) in 1928–1955, and *Tojikistoni Soveti* (Soviet Tajikistan) in 1955–1991. This central Tajik newspaper had analogous versions in Russian and **Uzbek**. The Russian version was named *Sovietskiy Tadzhikistan* (Soviet Tajikistan) in 1925–1955 and *Kommunist Tadzhikistana* (Communist of Tajikistan) in 1955–1991. The national newspaper in the Uzbek language had the names *Qizil Tojikiston* (Red Tajikistan) in 1928–1955 and *Sovet Tojikistoni* (Soviet Tajikistan) in 1955–1991. All were the most popular daily newspapers in Soviet Tajikistan.

Daily and weekly outlets were also published at the provincial and district levels throughout the Soviet period in the Tajik, Russian, Uzbek, and **Kyrgyz** languages. There were also numerous newspapers and magazines for **Komsomol** and trade union members. Soviet Tajikistan's press included publications focusing on **health, education, agriculture**, and other issues. Several were intended especially for children and women. Literary magazines were published in the Tajik, Uzbek, and Russian languages. The **Academy of Sciences of Tajikistan** published five scholarly journals.

Regardless of their established names, all media outlets were controlled by the Communist Party; all shared the motto "Proletarians of all countries, unite!" All were owned, funded, and distributed by the state. In 1940, for a population of 1.5 million Tajikistanis, there were 83 newspapers with a total circulation of about 45 million in the republic. Among them, 53 were published in Tajik, 17 in Uzbek, and 13 in Russian. Additionally, the people of Tajikistan received central newspapers and journals coming from Moscow and other parts of the Soviet Union.

Communist Party committees at various levels were charged with censoring media outlets. During perestroika, the party tolerated more criticism of the government in order to conciliate Tajik nationalists and encourage them to support efforts for change. The situation changed dramatically with independence in 1991, followed by Tajikistan's **civil war** (1992–1997). Most media enterprises were privatized, and their support from the state was discontinued. Major national newspapers managed to survive under new names. *Tojikistoni Soveti* changed its name to *Junhuriyat* (Republic), while its Russian counterpart *Kommunist Tadzhikistana* became *Narodnaya Gazeta* (People's Newspaper) and the *Sovet Tojikistoni* in Uzbek is known today as *Khalq Ovozi* (Voice of the People). All of them are state owned and published two or three times a week under the direct control of the government.

In 1991–1992, new newspapers appeared, representing independent journalists' groups, various foundations, cultural and religious groups, and opposition **political parties**. After the government of **Emomali Rahmon** came to power at the end of 1992, it cracked down on the press. Yet **Dodojon Atovulloev**'s *Charoghi Ruz* continued to publish from 1993 onward in Moscow. The **United Tajik**

Opposition (UTO) media continued to operate in exile; a radio station broadcast from refugee camps in northern **Afghanistan**, and at least two bulletins were published in **Pakistan**.

Print media has expanded since the signing of the **General Agreement on the Establishment of Peace and National Accord** in June 1997 and the lifting of a six-year ban on the activities of UTO parties and their media outlets in August 1999. Among the newer popular Tajik newspapers are *Sadoi Mardum* (Voice of the People), which is parliament owned and is published three times a week, in Tajik; *Asia-Plus*, a privately owned weekly published in Russian; *Kurier Tadzhikistana* (Tajikistan's Courier), a privately owned weekly published in Russian; *Tojikiston* (Tajikistan), privately owned and published in Tajik, three times a week; and *Nerui Sukhan* (Power of Speech), another privately owned weekly. Two popular Russian-language weekly newspapers, *Biznes i Politika* (Business and Politics) and *Vechernie Novosti* (Evening News), are nominally private but receive support from the **government**. Political party newspapers include *Minbari Khalq* (People's Tribune), a weekly published by the **People's Democratic Party of Tajikistan**, in Tajik; *Nidoi Ranjbar* (Call of Toiler), a weekly published by the Communist Party of Tajikistan, in Tajik; *Golos Tajikistana* (Voice of Tajikistan), a weekly published by the Communist Party of Tajikistan, in Russian; *Najot* (Salvation), a weekly published by the **Islamic Renaissance Party of Tajikistan**, in Tajik.

There is no daily newspaper in Tajikistan. The provincial (**veloyat**) and city newspapers are issued, as a rule, once or twice a month. In 2004, the Ministry of Culture had registered 362 publications, including 268 newspapers and 94 journals. Among them, only 24 newspapers and 21 journals were state owned. Most newspapers print just 3,000–4,000 copies a week and cannot reach rural areas, further limiting their circulation.

Nominally independent newspapers are owned by their editorial staffs and financed by private sponsors, political associations, or commercial groups. Most Tajik media outlets that emerged in 1991–2008 joined the Tojikiston, Kharkhi Gardun, and Asia-Plus media-holding companies.

The 1991 Law on Press Freedom and the 1994 **constitution** guarantee freedom of the press and citizens' access to the media. Tajikistan also ratified the International Covenant on Civil and Political

Rights (ICCPR) in 1998. Under the constitution, all forms of censorship are illegal. Nevertheless, the government exercises control over the media both openly through legislation and indirectly through "recommendations" to journalists. Heavy tax burdens introduced into law in January 1999 have been used as a device for controlling the media and increasing their dependence on the government. Media outlets are subject to 15 different national, regional, and local taxes. Tax evasion is widespread. Most editors have a dual accounting system, and some engage in offering bribes. This reality gives the government a powerful instrument to prosecute virtually any private media outlet for illegal activities. The country's sole publishing house for printing newspapers, *Sharqi Ozod* (Free Orient), is owned by the state, and this adds to government power.

The nongovernmental organization Freedom House rated Tajikistan as "Not Free" in the category of press freedoms beginning in 1992. Editors and journalists afraid of reprisals cautiously exercise self-censorship. Article 137 of Tajikistan's penal code stipulates that publicly insulting the Tajik president can lead to a punishment of up to five years in prison. Since 1994, criticism of the president and the ruling party has been taboo in the Tajik media. Journalists often are subject to persecution, pressure, and violence. Estimates for the number of journalists killed during and after the civil war vary from 70 to 80. By 2007, the murder of journalists had stopped.

In 2009, four domestic news agencies, including the private **Asia-Plus**, Avesta (in Dushanbe), and Varorud (**Sughd veloyat**) agencies, and the state-run Khovar (Dushanbe) were operating in the country, in addition to the Russian RIA Novosti agency. *See also* RADIO, TELEVISION, AND ELECTRONIC MEDIA.

MASSOUD, AHMAD SHAH (1953–2001). An Afghan leader of Tajik origin, born in the Jangalak district of Panjsher, Massoud waged **jihad** against the Soviet invaders of **Afghanistan** in 1979–1989. After their defeat, he became defense minister of Afghanistan in 1992 under President Burhanuddin Rabbani. Some **United Tajik Opposition** (UTO) military groups are reported to have been trained in Massoud's bases in Panjsher. Following the fall of Rabbani's government and the rise of the **Taliban**, Massoud became the military leader of the United Islamic Front for the Salvation of Afghanistan, known as the **Northern Alliance**. On 9 September 2001, Massoud was assassinated by alleged al-Qaeda agents. On 25 April 2002, he was officially proclaimed a national hero of Afghanistan. During Tajikistan's **civil war**, Massoud and Rabbani (ethnic Tajiks) were important brokers in the **Inter-Tajik Peace Talks**. *See also* KHOS DEH PROTOCOL; TAJIKS OF AFGHANISTAN.

MAVLANBEKOV, AHMADBEK (1897–1937). A Tajik revolutionary, Mavlanbekov was a Communist Party (CP) and state leader in **Uzbekistan** and Tajikistan. He fell victim to the Stalinist purges of the 1930s. Mavlanbekov was born in **Khujand** and joined the **Turkistan Communist Party** in 1918. From 1918 to 1921, he worked in the Khujand city soviet. In 1921–1923, he was chair of the emergency commission (Cheka) in the **Ferghana** province of Turkistan and fought against the **Basmachi** movement. In 1923–1924, he was first secretary of the central committee of the **Communist Party of Bukhara**. In 1927–1930, he was people's commissar of justice and prosecutor of the Uzbek Soviet Socialist Republic. In 1931–1933, Mavlanbekov attended the Institute of Red Professors in Moscow and subsequently headed the Agitation and Propaganda Department of the **Communist Party of Tajikistan**. Mavlanbekov was arrested in 1937, charged with counterrevolutionary activity, and executed. His reputation was rehabilitated in 1957.

MAZAR. A *mazar* is the burial place or mausoleum of a saint, holy person, or eminent religious scholar. It is traditional to perform a pilgrimage to a mazar to perform ritual actions there. It is believed that mazars have a magic curing power. *See also* ISLAM.

MAZHAB. A *mazhab* is a law, rule, bylaw, or system of manners. The term is also used for a religious opinion, confession, religion, or sect. *See also* HANAFIYA; ISLAM.

MINING. More than 500 ore deposits and fields have been identified in Tajikistan, from which about 100 mines are in operation. The biggest ore extracting mine is the **Anzob** mining mill, operating at the base of the Jijikrut deposit, with more than 6.2 million tons of mercury and 183,300 tons of surma. All products were sent to **Kyrgyzstan** for development. Tajikistan's isolation from world markets and major transportation links means that transport and infrastructure development costs are major factors in evaluating the practicability of mineral development. Tajikistan's mining industry also suffers from dilapidated equipment and a shortage of investment funds and qualified specialists. *See also* COAL; DARVOZ NOHIYA; ECONOMY; GOLD; SILVER; ZARAFSHON RIVER.

MIR. *See* AMIR.

MIRALIEV, AMIRSHO (1946–). Born in **Danghara nohiya**, Kulob veloyat, Miraliev graduated from the Tajik Institute of Agriculture in 1970 and started his working life as a bricklayer in Danghara. In 1972, he worked in the Kulob provincial organization of **Komsomol** and in 1985 was appointed first secretary of the Moskva nohiya's (**Hamadoni**) Komsomol committee. In 1990–1994, he was chair of the Moskva nohiya executive committee. In December 1994, Miraliev became adviser to the president on cadre policy and in 1995 was elected to the **Majlisi Oli**. He was elected to the **Majlisi Namoyandagon** in February 2000 and became chair of the Standing Committee on Ethics. From February 2001 to November 2004, he was chair of **Khatlon** veloyat. In December 2006, he became head of the executive office of the president of Tajikistan.

MIRSAIDOV, ULMAS (1945–). A Tajik scholar and **academician**, Mirsaidov was born in Uroteppa (**Istravshan**). He graduated from the Mendeleev Institute of Chemistry and Technology (Moscow) in 1967. In 1970, he started work at the Institute of Chemistry, **Academy of Sciences of Tajikistan**, as a research fellow, then became head of department, deputy director, and finally director of that institute. Mirsaidov was president of the Academy of Sciences of Tajikistan from 1995 to 2005.

MIRZOYEV, GHAFFOR (1956–). A military leader, Mirzoyev was born in **Kulob** and graduated from the Tajik Institute of Physical Education in 1978 and the High School of Militia, **Dushanbe**. He worked in a Kulob factory of technological equipment and then as a schoolteacher. In 1982–1985, he was deputy rector of management in Tajikistan's Institute of Physical Education. In 1986, he moved to Kulob, where he worked as a driver. Between 1989 and 1991, he served as chair of the Council of Trade Unions for Agricultural

Workers in the Kulob veloyat. During the political crisis of 1992, Mirzoyev formed a group and joined the **Sitodi Melli**. He controlled the Kulob region and also fought in **Gharm**, **Tavildara**, and Dushanbe.

When **Emomali Rahmon** came to power, Mirzoyev was appointed deputy commander of the Brigade of Special Destination in the Ministry of Internal Affairs. In January 1993, this brigade was removed from the Ministry of Internal Affairs command and formed the core of Tajikistan's presidential guard. In 1995, Major General Mirzoyev was appointed commander of the guard. In 1999, he was promoted to the rank of lieutenant general. He entered the **Majlisi Oli** in 1995. He was dismissed as head of the presidential guard in January 2004. From January to August 2004, Mirzoyev was director of the agency on drug control. In August 2004, he was dismissed and arrested under charges of **corruption**, murder, and **terrorism** and was later imprisoned.

MIRZOYEV, RAMAZON (1945–). Born in Sarsibuloq village, Kulob veloyat, Mirzoyev graduated from the Tajik Institute of Agriculture in 1967 and worked with different construction organizations in Kulob. In 1979, he was appointed deputy minister of agricultural construction. In 1983, he graduated from the Communist Party's Academy of Social Sciences and worked as the first secretary of the **Danghara** district committee of the **Communist Party of Tajikistan**. In 1986, Mirzoyev was elected to the **Supreme Soviet** of the **Tajik Soviet Socialist Republic**. Between 1989 and 1992, he was a member of the last Soviet parliament—the USSR Supreme Soviet. In 1991–1992, he worked in Tajikistan's presidential administration. In 1992, Mirzoyev was appointed manager of Tajikistan's Council of Ministers office. In January 1995, he was appointed Tajikistan's ambassador to the **Russian Federation**. In 2001, Mirzoyev became Tajikistan's ambassador to the Islamic Republic of **Iran**.

MISKAL. A measure of weight in medieval **Central Asia** that was used until the 1920s, a *miskal* varied from region to region. In the 17th–19th centuries, a miskal in **Bukhara** equaled 100 jau (5 grams).

MOGOLS. An ethnic group in Tajikistan and other parts of **Central Asia**, the Mogols (Mughuls) are turkified Mongols who, since the 15th-century **Timurid** dynasty, adopted Turkic language and culture and settled in the **Amu Darya** basin. Following the establishment of Soviet rule in 1921–1923, most Mogols migrated to **Afghanistan**. In 1924, 2,365 Mogols were registered in **Hisor** and **Kulob**. In the Soviet period, Mogols were often registered as **Uzbeks** or **Tajiks** in official censuses, and the Mogol category disappeared.

MOSQUES. Known as a *masjid* to **Tajiks**, a *mosque* is a Muslim place of prayer. The typical Tajik mosque is a flat building decorated by carved wooden columns. There is also an open yard with a small fountain or a water faucet. The biggest Tajik mosques are Mavlono Yaqubi Charkhi in **Dushanbe** and Sheikh Muslihiddin in **Khujand**. Very few Tajik mosques have *minarets*—the towers from which the faithful are called for prayer. The congregational mosques, *masjidi jome'i*, known as "Friday mosques" (larger facilities built for weekly Friday prayers), can be found today in all cities and big villages. There are also thousands of smaller mosques, *masjidi panjvaqta*, in villages and city blocks. In the *panjvaqta* mosques, everyday prayers are delivered. In the Soviet times, most mosques were closed and destroyed. People prayed in private houses and *chaikhanas* (tea houses).

In independent Tajikistan, Friday mosques must be registered with the department for religious affairs that is subordinate to the ministry of culture. Only one Friday mosque is authorized per 15,000 residents in a given geographic area. The number of such mosques rose from 17 in 1989 to 240 in 2000. In 2002, this number decreased to 152. In 2008, there were 262 congregational (Friday) mosques registered and 2,842 *panjvaqta* mosques for daily prayers. **Ismaili** *jamoatkhona* (places of worship) are not included in this number.

Some mosques have religious schools. As of 2008, at 44 Tajik mosques, about 2,000 children were receiving basic religious education. *See also* ISLAM; OFFICIAL MUSLIM CLERGY; SALAFIYA.

MOTOR ROADS. Despite their bad quality, motor roads are the most popular means of transportation in Tajikistan. The country is estimated to have about 13,000 kilometers of motor roads. In 1997, 90 percent of Tajikistan's total passenger traffic (about 130 million passengers) and 87 percent of freight traffic (14.6 million) traveled on motor roads. The distribution of road networks is not equal throughout the country. In the lowlands of northern Tajikistan, as well as in **Hisor** and Kulob nohiyas in the **Vakhsh valley**, the road network is relatively developed and properly surfaced with asphalt. The situation in the **Mountainous Badakhshon Autonomous Veloyat** (MBAV), **Gharm**, and **Zarafshon** valley is not comparable; the mountainous terrain has meant unpaved roads and a limited network. The **Dushanbe-Ayni** and Dushanbe-Qalai-Khumb roads, which connect the capital with **Sughd** and Badakhshon respectively, are open only six months a year due to the high altitude and severe climate, closing **Anzob** and Khaburobod passes to traffic. In winter, Dushanbe is linked with northern and eastern parts of the country via adjacent countries: **Uzbekistan** (Dushanbe-**Samarqand-Khujand**) and **Kyrgyzstan** (**Khorugh**-Osh).

In order to reinforce national security, Tajikistan built the **Istiqlol tunnel** under the Anzob Pass and the Kulob-Qalai-Khumb roads to ensure uninterrupted connections with Sughd and the MBAV. Tajikistan has also built the **Murghob-Kulma** motor road (32 kilometers) to connect Badakhshon with the bordering **Karakoram Highway** in **China**. In June 2006, Tajikistan and China signed a deal for the Dushanbe-Khujand-Chanak highway rehabilitation project, including construction of the Shahriston tunnel, aimed at improving road communications between Dushanbe, Khujand, and the Uzbek border town of Chanak. The cost is estimated at $296 million, including $281.2 million provided by the Chinese government in the form of a long-term loan.

MOUNTAINOUS BADAKHSHON AUTONOMOUS VELOYAT (MBAV).

The Veloyati Mukhtori Kuhistoni Badakhshon (Gorno-Badkhshanskaya Avtonomnaya Oblast, in Russian), or MBAV, was formed in 1925. The MBAV covers 63,700 square kilometers and accounts for 44.5 percent of Tajikistan's territory but only 3 percent of its population (about 234,000). The MBAV is the only autonomous province in Tajikistan, recognizing its distinct **Pamiri** inhabitants and reflecting its geographical isolation from the central government in **Dushanbe**. The MBAV assembly initiates legislation within its territory, and its consent is required for any alteration of MBAV territory. One of the deputy chairs of the **Majlisi Oli** is a member of MBAV parliament, and one of the judges of Constitutional Court is a representative of MBAV. **Tajik** is the official language of the province.

The MBAV's center is the city of **Khorugh**. The province consists of seven nohiyas: **Darvoz, Vanj**, Rushan, Rosht Kala, **Shughnon, Ishkashim**, and **Murghob**. There is one city and 42 rural **jamoats**. The population speaks mostly the **Shughni and Rushani**, Khufi, **Bartangi**, Roshorvi, **Sarikoli, Yazghulami, Vakhani**, and **Ishkashimi languages**, which have no script or written tradition and are used only as spoken languages in the region. **Pamirian languages** are eastern Iranian dialects, distinct from west Iranian **Tajik-Farsi**, but all inhabitants of the area use Tajik as their intercommunal and state language. Among them, the group of Shughnis and Rushanis dominates. The majority of the population belongs to the **Ismaili** branch of **Islam** and follows the **Aga Khan**. The MBAV also contains compact pockets of Tajik **Sunni Hanafi** in the two nohiyas of Darvoz and Vanj. Six percent of the MBAV population is Sunni **Kyrgyz** living in Murghob.

The MBAV is the least economically developed and the most isolated region of the republic. It depends on supplies brought in by **motor roads**. Badakhshon boasts a distinct identity from the rest of Tajikistan. Following the Soviet collapse and during the Tajik **civil war**, especially in 1992, calls for Badakhshon's independence heightened. The **La'li Badakhshon Association**, a nationalist organization, sided with the opposition movement to advance this cause. Since 1993, however, the Badakhshoni provincial government has declared its loyalty to Dushanbe and the separatist tendency has subsided.

MOVAROUNNAHR. A vast region of **Central Asia** between the **Amu Darya** and **Syr Darya** rivers, Movarounnahr was known to **Arab** invaders as the "transriver" land. **Bukhara** and **Samarqand** were part of this territory. The area is also known as Transoxiana, a reference to the Oxus River, an earlier name for the Amu Darya. To the south of the Amu Darya, Movarounnahr bordered **Khurasan**. These two regions constituted the core of Islamic Central Asia.

MOVEMENT FOR ISLAMIC REVIVAL IN TAJIKISTAN (MIRT). Harakati Nahzati Islomii Tojikiston, the Movement for Islamic Revival in Tajikistan, was formed by exiled Tajik opposition leaders at the end of 1993 in Taluqan (**Afghanistan**). The MIRT aimed to coordinate all exiled Tajik opposition activists and their military forces. Its leaders were **Said Abdullo Nuri** (chair), **Hoji**

Akbar Turajonzoda (first deputy chair), and **Muhammad Sharif Himmatzoda** (deputy chair). The **Islamic Renaissance Party of Tajikistan** was at the core of the MIRT and commanded between 8,000 and 15,000 fighters. In 1993–1996, the MIRT acted in effect as a government in exile.

In addition to leading the armed **jihad** in Tajikistan, the MIRT tried to perform active diplomatic functions. In 1995, MIRT leaders visited the **United States** and Western Europe and established contacts with the **United Nations**, the **Organization of Security and Cooperation in Europe**, and international nongovernmental organizations. A MIRT delegation also met with the **Aga Khan**, the leader of **Ismailis**. Close contacts were established with **Russia** and **Uzbekistan**. The MIRT leaders also visited Libya, **Iran**, and other Muslim countries and established close contacts with the Organization of the Islamic Conference. In 1994, the MIRT joined the **United Tajik Opposition** and entered the **Inter-Tajik Peace Talks**. In 1998, the MIRT's armed forces began to be integrated into Tajikistan's regular **army**, a process that took over a year to complete. *See also* CIVIL WAR; POLITICAL PARTIES.

MOVEMENT FOR NATIONAL UNITY AND REVIVAL IN TA-JIKISTAN (MNURT). Tajikistan's biggest government-sponsored political movement has been Harakati Vahdati Melli va Ehyoi Tojikiston, the Movement for National Unity and Revival in Tajikistan, chaired by President **Emomali Rahmon**. The MNURT was formed on 18 July 1997 and registered in August 1997. The movement incorporates representatives of all regions and a majority of **political parties** and associations loyal to the president, including the **People's Democratic Party of Tajikistan**. The MNURT is ruled by a general assembly of founding organizations and governed by an executive council that comprises elected and appointed representatives of all member organizations. The executive committee, elected by this council, is headed by a chair. The MNURT declared its aim in July 1997 to unify "different social segments and forces of Tajikistan" and establish "a stable civil accord, mutual trust, and agreement."

MUALLIM. A *muallim* is a teacher, educated person, or master of a trade or craft.

MUBORAKSHOEVA, NAZARBEGIM (1952–). Born in **Rushan**, Muborakshoeva graduated from the Tajik Agricultural Institute in 1974 and the Communist Party High School (Tashkent) in 1991. She started her professional career as an agronomist in a Shughnan **kolkhoz.** In 1975, she was recruited into the **Komsomol** organization. Between 1975 and 1983, Muborakshoeva was an instructor in the organizational department of the **Mountainous Badakhshon Autonomous Veloyat** (MBAV) Komsomol, then was first secretary of the Rushan and Khorugh Komsomol committees. In 1983–1987, she was an instructor at the Khorugh city Committee of the **Communist Party of Tajikistan** (CPT) and in 1987–1991 first secretary of the Rushan **nohiya** committee of the CPT. From 1991 to 1997, Muborakshoeva was chair of the executive committee of the Rushan nohiya Council of People's Deputies and in 1997 became chair of Rushan nohiya. She was appointed to the **Majlisi Melli** in 2000 by a presidential decree. At the first session of the Majlisi Melli, she was appointed its deputy chair. In December 2006, she became chair of the Khorugh city council.

MUDIR. The term *mudir* is used for an administrator, director, or editor.

MUFTI. The *mufti* is the highest religious authority and official leader of the Muslims in Tajikistan. Under Soviet rule, the seat of the mufti was in Tashkent (**Uzbekistan**). The mufti headed the Muslim Spiritual Board for Central Asia and Kazakhstan (Sredneaziatskoye dukhovnoye upravlenie musulman), or SADUM, formed in 1943 with jurisdiction over Muslim spiritual affairs in Kazakhstan, **Kyrgyzstan**, Tajikistan, Turkmenistan, and Uzbekistan. The mufti and the board operated under close state control. The central Soviet government in Moscow, through a myriad of bureaucratic structures, nominated and endorsed the appointment of muftis and their deputies. The mufti nominally appointed a *qazi* to head each of the republican Islamic clerical establishments, but these appointments were tightly controlled by central state agencies. The SADUM was the core of "official" **Islam** after **World War II**. It was charged with regulating the registration of **mosques**, appointing **imams**, and even dictating the content of sermons and the nature of "proper" Islamic practice. After the Soviet collapse in December 1991 and the emergence of independent states in **Central Asia**, the Central Asian office of the muftiyat disintegrated into five separate republican boards. In theory, muftis were elected by a *shoura-i ulamo* (council of religious scholars), but government control remained.

Under the leadership of Qazi-kalon (Great Qazi) **Hoji Akbar Turajonzoda**, the Islamic clerical establishment in Tajikistan took on a political role and was embroiled in the **civil war** that followed the Soviet collapse. With the departure of Turajonzoda from Tajikistan at the end of 1992, the government reestablished control over official Islam and replaced the qaziyat with the Soviet-type muftiyat. Between 1992 and 1996, the muftiyat in **Dushanbe**, through a newly organized Islamic Center, conducted all affairs in mosques and **madrasas** (secondary schools), and appointed local religious administrators (*imam khatibs*). However, following the murder of the pro-government Mufti **Fathullokhon Sharifzoda** in 1996, the government implemented a reformation of the muftiyat and abolished the office of the muftiyat. Religious authority at the present time is held by the *shoura*, which is headed by a *raisi-shoura* (council chair). The scope of authority of the **rais** is significantly narrower than his mufti predecessor's. The government controls all finances available to the *shoura* and does not allow the Islamic clergy to participate in politics. According to the Law on Religious Affairs, no **political party** can use either a mosque or madrasa for a political agenda. *See also* OFFICIAL MUSLIM CLERGY; SALAFIYA.

MUHABBATOV, SALAMSHO (1960–). Born in **Vanj**, in the **Mountainous Badakhshon Autonomous Veloyat**, Muhabbatov graduated from the Tajik Institute of Physical Education in 1983 and started work as a high school teacher in **Dushanbe**. At the outset of the **civil war** in 1992, he organized an armed group in Vanj and was forced to flee to **Afghanistan** in 1993. In 1994, **Said Abdullo Nuri** appointed him commander in chief of the **United Tajik Opposition** (UTO) forces in Badakhshon. Following the conclusion of the **Inter-Tajik Peace Talks**, in late 1997 Muhabbatov was appointed chair of the state committee on oil and gas and was a representative of the UTO in the **government**. In 2002, he became head of the state tourism company Sayoh.

MUHIDDINOV, FARIDUN (1951–). A manager and politician, Muhiddinov was born in **Vose**, Kulob veloyat. He studied at the Moscow Automobile and Road Economy Institute, graduating in 1972. Between 1975 and 1981, he was a foreman and then engineer in the **Dushanbe** Road Management Office. In 1981–1985, he was chief engineer and then head of the Dushanberemstroi enterprise. In 1985–1989, he worked for the Inzhdorstroi and Promstroi companies, and in 1989–1990 he was a department head in the Dushanbe city executive committee's communal economy office. In 1990–1993, he was deputy chair of the Dushanbe executive committee. In 1993–2000, Muhiddinov served as minister of transportation and road economy before being appointed vice premier in June 2000. From 2002 to 2008, he was chair of Shahmansur nohiya of Dushanbe city. He retired in January 2008.

MULLAH (MULLO). A *mullah* or *mullo* is a cleric graduate of a **madrasa**, a clergyman serving in a **mosque**, or a teacher or educator.

MULLO ABDUGHAFOR. *See* KHUDOIDODOV, ABDUGHAFOR.

MULLO ABDULLO. *See* RAHIMOV, ABDULLO.

MULLO ABDURAHIM. *See* KARIMOV, ABDURAHIM.

MUMINOBOD NOHIYA. Known as Leningrad **nohiya** between 1973 and 1997, this mountainous district is situated in the southeastern part of **Khatlon, Kulob** region, bordering **Afghanistan**. It was established in 1973 within Kulob. The district is 2,387 square kilometers, with a population of more than 72,300 (16,500 urban), mainly **Tajiks**, living in five **jamoats**. The distance from the district center, Muminobod **shahrak**, to Kulob is 42 kilometers, and to **Dushanbe** 244 kilometers. Average January and July temperatures can reach –4°C and 24°C respectively. The annual rainfall is 700–1,100 millimeters. Arable land amounts to 239,686 hectares. The main occupation is **agriculture**, including livestock breeding and vegetable gardening.

MUNJI (MUNJANI). One of the **Pamirian languages**, Munji is spoken in the Munjan valley of Afghan **Badakhshon**. Munji speakers

(Iidga dialect) can also be found in the adjacent Chitral area of **Pakistan**. Munji is close to **Yazghulami** as well as **Shughni and Rushani** in terms of phonetics, grammar, and vocabulary.

MURGHOB NOHIYA. Tajikistan's highest district in elevation, biggest in territory, and smallest in population, Murghob covers the eastern part of the **Mountainous Badakhshon Autonomous Veloyat** (MBAV), also known as Eastern **Pamir**. The district center, Murghob **shahrak**, is the highest urban settlement in Tajikistan and the former **Soviet Union** (3,650 meters above sea level). Murghob has a territory of 38,000 square kilometers (60 percent of the total territory of MBAV) and is situated along the M41 Osh-**Khorugh-Dushanbe motor road** that connects Murghob with the MBAV's capital, Khorugh, to the southwest, and to the **Kulma Pass, Karakoram Highway**, and the Chinese city of **Tashkurgan** to the east, as well as **Kyrgyzstan** to the north. The M41 is the highest motor road in the former Soviet Union (3,600–4,600 meters above sea level). Murghob is the least integrated region in terms of ethnicity. Its population is about 5,000, mostly **Kyrgyzs**. Kyrgyzs came to this territory in the 17th–18th centuries. Murghob is the most arid, the least forested, and the coldest area in **Central Asia**. Lake Karakul is the biggest water reservoir in Eastern Pamir. Average January and July temperatures are –16°C and 15°C respectively. Annual rainfall is 60–150 millimeters. The main occupation is livestock breeding. *See also* ALICHUR; ALICHUR VALLEY; ARKHAR.

MURID. A *murid*, a disciple of a Sufi **murshid**, renounces worldly ties and follows the example and the word of his chosen master. Murid devotion to Sufi masters remains an important practice in **Sufism**. *See also* ISLAM.

MURSHID. A *murshid* is a Sufi elder; the title is equal to sheikh, **ishan**, or **pir**. In **Sufism**, the murshid is a master of a **murid** (disciple). In the eyes of a murid, the murshid is a holy person, an intermediary between the individual and God. *See also* ISLAM.

MUSIC. Since the **Kushan** period (3rd–4th centuries), those who lived in the territory that stretches from **Iran** to **China** and **India** were familiar with basic types of wind, string, and percussion musical instruments and used them solo and in ensemble. The music of **Tajiks**, whose ancestors populated this region, has been conditioned by Middle Eastern (**Arab**, Persian, Turkish) and South Asian (**Afghan**, Indian) musical traditions. At the same time, the music of Tajiks is unique and quite uniform. The region's major Tajik populated cities—**Samarqand** and **Bukhara**—have served as cultural centers where the classical styles of music were developed and refined. In Bukhara, the oldest musical tradition, the **Shashmaqom**, had completed its formation by the16th century.

The major classical form is the *maqom* (musical poem). In the structure of the music and its mode, it is similar to classical Persian music as well as to Azeri *mugam* and Uighur *muqam*. Classic Tajik music is based on monody understood as a solo vocal style that has a single melodic line and musical accompaniment. The typical Tajik musical ensemble includes instruments such as the **dutar, nai, setor, rubob, tanbur, doira, ghijjak**, and **chang**. Traditional Tajik music is performed by singers and musicians (*hofiz, saroyanda*) of both sexes, by multiple voices in unison. Intervals of famous Sufi poetry are included. Tajik songs typically begin at a low register and gradually ascend to a culmination (*avj*) before moving down to the beginning tone. Perpetuation of the *maqom* style makes it difficult to introduce polyphony into Tajik music.

The folk music of Tajikistan can be divided into three types, representing the major regional and cultural groups: the **Pamiri**, performed by **Ismailia** Tajiks; the Kuhistoni, popular in **Hisor**, **Khatlon**, and **Gharm**; and the northern style of **Sughd veloyat**. The Pamiris are known for sung religious poetry called *maddoh* (veneration, worship) performed in accompaniment with various rubobs, setors, lutes, and dafs (drums similar to the *doira*). Featured prominently in the musical tradition of the Pamiris are the poet **Nasir Khusraw**, famous for having converted the ancestors of the Pamiris to Ismailism, and the great Sufi poet **Jalolidin Rumi** and his spiritual mentor Shams Tabrizi. The folk music of northern Tajiks (including Tajiks of Samarqand and Bukhara) is deeply rooted in classical *maqom* tradition, while the predominantly rural Tajiks of Pamir and Khatlon are not attached to sophisticated and urban *Shashmaqom*. Southern Tajiks are fond of more improvisatory **falak** and a musical epic called *Gurughli*. Northern Tajiks did not develop a strong falak tradition. Among the southern Tajiks and Pamiri, there are no prominent *shashmaqonkhon* (Shashmaqom performers).

During Soviet times, European musical forms and polyphony were introduced. Tajik composers who graduated from Russian conservatories, including **Ziyodullo Shahidi**, tried to incorporate Tajik musical forms and melodies into the broader classical forms. The Soviets did not completely dispel the traditional Tajik music; the Shashmaqom was preserved and even developed. But the introduction of European symphonic music, with its official, "academic" status, lowered the standing of Tajik traditional music. The falak and maddah survived by adapting to the new environment.

Virtually all folk singers in Tajikistan are amateurs who serve their communities by performing at weddings, circumcisions, funerals, and other important events. Some were given the rank of "people's singer" (*hofizi khalqi*) due to their popularity. People's singers like **Akasharif Juraev**, **Odina Khoshim**, Marufkhoja Bahodurov, and Fazliddin Shahobov were broadcast nationally beginning in the 1940s. Since the late Soviet period, Tajik folk-pop music mixed with Arab, Iranian, and Indian styles has been very popular in Tajikistan, **Uzbekistan**, and neighboring **Afghanistan**. The modern Tajik falak performer Davlatmand Khol is known in the Islamic Republic of Iran.

In the independent Tajikistan, the Kulobi-dominated **government** promotes the music of southern Tajiks, but not at the expense of Shashmaqom. To secure national consolidation, the government tries to promote a common, nationwide, Tajik cultural mainstream that will bring together the admirers of the two dominant but distinctive Tajik musical genres: classical and folk, the text-based and canonized Shashmaqom and the predominantly oral and spontaneous falak, which represent the urban north and the rural south. Symphonic music in Tajikistan is in decline; it cannot survive without outside support. *See also* BORBAD; OPERA AND BALLET THEATER; KHOJA ABDULAZIZ RASULOV; SHAHIDI, TOLIBKHON; SURNAY.

MUSOEVA, RAFIQA (1953–). A Tajik politician, Musoeva trained as an engineer and became a lecturer at the Tajik Polytechnical Institute. She received her engineering degree in 1979 from the Moscow Institute of Engineers of Civil Aviation. In 1980, she was appointed secretary of the central committee of the **Komsomol** of Tajikistan. She became first secretary of the central district of the Dushanbe

Communist Party of Tajikistan committee in 1987. Musoeva was first elected to Tajikistan's **Majlisi Oli** in 1989. In 1995, she was appointed chair of the Majlisi Oli state building committee. From January 2000 to January 2003, Musoeva served as minister of labor and social protection.

– N –

NABIEV, RAHMON (1930–1993). A president of Tajikistan, Nabiev was born in **Khujand**. He started his working life in 1946 as registrar in a **kolkhoz**. In 1953, he graduated from the Institute of Land Improvement and Mechanization Engineers in Tashkent. In 1954–1955, he was chief engineer in the machine tractor station in Isfisor, **Sughd veloyat**. In 1956–1960, he was chief engineer and then director of the machinery repair station of Khujand **nohiya**, head of the Ministry of Agriculture's chief office, and subsequently deputy chair of the Agricultural Machinery of Tajikistan Association (Tajikselkhoztekhnika).

In 1961, Nabiev started work in party organs: first deputy head and then head of the Department of the Central Committee (CC) of the **Communist Party of Tajikistan** (CPT), inspector of the Central Asian Bureau of the Communist Party of the Soviet Union, and inspector and head of the Agriculture Department of the CC CPT. He was a member of Tajikistan's **Supreme Soviet** from 1961 to 1992. In 1971–1973, he was Tajikistan's minister of agriculture and in 1973–1983 was chair of the Soviet of Ministers (prime minister). In 1982–1986, he was first secretary of the CC CPT.

In 1986, Nabiev was removed from Tajikistan's highest political and administrative positions and appointed chair of the newly established Central Council for Environmental Protection. He reemerged on the political stage in 1991, first being appointed chair of Tajikistan's Supreme Soviet in September, and then elected in the first openly contested presidential elections in November. Nabiev received 59 percent of the votes, defeating the opposition candidate, **Davlatnazar Khudonazarov**, and becoming Tajikistan's first president. In the turbulent days that followed the Soviet collapse, Nabiev proved inept as a politician and unable to prevent Tajikistan's descent into **civil war**. Although he retained the presidency in the **Government** of **National Reconciliation** agreed to in May 1992, he was forced to resign by an armed band of "youth of Dushanbe" in the capital's airport in September 1992. At the 16th session of Tajikistan's parliament, held in November 1992 in Khujand, he was not reinstated as president and officially retired from politics. Nabiev passed away in March 1993 in his native Khujand.

NAI. One of the oldest major wind instruments still in use among **Tajiks**, the *nai* is an end-blown, longitudinal flute. It has six finger holes and one thumb hole. *See also* MUSIC; SHASHMAQOM; SURNAY.

NAJMIDDINOV, SAFARALI (1951–). A minister of finance, Najmiddinov was born in **Vose** and received a degree in economics from the Tajik State University in 1973. He occupied different positions in organizations run by the Tajik Ministry of Finance. From 1993 to 2000, Najmiddinov worked as deputy minister of trade and material resources, then deputy chair of the state committee for trade. In 2000, he was appointed minister of finance.

NAMANGANI, JUMABOI (KHOJIEV, JUMABOI) (1969–2001). An Uzbek opposition leader and one of the founders of the **Islamic Movement of Uzbekistan** (IMU), Namangani was born in Khoja village, Namangan province, **Uzbekistan**, and studied at the Agricultural Technical College in Namangan. After graduation in 1987, he enlisted in the Soviet Army, air paratroopers division, and served until 1989. After completing his tour of duty in **Afghanistan**, he returned to his native Namangan. In 1992, he joined a militant Islamic group called Tawba (Repentance). Almost immediately, he was accused of criminal activity, including murder, in Uzbekistan. In 1992, he left for Tajikistan and joined the Tajik Islamic opposition movement, forming an armed band of Uzbek dissidents in Qarategin. In 1993, he was forced to escape Tajikistan into Afghanistan. He is reported to have traveled to **Iran** and **Pakistan** before returning to Tajikistan.

After the signing of the **General Agreement on the Establishment of Peace and National Accord** between the **United Tajik Opposition** (UTO) and the government of President **Emomali Rahmon**, Namangani was allowed to station his armed band in

Jirghatol. In August 1999, Namangani's band raided the Batken district of **Kyrgyzstan.** In May 2000, Namangani and his band left Tajikistan's territory for Afghanistan. His withdrawal was negotiated by UTO leader **Said Abdullo Nuri** and **Mirzo Ziyoev,** the minister of emergency situations, who was a former UTO commander. In Afghanistan, the IMU joined with the **Taliban** and the international **terrorist** network. Namangani was killed in Afghanistan in the fall of 2001 during the fighting to topple the Taliban regime.

NAQSHBANDIYAH. The biggest and most influential fraternity of orthodox Muslim mystics (Sufis) in **Central Asia,** the Naqshbandiyah order was named in honor of its founder, Baha ad-Din (1318–1389), nicknamed *an-Naqshband* (the Painter). The Naqshbandiyah played an important role in Muslim thought in the 17th–19th centuries. Most **ishans** in Tajikistan are affiliated with this order. *See also* ISLAM; SUFISM.

NASIR KHUSRAW (1004–1090). A Perso-Tajik poet, mystic, and philosopher, Nasir Khusraw was born in **Qubodiyon nohiya** and traveled throughout the Near and Middle East. He became a strong adept of **Ismailia** while in Egypt and, on returning to **Khurasan,** openly propagated Ismaili teachings. Compelled to flee religious persecution, he settled in **Badakhshon** and spent his time preaching Ismaili teachings and writing on history, geography, and philosophy. The rapid growth of the Ismaili sect in Badakhshon is attributed to his powers of persuasion and his popularity. He is regarded highly by all Tajiks. *See also* ISLAM; MUSIC.

NASIR KHUSRAW NOHIYA. Formerly known as Beshkent nohiya of **Khatlon** province, the district was later named after the poet **Nasir Khusraw.** It is situated in Beshkent valley, the southeast corner of Tajikistan. Beshkent is a lowland area 70 kilometers long and 5 kilometers wide. It is dry, without any reliable source of **water.** It is the warmest valley in Tajikistan, with average temperatures in January and July of 3°C and 31°C respectively. The average annual precipitation is 140 millimeters.

NATIONAL BANK OF TAJIKISTAN (NBT). The central bank of issue and reserve of the country, the National Bank of Tajikistan is charged with implementing monetary policy and issuing currency. The NBT was formally established as the central bank in 1991. By presidential decree in 1997, the NBT became independent. It takes part in the development of the economic policy of the country and reports to the **Majlisi Namoyandagon**. The NBT consists of the central administration and regional branches. As of mid-2009, the central administration includes two departments, 12 divisions, five independent offices, and the press center.

In March 2008, the International Monetary Fund (IMF) accused the NBT of providing incorrect data in 2002–2006 on the net international reserves of Tajikistan and net domestic assets of the NBT. This misreporting led to five disbursements (a total of $79 million) of the loan Tajikistan received from the IMF within the framework of the Poverty Reduction and Growth Facility program. The IMF ordered the NBT to repay $47.9 million and suggested that a special audit of the NBT be carried out.

Two months prior to this scandal, NBT chair **Murodali Alimardon** was accused of providing insufficient credit for **agriculture** and was removed from the position he had held since 1995. Sharif Rahimzoda became chair of the NBT in January 2008. *See also* BANKS; CORRUPTION; ECONOMY.

NATIONAL HOLIDAYS. According to Tajikistan's Labor Code (June 1997), national nonworking holidays are 1 January, New Year; 8 March, International Women's Day; 21–22 March, **Nawruz**; 1 May, International Workers Solidarity Day; 9 May, Victory Day in the Great Patriotic War; 9 September, Independence Day; 6 November, Constitution Day; **Idi Ramazon** or al-Fitr (a day determined by the Qamari **calendar**); **Idi Qurbon** or al-Adha (a day determined by the Qamari calendar).

NATIONAL MOVEMENT OF TAJIKISTAN (JUNBESH). *See* PARTY OF THE NATIONAL MOVEMENT OF TAJIKISTAN.

NAU NOHIYA. This district, established in 1926, is situated in **Sughd veloyat** in the western part of the **Ferghana** valley. The distance between the regional center and **Khujand** is 36 kilometers, and to **Dushanbe** 305 kilometers. The **Konibodom**-Dushanbe **railway** traverses Nau. This nohiya is 355 square kilometers, with a population of more than 99,200 (14,700 urban), **Uzbeks** and **Tajiks**, living in six **jamoats**. Average January and July temperatures can reach –1°C and 28°C respectively. The average annual rainfall is 250 millimeters. The main occupation is **agriculture**, including **cotton**, **grain**, and fruit production as well as livestock breeding.

NAWRUZ. An ancient festival of the Iranian people, Nawruz (new day) signifies the first day of spring and the beginning of the new year in the solar **calendar**. It falls on 21 March every year in the Gregorian calendar. This pre-Islamic tradition has been celebrated by all **Tajiks** for centuries, but it became an official **national holiday** only in 1997.

NAZAROV, RUSTAM (1959–). Born in **Dushanbe** to an **Uzbek** family, Nazarov graduated from the Omsk (**Russia**) high school of police under the Ministry of Internal Affairs of the Union of the Soviet Socialist Republics. From 1984 to 1985, he worked as a field police officer. In 1995, he was deputy minister of internal affairs. In October 1996, he was appointed chair of the state commission on drug control, renamed the Agency on Drug Control in 1999. From January to August 2004, Nazarov was deputy director of the agency, giving up his position to a **Kulobi** warlord, **Ghaffor Mirzoyev**, who was soon dismissed under charges of **corruption**, murder, and **terrorism** and later imprisoned. In August 2004, Nazarov was reappointed director of the Agency on Drug Control. *See also* DRUG TRAFFICKING.

NAZAROV, TALBAK (1938–). A Tajik politician and **academician**, Nazarov was born in **Danghara**, Kulob veloyat. He graduated from the Finance and Credit College in **Dushanbe** in 1956 and from Leningrad's Institute of Finance and Economics in 1960. Between 1960 and 1972, Nazarov worked his way up in the Department of Economics at the Tajik State University, first as a teacher and then as chair of finance and credit, deputy dean, and deputy rector. Between 1976 and 1982, he was dean of the Economics Department. In 1982, he was appointed rector of the Tajik State University. In 1986–1988, Nazarov chaired the **Supreme Soviet** of the **Tajik Soviet Socialist Republic** and then occupied the post of minister of education (1988–1990). He was elected to the People's Deputies Congress of the Soviet Union in 1989. In 1990, Nazarov was appointed first vice premier of the government and chair of the State Planning Office. In 1991, he was appointed vice president of the **Academy of Sciences of Tajikistan**. In 1994, President **Emomali Rahmon** appointed Nazarov head of the presidential apparatus; on 24 December 1994, he became minister of foreign affairs. Nazarov was elected twice to Tajikistan's **Majlisi Oli**. He retired in December 2006. In 2007, by a presidential decision, Nazarov was appointed chair of the National Charity Foundation.

NAZIROV, TOSHMAT (1953–). Born in Shurobod, Kulob veloyat, Nazirov graduated in 1979 from the Tajik Institute of Agriculture and worked as an instructor in the Kulob provincial **Komsomol** committee. In 1979, he was appointed first secretary of the Komsomol committee in the Sovet district. In 1983–1986, he was an instructor for the Department of Agriculture in the Kulob provincial committee of the **Communist Party of Tajikistan**, and in 1986–1987 he headed the department. In 1990, Nazirov was appointed chair of the Kulob provincial committee of people's control, then in 1991 chair of the Shurobod district executive committee. In 1992–1994, he was chair of the Kulob city executive committee. In 1994–1995, he was ambassador at large for Tajikistan's Ministry of Foreign Affairs. In 1995, he was appointed plenipotentiary and in 1996 ambassador to the Islamic Republic of **Iran**. Since 2001, he has been an ambassador at large.

NEGMATULLOEV, SABIT (1937–). A Tajik scholar and **academician**, Negmatulloev was born in Uroteppa (**Istravshan**), **Sughd veloyat**, and studied in the Tajik Polytechnical Institute, graduating in 1961. Later he worked as director of the Institute of Seismology and Seismologic Construction, the biggest institute in the Academy of Sciences. Negmatulloev was in charge of building the first experimental seismologic facility in the **Soviet Union**. He is the author of several monographs on seismology. He was president of the **Academy of Sciences of Tajikistan** in 1988–1995. In 1996, he returned to his position as director of the Institute of Seismology and Seismologic Construction.

NIYOZMAMADOV, ALIMAMAD (1943–). Born in **Khorugh**, Niyozmamadov studied mechanics at the Tajik Institute of Agriculture, graduating in 1965. He graduated from the Communist Party High School (Tashkent) in 1985. Between 1970 and 1980, he worked in Tadzhikselkhoztekhnika, Tajikistan's Agricultural Machinery Corporation. In 1980–1983, he chaired the **Shahritus nohiya** executive committee and was recruited in 1985 into the apparatus of the **Communist Party of Tajikistan** (CPT) in the **Qurghonteppa veloyat**. In 1988, he was appointed **Panj** district secretary of the party. With the onset of Tajikistan's **civil war** in 1992, Niyozmamadov moved to his native Khorugh and in 1994 was appointed chair of the **Mountainous Badakhshon Autonomous Veloyat** (MBAV). He was elected to the **Majlisi Oli** in 1995. Elected to the **Majlisi Melli** in March 2000, he became chair of the standing committee on coordination of activities between the Majlisi Melli and the **Majlisi Namoyandagon**. On 26 August 2007, he was replaced by **Qodir Qosimi** as chair of the MBAV.

NIYOZOV, JUMABOI (1947–). Born in **Khujand**, Niyozov chaired the **Sughd** provincial committee of the **Democratic Party of Tajikistan** (DPT) in 1991–1992. In 1993, he received a seven-year prison sentence for the illegal possession of firearms. In November 1994, following an agreement between the **government** of Tajikistan and the opposition (signed in Islamabad, **Pakistan**), Niyozov and 26 other political prisoners were released. Between 1994 and 1997, he lived in Khujand and chaired a splinter group, the **Democratic Party of Tajikistan Almaty Platform**. In 1999, Niyozov was replaced by **Mahmadruzi Iskandarov** as party leader. He was a member of the **United Tajik Opposition** and the **Commission for National Reconciliation**.

NIZOMOV, MIRZOKHUJA (1947–). A major field commander of the **United Tajik Opposition** (UTO), Nizomov was born in Novobod village, Gharm nohiya. He studied physical education at the Dushanbe Pedagogical Institute, graduating in 1970. He graduated from the militia school in Cheboksary (**Russia**) in 1979. Joining the security forces in 1980, he rose to head of the Department of Internal Affairs in his native Gharm nohiya. During Tajikistan's **civil war**, he led 500 troops and headed the military headquarters of the UTO. Nizomov fled to **Afghanistan** in 1993 but soon returned to Tajikistan. He was one of the first UTO commanders to accept contacts with the government of **Emomali Rahmon**. In the summer of 1999, he was appointed chair of the State Committee for Customs but was unexpectedly dismissed in 2002.

NOHIYA. A Tajik term for a district, *nohiya* appeared in official use after Tajikistan gained its independence in the 1990s. It was introduced into official jargon with the 1994 **constitution** of the Republic of Tajikistan. It replaced the Russian term *rayon*. Nohiyas are urban districts in major cities such as **Dushanbe** and **Khujand** and administrative subdivisions in **veloyats**. *See also* ADMINISTRATIVE STRUCTURE.

NOHIYAS UNDER REPUBLICAN CONTROL (NRC). The Nohiyahoi Tobei Jumhuri, one of Tajikistan's four territorial administrative areas, is located in the central part of the country. The NRC is composed of 13 **nohiyas**, four cities, nine towns, and 91 rural **jamoats**. As of 2006, the population was 1.6 million, excluding the capital, **Dushanbe**. Unlike **veloyats**, the NRC is not united administratively. Each nohiya is directly subordinate to the central government in Dushanbe. Five NRC municipalities are administrated separately by city administrations: Dushanbe, **Norak, Vahdat**, Roghun, and **Tursunzoda**.

The NRC stretches over 28,000 square kilometers and includes the **Rasht valley**, formerly Qarategin, the main producer of apples, potatoes, and wheat in the country. During the 1930s and the 1940s, when the **Soviet Union** launched **cotton** production in the south of Tajikistan, thousands of people were forced to migrate to the southern **Vakhsh valley** to work in the cotton fields. These settlers and other internally displaced people from the city of **Gharm**, who moved south after the devastating 1949 earthquake, make up the Gharmi population in the **Khatlon** veloyat. The NRC also includes the **Hisor** valley, which has a large **Uzbek** population (45 percent). Hisor is one of the most economically developed areas of the country. The Tajik Aluminum Plant, **TALCO**, is situated in the Hisor valley. Hisor is famous for its historical sites, among them the Hisor fortress. During Tajikistan's **civil war**, armed bands from the Hisor valley supported the **Kulobi** faction and helped bring **Emomali Rahmon** to power; Gharmis sided with the **United Tajik Opposition**. *See also* ADMINISTRATIVE STRUCTURE.

NONFERROUS METALLURGY. Nonferrous metallurgy is Tajikistan's main **industry**. It generated 40 percent of the total industrial production in 2007. It includes aluminum production and mining and processing **gold**, **silver**, lead zinc, copper molybdenum, wolfram, and mercury. The Tajik Aluminum Plant, **TALCO**, which was built in 1975, is the biggest branch of this industry. TALCO's production capacity exceeds 517,000 tons of aluminum per year, making it the third largest plant of its kind in the world. Yet due to a combination of factors, including the absence of accessible raw materials and expensive, unreliable electricity supplies, the plant has never run at full capacity. *See also* BARQI TOJIK; CORRUPTION.

NORAK. Norak is the name of a city and a **nohiya** in the northern part of **Khatlon** veloyat. The construction of **Central Asia**'s biggest hydroelectric station on the **Vakhsh River** in 1960 stimulated rapid growth in Norak village and surrounding villages. Norak's economic importance facilitated the village's upgrading to city status in 1993. Norak is on the **Dushanbe-Kulob motor road**. In 1992–1993, opposition forces in Tajikistan's **civil war** tried to block this road, cutting supplies to Kulob. After a change of government in 1993, Norak and adjoining territories of the **Vahdat** nohiya were demarcated into a nohiya within the Khatlon veloyat. The population of the Norak nohiya is 41,300 (including 19,200 urban dwellers in Norak city), mostly **Tajiks**. The distance from Norak city to Dushanbe is 68 kilometers. The main occupations are in the electric power industry and **agriculture**, including **cotton** production and livestock breeding. *See also* POWER GENERATION.

NORTHERN ALLIANCE. Also known as the United Islamic Front for the Salvation of Afghanistan (*Shura-i Nazar*), the Northern Alliance was a **Tajik**-dominated, anti-**Taliban** coalition of commanders affiliated with **Ahmad Shah Massoud** in the 1994–2002 struggle against the Taliban regime in **Afghanistan**. The name Northern Alliance was created by **Pakistan**'s intelligence agency to highlight the fact that this coalition was made up of northern, non-Pushtun regional and tribal leaders, as opposed to the collection of Pushtun commanders in the southern and eastern regions. The Northern Alliance was nominally led by the exiled president and ethnic Tajik Burhanuddin Rabbani. The Taliban claimed that the Northern Alliance had hidden motives and were receiving help from **Iran**, **Russia**, and the **United States**. In September 2001, Massoud died from wounds suffered in a suicide bombing, allegedly carried out by al-Qaeda, the **terrorist** organization with close ties to the Taliban. Following al-Qaeda's 11 September 2001 attacks in the **United States**, the Northern Alliance forces received support from the international coalition that led to the end of the Taliban regime. In early 2002, the Northern Alliance ceased to exist. *See also* KHOS DEH PROTOCOL; TAJIKS OF AFGHANISTAN.

NURI, SAID ABDULLO (1946–2006). Also known as Mullo Abdullo and Abdullo Saidov, Nuri was one of the key oppositional leaders during Tajikistan's **civil war** in 1992–1997. He was the officially recognized **United Tajik Opposition** (UTO) leader who put his signature to the **General Agreement on the Establishment of Peace and National Accord** along with President **Emomali Rahmon**. Nuri was a pioneer of political **Islam** in Tajikistan and one of the founders of the **Islamic Renaissance Party of Tajikistan** (IRPT). He was born in Oshtiyon village in Sangvor (**Tavildara**) nohiya and moved with his relatives and other **Gharmi** companions to the Turkmenistan **sovkhoz** in the **Vakhsh valley** in the 1960s. After graduating from high school and special courses, he worked as an engineer in the Bureau of Technical Stocktaking. He received his religious training at home from his father and an unofficial mullah, Ishan Qari Muhammadjon Rustamov, also known as Mavlavi Hindustani. Nuri's religious stature grew, and in 1974 he formed the illegal Islamic educational organization Nahzati Islomi (Islamic Movement).

Nuri and 40 other Tajik Islamists were arrested by Tajik authorities in 1986 for distributing religious propaganda in **Qurghonteppa** and sentenced to 18 months in jail. Nuri spent his term in the prison in Komsomol'sk-na-Amure (Russian Far East). Soon after gaining his freedom in 1988, he became chief editor of the newspaper *Minbari Islom* (Islam's Pulpit). He played a leading role in the formation of the IRPT and became chair of the **Movement for Islamic Revival in Tajikistan** (MIRT) during his Afghan exile in 1993. In 1997, he was elected chair of the **Commission for National Reconciliation**. In 1999, he replaced **Muhammad Sharif Himmatzoda** as head of the IRPT. Before Nuri died in August 2006, he gave his blessing to **Muhiddin Kabiri** to become a chair of IRPT.

NUROBOD NOHIYA. Known as Komsomolobod in 1936–1997 and Darband in 1997–2007, this mountainous district is situated in the **Nohiyas under Republican Control**, northeast of **Dushanbe** in the Obi Khingou river basin. Nurobod district lies east of **Roghun nohiya**, south of **Vahdat** and **Rasht** nohiyas, and west of **Tavildara**. It borders the **Khatlon** veloyat to the south. The nohiya was formed in 1936 but was combined with the Gharm nohiya in 1963. Since 1965, it has become a separate nohiya, with a territory of 7,130 square kilometers, a population of about 100,000, mostly **Tajiks**, and seven **jamoats**. The district center is Darband (population 1,100). The distance from Darband to Dushanbe is 135 kilometers. Average January and July temperatures can reach –4°C and 24°C respectively. The annual rainfall is 400–800 millimeters in the lowlands and up to 1,600 millimeters in the mountains. Arable land amounts to 4,096 hectares. Nurobod is a non-**cotton** district. The main occupation is **agriculture**, including **grain** production and livestock breeding.

– O –

OFFICIAL MUSLIM CLERGY. Institutionalized **Islam** in Tajikistan is served and administered by the official Muslim clergy. Under Soviet rule, this group was subordinated to state agencies and endorsed state policies. Official Muslim clergy in Tajikistan was administered by the muftiyat based in Tashkent, the Muslim Spiritual Board of Central Asia and Kazakhstan. **Hoji Akbar Turajonzoda** was head (*qazi-kalon*) of the Tajikistan branch of the Central Asian muftiyat (1988–1993), and he achieved a degree of independence for the religious institutions from the state. However, following the outbreak of Tajikistan's **civil war** and the disintegration of the Central Asian muftiyat into national organizations, the official Muslim clergy in Tajikistan were officially reorganized as an independent muftiyat in 1993.

Official clerics, or **mullahs**, in Tajikistan serve in legally registered **mosques**. From 1993 to 1996, they were under the close supervision of the government-appointed muftiyat. Officially, the *imam khatibs* were chosen by the congregation, and the candidate they chose was confirmed by the muftiyat. But in practice, the muftiyat acted on the instructions of the authorities, and an unwanted **imam** would be quickly removed.

In 1996, Tajikistan's muftiyat was replaced by the *shoura* (council) of religious scholars, chaired by a **rais**. Usually official clerics (five or six in each mosque) have tertiary religious **education**. Together with **unofficial mullahs**, they perform religious rituals such as *nikoh* (marriage) and *janoza* (funeral service). Since 1993, the political involvement of the official clergy has been very limited. They are loyal to the state authorities and the principle of the separation of church and state. Official and unofficial mullahs are often criticized by the **Islamic Renaissance Party of Tajikistan** for corruption, incompetence in religious affairs, and immorality. *See also* MUFTI.

OIL AND GAS. Tajikistan's first oil was extracted in 1905 in **Konibodom**. In 1913, Tajikistan produced 9,700 tons of oil. In 1940, oil production amounted to 30,000 tons. Production was 181,000 tons in 1970 and 330,000 tons in 1980. In 1985, Tajikistan extracted 389,000 tons of oil and 309 million cubic meters of natural gas. In the 1990s, output declined to 26,000 tons of oil and 47 million cubic meters of gas. Total deposits of oil and gas in Tajikistan are estimated to be 113 million tons and 875 billion cubic meters respectively. About 81 percent of the deposits are in the southwest: **Hisor, Kulob, Qumsangir, Vose**, and **Shahritus**. The remainder are in northern Tajikistan: **Isfara** and Konibodom. The depth of deposits (4–8 kilometers) and lack of investment are the main factors hampering oil and gas production. *See also* FUEL INDUSTRY.

OKNO. The space monitoring station Okno (which means "window" in Russian) is located in **Norak** nohiya. The construction of this unique component of the space control system started in 1979 but stopped after the demise of the **Soviet Union** in 1991. The work resumed after the end of Tajikistan's **civil war** in the late 1990s, and the facility was put on test duty in July 2002. Okno became fully operational in 2004. Situated at a height of 2,200 meters above sea level, Okno takes advantage of the area's fine weather conditions and atmosphere. The facility has the capability to track satellites, spacecraft, and small pieces of space debris up to 40,000 kilometers from Earth. The complex was constructed as a military facility but also implements peaceful tasks.

In 2008–2009, Tajikistan and **Russia** reached agreement on the regulation of Tajikistan's debt to Russia. Russia agreed to write off

$242 million in Tajik debt and take unilateral control of the Okno mountaintop facility.

OLIMOV, MUZAFFAR (1954–). Born in **Isfara, Sughd veloyat,** Olimov studied history at the Tajik State University, graduating in 1976, and pursued postgraduate courses at the Institute of Oriental Studies and the Academy of Sciences of the Union of Soviet Socialist Republics (Moscow), receiving his doctorate in history in 1994. In 1976–1984 and 1986–1993, Olimov was a research fellow at the Institute of Oriental Studies, **Academy of Sciences of Tajikistan.** In 1993–1998, he served as a department head, deputy director of science, and senior research fellow at the Institute of World Economy and International Relations at the Academy of Sciences. In 1995, Olimov was a professor of history and chair of world history at the Tajik State University and director of the Information and Analytical Center, Sharq. Olimov has specialized in the history of Sind in the 17th–19th centuries and in the ethno-political and religious makeup of Tajikistan.

OPERA AND BALLET THEATER. The Academic Opera and Ballet Theater named after **Sadriddin Ayni** is a leading musical theater in Tajikistan. It was established in Stalinobod (**Dushanbe**) in 1940 on the basis of the Tajik musical theater founded in 1936. The first Tajik ballet, *Du Gul* (Two Roses) was staged in 1941 by the eminent Russian choreographer Kasyan Goleizovsky. The music was composed by Alexander Lensky. In the spring of 1941, the theater participated in the Decade of Tajik Art in Moscow. It brought to Moscow the first Tajik operas—*Vose Rebellion* and *Kova the Smith* by Sergey Balasanyan (an Armenian) and a musical performance, *Lola*, by S. Balasanyan and S. Urbach.

From 1944 to the 1960s, several more new Tajik operas were staged, including *Takhir and Zuhra* (1944), *The Bride* (1946), *Pulat and Gulru* (1957) by Sharofiddin Saifiddinov (a Tajik from **Khujand**), and *Komde and Madan* (1960) by **Ziyodullo Shahidi** (a Tajik from **Samarqand**). In the 1950s and 1960s, the theater was joined by a new generation of professional Tajik singers, ballet dancers, choreographers, musicians, composers, and conductors who graduated from the Moscow Conservatory and from the Leningrad School of Choreography. The first national professional choreographers were

Ghaffor Valamatzadeh and Aziza Azimova, who started their work in the theater in 1951. Among Tajik ballet dancers, the most famous was Malika Sabirova (1942–1982). In 1969, Sabirova won a gold medal in an international ballet competition in Varna (Bulgaria).

From 1944 to 1992, the theater regularly staged Russian and European classical operas in Russian and **Tajik**. The ballet troop performed classical and Soviet ballets. During Tajikistan's **civil war**, many professional musicians, dancers, composers, and singers left the country. Since the demise of the **Soviet Union**, the repertoire of the theater has gotten poorer, and the orchestra and ballet troop are considerably smaller. There were only 13 dancers in the ballet troop of the theater in 2008. The reasons were outmigration, lack of financial resources, and decline of popular interest in opera and ballet in Tajikistan. *See also* ARTS; MUSIC.

OQILOV, OQIL (1944–). A Tajik prime minister, Oqilov (or Akilov) was born in **Khujand**. He graduated from the Moscow Institute for Engineering and Construction in 1967. Between 1960 and 1976, he worked at different engineering posts in the **Sughd veloyat**. From 1976 to 1993, he worked for the **Communist Party of Tajikistan**. He was appointed minister of construction in 1993. In 1994–1996, he acted as Tajikistan's vice premier. Oqilov returned to his native land as first deputy chair of the Sughd veloyat in June 1996. He was appointed prime minister of Tajikistan in December 1999.

ORGANIZATION FOR SECURITY AND COOPERATION IN EUROPE (OSCE). The OSCE, known before 1995 as the Conference on Security and Cooperation in Europe (CSCE), was joined by Tajikistan in February 1992. The OSCE Mission to Tajikistan was established on 1 December 1994, during Tajikistan's **civil war**. The OSCE and the Organization of the Islamic Conference (OIC) were observers at the **Inter-Tajik Peace Talks** in 1994–1997. In 1997–2000, the OSCE assisted with implementing the peace process, which culminated in Tajikistan's multiparty parliamentary **elections** in early 2000. As one of the guarantors of the **General Agreement on the Establishment of Peace and National Accord**, the OSCE was a key collaborator with the **United Nations** (UN) in Tajikistan. From 1997 to 2001, the OSCE promoted the development of democratic institutions, including organizing elections, helping to develop a new **constitution**, and monitoring **human rights**. It also supported Tajik authorities, helping them to return and reintegrate former combatants into society. In late 2002, the mandate of the OSCE Mission changed and it was renamed the OSCE Center in Dushanbe. In 2009, the center had 87 staff members, of whom 70 were Tajik nationals. The center's five field offices made up the largest OSCE presence in **Central Asia** in terms of personnel.

OSH. A main dish at dinner or lunch, *osh*, also known as *palov* (pilaf), is made of roasted meat, onions, and carrots steamed in bouillon and accompanied with seasoned rice. It is served at **tuis, khatmul qurons**, and other occasions. *See also* OSHI OSHTI.

OSHI OSHTI. A meal of reconciliation, an Oshi Oshti is a traditional ceremonial practice to signify the resolution of conflict between protagonists. In the spring and fall of 1992, two Oshi Oshti ceremonies were held in **Khorugh** and **Khujand** with the leaders of **Badakhshon, Kulob**, and Khujand to declare peace during Tajikistan's **civil war**, but the agreements were soon broken.

OVOZI TOJIK (TAJIK VOICE). A central **Tajik**-language newspaper in **Uzbekistan**, *Ovozi Tojik* was first published in **Samarqand** in 1924–1938 and then moved to Tashkent in 1950. Its first issue, under the name *Ovozi Tojiki Kambaghal* (Voice of the Poor Tajik), was published on 25 August 1924. This newspaper was an organ of the **Turkistan Communist Party**. On 10 December 1924, it became an organ of the Tajik Bureau of the Communist Party of Uzbekistan and the revolutionary committee of the **Tajik Autonomous Soviet Socialist Republic**. In June 1925, the paper became a joint organ of the Uzbekistan Communist Party and the government of Uzbekistan. In January 1931, the paper was renamed *Haqiqati Uzbekiston* (Truth of Uzbekistan), but it was suspended between 1938 and 1950. On 5 March 1950, the newspaper was reopened in Tashkent under the title *Uzbekistoni Surkh* (Red Uzbekistan). In 1964, the paper was again renamed, this time *Haqiqati Uzbekiston*, a title it retained until 1991. In 1991, the paper reverted to the name *Ovozi Tojik*.

Many Tajik writers and scholars wrote for the paper, among them **Sadriddin Ayni, Abulqasem Lahuti, Jalol Ikromi**, Sotim Ulighzoda, and **Bobojon Ghafurov**. A primary task of *Ovozi Tojik* was communist propaganda, but it also contributed to the development of Tajik **education**, teaching material on Tajik **literature**, and simplification of the Tajik **language**. *See also* MASS MEDIA.

– P –

PAKISTAN. The Islamic Republic of Pakistan was formed in 1947 as a result of the struggle by Muslims of the South Asian subcontinent for a separate homeland. With a population of 148 million, 35 percent of whom live below the poverty line, Pakistan is the sixth most populous country and the second largest Muslim population in the world. Geographically and culturally, Tajikistan is the closest Central Asian state to Pakistan; only a 15-kilometers-wide strip of high-altitude territory in **Afghanistan** separates the Tajik **Pamirs** from Pakistan. Karachi is the nearest port city for Tajikistan, and **Dushanbe** is only one hour's flight from Islamabad. Both nations share attachment to the unique Perso-Islamic culture of Muslim **India**. Sir Muhammad Iqbal (1877–1939), a great Muslim poet and the conceptual founder of Pakistan, said that Pakistan may be located in South Asia but that it faces toward **Central Asia**. In Tajikistan, Iqbal is revered as a national writer; in his poems written mostly in Persian rather than Urdu, he promoted ideas of greater Islamic political cooperation and unity, calling for the shedding of nationalist differences.

Pakistan is a nuclear power that has enormous potential and a growing **economy**. However, given the influence of **Russia, China,** and India in Central Asia, Pakistan appears less important and weaker than it actually is. Pakistan views Tajikistan in terms of its "strategic depth" policy, which aims to counterbalance India's influence in the region by strengthening economic, diplomatic, and military relations with Afghanistan and the wider Central Asia. Pakistan also wants Tajikistan and its Muslim-majority neighbors to regard Pakistan as a powerful Islamic leader in the region. With its limited energy resources, Pakistan is also eager to secure trade access to the hydrocarbon-rich Central Asia.

On 6 June 1992, Tajikistan and Pakistan established diplomatic relations. Pakistan's involvement in Tajikistan's **civil war** is unclear, but it is rarely viewed as a major player. Yet Pakistan was an official observer of the Inter-Tajik negotiations, and Islamabad hosted the third round of the **Inter-Tajik Peace Talks** in October–November 1994. At that meeting, the personal commitment of Pakistan's foreign minister, Asef Ali, made it possible to extend the cease-fire agreement. Groups based in Pakistan may have supplied weapons and other support to the Tajik opposition, perhaps with the involvement of government officials, but no firm evidence is available. Also Pakistan provided a shelter for a number of the **United Tajik Opposition** (UTO) members.

Until the early 2000s, relations between Pakistan and Tajikistan were not quite amicable. In the course of the 1980s and 1990s, the countries supported rival players in Afghanistan. Pakistan, which has an immense Pushtun minority, wanted Afghanistan to be controlled by a Pushtun-centered religious party malleable to Pakistan. Backed by the **United States**, the Pakistan army supported Afghan groups fighting against the Soviet Army in the 1980s. In 1994, Pakistan fostered the **Taliban** movement and helped them conquer almost all of Afghanistan by 1998. Tajikistan and Russia supported the **Northern Alliance**, which eventually helped to overthrow the Taliban regime in late 2001. In early 2002, after the ousting of the Taliban, the situation changed. Pakistan and Tajikistan both expressed their willingness to help the Afghan leader Hamid Karzai to extend peace and security throughout Afghanistan. Nevertheless, the Taliban and **Islamic Movement of Uzbekistan** still have their bases in Pakistan. Islamabad's inclination to use radical movements as a tool to boost its security creates a serious impediment for trust-building between the two states.

Tajikistan opened an embassy in Islamabad in February 2005. Pakistan and Tajikistan are member states of the **Economic Cooperation Organization** (ECO), and Pakistan is an observer in the **Shanghai Cooperation Organization** (SCO). Both governments have signed about 20 agreements, protocols, and memorandums of understanding to extend cooperation in energy, communications, insurance, investments and **industry**, air transport, banking and finance, **agriculture** and food industries, transport and road construction, science and technology, **education, health**, and tourism. Pakistan is interested in purchasing energy from Tajikistan and is ready to make investments in Tajik hydroenergy projects. Tajikistan is in need of access to Pakistani ports via the **Murghob-Kulma** road that connects Tajikistan with the trans-Asian **Karakoram Highway**. *See also* FOREIGN POLICY; GREATER CENTRAL ASIA.

PALOV. *See* OSH.

PAMIR. In the high-altitude region of southeast Tajikistan known as Pamir, or the Pamirs, several Central Asian mountain ranges emerge, namely the Hindu Kush, the **Karakoram**, the Kunlun, and the Tien Shan. Pamir extends into **Afghanistan, China, Pakistan,** and **Kyrgyzstan,** but most of this mountainous region lies within eastern Tajikistan. At the core of Pamir is the short Academy of Sciences mountain range (nearly 108 kilometers). Four mountain ranges—the Peter the Great, **Darvoz, Vanj,** and **Yazghulam**—separate from the Academy of Sciences range. The higher elevations feature glaciers.

With an altitude of about 6,100 meters, Western Pamir is characterized by narrow mountain ranges, sharp peaks covered with snowdrifts, and deep, turbulent river canyons. In Eastern Pamir, with altitudes of 5,000–5,500 meters, there are many vast valleys, quiet rivers, and relatively low mountain ranges, about 1,000–1,500 meters. To the north of Pamir lies the Zaalai (Trans-Alai) range (length 92 kilometers), which descends to the Alai valley. Zaalai's apex is the Lenin Peak (7,134 meters). The highest point in Pamir is the **Samanids** Peak (7,495 meters). The **Pamir Highway** connects **Khorugh** in the **Mountainous Badakhshon Autonomous Veloyat** with Kyrgyzstan. The **Sarikol** range (reaching 5,909 meters) in the eastern part of Pamir extends along the **China-Tajik border**. *See also* TAJIKS OF CHINA.

PAMIR HIGHWAY. The second (after **Karakoram**) highest **motor road** in the world, the **Pamir** Highway, part of the M41 highway, runs from **Dushanbe** east through **Khorugh** and **Murghob** in the **Mountainous Badakhshon Autonomous Veloyat** and ends at Osh, **Kyrgyzstan.** With a length of 710 kilometers, the Pamir Highway was built in 1931–1934. Its highest point is the Aq Baital Pass (4,655 meters above sea level). *See also* KULMA PASS.

PAMIRIAN BOTANICAL GARDEN. Situated in **Shughnon nohiya, Badakhshon,** 6 kilometers southeast of **Khorugh,** the Pamirian Botanical Garden opened in 1940 at the initiative of Anatoliy Gurskiy, who headed the garden from 1940 until his death in 1966. Of the total area of 612 hectares, 50 hectares are irrigated. Nearly 2,300 kinds of flora from **Central Asia,** East Asia, Europe, America, and other regions are grown. The garden has introduced 140 fruit plants and vegetables, more than 30 trees and bushes, and 55 kinds of meadow plants and herbs to the alpine conditions of **Pamir**. It has reciprocal relations with nearly 100 botanical gardens worldwide. *See also* ACADEMY OF SCIENCES OF TAJIKISTAN.

PAMIRIAN LANGUAGES. The Pamirian languages are East Iranian languages spoken in western and southern **Pamir**. Pamirian speakers include the **Shughnis** (some 80,000), Rushanis (20,000), **Vakhanis** (12,000–14,000), Bartangis (6,000), **Yazghulamis** (4,000), **Ishkashimis**, **Munjis**, Khufis, Sanglichis, Roshorvis (1,000–2,000 each), and others with approximately 150,000 living primarily in the **Mountainous Badakhshon Autonomous Veloyat** (MBAV) but also in **Afghanistan, China (Sarikol)**, and **Pakistan**. The different Pamirian languages are not mutually intelligible. For that reason, speakers of these vernaculars use **Tajik** in Tajikistan, Uighur in China, and Urdu in Pakistan as their lingua franca. The Pamirian languages have not been produced in writing, though there have been attempts to introduce Pamirian language teaching in local schools in the MBAV.

PANJ. The Panj nohiya and the city of Panj are located in the southern part of **Khatlon** veloyat, **Qurghonteppa** zone, bordering **Afghanistan**. The nohiya was established in 1930 as an administrative subdivision of Kulob veloyat. In 1998, the population of the Panj nohiya was 81,900 (9,100 urban dwellers), **Tajiks** and **Uzbeks**, living in five **jamoats** and one city. The territory of the nohiya is 880 square kilometers. The climate is dry subtropical. Average January and July temperatures are 0°C and 30°C respectively, and the annual precipitation is 200–500 millimeters. The main occupation is **cotton** production and cattle breeding. The city of Panj is linked by motorway to **Dushanbe** (206 kilometers), Kulob (123 kilometers), and Qurghonteppa (107 kilometers).

PANJ RIVER. *See* AMU DARYA.

PANJAKENT. Located in **Panjakent nohiya**, Panjakent was one of the prosperous cities of pre-**Arab Central Asia** and a major provincial capital of **Sogdiana**. The Divashtich monarch in Panjakent resisted the Arab invasion in 720–722, but his forces were overrun and the city was destroyed. In the 15th century, the city of Panjakent was rebuilt. The **Academy of Sciences of Tajikistan** conducts an ongoing archeology project in Panjakent.

PANJAKENT NOHIYA. Located in the **Sughd veloyat**, in the **Zarafshon** valley, Panjakent nohiya borders **Uzbekistan**. The nohiya was established in 1930. It is 3,670 square kilometers, with a population of more than 163,800, mostly **Tajiks** and **Uzbeks**, living in 14 **jamoats**. The center of this district is the city of **Panjakent**. The district is linked with the rest of the country by **motor road**. The distance from Panjakent to **Dushanbe** is 270 kilometers, to **Khujand** 282 kilometers, and to **Samarqand** 68 kilometers. Average January and July temperatures can reach –5°C and 30°C respectively. The average annual precipitation is 500–700 millimeters. Total arable land amounts to 22,218 hectares. The main occupation is **agriculture**, including tobacco, **grain**, rice, vegetables, and fruits. Panjakent produces 74 percent of the country's tobacco. Canned-food factories and tobacco production constitute the main industries. The famous Persian poet **Abuabdullo Rudaki** (858–941) was born in Panj Rud village near Panjakent city.

PARLIAMENT. *See* MAJLISI MELLI; MAJLISI NAMOYAN-DAGON; MAJLISI OLI; SUPREME SOVIET.

PARTY OF ECONOMIC REFORMS OF TAJIKISTAN (PERT). One of the eight registered **political parties** of Tajikistan, PERT has some 1,000 members. The party was formed in 2005 and registered without difficulty on 9 November 2005. It is headed by Olim Boboev, who won 6.2 percent of the votes in the **presidential elections of 2006**. Some experts call PERT a satellite of the ruling **People's Democratic Party of Tajikistan** (PDPT). The PERT chair is a rector of the Tajik Institute of Transport and therefore a government official directly subordinate to the president of Tajikistan. According to Tajik law, all rectors are appointed by the president.

PARTY OF THE NATIONAL MOVEMENT OF TAJIKISTAN (PNMT). Originating in November 1996 as the National Movement of Tajikistan, the PNMT held its inaugural congress on 27 February 1999. However, the party was not registered with the Ministry of

Justice. In August 1997, the party established the weekly *Junbesh* newspaper, published in **Tajik** and Russian. The PNMT favored a secular state and deplored "the use of religion to instigate national discord, ideological intolerance, hostility, and hatred between adherents of different confessions." The party was chaired by Hakim Muhabbatov. In October 1999, on the eve of the presidential election, the *Junbesh* weekly was banned, and by the end of the year the PNMT ceased to exist. *See also* POLITICAL PARTIES.

PARTY OF PEOPLE'S UNITY (PPU). Known as Hizbi Yagonagii Khalqi in **Tajik**, the PPU was formed in **Khujand** on 30 November 1994 and was registered on 16 December with a membership of 895. The PPU is popularly known as the party of **Abdumalik Abdullojonov**, its founder and chair. It has branches in **Sughd veloyat**, the **Mountainous Badakhshon Autonomous Veloyat** (MBAV), and **Dushanbe**, as well as in Somoni, **Tursunzoda**, and Shahrinav **nohiyas**. The PPU participated in the **Societal Council** and signed the **Agreement on National Accord** in 1996. But following an assassination attempt against President **Emomali Rahmon** in April 1997 and an armed uprising by a renegade general in November 1998, the PPT was banned in December 1998 due to the alleged involvement of its chair. *See also* POLITICAL PARTIES.

PARTY OF POLITICAL AND ECONOMIC REGENERATION OF TAJIKISTAN (PPERT). A small opposition party known as Hizbi Ehyoi Siyosi va Iqtisodii Tojikiston in **Tajik**, the PPERT was formed on 6 September 1993 in Chkalovsk, **Sughd veloyat**, and was registered with the Ministry of Justice on 5 April 1994 with a membership of 556. In 1993, Mukhtor Boboev, president of the Asian-American AAA company, was elected chair of the PPERT. After he was assassinated in 1996, his brother, Valijon Boboev, became president of the AAA company and chair of the party. In March 1996, the PPERT entered the **Agreement on National Accord** and joined the **Societal Council**. In April 1998, the PPERT withdrew from the National Accord and joined the **United Tajik Opposition** (UTO). In August 1998, Valijon Boboev was elected representative of the UTO to Sughd veloyat. In November 1998, the government refused PPERT's application for the renewal of its registration. *See also* POLITICAL PARTIES.

PEOPLE'S DEMOCRATIC PARTY OF TAJIKISTAN (PDPT).
Known as Hizbi Khalqi-Demokratii Tojikiston in **Tajik**, the PDPT is
Tajikistan's ruling **political party**. The party was formed on 10 December 1994 and registered with the Ministry of Justice within five
days. It was initially known as the People's Party of Tajikistan, but
at its third congress (25 June 1997), "Democratic" was added to the
title. The party membership is about 102,000. **Abdulmajid Dostiev**
headed the party from its inception until March 1998, when President
Emomali Rahmon formally joined it and was elected chair.

The organization of the PDPT resembles that of the **Communist
Party of Tajikistan**. The supreme organ of the party is its congress,
which should convene at least once every five years. The congress
is elected by members in primary cells, which operate in all regions,
and it in turn elects a **central executive committee** to manage the
party's daily affairs. The party launched the monthly magazine
Minbari Khalq (People's Platform) in Tajik, Uzbek, and Russian in
September 1996. The party is a founding member of the **Societal
Council** and the **Movement for National Unity and Revival in
Tajikistan**. It signed the **Agreement on National Accord** in March
1996. Five members of the PDPT were elected to the **Majlisi Oli** in
1995, and the party chair, the incumbent President Emomali Rahmon, was elected president in **presidential elections** of 1999 and
2006. In the 2005–2010 **Majlisi Namoyandagon**, the PDPT held 52
of the 63 seats.

The PDPT considers itself a centrist, parliamentary **political
party**, with the stated objective of "uniting all citizens of Tajikistan,
regardless of language, ethnic affinity, social status, or political
beliefs," and it supports "the establishment of the rule of law and a
sovereign, democratic, and secular state."

PEOPLE'S UPRISING IN CENTRAL ASIA IN 1916. The cause of
the uprising that enveloped most of **Central Asia** in 1916 was the
tsarist decision to mobilize non-Russian males age 19–43 in Siberia
and Central Asia to serve in the Russian army in World War I. The
revolt began in the summer of 1916 in **Khujand** and soon spread to
the rest of the country. The uprising was initially directed at local
authorities responsible for registering prospective conscripts, but it
soon developed into an anti-Russian revolt with nationalist under-
tones. The uprising was put down by the Russian army.

PIR. A *pir* is an elder, chief, holy man, clergy, or founder or head of a religious sect. *See also* ISLAM.

PO BASMACHU. The first newspaper published in Tajikistan, *Po Basmachu* (Against a Basmach) was established in 1923. It was an organ of the Red Army's 13th Infantry Regiment, published in Russian in **Dushanbe**. The newspaper reflected the Soviet regime's campaign against the **Basmachi** movement. Only a few issues were published. *See also* MASS MEDIA.

POLITICAL PARTIES. The first political party that appeared in Tajikistan was the Russian Social Democratic Party (RSDP) formed in 1900, when the area was part of tsarist **Russia**. Three years later, a split occurred within the party, resulting in the formation of the Bolshevik and Menshevik factions. The Bolshevik faction, led by Vladimir Lenin and formally called the RSDP (B), advocated a proletarian revolution and dictatorship by the proletariat. Between 1903–1905, the Bolshevik newspaper *Iskra* (Spark) found its way to the barracks of Russian soldiers stationed on the Afghan border. RSDP (B) party cells were formed in the region's industrial centers (mostly **Ferghana**, Tashkent, and **Khujand**), as well as along **railway** lines. The Russo-Japanese War and the revolution in 1904–1905 awakened some Bukharan and Turkistani intellectuals, who by 1917 joined the **Jadidia** movement.

The period between the fall of tsarism in Russia in February 1917 and the Bolshevik coup in October 1917 was the most pluralistic in the modern political history of Russia and its Central Asian colonies. During this time, central power in Russia was held by the Provisional Government, which was itself a coalition of various political parties. In March 1917, the **Young Bukharan Party** was formed by the Jadids in **Bukhara**. Concurrently, the **Shuroi Islomiya** and **Jamiyati Ulamo**, the first political organizations of Central Asian Muslims to take part in a democratic electoral process, appeared in **Turkistan**.

In November 1918, the Bolshevik takeover came to Tashkent, the center of Russian administration in **Central Asia**. The Tashkent Bolsheviks marginalized and defeated their rivals, including the Social Democrats (Mensheviks), the Constitutional Democrats (Kadets), and the Left Social Revolutionaries (Left SRs). The short-lived Shuroi Islomiya and Jamiyati Ulamo had already been marginalized at the end of 1917. Some of the Jadids managed to survive, however. In 1918, the Young Bukharan Party reached an agreement with the Russian Bolsheviks, and the **Communist Party of Bukhara** (CPB) was formed and charged with preparing the ground for a "people's revolution" in Bukhara. In the **Turkistan Soviet Socialist Republic** (TSSR), which was a member of the Russian Soviet Federated Socialist Republic (RSFSR), the **Turkistan Communist Party** (TCP) functioned during 1918–1924. The northern part of Tajikistan (currently **Sughd veloyat**) was part of the TSSR, and **Abdullo Rahimboyev**, from Khujand, was the secretary in charge of the CPT in 1920–1921. In February 1922, when General **Enver Pasha** invigorated the **Basmachi** movement in **Eastern Bukhara**, the Political Bureau (Politburo) of the Central Committee of the Russian Communist Party (Bolsheviks) decided to incorporate the CPB, thus putting a de facto end to the independent party of Bukharan reformers. From that time, Tajik politics was put under the strict control of the RCP (B).

The Union of Soviet Socialist Republics (USSR), or **Soviet Union**, was officially established in 1922. During the national delimitation of Central Asia in December 1924, the Communist Party of Bukhara and the Communist Party of Turkistan were dissolved, and five national communist parties were founded instead. Among them was the **Communist Party of Tajikistan** (CPT). From 1925 to 1929, Tajikistan was an autonomous republic within **Uzbekistan**, and its communist organization was subordinated to the Communist Party of Uzbekistan (Bolsheviks). In 1929, the CPT became part of the All-Soviet Communist Party (Bolsheviks). In 1952, the All-Soviet Communist Party (Bolsheviks) was renamed the Communist Party of the Soviet Union (CPSU). The CPSU exercised all effective power within the Soviet Union and was led by its Politburo, a group of mostly older Russian men.

The late Soviet period from the mid-1980s to December 1991, known as perestroika, was the most tolerant and politically relaxed period in Soviet history, though it ultimately led to the collapse of the USSR. A number of parties and organizations emerged in this period and were active through Tajikistan's **civil war** in 1992–1997. One was the popular movement **Rastokhez**, founded by young secular Tajik nationalists in September 1989. The **Democratic Party of Tajikistan** (DPT), the first opposition party in the country, was formed on 10 August 1990 by local intelligentsia. Rastokhez, the DPT, various discussion clubs, and other civic movements and associations were supported by Moscow democrats and anticommunist reformers. Tens of thousands of the Tajik members of the CPSU discontinued their party membership.

Perestroika also marked a rapid rise of political **Islam** in Tajikistan. Under the immediate influence of the Islamic revolution in **Iran** in 1979 and the Soviet-Afghan war in 1979–1989, the **Islamic Renaissance Party of Tajikistan** (IRPT) was created by an underground group of young Tajik Islamists on 6 October 1990. The national organization of **Pamiris, La'li Badakhshon**, was formed on 4 March 1991. This organization joined with Rastokhez, the DPT, and the IRPT to form an opposition coalition, called *mukholifin* in Tajik, in September 1991. The *mukholifin*, with the Islamists playing the leading role, were very visible and active during the mass demonstrations in the spring of 1992 in **Dushanbe** that led to violence in the southern and central parts of the country.

In the ensuing civil war, the nascent political debate was overwhelmed by the apolitical, regional confrontation of local post-communist power brokers who allied with the newly arisen amateur and criminal "people's generals" and field commanders. During the war, all Tajik political parties, including the Communist Party, lost connections with their electorate, and many political leaders joined the regional factions struggling for central power. Yet some political contexts remained intact during the war. The **Kulobi** and Leninobodi (Khujand) factions did not resist being viewed as a pro-communist, secular party confronting the "false democrats" and "radical Islamists." With the backing of Uzbekistan and Russia, the Kulobi faction was victorious in November 1992, but the war lasted into 1997. During the war, most *mukholifin* leaders went into exile and their parties were forbidden. The IRPT, DPT, La'li Badakhshon and some smaller parties formed the **United Tajik Opposition** (UTO) in June 1993 and entered the **Inter-Tajik Peace Talks** in April 1994 as a common opposition bloc.

Article 8 of the **constitution** adopted in November 1994 states: "In Tajikistan, public life is to develop on the basis of political and ideological diversity. No ideology, including religious ideology, is granted the status of state ideology." According to the Law on Public Associations adopted in May 1998, "Establishment and operation of public associations advocating racial, national, social and religious enmity or inciting a violent overthrow of the constitutional order or organization of military groups shall be prohibited." The Law on Political Parties of November 1998 asserts that "only country-wide political parties can be created" and are to be established "freely at the founding convention (conference, meeting) where the charter is adopted and the party's governing bodies are formed." To be officially registered as a political party, an organization must present a list with 1,000 or more names of party supporters.

A multiparty system started to form during the peace talks and the implementation of the provisions of the **General Agreement on the Establishment of Peace and National Accord** signed in June 1997. The **Party of Political and Economic Regeneration of Tajikistan** (PPERT) was formed on 6 September 1993 in the northern **Sughd veloyat** and was registered with the Ministry of Justice on 5 April 1994. On 10 December 1994, the **People's Democratic Party of Tajikistan** (PDPT) was formed. It has been the largest political party, chaired from March 1998 by President **Emomali Rahmon**. Among the minor parties that appeared in the course of the peace process were the **Socialist Party of Tajikistan** (SPT), founded by one of the key wartime leaders from the Sughd veloyat, **Safarali Kenjaev**, on 15 June 1996, and the **Adolatkhoh Party of Justice** (APJ), formed in **Konibodom**, Sughd veloyat, on 15 November 1995 and registered on March 1996. **Ittihod: Civil-Patriotic Party of Tajikistan** (ICPPT), a small party, was formed on 2 November 1994 and registered in April 1995. One more minor Tajik party, the **Agrarian Party of Tajikistan** (APT), was formed in July 1998 and registered in January 1999. The **Social-Democratic Party of Tajikistan** (SDPT) was formed in March 1998 by **Rahmatulloh Zoirov**, a liberal lawyer who was not involved in the war and has no regional support within Tajikistan. President Rahmon's main rival, **Abdumalik Abdullojonov**, formed the **Party of People's Unity** (PPU) in his native Khujand in November 1994. The party was registered on 16 December 1994. The PPU was banned in November 1998 for alleged involvement of its chair in an assassination attempt against the president of Tajikistan and an armed uprising by colonel **Mahmud Khudoiberdyev**. The **Party of the National Movement of Tajikistan** (PNMT) was formed in November 1996 but was not registered with the Ministry of Justice.

On the eve of the 2000 parliamentary **elections,** the first multiparty elections in the history of the country, the government started excluding some parties from the electoral process. In addition, party leaders Mukhtor Boboev (PPERT) and Safarali Kenjaev (SPT) were assassinated in 1996 and 1999 respectively. In 1998–1999, the PNMT, PPERT, APT, SDPT, and Ittihod were suspended and their applications for the renewal of their registration refused by the government. Lack of experience among the newest political parties served as an additional impediment to the development of political pluralism and a multiparty system in Tajikistan. As far as the major wartime opposition political parties are concerned, all of them managed to preserve their status. In November 1998, under the pressure of the international sponsors of the Tajik peace process, the constitutional clause that did not allow religious parties to act was amended, and in August 1999 the IRPT was registered. The DPT, banned by the Supreme Court on 21 June 1993, split in 1995. The faction known as the **Democratic Party of Tajikistan Tehran Platform** was registered in July 1995. The **Democratic Party of Tajikistan Almaty Platform,** which represented the DPT in the peace talks in 1994–1997 and was part of UTO, was registered in December 1999. This divide had more to do with geography than with ideology. It occurred mostly because the democrats were in exile since 1993, mostly in **Iran,** Russia, Kazakhstan, and **Kyrgyzstan.** While in exile, they formed two groups: one in Almaty and another in Tehran. After a peace accord was signed in June 1997, most of them returned to Tajikistan. In 1999, the members of both wings of the DPT reunited and elected **Mahmadruzi Iskandarov** chair. In December 1999, the Ministry of Justice lifted a ban on the activity of the DPT.

In the February 2000 parliamentary elections, only six out of 10 Tajik parties were registered by the Ministry of Justice and included in the list by the Central Commission for Elections and Referenda. These six parties—the PDPT (21 candidates on the party list), CPT (20 candidates), IRPT (15 candidates), DPT (19 candidates), Adolatkhoh Party of Justice (15 candidates), and SPT (18 candidates)—competed for 22 seats in the lower chamber, the **Majlisi Namoyandagon.** Tajikistan's electoral system represents a combination of the single-member constituency (41 seats) and proportional representation systems (22 seats). The official results of the party lists were PDPT 15 seats, CPT five seats, IRPT two seats. The results from the single-member and party lists gave an absolute majority to the People's Democratic Party of Tajikistan, 36 seats. The Communist Party was represented by 13 deputies and the IRPT by two. The remaining 18 deputies were elected as independent, self-nominated candidates. Four opposition parties, including those that failed to surpass the 5 percent threshold, accused the authorities of violating the law and stated that they did not recognize the election results.

In 2004, after being refused registration, the Adolatkhoh Party of Justice stopped its activities. In 2005, the split of the Socialist Party into two factions further weakened the SPT. At the end of 2005, a new party, the **Party of Economic Reforms of Tajikistan** (PERT) was registered, and the Agrarian Party of Tajikistan, which had been suspended in April 1999, was allowed to register.

Six political parties were registered and allowed to take part in the February 2005 parliamentary elections, including the People's Democrats, Communists, Islamists, Democrats, Socialists, and for the first time, the Social Democrats. The PDPT won 52 seats. The remaining seats were divided between the Communists (four seats), Islamists (two seats), and five independents, considered by many to be supporters of the president.

Four political parties nominated candidates for the November 2006 **presidential election**. Olimjon Boboev of the PERT won 6.2 percent of the votes; Amir Karakulov, a chair of the APT, received 5.3 percent; Ismoil Talbakov, a Communist, won 5.1 percent; and Abdualim Ghafforov, a Socialist, received 2.8 percent.

Tajikistan is a one-party-dominated state. The PDPT's chair, Emomali Rahmon, is the country's president, commander in chief of the armed forces, and chair of the security council. Virtually all other political parties remain outside of the political process. The president prefers coopting opponents instead of direct competition and open debate. Since his rule began in November 1992, he has never had meetings or discussions with the country's political party leaders and representatives.

As of early 2009, eight political parties are registered in Tajikistan. In addition to the ruling PDPT, there are two major parties: the Communists and the Islamists. Both have been represented in the parliament since 2000 and support President Rahmon on most issues. The Communists and Islamists have never thought of forming a united bloc due to their sharp ideological differences. Minor opposition parties with some influence include the DPT, SDPT, and SPT. The pro-governmental PERT and APT have no political weight. Tajik Democrats and Socialists refuse to cooperate with the Islamists and the Communists, tending instead to work and cooperate with each other. In March 2008, three opposition parties—the DPT, SDPT, and SPT—released a joint statement, "On the Critical Situation in Tajikistan and Ways out of It," but the IRPT and the Communist Party refused to sign the statement, while the PERT and APT ignored it.

POPULATION. The first systematic census covering **Central Asia** was conducted by the Russian administration in 1897, though Tajik-populated areas of the **Bukharan emirate** were not included. The first Soviet census in 1920 also overlooked most of Tajikistan. Quantitative data on Soviet nationalities, in which the categories of Tajikistan and Tajik ethnicity were included, can be found in the First All-Union Census of the **Soviet Union** in 1926. General Soviet censuses followed in 1937, 1939, 1959, 1970, and 1979. In 1989, the last Soviet census was conducted. In February 2000, Tajikistan carried out its first national census.

In general, the population of Tajikistan grew as a result of high birthrates and a sharp decline in mortality rates that started under Soviet rule. In 1989, the index of natural population growth in Tajikistan was the highest in the Soviet Union, exceeding the average rate by 5.6 times. The population of Tajikistan was more than 1 million (10 percent urban) in 1926, nearly 1.5 million (17 percent urban) in 1937, 5 million (33 percent urban) in 1989, 6 million (26.5 percent urban) in 2000, and more than 7 million in 2008.

In the last decade of the 20th century and in the first decade of the 21st century, population growth slowed. The birthrate decreased from 38.9 per 1,000 in 1991 to 21 per 1,000 in 2002–2008. In 1999, the average number of children born to a Tajik woman was 3.7, while in the middle of the 1970s this number was 6.3. The population's annual growth rate dropped from 2.9 percent in 1970–1990 to 1.4 percent in 1990–2006. In 2008, the fertility rate was 3.04 children born per woman. Infant mortality declined from 47 per 1,000 in 1993 to 31 per 1,000 in 1997. This improvement can probably be attributed to the end of the **civil war** and the decline in the number of children per woman. According to state statistics, life expectancy in Tajikistan declined from 70.5 years in 1991 to 66.1 years in 1994 and then rose to 68.4 years in 1998 and 70.6 years in 2005. The rise may be attributed to the end of the civil war. However, the United Nations Human Development Report claims that Tajikistan's life expectancy at birth was 66.3 years in 2005.

The average age of marriage in Tajikistan has traditionally been 20–24 for men and 20–21 for women. In 1991, 56,505 marriages were registered in Tajikistan, while in 1994 this number dropped to 38,820, and in 1997 to 28,836. This drop may be explained by the hard economic conditions in Tajikistan and a new registration fee for births, deaths, and marriages, which might have encouraged newlyweds to forgo official registration.

The 1989 and 2000 censuses indicate that Tajikistan's population grew despite human losses and outmigration of the non-Tajik population caused by the civil war. In the 1990s, emigration from Tajikistan reached 640,000 people, and about 50,000 Tajik men and women lost their lives. Nevertheless, the country's total population increased from 5 million to 6 million during this period. Another demographic feature worth mentioning is that since the fall of the Soviet Union, Tajikistan is becoming increasingly monoethnic. In 1989, ethnic Tajiks constituted 62.3 percent of the country's population, 69.1 percent in 1998, and 79.9 percent in 2000. The second biggest ethnic group, **Uzbek**, dropped from 23.5 percent of Tajikistan's total population in 1989 to 17 percent in 2000. Part of this drop results from the fact that groups such as the **Barlas, Laqais,** and **Qataghan** were recorded as Uzbeks by Soviet census takers but were registered as separate ethnic groups in the 2000 census. **Russians,** the third largest ethnic group in Tajikistan, decreased in number significantly, from 388,500 in 1989 to 68,200 in 2000.

One more important demographic trend is the remarkable decline of the urban population. Independent Tajikistan is the least urbanized republic of the former Soviet Union. In 1989, 32.5 percent of Tajikistanis lived in urban areas; in 2000, this figure decreased to 26.5 percent. The largest region of Tajikistan by population in 2000 was **Khatlon** veloyat, numbering 2 million people, including 373,900 urban dwellers (17.4 percent). In **Sughd**, a slightly less populated but more urbanized region of Tajikistan, the population is nearly 2 million, including 496,600 urban people (26.52 percent). In the **Nohiyas under Republican Control**, the population in 2000 was more than 1 million, including 166,200 urban people (12.43 percent). The population of **Mountainous Badakhshon Autonomous Veloyat** was 206,000, including 27,400 urban dwellers (13.3 percent).

Another tendency worth noting is the increase in the percentage of men in the population, from 49.7 percent in 1989 to 50.1 percent in 2000. In 2000, 42.7 percent of the population was under 14 years of age. The average size of a Tajik family in an urban area was 4.5 people, and 6.5 people in rural areas. The average density of the population in Tajikistan in 2008 was 50.4 persons per square kilometer, but this figure is misleading, since the majority of the population lives in valleys that constitute only 7 percent of Tajikistan's territory.

The number of people employed in 1998 was about 1.8 million, a 6.2 percent increase since 1992. During the same period, 59,000 people were unemployed and the official unemployment rate was 3.2 percent. The number of people employed in 2007 was 1.9 million. Of this number, 24.2 percent were employed by central and local government, state enterprises, and state farms. Some 22.9 percent worked in the public sector (publicly owned corporations, mostly **cooperative farms**) and 51.8 operated in the private sector. According to official data, in 2007, 67 percent of the population was engaged in **agriculture**, 25 percent in the service industry, and 8 percent in **industry** and construction. However, these official employment figures are not reliable. Many people employed in low-paid government institutions supplement their state salary with income from private business and commerce. With the practical collapse of the national **economy** and extensive unemployment, more than 1 million citizens can be classified as **labor migrants**, obtaining seasonal employment in Russia and other foreign countries.

POWER GENERATION. Since the 1930s, hydroelectric power stations have been the core of Tajikistan's power industry. The country's first power stations were constructed in the 1930s on the **Varzob** River. In 1956, Qairaqum power station on the **Syr Darya** River started to generate 126,000 kilowatt hours, servicing the whole country. In the 1960s, the Perepad, Golovnaiya, and Tsentralnaya stations were built on the **Vakhsh River**. In 1979, the **Norak** station, the biggest of its kind in **Central Asia**, started operating at full capacity, generating 2,700 megawatts. The Norak station, one of the world's 30 biggest power stations, has the highest embankment in the world: 300

meters. In the late 1980s, power generation in Tajikistan was 3,000 kilowatt hours per head, exceeding the European average rate. In the 1990s, the Baipazy station on the Vakhsh River was completed, and the Roghun, Sangtuda, and Shuroob stations were launched.

Since the 1990s, electric power generation is Tajikistan's second industry, after **nonferrous metallurgy**. It benefits from the abundance of hydroelectric energy resources and the effectiveness of electricity production. Electricity production in millions of kilowatt hours was 16,822 in 1992, 15,243 in 2002, and 17,500 in 2007. Despite extensive energy resources, however, the country has experienced energy deficits (up to 600 million kilowatt hours per year), which becomes a serious problem in the winter. Tajikistan meets its electricity needs by importing from neighboring Turkmenistan, **Uzbekistan**, and **Kyrgyzstan**.

The Tajik government intends to make Tajikistan a major exporter of hydropower in the region. To attract investors, the government transformed the Sangtuda station into the Sangtuda Joint Stock Company in 1996. An ambitious project is the Roghun hydroelectric station on the Vakhsh, which in 1999 needed $3 billion for its completion. With a capacity of 3,600 megawatts and an embankment of 350 meters, this station is expected to make Tajikistan the biggest exporter of electricity in the region.

Since 2004, Tajikistan has managed to attract **foreign investments** to its energy sector. **Russia, Iran, China,** Japan, the **United States,** some European states, and Kazakhstan expressed an interest in investing in Tajikistan's energy sector. When all projected hydropower plants are completed, the Roghun (3,600 megawatts), Sangtuda-1 (670 megawatts), Sangtuda-2 (220 megawatts) on the Vakhsh River, Zarafshan (150 megawatts) on the Zarafshon River, and the gigantic Dashtijum (4,000 megawatts) station on the Panj River will provide irrigation and power and will solve Tajikistan's energy problems. Exporting surplus energy to Russia, **Afghanistan, Pakistan,** China, and other neighboring countries will provide further economic benefits for Tajikistan. *See also* BARQI TOJIK; WATER.

PRESIDENTIAL ELECTIONS OF 1999. According to the **constitution** of the Republic of Tajikistan, citizens age 35–65 who speak **Tajik** and have lived in Tajikistan for no fewer than 10 years are eligible to be elected president of Tajikistan. Amendments to the constitution adopted in a general referendum on 26 September 1999 made the presidential term seven years and limited **presidents** to one term, but the limit on the number of terms was removed by referendum in 2003.

According to the electoral law, the presidential **elections** require the participation of more than half the registered voters in order to be valid. To win the presidential elections, a candidate's majority votes must be at least 50 percent of the participating electorate plus one vote. In the event that no candidate passes the 50 percent plus one vote threshold, a second round of voting becomes necessary.

The central electoral commission for the 1999 presidential elections was formed under directions from the **Majlisi Oli**, and it included members of the **United Tajik Opposition** (UTO). In the 1999 presidential elections, **Emomali Rahmon** was nominated by the **People's Democratic Party of Tajikistan**, **Davlat Usmon** by the **Islamic Renaissance Party of Tajikistan** (IRPT), Sulton Quvvatov by the **Democratic Party of Tajikistan Tehran Platform**, and **Saifiddin Turaev** by the **Adolatkhoh Party of Justice**.

Usmon, Quvvatov, and Turaev failed to collect the required 145,000 signatures (or 5 percent of the total number of registered voters) and were barred from entering the presidential race. On 8–9 October, they protested their exclusion, claiming that local authorities had prevented them from collecting signatures. Consequently, the UTO recalled its representatives from the **Commission for National Reconciliation** and the central electoral commission. But **Hoji Akbar Turajonzoda** rejected the UTO position and publicly supported Emomali Rahmon's candidacy. The central electoral commission later decided to allow Davlat Usmon's candidacy to proceed. Thus two candidates, Emomali Rahmon and Davlat Usmon, were listed on the ballots.

The central electoral commission organized 68 electoral districts and 2,700 polling stations. Polling stations were also established in Moscow, Minsk, Almaty, Ashkhabad, Bonn, and New York. According to official results, more than 2.8 million voters, 98.9 percent of the total eligible voters, took part in the presidential elections on 6 November 1999. Emomali Rahmon received 96.9 percent of the votes cast, while his opponent attracted only 2.1 percent. The regional breakdown was **Dushanbe** city, 95.2 percent for Rahmon to 3.5 percent for Usmon; **Nohiyas under Republican Control**, 96.7

percent to 2.4 percent; **Mountainous Badakhshon Autonomous Veloyat**, 97.7 percent to 1.7 percent; Sughd veloyat, 94.7 percent to 3.3 percent; and **Khatlon** veloyat, 99.6 percent to 0.2 percent.

The presidential elections were monitored by 62 observers from 12 states and international organizations, including Azerbaijan, Belorussia, **Iran**, Kazakhstan, **Kyrgyzstan, Russia, Uzbekistan**, Turkey, the Inter-Parliamentary Assembly of the **Commonwealth of Independent States** (CIS), and the secretariat of the executive committee of the CIS. In addition, 12,000 citizens of Tajikistan acted as observers. The election results were recognized by **Said Abdullo Nuri**, leader of the IRPT.

PRESIDENTIAL ELECTIONS OF 2006. In June 2003, constitutional provisions which would block President **Emomali Rahmon** from seeking further terms were removed by referendum. The elections were held on 6 November 2006. The candidates were President Rahmon, chair of the **People's Democratic Party of Tajikistan**; Abduhalim Ghafforov of the **Socialist Party of Tajikistan** (SPT); Amir Qoraqulov of the **Agrarian Party of Tajikistan** (APT); Olimjon Boboyev of the **Party of Economic Reforms of Tajikistan** (PERT); and Ismoil Talbakov of the **Communist Party of Tajikistan** (CPT). During the campaign, none of the four candidates opposing Rahmon publicly criticized him.

As a result of the elections, President Emomali Rahmon received 79.3 percent of all votes and won a third term in office. Boboyev received 6.2 percent of the votes, Karakulov 5.3 percent, Talbakov 5.1 percent, and Ghafforov 2.8 percent. The **Islamic Renaissance Party of Tajikistan**, the **Democratic Party of Tajikistan**, and the **Social-Democratic Party of Tajikistan** all boycotted the elections and criticized the electoral commission as untrustworthy. The **Organization of Security and Cooperation in Europe** (OSCE) condemned the elections, while the **Commonwealth of Independent States** (CIS) monitors declared the elections "legal, free, and transparent."

PRESIDENTS OF TAJIKISTAN. The presidency of Tajikistan was created in 1991. In March 1991, **Qahor Mahkamov** became president of the **Tajik Soviet Socialist Republic** (Tajik SSR), elected by the **Supreme Soviet** of the Tajik SSR. He was forced to resign on 31

August 1991 by public pressure. From 31 August 1991 to 23 September 1991, **Qadriddin Aslonov** was the acting president.

Rahmon Nabiev served as president of Tajikistan from 23 September 1991 to 7 September 1992. He had received 58 percent of the vote in the first direct general elections. He was forced to resign by an armed band. **Akbarsho Iskandarov** then served as acting president from 7 September until 19 November 1992. Political differences and violence escalated into the 1992–1997 **civil war**, and the presidency was abolished between November 1992 and November 1994.

On 19 November 1992, **Emomali Rahmon** was elected chair of Tajikistan's Supreme Soviet. On 6 November 1994, after the presidential system was reinstated, he was elected president. He was reelected in 1999 and 2006. *See also* PRESIDENTIAL ELECTIONS OF 1999; PRESIDENTIAL ELECTIONS OF 2006.

PRIME MINISTERS OF TAJIKISTAN. The office of prime minister was formed in January 1991. Izatullo Khayoyev served from 25 June 1991 to 9 January 1992. Akbar Mirzoyev served from 9 January 1992 to 21 September 1992. **Abdumalik Abdullojonov** was acting prime minister until 20 November 1992 and then prime minister until 18 December 1993. Abdujalil Samadov was acting prime minister until 27 December 1993 and then prime minister until 2 December 1994. **Jamshed Karimov** served from 2 December 1994 to 8 February 1996. **Yahyo Azimov** served from 8 February 1996 to 20 December 1999. He was succeeded by **Oqil Oqilov**.

PRIVATE FARMING. Peasant farms (*khojagii dehqonii fermeri*) are a new form of **agricultural** organization and ownership since 1992. A government-sponsored program to reorganize the **kolkhoz** (collective farm) and **sovkhoz** (state farm) forms of **cooperative farms** into private farms was initiated in 1996–1997. In the first year of the program, 8,110 private farms had title to 76,589 hectares of arable land. In 1999, nearly 12,500 private farms covered 112,000 hectares of arable land (some 20 percent of all arable land), contributing 30 percent to Tajikistan's total harvest. The Law on Dehqon (Farm) Economy of 10 May 2002 and the governmental decree "On Reorganization of Agricultural Enterprises and Organizations from 2002–2005" provided for transfer of lands of former kolkhozes and sovkhozes to

dehqons (farmers). In 2008 in Tajikistan, about 25,000 private farms cultivated almost 60 percent of the country's arable land.

Private farms suffer from an acute shortage of finance and credit support systems, training, and technical services. State representatives tend to interfere in farm operations, dictating to farmers what they should plant and what prices they can charge for their crops. The government provides no credit programs to private farms, leaving the private farmers without any means to restore the collapsing infrastructure of their farms. In 2007, the private farms produced only one-third of the value of crop production. Household plots with less than 20 percent of arable land are the dominant force in agriculture. They produced about 45 percent of the value of all crops and 90 percent of the value of livestock production in 2006.

PRIVATIZATION. In contrast to the **Russian Federation**, where all citizens were made holders of small shares of state property, in Tajikistan privatization checks were given to part of the population in 1995–1996 as a substitute for their outstanding salaries for 1994–1995. In the midst of the **civil war** (1992–1997), Tajikistan suffered from a lack of Russian rubles—the only **currency** used in the country at that time—and these checks were used as surrogate money. These checks were not equal to the exchange rate, however, and most Tajikistanis lost their savings. This contributed to the mass outmigration of half a million professionals, mostly **Russians**, from the country.

The 16 May 1997 law "On Privatization of State Property" determined the legal framework and basic terms for the privatization of state property in Tajikistan. In 1998, 80 percent of residential houses were privately owned. By 1999, 4,507 state enterprises were privatized, 350 stock companies and more than 1,223 enterprises were transferred to collective entities, and 1,866 ventures were given the right to own private property. By 2000, the privatization of small and medium enterprises from government ownership was complete. Because the privatization took place during the civil war and reconciliation period, 1992–2000, many ordinary citizens and potential international owners had limited access to these enterprises.

In **agriculture, sovkhozes** (state farms) and **kolkhozes** (collective farms) were defined as state property that should be privatized by **dehqons** (farmers). From 1996 to 2002, the number of sovkhozes dropped from 348 to 152, and kolkhozes from 387 to 185. As a result of this rush of privatization, most agricultural enterprises were in practice liquidated as economic entities. Formerly potent and effective kolkhozes crumbled into hundreds of small and weak **private farms**. In 2003, Tajikistan had 16,433 private farms, with 240,000 hectares of arable land. According to land reform legislation, including the Land Code of the Republic of Tajikistan of 13 December 1996 (amended in 1997, 1999, 2001, and 2004), members of a collective farm who want to withdraw their land and farm separately must assume part of the debt accrued by the former kolkhoz or sovkhoz.

Unfair manipulations by state authorities during the land allocation and the unpreparedness of Tajik peasants allowed a small and privileged class of former kolkhoz and sovkhoz members to become dominant landlords. In one 2004 study, only 7.8 percent of Tajik households interviewed knew how to apply for a private farm, and many did not know what a private farm was. Many prefer to lease their land from the collective farm to avoid taking on farm debt and to evade the high taxes levied on privately held land. Only one-third of Tajik peasants became leaseholders. The majority of farmers were left only with the option to rely on household plots. As a consequence of the privatization and breakdown of the kolkhoz system, more than 1 million dispossessed and underprivileged Tajik peasants were forced to migrate to cities and join the **labor migration** to **Russia** and Kazakhstan.

In 2007, 51.8 percent of the country's population worked in the private sector. According to the Tajik Committee of State Property, 430 large and medium enterprises as well as 10,000 smaller entities, all worth $1 billion, were privatized in Tajikistan by 2008. The most profitable resources were sold at low cost to elites, who hold an advantage in acquiring rights to former state property. Among them were regional leaders of **Kulobi** origin, former **United Tajik Opposition** (UTO) members, and field commanders from both sides of the civil war. In the opinion of **Rahmatulloh Zoirov**, chair of the **Social-Democratic Party of Tajikistan**, "under the cover of privatization, state property was squandered."

As of 2009, privatization of state property continues, and although there are no limitations on foreign investor participation in the privatization of state-owned assets, in many circumstances, the decisions are made in favor of politically connected interest groups through behind-the-scenes deals. The largest enterprises, mainly in Tajikistan's transportation infrastructure, **nonferrous metallurgy**, **power generation**, and maintenance sectors, are still government owned.

– Q –

QAHOROV, ABDULAHAD (1913–1984). A prime minister of Tajikistan, Qahorov (Kakharov) was born in **Konibodom**, graduated from the Pedagogical Institute of Leninobod (**Khujand**) via correspondence course in 1954, and completed the courses of the Central Committee of the Communist Party of the Soviet Union in 1956. Qahorov started his career in **Uzbekistan** as inspector of the labor department in the Kokand district administration in 1930. A year later, he returned to Konibodom, where he worked first as chair of the union of construction workers and then chair of the union of Konibodom Canning Combine until 1935, when he was appointed secretary of the **Komsomol** in **Panjakent**. He then held positions as head of the Transportation Agency, deputy chair of the nohiya's executive committee, and head of the department of agitation and propaganda (agitprop) in the city committee of the Communist Party. In 1942–1943, during **World War II**, he was the commissar of an infantry battalion in the Red Army. From 1943 to 1956, his posts included deputy head of the Central Committee of the Communist Party (CP) in Leninobod province and chair of the Leninobod provincial executive committee. In 1956, he was appointed deputy chair of the State Planning Committee of Tajikistan, and in 1961 he became chair of this organization. From 1961 to 1973, he was chair of the council of ministers (prime minister) and the minister of foreign affairs of Tajikistan. From his retirement in 1973 until his death in 1984, Qahorov worked as head of the Archives Department of the Tajik government. Abdulahad Qahorov was the father of **Abdurahim Qahorov**, a minister of internal affairs.

QAHOROV, ABDURAHIM (1951–). The son of **Abdulahad Qahorov**, Abdurahim Qahorov received a law degree from Tajik State National University in 1973 and graduated from the Academy of the Ministry of Internal Affairs of the Soviet Union in 1981. Beginning in 1974, he worked at various positions in Tajik militia until in

1983 he was appointed head of the Department of Internal Affairs of Oktiabr nohiya in **Dushanbe**. He was deputy minister of internal affairs in 1987–1992, and first deputy minister in 1992–1993 and 2000–2006. During 1993–2000, he headed the Academy of Internal Affairs of the Republic of Tajikistan. In 2006, he was appointed head of the Office of Internal Affairs in **Sughd** veloyat. In January 2009, he became Tajikistan's minister of internal affairs.

QAL'A. A *qal'a* is a fortress or citadel.

QALIN. Cash, livestock, and other goods that the bridegroom or his parents pay to the parents of a bride at the time of marriage are called *qalin (kalym)* in **Central Asia**. **Tajiks** often call this *haqqi shir* (milk money). This pre-Islamic tradition is widely practiced, especially in southern parts of Tajikistan. The amount of *qalin* varies from region to region and family to family. It is set by agreement between the two joining families and depends on their social and financial status. Qalin is usually divided into three parts: one part goes to the bride, another part to her parents, and the third is spent on the wedding ceremony. Qalin may be paid in two installments, before and after the wedding. Soviet rule failed to eradicate this practice.

QARATEGIN. *See* RASHT.

QARLUQ (QALLUGH, KARLIUK). An ethnic group in territories constituting present-day southern Tajikistan and northern **Afghanistan**, the Qarluq appeared mostly in the 8th century, after the breakdown of the Turkic kaganate but before the widespread migration of Turkic tribes to the region around the time of the Mongol advance. Qarluqs preserved their seminomadism and tribal-kinship structure, living side by side with sedentary **Tajiks**, although some Qarluqs settled and were assimilated by Tajiks. In terms of physical appearance, Qarluqs of Tajikistan are closer to Tajiks than to seminomadic **Uzbeks**. In the 1920s, Qarluqs numbered around 7,238 (4.3 percent of the total Uzbek population in southern Tajikistan) and lived mostly in **Hisor** and **Baljuvon**. Some Qarluq villages remain in the **Khatlon** veloyat, but their nomadic traditions have been lost. Their precise number is unknown; Soviet censuses recorded them mostly as Uzbek and sometimes as Tajik, according to their mother tongue.

QATAGHAN. A Turkic ethnic group in Tajikistan, the Qataghans were a seminomadic people originating from Dashti Qipchaq (steppe lands, currently in northern Kazakhstan) and appeared in southern Tajikistan and northern **Afghanistan** in the 16th century together with **Shaybanids**. In 1924, 8,935 Qataghans were registered in southern Tajikistan. Other Qataghans live in **Uzbekistan** (Navoi and **Samarqand** provinces). During the Soviet period, Qataghans were partly assimilated by **Uzbeks** and to a lesser extent by Kazakhs and **Kyrgyzs**. Their precise number in Soviet Tajikistan is unknown, as they were officially registered as Uzbeks. Several Qataghan villages may be found in the **Khatlon** veloyat. The 2000 census recorded 4,900 Qataghans living in Tajikistan.

QAZI (QADI). A judge appointed by a ruler or government, a *qazi* was to possess superior knowledge of Islamic law. *See also* ISLAM.

QAZIYAT. An office of high Muslim authority, the *qaziyat* (**qazi**'s seat) replaced the Soviet installed muftiyat in 1988 and served as the head office of the Islamic opposition to the pro-communist government. It existed until the ousting of the Islamic opposition from **Dushanbe** during Tajikistan's **civil war**, in February 1993, when the qaziyat was renamed the muftiyat and was returned to strict governmental control. **Hoji Akbar Turajonzoda** headed the qaziyat from 1988 to October 1992. The highest organ of the qaziyat was the collective assembly of the members of the council of experts (*shura*) as well as the faculty of the **Islamic University** and *imam-khatibs* (administrators of major **mosques**). *See also* IMAM; ISLAM; OFFICIAL MUSLIM CLERGY; MUFTI.

QODIRI, ABDURAHMON (1953–). Born in **Khujand**, Qodiri graduated from the Tajik Institute of Agriculture in 1975 and started his career as an economist with the collective farm in Khujand. Then he held agriculture-related managerial positions in the provincial government and communist party committee. He became director general of the Khujand agro-industrial enterprise in 1992 and later served as first deputy chair of Khujand city and first deputy chair of Sughd veloyat. In 2004–2006, he was chair of **Zafarobod nohiya**. Qodiri was minister of agriculture and environmental protection from December 2006 to January 2008.

QOIMDODOV, QOZIDAVLAT (1949–). Born in **Shughnon no-hiya**, **Mountainous Badakhshon Autonomous Veloyat** (MBAV), Qoimdodov studied animal genetics at the Tajik Institute of Agriculture, graduating in 1971; he graduated from the Communist Party High School (Tashkent) in 1986. During 1971–1972, he served in the Soviet army. Between 1973 and 1978, he was an instructor and head of the lecturers' group in the **Komsomol** committee of the MBAV. In 1978, he began work as an instructor in the Department of Agriculture and Food Industry in the Badakhshon committee of the **Communist Party of Tajikistan** (CPT). Qoimdodov was elected to Tajikistan's **Supreme Soviet** in 1990 and chaired the parliamentary committee on agricultural policy and provisions. In October 1991, he was appointed the first secretary of the party in **Khorugh**. In November 1992, he was appointed deputy chair of Tajikistan's Supreme Soviet. In April 1995, he became deputy chair of the **Majlisi Oli**. In January 2000, Qoimdodov was appointed vice premier of the government of Tajikistan by President **Emomali Rahmon**. During 2005–2009, he was Tajik ambassador to Turkmenistan. Qoimdodov is also a coordinator of the **Aga Khan** Foundation in Tajikistan. *See also* GOVERNMENT.

QOSIMI, QODIR (1961–). Born in **Vanj nohiya**, Qosimi (Qosimov) graduated from the agronomy department of the Tajik Institute of Agriculture in 1983. He then worked as an agronomist until he was appointed director of **sovkhoz** in his native Vanj in 1985. From 1986 to 1990, he worked as an instructor, then second secretary of the MBAV's **Komsomol** organization. In 1990–1996, Qosimi was deputy head of the agricultural department of the government of the **Mountainous Badakhshon Autonomous Veloyat** (MBAV). In 1996, he was appointed chair of Vanj nohiya and in 1999 became first deputy chair of the MBAV. In 2005–2006, he was deputy minister of agriculture in the government of Tajikistan. President **Emomali Rahmon** appointed Qodiri chair of the MBAV in February 2007. *See also* GOVERNMENT.

QOSIMOV, QOSIM (1964–). Born in **Khujand**, Qosimov graduated from the Tajik Institute of Agriculture in 1986 and the High Komsomol School (Moscow) in 1990. Qosimov started work as an agronomist in Khujand nohiya in 1986. In 1990, he was appointed second secretary of the **Komsomol** committee in Khujand nohiya and in 1991 became head of the organizational department of the **Sughd veloyat** Union of Youth. In 1994, Qosimov worked in the Sughd branch of the presidential electoral headquarters. After the elections in 1994, he was appointed chair of Khujand nohiya. He became chair of Sughd veloyat in 1996. Qosimov was elected to the **Majlisi Oli** in 1995 and to the **Majlisi Melli** in March 2000. He became chair of the parliamentary standing committee on economics and communications. On 2 December 2006, he was removed from the position of chair of Sughd veloyat. He then worked as chair of the **People's Democratic Party of Tajikistan** department in Sughd. In January 2008, Qosimov was appointed Tajikistan's minister of agriculture. *See also* GOVERNMENT.

QOSIMOV, SUHROB (1961–). A field commander in the **Sitodi Melli**, Qosimov was born in the Timurmalik (formerly Sovet) nohiya, Kulob veloyat, and graduated from the Moscow Pedagogical Institute in 1984. Qosimov was a physical trainer in boarding schools in **Dushanbe**, then worked in an automobile factory, and subsequently was head of a car repair shop in **Rudaki nohiya**. In May 1992, he joined the Sitodi Melli and fought against Islamic opposition forces in Tajikistan's **civil war**. He controlled the northern part of Dushanbe and fought in **Gharm** and **Tavildara**. After President **Emomali Rahmon** came to power, Qosimov's armed unit was incorporated into Tajikistan's regular **army**. Qosimov was elected to the **Majlisi Oli** in 1995. He fought against his former associates **Mahmud Khudoiberdyev** and **Yaqub Salimov** in 1998. Qosimov resigned on 17 March 2007. Since 2000, he has been president of the Soccer Association of Tajikistan.

QUBODIYON NOHIYA. A district in the **Khatlon** veloyat, **Qurghonteppa** zone, in southern Tajikistan, Qubodiyon nohiya is situated at the confluence of the Kofarnihon and **Amu Darya** rivers, adjacent to **Afghanistan**. Qubodiyon was formed in 1978, although a historical area by the same name has been known since the 7th century. In 1877, the **Amu Darya Treasures** were found in this area. The district is 1,878 square kilometers, with a population of more than 150,000, **Tajiks** and **Uzbeks**, living in six **jamoats**. The distance from Qubodiyon's administrative center to Qurghonteppa is 100 kilometers, and to **Dushanbe** 205 kilometers. Average temperatures in January and July are 1–3°C and 32–33°C respectively; the average annual precipitation is 157 millimeters. The main occupation is **agriculture**, including **cotton** production and livestock breeding (especially astrakhan sheep). Arable land amounts to 19,105 hectares.

QUMSANGIR NOHIYA. The Qumsangir nohiya is located in **Khatlon** veloyat, **Qurghonteppa** zone, in the **Vakhsh** and **Panj** river basins, bordering **Afghanistan**. The district, formed in 1936, is 1,313 square kilometers, and its population is more than 88,100 (8,000 urban dwellers), **Tajiks** and **Uzbeks**, living in five **jamoats**. The distance from Dusti, Qumsangir's center, to Qurghonteppa is 72 kilometers, and to **Dushanbe** 171 kilometers. Average temperatures in January and July can reach 0°C and 30°C respectively; the average annual precipitation is 200–500 millimeters. The main occupation is **agriculture**, including **cotton, lemon,** and rice production. Arable land amounts to 17,000 hectares.

QUNGHRATS. An ethnic group in Tajikistan and other parts of **Central Asia**, the Qunghrats descended from turkified Mongols of Dashti Qipchaq (present-day Kazakhstan), who appeared in Central Asia in the 16th century. The Qunghrats constituted the core military force of ruling dynasties. Not surprisingly, the Qunghrats were among the most resourceful **Basmachis** in 1921–1932. At the turn of the 20th century, the Qunghrats lived in the Kazakh steppes and Khorazm, **Samarqand,** and **Bukhara** in **Uzbekistan**, as well as southern Tajikistan. In 1924, the Qunghrats were the second largest Turkic tribe (37,148 people, or 22.4 percent of the total Uzbek population) in Tajikistan, after the Manghyts. Qunghrat villages may be found in **Hisor** valley. In the **Soviet Union**, they were officially registered as **Uzbeks.** The 2000 census recorded 15,100 Qunghrats in Tajikistan.

QURGHON. A *qurghon* is a fortress or city wall.

QURGHONTEPPA. A city and former province in southern Tajikistan, Qurghonteppa is situated in the fertile **Vakhsh valley,** bordering **Afghanistan** and **Uzbekistan**. The ancient fortress city of Qurghonteppa was historically located in **Eastern Bukhara** and was incorporated into the **Tajik Autonomous Soviet Socialist Republic**

in 1924. The city of Qurghonteppa became the administrative center of the newly formed Qurghonteppa veloyat in 1926. Qurghonteppa became the home of forcibly resettled communities, mostly from **Rasht**, in the 1930s.

In 1939, an administrative reorganization resulted in the elimination of the province. Qurghonteppa veloyat emerged again for a short period in 1944–1947 before disappearing for 30 years. The administrative reorganization of Tajikistan witnessed the reemergence of this province in 1977. After incorporating **Panj** nohiya in 1979, Qurghonteppa veloyat comprised 11 nohiyas.

During the political turmoil of 1992 and the ensuing **civil war**, Qurghonteppa became a scene of conflict, with devastating consequences for the agriculture of the region. Soon after the ascent of **Emomali Rahmon**, this province was merged with the neighboring Kulob veloyat to form the new **Khatlon** veloyat, with the city of Qurghonteppa as administrative center. In later years, this region was used by renegade General **Mahmud Khudoiberdyev** as a power base against **Dushanbe**. Qurghonteppa city is 91 kilometers from Dushanbe and is connected by **motor road**. The population of the Qurghonteppa zone in Khatlon veloyat is over 1.3 million, mostly **Tajiks** and **Uzbeks**.

QYSHLOQ. A *qyshloq* or *kishlak* is a village or rural settlement.

– R –

RADIO, TELEVISION, AND ELECTRONIC MEDIA. The first radio station in Tajikistan was established in 1924. By 1929, three stations were serving **Dushanbe, Khujand**, and Uroteppa. The first television studio started operation at the end of 1959 in Dushanbe. In 1967, a relay line was established between Dushanbe and Tashkent, which allowed viewers in Tajikistan to watch TV programs from Tashkent and Moscow. Since 1975, color broadcasts use the European SECAM system. With the help of space communication stations, the population of **Badakhshon** and other mountainous regions watched their first Moscow TV program (Channel 1) in 1977. In June 2006, Tajik television switched from analog to digital technology.

For a majority of the population, radio and television are the most important sources of information. In 2000, 97.2 percent of the population in Tajikistan had access to at least one TV channel. There is now only one republic-wide TV station, and it is state owned. Television and radio broadcasting is the monopoly of the State Television and Radio Broadcasting Company of Tajikistan, which is controlled by the Ministry of Communications. Major television stations include the state-run Shabakai Yakkum (First Channel) and Safina in Dushanbe, Sughd TV in **Sughd veloyat**, and Khatlon TV in **Khatlon** veloyat. The independent television company Somoniyon was operational from September 1992 to January 1994. In 2009, six government television stations and 18 private stations were in operation. None operate 24 hours a day. Most Tajik TV stations focus on entertainment. In March 2008, the three Persian-speaking, neighboring countries of **Iran**, **Afghanistan**, and Tajikistan agreed to set up a TV network in Dushanbe to prepare and broadcast programs in **Farsi** and Pushtun languages.

State and private radio stations broadcast in **Tajik**, Russian, and **Uzbek** throughout the country. In addition to the national radio and three provincial (**veloyat**) stations, Tajikistan has around 30 other radio stations. Several private radio stations operate in the national capital, veloyats, and cities. Dushanbe's first private station, **Asia-Plus**, opened in September 2002, after a four-year wait for a license. To obtain licenses, independent television and radio stations must work through the Ministry of Communications and the State Committee on Radio and Television.

In 2000 the total capacity of Tajikistan's 73 telephone stations was 247,000 numbers. On the national level, there were 4.1 telephones per 100 persons, the lowest in the Commonwealth of Independent States. Electronic media operators have been allowed to enter the telecom market since 1995. Mobile cell and paging communications (provided by Tajik Tel and Jahon Page joint stock companies) were introduced to Dushanbe in 1996. Between 1995 and 1998, the Central Asia Development Agency (CADA, a U.S. humanitarian organization) with the help of PERDKA, the Soros Foundation, and the Eurasia Foundation, started e-mail services in Dushanbe, Khujand, **Khorugh**, **Qurghonteppa**, and **Kulob**. In 1998, about 1,500 Tajikistanis were registered by CADA as Internet users. Full access to the Internet first became available in Dushanbe and Khujand in January 1999. Tajikistan's Internet country code is tj. There were more than 50,000 active Internet users in 2008 (about 1 percent of the population). The government has allowed a few Internet providers to operate, but high fees and limited capacity put access to the Web out of reach for most citizens. *See also* MASS MEDIA.

RAHIMBOYEV, ABDULLO (1896–1938). A Communist Party (CP) and state leader in Tajikistan and **Uzbekistan**, Rahimboyev was head of Tajikistan's government in 1933–1937. He was the only Tajik Bolshevik who personally met Vladimir Lenin. Rahimboyev fell victim to Stalin's purges in the 1930s. Rahimboyev was born in **Khujand**. He studied in the Khujand Russian native school, the **Samarqand** city high elementary college, and then in the Tashkent teachers' seminary between 1908 and 1917. After graduation, he was a teacher in Khujand, where he joined the CP in 1919. In September 1920, he was appointed chair of the Turkistan **central executive committee** (CEC) and then secretary in charge of the **Turkistan Communist Party**. In 1922 he met Lenin. Following his recommendation, Rahimboyev was elected to the Russian Communist Party (Bolsheviks) Central Committee (CC). In March 1921, he was appointed to the Russian Federation People's Commissariat of Nationalities Collegium but in August returned to his position of chair of the Turkistan CEC.

In 1923, Rahimboyev was appointed first secretary of the **Communist Party of Bukhara**; four months later, he was appointed second secretary of the Turkistan CP CC. He was a member of the commission for the national delimitation of **Central Asia**, then worked as a secretary of the Uzbekistan CP CC for several months. In 1925, he was sent to study at the Communist Academy, Moscow. In 1928, he was appointed chair of the Soviet publishing house Tsentroizdat, and in 1929 he joined the Russian Commissariat of Education, where he worked with Krupskaya (Lenin's spouse) until 1933. In December 1933, he was appointed chair of the Soviet of People's Commissars in the **Tajik Soviet Socialist Republic** and the Soviet Union's CEC. Rahimboyev was arrested in 1938, charged with counterrevolutionary activities, and sentenced to death by the military collegium of the Supreme Court in Moscow. Rahimboyev was executed in 1938.

His reputation was rehabilitated in 1957. *See also* COMMUNIST PARTY OF TAJIKISTAN.

RAHIMOV, ABDULLO. A military leader during Tajikistan's **civil war**, Rahimov, known also as Mullo Abdullo, operated as part of the **United Tajik Opposition** (UTO). In the 1990s, he committed a number of grave crimes in **Vahdat** and Faizabad nohiyas. He did not recognize the 1997 **General Agreement on the Establishment of Peace and National Accord** signed by Tajik government and opposition representatives, and he refused to lay down arms. In 1997–2000, Rahimov led an armed band that maintained a base in northern **Afghanistan** and made regular forays into Tajikistan, during which he allegedly murdered two policemen. In September 2000, the government offensive in the **Nurobod nohiya** destroyed most of his group, with over 40 fighters detained. Rahimov, who was captured in this encounter, was amnestied and released. Later he left for Afghanistan where, according to some accounts, he joined the **Taliban** and was captured by Afghan government forces in Qandahar province in 2002, after which little was heard of him. In March or April 2009, Mullo Abdullo crossed into eastern Tajikistan, allegedly from his hideout in **Pakistan**, bringing with him up to 100 militants. In May 2009, Tajik security forces launched a security operation nicknamed "Poppy 2009" in **Tavildara** and the adjacent **Rasht valley**. Some analysts believe this operation was designed to target civil war commanders such as Rahimov, whose whereabouts are unknown.

RAHIMOV, RASHID (1932–). A Tajik scholar and **academician**, Rahimov was born in **Khujand** and studied at the Plekhanov Institute of People's Economy in Moscow, graduating in 1953. In 1957–1958, he was assistant to the vice president of the **Academy of Sciences of Tajikistan**. In 1958, Rahimov was appointed head of the Industrial Department at the Institute of Economy, Academy of Sciences, becoming director in 1964. After Tajikistan gained its independence, some departments of the Institute of Oriental Studies combined with the Institute of Economy to establish the new Institute of World Economy and International Relations at the Academy of Sciences. Rahimov was the director between 1991 and 2000. In

January 2000, when the institute was reformed to create the Institute of Economy, Rahimov resigned.

RAHMON, EMOMALI (1952–). A president of Tajikistan, Rahmon, also known as Emomali Rakhmonov, was born in **Danghara nohiya**, Kulob veloyat. After graduating from a technical college as an electrician, Rahmon began work in the **Qurghonteppa** oil extraction factory in 1969. In 1971–1974, he served in the Soviet navy. After completing his military service, Rahmon returned to the Qurghonteppa oil extraction factory. In 1982, he received a degree in economics from the Tajik State University (correspondence course). In 1976–1988, he was secretary of administration and then chair of the trade union committee of the Lenin **kolkhoz** (collective farm) in Danghara. It became the Lenin **sovkhoz** (state farm) in 1988 and he was its director until 1992.

Rahmon was elected to Tajikistan's **Supreme Soviet** in 1990. On 2 November 1992, at the height of Tajikistan's **civil war**, he was appointed chair of the Kulob Provincial Soviet of People's Deputies. At the 16th session of the Supreme Soviet in Khujand on 19 November, Rahmon was elected chair of Tajikistan's Supreme Soviet. On 6 November 1994, after the presidential system was reinstated, he was elected president with 58.3 percent support (nearly 1.5 million votes). In March 1998, Rahmon joined the **People's Democratic Party of Tajikistan** and on 18 April was elected party chair. In July 1997, he also became the leader of the **Movement for National Unity and Revival of Tajikistan**. In the **presidential elections of 1999**, Rahmon received 96.9 percent of all votes. In the **presidential elections 2006**, he won a third term in office, with 79.3 percent of the votes. *See also* ELECTIONS; GOVERNMENT; PRESIDENTS OF TAJIKISTAN.

RAHMONOV, ABDUJABBOR (1959–). Born in **Kulob**, Rahmonov graduated from the Tajik State University and then was a professor and administrative official at the university from 1983 to 2000. Rahmonov served as an interpreter in **Afghanistan** in 1985–1987. In 2000, he was invited by President **Emomali Rahmon** to join the executive apparatus and became head of the translation department and then the department for culture. In 2004–2005, Rahmonov chaired the State Committee for Radio and Television and in December 2006 was appointed minister of **education**. Rahmonov is a **doctor of sciences** in philology. *See also* GOVERNMENT.

RAILWAYS. Due to Tajikistan's mountainous terrain, railways are underdeveloped, with none more than 954 kilometers in length. In 2009, there were 31 railway stations in the republic. Tajikistan has three major lines, each isolated from the others by neighboring **Uzbekistan**.

In the north, the major Andijon-**Samarqand** line joins **Konibodom** with Uzbekistan's Khavast station. In the south, with the construction of the line joining Termez (Uzbekistan) with **Dushanbe** and Kofarnihon (256 kilometers) in 1929, Tajikistan was incorporated into the **Central Asian Railway** network. The third, southernmost line also comes to Tajikistan from Uzbekistan. The Termez-**Qurghonteppa**-Yovon railway (264 kilometers) was constructed between 1966 and 1980. In 1999, rail passenger traffic amounted to 639,400 passengers (some 13 percent of rail services), and freight traffic reached 622,800 tons. From January to September 2008, Tajik railways carried 598,000 passengers; some 670,000 tons of cargo were exported from Tajikistan by rail, while rail imports over this period amounted to 3.161 million tons. Since 1994, Tajikistan's railways (TZD) are run by the state-owned Tajik Office of Railways (5,600 workers), which has 1,751 wagons, 351 passenger carriages, and 56 diesel locomotives.

Since independence, Tajikistan has faced difficulties because it has railway access to other countries only via Uzbekistan. The Qurghonteppa-**Kulob** railway (132 kilometers), completed in 1999, links Kulob with the **motor road** running through Qalai Khumb (**Darvoz**), **Khorugh**, **Murghob**, and the **Kulma Pass** and should improve state security. In the early 2000s, Tajikistan decided to build a new railway line between Dushanbe, **Gharm**, and **Jirghatol**, which will link the country with **Kyrgyzstan**, Kazakhstan, and **Russia**, skipping Uzbekistan. Tajikistan is also promoting construction of a railroad connecting Dushanbe with Mashad (**Iran**) via Herat (**Afghanistan**).

RAIS. The title *rais* is used for a ruler, leader, chair, or Muslim religious officer. It is also the title of the director of a **kolkhoz** or **sovkhoz** and the title of the president of Tajikistan (*raisi jumhur*).

RAJABOV, SAFARALI (1955–). Born in Faizobod (currently **Roghun**) nohiya, Rajabov graduated from the Dushanbe Pedagogical Institute in 1977 and the Tajik Agricultural Institute in 1989. In 1977, he started teaching at the Faizobod nohiya high school and served as director of the Faizobod sports-technical club (1977–1980). Between 1980 and 1986, he was a director of interschool training and industry in Faizobod. In 1986, Rajabov was appointed director of Faizobod's professional-technical college. In 1990, he was elected to the parliament and served as secretary, deputy chair, and finally chair of the **Supreme Soviet** committee on legislature, **human rights**, and appeals. Following a recommendation from President **Emomali Rahmon**, the **Majlisi Oli** elected Rajabov its chair in 1995. In January 2000, he was appointed minister of **education**. In February 2005, he was elected to the **Majlisi Namoyandagon** and became chair of the standing committee on state administration and local governance.

RAKHMONOV, EMOMALI. *See* RAHMON, EMOMALI.

RAMAZON (RAMADAN). The ninth month of the Islamic **calendar**, Ramazon commemorates the blessed month when the Quran was revealed to the Prophet Muhammad. Fasting (**ruzah**) during Ramazon is one of the five pillars of **Islam**. The starting date of Ramazon is determined by the lunar calendar.

RANOV, VADIM ALEKSANDROVICH (1924–2006). An **academician**, historian, and expert on the Stone Age in **Central Asia**, Ranov was born in Verkhotura, Sverdlovsk province (**Russian Federation**). He graduated from the Tajik State University in 1954 and started work at the Institute of History at the **Academy of Sciences of Tajikistan**. In 1971, Ranov was appointed head of the Archeology Department at the institute. He authored numerous books and articles on the chronology of the Stone Age in and relations between ancient Central Asia and adjacent regions. In the 1970s, he headed excavations in southern Tajikistan. Ranov was a veteran of **World War II**.

RASHT NOHIYA. One of the **Nohiyas under Republican Control**, Rasht has also been called Qarategin and Gharm nohiya. It is situated in the **Rasht valley** between **Vahdat** nohiya on the west and **Jirgha-**

tol nohiya on the east. To the south, it borders **Nurobod, Tavildara,** and **Tojikobod** nohiyas; its northern border runs along the eastern part of **Sughd veloyat** and along the border with **Kyrgyzstan.** By early 1921, **Gharm** township was a center of Qarategin *bekigari* (a province ruled by a **bek**) in the **Bukharan emirate.** This mountainous nohiya, with a territory of 5,346 square kilometers, was formed in 1931. In April 2001, Gharm nohiya was renamed Rasht nohiya.

The district has a population of more than 103,057 people (12,000 urban dwellers), almost exclusively **Tajiks,** in two **shahraks** (townships) and 14 **jamoats.** The distance from Rasht's administrative center, Gharm, to **Dushanbe** is 193 kilometers. Temperatures in January and July can reach –5°C and 25°C respectively, and the average annual precipitation is 500–900 millimeters. The main occupation is **agriculture,** including potato and apple cultivation and livestock breeding. Arable land amounts to 10,281 hectares.

RASHT VALLEY. A mountainous area in the Surkhob river basin, the Rasht valley covers the **Rasht, Tojikobod, Tavildara, Jirghatol,** and **Nurobod nohiyas.** This area was known as Rasht in Arabic chronicles but became known as Qarategin in **Timurid** times (15th century). **Tajiks** were the traditional inhabitants of this region. In 1635–1636, several thousand **Kyrgyz** families settled in what is now Jirghatol. In the 18th and early 19th centuries, Qarategin was a quasi-independent region in **Eastern Bukhara.** Following the incorporation of north **Turkistan** into the Turkistan general gubernatorial, Russian help was offered to the **Bukharan emirate** to subdue the rebellious Eastern Bukhara. Soviet power was established in Qarategin in July 1923, nearly two and a half years later than in **Dushanbe.** This was due to the remoteness of the region and the resistance of the **Basmachis.** In the 1920s–1940s, the Soviet regime resettled many Qarateginis in valleys, mostly in the **Vakhsh valley.** In 1949, **Gharm** suffered a devastating earthquake. During the Tajik **civil war,** Gharm was one of the strongholds of the **United Tajik Opposition.**

The population of the five nohiyas of the Rasht valley is 251,988, and the area covers 17,055 square kilometers. It has Tajikistan's highest **labor migration** and lowest level of urbanization: 10 percent of the people live in cities. The region has 23,000 hectares of irrigated land and 308 hectares of rain-fed lands. The valley is famous for its potatoes and apples.

RASTOKHEZ. A civil movement, Rastokhez was formed in 1989. The name may have been chosen to echo the Rastokhez-i-Milli (National Renaissance) party founded by the shah of **Iran** in 1975 to counterbalance Islamic forces. Rastokhez was concerned with the revival of the **Tajik language** and culture and enjoyed the tacit endorsement of the **Communist Party of Tajikistan** (CPT), which was trying to harness the growing tide of Tajik nationalism. Rastokhez attracted members of the Tajik intelligentsia. **Tohir Abdujabbor**, an economist and research fellow at the **Academy of Sciences of Tajikistan**, was elected chair of the movement at its inaugural conference. Rastokhez had no fixed membership, but its members and supporters were estimated to number around 10,000 in 1989–1990.

On the eve of the collapse of the **Soviet Union**, with the control of the CPT weakened, Rastokhez became very critical of the regime and joined the opposition movement on nationalist and democratic grounds. In 1991, Rastokhez formed an anticommunist bloc with the **Islamic Renaissance Party of Tajikistan** and the **Democratic Party of Tajikistan**, and it actively participated in antigovernment rallies in **Dushanbe** in 1992. Following the outbreak of the **civil war** in Tajikistan and the emergence of regional conflicts, Rastokhez leaders were forced to go into exile and the movement lost its political weight. Rastokhez was banned by the government of **Emomali Rahmon** in 1993.

RASULOV, JABBOR (1913–1982). A Communist Party leader born in **Khujand**, Rasulov received his higher education in the Central Asian Cotton Production Institute (Tashkent), graduating in 1934. He worked as an agronomist in 1934–1938 and as head of a department in the People's Commissariat of Farming in the **Tajik Soviet Socialist Republic** (Tajik SSR) in 1938–1941. He represented the Union of Soviet Socialist Republics (USSR) People's Commissariat of Procurement in Tajikistan in 1941–1945, and in 1945–1946 became Tajikistan's People's Commissar of Farming, later renamed the People's Commissar of Industrial Farming. Rasulov served in the **Supreme Soviets** of the USSR and the Tajik SSR in the 1940s–1970s. In 1946, he became chair of the Tajik SSR Soviet of Ministers, but he left that post in 1955 for Moscow, where he was appointed the USSR deputy minister of **agriculture**. In 1958, he was appointed secretary of the central committee of the

Communist Party of Tajikistan (CPT). He served as the Soviet ambassador to Togo in 1960–1961. From 1961 until his death, Rasulov was the first secretary of the CPT.

RASULZODA, QOHIR (1961–). Born in **Bobojon Ghafurov nohiya**, Rasulzoda (Rasulov) graduated from the Tajik Institute of Agriculture with a degree in engineering and hydrotechnics in 1982. He then worked as a technician, engineer, and head of the Tajik-irsovkhozstroii company for construction of irrigation systems for **sovkhozes** in **Khujand**. From 2000 to 2006, he was minister of soil improvement and water economy. In December 2006, Rasulzoda was appointed chair of **Sughd veloyat**.

RELIGIONS. Prior to the **Arab** conquest in the beginning of the 7th century, the most common religions of people living in the territory of Tajikistan were Zoroastrianism, Manichaeism, **Buddhism**, Hinduism, Nestorian Christianity, and Judaism. Nearly all **Tajiks** were Islamized by the 8th century. **Islam** became the official religion of Tajiks under the **Samanid** state (875–999). In the 12th–14th centuries, the first Sufi brotherhoods were established. The best-known among them are the **Naqshbandiyah**, Qadiriya, Kubravia, and Yasaviya. In Soviet Tajikistan, Islam survived in spite of the atheistic policies of the Soviet leadership.

Some 95 percent of independent Tajikistan's indigenous population (**Tajik, Uzbek, Kyrgyz, Turkmen**) adhere to Islam of the **Sunni Hanafiya** variety, while about 5 percent follow **Ismaili Shiism** (in **Badakhshon**). The second-largest religious community in Tajikistan is the Russian Orthodox. In 1991, there were about 400,000 Christians in Tajikistan, the majority of them **Russians**. St. Nicholas Cathedral in **Dushanbe** serves the Orthodox community. By the end of the Soviet era, Tajikistan also was home to small numbers of people belonging to other Christian denominations, including some 30,000 Roman Catholics (most of whom were **German**). There were also some 15,000 **Jews**, about 6,000 followers of the **Armenian** Apostolic (Gregorian) Church, and about 14,000 **Korean** Protestants. The number of adherents to these minority religions decreased sharply in the 1990s because of the wave of emigration from Tajikistan during the **civil war**. As a consequence of the brutal civil conflict, economic collapse, and ethnic tensions, the number of Russians decreased from

388,500 in 1989 to some 70,000 in 2009. The exodus of non-Muslims had little to do with religious persecution.

Since 1991, religious tolerance characterized societal and legal attitudes toward the practices of Islam, Russian Orthodoxy, and other religions. The 1994 **constitution** and the law "On Religion and Religious Organizations" of 1 December 1994 (amended in 1997) provide for freedom of religion and protect the right of individuals to choose and change their religion. Although the registration of religious communities is not compulsory, as a rule, religious communities are registered by Tajikistan's Culture Ministry. Around 85 registered religious associations were functioning in Tajikistan in 2009. Some 100,000 Christians (mostly Russians) constituted the largest non-Muslim religious community in Tajikistan. There were about 4,000 Protestants in Tajikistan. The Jehovah's Witnesses charter was registered in 1994 and reregistered in 1997. The Ehyo Protestant Church charter was registered in 2001, and the Abundant Life Christian Center charter was registered in 2003. Of 16 churches belonging to the Protestant Hope Reformed Church, 11 were registered. The Protestant Grace Sonmin had five churches, three of them registered. Other religious groups are the Bahais (four registered organizations), Hare Krishnas (one group registered), and Zoroastrians (no data available). The Lutheran Church and Seventh-Day Adventists each had one congregation in Dushanbe. The Baptist community's membership was around 1,000. Unregistered churches do not encounter significant difficulties. Nearly all of the non-Muslim groups are based in Dushanbe and Khujand.

It is legal to distribute Christian literature, and there generally is accord between Muslims and Christians. Compared to the Uzbek authorities, the Tajik government follows a much more moderate policy toward unregistered non-Muslim religious communities. The government of **Emomali Rahmon** is mainly concerned with controlling **mosques** and the **Islamic Renaissance Party of Tajikistan** (IRPT), as well as with campaigning against **Hizb-ut-Tahrir**, **Wahhabiya**, and **Salafiya**. In May 1998, the parliament passed a law prohibiting the founding of **political parties** with a religious orientation. But a 1999 constitutional amendment permitted religiously based political parties to operate. The legislation does not allow IRPT members to practice as clergy members. Also, according to the law on political parties, "political parties and their members have no right to make use of religious organizations in their activity." On the basis of this law, authorities closed several mosques and dismissed a number of *imam khatibs* (religious administrators) in **Isfara nohiya** in May–June 2003.

Missionary activity by permitted religious groups is not restricted by law. Several Christian missions from foreign countries have come to Tajikistan since 1992. In 2005, the government estimated there were 3,000 Christian converts. No reports of forced religious conversion were registered.

In January 2006, the Committee for Religious Affairs proposed a draft of a new law, "On Freedom of Conscience, on Religious Associations and Other Religious Organizations," which was described by religious denominations and **human rights** activists as "anti-democratic." The **Organization for Security and Cooperation in Europe** (OSCE) was critical of the draft law's "over-intensive state control on religion and religious activities." In March 2009, the draft was approved by the parliament's lower chamber.

ROGHUN NOHIYA. Situated in the **Vakhsh** river basin, within the **Nohiyas under Republican Control**, the Roghun nohiya was established in 1996 at the expense of the two nohiyas of Darband and Faizobod. It was named after the Roghun hydroelectric station on the **Vakhsh River**, the construction of which was halted in 1993. The city of Roghun is the administrative center of the district. The population of Roghun nohiya is more than 21,600 (including 9,100 in Roghun city), mostly **Tajiks**. The distance from the city of Roghun to **Dushanbe** is 100 kilometers. Average January and July temperatures can reach –4°C and 24°C respectively. The annual precipitation is 400–800 millimeters in the lowlands and 1,200–1,600 millimeters in the mountains. The main occupation is **agriculture**, including **grain**, vegetables, fruits, and livestock breeding. *See also* POWER GENERATION.

RU BA RU. A political club formed in 1988 at the initiative of the **Communist Party of Tajikistan** (CPT) youth organization, Ru Ba Ru (Face to Face) aimed to mobilize social support for Mikhail Gorbachev's reform policies. Intellectual Tajik youth formed the core of the association and engaged in discussions with the CPT leadership over social and political issues. With the collapse of the

Soviet Union and the isolation of the CPT, Ru Ba Ru ceased its activities in 1991.

RUBOB. An instrument in the lute family, the *rubob* originated in **Central Asia** no later than 8 CE. In Tajikistan, the rubob is found in three types. The Qashqari (Kashgarian) rubob has two double strings and one thick string and is commonly played in northern Tajikistan. The Badakhshoni or Afghani) rubob, popular in the 17th and 18th centuries, has five strings plus a second set of 8–10 strings. The **Pamiri** rubob is a three-string instrument and combines features of the Qashqari and Badakhshoni rubobs. It is commonly played in Badakhshon. *See also* MUSIC; NAI; SHASHMAQOM.

RUDAKI, ABUABDULLO (858–c. 941). A poet and founder of Perso-Tajik classical literature, Rudaki has been called "the Adam of poets of the Orient." He was the first and greatest literary genius of **Ajam**, the Persian-language world. Born in Rudak (Panj Rud) village near **Panjakent**, Rudaki was court poet to the **Samanid** rulers in **Bukhara** but fell out of favor. Of the more than 1 million verses attributed to him, only 52 poems survive. Among the most famous are *Kalila and Dimna* and various odes and epigrams. Rudaki is buried in his native Panj Rud. In 2008, Tajikistan celebrated the 1,150th anniversary of his birth.

RUDAKI NOHIYA. One of the **Nohiyas under Republican Control**, Rudaki nohiya is located in the **Varzob** and Kofarnihon valleys, south of the capital, **Dushanbe**. One of the biggest Tajik districts in population, it was established in 1935 and was known as Stalinobod district until 1961. In 1996, the district was divided into two separate districts: Varzob, north of Dushanbe, and Lenin, south of Dushanbe. The nohiya center is the township of Somoniyon (formerly known as Koktash, Karakhan Sardarov, and Leninskiy). The distance from Somoniyon to Dushanbe is 17 kilometers. The district territory is 1,800 square kilometers, with a population of more than 274,500 (including 23,300 urban dwellers), mainly **Tajiks** and **Uzbeks**, living in 18 **jamoats**. Average January and July temperatures are 1°C and 29°C respectively. The annual precipitation is 500–700 millimeters. The main occupation is **agriculture**, including **cotton**,

grain, and vegetable production as well as livestock breeding. Arable land totals 31,816 hectares.

RUMI, JALOLIDIN (1207–1273). Known also as Jala ad-Din ar-Rumi and as Balkhi, Rumi was of Persian/Tajik origin, born presumably in what is now **Jalolidin Rumi nohiya** in the **Vakhsh valley**. He left at an early age with his father for Konya, Turkey. Rumi was one of the greatest mystics of **Islam**, famous for the Mevlevi, or the order of Whirling Dervishes. He had a powerful spiritual influence on the Persian-speaking world, including Tajikistan, but also on Turks and Indian Muslims. The Tajik **government** venerates Rumi as a great Tajik poet. *See also* LITERATURE; SUFISM.

RUSHANI. *See* SHUGHNI AND RUSHANI.

RUSSIA. By territory, Russia is the largest country in the world, with more than 17 million square kilometers. By population, it is the ninth largest, with 142 million people. It possesses the largest stockpile of nuclear weapons in the world. Russia also has the world's largest natural gas reserves and the eighth largest oil reserves. For about 150 years, **Tajiks** have considered this country, successively, as an aggressive superior, a generous "older brother," and since 1991 the closest strategic partner. Tajikistan is separated from Russia by **Kyrgyzstan**, **Uzbekistan**, and Kazakhstan. For Russia, Tajikistan has always been on the remotest Central Asian periphery and of little significance.

Russian control over Tajik-populated territories in **Central Asia** was established in the second half of the 19th century. The northern part of Tajikistan (**Sughd veloyat**) and the western **Pamir** were part of the governorate-general of **Turkistan** (Turkistanskii Krai) within the Russian empire from 1867. The Tajik south, as part of the **Bukharan emirate**, was a Russian protectorate until September 1920. Russia's position in Central Asia deteriorated after the Russian Revolution of 1917 and the **Bukharan Revolution** of 1920. From 1918 to 1932, Russian domination in Tajikistan was fiercely contested by the **Basmachis**.

The Russian Soviet Federated Socialist Republic was the largest republic in the Union of the Soviet Socialist Republics, or **Soviet**

Union, which collapsed in 1991. Subsequently known as the Russian Federation, it became a member of the **Commonwealth of Independent States** (CIS).

At the start of Tajikistan's **civil war** in 1992, President **Rahmon Nabiev** continued to rely on Moscow to secure his rule and settle the emerging conflict. The Islamist and nationalist opposition groups also continued to view Russia as the ultimate and legitimate arbiter of the inter-Tajik conflict. At that time, Russia ceased to subsidize the Tajik **economy**. Reform-minded advisers to the Russian president were preoccupied with reinforcing their ties to the West and called for the severance of all residual colonial ties to the former Soviet republics, including Tajikistan. Former Soviet troops stationed in Tajikistan, namely the 201st Motorized Rifle Division and the **Frontier Guard of the Russian Federation**, represented Russian power in Tajikistan and advised the Tajik **government** during the civil war. Beginning in 1993, many members of the opposition, particularly those from the **Democratic Party of Tajikistan**, were given refuge in Moscow. Russia served as a key sponsor and observer of the **Inter-Tajik Peace Talks**. The Kremlin hosted several of the most important rounds of negotiations—the first one and the final two—as well as one consultative meeting and two meetings between President **Emomali Rahmon** and the **United Tajik Opposition** leader **Said Abdullo Nuri**. The **General Agreement on the Establishment of Peace and National Accord** was signed in Moscow and witnessed by Russian President Boris Yeltsin on 27 June 1997.

Tajik-Russian diplomatic relations were established on 9 April 1992, and by the beginning of 2009, about 180 bilateral agreements had been signed. The most important among these is the "Treaty on Friendship, Cooperation, and Mutual Assistance" dated 25 May 1993 and the "21st Century Oriented Ally Cooperation Treaty" of 16 April 1999. Both countries are members of the **Collective Security Treaty Organization** (CSTO), the **Eurasian Economic Community** (Eurasec), the **Conference on Interaction and Confidence-Building Measures in Asia** (CICA), the **Shanghai Cooperation Organization** (SCO), and other interstate organizations.

Tajikistan is closely linked to the Russian economy within the framework of the **Customs Union** and Eurasec. From 1990 to 2000, Russian trade with Tajikistan fell by 4 percent, while the decline of Tajik trade on the average with the CIS was 20 percent. Nevertheless, between 1997 and 2007, Russia accounted for 80 percent of Tajikistan's trade with the CIS. Russia is Tajikistan's principal **foreign trade** partner. In 2008, 15 percent of Tajik commodity turnover was with Russia. Russian-Tajik bilateral trade reached $1 billion by the end of 2008. And Russia is the biggest foreign investor in Tajikistan. From 2005 to 2008, Russia's direct investment in Tajikistan soared from $93 million to $300 million. In 2008, it represented 75 percent of all **foreign investment** in Tajikistan. As of late 2007, more than 113 Tajik-Russian joint ventures were operating in Tajikistan. Unified Energy Systems of Russia has taken an active part in the construction of the Sangtuda-1 hydroelectric power station in Tajikistan. In November 2008, the third unit of the Sangtuda-1 hydropower plant was put into operation. The Sangtuda-1 is a joint Tajik-Russian project: Russia holds 75 percent of the shares and the remaining 25 percent is held by Tajikistan. Construction of the **Roghun** hydroelectric plant was another joint Tajik-Russian project, but Russia requested more than 50 percent of Roghun's shares, a demand which made Tajikistan opt out of the proposal. Russia has adopted the same policy of near-universal control with regard to the military airport in **Ayni (Hisor** valley), while Tajikistan proposes joint use. President Emomali Rahmon remains firm in his intention "not to allow any foreign bases on the territory of Tajikistan, other than Russian ones."

Political and military cooperation between the two states is more important than their economic and cultural ties. Russia runs several strategic facilities in Tajikistan, including a **Russian military base**, the optics and electronic system **Okno**, and an airbase in Ayni. In exchange for the base and the Okno facility, Russia agreed to write off $242 million of Tajik debt.

The population of Russia has shrunk (from more than 148 million in 1991 to 142 million in 2008), while the number of **labor migrants** from former Soviet states, including those from Tajikistan, grows. Russia is home to 15–20 million Muslims, including some 3–4 million migrants from Tajikistan, Uzbekistan, Kyrgyzstan, and Azerbaijan. See also FOREIGN POLICY.

RUSSIAN MILITARY BASE IN TAJIKISTAN. An agreement for the establishment of a Russian base in Tajikistan was signed by the presidents of **Russia** and Tajikistan in Moscow on 16 April 1999, and the base was officially established in October 2004. The agreement provides for the stationing of 8,500 Russian troops in **Dushanbe, Qurghonteppa**, and **Kulob**. It exempts Russia from paying rent to Tajikistan. This bilateral agreement, ratified by the Russian parliament (Duma) in the second half of 1999, is valid for 10 years and is renewable. The arrangement received the endorsement of the Moscow summit of the **Commonwealth of Independent States** (CIS), following the completion of the CIS collective peacekeeping mission in Tajikistan. The Russian base provided assistance to Tajik border guards protecting the Tajik-Afghan border, for which Tajikistan assumed responsibility in 2005. The base also would provide support to the Tajik **army** in case of invasion.

The military base in Tajikistan is Russia's biggest base abroad. The 201st Gatchina Twice Red Banner Motorized Rifle Division that had been stationed in Tajikistan since Soviet times forms the core of this force. It comprises three infantry regiments: the 92nd stationed in Dushanbe, the 149th in Kulob, and the 191st in Qurghonteppa. The division has about 100 tanks and 300 various armored cars and anti-aircraft artilleries. The air force includes the 670th aviation group (five SU-25 attack aircraft) and the 33rd helicopter squadron (four MI-24s and four MI-8s) in **Ayni** airfield, in addition to several supply and maintenance battalions and commands. In July 2009, Major General Alexei Zavizion was replaced by Colonel Igor Krasin as commander of the Russian military base in Tajikistan. Russia's only other permanent base in the Central Asian region is in **Kyrgyzstan**. *See also* COLLECTIVE PEACEKEEPING FORCE IN THE REPUBLIC OF TAJIKISTAN.

RUSSIANS IN TAJIKISTAN. The first Russian settlement in Tajik-populated areas of **Central Asia** occurred in the 1860s. By 1871, 2,045 Russians (including 1,529 troops) lived in the **Khujand** district. Russian settlements also appeared in **Uroteppa, Khorugh**, and **Murghob**. Early Russian settlers included peasants who left **Russia** for the Central Asian oases in search of a better life after the abolition of serfdom in 1861. At the time of the Russian Revolution in 1917, about 7,000 Russian peasants were living in their villages in the Khujand district. Russian peasant settlement was interrupted by the revolution and the subsequent civil war and **Basmachi** uprising. But the consolidation of Soviet rule led to a new wave of Russian settlement. After the second half of the 1920s, Russian professionals and trained workers were sent to Tajikistan to build the **economy**. During **World War II**, many industrial enterprises were evacuated from Russia and moved to Tajikistan together with their professional workforce and their families. In the 1960s, Tajikistan witnessed the last wave of Russian migration, which brought mostly trained industrial workers and engineers to accelerate the construction of new **industries**.

With growing political tensions in the 1980s and the demand for **Tajik** to become the **language** of the state, many Russian residents felt uneasy about their future. The Russian population in Tajikistan dropped markedly in the last decade of the 20th century. The Russian population in 1926 stood at 8,200 (0.8 percent of the total population); in 1959, it was 262,600 (13.3 percent); in 2000, it was 68,200 (1.0 percent). *See also* RUSSIAN MILITARY BASE IN TAJIKISTAN.

RUZAH. A Persian-Tajik term, *ruzah* (Arabic *sawm*) refers to a fast. During ruzah, Muslims do not eat or drink from daybreak until the sun has set. They must also abstain from sexual enjoyment. It is common among Tajik Muslims to have a joint breakfast called *iftar*. The ban on ruzah introduced by the Soviets in the late 1920s was lifted after Tajikistan became independent in 1991. *See also* ISLAM; RAMADAN.

– S –

SADRI ZIYO (MUHAMMAD SHARIFJON MAHDUM) (1867–1932). A Tajik writer, historian, and literary critic, Sadri Ziyo was born and educated in **Bukhara**. He supported the **Jadid** movement and held regular meetings at his home, known as **majlisi** Sadri Ziyo. **Sadriddin Ayni** often attended these meetings and enjoyed the moral and financial support of Ziyo. In 1893, Sadri Ziyo graduated from a **madrasa** and was a **qazi** (judge). In March 1917, he was appointed *qazi kalon* (chief judge) of the **Bukharan emirate**, but he was soon removed for his reformist tendencies and exiled. In 1918, he was imprisoned and his properties were confiscated. After the **Bukharan Revolution**, he reproduced some of his writings, which had earlier been destroyed by emir **Said Alim Khan**. Most of Sadri Ziyo's writings are held at the Institute of Oriental Studies in **Uzbekistan**. Sadri Ziyo was the father of **Muhammadjon Shu-kurov**. *See also* LITERATURE.

SADULLOEV (ASADULLOZODA), HASAN (1968–). Born in **Bokhtar nohiya** to a **Kulobi** family, Sadulloev started his career as a village gas-station attendant. His sister Azizamoh married **Emomali Rahmon**, who has served as President of Tajikistan since 1994. Sadulloev, known as Hasan Asadullozoda since 2008, heads the country's leading commercial **bank**, Orienbank, and, allegedly, also runs CDH Investments Corporation, an offshore company that controls the smelter **TALCO**'s profits. In addition, Sadulloev owns some 60 large companies in Tajikistan, including several factories, **cotton** mills, and food-processing enterprises. His holding company Ismail Samani–21st Century and the Orioyon International trust company also extend his influence into real estate development, transport, **media**, insurance, and banking.

Rumors have circulated that in May 2008 Sadulloev was shot and seriously wounded by his nephew Rustam, president Rahmon's elder son, in a family feud. Some reports claim that Sadulloev was killed, and that his twin brother, Hussein, now appears in public as Hasan Sadulloev. *See also* CORRUPTION.

SAFAROV, SAFAR (1947–). Born in **Danghara nohiya**, Safarov graduated from the Tashkent Polytechnical Institute in 1970 and the Tashkent Communist Party High School in 1983. In 1971, he started work as an engineer in a **Kulob cotton** cleaning factory, but he was soon promoted to chief engineer of state control over agricultural equipment in the Danghara nohiya executive committee. In 1974, he was recruited into the **Communist Party of Tajikistan** (CPT) and by 1981 had worked as second secretary of Danghara nohiya **Komsomol**, and as an instructor and head of the **Qurghonteppa** veloyat Komsomol committee. In 1988–1989, Safarov became second secretary of the CPT in Qurghonteppa city, and then first secretary of Sovet (Timurmalik) nohiya. In 1990, he was elected to Tajikistan's **Supreme Soviet**, where he served as deputy chair of the committee on the **economy** and budget. In 1994, he was elected again to Tajikistan's parliament. Between 1995 and 2000, Safarov was chair of the **Majlisi Oli** committee on the economy and budget.

He was appointed head of the presidential apparatus in May 2000. From 2001 to 2006, he was Tajik ambassador to Russia. In 2007, he was elected to the **Majlisi Namoyadagon** and was appointed its first deputy chair.

SAFAROV, SANGAK (1927–1993). A militia commander and leader of the **Sitodi Melli**, Safarov was born in Khovaling, Kulob veloyat. In 1950, he was imprisoned for theft and murder. He was released in the mid-1970s. Safarov made his political debut in April 1992, when he formed a band in **Kulob** against the Islamic opposition movement. In May, he led a rally in support of **Rahmon Nabiev** in Ozodi (Dusti) Square in **Dushanbe** and won the epithet "people's general." After the rally, Safarov and two of his companions were reportedly attacked and detained by Islamists for a short while. After that experience, he organized and led the Sitodi Melli and in December 1992 seized Dushanbe from the government. On 29 March 1993, he was killed in an exchange of fire with another Kulobi field commander, **Faizali Saidov**, in **Bokhtar nohiya**. *See also* CIVIL WAR; GOVERNMENT.

SAFAVIDS (1501–1732). An Iranian Shia dynasty of Azeri origin, the Safavids made Twelve-Imam **Shiism** the state religion and established the great Iranian empire. By doing so, the Safavids reasserted the Iranian identity that had been weakened by the **Arab** invasion. But making Shiism the official religion isolated Persia from its **Sunni** neighbors in **Central Asia**, including the **Tajiks**, and heightened tension between the two major Islamic currents. In Persia, the Safavids were followed by the Afsharids.

SAFFARIDS (873–903). A Muslim dynasty of Iranian origin, the Saffarids ruled Sistan in southeastern Persia and southwestern **Afghanistan**. The Saffarid capital was in Zaranj (now in Afghanistan). This empire collapsed when Amr ibn Layth Saffarid, trying to wrest **Movarounnahr** from the **Samanids**, was defeated and captured by Ismail Samani in 900.

SAID ALIM KHAN (1880–1944). Emir Mohammed Alim Khan, the son of Abdulahad Khan, was the last ruler of the **Uzbek** Manghyt dynasty, the last ruling dynasty of the **Bukharan emirate**. From 1893 to 1896, Alim Khan was in St. Petersburg, **Russia**, studying the Russian language and government and military disciplines at the tsar's court. In 1910, he became emir of Bukhara. In September 1920, as a result of the **Bukharan Revolution**, he was overthrown and was forced to flee to his base at **Dushanbe**. After vain attempts to stop the Red Army's advance with the help of **Basmachis**, in March 1921 Alim Khan escaped to **Afghanistan**. In Kabul, Emir Amanulla Khan provided him with a residence and pension. Alim Khan died in Kabul in April 1944. *See also* BACHAI SAQQAO; IBRAHIMBEK; KOLESOV'S MARCH; YOUNG BUKHARANS.

SAIDOV, FAIZALI (1963–1993). A militia commander and a leader of the **Sitodi Melli**, Saidov was born to a Kulobi family in **Bokhtar nohiya**, **Qurghonteppa** veloyat, and studied at the technical college in Qurghonteppa. In 1981–1983, Saidov served in the Soviet army. In 1992, he joined the Sitodi Melli and commanded one of its core brigades. In March 1993, Saidov was shot dead in an exchange of fire with another field commander, **Sangak Safarov**, in Bokhtar nohiya. *See also* CIVIL WAR.

SAIDOV, ZAFAR (1962–). A Tajik journalist and press secretary, Saidov graduated from the Tajik State University with a degree in history in 1983. Between 1983 and 1987, he lectured at the university and in 1989 was awarded a **candidate** degree in social philosophy. In 1987, Saidov began work in the Central Committee of Tajikistan's **Komsomol** as an instructor in the Department of Ideology. In 1988, he was appointed to the Committee on Youth Affairs in Tajikistan's **Supreme Soviet**. Saidov was press secretary for President **Qahor Mahkamov** for one week in August 1991 and for President **Rahmon Nabiev** in 1991–1992. After Nabiev resigned in August 1992, Saidov taught at the Tajik State University. At the end of 1993, he was appointed director of the Department of Information at the Ministry of Foreign Affairs. Saidov was appointed press secretary by President **Emomali Rahmon** in November 1995. From December 2003 to February 2008, he headed the Khovar National Information Agency. He then became a senior adviser to the president on **foreign policy**. Saidov has authored eight books about his patron, Emomali Rahmon. *See also* MASS MEDIA.

SALAFIYA. The Salafiya movement within **Islam**, which began in the early 20th century in Europe and Egypt, has had a profound influence all over the Muslim world. While the Salafiya movement harks back to the earliest days of Islam (the name is derived from *salaf as-salihin*, "the pious ancestors"), it is a reformist and modernist movement. It proposes a common Islamic identity to replace existing mixed, fragmented, or weak religious and ethno-political identities. In particular, Salafism calls for the suspension of the four schools of law (**mazhabs**) in Islam, and for the institution of an integrated law which would incorporate modifications to conform to the demands of modern times. Salafi is not welcomed by most Muslims as it propagates *takfir*: the right to declare as unbelievers or heretics those who, in the opinion of Salafits and Wahhabits, violate norms of true Islam.

An ultra-strict Salafiya is not a mainstream vision among Muslims in Tajikistan. The movement, in part, was imported by Tajiks who temporarily sought refuge in **Pakistan** during Tajikistan's **civil war**. Salafits state that their number reached 20,000 in 2009. They oppose the **Islamic Renaissance Party of Tajikistan** (IRPT), claiming that there should be no parties in Islam. Salafi missionary activities within Tajikistan and among **labor migrants** outside the country (particularly in **Russia**) have been met with fierce resistance by the religious authorities and most Tajik Muslims. Traditional **mullahs** do not want Salafits to attend Tajiks **mosques** due to their different performance of rites. Referring to their attack on **Hanafi** traditions and hostility to **Iran** and to **Shiism**, the traditional Tajik Muslims who, except for a small number of **Ismailis** are followers of Hanafi, claim that Salafits pose a threat to the integrity of the established Muslim identity in Tajikistan. Most Tajik Muslims, including **Sufis**, view Salafiya as hostile to local views, often labeling it **Wahhabism** to indicate its foreign (Saudi) origin. Some even regard the Salafits as a tool of foreigners, including the Americans and Saudis, striving to target Shia Iran from Tajik soil.

The government of Tajikistan was initially tolerant of the Salafiya, referring to its nonviolent character, and some local religious authorities believed that Tajik Salafits enjoyed hidden support from the government. At the end of 2008, however, the ruling National Democratic Party of Tajikistan made a sudden turn, calling on Muslims to oppose Salafism in Tajikistan. On 8 January 2009, following an appeal from the prosecutor general, the supreme court outlawed the Salafiya religious movement. *See also* MUFTI; OFFICIAL MUSLIM CLERGY; RELIGIONS; SUFIS; UNOFFICIAL MULLAHS.

SALIKHOV, MAHMADNAZAR (1957–2009). Born in the Vakhsh nohiya, to a **Kulobi** family, Salikhov received a law degree from the Tajik State University in 1980. Salikhov became a lieutenant general of police and worked in different judicial positions, including assistant prosecutor of Frunze nohiya in **Dushanbe** and prosecutor of **Konibodom**. At the end of 1992, he was appointed by **Emomali Rahmon** as Tajikistan's prosecutor general. In 1994–2003, he worked as deputy minister of internal affairs, head of the executive apparatus of the president of Tajikistan, chair of the constitutional court, and head of the **Council of Justice**. In 2003–2006, he again headed the executive apparatus of the president. In December 2006, Salikhov became minister of internal affairs. He was fired from this position in February 2009. In June 2009, he committed suicide.

SALIMOV, SHERKHON (1957–). Born in Timurmalik (formerly Sovet) nohiya, **Kulob** zone, Salimov received a law degree from the Tajik State University and served in the Soviet Army. From 1980 to 2002, he held various positions: lawyer in the Selkhozkhimiya state company; senior assistant to the prosecutor, then chief detective in the prosecutor's office of the **Mountainous Badakhshon Autonomous Veloyat** (MBAV); instructor of the MBAV Communist Party Committee; head of the law department of the Kulob veloyat Communist Party Committee; prosecutor of **Shurobod nohiya**; department head in the Tajikistan prosecutor general's office; prosecutor of the Frunze district of **Dushanbe** city; deputy prosecutor general of Tajikistan. In 2002 and 2005, he was elected to the **Majlisi Namoyandagon**. In January 2007, President **Emomali Rahmon** appointed him head of the newly established Agency on Combating Corruption and Economic Crimes.

SALIMOV, YAQUB (1958–). A **Sitodi Melli** field commander, Salimov was born in the Vakhsh nohiya to a **Kulobi** family. He graduated from the Tajik State University and the Tajik Institute of Physical Education and worked as a high school teacher in **Du-**

shanbe. At the onset of Tajikistan's **civil war** in 1992, he joined the Sitodi Melli and soon became one of the most influential field commanders in Dushanbe and the **Vakhsh valley**. At the 16th session of the **Supreme Soviet** in **Khujand** in November 1992, Salimov was appointed minister of internal affairs. In 1995, he was appointed Tajikistan's ambassador to Turkey and in 1997 became chair of the state customs committee. In 1998, when Salimov was accused of supporting the armed insurgency by **Mahmud Khudoiberdyev** in the **Sughd veloyat**, he left Tajikistan for exile. In 2003, he was arrested in Moscow, extradited to Dushanbe, and imprisoned.

SAMANIDS (875–999). The Samanids were the first Islamic dynasty in **Central Asia** independent of the **Arab** caliphate. Saman, a noble from Balkh, founded the dynasty and appointed his grandsons governors of four areas: Ahmad in **Ferghana**, Yahya in Shash (Tashkent area) and **Istravshan**, and Ilias in Herat (northwestern **Afghanistan**). His eldest son, Nuh, was made responsible for the external affairs of the family, strengthening the dynasty. After Nuh's death, Ahmad took over his responsibilities. Ahmad's son, Nasr, who ruled **Samarqand**, inherited the mantle of dynastic leadership after Ahmad's death in 864. In 875, the reigning Arab caliph in Baghdad recognized Nasr as the ruler of **Movarounnahr**, marking the formal inauguration of Samanid rule with Samarqand as the capital.

In 892, after the death of Nasr, his brother Ismail became head of the Samanid dynasty and moved the seat of power to **Bukhara**. Ismail strengthened his estate considerably and defended its independence against claims from the ruler of **Khurasan** in the south, Amr ibn Layth **Saffarid**, and nomadic incursions from the north and northeast. Samanid rule under Ismail extended to most parts of Movarounnahr and Khurasan, as well as to eastern and northern parts of **Iran**. The Samanid dynasty revived **Sassanid** traditions of empire building and introduced a monarchical regime to Central Asia. A hierarchical pyramid with the ruler at its apex replaced the amorphous federation of fiefdoms and quasi-states of the pre-Islamic era.

The Samanids cultivated Persian traditions and the Islamic faith. They played a crucial role in reviving classical poetry in **Dari-Farsi** after the Arab invasion. Their court was the focal point of continuity of old Persian culture and the staging place for the renewal of Perso-Tajik **literature**. Science and the **arts** flourished. The Samanids were the last Iranian ruling dynasty in Central Asia. In 999, they were replaced by the Turkic dynasty of Karakhanids.

Many scholars and writers of the Samanid period are still very highly regarded, notably **Abuabdullo Rudaki** and **Abuali ibn Sino** (Avicenna). The modern state of Tajikistan considers that the Tajik identity was fully formed during the Samanid period.

SAMARQAND. Originating in the ancient city of **Afrasiab**, Samarqand is one of the centers of Tajik culture and history. At the time of the Soviet delimitation of **Central Asia** in 1924, Samarqand was included in **Uzbekistan**, where it is a provincial center. The city is linked with Tajikistan by **railway** and **motor road**.

Samarqand, also known as Marakanda, was a **Sogdian** capital. It was captured by **Alexander the Great** in 329 BCE. With its location on the **Zarafshon** River and along the legendary Silk Road, Samarqand was at the crossroads of civilizations and cultures. In 712, Muslim **Arabs** conquered the city, although Sogdian resistance lasted for another century. At the end of the 9th century, Samarqand was incorporated into the **Samanid** empire and grew in fame, after **Bukhara**, as a center of science and **Farsi-Tajik literature**. Turkic rule over Samarqand (Karakhanids, Seljuks, Karakidans) from the 11th century marked the city's gradual decline as a center of power and learning. In 1212, Muhammad Khorazm Shah captured the city and tried to establish his capital there but was soon overpowered by Genghiz Khan.

The Mongol invasion in 1220 destroyed the city and led to the loss of many lives, an era known in folklore and songs as the Mongol plague. In 1370, **Timur** established his empire in Central Asia with Samarqand as its center. Samarqand experienced a respite from decline under **Timurid** rule as many architectural monuments were built or restored. In 1500, **Shaybani** Khan captured Samarqand and made it the capital of the Shaybanids. The **Bukharan emirate** rose on the ruins of the disintegrated Shaybani rule, and it included Samarqand as an important, albeit fading, center of culture and commerce. Samarqand declined further as the Bukharan emirate was raided by Turko-Mongol tribes (Astarkhanids and Mangyts) in the 17th–19th centuries. In May 1868, Samarqand was seized by tsarist troops and incorporated into the Russian empire. In 1886, Samarqand, Kattaqurghan, and **Panjakent** composed the Zarafshon province (oblast). Samarqand was later included in the **Turkistan Soviet Republic**. Between 1924 and 1930, Samarqand was the capital of Uzbekistan, and it continues to be the second most industrialized city in that republic.

SAMBUSA. A popular Tajik appetizer, *sambusa* is a small triangular or round pastry stuffed with ground meat or vegetables (often pumpkin) and fried in oil or baked in a **tanur**.

SANGINOV, HABIBULLO (1950–2001). Born in **Gharm**, Sanginov graduated from the Tajik Polytechnical Institute in 1973 and worked at the Ministry of Internal Affairs of Tajikistan. In 1987, he completed his higher education at the Academy of the Ministry of Internal Affairs of the Union of Soviet Socialist Republics (USSR) and was appointed chief of Tajikistan's traffic police, where he remained until 1991. Sanginov was elected to the Republican Assembly in 1990. At the outset of Tajikistan's **civil war** in 1992, Sanginov left his post at the Ministry of Internal Affairs and settled in Moscow. In exile, he chaired the Umed Foundation to assist Tajik refugees and forcibly displaced persons. In 1997, Sanginov, as a member of the **United Tajik Opposition** (UTO), was included in the **Commission for National Reconciliation**, on the subcommission of military affairs. In accordance with the 30 percent quota for the UTO, negotiated between the Tajik opposition and the government in 1997, Sanginov was appointed first deputy minister of internal affairs in June 1999. He was assassinated in **Dushanbe** on 11 April 2001.

SAREZ LAKE. One of the biggest embankment lakes in the world, Sarez Lake was formed in 1911 at 3,265 meters altitude as a result of a massive landslide. The lake is located in the central part of **Badakhshon**, near Ysoi **qyshloq**, on the Murghob River. The earthen dam known as the Ysoi slope covers 2.2 square kilometers and is 650 meters high. The lake is 60 kilometers long, up to 500 meters deep, and the average width is 1.4 kilometers. Landslides and the erosion of the dam continue to endanger the Ysoi slope. If the dam were to break, 17 billion cubic meters of water could cover **Khatlon** and Badakhshon as well as parts of neighboring **Afghanistan**, **Uzbekistan**, and Turkmenistan for several days. Five million people could be affected.

The government of Tajikistan launched a campaign in 1995 to attract international assistance to deal with this impending catastrophe.

SARIKOL (SARIQUL, ZORKUL). The Sarikol region includes a lake, mountain range, and plateau in the **Pamir** region. The Sarikol kingdom had its capital at **Tashkurgan**, a homeland of the **Tajiks of China**. The area may have been settled by Saka nomads of Iranian origin, who first inhabited the Pamirs in the first millennium BCE. The Sarikoli language, which is unique and not spoken outside of **China**, belongs to the East Iranian languages and is close to the **Pamirian languages** of Tajikistan. It is not a written language; children learn and study in the Uighur (Turkic) language using Arabic script, but more highly educated people, as well as the communal and religious leaders of Sarikoli Tajiks, can speak some **Farsi-Tajik**.

Traditional occupations have been in **agriculture**, including farming and animal husbandry, with cyclic exploitation of Pamir pastures. Sarikolis usually moved their flocks within the Taghdumbash Pamir and paid tribute to the ruler of Hunza, in northern **Pakistan**, who exercised control over these pastures until 1937. In October 1949, Sarikol was incorporated into Communist China. *See also* CHINA-TAJIK BORDER; TASHKURGAN TAJIK AUTONOMOUS COUNTY.

SART. The Sanskrit term *sart*, meaning "merchant" or "caravan head," was used by nomadic **Turks** to identify sedentary **Sogdians** and their descendants, the **Tajiks**. In the time of Genghiz Khan, the population of **Central Asia** was divided into sedentary Tajik-speaking Sarts and nomadic Turks. In time, some Turks adopted a sedentary way of life and became Turkic-speaking Sarts. When **Russia** established control in the area, the tsarist administration used the term to identify sedentary populations of the oases of Central Asia (both Tajik and Turkic speakers). In the 1920s, the term disappeared, such people being classified in subsequent Soviet censuses as either Tajiks or **Uzbeks**.

SASSANIDS (220–651). This centralized Iranian empire was formed by the Persian Zoroastrian aristocracy on the ruins of Parthia. The empire's territory encompassed present-day **Iran**, Iraq, Armenia, **Afghanistan**, eastern parts of Turkey, and parts of **India**, Syria, **Pakistan**, and other regions. The Sassanids had some success in establishing control over **Bactria**, but their hold was tenuous as nomadic tribes continued to make inroads into **Central Asia** in the 5th century. Much of what later became known as Islamic culture was taken mainly from the Sassanids into other parts of the Middle East as well as Western Europe, Africa, **China**, and **India**. The Sassanids were defeated by the **Arab** invasion in the middle of the 7th century.

SATTOROV (SATTORZODA), ABDUNABI (1941–). A Tajik politician and academic, Sattorov was born in the **Panjakent nohiya, Sughd veloyat**, and received a degree in philology from the Tajik State University in 1963. Between 1967 and 1969, Sattorov was head of the Department of Literary Criticism, which included *Sadoi Mardum* magazine. He was a lecturer at the university and then head of Tajik classic **literature** (1969–1990). He obtained his doctorate in philology in 1985. Sattorov joined the **Democratic Party of Tajikistan** in 1991 and lived in exile between 1993 and 1997. In 1997, he was appointed to the **Commission for National Reconciliation**, on the subcommission for political issues. Sattorov was deputy chair of the **Democratic Party of Tajikistan Almaty Platform**. He was appointed deputy minister of foreign affairs in March 1999 after the signing of the **General Agreement on the Establishment of Peace and National Accord**, under which 30 percent of government positions were to be filled from the United Tajik Opposition. In 2006, Sattorov became head of the Foreign Policy and Foreign Economic Development Administration of the Strategic Studies Center under the president of the Republic of Tajikistan.

SAVRIDINOVA, GULAFZO (1947–). Born in **Isfara, Sughd veloyat**, Savridinova graduated from the Moscow Institute of Agriculture in 1969 and the Tashkent Communist Party High School in 1985. She started her career in 1969 as a salesperson in her native Isfara. In 1972–1977, she chaired the local industry's trade unions. In 1977, she was appointed deputy chair of the Isfara district executive committee. In 1980, she became secretary of the **Communist Party of Tajikistan** (CPT) in Isfara city. Savridinova chaired the Isfara district executive committee between 1982 and 1985. In 1985, she moved to **Dushanbe** and headed the Department of Trade and Communal Services in the CPT central committee. She returned to Isfara in 1988 as the city secretary of the CPT. In 1991–1994, she again chaired the Isfara district executive committee and in 1994–1996 chaired the Isfara city committee. She was elected to Tajikistan's parliament in 1990, 1995, and 2000. From 1995 to 2000, Savridinova was deputy chair of the **Majlisi Oli**, a post she retained in the newly elected **Majlisi Namoyandagon**. She retired in 2005.

SEMENOV, ALEXANDER (1873–1958). A Russian/Soviet historian and **academician**, Semenov was the first director of the Institute of History at the **Academy of Sciences of Tajikistan**. He graduated from the Tambov Teacher's Institute (1895) and the Moscow Institute of Oriental Languages (1900). In 1906, Semenov started work as an official in the **Turkistan** general gubernatorial. In 1917, he was an adviser to the Russian plenipotentiary in **Bukhara**. After the 1917 revolution, he worked in various scientific institutes in **Russia**, **Uzbekistan**, and Tajikistan. From 1951 until his death, Semenov was the director of the Institute of History at the Academy of Sciences of Tajikistan. He specialized in archeology, ethnography, **art**, and **Islam**, and he published more than 300 works on medieval manuscripts, translations, and interpretations.

SETOR. The *setor* (from Tajik *se tor*, meaning "three strings") is a Perso-Tajik musical instrument of the lute family. In Tajikistan, the Pamiri setor, which has metal strings and is played with fingerpicks, is popular. *See also* MUSIC.

SHA (SHAH). The title *sha*, or *shah*, was used for the hereditary rulers of Qarategin, **Darvoz**, and **Badakhshon** in the 15th–20th centuries.

SHABDOLOV, SHODI (1943–). Born in **Khorugh, Mountainous Badakhshon Autonomous Veloyat** (MBAV), Shabdolov graduated from the Tajik Polytechnic Institute in 1965 and started working for the Communist Party in the MBAV and the Central Committee in **Dushanbe**. Shabdolov was elected chair of the **Communist Party of Tajikistan** (CPT) in September 1991. He was first elected to Tajikistan's parliament in 1990.

SHADUNTS, SUREN (1898–1940). Born in Azerbaijan to Armenian parents, Shadunts joined the Communist Party in 1917. In 1931–1932, he chaired the Central Asian Cotton-growing Company and in 1932–1934 worked as secretary of the Central Asian Bureau of the All-Soviet Communist Party. In 1935, Shadunts was appointed first secretary of the **Communist Party of Tajikistan**. In 1936, he went to Moscow, where he worked in the party control committee. Later he was arrested and charged with counterrevolutionary activity. He was sentenced to death by the military collegium of the USSR Supreme Court and was executed in 1940. In 1957, his reputation was rehabilitated.

SHAGADAEV, MINOVAR (1898–1950). Born in **Gharm**, Shagadaev (Shogadoev) joined the **Communist Party of Tajikistan** in 1925 and graduated from the courses of Marxism-Leninism in Stalinobod (**Dushanbe**) in 1936. In 1936–1937, he chaired the executive committee of Hoit districts. In October 1937, he was appointed chair of Tajikistan's **central executive committee**. From 15 July 1938 to 29 July 1950, he chaired the Presidium of the **Supreme Soviet** of Tajikistan. He was elected three times to the **Soviet Union**'s supreme assembly and twice to that of Tajikistan.

SHAHIDI, TOLIBKHON (1946–). A modern Tajik composer, Shahidi was born in **Dushanbe** to the family of composer **Ziyodullo Shahidi**. He graduated from the Musical College in Dushanbe in 1965 and the Moscow Tchaikovsky State Conservatory (the class of Aram Khachaturian) in 1972. Shahidi works in a number of different genres, including theater and cinema, representing a fusion of the Tajik and European musical traditions. *See also* MUSIC; OPERA AND BALLET THEATER.

SHAHIDI, ZIYODULLO (1914–1985). One of the founders of modern Tajik symphonic music, Shahidi was born in **Samarqand** and moved to **Dushanbe**, the capital of Tajikistan, at the age of 18. He was already an adult and popular composer when he joined the Moscow State Conservatory. A great admirer of the Tajik **Shashmaqom**, he went further, bringing Tajik classical melodies into modern symphonic **music**. From the 1940s to 1985, Shahidi composed lyric songs as well as music for theaters and cinema. He also authored the first Tajik musical comedies, symphonies, and operas. The Ziyodullo Shahidi Museum was established in Dushanbe in 1989. *See also* OPERA AND BALLET THEATER; SHAHIDI, TOLIBKHON.

SHAHRAK. A *shahrak* is a township or rural settlement with some urban elements. The shahrak and **deh** are at the lowest (**jamoat**) level of local government. *See also* ADMINISTRATIVE STRUCTURE.

SHAHRISTON NOHIYA. Situated in the south of the **Sughd veloyat**, the Shahriston nohiya was formed in 1991 at the expense of the **Uroteppa** nohiya. Shahriston's population is more than 29,400, **Tajiks** and **Uzbeks**. The distance from the administrative center, the village of Shahriston, to **Khujand** is 144 kilometers. Arable land amounts to 10,200 hectares. The main occupation is **agriculture**, including fruit, vegetable, and **cotton** production. The Shahriston mountain pass, on the **Turkistan** ridge, is 3,378 meters high and connects **Dushanbe** with Khujand. The pass is open to traffic only between May and November.

SHAHRITUS NOHIYA. Located in the **Khatlon** veloyat, **Qurghonteppa** zone, the Shahritus nohiya is adjacent to the Surkhan Darya province of **Uzbekistan** and the Qunduz province of **Afghanistan**. The district was formed in 1930. It is 2,336 square kilometers with a population of 79,100 (9,600 urban dwellers), **Tajiks, Uzbeks**, and **Arabs**, living in five **jamoats**. The distance from the administrative center, the village of Shahritus, to Qurghonteppa is 112 kilometers and to **Dushanbe** 195 kilometers. The climate is subtropical. July temperatures can reach 39°C or even 46°C, and the average annual precipitation is 200 millimeters. The main occupation is **agriculture**, including **cotton** production and livestock breeding, especially astrakhan sheep. The Termez-Qurghonteppa **railway** traverses this nohiya.

SHAIDON. This settlement is the center of the **Asht nohiya, Sughd veloyat**. The distance from Shaidon to **Khujand** is 107 kilometers, and to **Dushanbe** 448 kilometers. The closest railway station is Rapqon (35 kilometers). The population is about 11,800, consisting of **Tajiks** and **Uzbeks**. The main industrial enterprise in Shaidont is a fruit conservation plant.

SHANGHAI COOPERATION ORGANIZATION (SCO). An intergovernmental security organization initially formed to deal with border issues between China and its post-Soviet neighbors, the SCO is rooted in a treaty signed by the presidents of **China**, Kazakhstan,

Russia, **Kyrgyzstan**, and Tajikistan in Shanghai on 26 April 1996. The treaty stipulates the withdrawal of armed forces and armaments, except border guards, 100 kilometers away from state borders; the cessation of military exercises directed against any signatory to the treaty; and limitations on the size and the forces involved in military exercises, as well as the need for the signatories to inform one another about such exercises. The treaty also established a mechanism for making contact between border troops and provided for mutual invitation of observers to military exercises. After the inclusion of **Uzbekistan**, the group was renamed the Shanghai Cooperation Organization on 15 June 2001. Its working languages are Chinese and Russian.

By 2002, all border issues, including the **Tajik-China border** dispute, were resolved. The SCO's main concerns include combating **terrorism**, separatism, and extremism. At the SCO summit in Tashkent in June 2004, the Regional Antiterrorism Structure was established.

A Framework Agreement to boost economic cooperation was signed by the SCO member states on 23 September 2003, and China proposed a free trade area. The SCO supports joint energy projects in the oil and gas sectors. It also engaged in exploration for new hydrocarbon reserves and sought joint use of water resources. In November 2006, Russia announced it was developing plans for an SCO "Energy Club."

The economic focus of the SCO is useful for China. But Russia is eager to turn the organization into a military-political bloc confronting the North Atlantic Treaty Organization (NATO) and would like the SCO to merge with the **Collective Security Treaty Organization** (CSTO). In October 2007, the SCO signed an agreement with the CSTO, in **Dushanbe**, to broaden cooperation on issues such as security, crime, and **drug trafficking**. There have been a number of SCO joint military exercises. Cultural cooperation also takes place. The culture ministers of the SCO met for the first time in Beijing in April 2002 and signed a joint statement for ongoing cooperation.

Among other nations of Eurasia, Mongolia became the first country to receive observer status to the SCO in 2004. **Pakistan**, **India**, and **Iran** received observer status in 2005. Mongolia, Pakistan, and Iran have since applied for full membership to the organization. Belarus has applied for observer status. The **United States** applied for observer status but was rejected in 2005. The territory of the SCO member states constitutes 60 percent of Eurasia's territory and a population of approximately 1.5 billion. Together with the four SCO observers, this growing organization represents a strong alliance of states with huge energy resources as well as nuclear weapons. *See also* FOREIGN POLICY.

SHARIFZODA, FATHULLOKHON (1941–1996). Born in **Hisor** to an influential religious family, Sharifzoda (Sharifov) received his education at home. He preached in Hisor **mosques** and by the 1980s was a respected religious authority. In February 1993, following the departure of **Hoji Akbar Turajonzoda** from Tajikistan, a Muslim conference in Dushanbe decided to break with the Central Asian Office of the Muftiyat in Tashkent and establish a national authority. Sharifzoda was appointed the first **mufti** of Tajikistan. In January 1996, he was assassinated by unknown assailants. *See also* OFFICIAL MUSLIM CLERGY; UNOFFICIAL MULLAHS.

SHARIK. A form of communal work in **agriculture**, *sharik* (coworker) is an arrangement to pool together land, working animals, equipment, and seeds for common use. With the launch of **collectivization** in the 1930s, sharik arrangements ceased.

SHASHMAQOM. A six-step cycle of Tajik classical songs and melodies arranged in a definite order, the Shashmaqom was formed in **Bukhara, Samarqand, Khujand**, and other Persian-speaking urban centers of **Central Asia** about 9–16 CE. Born as a classical court style, the Shashmaqom became extremely popular among northern Tajiks and later **Uzbeks**. The form comprises six (*shash*) *maqoms* (musical poems): *buzruk, rost, navo, dugoh, segoh*, and *iroq*. Texts include poems of Perso-Tajik poets **Abuabdullo Rudaki**, Hafiz, **Abdurahmon Jomi**, Kamoli Khujandi, Saadi Shirazi, Badriddin Hiloli, Zebunisso, Abdulqadir Bedil, Fuzuli, and others. The main musical instruments used by Shashmaqom performers are the **tanbur, doira, ghijjak, dutar, chang**, and **nai**. In Tajikistan and **Uzbekistan**, Shashmaqom is often performed along with female **dances**. **Khoja Abdulaziz Rasulov** and Levi Babakhanov were among the best performers of Shashmaqom in prerevolutionary Bukhara and Samarqand.

The first records of Tajik Shashmaqom were collected in Bukhara in 1923 by the Russian musicologist Viktor Uspenskiy and Tajik singers Ota Ghiyos and Ota Jalol. From 1950 to 1967, Fazliddin Shahobov, Boboqul Faizulloev, and Shohnazar Sohibov transcribed and taped the main bulk of Shashmaqom. In 1966 in **Dushanbe**, by government decision, a group of professional Shashmaqom performers was formed. The Academy of Shashmaqom was opened in Dushanbe in 2000. Shashmaqom is also popular among the **Bukharan Jews** residing since the end of the 1980s in Israel and the **United States**. *See also* FALAK; MUSIC.

SHAYBANIDS (1500–1599). A Turkic dynasty that ruled over **Khurasan** and **Movarounnahr** in the 16th century, the Shaybanids traced their lineage to Shayban, a grandson of Genghiz Khan. At the beginning of the 16th century, Muhammad Shayban Khan defeated the **Timurids** and established the Shaybanid dynasty. This victory heralded the arrival of other Turkic tribes in **Central Asia**, such as the **Qunghrats**, **Laqais**, and **Qataghans**, which accelerated the Turkification of the region and gave rise to the **Uzbek** identity. At the end of the 16th century, the Shaybanids were removed by the Janids, another Turkic dynasty with a lineage from Genghiz Khan.

SHIISM. A branch in **Islam** with doctrines different from those of the orthodox **Sunni** majority, Shiism recognizes only the fourth caliph, Ali, and his descendants as the lawful heirs of the Prophet Muhammad. Of the three principal Shiite groups, only **Ismailia** is present in Tajikistan. Roughly 5 percent of Tajikistan's Muslims subscribe to Ismailism. Twelve-Imam Shiism, which is the official religion of **Iran**, and the Five-Imam Shiism found in Yemen are not recorded in Tajikistan.

SHIRINOV, ABDUJABBOR (1953–). Born in **Khatlon** veloyat, Shirinov received a degree in mathematics from the Tajik State National University in 1974 and began working as a computer software programmer at the Tajik State University. In 1992–1998, he was director of the Settlement Department of the **National Bank of Tajikistan**. In 1998 to 2000, he was first deputy chair of the executive board of the Joint Stock Commerce Agro-Industrial Investment

Bank. In 2000–2006, he was first deputy chair of the National Bank. In 2006, Shirinov chaired the Committee for State Financial Control of Tajikistan. At the end of January 2007, the committee was abolished and Shirinov was appointed first deputy director of the Agency for State Finance Control and the Struggle against Corruption. On 1 February 2007, Shirinov was appointed ambassador extraordinary and plenipotentiary of the Republic of Tajikistan to the **United States**. *See also* BANKS; CORRUPTION.

SHISHLIANNIKOV, ALEXANDER (1950–). Born in Tashkent, Shishliannikov graduated from the Tashkent Tank High College in 1972. Between 1973 and 1990, he served in the Soviet Army in Czechoslovakia and Turkmenia. In 1991, he was head of the headquarters operation of a large military unit. In 1992, he enlisted in the **Uzbekistan** national army and in January 1993 was appointed minister of defense in Tajikistan. In 1995, Shishliannikov was replaced by **Sherali Khairulloev**.

SHOHNOMA. A collection of medieval stories on the history of the Iranian people, *Shohnoma*, or *Shahnameh* (King's Story), was a work by **Abulqasem Firdawsi** (940–1025). It purports to describe the history of the Iranian kings from ancient times until the fall of the last **Sassanid** king, Yazdigurd III (7th century). Written in **Farsi-Dari**, it records the renewal of Farsi after the **Arab** invasion. *Shohnoma* was completed in 994. The first edition is believed to have been lost; the second edition, which appeared in 1010–1014, contains 52,000–55,000 rows. *Shohnoma* has inspired movies, poems, novels, and dramas in Tajikistan, **Iran**, and **Afghanistan**. In the **Tajik**/Dari/ Farsi speaking world, *Shohnoma* is considered an important cultural treasure and a precious part of the oral and written heritage and national historiography.

SHOTEMUR, SHIRINSHO (1899–1937). A leader of the **Communist Party of Tajikistan** (CPT), Shotemur was born in **Shughnon nohiya, Badakhshon**. He started his political activity in 1921, when he was appointed a member of the **Pamiri** military-political commission. In 1921–1923, he was chair of the Pamir Revolutionary Committee (Commission, in 1922–1923). In 1923–1924, he worked in the

Turkistan Communist Party. In 1926, he was appointed people's commissar of finance in Tajikistan. In 1929, he graduated from the University of the Toilers of the East (Moscow). In 1929–1932, he became second secretary of the Central Committee of the CPT. Then he was sent to the Institute of the Red Professorship in Moscow. In 1933, after the removal of **Nusratullo Maqsum**, Shotemur was criticized for deviating from the party line, but he was appointed chair of the **central executive committee** of the **Tajik Soviet Socialist Republic** in December 1933. In 1937, he was charged with counter-revolutionary activity, sentenced to death by the military collegium of the Soviet Supreme Court, and executed. In 1957, his reputation was rehabilitated. In 1964, he was reinstated in the Communist Party of the Soviet Union.

SHU'LAI INQILOB. The first Soviet newspaper in the **Tajik** language, *Shu'lai Inqilob* (Fire of Revolution), an eight-page weekly, started in April 1919 but ceased publication in December 1921. *Shu'lai Inqilob* was the organ of the **Turkistan Communist Party** and was published in **Samarqand**. It propagated the Communist Party's position on politics, **religion**, and **women's issues**, as well as Tajik **literature**. Famous Tajik literary figures such as **Sadriddin Ayni**, Alizoda, Raji, and others contributed to *Shu'lai Inqilob. See also* MASS MEDIA.

SHUGHNI AND RUSHANI. Two **Pamirian languages**, Shughni and Rushani are spoken by the inhabitants of Shughnon, Rushan, and Rosht Qal'a **nohiyas** in the **Mountainous Badakhshon Autonomous Veloyat**. Shughni and Rushani speakers number around 100,000.

SHUGHNON NOHIYA. Located in the basin of the Ghund and Shahdara rivers, in the **Mountainous Badakhshon Autonomous Veloyat** (MBAV), the Shughnon nohiya was formed in 1932. It is the most populated district of the MBAV. **Khorugh** is the administrative center. The district encompasses 8,851 square kilometers, with a population of 39,900, mostly Shughni-speaking **Ismaili Tajiks**. The nohiya borders **Afghanistan**. Average temperatures in January and July are –8°C and 22°C respectively. The main occupation is animal husbandry and **grain** cultivation.

SHUKUROV, MUHAMMADJON (1926–). A Tajik literary critic and **academician**, Shukurov was born in **Bukhara** to the family of Muhammad Sharifjon Mahdum (**Sadri Ziyo**) and graduated from the Tajik Pedagogical Institute in 1945. In 1951, Shukurov started work at the Institute of (Tajik) Language and Literature in the **Academy of Sciences of Tajikistan** as a research fellow. In 1959, he was appointed head of the Department of Tajik Modern Literature. Shukurov has written a number of works on the history of Soviet Tajik literature. In the mid-1980s, he started his ardent campaign in defense of the Tajik language and proposed an Iranian cultural unity.

SHUROBOD NOHIYA. Located in the **Khatlon** veloyat, the Shurobod nohiya was created in the Kulob veloyat in 1939 but merged with neighboring districts in 1955. In 1991, it was formed again at the expense of **Muminobod** nohiya (Dashtijum and Shurobod **jamoats**) and Moskva nohiya (Sarichashma jamoat). Shurobod's population is about 39,200, mostly **Tajiks** and **Uzbeks**. The distance from the district center, Shurobod, to **Kulob** is 35 kilometers and to **Dushanbe** 237 kilometers. Average January and July temperatures are –4°C and 22–24°C respectively. Annual precipitation is 700–1,100 millimeters. The main occupation is **agriculture**, including **cotton** and **grain** production, gardening, and livestock breeding.

SHUROI ISLOMIA (ISLAMIC COUNCIL). A Muslim political organization, the Shuroi Islomia was formed in March 1917 under the leadership of Munavvar Qari Abdurashidkhanov. The organization supported Turkistan's provisional government, insisting on national and religious autonomy for **Turkistan** within the framework of a democratic **Russia**. The Shuroi Islomia was supported by **Jadid** leaders, but in June 1917 it joined forces with the conservative **Jamiyati Ulamo** against the Bolshevik takeover in October 1917. This resulted in the banning of the Shuro by Soviet authorities at the end of 1917. The Shuroi Islomia nonetheless continued to be active and to question the legitimacy of the **Turkistan Soviet Republic** in Tashkent. It formed an alternative government in 1918 known as the Kokand Autonomy and supported the **Basmachi**. *See also* POLITICAL PARTIES.

SHUROI ULAMO. Tajikistan's highest religious authority, the Shuroi Ulamo replaced the Muftiyat in 1996. The Shuroi Ulamo controls all of the country's **mosques**. It approves or rejects **imams** elected by parishioners, collects taxes from mosques, and administers the **hajj** together with the Department of Religious Affairs in the Ministry of Culture. In 2004, the Shuroi issued an unpopular *fatvo* (opinion) barring women from attending mosques. The **Islamic Renaissance Party of Tajikistan** criticizes the Shuroi Ulamo for its submission to the **government**. Since June 1996, Hoji Amonullo Nematzoda heads Tajikistan's Shuroi Ulamo. *See also* ISLAM; MUFTI; WOMEN'S ISSUES.

SILVER. Tajikistan possesses large deposits of silver, with estimated reserves of 57.4 million tons—the largest in the world. The biggest mine, Bolshoi Koni Mansur (51.2 million tons of reserves), is located in the **Sughd veloyat**. During 2002–2009, Tajikistan produced 5 metric tons of silver a year.

SITODI MELLI. This armed group, a predominantly **Kulobi** force, brought **Emomali Rahmon** to power. The Sitodi Melli (Popular Front) emerged in May 1992 during pro-communist rallies in **Dushanbe's** Ozodi Square, when President **Rahmon Nabiev** founded the Presidential Guard by distributing weapons to pro-governmental demonstrators. Nabiev was forced to disband this guard shortly after its creation, but a number of Kalashnikov rifles were taken away by Kulobis. In the summer of 1992, the Sitodi Melli emerged in Kulob and later in **Hisor nohiya**, led by **Sangak Safarov** and **Faizali Saidov**. The group received substantial support from sources including **Uzbekistan** and **Russia**.

At the 16th session of the **Supreme Soviet**, held in **Sughd veloyat** in November 1992, Sitodi Melli's military victory was rewarded by naming its choice, Emomali Rahmon, head of state. The government placed Kulobis in key positions but disbanded the Sitodi Melli, incorporating its armed units into the national **army**.

SOCIAL-DEMOCRATIC PARTY OF TAJIKISTAN. Tajikistan's Party of Justice and Progress was formed in March 1998 and registered in February 1999, but the registration was not renewed in

April 1999. The party then regenerated itself under its current name, Social-Democratic Party of Tajikistan (Hizbi Social-Demokratii Tojikiston in **Tajik**), in October 1999. The party was led by a collective of intellectuals with no apparent regional affiliation. The party chair, **Rahmatulloh Zoirov**, is a professor of law. The party was unable to enter **elections** for the **Majlisi Namoyandagon** in 2000 and 2005. *See also* POLITICAL PARTIES.

SOCIALIST PARTY OF TAJIKISTAN (SPT). The Socialist Party of Tajikistan (Hizbi Socialisti Tojikiston in **Tajik**) held its inaugural congress in **Khujand** on 15 June 1996 under the leadership of **Safarali Kenjaev**. The SPT was registered on 6 August 1996 and operates in almost all regions of the republic, with its biggest branch in **Sughd** (8,600 members). Party membership in 2000 was 24,000. Between 1996 and 1999, the SPT published the *Ittihod* newspaper in Russian, Tajik, and Uzbek. The Sughd provincial branch of the SPT led the party in joining the **Agreement on National Accord**, signed in March 1996, and plays a leading role in the **Societal Council**.

Kenjaev's assassination in 1999 seriously undermined the party. Safarali Kenjaev's son, Sherali Kenjaev, became acting chair in 1999. The party advanced a list of 19 candidates in the parliamentary **elections** of February 2000 but received only 32,223 votes (1.24 percent of all votes) and was consequently unable to enter the **Majlisi Oli**. In 2006, the SPT again lost in the parliamentary elections. In the 2006 presidential election, SPT candidate Abdualim Ghafforov received 2.8 percent of the vote. *See also* POLITICAL PARTIES.

SOCIETAL COUNCIL. Formed as a consultative organ of the signatories to the **Agreement on National Accord**, signed in March 1996, the Societal Council included representatives of the **government** and 30 public organizations. The Societal Council ceased its activity in the second half of 1997, following the signing of the **General Agreement on the Establishment of Peace and National Accord** and the formation of the **Commission for National Reconciliation**. *See also* CIVIL WAR.

SOGDIANA. An Ancient territory of **Central Asia**, Sogdiana was centered around the **Zarafshon** and Qashqa Darya river basins in the

7th century BCE through 8th century CE. In this period, Sogdiana (**Sughd** in **Tajik**) was ruled by the **Achaemenids, Alexander the Great**, Greco-**Bactrians**, and **Kushans. Samarqand** was the center of Sogdiana. The Tajik people have their roots in the Sogdian-speaking inhabitants of this land, and Bactrians. In the first decades of the 8th century CE, **Arab** invaders reached Sogdiana and incorporated it into the Muslim world. By the 10th century, the Sogdian language was replaced by **Dari**.

SOIL. In Tajikistan, a mountainous country, there are four belts of soil, depending on altitude. The plain and low-mountain belt (300–1,600 meters above sea level) is an area of gray soil. The mid-mountainous belt (1,600–2,800 meters) is an area of brown soil. The high-mountainous belt (2,800–4,600 meters) encompasses alpine-steppe, steppe, and desert-steppe soil. The highest alpine level is the nival belt (higher than 4,600 meters). The **Tajiks** adapted to life in mountainous regions and cultivated alpine lands. They were aware of the ecological capacity of these territories. Under Soviet rule, however, modern **agriculture** upset the harmony between traditional cultivation practices and the mountainous terrain. The Soviet irrigation system resulted in the pollution of collector networks and a rise in the level of bottom waters.

SOKH (SUKH). An area and village that form a Tajik-populated **Uzbek** enclave within **Kyrgyzstan**, Sokh covers 325 square kilometers in the **Ferghana** valley. The population of up to 29,000 is composed predominantly of **Tajiks**, with about 5 percent **Kyrgyzs**.

SOLIEV, HAKIM (1946–). Born in **Rudaki nohiya**, Soliev graduated from the Trades College, **Dushanbe**, in 1965 and the Far Eastern Institute of Soviet Trade in 1997. In 1968–1977, he was director of the Food Department at the Vladivostok railway station (**Russia**). In 1977–1978, he was director of the Varzob restaurant in Dushanbe. At the end of 1992, he was appointed minister of trade and material resources, and he became chair of the state committee on trade and contracts in 1994. Soliev was appointed minister of economics and trade in January 2001. From November 2006 until his retirement in January 2009, Soliev served as chair of the tax committee.

SOVIET OF PEOPLE'S DEPUTIES. In January 1922, the extraordinary dictatorial commission on Eastern Bukharan affairs (Chedeka) of the All-Bukharan **central executive committee** (CEC) was formed. It had legislative, executive, and legal powers in Tajikistan. At local levels, state power was held by revolutionary committees. In June 1924, it was abolished and its functions were transferred to the provisional CEC of **Eastern Bukhara**. A year later, the Eastern Bukhara Soviet ceased to exist, passing its responsibilities to the revolutionary committee of the **Tajik Autonomous Soviet Socialist Republic**. In 1938, the first election to the **Supreme Soviet** of the **Tajik Soviet Socialist Republic** was held, electing 182 deputies (including four women). The Supreme Soviet elected a presidium, a permanently acting body to rule between sessions of the Supreme Soviet. Deputies to the Soviet were elected for a period of five years from the electoral districts of equal population. The Supreme Soviet was the supreme representative and legislative body in the state. In February 1995, parliamentary elections were held, and the Supreme Soviet was renamed **Majlisi Oli** in April of that year.

SOVIET UNION. The Soviet Union (Ittifoqi Soveti in **Tajik**, Sovetskiy Soyuz in Russian), or Union of Soviet Socialist Republics (USSR), emerged from the Russian empire after the Russian Revolution in 1917. It was officially proclaimed on 30 December 1922 as a union of four Soviet republics by the Congress of Soviets, which was headed by the leaders of the Russian Communist Party (Bolsheviks). At that time, the **Turkistan Soviet Republic**, including what is now northern Tajikistan, was part of the Russian Soviet Federated Socialist Republic, or Russian Federation, the largest and most populous constituent state of the Soviet Union. In 1924, the **Tajik Autonomous Soviet Socialist Republic**, covering what are now the southern and central regions of Tajikistan, joined the Soviet Union as part of the Uzbek Soviet Socialist Republic. From 1922 to 1940, the USSR grew to include 15 constituent soviet socialist republics, including the **Tajik Soviet Socialist Republic**, which was formed in 1929. The Soviet Union stretched from Eastern Europe across northern Asia to the Pacific Ocean. With its collapse in 1991, Tajikistan and a number of other states in **Central Asia** established their independence. *See also* COMMONWEALTH OF INDEPENDENT STATES; RUSSIA.

SOVKHOZ. *Sovkhoz* is an acronym for *sovetskoye khoziaistvo* (soviet farm). The sovkhoz farms were an important and widespread form of agricultural organization in Tajikistan since the 1930s. In contrast to **kolkhoz** farms, sovkhoz property did not belong to the members but to the state. Sovkhoz farms were considered state enterprises, and their members were agricultural workers. *See also* AGRICULTURE; COOPERATIVE FARMS.

SPITAMEN (SPITAMAN) (d. 328 BCE). A warlord of **Sogdiana**, Spitamen mobilized military resistance against the advancing forces of **Alexander the Great** in the 320s BCE. Spitamen was the only general in history to defeat a part of the Macedonian army. The Order of Spitamen has been a high military award in Tajikistan since 1996.

SPORTS. Since antiquity, physical exercises (*varzish*) such as walking and riding have been an important part of the daily life of the **Tajiks**. Generations of Tajiks have remained attached to the masculine image and code of conduct advocated by the legendary strongman of the **Shohnoma** epic, Rustam. The national sports **gushtingiri** (wrestling) and **buzkashi** (polo can be traced back to the time of Zoroastrianism. Since the Tajiks are not only Persians but also Muslims, they consider it permissible and even required to relax the mind and body in exercise. Activities associated with defending and protecting **religion** and country, like archery, wrestling, swimming, and riding, are *mustahab* (praiseworthy) and essential, while anything done simply for "futile, meaningless pleasures" is *makhrooh* (abominable), according to Muslim teachings.

Soviet authorities promoted the policy of "physical culture and sport," and various sports clubs and societies such as Dinamo, Spartak, Lokomotiv, and Trudovye Rezervy operated all over the **Soviet Union**, including in Tajikistan. Modern stadiums were built in cities and district centers, and athletic fields were provided for every school. The Tajik Institute of Physical Culture was established in the early 1970s, and the Pamir team was among the top 10 Soviet soccer teams in the 1980s. Since 1960, Tajiks have been involved in international athletic competitions like the Olympic Games and have achieved some noteworthy results. Ibrahim Hasanov was a multiple champion of the Soviet Union and Tajikistan in canoeing and was the first Tajik participant in the Olympic Games in Rome in 1960.

Zebinisso Rustamova, an archer, won the gold medal in the world championship in 1975 and the bronze medal at the 1976 Montreal Summer Olympic Games in individual archery. Saimumin Rahimov, a famous Tajik *gushtingir* (wrestler), became the world champion in the Russian martial art of *sambo* in 1975. From the mid-1960s onward, alpine skiers from all over the Soviet Union came to the Rui Dasht and Safed Dara plateaus in **Varzob** canyon for downhill skiing and competitions.

Developments in Tajik sports were interrupted during the civil war (1992–1997). More than 300 coaches, managers, and trainers and around 200 high-class athletes left Tajikistan. Most of them were **Russians**. Cycling, pentathlon, water polo, fencing, and other sports ceased to exist in the country. The oldest stadiums in Tajikistan, Dinamo and Spartak in **Dushanbe**, were destroyed.

During Tajikistan's time as a constituent republic of the Soviet Union, Tajik athletes competed for the Soviet team, and four of them won Olympic medals from 1960 to 1992. On 5 May 1992, the Olympic Committee of the Republic of Tajikistan was formed. However, Tajik athletes were still part of the last united team of the former Soviet republics in the 1992 Olympics. At the Barcelona Summer Olympics of 1992, Andrey Abduvaliev from Dushanbe won the gold medal in the hammer throw. The Atlanta Summer Olympics of 1996 were Tajikistan's independent debut in the Olympic Games. Four Tajik athletes participated. In 2000, four Tajik athletes took part in the Sidney Olympics. In 2004, seven went to the Athens Olympics. None of them won medals.

In 2008, Tajikistan's sports program entered a phase of stabilization. In the Beijing Olympics, the country was represented by 14 athletes who took part in five sports: boxing, judo, swimming, hammer throw, and freestyle wrestling. Rasul Boqiev won the bronze medal in judo. It was the first independent Tajik Olympic medal. Another Tajik athlete, Yusuf Abdusalomov, was the silver medalist in wrestling. Tajikistan participated without success in the winter Olympics of 2002 and 2006. In February 2009, President **Emomali Rahmon** was elected president of the National Olympic Committee.

The country has slowly restored its sports infrastructure but needs sports schools, stadiums, athletic fields, and qualified coaches. Tajik sports need more autonomy but cannot survive without state support. The existing economic system cannot afford the construction of modern stadiums and sport facilities, not to mention the cost of camps abroad to train world-class athletes. The poverty of the population leads to poor nutrition, with bread being a major element of the Tajik diet. Dietary deficiencies decrease participation in sports and regular physical exercise.

STALINOBOD. *See* DUSHANBE.

STATE HYMN. Tajikistan's state hymn was accepted by the **Supreme Soviet** in September 1994. The author of the verses is a modern poet, Gulnazar Keldy. The melody remains that of the previous hymn of Soviet Tajikistan, written in the 1930s by Sulaimon Iyudakov, a **Bukharan Jew**. *See also* FLAG; MUSIC.

SUFISM. A mystical tradition within **Islam**, Sufism is also known as *tasawwuf* ("to dress in wool" in Arabic). The movement was founded in the 8th century. Sufism teaches Islamic esoterics and has influenced local traditions over the years. The great poet **Jalolidin Rumi** was a Sufi mystic. *See also* MURID; MURSHID; NAQSHBANDI-YAH; RELIGIONS.

SUGDIAN LANGUAGE. The Sugdian (Sogdian) language belongs to the East Iranian division of the Indo-Iranian group of languages. In the 4th–7th centuries, Sugdian was widely used in the **Zarafshon** and **Ferghana** valleys, as well as in the Tashkent oasis and **Samarqand**. In the 7th–10th centuries, Sugdian was gradually replaced by **Dari**. Sugdian continued to be used in remote mountain villages up to the 14th century. A derivation of the Sugdian language known as **Yaghnobi** is spoken by the indigenous population of Yaghnob. *See also* LANGUAGES.

SUGHD VELOYAT. Sughd is the most economically advanced province in Tajikistan. The provincial center is the city of **Khujand**. The region was known as Khujand *uezd* in 1918–1924, within the boundaries of the **Samarqand** province of the **Turkistan Soviet Republic**. In 1924–1929, the territory constituted part of the **Uzbek** SSR, but in 1929 Khujand *uezd* was transferred to Tajikistan. In 1936, Khujand was renamed Leninobod, and in 1939 Leninobod province was formed (known as Leninabad oblast at the time). The province was abolished in 1962 but was reestablished in 1970. It was renamed the Sughd veloyat in July 2000.

Sughd's territory is 26,100 square kilometers, with a population of more than 1.9 million (531,100 urban dwellers), mainly **Tajiks** with a minority of **Uzbeks** (around 30 percent). Sughd includes 14 **nohiyas**, 10 cities, and 21 villages. Surrounded by **Uzbekistan** and **Kyrgyzstan**, the province is separated from the rest of the country by the mountain ranges of **Turkistan, Zarafshon**, and **Hisor**. The Trans-Tajik Railway from **Konibodom** to **Dushanbe** runs through Uzbekistan, connecting the province with southern Tajikistan. Sughd includes an exclave around the town of **Vorukh**, surrounded by Kyrgyzstan. Average January and July temperatures in the valleys are −1°C and 29°C respectively, and the average annual precipitation is 400 millimeters. There are deposits of oil, gas, coal, wolfram, rare metals, copper, and salt in northern Tajikistan. Total arable and pasture lands amount to more than 1 million hectares. Industrial activity in Sughd started before the 1917 Russian Revolution. In the 1980s and 1990s, the province contributed around 35 percent of Tajikistan's gross industrial production, which included 100 percent of coal, 99 percent of carpets, 93 percent of silk fabrics, and 93 percent of gas. Sughd produces 30 percent of the country's agricultural production, including 27 percent of **cotton**, 50 percent of silk cocoon, 89 percent of tobacco, and 50 percent of vegetable products.

Sughd's economic weight facilitated its political prominence in the republic. After **World War II**, leading figures from Sughd headed the **Communist Party of Tajikistan** (CPT). **Rahmon Nabiev** was the last Sughdi figure to lead Tajikistan. In the **civil war**, Sughd supported **Kulobi** forces against the opposition, and the province remained largely untouched by fighting. In November 1998, however, **Mahmud Khudoiberdyev** and his forces raided Sughd from the territory of neighboring Uzbekistan.

SUMALAK. A meal made from the juice of wheat sprouts, *sumalak* is served during the **Nawruz**. The making of sumalak is a ritual, as the women who prepare it recite poetry, sing, and **dance**.

SUNNISM. The largest denomination in **Islam**, Sunnism claims the majority of Muslims worldwide, and 95 percent of **Tajiks** adhere. The remaining 5 percent of Tajik Muslims follow **Shia Ismailism**.

Sunnis recognize the first four caliphs and, unlike Shiites, attribute no special function to the descendants of Ali, the Prophet Muhammad's son-in-law. There are four Sunni schools of law (**mazhabs**). The Tajiks follow the largest, the Sunni **Hanafi** school. *See also* RELIGIONS; SALAFIYA.

SUPREME SOVIET. The Supreme Soviet was the highest legislative and representative body in Tajikistan between 1938 and 1995. The first general **elections** to the Supreme Soviet of Tajikistan were held in June 1938, and 99.5 percent of the country's eligible voters took part. The Supreme Soviet was known as *Verkhovnyi Sovet* in Russian and as *Soveti Oli* in **Tajik**. It was headed by the presidium. In accordance with the **constitution** of 1994, the **Majlisi Oli** was formed to replace the Supreme Soviet as the supreme representative and legislative organ of the state. Traditionally, the chair of the presidium of the Supreme Soviet, as surrogate president, came from the **Gharmis**. Among those serving as chair of the Supreme Soviet's presidium were **Minovar Shagadaev** (July 1938–July 1950), **Nazarshoh Dodkhudoev** (July 1950–May 1956), **Qahor Mahkamov** (April 1990–November 1990), **Qadriddin Aslonov** (November 1990–September 1991), **Rahmon Nabiev** (September 1991–December 1991), **Safarali Kenjaev** (December 1991–April 1992), **Akbarsho Iskandarov** (August 1992–November 1992), **Emomali Rahmon** (November 1992–November 1994), **Safarali Rajabov** (April 1995–March 2000), and **Sadulloh Khairulloev** from March 2000. *See also* SOVIET OF PEOPLE'S DEPUTIES.

SURNAY. A musical instrument in the form of a long wooden tube (approximately 500 millimeters), the *surnay* produces a loud sound in high registers. It is played in ensemble with **karnai** and drums outdoors at mass public events. *See also* MUSIC.

SUZANI (SUZANE). Persian for "needle," *suzani* is traditional needlework, embroidered carpet using silk, satin, or velvet. Suzani is a medieval craft still practiced in Tajikistan. Suzani needleworks are used to decorate walls in Tajik houses.

SYR DARYA. The ancient Jaxartes River is currently known as Syr Darya and runs through the republics of **Uzbekistan**, Tajikistan, and

Kazakhstan. It is interchangeably referred to as Daryoi Sir or Sirdaryo in **Tajik**. The Syr Darya is the longest river in **Central Asia** (2,684 kilometers), but it carries less water than the **Amu Darya**. The Syr Darya is formed by the joining of the Naryn and Qara Darya rivers in the eastern parts of the **Ferghana** valley. It then flows northwest and empties into the Aral Sea. There are a number of hydroelectric power stations on the Syr Darya, including a station in Qairaqum near **Khujand**. A large volume of the Syr Darya's water in the Ferghana valley, including in the **Sughd veloyat**, is used for irrigation, with serious consequences for the river. *See also* WATER.

– T –

TAJIK. An Iranian **language** used by Tajiks in **Central Asia**, Tajik is the national language of Tajikistan and is also used in **Afghanistan**, **Iran**, and western **China**. Tajik is closely related to other Iranian languages, **Dari** and **Farsi**, in phonetics, grammar, and lexicon. Tajik, known interchangeably as Farsi or Dari, flourished in the 9th–10th centuries, when the **Samanids** founded their dynasty centered in **Samarqand**. Dari, which used Arabic script, displaced the Arabic language in the Samanid court. Dari was used in official recordkeeping, science, and **literature**. In spite of conflicts between the rulers of Iran, Afghanistan, and Central Asia, Dari was commonly used by the people of these regions. A common literary heritage binds these people together. Among the most renowned literary treasures of this language are the writers **Abuabdullo Rudaki** (858–941) and **Abulqasem Firdawsi** (940–1025).

In the 16th–20th centuries, Dari in Central Asia was influenced by Turkic languages, primarily Uzbek. The Central Asian variant therefore grew apart from other Iranian languages in Iran and Afghanistan. In the same period, classical Dari grew closer to dialects in everyday usage and was increasingly defined as Tajik.

In the wake of the October 1917 revolution in **Russia**, the formation of the Tajik republic brought a boost for Tajik. Under Soviet rule, Tajik was promoted as a national language of the **Tajiks** with emphasis on differences between Tajik, Dari, and Farsi—a policy aimed at instilling a separate sense of national identity from other Iranian-speaking communities beyond Soviet borders. The Soviet system of

education in Tajikistan made significant strides in unifying Tajik dialects and simplifying classical literary texts for wide usage. Tajik, however, suffered two breaks in continuity. In the 1920s, Arabic script was replaced with modified Latin script. In 1940, it was replaced with modified Cyrillic script, which contains 39 letters, six more than Russian Cyrillic. The Soviet-imposed shifts deprived new generations of access to classical and religious manuscripts in Dari.

In spite of the apparent promotion of Tajik, Russian was the dominant language under Soviet rule. All party and state affairs were conducted in Russian. In the 1980s, growing national awareness among Tajiks led to demands for a reassessment of the status of the Tajik language. Tajik was proclaimed the official language of the state in the first post-Soviet **constitution** of the Republic of Tajikistan. Tajik is currently taught in modified Cyrillic script at schools, though the state expects to replace this script with Arabic. Russian remains widely used in the public sphere, especially in the media.

TAJIK ALUMINIUM PLANT. *See* TALCO.

TAJIK AUTONOMOUS SOVIET SOCIALIST REPUBLIC (TAJIK ASSR) (1924–1929). Following the Soviet national delimitation of **Central Asia**, the first modern Tajik state was created in September 1924 as part of the Uzbek Soviet Socialist Republic. The Tajik ASSR included 12 *volosti* (districts) of the **Turkistan Soviet Republic** (with a population of 135,665 people) and almost all the eastern territory of the **Bukharan People's Soviet Republic** (population 603,838). The Tajik ASSR also included a part of the Uzbek Soviet Socialist Republic (a population of 739,503, 65.4 percent **Tajiks** and 32.4 percent **Uzbeks**). The **Mountainous Badakhshon Autonomous Veloyat** formed a separate part of the newborn republic. The capital was established in **Dushanbe**. In November 1924, the first government of Tajikistan (known as the revolutionary committee) was formed and was headed by **Nusratullo Maqsum**.

Consolidation of the administrative and state structures in Tajikistan was hampered by the struggle against **Basmachi** rebels. The newborn republic also experienced a lack of professional cadres. The majority of trained technical and political professionals were **Russian** (82.6 percent), while 80 percent of the low-level local administrators were former officials of the **Bukharan emirate**. The first general **elections** in Tajikistan were held in August 1926, although "members of hostile classes" were excluded. About 40 percent of the total eligible electorate, mostly poor peasants, took part in elections, leading to the replacement of ad hoc revolutionary committees (Revkoms) by elected Soviet organs. Subsequently the republican power structure consisted of six **veloyat** soviets (**Gharm, Dushanbe, Kulob, Qurghonteppa, Panjakent**, and **Uroteppa**), 17 *tumen* (district) soviets, 75 *kent* (town) soviets, and 253 **qyshloq** soviets. The inaugural congress of the Soviets of the Tajik ASSR (December 1926) adopted a declaration on the formation of the Tajik ASSR. It formed the **central executive committee** and the government: Soviet of People's Commissars. The Tajik ASSR gave way to the **Tajik Soviet Socialist Republic** in November 1929.

TAJIK COTTON. The Tajik Cotton Corporation (Korpotatsiyai Respublikavii, or Pakhtai Tojik) was established in September 1997 to improve the **cotton** processing **industry**, which encompasses 20 cotton processing mills throughout the country. Sixty percent of the corporation's assets are held by the state. *See also* AGRICULTURE; ECONOMY.

TAJIK SOVIET ENCYCLOPEDIA (TSE). The Tajik Soviet Encyclopedia (Entsiklopediai Sovetii Tojik), a general encyclopedia, was published in 1978–1988. The TSE is written in **Tajik** and consists of eight volumes, with 23,000 entries. It is modeled on the Bol'shaya Sovetskaya Entsiklopedia (Grand Soviet Encyclopedia). Nearly 20,000 copies of the TSE were printed. The president of the **Academy of Sciences of Tajikistan, Muhammad Asimov**, acted as the chief editor.

TAJIK SOVIET SOCIALIST REPUBLIC (TAJIK SSR) (1929–1991). In November 1929, the **Tajik Autonomous Soviet Socialist Republic** was upgraded into a full **Soviet Union** republic and removed from the jurisdiction of **Uzbekistan**. This transition was made possible with the allocation of the economically developed and culturally advanced **Khujand** province from Uzbekistan to Tajikistan. The transfer of 16 districts and three towns in the province of Khujand enlarged Tajikistan's territory by more than 26,000 square kilometers and 205,800 people. In 1929, the population of Tajikistan was about 1.2 million (78 percent Tajik).

From its inception in 1929 until 1936, the Tajik SSR was divided into eight provinces (*okrug*) and the **Mountainous Badakhshon Autonomous Veloyat** (MBAV) for administrative purposes. After the introduction of the *oblast* (provincial) administrative division by the 1936 Soviet constitution, Tajikistan was restructured (1939). This resulted in the formation of the provinces of Leninobod (23,300 square kilometers, 502,000 people), Stalinobod (24,100 square kilometers, 491,000 people), **Kulob** (10,600 square kilometers, 203,000 people), **Gharm** (19,000 square kilometers, 163,000 people), plus the MBAV (66,900 square kilometers, 50,000 people). Each province (**veloyat** in **Tajik**) was subsequently divided into administrative structures based on cities, *rayons* (districts), towns, and village soviets.

In 1951, the Stalinobod province was abolished, followed by Gharm and Kulob (1955), and Leninobod (1962), and the territory was brought under direct central control from **Dushanbe**. This was aimed at unifying and strengthening agricultural regions. In 1959, some 600 square kilometers of virgin lands in Dashti Tashnalab, Uzbekistan, were transferred to Tajikistan. The Leninobod veloyat was reinstated in 1970, followed by Kulob (1973) and **Qurghonteppa** (1977). In September 1991, after the collapse of the Soviet Union, Tajikistan declared its independence and the Tajik Soviet Socialist Republic ceased to exist.

TAJIKISTAN MOVEMENT FOR NATIONAL UNITY AND REVIVAL. The Movement for National Unity and Revival (Harakati Baroi Yagonagii Melli va Ehyoi Tojikistan) was established in July 1997 at the government's initiative, immediately after the signing of the **General Agreement on the Establishment of Peace and National Accord** that brought an end to Tajikistan's **civil war**. The movement declared itself to be a nonpolitical and nongovernmental association aiming to contribute to peace in the republic. It has declared its membership to be 1 million. President **Emomali Rahmon** leads the association.

TAJIKISTAN STATE AWARDS. The **Majlisi Oli** approved the following state awards in May 1997: Gold Medal of Zarrin Tojik

(Golden Tajik), Order of Sitorai Prezidenti Tojikiston (Tajikistan President's Star), Order of Ismail Samani, Order of Dusti (Friendship), Order of **Spitamen**, Order of Sharaf (Glory), Medal of Jasorat (Heroism), Medal of Khizmati Shoista (Renowned Service), Medal of Shavqat (Compassion), Medal of Marzboni Shujoi Tojikiston (Tajikistan's Courageous Border Guard), and the Decorations for the People's Writer of Tajikistan, Tajikistan's Science and Technology Figure, and Tajikistan's Renowned Artist.

TAJIKISTAN UNION OF WRITERS. A voluntary association of professional writers, the Tajikistan Union of Writers (Ittifoqi Navisandagoni Tojikiston) was formed under the patronage of the **Communist Party of Tajikistan** in 1934. It united writers on the ideological basis of "socialist realism," closely following the **Soviet Union**'s Union of Writers in Moscow. Chairs of the board of the union have included **Abulqasem Lahuti** (1934–1946), **Mirzo Tursunzoda** (1946–1977), Mumin Qanoat (1977–1991), Askar Hakimov (1991–2004), and Mehmon Bakhti (since 2004). The union publishes two **Tajik**-language periodicals, *Sadoi Sharq* (Voice of the East) and *Madaniyati Tojikiston* (Tajikistan's Culture), and *Pamir* magazine in Russian. *See also* LITERATURE.

TAJIKS. The titular national group in Tajikistan, the Tajiks are of Iranian stock and speak an Iranian **language, Tajik**. Tajiks also live in **Uzbekistan, Afghanistan, China**, and other parts of the region. The Tajiks were the first to settle in **Central Asia**, but subsequent migrations of Turco-Mongolian groups changed the demographic landscape and reduced the Tajiks to a minority.

Most Tajik scholars believe that the word *Tajik* is derived from *toj* ("crown" from Tajik-**Farsi**). Some Western and Russian Orientalists suggest that it was originally the name of an **Arab** tribe (*Taj*, or *Tazik*) that invaded Central Asia in the 7th–8th centuries. In the medieval Tajik-Farsi **literature** and historical chronicles, the word *Tajik* was used to distinguish Persians from Turks. The whole population was called "Turku-Tojik." In the Russian usage of the 16th century and later, *Tajik* was applied to the urban population of Central Asia, distinct from Uzbek nomads. By the early 20th century, the term was used for mountainous Tajiks (the population of Qarategin, Mastchah, **Darvaz**, and **Badakhshon**), while Tajik speakers of the plains were called **Sart**. With the establishment of Soviet rule in Central Asia and the formation of the **Tajik Autonomous Soviet Socialist Republic**, the term acquired a distinct ethnic connotation and is now applied to Tajik speakers of Central Asia.

The Tajiks are Muslims, predominantly **Sunnis (Hanafi** school). Some 150,000 Tajiks (about 5 percent of the Muslim population) are **Shia Ismailis**. The Tajiks speak different Iranian languages. In addition to western Iranian Tajik and **Dari**, the Tajiks in Tajikistan, Afghanistan, and China speak eastern Iranian languages (**Pamiri** and **Yaghnobi**). Tajiks may be divided into three subcategories: those living in the valleys of the northern part of the country, those in the foothills and mountains of central and southern Tajikistan, and those in the vast alpine country of Pamir. These subgroups are distinguishable by their political culture, physical appearance, dialects, customs, **music**, and folklore.

The valley dwellers of the north are representatives of the rich urban civilization of **Samarqand, Bukhara, Khujand**, and **Ferghana**. The national delimitation of 1924 divided the Tajik descendants of these cultural centers. The Tajiks of the Leninobod (**Sughd**) veloyat, known as Leninobodis (including dwellers of Tajik cities of the Ferghana valley) live almost exclusively in Tajikistan, while the largest part of the Bukharan and Samarqandi Tajiks live in Uzbekistan. Tajiks also live in **Sokh**, an Uzbek enclave within Kyrgyzstan.

The Tajiks of the center and south, living in narrow valleys, foothills, and mountains of the **Khatlon** veloyat and **Nohiyas under Republican Control**, in contrast to northern Tajiks, were mostly separated from outside influences and lived almost independently of other Tajiks until the 20th century. Kulobi, Gharmi, Qarategini, and Hisori Tajiks are the biggest groups in this subcategory. These communities are strongly attached to their places of origin.

The Pamiri Tajiks live in Badakhshon. They are officially registered as Tajiks, although they are distinct from other Tajiks in language and **religion**. Pamiri Tajiks are generally Ismailis and speak different **Pamirian languages**, some of which are incomprehensible to other Tajiks. In addition to those in Tajikistan, nearly 100,000 Pamiris live in the adjacent mountain regions of Afghanistan, China, and **Pakistan**.

The population of Tajiks in Tajikistan in 1926 was 738,100 (or 71.5 percent of the total population), 884,000 (59.6 percent) in 1939,

3.1 million (62.3 percent) in 1989, and nearly 6 million (82 percent) in 2008. The diversity among Tajiks has proven to be the principal obstacle to consolidation of a unified Tajik state. *See also* TAJIKS OF AFGHANISTAN; TAJIKS OF CHINA.

TAJIKS OF AFGHANISTAN. Tajiks are the oldest ethnic group in **Afghanistan**. In the 18th–19th centuries, Afghan feudal lords defeated the Tajiks of Qandahar, Kabul, and Ghazni. In the 1880s, the Afghan emir Abdur Rahman (a Durrani Pushtun) succeeded in finally breaking the Tajik resistance in the northern provinces of Herat, Qataghan, and **Badakhshon**. Subsequently, Afghan rulers from the 1880s to 1970 resettled Pushtun dissidents from rebellious eastern and southern provinces to the Tajik-dominated north. These Pushtun newcomers (*nakilin*) were exempted from taxes. Thus, Tajiks were crippled economically and ostracized politically in Afghanistan.

Compact masses of the Tajik population live in the center of the country—in Kabul province, areas of Charikar, Istalif, Panjsher, Gurband, Salang, and the southern and northern slopes of the Hindu Kush. Another large group of Tajiks live in western Afghanistan in Herat, Ghor, and partly in Nimroz and Farakh provinces. Tajiks constituted the largest ethnic group in northeastern Baghlan, Takhor, Qunduz, and Badakhshon provinces. In the northern provinces, Tajiks live together with **Uzbeks** and **Turkmens**. Estimates of the share of Tajiks in Afghanistan vary widely, from 25 percent to 50 percent or more of the total population. According to official data in 1987, Afghanistan's total population was about 16 million. Thus, on the eve of the Soviet invasion in 1989, Afghan Tajiks could have numbered 4–8 million, whereas the number of Tajiks in Tajikistan was about 4 million in 1998.

Compared to other ethnic groups, the Tajiks of Afghanistan are socially and economically more developed and urbanized. They ruled Afghanistan only two times: in 1929 (Habibulla **Bachai Saqqao**) and 1992–1996 (President Burhanuddin Rabbani). Tajik-Pushtun relations were not hostile. In Afghanistan, tribal, clan, and other kin-based institutions often play more important roles than ethnicity or nationality. The ruling Pushtuns used to rely more on Tajiks than on disunited Pushum compatriots. *See also* KHOS DEH PROTOCOL; MASSOUD, AHMAD SHAH; TAJIKS OF CHINA.

TAJIKS OF CHINA. In the People's Republic of **China, Tajiks** are recognized as one of the country's 56 nationalities forming a common unity called the "Chinese people." In 2000, there were 41,028 Tajiks living in China, about 33,000 of them in compact communities in the **Tashkurgan Tajik Autonomous County** of the Xinjiang-Uighur Autonomous Region. Smaller groups of Tajiks are scattered over some areas in southern Xinjiang, including Kashghar, Shache, Zepu, Yecheng, Pishan, and Hotan, where they live alongside Uighurs (a major minority group of Turkic descent), Kazakhs, **Kyrgyzs**, Dungans, Hans, and other ethnic groups.

The Tajiks of Xinjiang represent the only indigenous ethnic group of Indo-European origin in China. Like most of the Tajiks of the **Mountainous Badakhshon Autonomous Veloyat** (MBAV), the Tajiks of the Chinese Pamir follow the **Shia Ismaili** sect of **Islam**. Tajiks of Tajikistan and **Afghanistan** as well as the Persians of **Iran** view them as the northeasternmost outpost of Iranian people. Because of their isolation, they are culturally and linguistically distinct from their closest Tajik brethren—the Shughnis and Rushanis of the MBAV. However, physically, the Tajiks of China show all the racial characteristics of the Tajiks who form the bulk of the population in Tajikistan and Afghanistan. Ethnically, the Tajiks of China form a collection of small East Iranian ethnic groups with the **Vakhani** (Wakhi) as a separate faction. With the permission of the Chinese authorities in the early 20th century, the Vakhanis founded their settlement of Dafdar, south of Tashkurgan. A more sizable faction of Tajiks of China are the **Sarikoli**. Like other minorities, the Tajiks receive special consideration on their exams for entrance to middle school, high school, and college. Nevertheless, the Tajiks remain the least educated Muslim minority in China. In 1982, only 51 percent of them were literate.

From a religious standpoint, the Tajiks of China are different from their closest Muslim neighbors, Uighurs and Kyrgyzs, as well as the other Muslims of China who are **Sunnis**. As Ismailis, the Sarikoli and Vakhani Tajiks do not attend Sunni **mosques** and used to perform their worship at special houses called *jamoatkhona* (communion houses). The Ismaili Tajiks never revealed any religious zeal and did not participate in mass uprisings of local Muslims against Chinese rule in the 1920s–1930s and later. As Shiites who live in a non-Shiite environment, the Tajiks of China accept *taqiya*, the Islamic practice of "dissimilation" for the sake of avoiding persecution or imminent harm. *Taqiya*, according to which Islam may be ignored in life-threatening situations, allows Tajiks to preserve their unique culture in China. Mainly because of this, no complaints of mistreatment of Tajiks by Chinese authorities have been recorded.

The People's Republic of China pursued a "united front" nationality policy in its domestic affairs. Prominent local elites of Tajiks were included in the formal political structures. These policies of tolerance toward religious and ethnic minorities gained much support for the communists. During the Great Leap Forward of 1958, the policy shifted, and the Chinese authorities lessened their attention to ethnic and religious concerns of non-Han people. In the Cultural Revolution (1966–1976), no attention was paid to minority cultures, religion was persecuted, and the Tajiks were expected to accept the majority Han culture. During the rule of Deng Xiaoping, the approach to religion and minorities became more tolerant, and Islam was defined as one of the five official religions recognized within China. Then, an unparalleled Han migration into Xinjiang began and the ratio of Han Chinese to local Muslims increased in favor of the former. Also, the traditionally backward and poor western China became an area of large-scale investment.

Despite their closeness to the Turkic majority of Xinjiang, the Tajiks of China are not supportive of Uighur separatism and have no nationalist intentions. Tajikistan's **civil war** had no spillover effect in the Tajik-populated areas of Xinjiang. Conscious of Beijing's sensitivity with regard to interference in China's internal affairs, Tajikistan has largely avoided questions related to the Tajiks of China. The Ismaili leader **Aga Khan** and his agencies are not operational in China. *See also* RELIGION; CHINA-TAJIK BORDER.

TALCO. The Tajikistan Aluminum Company, or TALCO, is one of the world's largest smelters and Tajikistan's chief industrial asset. The enterprise is headquartered in the city of **Tursunzoda** and was formerly known as the Tajikistan Aluminum Plant, or TadAZ. It started producing aluminum sheets and other related products in 1975. In April 2007, it was renamed TALCO. This enterprise is 100 percent state owned. It consumes 40 percent of the country's electrical power and is the nation's most valuable exporter. TALCO's export earnings in 2006 amounted to $184 million out of Tajikistan's total export revenue of $383 million. In 2002–2007, it produced roughly 400,000–450,000 tons of aluminum per year. The plant is responsible for air and water pollution in the region, which is adjacent to **Uzbekistan**. A group of companies called TML (TALCO Management Limited) manages TALCO's financial operations.

The director of TALCO reports only to President **Emomali Rahmon**. Alleged **corruption** involving TALCO as well as costly lawsuits have undermined Tajikistan's credibility among government donors and international bank lenders. *See also* INDUSTRY; NONFERROUS METALLURGY.

TALIBAN. An Islamist, **Sunni**, Pushtun-dominated movement, the Taliban governed **Afghanistan** from 1996 to 2001. Having emerged as a purist party of **madrasa** *talibs* (students), the Taliban became a radical fundamentalist movement and instituted a repressive rule in most of Afghanistan. They were resisted by the Tajik-dominated **Northern Alliance**. The Taliban regime was defeated by the Northern Alliance in late 2001 with the support of a U.S.-led coalition that targeted the Taliban for its support of al-Qaeda terrorists. The Taliban subsequently launched an insurgent war, including acts of **terrorism**.

The Taliban were supported neither by the Tajik government nor by its Islamist opponents. Although the exiled **United Tajik Opposition** (UTO) leader **Said Abdullo Nuri** had contacts with the Taliban chief Mulla Omar in the mid-1990s, the sides did not come to an agreement. Tajik Islamists did not approve of the Pushtun nationalism and strict interpretation of **Islam** promoted by Taliban leaders, whom they perceived as ignorant **mullahs** from Pakistan-based madrasas. The Taliban were suspicious of the UTO's close links with **Iran** and its affiliation with the predominantly ethnic Tajik and **Uzbek** political and military leaders in northern Afghanistan. Along with Iran and **Russia**, the leaders of the Northern Alliance were among the major brokers of the **Inter-Tajik Peace Talks**. From 1994 to 2001, with Russia's consent, Tajikistan served as a base for provision of support to anti-Taliban Afghan factions. As a result of its support of the military operations of the Northern Alliance in 1996–2001, the Taliban charged the Tajik government with interference in Afghanistan's internal affairs and threatened retaliation.

See also KHOS DEH PROTOCOL; MASSOUD, AHMAD SHAH; TAJIKS OF AFGHANISTAN.

TAMERLANE. *See* TIMUR.

TANAB. A square measure in medieval **Central Asia** that was still used in the 1920s, the *tanab* varied in different regions. One tanab in **Bukhara** in the 19th and early 20th centuries was equal to 0.25 hectares.

TANBUR (TAMBUR). A metal-stringed lute used in Tajik folk and classical **music**, the *tanbur* has a pear-shaped resonator, a long neck, and three (sometimes four) strings. It is played with a metal implement called a *nokhun* (nail).

TANUR. A clay stove, the *tanur* is used for baking bread and **sambusa**.

TAR. A kind of lute, the *tar* is popular in **Iran**, the Caucasus, and **Central Asia**. *See also* MUSIC.

TARBIYAI ATFOL. A secret society of **Jadids**, Tarbiyai Atfol was formed in **Bukhara** in 1910 to further the **education** of young people. The founding members were Tajik intellectuals and liberal merchants, including Mirzo Abdulvohid Burkhanov (Munzim), Khomidkhoja Mehri, Akhmadjon Maqdum Abdusaidov (Hamdi), Khoji Rofe, and Mukammal Maqdum Burkhanov (Burkhonzoda). Later, **Sadriddin Ayni**, Mirzo Abdulqadir Muhiddinov, and others joined this clandestine organization. Of the 28 members, 14 were **mullahs** and sons of mullahs, and three were *mudarris* (teachers). The society propagated the introduction of *maktabi Jadid* (new method schools) as well as the teaching of arithmetic, native **languages**, geography, and other secular disciplines in addition to religious instruction. Tarbiyai Atfol sent Bukharan youth to Turkey to receive modern education. Despite the Tajik ethnicity of most members of Tarbiyai Atfol, they were very receptive to pan-Turkist ideas.

TASHKURGAN TAJIK AUTONOMOUS COUNTY. Part of the Kashgar prefecture in the Xinjiang-Uighur Autonomous Region of the People's Republic of **China**, the Tashkurgan Tajik Autonomous

County is a homeland of the **Tajiks of China**. The county was established in 1954 in the eastern part of the **Pamir** plateau, bordering **Afghanistan**, Tajikistan, and **Pakistani**-controlled Kashmir. The county's administrative center is Tashkurgan. In Turkic, *tashkurgan* means "stone fortress." One of the preserved Tashkurgan convents of **Kushan** times connects this area with **Buddhism** in **India**. Local tradition in Pamir asserts an Iranian origin and claims that the town of Tashkurgan town, known earlier as Varshadek, was founded by Afrasiab, the king of **Turan**, who is depicted in the Persian epic *Shohnoma*.

China established its protectorate over this area, known as **Sarikol**, in 713–741 and set up the Tsungling military post in Tashkurgan. The hereditary chiefs of Sarikol, descendants of a noble family from Kashghar, paid nominal tribute to the Chinese authorities and received compensation in gold and silver for the protection of the frontier toward the Pamirs in the west and Gilgit (today the Pakistani-controlled part of Kashmir) in the south. In the 14th century, Tashkurgan was controlled by the Mongols, who built a mud-brick fortress there. A new fort was erected in 1892 by three Manchu military expeditions, as a token of Chinese supremacy in Sarikol while **Russia** and Great Britain debated about control over the Pamirs.

The territory of the county is 52,400 square kilometers, and the whole area lies at an average altitude above 4,000 meters. Summer temperatures can reach 32°C, and winter minimums are around –39°C. The average precipitation is 68.3 millimeters. The total population is about 33,000, which includes 27,000 **Tajiks**. The nonagricultural population is about 9,300. *See also* KARAKORAM HIGHWAY.

TAVILDARA NOHIYA. Located in the Obi Khingou river basin in eastern Tajikistan, Tavildara nohiya is part of the **Nohiyas under Republican Control** (NRC). It was formed in 1939 as a part of the **Gharm** veloyat. In 1953, the Gharm veloyat was divided and Tavildara was joined to the NRC. In 1991, the Tavildara nohiya was reinstated at the expense of Darband nohiya and encompasses Sangvor and Tavildara **jamoats**. Its population is about 13,000 people. Average January and July temperatures can reach –4°C and 24°C respectively. The main occupation in this mountainous district is **agriculture**, including **grain** cultivation and livestock breeding. The distance from Tavildara to **Dushanbe** is 207 kilometers. The annual precipitation is 400–800 millimeters in the lowlands and 1,200–1,600 millimeters in the mountains. Tavildara borders the **Badakhshon** region of **Afghanistan**. During Tajikistan's **civil war**, opposition forces based in Afghanistan periodically conducted incursions across the Amu Darya into Tavildara.

TERRORISM. Terrorism-related violence in Tajikistan is low and the number of injuries insignificant. The main reason for the low level of terrorist activity is a Soviet legacy of zero tolerance for organized nonstate violence and weapons possession. Since the elimination of **Basmachism** in the early 1930s, the Soviet state successfully demilitarized Tajik society and secured the exclusive right to apply violence. Most violent acts in post-Soviet Tajikistan have been associated with the political opposition that opposed the government of **Emomali Rahmon** during and after Tajikistan's **civil war** (1992–1997). During the war, agents of various fundamentalist organizations from Africa, the Near and Middle East, northern Caucasus, and South Asia sponsored the military activities of the **United Tajik Opposition** (UTO) and taught its fighters how to carry out terrorist acts. The government and the UTO signed the **General Agreement on the Establishment of the Peace and National Accord** in June 1997, and the UTO was dissolved in January 2000.

Some dissident Islamist groups continued terrorist activities in 1997–2001. Remnants of the UTO allied with **Jumaboi Namangani** of the **Islamic Movement of Uzbekistan** (IMU) and used remote parts of Tajikistan as a base for armed incursions into **Kyrgyzstan** and **Uzbekistan**. After a February 1999 bombing in Tashkent, Uzbekistan, the IMU made an incursion into Batken in southern Kyrgyzstan from Tajik territory. Also, a number of important political figures, including government officials, religious leaders, party leaders, journalists, and scholars on both sides of the conflict, were assassinated in Tajikistan during 1997–2001. The overall situation stabilized by the end of 2001. In October 2001, Tajikistan joined the international coalition in its fight against terrorism. Coalition forces used Tajik airspace and facilities for operations in **Afghanistan** directed against al-Qaeda terrorists and the **Taliban** regime. Several humanitarian organizations based in Afghanistan delivered humanitarian goods through Tajikistan.

A small bomb causing no injuries or serious damage exploded outside the supreme court of Tajikistan on 17 June 2007. Another bomb was detonated at a conference hall on 14 November, killing one person. Except for this, there have been no significant violent incidents of a political or terrorist nature from 2001 to 2009 in Tajikistan. Tajikistan is not known to harbor terrorist groups like al-Qaeda, but extremists have crossed to and from Afghanistan to Tajikistan via the 1,400-kilometer Tajik-Afghan border. Since 2004, authorities have arrested tens of suspected IMU members in Tajikistan, mostly in **Sughd veloyat**. The extremist group **Hizb-ut-Tahrir** is also operational, mostly in northern Tajikistan, adjacent to the Uzbek part of the **Ferghana** valley.

Tajikistan has participated in the counterterrorist activities of the **Shanghai Cooperation Organization** (SCO), the **Collective Security Treaty Organization** (CSTO), and the CIS Counterterrorist Center. Tajikistan also endorsed the Global Initiative to Combat Nuclear Terrorism, co-chaired by the **United States** and **Russia**.

In an attempt to secure a partnership with the United States and European countries, President Rahmon has promoted Tajikistan as a stable country with a strong centralized government. The government is increasingly worried about radical religious doctrines capable of destabilizing the country. On 15 January 2007, the supreme court proclaimed 10 organizations and **political parties** to be terrorist in nature and banned their activities in Tajikistan. Among them are the IMU, the Islamic Party of Turkistan, the Tabligot Movement and Tabligot Society, Bayat, al-Qaeda, and the opposition party Tojikiston-i Ozod (Free Tajikistan). *See also* GOVERNMENT; SALAFIYA.

TIMUR (1336–1405). The last great nomadic conqueror in **Central Asia**, Timur is known among **Tajiks** and Iranians as Timuri Lang, literally the Lame Timur. He is called Tamerlane in the Russian- and English-speaking worlds. Timur was born in Shahrisabz, near **Samarqand**, into a family of the **Barlas** Turks who had descended from the Golden Horde of Genghiz Khan. Between 1382 and 1405, Timur conquered vast territories from Delhi to Moscow and from Kashgar to Herat. He constructed a centralized government and imposed a rigid tribal, hierarchical structure with himself at the apex. Timur made Samarqand *Markazi Rui Zamin*, the "Center of the World." An estimated 17 million people may have died from his conquests in Central Asia, **Iran**, Caucasus, **Afghanistan**, **India**, **Russia**, Asia Minor, and Mesopotamia. By adopting **Islam**, Timur and the **Timurids** also adopted the Perso-Tajik literary and high culture, which has dominated **Khurasan** and **Movarounnahr** since the early days of Islamic influence.

TIMURIDS (1405–1506). A dynasty of Turkic-Mongol origin, the Timurids were founded by **Timur**. Shoh Rukh, Timur's son (1377–1447), made Herat (**Afghanistan**) his capital. His son, Timur's grandson, Ulugh Bek (1394–1449) was a governor of **Samarqand**. The Timurids are renowned for their brilliant revival of the **arts** and sciences in **Iran** and **Central Asia**. Timurid rulers were sympathetic to Persian culture. Shoh Rukh and other Timurids made Mashad (Iran), Herat, and Samarqand centers for architectural innovation in the first half of the 15th century. A library was founded at Herat, and the schools of miniature painting at Shiraz, Tabriz, and Herat flourished. The most famous artist was Kamoluddin Behzod (d. 1552). The most famous poet of the Timurid era was **Abdurahmon Jomi** (1414–1492). Persian was the primary language of administration and literary culture, and Persian **literature**, especially poetry, played a central role in assimilation of the Timurid elite to the Perso-Islamic culture. Based on the established Persian literary tradition, in the 15th century, a national Turkic literature in the **Chaghatais** language was developed, with Alisher Navoi (1441–1501) as the most prominent poet.

The Timurid rule in **Movarounnahr** was discontinued by the rising power of the **Shaybani Uzbeks** in 1506. One of Timur's descendants, Babur, was defeated by Uzbeks. In 1526, he founded the Mughal empire in **India**. Bahadur Shah II (1837–1857) was the last Mughal ruler of the Timurid dynasty.

TOJIKOBOD NOHIYA. A mountainous district, the Tojikobod nohiya is located within the **Nohiyas under Republican Control** in the Qarategin valley, Surkhob river basin. Formed in 1991 at the expense of the **Gharm** nohiya, it incorporates Qalai Labi Ob, Langarishoh, Nushor, and Shagadaev **jamoats**. The population is about 49,000 people, mostly **Tajiks**. The distance from the district center, Tojikobod, to **Dushanbe** is 235 kilometers. Arable land amounts to

2,200 hectares. The main occupation is **agriculture**, including **grain**, potatoes, apples, and livestock.

TOQI. A Tajik national headdress worn by men and women, the *toqi* or *tuppi* is a circular or quadrangular head covering often decorated with embroidery. Each region has its own traditional design for the local toqi, complete with locally preferred fabrics and colors. The most popular toqi worn by men is a quadrangular head covering of black fabric with white decorations.

TRADITIONAL INSTITUTIONS. *See* AVLOD; HASHAR; MAHALLA; MASHVARAT; OSHI OSHTI; SHARIK.

TRANSPORTATION. *See* AIRLINES; DUSTI BRIDGE; ISTIQLOL TUNNEL; MOTOR ROADS; RAILWAYS.

TUI. Private parties that involve friends, relatives, neighbors, colleagues, and community leaders, *tuis* are typically held on the occasion of weddings (*tui arusi, nikoh*) and circumcisions (*tui khatna*). The celebration includes food, **music**, poetry recitation, and **dance**. Some rich families also organize **gushtingiri** (wrestling) and the polo-like sport **buzkashi**. In Tajikistan, a tui is a private and secular event. A traditional Tajik tui lasts several days. Women had their own colorful banquet with music and dances called *oshi zanon* (women's meal), in which men were not allowed to participate. The *nikoh* gathering, which brought hundreds of guests together, sealed the tui. However, this practice was stopped at the end of the 1950s when Soviet authorities aiming to "fight religious prejudices" introduced the *tui komsomoli* (**komsomol** wedding).

Since that time, the tui usually comprises two events. On the first day of the tui, the bride's family (at the expense of the groom's) serves a morning feast called an *osh* to neighbors, elders, remote relatives, and some friends. A famed dish called **palov** (pilaf) is traditionally served. The next day, a European-style *tui arusi* unites the main bulk of the guests. During this part, people of both sexes often sit at the same table and dance together. Serving alcohol (mostly vodka for males) has become a rule since the 1950s. Since the end of Tajikistan's **civil war**, most Tajiks prefer renting modern restaurants to using home facilities for tuis, birthday parties, and even funeral ceremonies.

The tui is a central event and the most important means of socializing among Tajiks. In 2006, Tajikistanis spent around $1.5 million on various private gatherings. On 8 June 2007, at the initiative of President **Emomali Rahmon**, the government imposed a law limiting the number of guests, meals, and cars in order to stop Tajiks from bankrupting themselves by throwing big tuis. According to the new rules, any *tui arusi* or *tui khatna* cannot have more than 150 guests and must not last more than three hours. Special governmental commissions were set up to monitor the implementation of the rules and levy heavy fines ($600 for ordinary citizens and up to $1,500 for civil servants) for overspending. The government claimed that the implementation of the law "On Regulation of Traditions, Celebrations, and Rituals" saved $340 million and 34,000 heads of cattle from January to October 2008. In 2008, a normal *tui arusi* (including, *osh* expenses, gifts, and other items) cost a groom's family about $5,000, while the gross domestic product (GDP) per capita was $1,356 and 58 percent of the population lived below the poverty line in Tajikistan. *See also* ETIQUETTE; KHATMUL QURON.

TUMOR. A *tumor* is an amulet or magical charm. Such talismans, originating in past shamanic and animalistic religions, are used everywhere in the Islamic world. Most often they are inscribed with passages from the Quran and sealed in a leather case worn around the neck or body.

TURAEV, SAIFIDDIN (1945–). Born in **Uroteppa**, Turaev graduated from the Textile Institute (Moscow) in 1973 and the Academy of People's Economy at the Council of Ministers of the Soviet Union in 1991. Between 1973 and 1986, he worked in a Uroteppa knitwear factory as master of an industrial workshop, and then as chief engineer and director. In 1986, he was appointed Tajikistan's minister of consumer services, which in 1988 was transformed into Shirkat State Stock Company. In 1991–1992, he was the first deputy of Tajikistan's **Supreme Soviet**. In September 1992, he was elected chair of the short-lived National Unity Congress, but he resigned that post in November 1992 when **Emomali Rahmon** was elected chair of the Supreme Soviet. At the end of 1992, Turaev left **Dushanbe**

for his native Uroteppa, where he became president of the Istravshan International Scientific-Industrial Trade Corporation.

In 1995, Turaev was elected co-chair of the **Congress of National Unity of Tajikistan** (CNUT), but the CNUT could not support Turaev's candidacy in the **presidential elections of 1999**. Instead, Turaev was nominated in the presidential race by the **Adolatkhoh Party of Justice**, which failed to pass the 5 percent minimum requirement hurdle. He was elected to Tajikistan's parliament in 1990 and 1995.

TURAJONZODA, HOJI AKBAR (1954–). A Tajik politician and religious leader also known as Akbar Qaharov, Turajonzoda was born in Kofarnihon (**Vahdat**) nohiya into the family of the influential Ishan Turajon. The Turajon family follows the Qadiriya **Sufi** brotherhood. Turajonzoda received religious training in the **Bukharan madrasa** (high school), followed by studies at the Islamic Institute in Tashkent and Amman University in Jordan in the late 1970s and early 1980s. He then began work in the Department of International Relations in the spiritual administration of the Muslims of Central Asia in Tashkent (1985–1987). In 1988, he was appointed the official leader of Tajikistan's religious institutions, with the title of *qazi kalon*, or supreme judge. In 1990, he was elected to Tajikistan's **Supreme Soviet**. Under Turajonzoda, the **Qaziyat** got the right to hire and fire **imams** and heads of **mosques**.

Turajonzoda's attitude to the formation of the **Islamic Renaissance Party of Tajikistan** (IRPT) in 1990 was not positive, but during Tajikistan's **civil war**, he entered into an alliance with this party. In May 1992, after the Islamic opposition was expelled from **Dushanbe**, Turajonzoda was dismissed as *qazi kalon*. He was forced to flee Tajikistan at the end of 1992. In 1993, he joined the **Movement for Islamic Revival in Tajikistan** (MIRT) and was appointed its first deputy chair as well as deputy chair of the IRPT. In 1995, Turajonzoda traveled to **Iran**, the **Arab** states, the **United States**, Europe, **Russia, Uzbekistan**, and other countries to garner support for the opposition cause. Turajonzoda participated in the **Inter-Tajik Peace Talks** between 1995 and 1997 as part of the **United Tajik Opposition** negotiation team.

Following the signing of the **General Agreement on the Establishment of Peace and National Accord**, President **Emomali**

Rahmon appointed Turajonzoda Tajikistan's first vice premier responsible for relationships with the **Commonwealth of Independent States** in March 1998. Turajonzoda supported Rahmon's candidacy in the **presidential elections of 1999**. He declared that the IRPT had lost its vision and was bogged down in petty partisan squabbles. This led to his dismissal from the party post of IRPT deputy chair, which caused a rift within the party; some members in the **Sughd veloyat** openly supported his position. He was released from the position of vice premier and appointed a member of the **Majlisi Oli** in 2005. In 2008–2009, Turajonzoda publicly criticized the **Salafites** and the economic policy of the Tajik government. *See also* MUFTI; OFFICIAL MUSLIM CLERGY.

TURAN. An ancient Iranian name for **Central Asia**, *Turan* comes from "Land of Tur." Tur was one of the sons of the emperor Faridun, according to Iranian mythology. As described in ***Shohnoma***, Tur ruled the region north from the Jaihun (**Amu Darya**) populated by Iranian people. Culturally, Turanians are not connected to the Turks, but in the early 20th century, Central Asian and Turkish nationalists used *Turan* in connection with pan-Turkism, also called Turanism.

TURKISTAN. The name Turkistan was applied to an area of **Central Asia** that included Tajik and other lands. But use of the term and the extent of the territory covered have changed over time. The territory of **Movarounnahr**, northern **Afghanistan**, and the adjacent part of Xinjiang province of **China** was often called Turkistan (Land of the Turks) in historical narratives. However, in ancient and medieval times, its population spoke mostly Iranian **languages**. In the 9th–10th centuries, **Arab** and Persian writers applied the term only to the area northeast of the **Syr Darya**. Later, the number of Turkic tribes moving into the region increased, and they founded powerful ruling dynasties there, most notably the empire established by **Timur** (Tamerlane) in the 15th century. As a result of this political domination, Turkistan was widely used in the court historiography of the **Timurids** and following Turkic-Mongol rulers, particularly those who dreamed of the reemergence of Timur's empire in the 16th–19th centuries. An Iranian-speaking population dominated the major cities, river valleys, and mountainous areas of the region. Until the Russian conquest in the 19th century, the Iranian cultural and historical component prevailed in urban Central Asia, and the territory was never ethnically homogeneous.

The region is now thought of as three areas: Western or Russian Turkistan, Southern or Afghan Turkistan (northern Afghanistan), and Eastern or Chinese Turkistan (southern part of Xinjiang-Uighur Autonomous Region of China). In the Russian part of Turkistan, the Governor-Generalate of Turkistan was formed in 1867. In 1886, it was renamed the Turkistanskii Krai. In 1918–1924, the **Turkistan Soviet Republic** functioned as a constituent member of the Russian Soviet Federated Socialist Republic. *See also* TURAN.

TURKISTAN COMMUNIST PARTY (TCP). The Turkistan Communist Party was organized after the establishment of Soviet rule in Tashkent, in present-day **Uzbekistan**. At the time, the Turkistan area included part of what is now Tajikistan. The inaugural congress of **Turkistan** Bolshevik organizations was held in June 1918. The **Khujand** Bolshevik organization was also present. The structure of the TCP was formalized at its second congress in December 1918. After the October 1917 revolution, Turkistan was cut off from the central provinces of **Russia** until October 1919, as the **railways** were controlled by White Russians. Sporadic contacts with Moscow meant that the TCP was badly organized and often diverged from Kremlin policies. In October 1919, after the White Russians' defeat and the reestablishment of links with Moscow, the Russian Communist Party (Bolsheviks), or RCP (B), and the Soviet government dispatched to Tashkent the commission on Turkistan affairs, or *Turkomissia*, which was later renamed the Central Asian Bureau, or *Sredazbiuro*. The Turkistan commission was granted extensive authority over local communist organizations.

The defeat of the anti-Bolshevik White Russian forces meant that Turkistan could be united with Soviet Russia. In October 1919, the **Turkistan Soviet Republic** reaffirmed its affiliation with the Russian Soviet Federated Socialist Republic. The Communist Party of Turkistan and those of **Bukhara** and Khorazm were restructured as regional branches of the RCP (B). The 1924 national delimitation of **Central Asia** led to a further restructuring of the Communist Party networks in Central Asia. The TCP ceased to exist.

The first social-democratic organization in northern Tajikistan appeared in 1905–1907. In October 1918, there were 300 Bolsheviks in northern Tajikistan; by the end of 1918, there were 2,117. In October 1924, the RCP (B) Politburo decided that "the Tajik provincial party organization should be linked to the RCP via the central committee of the Uzbek organization." In December 1924, therefore, the Organizational Bureau of the Uzbekistan central committee in the **Tajik Autonomous Soviet Socialist Republic** was formed. In October 1927, the **Communist Party of Tajikistan** was formed with direct lines of communication with Moscow. *See also* POLITICAL PARTIES.

TURKISTAN SOVIET REPUBLIC (1918–1924). The Turkistan Soviet Republic (TSR) was formed in April 1918 as a constituent member of the Russian Soviet Federated Socialist Republic (RSFSR). The TSR government was based in Tashkent, administering a territory of 1.7 million square kilometers and a population of more than 5 million. The TSR covered present-day **Kyrgyzstan**, Turkmenistan, most of **Uzbekistan** (excluding the steppe land to the east of the Caspian Sea), northern Tajikistan, and the southern half of Kazakhstan. The national composition of the TSR was 41 percent **Uzbeks**, 13.3 percent Kazakhs, 10.8 percent **Kyrgyzs**, 7.7 percent **Tajiks**, 4.7 percent **Turkmens**, 1.4 percent Karakalpaks, and 21.1 percent others. Some 85 percent of the population lived in rural areas. The TSR lost direct communication with the RSFSR between early 1918 and the end of 1919, as the Tashkent-Orenburg railway was controlled by anti-Bolshevik White Russians.

Following complaints about Russian chauvinism by Muslim Central Asians in the TSR, Moscow dispatched a commission on Turkistan affairs, or *Turkomissia*, to Tashkent at the end of 1919 to investigate and ensure the implementation of Bolshevik policies. At the same time, the Russian Communist Party criticized Muslim communists for their "nationalist tendencies." Turar Ryskulov, Nizameddin Khojaev, and others were criticized for their attempt to separate Turkistan from the Russian Federation and establish a Turkic republic and a Turkic Communist Party. Attempts at forming a Muslim army in Turkistan were also foiled. In September 1920, the TSR was renamed the Turkistan Soviet Socialist Republic (TSSR). In 1924, 53 Soviet newspapers were published in Soviet Turkistan. In October 1924, following the national delimitation of **Central Asia**, the TSSR was replaced with two socialist republics, two autonomous republics, and two autonomous regions.

TURKMENS. An ethnic group in Tajikistan, Turkmens transmigrated from the Turkmen steppes to the **Bukharan emirate** and settled in the Labi Ob (Near the Water) area of the **Amu Darya** in the 17th–19th centuries. Some Turkmen tribes settled in southern Tajikistan on the **Jilikul** plateau in the 1860s. In March 1996, the Society of Turkmens of Tajikistan signed the **Agreement on National Accord** and entered the **Societal Council**. In the 1990s, Turkmens started to emigrate from Tajikistan to Turkmenistan. The Turkmen population in Tajikistan in 1926 was 4,200 (0.4 percent of the total population), and it was 20,300 (0.3 percent) in 2000.

TURKS. An ethnic group in Tajikistan and other parts of **Central Asia**, Turks are descendants of Turkic nomadic tribes that migrated to Central Asia before the Mongol invasion in the 12th century. Turks in Central Asia adopted a sedentary lifestyle and were gradually assimilated by the **Tajiks** and **Uzbeks**. The 2000 census recorded 936,700 Central Asian Turks living in Tajikistan. *See also* MOGOLS.

TURSONZOD (TURSUNOV), AKBAR (1939–). A Tajik scholar and politician, Tursonzod was born in **Konibodom**. He graduated from the Tajik State University in 1961 and received a **candidate** degree in 1968 and a doctorate in philosophy in 1982 from the Institute of Philosophy, Academy of Sciences of the Soviet Union. In 1987, Tursonzod became a member of the **Academy of Sciences of Tajikistan**. Between 1986 and 1992, he was director of the Institute of Oriental Studies, Academy of Sciences of Tajikistan. In 1992, he was appointed deputy director of the Institute of World Economy and International Relations. In 1993, he initiated the National Association of Political Scientists of the Republic of Tajikistan and was elected its president. Tursonzod's research interests cover the foundations of modern cosmology, Oriental studies, ethnology, cultural studies, and international relations. He took part in forming the **Rastokhez** movement in 1989. In the spring of 1992, he mediated between the government and opposition forces, advancing the idea of a **Commission for National Reconciliation**, which was subsequently formed on 7 May 1992. In 1994, Tursonzod left Tajikistan for the **United States**. In 1996, he became a visiting curator for Central Asian ethnology at the University of Pennsylvania (Philadelphia).

TURSUNZODA. Situated in the westernmost part of central Tajikistan, Tursunzoda nohiya is part of the **Nohiyas under Republican Control.** The district includes the city of Tursunzoda, formerly known as Regar, which is located in **Hisor** valley, 60 kilometers west of **Dushanbe.** In 1978, the town and nohiya were renamed in honor of **Mirzo Tursunzoda.** The rail station is still called Regar. Fruits, including grapes, pomegranates, and **lemons**, are grown in the nohiya, which is also a major rice-growing area. The city of Tursunzoda is one of the industrial centers of Tajikistan, known for its aluminum smelting plant, **TALCO.** Tursunzoda is one of the eight major cities of Tajikistan. Its population was 40,600 in 1989, falling to 37,000 in 2006.

TURSUNZODA, MIRZO (1911–1977). A Tajik Soviet writer and a national hero of Tajikistan, Tursunzoda was born in the village of Qaratogh (**Hisor**) and in 1930 graduated from the Tashkent Pedagogical Institute. From 1946 until his death, he headed the **Tajikistan Union of Writers.** His poetic works include "Qissai Hinduston" (Story of India), "Khasani Arobakash" (Hassan the Cart Driver), and others. Tursunzoda was the recipient of various state awards. Alongside **Sadriddin Ayni** and **Bobojon Ghafurov**, he was recognized as a Tajikistan National Hero in 2001. *See also* LITERATURE.

– U –

UBAIDULLOEV, MAHMADSAID (1952–). One of the most influential Tajik politicians, Ubaidulloev was born in Farkhor, Kulob veloyat, and studied in the Kharkov (Ukraine) Polytechnical Institute. After graduation in 1974, he started work at the Provincial Statistics Agency in **Kulob.** Between 1979 and 1985, he worked in organs of the **Communist Party of Tajikistan.** In 1985, he was appointed deputy head of Tajikistan's Central Statistics Agency. In 1986, Ubaidulloev returned to party work and in 1988 was appointed head of the Statistics Department in the **Qurghonteppa** veloyat. In 1990, he served as deputy chair of the Kulob provincial executive committee. In November 1992, he was appointed deputy chair of the government and in December 1994 became first vice premier. He was elected to the **Majlisi Oli** in 1995 and in April 1996 was appointed mayor of **Dushanbe**. In April 2000, Ubaidulloev became chair of the **Majlisi Melli**. *See also* GOVERNMENT.

ULJABAEV, TURSUNBOI (1916–1988). Born to an **Uzbek** family in **Asht**, northern Tajikistan, Uljabaev completed his studies at the Communist Party High School in 1950. He started his career in 1935 as a high school teacher, then secretary of the Asht district committee of **Komsomol** and secretary of the Komsomol Central Committee. He served as first secretary of the Leninobod provincial committee of the **Communist Party of Tajikistan** (CPT), secretary of the CPT Central Committee, and chair of the republican Council of Ministers. In 1956, he was appointed first secretary of the CPT Central Committee. He was later charged with "antiparty and antistate activity" and removed from his party post in 1961. Between 1961 and 1988, Uljabaev directed a **sovkhoz** in **Qurghonteppa** veloyat.

UMAROV, SULTAN (1908–1964). A Tajik scientist and **academician**, Umarov was born in **Khujand**. He studied in the **Samarqand** Pedagogical Academy, graduating in 1927, and started his career at the Central Asian State University (Tashkent), working his way up from research fellow to rector of the university (1927–1943). In 1943–1945, Umarov served as deputy chair of **Uzbekistan**'s soviet of ministers. Between 1945 and 1957, he was again rector at the Central Asian University as well as director of the Physico-Technical Institute, Uzbekistan's Academy of Sciences. In 1957, Umarov moved to Tajikistan and was appointed president of the **Academy of Sciences of Tajikistan**.

UNION OF SOVIET SOCIALIST REPUBLICS (USSR). *See* SOVIET UNION.

UNITED NATIONS (UN). On 2 March 1992, the General Assembly of the United Nations unanimously resolved to admit Tajikistan to the UN. At the time, Tajikistan was engulfed in violent conflict that devolved into **civil war**. The UN response to Tajikistan's civil war began with an appeal from **Uzbek** President Islam Karimov. This was supported a few days later by Mauno Koivisto, president of Finland. In response to these appeals, UN Secretary-General Boutros Boutros-Ghali dispatched a first mission to Tajikistan in September

1992 to observe the situation on the ground. On 2 October 1992, the secretary-general conveyed the mission's results to the Security Council. A second mission visited Tajikistan in 1–14 November, initiating the active involvement of key UN humanitarian agencies: the UN High Commission for Refugees (UNHCR), World Food Program (WFP), UN Children's Fund (UNICEF), and World Health Organization (WHO).

In December 1992, the secretary-general decided to establish a small political mission in **Dushanbe**, with the agreement of the Tajik government. A UN unit of officers was sent to Dushanbe, and Liviu Bota of Romania was appointed to head the United Nations Mission of Observers in Tajikistan (UNMOT), which started its work on 21 January 1993. On 26 April 1993, the secretary-general appointed Ambassador Ismat Kittani of Iraq as a full-time special envoy to Tajikistan. Kittani had a mandate to achieve a cease-fire and to establish the process of negotiations for a political solution. In January 1994, Kittani was succeeded by Ambassador Ramiro Piriz-Ballon of Uruguay. The internationally facilitated **Inter-Tajik Peace Talks** under the aegis of the UN began on 5 April 1994. The special envoys were succeeded in May 1996 by special representatives resident in Tajikistan.

Representatives of **Afghanistan, Iran**, Kazakhstan, **Kyrgyzstan, Pakistan, Russia, Uzbekistan**, and later Turkmenistan as well as the **Organization for Security and Cooperation in Europe** (OSCE) and the Organization of the Islamic Conference (OIC) were invited by the UN mediation team to participate as observers in the inter-Tajik negotiations. Also, they consulted with important members of the Security Council, such as the **United States** and **China**, as well as key nonobserver countries in the region, including Turkey and Saudi Arabia. The UN mission was responsible for designing the negotiation process. The special envoys and representatives served as mediators and worked with the Tajik government and the opposition to arrange the peace talks and draft protocols for an agreement.

Between April 1994 and June 1997, the UN brought together the government of **Emomali Rahmon** and the **United Tajik Opposition** (UTO) for eight rounds of talks that yielded the **General Agreement on the Establishment of Peace and National Accord**, which formally ended the civil war. Sporadic fighting between rogue factions, however, continued in the following months. The UNMOT oversaw political and military reforms and supported humanitarian missions.

On 20 July 1998, four UNMOT staff members were killed during a patrol in **Gharm**. From June 1997 to March 2000, the UN special envoys and representatives worked in close cooperation with the **Commission for National Reconciliation** (CNR) made up of Tajik government and UTO representatives. The UN maintained close contact with the International Committee of the Red Cross (ICRC), **Aga Khan Foundation**, Doctors without Borders, and Helsinki Watch/Human Rights Watch and sought to orchestrate international efforts to help restore peace.

The UNMOT was officially terminated on 15 May 2000 and was replaced by the UN Tajikistan Office of Peace Building (UNTOP). UNTOP was the lead organization responsible for supporting the implementation of the Tajik peace agreement. The UN resident representative was the head of UNTOP. This UN office redirected its efforts to include wider conflict prevention and stability promotion. By 2002, most refugees and internally displaced persons returned. In July 2006, the Tajiks who fled the civil war, including those living in neighboring Central Asian republics, were no longer considered refugees. UNTOP was terminated in July 2007.

The United Nations Development Program (UNDP) has been present in Tajikistan since December 1993. In 2001, UNDP shifted its focus from post-conflict rehabilitation to development. A number of projects were implemented in partnership with the national government, key donors, and civil society. By early 2009, UNDP was present in all regions of Tajikistan. The programs supported by UNDP include local governance, action on land mines, improving rural livelihoods, curbing HIV/AIDS growth, environment and disaster mitigation, efforts against **corruption**, and border management.

UNITED STATES. The United States of America, a superpower 7,000 miles away from Tajikistan, recognized Tajikistan's independence on 25 December 1991, the day the **Soviet Union** ceased to exist. Diplomatic relations between the two countries were established on 14 February 1992. The United States was the second nation, after **Iran** and followed by **Russia**, to open an embassy in **Dushanbe** in March 1992. In October 1992, in the midst of Tajikistan's **civil war**, the U.S. embassy was evacuated to Almaty (Kazakhstan). It was reopened in March 1993. Tajikistan opened its embassy in Washington, D.C., in December 2002.

Unlike Russia and **China**, the United States has no legacy of conflict or colonialism in **Central Asia**. Throughout the 1990s, the American approach toward Tajikistan was modest. In 1993, Tajikistan and the United States did only $23 million in bilateral trade, 2.7 percent of Tajikistan's total turnover in external trade. In 2000, this figure dropped to $1.9 million (0.5 percent). America was not directly involved in the **Inter-Tajik Peace Talks** but appeared sympathetic to the joint effort of the **United Nations**, **Iran**, **Russia**, and other regional governments and interstate organizations to stop the civil war. America also provided sizable humanitarian assistance to Tajikistan during and after the war.

The **terrorist** attacks by al-Qaeda against the United States on 11 September 2001 and the subsequent U.S. actions and policies had a profound impact on Tajikistan. Initially, the terrorist acts generated sympathy toward America and Americans. Signals of solidarity came from the government and the public. Polls conducted in late September found that 99 percent of respondents approved punitive measures against the **Taliban** regime in **Afghanistan** that supported al-Qaeda. However, the U.S. air strikes in Afghanistan were criticized by some politicians and caused dismay among some Tajiks, including the leaders of the **Islamic Renaissance Party of Tajikistan**. At the end of September, Tajikistan officially stated that it was not considering permission for the use of its territory for U.S. strikes against Afghanistan. But on 2 October 2001, there were reports that 1,000 U.S. troops had been deployed on the Afghan border of **Uzbekistan** and Tajikistan to provide ground security for airforce fighters and combat search-and-rescue units. On 8 October, a day after the first air raids and cruise-missile attacks on targets in Kabul and other major Afghan cities, the Tajik government admitted to the presence of U.S. forces in Tajikistan and offered support to the U.S.-led air strikes in Afghanistan. Since late September 2001, Tajikistan has provided its air space for carrying out humanitarian and rescue operations in Afghanistan. Tajikistan also promised to forbid use of bank accounts and property by international terrorist organizations in its territory.

Tajikistan considered that by opening the country to a Western military presence, it could attract vitally important **foreign investment** to strengthen the country's ruined **economy**. Tajiks also believed that the American presence in Tajikistan would help fight

corruption, illegal trafficking, and other problems. Democratically minded Tajiks believed that direct influence of the world's most successful democracy and richest and powerful society would bring more justice and prosperity.

On 23 November 2001, Tajikistan was excluded from the international list of countries suspected of illegal traffic in arms and smuggling of drugs. In September 2002, President George W. Bush pledged to make the promotion of democracy abroad a primary objective of U.S. **foreign policy**. In Tajikistan, the core of this policy was engagement aimed at both cooperation and gradual change of the illiberal but friendly regime internally, by providing humanitarian aid and a wide array of assistance projects. Thus the United States has been involved in improving Tajikistan's electoral and judiciary systems and supporting civil society organizations. There has also been heavy funding to reequip and train military forces, given concerns about security and stability in Tajikistan, as some predicted that this weakest and poorest Central Asian state could serve as a haven for international terrorist groups. The U.S. government has therefore substantially supported the government of President **Emomali Rahmon**.

The U.S. is a major donor to development and security programs in Tajikistan. The amount of grants made to Tajikistan between 2003 and 2006 reached $250 million. The total volume of humanitarian assistance from 1992 to 2007 was $700 million, while total turnover in bilateral trade was $263 million. In 2004–2006, the U.S. government provided $40 million for the reconstruction, renovation, and equipping of 15 stations on the Afghan border as well as training and equipment for the Tajik border forces. In the framework of the **Greater Central Asia** strategy, the United States and Tajikistan opened the U.S.-funded ($36 million) **Dusti Bridge** over the Panj River in August 2007. The first bridge connecting the **Mountainous Badakhshon Autonomous Veloyat** (MBAV) and the province of Badakhshon in Afghanistan entered into operation in November 2002. The bridges connecting Tajikistan with Afghanistan contribute to emerging Eurasian transport corridors and communication networks between Europe, Central Asia, **India**, and East Asia, as well as various pipelines. In June 2006, Tajikistan and the United States signed an agreement on renovation of transmission lines to supply electricity to Afghanistan. In October 2006, Tajikistan, Afghanistan,

Kyrgyzstan, and **Pakistan** signed a memorandum of understanding for a model project to trade 1,000 megawatts of electricity. Supported by the World Bank and Asian Development Bank, the project should allow electricity to be traded with South Asia.

These developmental initiatives, abundant humanitarian aid, and other projects, make cooperation with the Unites States attractive for Tajikistan. Since the collapse of the Soviet Union, Tajiks feel ambivalent about Russia's role in the country's destiny. They are keen to explore options and to diversify their foreign policy. However, Russia's role has been too essential for it to lose influence overnight. The Tajiks are hesitant about the United States rising as a major power and security manager in Central Asia and doubt that the United States and other Western nations are willing to play a role as significant as Russia's in the past.

In Tajikistan, the United States pursues a more liberal policy that encourages confidence-building and multifaceted cooperation between the states of Central Asia and South Asia. The United States and its Western allies promote impartial border management, additional bridge building, new transport corridors, and development of cross-border peaceful communities. Many of these U.S. strategic perspectives, particularly the breakthrough to South Asia and gaining direct access to the international market, coincide with nationally defined priorities for Tajikistan. However, there are many obstacles. The illegal drug business is booming, and a Taliban insurgency remains active in Afghanistan. Pakistan is another source of regional instability and a breeding ground for radical jihadi movements. *See also* DRUG TRAFFICKING; FOREIGN TRADE.

UNITED TAJIK OPPOSITION (UTO). The main opposition **political parties** banned by the government of **Emomali Rahmon** came together in 1994, during Tajikistan's **civil war**, to form the United Tajik Opposition. The UTO was headed by **Said Abdullo Nuri** and included the **Islamic Renaissance Party of Tajikistan** (IRPT), the **Democratic Party of Tajikistan** (DPT), the Coordination Center of Opposition Forces (formed in Moscow in 1993), Umed association of refugees, and some other opposition movements. After a 1994 split in the DPT, the **Democratic Party of Tajikistan Tehran Platform** left the UTO. **La'li Badakhshon** joined the UTO in 1997. In 1994–1997, the UTO took part in the **Inter-Tajik Peace Talks**, which resulted in the signing of the **General Agreement on the Establishment of Peace and National Accord** in June 1997, bringing an end to the war. According to this agreement, UTO representatives were included in the **Commission for National Reconciliation** (CNR), and Said Abdullo Nuri was appointed its head.

In 1998–1999, the UTO suspended its activity in the CNR on several occasions due to the failure of the government to honor its responsibilities as postulated in the General Agreement. On the eve of the **presidential elections of 1999**, the UTO suffered a number of serious setbacks which undermined its continued activity. **Hoji Akbar Turajonzoda** endorsed the candidacy of incumbent President Emomali Rahmon, thus openly opposing the IRPT's leadership. Soon afterward, the **Democratic Party of Tajikistan Almaty Platform** left the UTO, followed by La'li Badakhshon's departure in December 1999. In January 2000, the UTO effectively ceased to exist, as it only included the IRPT.

UNOFFICIAL MULLAHS. Clerics of Tajikistan's "people's **Islam**" are not registered with state authorities. Unofficial **mullahs** in Tajikistan are often seen as closely tied to local traditions, often representing pre-Islamic beliefs, which ensured the survival of national practices under Soviet rule. Unofficial mullahs have focused on preserving and strengthening Islam at the level of the family, tribe, and region.

As a rule, unofficial clerics do not have formal religious training. They are often self-taught and disciples of **Sufi** mentors (*ishans, shaikhs, makhsums*). Almost every village under Soviet rule had a tea house (*choi khona*) at which unregistered Islamic congregations were led by unofficial mullahs, conducting all religious and traditional rituals for the community. Unofficial mullahs have played an important role in preserving pre-Islamist beliefs and practices such as the cult of holy places: numerous Sufi-related *mazars* (burial grounds), mausoleums, shrines, stones, and trees. In 1990, there were about 1,400 unofficial mullahs operating in Tajikistan. Many of these were incorporated into the official religious structure under the leadership of **Hoji Akbar Turajonzoda** in 1988–1992. More recently, unofficial mullahs are often criticized by more educated Tajik Islamists from the **Islamic Renaissance Party of Tajikistan** as well as **Wahhabis** and **Salafis**. *See also* OFFICIAL MUSLIM CLERGY.

UROTEPPA NOHIYA. *See* ISTRAVSHAN NOHIYA.

USMANOV, ZAFAR (1937–). A Tajik **academician** who specialized in mathematics, Usmanov was born in **Dushanbe** and graduated from the Moscow State University in 1961. He defended his **candidate** dissertation in 1966 and **doctoral** dissertation in 1973 at the university. Usmanov worked at the Institute of Physics and Techniques of the **Academy of Sciences of Tajikistan** from 1962 to 1970 as a research fellow, then as head of the laboratory for calculus mathematics. He has worked at the Institute of Mathematics of the National Academy of Sciences as deputy director (1970–1976), head of the Calculation Center (1976–1984), and director (1988–1999), and he has been a member of the Tajik Academy since 1981.

USMON, DAVLAT (1958–). A Tajik Islamist and politician, Usmon is also known as Davlat Usmonov. He was born in Boshkala village, in the **Qubodiyon nohiya** of **Qurghonteppa**, to a family of **sovkhoz** workers of **Gharmi** origin. He worked in **Yovon nohiya** and then in the **Dushanbe cotton**-selling base as an electrician, and subsequently as a warehouse head. He also worked as deputy head of the Department of Construction in the silkworm breeding company for two years. In 1981, Usmon received a law degree from the Tajik State University (correspondence course). He was active in forming the **Islamic Renaissance Party of Tajikistan** (IRPT) in 1990 and was elected the party's deputy chair at the inaugural congress. Usmon was appointed vice premier in the **Government of National Reconciliation** in 1992 and was responsible for the armed forces, security, and police.

When the government collapsed, Usmon was forced to flee to **Afghanistan** in January 1993 and then to **Pakistan**. He was appointed head of headquarters of the Tajik opposition in 1993. He returned to Tajikistan in December 1996 as chair of the military-political commission on the realization of the **Khos Deh Protocol**. In February 1998, he was appointed minister of economics and external economic relations. The IRPT nominated Usmon as a candidate in the **presidential elections of 1999**, but he withdrew from the race to protest restrictions on his campaign. Nonetheless, his name appeared on the ballot and he received 59,857 votes (2.1 percent of all votes). Usmon left his ministerial post in March 2000 to study at the Russian

Academy of External Trade in Moscow. Since 2007, he has been a research fellow at the Tajik **Academy of Sciences**.

USMONOV, IBRAHIM (1947–). A Tajik politician and scholar, Usmonov was born in **Asht**, Leninobod veloyat. He graduated from the Tajik State University with a degree in journalism in 1971 and started work as a reporter with the *Tojikistoni Soveti* newspaper. He obtained a **candidate of science** degree in journalism from the Moscow State University in 1976 and defended his **doctor of science** dissertation at the end of the 1980s. Between 1976 and 1993, Usmonov worked as assistant, lecturer, docent, professor, and dean of the faculty of journalism at the Tajik State University. In 1993, he was appointed minister of communications. In 1995, he was state adviser to the president. Usmonov was elected to the **Majlisi Oli** in 1994. Between 1995 and 2000, he chaired the parliamentary committee on international affairs, interethnic relations, and culture. In February 2000, he was elected to the **Majlisi Namoyandagon** and became chair of the standing committee on international affairs, public organizations, and information. In January 2000, Usmonov left the Central Committee of the **Communist Party of Tajikistan** and joined the **People's Democratic Party of Tajikistan**. From 2001 to 2004, he worked as state adviser to the president on public relations. In April 2004, he was appointed first deputy minister of culture. Since 2007, Usmanov has been the chair of international journalism in the Tajik National University.

USTOD. The title *ustod* is used for a highly respected master, teacher, or mentor (e.g., Ustod **Rudaki**, Ustod **Ayni**).

UZBEKI. Spoken by more than 1 million **Uzbeks**, or a quarter of Tajikistan's total population, Uzbeki has been in use from the 13th century in the territory that makes up the current state of Tajikistan, especially in the lowlands of the north and south as well as in the **Hisor** valley. Modern Uzbeki is related to the southeastern Central Asian, or Qarluq, group of Turkic languages. Uzbeki contains many **Tajik** and **Arab** loanwords, and it was written in Arabic script until 1927. It was written in Latin between 1928 and 1940, and then Cyrillic. Uzbeks in Tajikistan use the Cyrillic script, as do Tajiks, but the government of **Uzbekistan**, following the Soviet collapse, reverted to the Latin script. Uzbeki is a language of instruction in schools and high schools in Uzbek-populated neighborhoods, as well as at universities. Some **mass media** in Tajikistan use Uzbeki. *See also* LANGUAGES.

UZBEKISTAN. Tajikistan shares its longest border, 1,363 kilometers, with Uzbekistan, a former republic within the **Soviet Union**. Uzbekistan covers an area of 447,000 square kilometers. With a population of nearly 28 million, Uzbekistan is the most populous republic in **Central Asia**, with about four times the population of Tajikistan. According to official sources, **Uzbeks** form 80 percent of the population. Other Central Asian ethnic communities also live in Uzbekistan, including **Tajiks** (5 percent), Kazakhs (3 percent), and Karakalpaks (2.5 percent). The actual number of Tajiks in Uzbekistan is believed to be much higher than the officially stated 135,000.

Uzbeks and Tajiks belong to the **Sunni Hanafi** branch of **Islam**, and for centuries they lived next to each other in the oases of Central Asia. With the establishment of Soviet power in Central Asia, the **Tajik Autonomous Soviet Socialist Republic** was created as part of the Uzbek Soviet Socialist Republic in September 1924. This arrangement lasted until 1929, when Tajikistan became a Soviet member in its own right. The Uzbek nation is 88 percent Sunni Muslim and has a minor **Shia** community (5 percent). **Uzbeki** is the only official state language. Russian serves as a major language for interethnic communication, and **Tajik** is used in Tajik-populated areas, including **Samarqand** and **Bukhara**. Uzbek laws have upgraded the status of Uzbek without giving similar support to Tajik and Russian.

Tashkent, the nation's capital and the largest city in Central Asia, is only a three-hour drive from **Khujand** in Tajikistan. The **Central Asian Railway**, inherited from the Soviet Union, connects many towns within Uzbekistan as well as neighboring Tajikistan. Uzbekistan is rich in natural resources. Since 1991, this country is the world's fourth largest producer of **cotton** and the seventh largest producer of **gold**. It also has significant deposits of natural gas, coal, copper, oil, **silver**, and uranium.

Uzbekistan has the largest army in Central Asia (65,000 people), and the government spends about 3.7 percent of the gross domestic product (GDP) on the military. Following the 11 September 2001 terrorist attacks by al-Qaeda in the United States, Uzbekistan became a key U.S. ally. To support military operations in neighboring Afghanistan, the government provided the U.S. military with access to the Karshi-Khanabad airbase in southern Uzbekistan. In 2004, the country received $500 million in U.S. aid. However, tensions arose when the Uzbek government used force against civil unrest in Andijon, in the Uzbek part of the Ferghana valley, which resulted in several hundred deaths in May 2005. The United States, European Union, United Nations, and Organization for Security and Cooperation in Europe (OSCE) requested an independent investigation of the events, but the government maintained it had simply conducted an antiterrorist operation, exercising only necessary force. Claiming that "enemies of Uzbekistan" had supported the insurgents, the government asked the U.S. military to leave. The U.S. troops left Uzbekistan by November 2005.

Like Tajikistan, Uzbekistan joined the Commonwealth of Independent States (CIS) in December 1991. However, it withdrew from the CIS collective security arrangement in 1999. Uzbekistan is a member of the UN, the Euro-Atlantic Partnership Council, Partnership for Peace, OSCE, Organization of the Islamic Conference (OIC), Shanghai Cooperation Organization (SCO), Central Asian Cooperation Organization (CACO), and Economic Cooperation Organization (ECO). In 1999, Uzbekistan joined the GUAM alliance (Georgia, Ukraine, Azerbaijan, and Moldova), an alternative to the Russia-dominated CIS, but left the organization in 2005.

Some tensions between Tajikistan and Uzbekistan began in Soviet times. As a result of the national delimitation of Central Asia, Tajik-populated Samarqand and Bukhara became part of Uzbekistan in 1924, Tajik intellectuals have criticized Uzbekistan for unfairness against its Tajik minority. Both nations have divergent national historiographies and opposing interpretations of major historical figures and events. The official Uzbek vision of history tends to view Tajiks as a part of the Turkic world, subject to Iranian influence and unlawfully alienated from Uzbekistan during the national delimitation in 1924–1929. It rejects Tajikistan's effort to extend its history beyond the geographical borders of the Tajik republic. Uzbek authorities were displeased by Tajikistan's celebration in 1999 of the 1,100th anniversary of the **Samanid** dynasty, whose capital was Bukhara—now a provincial capital in Uzbekistan. Uzbek historiography questions the Tajik nature of the Samanids. For Tajikistan, the Samanids are a point of departure for national history and a cultural symbol of Tajik civilization. Tajik official historians regard the dynasties of Turkic and Genghis origin that ruled **Movarounnahr** since the fall of the Samanids in 999 as foreign invasions and a despotic yoke imposed on the indigenous Aryan-Tajik nation.

Uzbekistan has played a significant, sometimes controversial role in Tajikistan, especially during Tajikistan's **civil war.** The Uzbekistan-backed militias of ethnic Uzbeks in the **Khatlon** and **Hisor** areas were part of the pro-government **Sitodi Melli.** Fearing the spread of the insurgency, Uzbekistan provided military support to pro-government forces against the opposition forces in 1992–1993, which proved crucial for the rise of **Emomali Rahmon.** At the request of the Tajik government, the Uzbek air force bombarded the zone in central Tajikistan that was controlled by the **United Tajik Opposition** (UTO) in 1993–1994. In September 1992, President Islam Karimov of Uzbekistan appealed to the UN secretary-general for international involvement in peacemaking in Tajikistan. Representatives of Uzbekistan participated as observers in the **Inter-Tajik Peace Talks** in 1994–1997. None of the eight rounds of the peace talks were held in Uzbekistan.

In 1995, Uzbekistan's attitude toward President Rahmon's leadership changed, mostly because of the continued presence of Russian military forces in Tajikistan. In November 1998, Colonel **Mahmud Khudoiberdyev** launched an incursion into **Sughd veloyat** from the territory of Uzbekistan. Tensions between the two states escalated further in 1999–2000 as Uzbekistan accused Tajikistan of harboring the militant **Islamic Movement of Uzbekistan** (IMU). The two states have opposite approaches to regional security affairs. In the late 1990s, Tajikistan and Russia supported the anti-**Taliban** alliance in Afghanistan and advised Uzbekistan to enter into negotiations with the IMU. Uzbekistan and **Kyrgyzstan** have strictly denounced the Tajikistan government for not doing enough to demolish the IMU bands. In November 2000, Uzbekistan introduced a visa regime with Tajikistan, creating obstacles at border posts. Tajikistan and Uzbekistan have not completed border demarcations, and the Uzbek authorities question the legitimacy of the existing border, undertaking unilateral demarcations. Some sections of the border have been mined by Uzbekistan, leading to a number of deaths among the civilian Tajik population. During 2003–2009 in Tajikistan, numerous ethnic Uzbek men were sentenced to long prison terms on charges of espionage and supporting Khudoiberdyev.

Another disputed issue is the allocation of water resources of the **Amu Darya, Zarafshon,** and **Syr Darya** rivers. Tajikistan remains at the mercy of Uzbekistan for transport and energy, while Uzbekistan depends on Tajikistan's water. Since 2002, some improvements in governmental relations have been observed. In February 2002, four documents on cooperation with regard to use of water and energy resources, crossing points on the Tajik-Uzbek border, restructuring of Tajik debt, and transportation of cargo, gas, and fuel were signed. On 6 October 2002 in Dushanbe, presidents Karimov and Rahmon signed an agreement on the demarcation of most of the shared border. The remaining undemarcated border is in the Sughd region. In October 2007, Uzbekistan agreed to transmit Turkmen electricity to Tajikistan, and in January 2008 the sides agreed on prices of Uzbek natural gas supply to Tajikistan. Still, as of early 2009, Tajikistan's northern and western border with Uzbekistan has remained mined.

Uzbekistan is Tajikistan's second trading partner after Russia. Trade with Uzbekistan in 1999 constituted 32.9 percent of Tajikistan's total **foreign trade**. It stood at $278 million in 2007. *See also* FOREIGN INVESTMENT; FOREIGN POLICY; LAND MINES; SOKH; WATER.

UZBEKS. A Turkic ethnic group in Tajikistan, and the largest in **Central Asia**, the Uzbeks accounted for 15 percent of Tajikistan's population in 2008, or more than 1 million people. Uzbek minorities are found in all regions of Tajikistan, except for Qarategin and **Badakhshon**. They are especially visible in the valleys of **Sughd veloyat**, the western part of **Khatlon** veloyat, and west of the **Hisor**. The Uzbeks may be divided into four groups. One is composed of seminomadic Turkic descendants of pre-Uzbek Turkic tribes: **Qarluqs**, **Mogols**, and others. This group was not known as Uzbek before 1924. A second group, Turkified Mongol tribes, are descendants of nomads from the Kazakh Dashti Qipchaq steppes (a wide zone from the Caspian Sea east to the Altai mountains), who migrated to Central Asia with **Shaybani** Khan in the 16th century, and later **Qunghrats**, **Laqais**, **Qataghans**, Durmens, and others. In a third group are Turkic-speaking peoples with no tribal structure: **Chaghatai**. A fourth group are turkified Tajik-speaking sedentary populations of the oases: **Sarts**. In early Soviet times, all these groups were included in the now official Uzbek identity.

The Uzbeks in Tajikistan live in compact enclaves and maintain their traditional social structures and institutions: tribes, **avlods**, **mahallas**. The Uzbeks of Tajikistan mostly did not support the **United Tajik Opposition** in Tajikistan's **civil war** (1992–1997). Since 2000, there are almost no Uzbeks in high government positions. Since 2002, Tajikistan's government promotes a policy of bringing Tajiks into strategic areas traditionally inhabited by members of the Uzbek minority. During 2002–2007, several thousand Tajik families were resettled from Kulob to **Tursunzoda** and **Shahritus** nohiyas bordering **Uzbekistan**. *See also* UZBEKI.

– V –

VAHDAT. The city of Vahdat is the administrative center of **Vahdat nohiya**. Registered as a city in 1965, it was earlier known as Yangi Bazar (1927–1936), Ordzhonikidzeobod (1936–1993), and Kofarnihon (1993–2006). Vahdat is located on the left bank of the Kofarnihon River, 21 kilometers east of **Dushanbe**. Its population is about 49,100 people, primarily **Tajiks** and **Uzbeks** but also Tatars and **Russians**. Vahdat's railway station was constructed in 1930. **Cotton** ginning industries dominate Vahdat.

VAHDAT NOHIYA. Earlier known as Yangi Bazar (1927–1937), Ordzhonikidzeobod (1937–1993), and Kofarnihon (1993–2006), Vahdat nohiya falls within the jurisdiction of the **Nohiyas under Republican Control** and is located in the Kofarnihon river basin. The eastern part of the nohiya is in the mountainous Romit canyon area. The district covers a territory of 3,900 square kilometers, and its population is about 200,000 (49,100 urban), primarily **Tajiks** and **Uzbeks**. The main occupation in Vahdat is **agriculture**, including **cotton**, **grain**, fruit, and poultry production. Arable land amounts to 18,036 hectares. The city of **Vahdat** is the administrative center. Vahdat is connected by **motor road** to **Dushanbe** (21 kilometers) and is on the important motor road between Dushanbe, **Gharm**, **Kulob**, and **Khorugh**. Average July and January temperatures can reach

25C° (in valleys) and –5°C respectively. Average annual precipitation is 700–900 millimeters.

VAKHAN VALLEY. The valley of Vakhan (Wakhan) is situated in the southern part of the **Mountainous Badakhshon Autonomous Veloyat** and northeast **Afghanistan**. The valley shares its name with a mountain range and a river. Vakhan was part of the Greco-**Bactrian** empire in the 3rd–2nd centuries BCE, Tokharistan in the 6th–8th centuries, and the Gurids in the 12th century. The Silk Road passed through the Vakhan valley. In 1895, the valley was divided into Russian and Afghan parts following the delimitation by **Russia** and Great Britain. *See also* VAKHANI.

VAKHANI. Residents of the **Vakhan valley** speak Vakhani, which belongs to the **Pamirian languages** subgroup of East Iranian languages. Vakhani is a vernacular language with no written form and is generally used at the family and communal level. About 8,000 Vakhani speakers live in Tajikistan. Comparable communities in **Afghanistan** are about 8,000, in **China** 7,000, and in Pakistan 10,000. Vakhani speakers are **Ismaili** Muslims. *See also* TAJIKS OF AFGHANISTAN; TAJIKS OF CHINA.

VAKHSH RIVER. The Vakhsh is the main river of the Republic of Tajikistan. In ancient Iranian, *vakhsh* means "streaming waters," while Hindi sources use that name for the **Amu Darya**. Vakhsh is 524 kilometers long. Merging with the Panj River, it forms Amu Darya, the biggest river of **Central Asia**. This river springs in the **Pamir** glaciers and runs west; upstream it is known as Surkhob. The Vakhsh River is only formed after the Surkhob joins the Obi Khingou River. Some 170 kilometers from the headwaters, the river enters the wide **Vakhsh valley** and joins the Panj River south from Dusti village in the **Khatlon** veloyat. The Vakhsh has a basin area of 39,160 square kilometers, almost a quarter of Tajikistan.

Tajikistan's biggest hydroelectrical stations, including **Norak, Roghun**, Sangtuda, and Baipaza, operate on the Vakhsh River. Potential power resources of the Vakhsh are about 28.6 million kilowatts; it can provide up to 250 billion kilowatt hours of electric power per year. *See also* POWER GENERATION; WATER.

VAKHSH VALLEY. Situated in southwestern Tajikistan, the Vakhsh valley is in the lower stream of the **Vakhsh River**. It covers the whole territory of the **Qurghonteppa** zone in the **Khatlon** veloyat. The valley is surrounded by mountain ranges on three sides (Tuiyn Tagh, Aq Tagh, Rangan, Qara Tagh, and Terekli Tagh) and borders **Afghanistan** to the south. The valley is 300–500 meters above sea level. The Vakhsh valley extends for 110 kilometers, with a width of up to 30 kilometers. It was irrigated in the 1930s by forcibly resettled communities from different regions in Tajikistan, notably **Gharm**. In 1992, the valley was ravaged by Tajikistan's **civil war**. The climate is hot, with average temperatures in January and July reaching 1°C and 31°C respectively. Annual precipitation is 200–300 millimeters.

VANJ NOHIYA. Established in 1933 in the **Mountainous Badakh-shon Autonomous Veloyat** (MBAV) in western **Pamir**, between the **Darvoz** and the **Yazghulam** mountain ranges, the Vanj **nohiya** borders **Afghanistan** to the west. The distance from the center of the district, the city of Vanj, to **Khorugh** is 171 kilometers, and to **Dushanbe** 387 kilometers. The nohiya is 4,430 square kilometers in size; its population is about 27,600, **Sunni** and **Ismaili**, in five **ja-moats**. The altitude ranges from 6,083 meters (Arnavad qyshloq) to 1,400 meters, where the Panj river valley is located. Average January and July temperatures can reach –8°C and 24°C respectively, and the annual precipitation is 200–300 millimeters. The main occupation is **agriculture**, including livestock breeding and **grain** production.

VAQF. Religious endowments, lands, and estates donated to religious institutions are known as *vaqf*. The practice was ended in **Central Asia** under Soviet rule in the late 1920s but began to reemerge following the Soviet collapse in 1991.

VARZOB. A canyon north of **Dushanbe**, Varzob is more than 50 kilometers long and ranges from 100 meters to 700 meters wide. Average temperatures in January and July can reach –11°C and 24°C respectively; the annual precipitation is 1,600–1,800 millimeters. The **motor roads** between Dushanbe and **Khujand** and Dushanbe and **Samarqand** traverse this canyon. A popular health resort and the Khoja Obi Garm ski camp (altitude 1,800 meters) are located here. *See also* SPORTS.

VARZOB NOHIYA. One of the **Nohiyas under Republican Control,** Varzob nohiya is situated in the Varzob river basin. It was established in 1991 at the expense of the Lenin nohiya and the October nohiya of **Dushanbe.** The population is about 54,800 (2,200 urban dwellers), mostly **Tajiks,** living in seven **jamoats.** The nohiya center is the city of Varzob, 21 kilometers from Dushanbe. Average January and July temperatures are $-2°C$ and $25°C$ respectively. The Varzob nohiya covers 2,503 square kilometers of mountainous territory north of Dushanbe, up to the **Anzob** Pass. The main occupations include gardening, livestock breeding, and **mining.** The Takob mining mill and Khoja Obi Garm health resort are located in Varzob.

VATAN. The term *vatan* means "homeland."

VATANDOR. An opposition political movement, Vatandor (Patriot) formed in Moscow in February 2007. Its chair and founder, the dissident journalist **Dodojon Atovulloev,** declared that the organization includes former members of the parliament, ex-premiers of Tajikistan, regional and student movement leaders, opposition party members, and representatives of the clergy. Vatandor hopes to gain support from the approximately 1.5 million Tajik migrant workers in **Russia** and other countries. Seeking the resignation of President **Emomali Rahmon,** Vatandor claims it has plans to orchestrate a "violet revolution" similar to the color revolutions in Georgia and Ukraine, to overthrow the ruling regime. As of 2009, the movement did not show any political activity. *See also* POLITICAL PARTIES.

VAZIR. A *vazir* (*wazir*) is a high minister of the state.

VAZIROV, ZAKIR (1948–). Born in Urfad village in the Vakhie valley, **Tavildara nohiya,** Vazirov graduated from the **Dushanbe** Pedagogical Institute with a degree in history in 1970. He became a lecturer at the institute and then head of philosophy. In 1991–1992, he worked in the Tajikistan Ministry of Education as head of the Department of Higher Education. He received his **doctorate** in Islamic philosophy in 1995. Early in the 1990s, Vazirov joined the opposition movement and served as minister of education in the **Government of National Reconciliation.** In 1993–1994, he was chair of the state book chamber and of philosophy and cultural studies at the Tajik

Institute of Commerce. Vazirov was appointed vice premier in October 1998, following the signing of the **General Agreement on the Establishment of Peace and National Accord**, which provided for the allocation of 30 percent of government posts to the **United Tajik Opposition**. Vazirov's portfolio was the social sphere and local self-government. He left in 1999. From February 2005 to November 2006, he served as minister of labor and social protection. In December 2006, he was appointed rector of the Institute of Entrepreneurship and Service.

VELOYAT. The Tajik term *veloyat* (territory, province) replaced the Russian term *oblast*. In 2009, there were three veloyats in Tajikistan: **Khatlon, Sughd**, and the **Mountainous Badakhshon Autonomous Veloyat** (MBAV). Veloyats consist of **nohiya** subdivisions. Heads of veloyats are appointed by the president. *See also* ADMINISTRATIVE STRUCTURE.

VORUKH. A *shahrak* (rural settlement) and *jamoat* (self-governing community) in **Isfara nohiya**, Vorukh is a Tajik enclave within the borders of **Kyrgyzstan** that encompasses 130 square kilometers with a population of up to 29,000 (95 percent **Tajiks** and 5 percent **Kyrgyzs**), living in 17 villages. Vorukh is located 45 kilometers south of Isfara within the territory of Batken province, Kyrgyzstan. During 1975–2008, Vorukh and Batken witnessed several violent disputes over land, irrigation water, and property rights along the border between the Tajik and Kyrgyz communities. *See also* WATER.

VOSE (1845–1888). A national hero known also as Abdulvose and Mullo Vosecha, Vose was born in Darai Mukhtor village in Khovaling, Kulob veloyat. He was the leader of the 1886 popular rebellion against the **Bukharan** emir in Baljuvon. Vose was captured and executed by the emir's authorities in 1888. **Vose nohiya** was named after him.

VOSE NOHIYA. Established in 1957 as Aral nohiya in the Kulob veloyat, the district was renamed Vose nohiya in 1960 after the national hero **Vose**. The territory includes 3,600 square kilometers and borders **Tavildara** and **Norak** in the northeast and west, and **Muminobod** and **Kulob** in the south. The distance from the district center, the city of Vose, to **Dushanbe** is 184 kilometers, and to Kulob 18 kilometers. Vose is connected by rail to Kulob, **Qurghonteppa**, and Dushanbe. The population of the district is about 144,300 (18,100 urban), with 82 percent **Tajiks** and 15 percent **Uzbeks** in 10 **jamoats**. Average January and July temperatures can reach –2°C and 30°C respectively. Tajikistan's largest rock salt depository, Khoja Mumin, is located in Vose nohiya. The main occupation is **agriculture**, including **cotton**, cereals, and livestock breeding.

VOSTOKREDMET. The Vostokredmet enterprise operates Tajikistan's sole **gold** refinery. The name comes from a Russian phrase for "East Rare Metals." Originally constructed in the Soviet period to process uranium, which was mined across the northern border in Kazakhstan and shipped south through **Uzbekistan**, the refinery ceased work when Kazakhstan halted uranium shipments and Uzbekistan blocked transit. In the late 1990s, additional gold refining capacity was added at Vostokredmet. *See also* MINING.

– W –

WAHHABIYA. A puritanical movement within the **Sunni** branch of **Islam**, the Wahhabiya formed in Arabia in the 18th century. Its founder was Abd al-Wahhab (1703–1787). Now the dominant sect in Saudi Arabia and Qatar, Wahhabism teaches a return to the origins of Islam as practiced by the Prophet Muhammad. Wahhabism rejects mysticism and the idea of saints. There is no apparent support for Wahhabism in Tajikistan, although some features of Wahhabi teachings (including strict observance of Islam and rejection of excessive display of wealth) are appealing to Islamic activists. *See also* SALAFIYA.

WATER. Water issues are the core of a number of environmental, political, and economic problems in Tajikistan and wider **Central Asia.** The **constitution** of Tajikistan and the Water Code approved in November 2000 stipulate exclusive state ownership of water and the state's guarantee of its effective use and protection in the interests of citizens. General water use in Tajikistan is free of charge, but special water use should be paid for. In Tajikistan, water resource control and management functions are divided among various agencies. The Ministry of Soil Improvement and Water Economy is the main organization.

Out of 130 cubic kilometers of annual surface water in Central Asia, 40 percent is formed in Tajikistan, 30 percent in **Kyrgyzstan**, and 5 percent in **Uzbekistan**. Since the collapse of the **Soviet Union**, the region's governments have failed to agree on water management issues due to conflicting interests among the states located upstream and downstream of the main rivers, the **Amu Darya** and **Syr Darya**. Downstream Uzbekistan consumes almost 50 percent of Amu Darya and Syr Darya water, and Kazakhstan needs water in the summer for irrigation. The energy-poor upstream Kyrgyzstan and Tajikistan use water in winter for electricity production. During the Soviet period, the allocation of water among the Central Asian republics was based on quotas and special regulations, approved by the central government. Tajikistan was tasked to collect water in its reservoirs in winter and discharge it downstream to Uzbekistan in the spring. Uzbekistan was instructed to provide Tajikistan with the fuel and natural gas needed for the winter. This barter system proved inefficient in the 1990s and later.

In independent Tajikistan, electricity is a main energy source. The country is experiencing a drastic decline in water levels. It believes that the water allocation system does not provide for sufficient irrigation farming to satisfy food requirements. Nor is the construction of hydropower stations sufficient to cover the need for electricity. Tajikistan seeks to become a leading power exporter, but the construction of hydropower stations in upstream Tajikistan was always a headache for Uzbekistan. This downstream country asked for guarantees that the construction of new hydroelectric stations would not harm the interests of the downstream states.

The poor irrigation systems used in the region further aggravate water shortages. Per capita water consumption in Central Asia is on average twice that of Organization for Economic Cooperation and Development countries. Yet the supply of safe drinking water remains poor. About 40 percent of the Tajik population uses water from open sources. Many Tajik citizens, even in **Dushanbe**, lack clean drinking water. Water quality is affected by discharges of contaminated municipal and industrial waste water and return flow from **agriculture**.

The shortage of water resources and poor management may result in conflicts among Central Asian countries and within them, particularly in the **Ferghana**, **Vakhsh**, and **Zarafshon** valleys. In the future, water allocation may become more problematic due to the growing needs of **Afghanistan** as it gradually recovers from political instability and may claim a bigger share of water for the economic development of its northern provinces. *See also* POWER GENERATION.

WOMEN'S ISSUES. From the 8th century, **Tajiks** lived in a Muslim society where all authority and power was assigned to men by Islamic law. The unquestionable principle of male domination became central in **adat** (unwritten regional customs), and men have always controlled leadership and decision-making in Tajik communities. But Tajik women have traditionally played a central role in the private sphere of the family. Women serve as guardians of traditional culture, preservers of the Tajik **language**, and transmitters of religious knowledge and experience. Under the **Soviet Union**, Tajik women and men were given equal civic rights. The **hujum** campaign in the late 1920s was designed to prohibit the wearing of coverings such as **faranji** and to liberate women overnight.

In 1991, women made up 40 percent of the Tajik labor force. They enjoyed various benefits related to child care. In addition to state-run medical and **educational** facilities, the enterprises and **kolkhozes** (collective farms) where women worked had their own nurseries, kindergartens, clinics, and even health resorts. However, compared to the other Soviet republics, the modernization process was least successful in Tajikistan. Tajikistan managed to preserve its fundamental traditions and Islamic identity. Living in an **avlod** (extended family) is still the norm for Tajiks, and most marriages are arranged. Men have to accumulate sufficient wealth in order to afford marriage, since it often includes **qalin** (payment of the bride price). In the family, parents often see their sons as potential breadwinners while girls are considered temporary (and sometimes unwanted) members of the family. Upon marriage, women become members of their husband's family, where they have a low status.

The collapse of the Soviet Union in 1991 led to the end of most of the state-funded institutions and services that supported women, such as universal child allowances and extensive child-care facilities. The textile and manufacturing industries as well as **agriculture** that employed mostly women laborers collapsed, and Tajik women were among the first who lost their jobs. During Tajikistan's **civil war** in 1992–1997, women were subject to various forms of violence, including rape, torture, kidnapping, and verbal abuse. As a result of the civil war, many men died, leaving 55,000 orphans and 25,000 widows. The ensuing **labor migration** resulted in the additional outflow of hundreds of thousands of young Tajik men from their families. Some labor migrants send money back home, while others do not. Many marry or remarry (legally or otherwise) in **Russia** and discontinue their relations with their families in Tajikistan. As a result, the number of households headed by females has increased. The postwar period has seen the revival of the pre-Soviet, Muslim custom of Tajik men taking a second wife. These marriages, called *nikoh*, are "registered" by mullahs only. Children born to second wives are not protected by law, as the government does not consider the *nikoh* legal. Finding a well-paying job is especially hard for women in Tajikistan, and the number of women forced into prostitution and **drug-trafficking** is increasing.

Tajikistan was the first **Central Asian** country to ratify the United Nation's Convention on the Elimination of All Forms of Discrimination against Women on 26 October 1993. In 2005, Tajikistan adopted a gender equality law. In 2007, the country was ranked 62nd out of 189 countries classified by the Inter-Parliamentary Union in terms of the representation of women in parliament. In 2006–2009, women accounted for 17.5 percent (11 seats) in the 63-seat **Majlisi Namoyandagon**, some 12.5 percent in the **Majlisi Melli**, and 11.5 percent in local *majlises*. There is a State Committee on Women and the Family within the government. It has branches in all **veloyats** and **nohiyas** and is charged with the protection of women's rights and implementation of the National Plan of Action for the Advancement of Women. But the committee lacks funding and real power.

Despite the president's attempt to shape Tajikistan as a secular state, there has been a revival of Islamic practices and a definite withdrawal of women from social and political life. Women occupy around 7 percent of senior posts within government ministries. There were only three women in ministerial posts in 2009. The representation of women at lower levels of administration and in legislatures, particularly in local *majlises*, is more significant. In 2007, 7 women (9 percent) were city and **nohiya** chairs, and 93 women (23 percent) headed **jamoats**. The number of women among deputy chairs of cities and nohiyas has increased up to 33.9 percent and up to 43 among deputy chairs of jamoats. In 2007, women accounted for 20 percent of the total number of judges in Tajikistan. Very few women occupy senior positions in **political parties**, while no women's faction exists in the **Majlisi Oli**. Women are active in the nongovernmental sphere. They constitute 35 percent of the heads of all nongovernmental organizations, though 17.5 percent of parliamentarians.

Since the end of the civil war, the fertility rate has fallen from 4.17 children in 1998 to 3.04 in 2008. The marriage rate is also in decline, due to poor living conditions, lack of necessary finances, and the predominantly male labor migration. These trends put women under harsh economic, social, and psychological stresses, especially since family and a large number of children are essential to traditional Tajik women. *See also* BIOTUN; HIJAB; KADBONU.

WORLD WAR II (1939–1945). The general conscription of **Tajiks** into the army of the **Soviet Union** started in 1939. During World War II, about 260,000 people from Tajikistan served in the Soviet Army. Some Tajiks fought against Finland in 1939–1940 and Japan in 1945, but most of them took part in the war against Nazi Germany in 1941–1945, the Great Patriotic War. About 60,000 citizens of Tajikistan lost their lives in the war. Fifty-four Tajikistanis received the highest award—Hero of the Soviet Union. Light **industries** and food processing plants were evacuated from the central parts of the Soviet Union to Tajikistan in 1941–1943. On the eve of the 21st century, Tajikistan had about 13,000 war veterans.

– Y –

YAGHNOBI. Sometimes called the new Sogdian **language**, Yaghnobi is an East Iranian language, spoken only by **Yaghnobis**. *See also* KHROMOV, ALBERT.

YAGHNOBIS. Members of a Tajik ethnic group, Yaghnobis are the traditional inhabitants of the narrow Yaghnob river valley in central Tajikistan. The valley is 2,000–3,000 meters above sea level and is located between **Hisor** and the **Zarafshon** valley. It is 100 kilometers north of **Dushanbe**. Until 1970, there were 33 **qyshloqs** (villages) with a total population of 3,000 in the Yaghnob valley. But in the 1970s, almost all the Yaghnobis were forcibly resettled in the Zarafshon nohiya of the **Sughd veloyat** to accelerate **cotton** production. After the Soviet collapse, over 300 Yaghnobis returned to the Yaghnob area. *See also* KHROMOV, ALBERT; YAGHNOBI.

YAKUB BEG (1820–1877). A Muslim leader who ruled Kasgharia (southern Xinjiang) from 1864 to 1877, Yakub Beg (Yaqub Bek) was also known as Ataliq and Badavlet. He was born probably to a Tajik family in Pskent (Tashkent oasis) or in **Khujand**. Yakub Beg was an officer in the **Kokand** army and a commander of the fort until it was captured by the Russian army in 1853. He fled to **Bukhara** but returned to Kokand in 1863. Taking advantage of the anti-Chinese uprisings of Muslims in Xinjiang, the Kokandis sent an expedition to Kashghar in 1864, and Yakub Beg arose there as a powerful leader. By the beginning of the 1870s, he managed to control Kashgaria and set up a strong emirate.

Yakub Beg's rule took place at the height of the "Great Game," the competition between major world powers for control in the region, and he exploited the situation. Having concluded treaties with Great Britain and **Russia**, and receiving the support of the Ottoman empire, he sought backing from all sides involved in the competition. The aid offered by the British proved insufficient, and Russia decided to support the Chinese, helping them to destroy independent Kashgaria. The circumstances of Yakub Beg's death on 30 May 1877 remain unclear. some say he was killed in battle or was poisoned; others say he committed suicide or had a stroke. His followers were brutally massacred by the Chinese. But Yakub Beg set a precedent for subsequent generations of Xinjiangese Muslims by calling for independence from foreign domination. In the view of **China**, however, the Kashghar emirate established by Yakub Beg was a foreign invasion.

YARMATOV, KAMIL (1903–1978). A Tajik/Uzbek filmmaker and actor, Yarmatov was born in **Konibodom** and was a member of the people's militia in 1918–1923 in Tajikistan. Yarmatov graduated from the Chaikovskiy Art Studio in Moscow in 1926 and the State Institute of Cinematography in Moscow in 1931. He made the first Tajik film, *Emigrant*, in 1934. In 1934, he moved to Tashkent, where he continued to make films. The **Uzbekistan** film studio bore his name until the mid-1990s.

YAZGHULAMI. One of the **Pamirian languages**, Yazghulami is spoken by the inhabitants of the Yazghulam valley, **Vanj nohiya**, in the **Mountainous Badakhshon Autonomous Veloyat**. Some Yazghulamis were resettled in the **Vakhsh valley** in the 1950s and 1960s. In 1999, the total number of Yazghulami speakers was around 4,000.

YOUNG BUKHARANS. A revolutionary Bukharan organization, the Young Bukharans was formed following the **February 1917 revolution** from the ranks of the **Jadids** in the **Bukharan emirate**. Young Bukharans, headed by **Faizullo Khojaev**, aimed to overthrow the Bukharan emir **Said Alim Khan** and establish a democratic republic. After the defeat of **Kolesov's March**, Young Bukharans were forced to flee prosecution by taking refuge in the **Turkistan Soviet Republic**. The Young Bukharans joined the **Communist Party of Bukhara** (CPB) on the eve of the September 1920 **Bukharan Revolution**. Former Young Bukharans, now members of the CPB, staffed the newly formed **Bukharan People's Soviet Republic**.

YOVON NOHIYA. Formed in 1934, Yovon nohiya is situated in dry lowland on the **Vakhsh River** in **Qurghonteppa** veloyat. The district is 976.2 square kilometers, with five **jamoats** and two towns, populated by descendants of nomadic and seminomadic **Uzbek** tribes, **Laqais**, **Qarluqs**, sedentary **Tajiks**, and migrant settlers from other parts of the republic, totaling about 134,900 (28,700 urban). The district center, the city of Yovon, is connected by rail to Qurghonteppa, a distance of 88 kilometers. The distance to **Dushanbe** is 59 kilometers. Average temperatures in January and July are 4°C and 30°C respectively, and the annual precipitation is 683 millimeters. Arable land amounts to 2,800 hectares. The largest electrochemical plant in **Central Asia** is located in Yovon.

YUSUF (YUSUPOV), SHODMON (1949–). A Tajik opposition leader, Yusuf was born in Darband nohiya. He graduated from Saratov State University in **Russia** in 1972 and later completed postgraduate studies at the Institute of Philosophy, Academy of Sciences, Moscow. In 1977, Yusuf became a research fellow and the Communist Party's organizer in the Department of Philosophy, **Academy of Sciences of Tajikistan**.

On 10 August 1990, Yusuf was appointed chair of the newly organized **Democratic Party of Tajikistan** (DPT). In March–May 1992, the DPT under his leadership joined with the **Islamic Renaissance Party of Tajikistan** (IRPT) in organizing a 52-day rally in Shahidon Square, **Dushanbe**. After the onset of the **civil war**, Yusuf left Tajikistan. In June 1994, at the DPT congress in Almaty, a split occurred in the party, leading to the formation of the **Democratic Party of Tajikistan Almaty Platform**. Yusuf and his followers organized the **DPT Tehran Platform** in June 1995. Yusuf officially declared his allegiance to the government of **Emomali Rahmon**, and in January 1996 President Rahmon granted Yusuf and his party colleagues amnesty. Nevertheless, Yusuf did not return to Dushanbe. In July 1999, Yusuf was removed as chair of the DPT Tehran Platform.

– Z –

ZAFAROBOD NOHIYA. The Zafarobod nohiya was established in 1965 in the western part of Leninobod veloyat to irrigate the Tajik part of the Mirzachul steppes. The distance between the center of the nohiya, the city of Zafarobod, and **Khujand** is 105 kilometers. Zafarobod is one of the smallest districts in Tajikistan, with a territory of 441 square kilometers. The population is about 49,900 (28,700 urban), comprising **Tajiks**, **Uzbeks**, and forcibly resettled **Yaghnobis** who live in three towns. Average January and July temperatures can reach –1°C and 29°C respectively; the average annual precipitation is 250–300 millimeters. Arable land amounts to 44,094 hectares. The main occupation is **agriculture**, including **cotton** and **grain** production, livestock breeding, and fruit and vegetable gardening. Local **industries** include a fruit conservation plant and a salt plant.

ZARAFSHON RIVER. The Zarafshon River traverses the territories of Tajikistan and **Uzbekistan**, giving its name to a valley and a mountain range. The river is 782 kilometers long. It springs up in the Zarafshon glacier and flows west, passing through **Kuhistoni Mastchoh**, **Ayni**, and **Panjakent**. It then crosses into Uzbekistan and flows through **Samarqand** and **Bukhara**, ending in the Qizil

Qum desert sands. The Zarafshon basin is considered the original homeland of the **Sogdians**.

ZARIFI (ZARIPOV), HAMROKHON (1948–). Born in **Vose nohiya**, Zarifi studied at the **Kulob** State Pedagogical Institute and in 1971–1972 taught physics there. In 1973, he became a research fellow at the Physico-Technical Institute of the **Academy of Sciences of Tajikistan**. Between 1974 and 1993, he worked in various branches of the **Communist Party of Tajikistan** and State Security Committee (KGB). In 1993, he was appointed deputy head and then head of the cadre department at the Ministry of Foreign Affairs. In 1995, he was appointed deputy minister of foreign affairs. In October 1996, he became the representative of Tajikistan to the **Organization of Security and Cooperation in Europe** and other international organizations as well as ambassador to Austria. From 2002 to 2006, he served as the first Tajik ambassador to the **United States**. Zarifi became minister of foreign affairs in December 2006.

ZIYOEV, MIRZO (1960–). Nicknamed "Djaga," Ziyoev was born in Khojai Khiloj village, **Panj** nohiya, **Qurghonteppa** veloyat, to a **Gharmi** family. Between 1977 and 1980, he served in the Soviet navy. In 1984, he graduated from the **Dushanbe** Industrial College and worked as technician-topographist in his native Panj until 1992. With the onset of Tajikistan's **civil war**, Ziyoev organized 100 volunteers and fought against **Sitodi Melli** bands. At the end of 1992, he fled to **Afghanistan** with his group and was appointed commander of oppositional military forces of the **United Tajik Opposition** (UTO). He was one of the most influential of the civil war commanders, with some 2,000 fighters in 1997. He and his troops are reported to have been trained in Afghanistan in **Ahmad Shah Massoud**'s camp. After the signing of the **General Agreement on the Establishment of Peace and National Accord** in June 1997, Ziyoev and his detachment returned to Tajikistan and located in the **Tavildara nohiya**. According to some reports, the **Islamic Movement of Uzbekistan** (IMU) leader **Jumaboi Namangani** was under Ziyoev's direct command during the civil war. The UTO insisted on Ziyoev's appointment as the minister of defense, but President **Emomali Rahmon** resisted. In June 1999, Ziyoev was promoted to general and appointed minister of emergency situations with the right to form military groups. In May 2000, he negotiated and oversaw the withdrawal of the IMU forces from central Tajikistan to Afghanistan. In December 2006, Zioyev was fired from his position by presidential decree. In July 2009, he joined with former UTO military leader **Abdullo Rahimov** in Tavildara and was killed in a skirmish between governmental forces and local insurgents.

ZOIROV, RAHMATULLOH (1958–). Born in Tashkent province, **Uzbekistan**, Zoirov served in the Soviet Army in 1977–1979 and then studied at the Kharkov Juridical Institute (Ukraine). Upon his graduation in 1983, Zoirov lectured at the institute until 1986. Between 1986 and 1993, he lectured at the Tajik State University. In 1993–1994, he was a member of Tajikistan's Constitutional Control Committee. In 1993–1997, he was the head of the International Law Department at the Institute of World Economy and International Relations, attached to the **Academy of Sciences of Tajikistan**. In 1998, he became head of the Law Department at the Tajik State Pedagogical Institute. Zoirov has authored numerous books and articles. He drafted an alternative **constitution** for Tajikistan in 1994 and has participated in the preparation of more than 20 laws. Zoirov launched the **Social-Democratic Party of Tajikistan** in March 1998. He was a presidential adviser on legal issues from 2001 until he resigned in protest in June 2003 over changes to the constitution allowing the president to seek more terms in office. *See also* ELECTIONS; GOVERNMENT.

ZUHUROV, SAIDAMIR (1951–). Born in Farkhor, Kulob veloyat, Zuhurov served in the Soviet Army in 1969–1971. In 1975, he received a degree in history from the Dushanbe Pedagogical Institute. In 1975–1977, he was a high school teacher in Farkhor, and in 1977 he joined the security services. In 1978, he was trained at the committee for state security (KGB) in Moscow and started work in the State Security Department in what is now **Muminobod nohiya**. In 1981–1982, he studied at the KGB high school and in 1983–1985 served as the KGB representative in Kabul, **Afghanistan**. Between 1985 and 1990, Zuhurov worked in the Kulob provincial department of Tajikistan's KGB, rising to deputy chief of the department. In 1990–1991, he was an officer with the KGB First Department (Chief Political Department) in Moscow.

In 1992, Zuhurov became deputy chief of Kulob provincial administration of the republican KGB. In November 1992, he was appointed chair of Tajikistan's Committee for National Security by President **Emomali Rahmon** and became minister of national security in 1993. In August 1995, he was appointed minister of internal affairs but in November 1996 returned to his earlier position as minister of national security. From December 1999 to January 2005, Zuhurov served as vice premier until he was appointed chair of the Committee of Border Protection. Since December 2006, Zuhurov has been head of the Department of Protection of State Secrets attached to the government of Tajikistan.

ZUHUROV, SHUKURJON (1954–). Born in the **Panj** nohiya, **Qurghonteppa** veloyat, to a **Gharmi** family, Zuhurov graduated from the Moscow Institute of Engineers of Land Tenure in 1976 and the Russian Academy of Management in 1992. He started his working life as an engineer of land tenure in Qurghonteppa and the Moskva nohiya. In 1979, he moved to **Dushanbe**, where he worked in the central apparatus of the **Komsomol**. In 1986, he was appointed chair of the nohiya executive committee in Komsomolobod (now **Darband**). In 1991, he was appointed chair of the State Committee on Labor and Worker Cadre Preparation. He served as minister of labor and worker cadre preparation in 1993–1998. In February 1998, Zuhurov was appointed director of the World Bank's Center for Coordination of Credits on Postconflict Rehabilitation. He took part in the 1994–1997 **Inter-Tajik Peace Talks**, and in 1997 he was appointed secretary of the subcommittee on refugees in the **Commission for National Reconciliation**. From 1992 to 2005, he served as minister of labor and employment. In February 2005, Zuhurov was elected to the **Majlisi Namoyandagon**. In December 2006, he became minister of labor and social protection of the population.

Appendix 1. Main Macroeconomic Indicators of Tajikistan as % of the Previous Year

	1995	1996	1997	1998	1999	2000	2001	2002	2003	2004	2005	2006	2007	2008
Gross domestic product	87.6	83.3	101.7	105.3	103.7	108.3	109.6	110.8	111.0	110.3	106.7	107.0	107.8	107.9
Industrial production	86	76	98	108	106	110	115	108	110	115	110	105	109.9	96.0
Agricultural production	84	91	100.2	106	103	113	107	117	109	111	102	106	106.5	107.9
Capital investments	—	—	—	—	—	—	—	—	—	150	112	170	203.6	160.8
Freight carried	74	71	105	126	89	105	100.8	99.3	121	117	115	110	116.7	109.8
Retail trade turnover	77	94	109	109	104	79	102	118	125	123	110	111	105.2	113.5
Industrial producers price index	376	355	178	130	144	144	127	109	115	117	99.0	122	118.4	116.3
Consumer price indices	543	370	172	143	126	124	137	110	117	107	108	112	121.5	120.4
Export to CIS countries	272	132	82	74	155	119	57	89	74	115	112	105	123.0	98.47
Export to other countries	124	88	108	83	95	110	107	125	120	115	97	166	102.2	95.30
Import from CIS countries	205	80	126	93	115	109	96	102	109	129	112	127	138.1	113.81
Import from other countries	106	86	94	99	56	78	130	116	163	148	112	134	149.7	153.42

Source: www.cisstat.com/eng/tad.htm

Appendix 2. Tajikistan in World Economic Outlook Database, International Monetary Fund, April 2009

	2006	2007	2008	2009
Gross domestic product, current prices, billions USD	2.811	3.712	5.135	5.383
Gross domestic product per capita, current prices, USD	440.575	578.294	795.108	828.580
Gross domestic product based on purchasing-power-parity (PPP) valuation of country GDP, USD	10.685	11.829	13.041	13.425
Gross domestic product based on purchasing-power-parity (PPP) per capita GDP, USD	1,674.495	1,842.646	2,019.335	2,066.493

Source: www.imf.org/external/pubs/

Appendix 3. Export of Goods, 1993–2007

	1993	1994	1995	1996	1997	1998	1999	2000	2001	2002	2003	2004	2005	2006	2007
Export total,															
million USD	456	559	779	769	746	597	689	784	652	739	797	915	909	1399	1468
Cotton	117	155	212	157	167	98	82	84	62	128	193	162	144	129	138
Electricity	30	29	123	175	155	114	175	92	79	67	55	58	53	49	60
Other	309	375	443	438	424	385	432	608	511	544	549	695	712	1221	1270
Export volume															
Cotton,															
thousand tons	150	126	121	104	108	81	86	74	68	137	149	133	133.0	120	120
Electricity, million															
kilowatt hours	4,827	4,062	2,704	3,139	3,889	3,346	3,831	3,908	4,047	3,874	4,597	4,451	4,258	4,231	4,259
Cotton price,															
thousand USD															
per ton					1.54	1.21	0.95	1.14	0.91	0.93	1.30	1.21	1.08	1.06	1.14
Electricity price,															
USD per one															
kilowatt hour					0.04	0.03	0.05	0.02	0.02	0.02	0.01	0.01	0.01	0.01	0.01

Source: www.stat.tj

Appendix 4.   Import of Goods, 1993–2007

	1993	1994	1995	1996	1997	1998	1999	2000	2001	2002	2003	2004	2005	2006	2007
Import total,															
million USD	648	693	838	668	750	711	663	675	688	721	881	1,191	1,330	1,725	2,547
Natural gas	48	84	70	38	40	40	36	35	27	22	24	28	27	35	65
Oil products	53	79	80	61	60	77	54	48	78	73	73	107	126	191	275
Electricity	26	19	164	133	180	128	179	119	98	82	61	65	58	67	66
Cereal	95	113	46	54	24	43	46	45	38	36	33	48	76	77	135
Other	426	398	478	169	446	423	348	428	447	508	690	943	1,043	1,355	2,006
Import volume															
Natural gas, million cubic meters	1,345	994	856	600	733	758	750	729	565 2	486	532	622	630	641	647
Oil products, thousand tons	685	421	394	311	312	390	318	215	293	337	305	357	308	379	519
Electricity, million kilowatt hours	3,694	3,579	3,366	2,898	3,987	3,592	3,641	5,243	5,396	4,660	4,605	4,810	4,508	4,839	4,361
Cereal, thousand tons	1,521	655	391	158	83	251	278	321	266	295	153	125	289	276	283

Source: www.stat.tj

Appendix 5.   Direction of Trade, 1992–2007 (in million USD)

	1992	1993	1994	1995	1996	1997	1998	1999	2000	2001	2002	2003	2004	2005	2006	2007
Exports																
total	29.3	349.8	491.9	748.6	771.5	803.4	596.6	688.7	770.0	652.9	736.9	797.1	914.9	908.7	1398.9	979.0
Netherlands	—	1.1	147.6	255.2	218.0	229.4	221.4	222.3	178.2	194.4	216.9	200.8	379.2	423.4	569.4	26.0
Turkey	—	5.2	7.6	8.1	1.9	8.2	0.4	1.0	58.4	75.1	118.5	193.2	139.7	143.4	442.8	130.3
Uzbekistan	—	20.3	22.7	132.0	190.7	172.5	125.7	181.0	97.8	87.2	72.9	67.1	65.9	66.5	67.4	80.5
Russia	—	62.5	46.2	95.3	79.0	63.5	47.8	115.1	258.8	104.7	87.5	52.2	60.5	82.8	65.4	85.8
Iran	—	—	1.4	0.7	1.7	3.5	13.6	13.5	12.5	29.9	28.4	51.4	29.6	36.7	76.1	99.1
Latvia	—	7.2	3.4	21.0	9.5	64.0	1.9	8.3	—	11.7	30.9	78.0	64.8	44.2	35.1	0.8
Switzerland	0.4	5.8	44.9	37.2	83.5	140.7	94.9	75.1	72.2	52.2	68.7	77.0	63.4	27.0	24.5	27.1
Norway	—	—	12.1	5.4	0.6	—	0.0	0.2	—	—	—	—	—	—	—	152.4
Italy	6.8	2.5	0.4	2.4	6.6	7.8	9.8	5.1	21.4	5.7	6.9	8.4	11.4	15.6	16.5	99.4
Kazakhstan	—	16.3	10.1	7.0	24.3	10.0	10.0	3.6	5.7	3.1	3.5	4.6	3.5	19.7	27.8	33.2
Imports																
total	72.9	532.1	547.0	809.9	668.1	750.3	711.0	663.0	670.5	693.5	720.5	907.5	1191.1	1330.0	1725.3	2384.6
Russian Federation	—	83.8	60.7	136.0	74.4	115.1	102.2	92.4	105.1	129.4	163.5	178.1	240.8	256.5	423.7	503.5
Uzbekistan	—	65.4	83.2	251.4	198.9	261.6	227.3	264.4	185.6	150.7	132.4	132.7	168.8	152.9	176.4	210.5

Source: www.adb.org/Statistics

Appendix 6.   Agricultural Production, 1990–2007 (in thousand tons)

	1990	1991	1992	1993	1994	1995	1996	1997	1998	1999	2000	2001	2002	2003	2004	2005	2006	2007
Cotton	842	826	515	524	531	412	318	353	383	313	335	453	515	537	557	448	438	420
Grain	318	304	276	273	229	249	548	559	500	482	550	494	596	730	734	935	773	801
Sweet corn	85	60	32	33	18	19	90	30	36	36	38	42	55	95	95	156	139	130
Field corn	1,222	1,150	727	599	498	436	191	186	170	180	226	241	299	294	295	339	407	457
Rice	29	26	20	23	23	24	21	44	40	47	82	39	50	59	59	62	49	51
Potatoes	207	181	167	147	134	112	108	128	175	240	303	308	357	473	527	555	574	662
Vegetables	528	628	543	485	483	491	397	351	322	385	354	397	473	583	679	718	760	835
Fruits	220	177	183	149	148	149	126	113	97	78	169	144	147	89	144	148	209	157
Grapes	190	121	100	88	80	96	122	127	46	54	110	110	81	28	93	91	107	117
Hay	1,521	1,486	1,212	1,112	1,014	931	315	379	359	304	290	275	376	356	443	219	231	256

Source: www.stat.tj

Appendix 7. Tajikistan's Population and Labor Force, 1990–2008

	1990	1991	1992	1993	1994	1995	1996	1997	1998	1999	2000	2001	2002	2003	2004	2005	2006	2007	2008
Population																			
in millions	5.30	5.43	5.54	5.57	5.61	5.67	5.74	5.82	5.94	6.06	6.19	6.31	6.44	6.57	6.71	6.85	6.99	7.13	7.21
Persons per square kilometer	37	38	39	39	39	40	40	41	41	42	44	45	46	47	48	49	49	50	50
% annual change	2.3	2.5	1.9	0.7	0.6	1.1	1.2	1.5	2.0	2.1	2.1	2.0	2.0	2.1	2.1	2.1	2.1	2.1	0.9
% urban	32.1	31.3	30.8	29.7	28.9	28.1	27.4	26.8	26.7	26.6	26.5	26.6	26.4	26.5	26.4	26.4	26.4	26.3	26.3
Labor force																			
in thousands	1939	1971	1917	1877	1887	1890	1777	1842	1855	1791	1794	1872	1904	1932	2132	2154	2185	—	
Employed	1939	1971	1909	1855	1855	1853	1731	1791	1796	1737	1745	1829	1857	1885	2090	2112	2137		
In agriculture	833	881	892	949	1002	1095	1026	1145	1090	1118	1133	1218	1255	1275	1391	1425	1432		
In industry	244	404	382	335	315	264	249	216	200	176	157	156	153	115	118	121	118		
Other	717	686	635	571	529	494	456	430	506	443	454	455	449	495	581	566	587		
Unemployed	—	—	8	22	28	33	49	48	59	40	49	43	47	47	42	42	48		
% unemployment	—	—	0.4	1.2	1.5	1.7	2.7	2.6	3.2	2.2	2.7	2.3	2.5	2.4	2.0	2.1	2.2		
% annual change	8.3	1.7	-2.7	-2.1	0.5	0.2	-6.0	3.7	0.7	-3.5	0.2	4.3	1.7	1.5	10.4	1.0	1.4		
% participation	77.3	75.5	73.6	75.9	73.6	70.9	65.4	62.9	61.3	57.3	55.3	55.4	53.4	53.0	56.0	55.0	54.0		

Source: www.adb.org/

Appendix 8. Tajikistan's National Accounts, 1991–2007 (in million somoni, at current prices)

	1991	1992	1993	1994	1995	1996	1997	1998	1999	2000	2001	2002	2003	2004	2005	2006	2007
GDP by industrial origin at current market prices	0.1	0.6	7.1	17.9	69.8	308.5	518.4	1025.2	1345.0	1786.7	2563.8	3375.3	4761.4	6167.2	7206.6	9335.2	12,779.7
Agriculture	0.0	0.2	1.5	3.4	25.6	111.1	165.9	257.4	341.5	448.8	610.2	750.0	1150.3	1184.1	1526.7	2001.7	2525.9
Manufacturing	0.0	0.2	2.1	3.7	23.8	79.3	114.0	206.1	592.3	858.0	1117.2	1440.2	1644.4	1645.1	1987.0	1966.9	—
Electricity, gas, and water	0.0	0.1	0.9	2.2	—	—	—	—	—	—	—	—	—	—	—	—	—
Construction	—	—	—	—	2.2	7.9	14.2	39.5	72.9	38.0	69.7	68.9	136.6	262.3	327.1	567.5	1115.6
Trade	—	—	—	—	5.3	45.1	106.2	226.4	265.3	193.9	274.7	394.6	543.7	1017.0	1191.1	1592.8	2529.3
Transport and communications	—	—	—	—	3.1	12.4	15.1	42.6	99.0	85.0	127.6	185.7	260.2	409.0	533.3	673.1	646.4
Finance	0.0	0.2	1.9	5.0	—	—	—	—	—	17.8	21.7	31.9	47.3	62.2	81.1	140.0	46.3
Public administration	—	—	—	—	6.7	29.2	53.0	177.4	176.7	43.2	59.8	65.0	100.2	117.1	205.0	268.5	297.3
Other	—	—	—	—	—	—	—	—	—	218.0	311.8	429.2	574.5	791.4	866.0	1045.0	2132.3
Taxes less subsidies on products	0.0	-0.1	0.7	3.6	3.2	23.4	49.8	77.8	98.0	149.7	230.3	332.8	508.3	679.7	831.2	1059.6	1519.7
Net factor income from abroad	—	—	-0.0	-0.3	-2.2	-20.3	-22.6	-43.9	-68.4	-104.3	-789.9	-158.1	-215.1	-170.8	-127.6	-216.5	—
GNI at current market prices	0.1	0.6	7.1	17.6	67.6	288.2	495.7	981.3	1276.5	1682.4	1773.9	3217.2	4546.3	5996.4	7079.0	9118.7	—

Source: www.adb.org

Appendix 9. National Composition of Tajikistan According to State Censuses, 1926–2000 (in thousands)

	1926	1937	1939	1959	1970	1979	1989	2000
Total population	827.2	1,383.5	1,484.4	1,980.5	2,899.6	3,806.2	5,092.6	6,127.5
Tajik	619.0	840.6	884.0	1,051.2	1,629.9	2,237.0	3,172.4	4,898.4
Central Asian Turk	0.8		6.0	455.0	665.7	873.2	1197.8	936.7
Uzbek	175.6	332.3	353.5					
Laqai								51.0
Qunghrat								15.1
Qataghan								4.9
Barlas								3.7
Jiuz								1.1
Russian	5.6	114.9	134.9	262.6	344.1	395.1	388.5	68.2
Kyrgyz	11.4	26.4	28.0	25.7	35.5	48.4	63.8	65.5
Turkmen	4.1	3.2	4.0	7.1	11.0	14.0	20.5	20.3
Tatars	1.0	16.6	18.3	56.9	70.8	79.5	79.4	19.0
Crimean Tatars	—	—	—				7.2	0.1
Arab	3.3	2.3	2.3				0.3	14.5
Afghan	0.7	1.0	0.55				2.1	4.7
Gypsy	0.19		1.2	1.6			1.8	4.3
Ukrainian	1.1	12.5	17.4	26.9	31.7	35.8	41.4	3.8

(continued)

Appendix 9. (*continued*)

	1926	1937	1939	1959	1970	1979	1989	2000
Korean	0.06		0.04	2.4	8.5	11.2	13.4	1.7
German	0.17		2.0	32.6	37.7	38.9	32.7	1.1
Armenian	0.15		1.3	2.9	3.8	4.9	5.7	1.0
Ossetian			1.7	4.5	5.8	7.7	7.9	1.0
Kazakh	1.6	12.4	12.7	12.6	8.3	9.6	11.4	0.9
Boshkort	0.17		1.4	3.9	4.8	6.1	6.8	0.9
Azerbaijan					1.6	2.2	3.6	0.8
Turks	0.004		0.1				0.8	0.7
Byelorussian	0.06		1.0	2.8	4.0	5.1	7.2	0.5
Moldovan	0.003		0.04		0.4	0.6	0.9	0.3
Mordva	0.18		4.8	6.7	7.0	6.5	5.5	0.3
Jewish	0.2		5.2	12.4	14.6	14.7	14.8	0.2
Bukharan Jewish	0.08			0.8	6.2		4.9	0.02
Chuvash	0.02		0.5	1.7			2.5	0.2
Georgian	0.03		0.4		0.7	0.8	1.0	0.2
Lak			0.05		0.9		1.4	0.14
Polish	0.07		0.6				0.7	0.07
Bulgar			0.04				1.1	0.07
Others	1.3		2.3				7.2	6.3
Ethnicity undefined	0.4		0.1				0.05	0.01

Source: www.demoscope.ru

Appendix 10
Governments of Tajikistan

1991–1992

Izzatulloh Hayeev, prime minister
Jamshed Karimov, first deputy prime minister
Sadulloh Khairulloev, deputy prime minister
Abdujalil Samadov, deputy prime minister
Habibulloh Sayidmuradov, deputy prime minister

Ministers

Faizulloh Abdoulloev, justice
Muhabbat Abdurahmona, social security
Tamara Abdushukurova, culture
Ismoil Davlatov, education
Yulbars Egamberdiyev, trade
Jura Inomov, health
Yuri Kostarev, housing and communal management
Mirzotimur Mirzoyev, external economic relations
Mamadayoz Navjuvanov, internal affairs
Akhtam Nurov, soil improvement and water management
Yuri Ponosov, construction
Lakim Qayumov, foreign affairs
Normat Unusov, finance
Ibrahim Usmonov, communications
Vahob Vahidov, agriculture

State Committee Chairs

Tursunboi Abdoulloev, construction and architecture
Kholmahmad Azimov, material and technical security

Ismatulloh Karimov, state property management
Georgiy Koshlakov, economy
Bobokhon Mahmadov, press and information
Khudoikul Mahmudov, oil products security
Munavvar Nazriev, environmental protection
Zebinisso Rustamova, sports and tourism
Otakhon Saifullaev, radio and television
Abdujabbar Sattarov, youth affairs
Anatoli Stroikin, state security
Shukurjon Zuhurov, labor and worker cadre preparation

MAY–NOVEMBER 1992

Akbar Mirzoyev, prime minister
Tukhtaboi Ghaforov, first deputy prime minister
Jamshed Karimov, first deputy prime minister
Sadulloh Khairulloev, deputy prime minister
Habibullo Saidmuradov, deputy prime minister
Davlat Usmon, deputy prime minister

Ministers

Faizulloh Abdoulloev, justice
Tursunboi Abdoulloev, construction and architecture; replaced in
    October by Bahovaddin Zuhurdinov
Muhabbat Abdurahmona, social security
Khol Akbarov, agriculture
Kholmahmad Azimov, statistics
Ismoil Davlatov, economy and finance
Jura Inomov, health
Ismatulloh Karimov, state property management
Ato Khojaev, culture
Khudoberdy Kholiknazarov, foreign affairs
Bobokhon Mahmadov, press and information
Mirbobo Mirrahimov, Tajikistan State Radio and Television Broad-
    cast Company; transformed in October into state committee on
    radio and television broadcasting, headed by Davron Ashurov

Mamadayoz Navjuvanov, internal affairs; replaced in June by Guldastashoh Imronshoyev
Munavvar Nazriev, environmental protection
Akhtam Nurov, soil improvement and water management
Bahrom Rahmonov, defense
Zebinisso Rustamova, sports and tourism
Bobo Safarov, transportation
Alijon Salibayev, state security; replaced in August by Shahob Sharipov
Hakim Salibayev, trade and material resources

State Committee Chairs

Shavkat Umarov, industry
Ibrahim Usmonov, communications
Zakir Vazirov, education
Shukurjon Zuhurov, labor and worker cadre preparation

1993

Abdumalik Abdullojonov, prime minister
Mahmadsaid Ubaidulloev, first vice premier
Zebo Amin Zoda, vice premier
Alexander Eliseev, vice premier
Rashid Makhkamov, vice premier
Munavvar Mazriev, vice premier
Abdurahim Mukhtashev, vice premier
Abdujalil Samadov, vice premier

Ministers

Alamkhon Ahmedov, health
Rashid Alimov, foreign affairs
Ismoil Davlatov, economy and finance
Basgul Dodkhudoeva, education
Narzulloh Dustov, transportation
Abdusator Jabbarov, social protection
Sadulloh Khairulloev, environmental protection
Ato Khojaev, culture

Bobokhon Mahmadov, press and information
Oqil Oqilov, construction
Mahmud Sabirov, grain products
Hakim Saliev, trade and material resources
Yaqub Salimov, internal affairs
Vohid Shafoev, soil improvement and water management
Alexander Shishliannikov, defense
Habibulloh Tabarov, agriculture and land reform
Shavkat Umarov, industry
Ibrahim Usmonov, communications
Shukurjon Zuhurov, labor and worker cadre preparation

State Committee Chairs

Kholmahmad Azimov, statistics
Khudoiqul Hamroqulov, customs
Izatulloh Hayeev, foreign trade; upgraded to a ministry in February
Bobojon Ikromov, radio and television broadcast
Ismatulloh Karimov, state property management (died in March)
Zebinisso Rustamova, sports and tourism
Bahovaddin Zuhurdinov, construction and architecture
Saidamir Zuhurov, national security

1994

Emomali Rahmon, president and chair of the government
Jamshed Karimov, prime minister
Mahmadsaid Ubaidulloev, first vice premier
Basgul Dodkhudoeva, vice premier
Qardiddin Ghiesov, vice premier
Jamoliddin Mansurov, vice premier
Oqil Oqilov, vice premier
Kholis Temurjonov, vice premier (until June)

Ministers

Alamkhon Ahmedov, health
Ismoil Davlatov, environmental protection
Ismat Eshmirzoev, soil improvement and water economy

Tukhtaboi Ghaforov, economics and external economic relations
Munira Inoyatova, education
Shavkat Ismoilov, justice
Abdusattor Jabbarov, social security
Sherali Khairulloev, defense
Bobokhon Mahmadov, culture and information
Farukh Muhiddinov, transportation and road economy
Anvarsho Muzaffarov, finance
Talbak Nazarov, foreign affairs
Yaqub Salimov, internal affairs
Qurbon Turayev, agriculture
Bobomurod Urokov, corn products
Ibrahim Usmonov, communications
Shukurjon Zuhurov, labor and worker cadre preparation
Saidamir Zuhurov, state security

State Committee Chairs

Matlubkhon Davlatov, state property management
Ghaforkhon Muhiddinov, industrial affairs
Hakim Saliev, contracts and trade

1996–1997

Emomali Rahmon, president and chair of the government
Yahyo Azimov, prime minister
Yuriy Ponosov, first vice premier
Basgul Dodkhudoeva, vice premier
Ismat Eshmirzoev, vice premier
Qardiddin Ghiesov, vice premier
Jamoliddin Mansurov, vice premier
Kholis Temurjonov, vice premier

Ministers

Alamkhon Ahmedov, health
N. Ashurov, soil improvement and water management
Muso Barotov, agriculture

Ismoil Davlatov, environmental protection
Tukhtaboi Ghaforov, economy and external economic relations
Munira Inoyatova, education
Shavkat Ismoilov, justice
Abdusattor Jabbarov, social protection
Saidanvar Kamolov, national security
Sherali Khairulloev, defense
Bobokhon Mahmadov, culture and information
Faridun Muhiddinov, transportation and road management
Nuriddin Muhiddinov, communications
Anvarsho Muzaffarov, finance
Talbak Nazarov, foreign affairs
Saidamir Zuhurov, internal affairs
Shukurjon Zuhurov, labor and employment

State Committee Chairs

Matlubkhon Davlatov, state property management
Gaforkhon Muhiddinov, industrial affairs
Hakim Saliev, contracts and trade

1998–1999

Emomali Rahmon, president and chair of the government
Yahyo Azimov, prime minister
Hoji Akbar Turajonzoda, first vice premier (UTO)
Abdurahmon Azimov, vice premier
Basgul Dodkhudoeva, vice premier
Ismat Eshmirzoev, vice premier
Jamoliddin Mansurov, vice premier
Abdurahim Rasulov, vice premier
Zakir Vazirov, vice premier (UTO)

Ministers

Alamkhon Ahmedov, health
Munira Inoyatova, education
Shavkat Ismoilov, justice

Abdusattor Jabbarov, social protection
Shodi Kabirov, agriculture (UTO)
Sherali Khairulloev, defense
Khudoiberdy Khaliknazarov, labor and employment (UTO)
Bobokhon Mahmadov, culture and information
Davlatbek Makhsudov, soil improvement and water economy
Faridun Muhiddinov, transportation and road economy
Nuriddin Muhiddinov, communications
Anvarsho Muzaffarov, finance
Talbak Nazarov, foreign affairs
Humdin Sharipov, internal affairs
Usmonqul Shokirov, environmental protection
Davlat Usmon, economics and external economic relations (UTO)
Mirzo Ziyoev, emergency situation (UTO), from September 1999
Saidamir Zuhurov, national security

State Committee Chairs

Said Ahmedov, religious affairs
Aiub Aliev, state control over work safety in industry and mining
Matlubkhon Davlatov, state property management
Habib Ghaibullaev, state statistics agency
Saidanvar Kamolov, state borders protection
Sadulloh Khairulloev, land resources and land tenure
Faizulloh Kuvvatov, food and food processing industry
Khol Mashrabov, taxation
Salamsho Muhabbatov, oil and gas (UTO)
Gaforkhon Muhiddinov, defense industry
Sarabek Murodov, precious metals (UTO)
Latofat Nasreddinova, women and family
Mirzokhuja Nizomov, customs (UTO), from June 1999
Hikmat Odinayiev, special property supply
Rajab Qadirov, precious stones and raw gemstones
Ibod Rahimov, youth affairs
Saifullo Rahimov, radio and television
Saimumin Rahimov, physical education and sports
Zaid Saidov, industrial affairs (UTO)
Hakim Saliev, contracts and trade
Bahovaddin Zuhurdinov, architecture and construction

2000–

Emomali Rahmon, president and chair of the government
Oqil Oqilov, prime minister
Hoji Akbar Turajonzoda, first vice premier (UTO), until March 2005
Qozidavlat Qoimdodov, vice premier, until 5 January 2005
Abdurahim Rasulov, vice premier
Nigina Sharopova, vice premier, until 19 January 2004
Zakir Vazirov, vice premier (UTO), until 3 February 2005
Saidamir Zuhurov, vice premier

Ministers

Khairiddin Abdurahimov, security
Alamkhon Ahmedov, health, until 18 January 2003
Yahyo Azimov, economics and external economic relations
Shavkat Ismoilov, justice; replaced by Khalifabobo Khamidov in
    2001
Shodi Kabirov, agriculture (UTO); replaced by Tursun Rahmatov in
    2001
Sherali Khairullaev, defense
Bobokhon Mahmadov, culture; replaced by Abdurahim Rahmonov
    in 2001
Faridun Muhiddinov, transportation and roads
Nuriddin Muhiddinov, communications
Rafiqa Musoeva, labor and employment
Safarali Najmiddinov, finance
Talbak Nazarov, foreign affairs
Abduqahor Nazirov, soil improvement and water economy
Safarali Rajabov, education
Qimat Rustamova, social security
Humdin Sharipov, internal affairs
Usmonqul Shokirov, environmental protection
Mirzo Ziyoev, emergency situation (UTO)

State Committee Chairs

Said Ahmedov, religious affairs
Aiub Aliev, safe work conditions

Matlubkhon Davlatov, state property management
Saidanvar Kamolov, state borders protection
Sadulloh Khairulloev, land resources and land tenure
Faizulloh Kuvvatov, food and food processing industry
Khol Mashrabov, taxation
Salamsho Muhabbatov, oil and gas (UTO)
Gafarkhon Muhiddinov, defense industry
Sarabek Murodov, precious metals (UTO)
Latofat Nasreddinova, women and family
Mirzokhuja Nizomov, customs (UTO)
Hikmat Odinayiev, special property supply
Qadirov Rajab, precious stones and raw gemstones
Saimumin Rahimov, physical education and sports
Ibod Rahimov, youth affairs
Saifullo Rahimov, radio and television; replaced by Ubaidullo Raja-
bov in June 2000
Zaid Saidov, industry affairs (UTO)
Hakim Saliev, contracts and trade
Bahovadin Zuhurdinov, architecture and construction

2002–2009

Heads of Organs of Direct Presidential Power

Oqil Oqilov, prime minister
Asadullo Ghulomov, first vice premier
Khayrinisso Iusufi, vice premier; replaced by Rukiya Qurbonova in
January 2008
Sherkhon Salimov, Agency on Combating Corruption and Economic
Crimes; replaced by Fattoh Saidov in June 2009
Rustam Nazarov, Agency on Drug Control

Ministers

Ranokhon Abdurahmonova, health; replaced by Nusratullo Salimov
in January 2009
Abdurahim Ashurov, transport and communications
Mirzoshohruh Asrorov, culture

Ghulomjon Boboev, economy and trade; replaced by Farukh Hamraliev in October 2009
Sherali Gul, energy and industry
Masaid Homidov, soil improvement and water economy
Sherali Khayrulloyev, defense
Bakhtiyor Khudoyorov, justice, from December 2006
Safarali Najmiddinov, finance
Abdurahmon Qodiri, agriculture and environmental protection; replaced by Qosim Qosimov in January 2008
Abdujabbor Rahmonov, education
Mahmadnazar Solehov, internal affairs; replaced by Qahorov Abdulahad in February 2009
Hamrokhon Zarifi, foreign affairs
Shukhurjon Zuhurov, labor and social security

State Committees

Khairiddin Abdurahimov, national security
Sharif Rahimzoda, investment and state property
Mirgand Shabozov, statistics

ORGANS UNDER GOVERNMENTAL POWER

Committees

Mehrinisso Nasyrova, women and family
Asadullo Rahmonov, television and radio
Davlatali Saidov, youth, sport, and tourism
Hakim Soliev, taxation
Gurez Zaripov, custom
Mahmadtohir Zokirov, extraordinary situations and civil defense

Agencies

Davlatsho Gulmahmadov, land management, geodesy, and cartography
Davlatali Khotamov, standardization, metrology, certification, and trade inspection
Abduvali Komilov, construction and architecture

Offices

Ibrohim Azim, geology
Murod Dzhumaev, state control for work safety in industry and mining
Shahlo Negmatova, archives
Saidamir Zuhurov, state secrets protection

Councils

Amirqul Azimov, security
Shermahmad Shoev, justice

Bibliography

CONTENTS

INTRODUCTION

This historical dictionary focuses mostly on modern Tajikistan. The establishment of colonial rule signaled the beginning of the modern period. It is not surprising that Western academic interest in Central Asia coincided with colonial advances in that region. Ethnic and cultural features of the people of Central Asia held an enigmatic fascination for British travelers and Russian researchers who arrived in the region following the Russian conquest in the late 19th century. The most comprehensive historical and ethnographical manuscript of that period was drafted by L. N. Logofet in his *Bukharskoye Khanstvo Pod Russkim Protektoratom* (Bukharan Khanate under Russian Protectorate), 2 vols. (1911). Another Russian author, A. P. Shishov, published an extensive manuscript on Russian and British research on Tajiks of Central Asia, *Tadzhiki: Etnograficheskie i Antropologichekie Issledovania* (The Tajiks: Anthropological and Ethnographical Research) in 1910. Famed Russian historian and anthropologist

Vasiliy Bartold made valuable contributions to the study of Islam and the social and cultural history of the Tajiks. His major works were published in nine volumes. English translations include *Four Studies on the History of Central Asia*, 3 vols. (1956–1962) and *Turkestan down to the Mongol Invasion* (1928). British army officer Alexander Burnes traveled from India via Balkh to present-day Tajikistan in 1832–1834; his *Travels into Bokhara* was published in 1834.

One of the first records of the Tajiks in Central Asia by a Tajik author was written by Ahmad Donish. He wrote his *Risola-yi Tarikhi* (Historical Essay), known also as *Ta'rikh-i Sulola-i Manghitia* (History of the Manghyt Dynasty) in 1897. It was translated into Russian and published as *Istoria Mangitskoy Dinastii* in 1960. Donish's writing inspired later studies on the cultural heritage of the Tajiks, who were being reorganized on the model of modern nations in the 1920s. Sadriddin Ayni was by far the most influential Tajik author to uphold the mantle of national identity and propagate the newborn Tajik identity. His anthology of Tajik literature, *Namunahoi Adabyoti Tojik* (The Examples of Tajik Literature), was published in Moscow in 1925. It glorified the cultural history of the Tajiks from the 10th to 20th centuries. Bobojon Ghafurov shared Ayni's passion and dedication to the Tajik nation and became in effect the architect of modern Tajik historiography. He published his seminal *Ta'rikhi Mukhtasari Khalqi Tojik* (Brief History of the Tajik People) in 1947. This document continues to be regarded as the most authoritative account on Tajik history and is adopted as the official historiography of Tajik culture and traditions. Ghafurov traced the origin of the Tajiks to the first settlements of Central Asia in the Paleolithic period and presented the Samanid dynasty as the first Tajik state. Ghafurov's book served as a model for later publications by the Academy of Sciences of Tajikistan, *Istoria Tadzhikskogo Naroda* (History of the Tajik People), 3 vols., published in the 1960s. In 1972, Ghafurov published his most famous historical account, *Tojikon: Ta'rikhi Qadimtarin, Qadim, Asri Miyona Va Davrai Nav* (The Tajiks: Early Ancient, Ancient, Medieval, and Modern History), 2 vols. The book was first published in Russian in 1972 and later in Tajik and Farsi. The English version was published in Delhi in 2005 under the title *Central Asia: Prehistoric to Pre-modern Times*.

At the end of the Soviet period, the Tajik Academy of Sciences launched the second edition of *History of Tajik People*, which was projected to be six volumes, but the collapse of the Soviet Union and ensuing war made the publication difficult. During 1998–2009, only three volumes were published (first, second, and fifth), focused on ancient history, early medieval history, and early Soviet period. It is unclear if the remaining volumes will be published, as most of the authors (including Russians and Tajiks) who started the project left the country during and after the civil war.

Western historians of the Cold War years paid little attention to Soviet Tajikistan as distinct from the rest of Central Asia. Until 1990, only two books were exclusively devoted to Tajikistan. The first, *Russia and Nationalism in Central Asia: Case of Tajikistan*, published in 1970, was by Teresa Rakowska-Harmstone, who used scarce Soviet sources to present a comprehensive account of emerging Tajik nationalism. In 1989, Muriel Atkin published a thoughtful study on the perceived threat of Islam: *The Subtlest Battle: Islam in Soviet Tajikistan*. Among other important publications for students of Tajikistan are *Central Asia: A Century of Russian Rule*, edited by Edward Allworth, and *Islam and the Russian Empire: Reform and Revolution in Central Asia*, by Helene Carrere d'Encausse.

With the collapse of the Union of Soviet Socialist Republics in 1991, English-language literature on Tajikistan increased enormously. It deals mostly with topics related to the civil war and the reconciliation, political Islam, the economy, social and political reforms, and foreign relations. During 1992–2000, publications on Tajikistan were more likely to be chapters in edited volumes or academic journals. In some cases, these separate chapters were brought together to form an edited volume, such as *Tajikistan: The Trials of Independence* (1997), by Mohammad-Reza Djalili, Frederic Grare, and Shirin Akiner. In the first decade of the 2000s, three English-language monographs on Tajikistan were published: Shirin Akiner's *Tajikistan: Disintegration or Reconciliation?*; Lena Jonson's *Tajikistan in the New Central Asia: Geopolitics, Great Power Rivalry, and Radical Islam*; and Paul Bergne's *The Birth of Tajikistan: National Identity and the Origins of the Republic*. Unlike Rakowska-Harmstone and Atkin, who due to Cold War constraints were not able to visit Tajikistan, these three authors collected a great deal of firsthand documents and interviewed many Tajiks during numerous trips to Central Asia.

Despite growing attention, there are still plenty of blanks in Tajikistan's history that have not been filled in by Western scholars. This bibliography therefore includes important sources in Russian and Tajik that may be of interest to students familiar with these languages. However, it excludes some items published in the first edition. Its aim is to encourage the reader's interest in further literature on Tajiks and Tajikistan.

GENERAL

Bibliography

Belan, V. G. *Tajikistan v literature na inostrannykh yazykakh*, 1961–65 [Tajikistan in Foreign-Language Literature]. Dushanbe: Biblioteka Firdawsi, 1969.
———. *Tajikistan v literature na inostrannykh yazykakh*, 1966–70 [Tajikistan in Foreign-Language Literature]. Pts. 1–2. Dushanbe: Biblioteka Firdawsi, 1972.

————. *Tajikistan v literature na inostrannykh yazykakh*, 1971–75 [Tajikistan in Foreign-Language Literature]. Pts. 1–3. Dushanbe: Biblioteka Firdawsi, 1978.
————. *Tajikistan v literature na inostrannykh yazykakh*, 1976–80 [Tajikistan in Foreign-Language Literature]. Pts. 1–3. Dushanbe: Biblioteka Firdawsi, 1983.
Bibliography of Central Asia Studies in Japan, 1879–1987. 2 vols. Tokyo: Toyo Bunko, 1989.
Stavisky, D. I., B. I. Vainberg, N. G. Gorbunova, and E. A. Novgorodova. *Soviet Central Asian Archeology and the Kushan Problem: An Annotated Bibliography*. Moscow: Nauka, 1968.

Yearbooks

Republic of Tajikistan. *Human Development Report 1995*. Dushanbe: UNDP, 1995.
————. *Human Development Report 1996*. Dushanbe: UNDP, 1996.
————. *Human Development Report 1997*. Dushanbe: UNDP, 1997.
————. *Human Development Report 1998*. Dushanbe: UNDP, 1998.
————. *Human Development Report 1999*. Dushanbe: UNDP, 1999.
————. *Human Development Report 2001–2002*. Information and Communications Technology for Development. Dushanbe: UNDP, 2002.
————. *Human Development Report 2003*. Tapping the Potential for Improving Water Management in Tajikistan. Dushanbe: UNDP, 2003.

Statistics

Chislennost' naselenia Respubliki Tadzhikistana [Population of the Republic of Tajikistan]. Dushanbe: Gosudarstvennoye statisticheskoye agenstvo pri pravitel'stve Respubliki Tadzhikistan. 1998, 1999, 2000, 2001, 2002, 2004.
Chislennost' naseleniya soyuznykh respublik po gorodskim poseleniyam i rayonam [Size of the Population of the Union Republics by Urban Settlement and District]. Moscow: Informatsionno-izdatel'skiy tsentr Goskomstata SSSR, 1991.
Demograficheskiy ezhegodnik SSSR 1990 [Demographic Yearbook of the USSR 1990]. Moscow: Finansy i statistika, 1990.
Ezhegondnik Respubliki Tadzhikistan 2003 [Yearbook of the Republic of Tajikistan 2003]. Dushanbe: Gosudarstvennoye statisticheskoye agenstvo pri pravitel'stve Respubliki Tadzhikistan, 2003.
Gendernaya statistika v Respublike Tadzhikistan [Gender Statistics in the Republic of Tajikistan]. Dushanbe: Gosudarstvennoye statisticheskoye agenstvo pri pravitel'stve Respubliki Tadzhikistan, 1999.
Living Standards of the Population of the Republic of Tajikistan (on the Basis of the Findings of the Survey of Randomly Selected Households). 1999

Statistical Data Collection. Dushanbe: Gosudarstvennoye statisticheskoye agenstvo pri pravitel'stve Respubliki Tadzhikistan, 1999.

Promyshlenost' Respubliki Tadzhikistan [Industry of the Republic of Tajikistan]. Dushanbe: Gosudarstvennoye statisticheskoye agenstvo pri pravitel'stve Respubliki Tadzhikistan, 1999–2008.

Regiony Tadzhikistana: Statisticheskiy sbornik [Regions of Tajikistan: Statistical Yearbook]. Dushanbe: Gosudarstvennoye statisticheskoye agenstvo pri pravitel'stve Respubliki Tadzhikistan, 1999, 2004.

Sel'skoye Khoziaystvo Tadzhikistana [Agriculture of Tajikistan: Statistical Yearbook]. Dushanbe: Gosudarstvennoye statisticheskoye agenstvo pri pravitel'stve Respubliki Tadzhikistan, Tsentr strategicheskikh issledovanii pri prezidente Tadzhikistana. Statisticheskiy Sbornik, 1999–2008.

Sovetskii Tadzhikistan za 50 Let: Sbornik Statisticheskikh Materialov [Fifty Years of Soviet Tajikistan: Collection of Statistical Material]. Dushanbe: Irfon, 1975.

Soyuznyye respubliki: Osnovnyye ekonomicheskiye i sotsial'nyye pokazateli [The Union Republics: Basic Economic and Social Indicators]. Moscow: Informatsionno-izdatel'skiy tsentr Goskomstata SSSR, 1991.

Tadzhikistan: Fakty i tsifry. Statisticheskoye obozrenie [Tajikistan: Facts and Numbers. A Statistical Survey]. Dushanbe: Gosudarstvennoye statisticheskoye agenstvo pri pravitel'stve Respubliki Tadzhikistan, 1999.

Tadzhikistan: 15 let gosudarstvennoi nezavisimosti. Statisticheskiy Sbornik [Tajikistan: 15 Years of State Independence. Collection of Statistical Data]. Dushanbe: Gosudarstvennoye statisticheskoye agenstvo pri pravitel'stve Respubliki Tadzhikistan, 2006.

Tajikistan: Country Report, March 2004. London: Economist Intelligence Unit, 2004.

Tajikistan: Country Report, 2005. London: Economist Intelligence Unit, 2005.

Vneshneekonomicheskaya deyatel'nost' respubliki Tadzhikistan: Statisticheskii sbornik [Foreign Trade of the Republic of Tajikistan]. Dushanbe: Gosudarstvennoye statisticheskoye agenstvo pri pravitel'stve Respubliki Tadzhikistan, 2004.

Travel and Description

Auzias, Dominique, Séverine Bardon, Patricia Chichmanova, Jean-Paul Labourdette, and Hervé Kerros. *Asie centrale: Kazakhstan, Kirghizistan, Ouzbékistan, Tadjikistan, Turkménistan.* Le Petit Futé, 2007.

Bradley, Mayhew, Greg Bloom, John Noble, and Dean Starnes. *Central Asia.* London: Lonely Planet, 2007.

Frith, Maier. *Trekking in Russia and Central Asia: A Traveler's Guide.* Seattle, Wash.: Mountaineers Books, 1997.

Middleton, Robert, Markus Hauser, Huw Thomas, and Monica Whitlock. *Tajikistan and the High Pamirs: A Companion and Guide.* Hong Kong: Odyssey, 2008.

Travel through Tajikistan. Dushanbe: Status, 2006.

Vambery, Arminius. *Travels in Central Asia.* 1865. Reprint, New York: Arno, 1970.

———. *Sketches of Central Asia: Additional Chapters on My Travels, Adventures, and on the Ethnology of Central Asia.* London: W. H. Allen, 1868.

Wood, John. *A Journey to the Source of the River Oxus.* 1872. Reprint, New York: Oxford University Press, 1976.

Maps, Atlases, and Guides

Afghanistan–Pakistan–Tajikistan. Gizi Map.

Atlas Tadzhikskoy Sovetskoy Sotsialisticheskoy Respubliki [Atlas of the Tajik Soviet Socialist Republic]. Dushanbe-Moscow: Glavnoye upravlenie geodezii i kartografii SSSR, 1968.

Central Asia. Nelles Map.

Frye, R., and E. Naby. *Tajikistan 1994.* Benson, Vt.: Chalidze, 1994.

Tajikistan: 500K Regional Maps. Gecko Maps (formerly Karto-Atelier).

CULTURE

General

Bartold, V. V. *Istoria culturnoy zhizni Turkestana* [The History of the Cultural Life of Turkestan]. Leningrad, 1927.

Istoria kul'turnogo stroitel'stva v Tadzhikistane (1917–1977) [The History of Cultural Construction in Tajikistan]. Dushanbe: Donish, 1979.

Shakuri, Muhammadjon (Shukurov Mauhammadjon). *Istiqlol va khudshinosii ijtimoivu ma'navi* [Independence and Shaping of Social and Spiritual Identities]. Dushanbe: Oli Somon, 1999.

Shukurov M. R. *Istoria kul'tunoi zhizni Sivetskogo Tadzhikistana (1917–1941)* [The History of Cultural Life of Soviet Tajikistan]. Dushanbe: Donish, 1970.

Dictionaries and Encyclopedias

Conroy, Joseph. *Tajik-English/English-Tajik Dictionary and Phrasebook.* New York: Hippocrene, 1998.

Ensiklopediyai Sovetii Tojik [Soviet Tajik Encyclopedia]. Vols. 1–8. Dushanbe: Sarredaktsiyai ilmii ensiklopediyai Sovetii Tojik, 1978–1987.

Farhangi Zaboni Tojiki [Dictionary of the Tajik Language]. Vols. 1–2. Moscow: Sovetskaya Entsyklopedia, 1969.

Frank, Allen J., and Mamatov, Jahangir. *Dictionary of Central Asian Islamic Terms.* Springfield, Va.: Dunwoody, 2002.

Jilani, Jon. *Practical Dictionary: Tajik-English/English-Tajik.* New York: Hippocrene, 2008.

Mamatov, Jahangir, S. J. Harrell, and Kathy Kehoe. *Tajik-English Dictionary.* Springfield, Va.: Dunwoody, 2005.

Mukhtorov, A., and A. Egani. *Tadzhiksko-Russkiy slovar' po istorii* [Tajik-Russian Historical Dictionary]. Dushanbe: Donish, 1986.

Russko-Tadzhikskiy slovar' [Russian-Tajik Dictionary]. Moscow-Stalinabad: Gosizdat, 1949.

Tursunov, Naim. *Kratkii russko-tadzhikskii slovar' pedagogicheskikh terminov* [Short Russo-Tajik Dictionary of Pedagogical Terms]. Dushanbe: Donish, 1979.

Arts

Akhrorov, A. *Tadzhikskoye kino, 1929–1969* [Tajik Cinema]. Dushanbe: Donish, 1971.

Ashrafi, M. M. *Persidsko-tadzhikskaya poeziya v miniatiurakh 14–17 vekov: Iz sobranii SSSR* [Tajik-Persian Poetry in 14th–17th Centuries' Miniatures. From the USSR Depositories]. Dushanbe: Irfon, 1974.

Chvyr', L. A. *Tadzhikskie iuvelirnye ukrasheniia: Materialy k istoriko-kul'turnomu raionirovaniiu Tadzhikistana* [Tajik Jewelry: Materials on Historical and Cultural Mapping of Tajikistan]. Moscow: Nauka, 1977.

Iskusstvo Tadzhikskoy SSR [Arts in the Tajik SSR]. Leningrad: Album, 1972.

Nurjonov, Nizom. *Dramai Khalqii Tojik* [Tajik Peoples' Drama]. Dushanbe: Donish, 1985.

———. *Teatral'naya i muzykal'naya zhizn' stolitsy gosudarstva Samanidov (XIX–XX vv.)* [Drama and Music in the Capital City of the Samanids in the 19th–20th Centuries]. Dushanbe: Donish, 2001.

Ocherki o khudozhnikakh Tadzhkistana [Essays about Artists of Tajikistan]. Dushanbe: Donish, 1975.

Rice, T. T. *Ancient Arts of Central Asia.* New York: Praeger, 1965.

Zhivopis drevnego Pendzhikenta [Painting of the Ancient Panjakent]. Moscow: Izdatelstvo Akademii Nauk, 1954.

Language and Script

Ayni, Sadriddin. "Mas'alahoi zaboni Tojiki" [Problems of the Tajik Language]. *Kulliyot* 11, no. 2 (1964).

Clifton, John M., ed. *Studies in Languages of Tajikistan.* Dushanbe and St. Petersburg: National State University of Tajikistan and North Eurasia Group, SIL International. 2005.

Dodykhudoev, Rahim. *Materialy po istoricheskoy phonetike shugnanskogo yazyka* [Materials on Historical Phonetics of the Shughni Language]. Dushanbe: Vazorati maorifi khalqii RSS Tojikiston, universiteti davlatii Tojikiston ba nomi V. I. Lenin, 1962.

Khojayori, Nasrullo. *Tajiki: An Elementary Textbook.* Bloomington: Indiana University Press, 2006.

Khromov, A. L. *Yagnobskiy Yazyk* [The Yaghnobi Language]. Dushanbe: Donish, 1972.

Landau, Jacob M., and Barbara Kellner-Heinkele. *Politics of Language in the Ex-Soviet Muslim States: Azerbaijan, Uzbekistan, Kazakhstan, Kyrgyzstan, Turkmenistan, and Tajikistan.* Ann Arbor: University of Michigan Press, 2001.

Perry, John R. *A Tajik Persian Reference Grammar.* Leiden: Brill, 2005.

Rastorgueva, V. S. *A Short Sketch of Tajik Grammar.* Ed. and trans. Herbert H. Paper. Bloomington: Indiana University Press; The Hague, Netherlands: Mouton, 1963.

Rozenfeld, A. Z. *Badakhshanskiye govory tadzhikskogo yazyka* [Badakhshani Dialects of the Tajik Language]. Leningrad: Izdatel'stvo Leningradskogo universiteta, 1971.

Shorish, Mobin M. "Planning by Decree: The Soviet Language Policy in Central Asia." *Language Problems and Language Planning* 8, no. 1 (1984).

Literature

Adibov, A., and A. Afsakhzod. *Az tarikhi adabieti tojik dar Badakhshon: Asri XIX va avvali asri XX* [From the History of Tajik Literature in Badakhshon: Nineteenth Century and the Beginning of the Twentieth Century]. Dushanbe: Donish, 1971.

Ayni, Sadriddin. *Namunahoi adabiyoti tojik* [The Examples of Tajik Literature]. Moscow, 1925.

———. *Alisher Navoi* [Alisher Navoi]. Stalinobod: Nashriyoti Davlatii Tojik, 1948.

———. *Mirzo Abdulqodiri Bedil* [Mirzo Abdulqadir Bedil]. Dushanbe: Nashriyoti Davlatii Tojik, 1954.

———. *Ustod Rudaki: Epoch, Life, and Activity.* Moscow, 1959.

———. *Margi sudkhur* [The Death of a Moneylender]. *Kulliyot* 4 (1961).

Becka, Jiri. "The Tajik Soviet Doston and Mirzo Tirsunzoda: On the Sixty-fifth Birth Anniversary of the Poet." *Archiv Orientalni* (Czechoslovakia) 44, no. 3 (1976).

———. *Sadriddin Ayni: Father of Modern Tajik Culture.* Naples: Instituto Universitario Orientale Seminario di Studi Asiatici, 1980.

————. "On the Friendship between a Tajik Poet and a Czech Doctor in Bukhara in 1918–1920." *Archiv Orientalni* (Czechoslovakia) 54, no. 3 (1986).

————. "Literature and Men of Letters in Tajikistan." *Journal of Turkish Studies* 18 (1994).

Berg, Gabrielle Rachel van den. *Minstrel Poetry from the Pamir Mountains: A Study on the Songs and Poems of the Ismailis of Tajik Badakhshan.* Wiesbaden: Reichert, 2004.

Encyclopedia persidsko-tadzhikskoy prozy [Encyclopedia of Persian-Tajik prose]. Dushanbe: Glavnaya nauchnaya redaktsia sovetskoy entsyclopedii, 1986.

Hakim, Askar. "The River Was Once a Drop of Water: Tajik Poetry in the Past Six Years." *World Literature Today* (Summer 1996).

Hodizoda, Rasul, et al. *Poety Tadzhikistana* [Poets of Tajikistan]. Leningrad: Sovetskii pisatel' Leningradskoe otdelenie, 1972.

————. *Adabiyati Tojik dar nimai duiumi asri XVIII va avvali asri XIX* [Tajik Literature in the Second Half of the Eighteenth Century and the Beginning of the Nineteenth Century]. Dushanbe: Donish, 1974.

Huseinzoda, Sh. *Guftor az ganji sukhan* [Samples from the Literary Treasure]. Dushanbe: Irfon, 1985.

Naby, Eden. "Bobodzhon Gafurovich Gafurov, 1908–1977." *Slavic Review* (June 1978).

Perry, John R. "Tajik Literature: Seventy Years Is Longer than the Millennium (Literatures of Central Asia)." *World Literature Today* (Summer 1996).

Rahmatova, Salomat. *Vohidhoi Khulosakunanda dar zaboni adabii hozirai tojik* [Summary Points on the Contemporary Tajik Literary Language]. Dushanbe: Donish, 1976.

Rypka, Jan. *History of Iranian Literature.* Dordrecht: D. Reidel, 1968.

Sattorzoda, Abdunabi. *Chahor-kitob* [Four Books]. Dushanbe: Adib, 1990.

Sports

Babadzhanov, A. *Sportivnyi Vek Tadzhikistana* [A Century of Tajikistan's Sports]. Dushanbe, 1998.

Mahmadrasulov, B. *Vydaiyshiesia mastera sporta Tadzhikistana* [The Prominent Sportsmen of Tajikistan]. Dushanbe, 2000.

Rasulzade, B. *Tadzhikistan Olimpiiski* [The Olympic Tajikistan]. Dushanbe: Paivand, 1996.

Music

During, Jean. *Tajik Music of Badakhshan: Musique Tadjike du Badakhshan.* Auvidis, Ivry-sur-Seine, 1993. Sound disc, 79 mins.

Levin, Theodore Craig. *The Hundred Thousand Fools of God: Musical Travels in Central Asia*. Bloomington: Indiana University Press, 1996.

Music of Central Asia: Tadjikistan. Tokyo: King Records and Seven Seas, 1992. Sound disc, 57 min.

Nizomov, Asliddin. *Tarikh va nazariyai shashmaqom* [History and Theory of Shashmaqom]. Dushanbe: Irfon, 2003.

Rajabov, Askarali, and Abduvali Abdurashidov. *Bayozi shashmaqom* [Anthology of Shashmaqom]. Dushanbe: Kontrast, 2008.

ECONOMY

Bliss, Frank, Nicola Pacult, and Sonia Guss. *Social and Economic Change in the Pamirs (Gorno-Badakhshan, Tajikistan)*. London: Routledge, 2006.

Country Report: Kyrgyz Republic, Tajikistan. London: Economist Intelligence Unit, 1998.

Dowling, Malcolm, and Ganeshan Wignaraja. *Central Asia's Economy: Mapping Future Prospects to 2015*. Silk Road Paper, July 2006. Available at: www.silkroadstudies.org/new/docs/Silkroadpapers/0607Wignaraja.pdf.

Gerhard, Hans, and Kenneth Warwick, eds. *International Monetary Fund: Tajikistan*. Washington, D.C.: International Monetary Fund, 1992.

Gleason, Gregory. *Markets and Politics in Central Asia: Structural Reform and Political Change*. New York: Routledge, 2003.

Gurgen, Emine, et al. *Economic Reforms in Kazakhstan, Kyrgyz Republic, Tajikistan, Turkmenistan, and Uzbekistan*. Occasional Paper 183. International Monetary Fund, 1999.

Lubin, Nancy. *Labour and Nationality in Soviet Central Asia: An Uneasy Compromise*. London: Macmillan, 1984.

Olimova, Saodat, and Igor Bosc. *Labour Migration from Tajikistan*. Dushanbe: Mission of the International Organization for Migration, 2003.

Pomfret, Richard W. T. *The Economies of Central Asia*. Princeton, N.J.: Princeton University Press, 2006.

Rumer, Boris. *Central Asia: The Challenge of Independence*. Armonk, N.Y.: M. E. Sharpe, 1998.

———. *Central Asia and the New Global Economy: The Year 2000 and Beyond*. Armonk, N.Y.: M. E. Sharpe, 2000.

Tajikistan: Country Report, March 2004. London: Economist Intelligence Unit, 2004.

Tajikistan: Country Report, 2005. London: Economist Intelligence Unit, 2005.

Usmon, Davlat. *Tajikistan Investment Projects*. Dushanbe, 1998.

Vneshneekonomicheskaya deyatel'nost' respubliki Tadzhikistan; Statisticheskii sbornik [Foreign Trade of the Republic of Tajikistan. Collection of Statistical Data]. Dushanbe: Statistics Agency, 2004.

HISTORY

General

Adshead, Samuel Adrian M. *Central Asia in World History.* New York: St. Martin's, 1993.

Brinton, William M. *An Abridged History of Central Asia.* 1998. Available at: www.asian-history.com/the_frame.html.

Ghafurov, Bobojon. *Ta'rikhi mukhtasari khalqi tojik* [Brief History of the Tajik People]. Vol. 1. Stalinobod: Gosizdat, 1947.

———. *Istoria Tadzhikskogo naroda* [History of the Tajik People]. Vols. 1–3. Moscow: Izdatel'stvo vostochnoi literatury, 1963–1965.

———. *Tojikon: Ta'rikhi qadimtarin, qadim, asri miyona va davrai nav* [The Tajiks: Early Ancient, Ancient, Medieval, and Modern History]. Vols. 1–2. Dushanbe: Irfon, 1998.

Istoria Tadzhikskogo naroda [History of the Tajik People]. Vols. 1, 2, 5. Dushanbe: Donish, 1997–1998.

Kolarz, Walter. *Russia and Her Colonies.* Hamden, Conn.: Archon, 1967.

Rakowska-Harmstone, Teresa. *Russia and Nationalism in Central Asia: Case of Tajikistan.* Baltimore, Md.: Johns Hopkins University Press, 1970.

Pre-Islamic Period

Bartold, V. V. "O khristianstve v Turkestane v domongolskiy period" [On Christianity in Turkestan in the Pre-Mongol Period]. *Zapiski Vostochnogo Otdelenia Russkogo Archeologicheskogo Obshchestva* 8, nos. 1–2 (1893).

Central Asia in the Kushan Period: Proceedings of the International Conferences. Vols. 1–2. Moscow: Nauka, 1975.

Holt, Frank. *Alexander the Great and Bactria: The Formation of a Greek Frontier in Central Asia.* Leiden: Brill, 1988.

Mukhtorov, Ahror. *Epigraficheskie pamiatniki Kukhistana* [Epigraphical Relics of Kuhistan]. Dushanbe: Donish, 1978.

Piankov, I. V. *Bakrtia v antichnoy traditsii* [Bactria in Antique Traditions]. Dushanbe: Donish, 1982.

Ranov, V. A. *Kamenny vek Tadzhikistana* [Tajikistan's Stone Age]. Dushanbe: Academy of Sciences of Tajikistan, 1965.

Trinkaus, E., et al. "Middle Paleolithic Human Deciduous Incisor from Khudji, Tajikistan." *Journal of Human Evolution* (April 2000).

Islamic Period

Amir, Olimkhon. *Ta'rikhi Huzn al-Millal-i Bukhoro* [The History of Wounded Bukhara]. Tehran: Markaz-i Mutole'ot-i Iron, 1994.

Ayni, Sadriddin. *Is'yoni Muqanna: Ocherki ta'rikhi-tadqiqoti* [The Muqanna's Mutiny: The Historical Essay]. Stalinobod: Redaktsiyai ta'rikhi tojikon va Tojikiston, 1944.

———. "Eddoshtho" [Memoirs]. *Kulliyot* 6–7 (1962–1963).

———. "Ta'rikhi Amironi Manghytiai Bukhoro" [The History of the Bukharan Manghyts]. *Kulliyot* 10 (1966).

———. *Ta'rikhi Inqilobi Bukhoro* [The History of the Bukharan Revolution]. Dushanbe: Adib, 1987.

———. *Yaddashtha.* Tehran: Agah, 1983.

Baljuvoni, Muhammadali ibn Muhammad Sayyid. *Tarikh-i Nofe'-i* [The Instructive History]. Dushanbe: Irfon, 1994.

Barfield, Thomas J. *The Central Asian Arabs of Afghanistan: Pastoral Nomadism in Transition.* Austin: University of Texas Press, 1981.

Bartold, V.V. *Turkestan Down to the Mongol Invasion.* London: Oxford University Press, 1928.

———. *Four Studies on the History of Central Asia.* 3 Vols. Leiden: Brill, 1956–1962.

———. "Istoria izuchenia Vostoka v Evrope i Rossii" [History of Oriental Studies in Europe and Russia]. *Sochinenia* 9 (1977).

Becker, Seymour. *Russia's Protectorates in Central Asia: Bukhara and Khiva, 1865–1924.* Cambridge, Mass.: Harvard University Press, 1968.

Burnes, Alexander. *Travels into Bokhara.* London: Murray, 1834.

Burton, Audrey. *The Bukharans: A Dynastic, Diplomatic, and Commercial History, 1550–1702.* New York: St. Martin's, 1997.

Bregel, Yuri. "Notes of the Study of Central Asia." *Vostok* 5–6 (1997).

Canfield, Robert L., ed. *Turko-Persia in Historical Perspective.* Cambridge: Cambridge University Press, 1991.

Chekhovich, O. D. *Samarkandskie Dokumenty XV–XVI vv* [The Samarqand Documents, 15th–16th Centuries]. Moscow: Nauka, 1974.

Defremery, Charles F. *Histoire des Samanides: A.D. 892–999 par Mirkhond (Mohammad ibn Khwand-Shah ibn Mahmoud).* Amsterdam: Oriental, 1974.

Donish, Ahmad. *Istoria Mangitskoy Dinastii* [History of the Manghyt Dynasty]. Dushanbe: Donish, 1967.

Frye, Richard N. *The History of Bukhara.* Translated from a Persian Abridgement of the Arabic Original by Narshakh'i. Cambridge, Mass.: Mediaeval Academy of America, 1954.

———. *Bukhara: The Medieval Achievement.* Costa Mesa, Calif.: Mazda, 1996.

Gankovsky, Yuri V. "Ibrahim Beg Lokai (1889–1932)." *Pakistan Journal of History and Culture* 17, no. 1 (1996).

Ghafurov, Bobojon. *Central Asia: Prehistoric to Pre-modern Times*. 2 vols. Delhi: Maulana Azad Institute of Asian Studies, Kolkata, Shipra Publications, 2005.

Gibb, H. A. R. *The Arab Conquest in Central Asia*. London: Royal Asiatic Society, 1923.

Holdsworth, Mary. *Turkestan in the Nineteenth Century: A Brief History of the Khanates of Bukhara, Khokand, and Khiva*. London: Oxford University Press, 1959.

Khalfin, N. A. *Politika Rossii v Srendei Azii (1857–1868)* [Russia's Central Asian Politics]. Moscow: Nauka, Izdatel'stvo vostochnoi literatury, 1960.

Khanykov, N. *Bokhara: Its Amir and People*. London, 1845.

Litvinskii, B. A. *Tepai-shakh: kultura i sviazi Kushanskoi Baktrii* [Teppai-Shah: Culture and Relations of Kushan Bactria]. Moscow: Nauka, Izdatel'stvo vostochnoi literatury, 1983.

————. *Srednevekovaia kultura Tokharistana v svete raskopok v Vakhshskoi doline* [Medieval Culture of Tokharistan in the Light of Excavations in the Vakhsh Valley]. Moscow: Nauka, 1985.

Logofet, L. N. *Bukharskoye khanstvo pod russkim protektoratom* [The Bukharan Khanate under Russian Protectorate]. St. Petersburg: V. Berezovsky, 1911.

Mashitskii, A. "K istorii revolyutsii v Bukhare [History of the Revolution in Bukhara]." *Vestnik Narodnogo Komissariata Inostrannykh Del* 6 (July 1921).

McChesney, R. D. *Waqf in Central Asia*. Princeton, N.J.: Princeton University Press, 1991.

Meyendorf, Georges. *Voyage d'Orenbourg à Boukhara, fait en 1820, à travers les steppes qui s'étendent à l'est de la mer d'Aral et au-delà de l'ancien Jaxartes*. Paris: Dondey-Dupru, 1826.

Olufsen, O. *The Emir of Bokhara and His Country*. Copenhagen, 1911.

Paquier, J. B. *Le Pamir: Étude de Géographie Physique et Historique sur L'Asie Centrale*. Paris: Maisonneuve, 1876.

Pierce, Richard. *Russian Central Asia 1867–1917: A Study in Colonial Rule*. Berkeley: University of California Press, 1960.

Postnikov, A. V. *Skhvatka na "Kryshe mira": Politiki, razvedchiki i geografy v bor'be za Pamir v XIX veke* [Struggle on the "Roof of the World": Politicians, Spies, and Geographers in the Contest for the Pamir in the 19th century]. Moscow, 2001.

Schuyler, E. *Turkistan: Notes of a Journey in Russian Turkistan, Khokand, Bukhara, and Kuldja*. New York: Scribner Armstrong, 1876.

Skrine, Francis Henry, and Edward Denison Ross. *The Heart of Asia: A History of Russian Turkestan and the Central Asian Khanates from Earliest Times*. London, 1899.

Trotter, J. M. *Central Asia, Part 6: Khanate of Bokhara*. Calcutta: Government of India, 1873.

Wheeler, Geoffrey. *The Modern History of Soviet Central Asia*. London: Weidenfeld and Nicolson, 1964.

Wolff, Joseph. *Narrative of a Mission to Bokhara*. London, 1845.

Soviet Period

Abdullaev, Kamoludin. "Central Asian Émigrés in Afghanistan: First Wave (1920–1931)." *Central Asia Monitor* 1, nos. 4–5 (1994).

———. *Ot Sintsiana do Khorasana. Iz Istorii Sredneaziatskoi Emigratsii 20 veka* (From Xingjiang to Khurasan: From the History of the 20th Century Central Asia's Emigration), Dushanbe: Irfon, 2009.

Allworth, Edward, ed. *Central Asia: A Century of Russian Rule*. New York: Columbia University Press, 1967.

———. *Nationalities of the Soviet East: Publications and Writing Systems*. New York: Columbia University Press, 1971.

Atkin, Muriel. *The Subtlest Battle: Islam in Soviet Tajikistan*. Philadelphia, Pa.: Foreign Policy Research Institute, 1989.

Bacon, Elizabeth E. *Central Asia under Russian Rule*. Ithaca, N.Y.: Cornell University Press, 1966.

Bergne, Paul. *The Birth of Tajikistan: National Identity and the Origins of the Republic*. London: I. B. Tauris, 2007.

Carrere d'Encausse, Helene. *Islam and the Russian Empire*. Berkeley: University of California Press, 1988.

———. "Civil War and New Government." In *Central Asia, One Hundred and Thirty Years of Russian Dominance: A Historical Overview*, ed. Edward Allworth. Durham, N.C.: Duke University Press, 1994.

———. "The National Republics Lose Their Independence." In *Central Asia, One Hundred and Thirty Years of Russian Dominance: A Historical Overview*, ed. Edward Allworth. Durham, N.C.: Duke University Press, 1994.

Dodkhudoev, Nazarsho. *Tajikistan, Land of Sunshine*. London: Soviet Booklets, 1959.

Fraser, Glenda. "Basmachi-i." *Central Asian Survey* 6, nos. 1–2 (1987).

———. "Alim Khan and the Fall of the Bokharan Emirate in 1920." *Central Asian Survey* 7, no. 4 (1988).

Irkaev, Mullo. *Istoria Grazhdanskoy Voiny v Tadzhikistane* [History of the Civil War in Tajikistan]. Dushanbe: Irfon, 1971.

Iskandarov, B. I. *Vostochnaya Bukhara i Pamir v period prisoedineniya k Rossii* [Eastern Bukhara and Pamir in the Period of Joining Russia]. Dushanbe: Tadzhikgosizdat, 1960.

Istoria Bukharskoy i Khorezmskoy Narodnykh Sovetskikh Respublik [History of the Bukharan and Khorezm People's Soviet Republics]. Moscow: Nauka, 1971.

Keller, Shoshana. *To Moscow, Not Mecca: The Soviet Campaign against Islam in Central Asia*. Westport, Conn.: Praeger, 2001.

Khalid, Adeeb. *The Politics of Muslim Cultural Reform: Jadidism in Central Asia*. Berkeley: University of California Press, 1998.

Khodzhaev, Faizulla. "O Mlado-Bukhartsakh" [About Young Bukharans]. *Istorik Marksist* 1 (1926).

Luknitsky, Pavel. *Soviet Tajikistan*. Moscow: Foreign Languages Publishing House, 1954.

Nourzhanov, Kirill. *Tajikistan: The History of an Ethnic State*. London: Hurst, 1999.

Olcott, Martha Brill. "The Basmachi or Freemen's Revolt in Turkestan, 1918–24." *Soviet Studies* (July 1981).

Osimi, Muhammad. *Tajikistan: Socialist Republics of the Soviet Union*. Moscow: Novosti Press Agency, 1987.

Park, Alexandre G. *Bolshevism in Turkestan, 1917–1927*. New York: Columbia University Press, 1957.

Rakowska-Harmstone, Teresa. *Russia and Nationalism in Central Asia: The Case of Tadzhikistan*. Baltimore, Md.: Johns Hopkins University Press, 1970.

Ro'i, Yaacov. "Central Asian Riots and Disturbances, 1989–1990: Causes and Context." *Central Asian Survey* 10, no. 3 (1991).

Rumer, Boris Z. *Soviet Central Asia: "A Tragic Experience."* London: Unwin Hyman, 1990.

Rywkin, Michael. *Moscow's Muslim Challenge*. London: Hurst, 1982.

Sarfraz Khan. *Muslim Reformist Political Thought: Revivalists, Modernists, and Free Will*. London: Routledge, 2003.

Symon, L. "Tadzhikistan: A Developing Country in the Soviet Union," *Asian Affairs* 61, no. 3 (1974).

Vaidyanath, R. *The Formation of the Soviet Central Asian Republics*. New Delhi: People's Publishing House, 1967.

Yamauchi, Masayuki. *The Green Crescent under the Red Star: Enver Pasha in Soviet Russia, 1919–1922*. Tokyo: Tokyo University of Foreign Studies, 1991.

Post-Soviet Period

Abashin, S. N., and V. I. Bushkov. *Tadzhikistan: Nekotorye posledstvia tragicheskikh let* [Tajikistan: Some Consequences of the Tragic Years]. Moscow: Academy of Sciences, 1998.

Abazov, Rafis. "Independent Tajikistan: Ten Lost Years." In *Oil, Transition, and Security in Central Asia*, ed. Sally N. Cummings. London; John Murray, 2002.

Abdullaev, Kamoludin. "The Civil War in Tajikistan." *Peace and Policy: Journal of the Toda Institute for Global Peace and Policy Research* 3, no. 1 (1998).

Abdullaev, Kamoludin, and Catherine Barnes, eds. *Politics of Compromise: The Tajikistan Peace Process*. London: Conciliation Resources, 2001. Available at: www.c-r.org/our-work/accord/tajikistan/contents.php.

Abdullaev, Kamoludin, and Sabine Frasier. *What Peace Five Years after the Signing of the Tajik Peace Agreement? Strategic Conflict Assessment and Peace Building Framework, Tajikistan*. Brussels: UK Government Global Conflict Prevention Pool, December 2003.

Akbarzadeh, Shahram. "Why Did Nationalism Fail in Tajikistan?" *Europe-Asia Studies* (Formerly *Soviet Studies*) (November 1996).

———. "The Political Shape of Central Asia." *Central Asian Survey* (December 1997).

Akhmedova, Fatima. "Women's Place in Tajik Society." *Central Asia Monitor* 8, no. 6 (1998).

Akiner, Shirin. *Tajikistan: Disintegration or Reconciliation?* London: Royal Institute of International Affairs, 2001.

Allison, Roy. *Peacekeeping in the Soviet Successor States*. Chaillot Paper no. 18. Paris: Institute for Security Studies, Western European Union, November 1994.

———. "Regional Threat Perceptions and Risks of Military Conflict." In *Energy, Wealth, Governance, and Welfare in the Caucasus and Central Asia: Lessons Not Learned*, ed. Richard Auty and Indra De Soysa. London: Routledge, 2005.

Allison, Roy, and Lena Jonson, eds. *Central Asian Security: The New International Context*. London: Royal Institute of International Affairs and Brookings Institution, 2001.

Babadzhanov, Bakhtiar. "Islam in Uzbekistan: From the Struggle for 'Religious Purity' to Political Activism." In *Central Asia: A Gathering Storm?* ed. Boris Rumer. Armonk, N.Y.: M. E. Sharpe, 2002.

Bashiri, Iraj. "Muslims and Communists Vie for Power in Tajikistan." *AACAR Bulletin* 6, no. 1 (1993). Available at: www.ilasll.umn.edu/bashiri/Muslims%20Comm%20Taj%20folder/frame.html.

Bitter, Jean-Nicolas, et al., eds. *From Confidence Building towards Cooperative Co-existence: The Tajik Experiment of Islamic-Secular Dialogue*. Baden-Baden: Nomos, 2005.

Bushkov, V. I., and D. V. Mikulskiy. *Istoriya grazhdanskoy voiny v Tadzhikistane* [The History of the Civil War in Tajikistan]. Moscow: Institut etnologii i antropologii RAN, 1996.

———. *Anatomia grazhdanskoy voiny* [The Anatomy of the Civil War]. Moscow: RGNF, 1997.

Chatterjee, Suchandana. *Politics and Society in Tajikistan in the Aftermath of the Civil War.* London: Greenwich Millenium, 2002.

Djalili, Mohammad Reza, Frédéric Grare, and Shirin Akiner. *Tajikistan: The Trials of Independence.* New York: St. Martin's, 1997.

Dudoignon, Stéphane A. *Communal Solidarity and Social Conflicts in Late Twentieth-Century Central Asia: The Case of the Tajik Civil War.* Tokyo: Islamic Area Studies Project, 1998.

Dudoignon, Stéphane A., and Hisao Komatsu, eds. *Islam in Politics of Russia and Central Asia (Early Eighteenth to Late Twentieth Centuries).* London: Kegan Paul, 2001.

Everett-Heath, Tom. *Central Asia Aspects of Transition.* London: Routledge, 2003.

Ferghana Valley Working Group. *Calming the Ferghana Valley: Development and Dialogue in the Heart of Central Asia.* New York: Century Foundation Press, 1999.

Fuller, Graham E. "Central Asia: The Quest for Identity." *Current History* (April 1994).

Greene, Thomas. "Turmoil in Tajikistan: Addressing the Crisis of Internal Displacement." In *The Forsaken People: Case Studies of the Internally Displaced,* ed. Roberta Cohen and Francis Deng. Washington, D.C.: Brookings Institution, 1998.

Gretsky, Sergei. "Qadi Akbar Turajonzoda." *Central Asia Monitor* 3, no 1 (1994).

Harris, Colette. *Control and Subversion: Gender Relations in Tajikistan.* Sterling, Va.: Pluto, 2004.

———. *Muslim Youth: Tensions and Transitions in Tajikistan.* Boulder, Colo.: Westview, 2006.

Horsman, Stewart. "Water in Central Asia: Regional Cooperation or Conflict?" In *Central Asian Security: The New International Context,* ed. Allison Roy and Lena Jonson. London: Royal Institute of International Affairs and Brookings Institution, 2001.

Human Rights Watch. *Conflict in the Soviet Union, Tadzhikistan: A Helsinki Watch Report.* New York: Human Rights Watch, 1991.

Jahangiri, Guissou. "Anatomie d'une crise: Le poids des tensions entre régions au Tadjikistan." *Cahiers d'études sur la Méditerrané orientale et le monde turco-iranien (CEMOTI)* (July–December 1994).

Kenjaev, Safarali. *Tabadduloti Tojikiston* [Coup d'état in Tajikistan]. Dushanbe: Fondi Kenjaev, 1993.

———. *Perevorot v Tadzhikistane* [Coup d'état in Tajikistan]. Dushanbe: Poligrafcombinat, 1996.

Khalid, Adeeb. *Islam after Communism: Religion and Politics in Central Asia.* Berkeley: University of California Press, 2007.

Kraeutler, Kirk. "Enfranchisement Wanted: Tajikistan." In *Breaking the Cycle*, ed. Roderick K. Von Lipsey. New York: St. Martin's, 1997.

Krauze, J. "Les troupes russes vont rester au Tadjikistan." *Le Monde*, 12 October 1992.

———. "La Russie va accroître son engagement militaire au Tadjikistan." *Le Monde*, 10 August 1993.

Mamadazimov, A. *Politicheskaya istoriya tadzhikskogo naroda* [Political History of the Tajik People]. Dushanbe, 2000.

Mezhtadzhikskiy conflict: put' k miru [Inter-Tajik Conflict: Path to Peace]. Moscow: Academy of Sciences, Shark, 1998.

Nassim, Jawad, and Shahrbanou Tadjbakhsh. *Tajikistan: A Forgotten Civil War*. London: Minority Rights Group, 1995.

Naumkin, Vitalii. *Radical Islam in Central Asia: Between Pen and Rifle*. Lanham, Md.: Rowman & Littlefield, 2005.

Negmatov, Numon. *Tadzhikskiy fenomen: Istoria i teoria* [The Tajik Phenomenon: History and Theory]. Dushanbe: Oli Somon, 1997.

Olimov, Muzaffar. "Ob etnicheskoy i konfessionalnoy situatsii v Tadzhikistane" [On the Ethnic and Confessional Situation in Tajikistan]. *Vostok* 2 (1994).

Rahmon, Emomali. *Tojikon dar oinai ta'rikh* [Tajiks in the Mirror of History]. 3 vols. Moscow: Flint River, 1999–2006.

———. *Istiqloliyati Tojikiston va eh'yoi millat* [Tajikistan's Independence and Revival of the Nation]. 8 vols. Dushanbe, 2002–2009.

Rakhmonov, Emomali. *Tajikistan na poroge budushego* [Tajikistan on the Threshold of the Future]. Moscow: ITAR TASS, 1997.

Rashid, Ahmed. "Tournament of Shadows: Opposition Skeptical over Latest Efforts to End Tajik War." *Far Eastern Economic Review*, 16 September 1993.

———. "Push for Peace: Neighbors Gear Up to Broker a Tajik Settlement." *Far Eastern Economic Review*, 3 February 1994.

Roy, Olivier. *The Civil War in Tajikistan: Causes and Implications*. Washington, D.C.: U.S. Institute of Peace, December 1993.

———. *The New Central Asia: The Creation of Nations*. New York: New York University Press, 2000.

Rubin, Barnett R. "The Fragmentation of Tadjikistan." *Survival* (Winter 1993–1994).

Schoeberlein, John S. "Conflict in Tajikistan and Central Asia: The Myth of Ethnic Animosity." *Harvard Middle Eastern and Islamic Review* 2, no. 1 (1995).

Shin, Milbert, and Human Rights Watch/Helsinki. *Tajikistan: Tajik Refugees in Northern Afghanistan, Obstacles to Repatriation*. New York: Human Rights Watch/Helsinki, 1996.

Shukurov, Sharif. *Tadzhiki: Opyt natsionalnogo avtoriteta* [The Tajiks: An Experience of National Authority]. Dushanbe, 1993.

Svante, Cornell. "The Interaction of Narcotics and Conflict." *Journal of Peace Research* 42, no. 6 (2005).

Tadjbakhsh, Shahrbanou. "The Bloody Path of Change: The Case of Post-Soviet Tadjikistan." *Harriman Institute Forum*, July 1993.

———. "Causes and Consequences of the Civil War." *Central Asia Monitor* 2, no. 1 (1993).

———. "National Reconciliation: The Imperfect Whim." *Central Asia Survey* (December 1996).

———. "The Tajik Spring of 1992." *Central Asia Monitor* 2, no. 2 (1993).

———. "Women and War in Tajikistan." *Central Asia Monitor* 3, no. 1 (1994).

Tajikistan: Refugee Reintegration and Conflict Prevention. New York: Open Society Institute, 1998.

Tetsuro, Iji. "Cooperation, Coordination, and Complementarity in International Peacekeeping: The Tajikistan Experience." *International Peacekeeping* 12, no. 2 (2005).

United Nations Department of Public Information. *The United Nations and the Situation in Tajikistan*. New York: United Nations, 1995.

United States Department of Justice. "Tajikistan." *Alert Series: Political Conditions in the Post-Soviet Era*. Washington, D.C.: INS Resource Information Center, 1993.

Wagner, S. *Public Opinion in Tajikistan, 1996*. Washington, D.C.: International Foundation for Electoral Systems, 1996.

Whitlock, Monica. *Beyond the Oxus: The Central Asians*. London: John Murray, 2002.

Yusuf, Shadmon. *Tajikistan: Bahaye Azadi* [Tajikistan: The Price of Freedom]. Tehran: Daftar Nashr Farhang Islami, 1994.

POLITICS

Parties and Movements

Grazhdanskiye politicheskiye dvizhenia Tadzhikistana, 1989–mart 1990 [Civil Political Movements of Tajikistan]. Dushanbe: Tsentralniy komitet komsomola Tadzhikistana, 1990.

Olimova, S. "Politicheskie partii i mnogopartinost v Tadzhikistane" [Political Parties and Multipartism in Tajikistan]. In *Na putiakh politicheskoy transformatsii (politicheskie partuu i politicheskie elity postsovetskogo perioda)*. Moscow: Moskovsky nauchny fond, 1997.

Olimova, S., and M. Olimov. *Tadzhikistan na poroge peremen* [Tajikistan at the Onset of Changes]. Moscow: Tsentr Strategicheskikh i politicheskikh issledovanii, Nauchno-analiticheskiy tsentr Sharq, 1999.

"Programma Agrarnoy Partii Tadzhikistana" [Program of the Agrarian Party of Tajikistan]. *Junbesh* 13 (1998).

"Programma Kommuisticheskoy partii Tadzhikistana" [Program of the Communist Party of Tajikistan]. *Golos Tadzhikistana*, 24–30 January 1997.

"Programma Sotsialisticheskoy partii Tadzhikistana" [Program of the Socialist Party of Tajikistan]. *Ittihod* 8 (1998).

"Programmnye tseli i printsipy Narodno-demokraticheskoy partii Tadzhikistana" [Programmatic Aims and Principles of the People's Democratic Party of Tajikistan]. *Minbari Khalq*, 30 July 1998.

Usmonov, I., Z. Aliev, and Kh. Khudoerov. *Dorogi mira: Dokumenty mezhtadzhikskikh peregovorov* [Paths of Peace: Documents of the Inter-Tajik Peace Talks]. Dushanbe, 1997.

"Ustav Kommunisticheskoy partii Tadzhikistana" [Rules of the Communist Party of Tajikistan]. *Golos Tadzhikistana*, 24–30 January 1997.

"Ustav Narodno-demokraticheskoy partii Tadzhikistana" [Rules of the People's Democratic Party of Tajikistan]. *Partii i dvizhenia Tadzhikistana* 3 (1998).

"Ustav Partii Politicheskogo i ekonomicheskogo obnovlenia" [Rules of the Party of Political and Economic Regeneration of Tajikistan]. *Tojikiston* 15–16 (1998).

Defense

Brown, Bess. "National Security and Military Issues in Central Asia." In *State Building and Military Power in Russia and the New States of Eurasia*, ed. Bruce Parrott. Armonk, N.Y.: M. E. Sharpe, 1995.

Clark, Susan L. "The Central Asian States: Defining Security Priorities and Developing Military Forces." In *Central Asia and the World: Kazakhstan, Uzbekistan, Tajikistan, Kyrgyzstan, and Turkmenistan*, ed. Michael Mandelbaum. New York: Council on Foreign Relations, 1994.

Foreign Relations

Alimov, R., A. Lebedev, and J. Sharipova. *Diplomatia Tadzhikistana* [Diplomacy of Tajikistan]. Dushanbe, 1994.

Arunova, M. R., and O. M. Shumilova. *Ocherki Istorii Formirovania Gosudarstvennikh Granits Mezhdu Rossiei, SSSR i Afghanistanom* [Essays on the History of Forming of State Frontiers between Russia, USSR, and Afghanistan]. Moscow: Institut Vostokovedenia, 1994.

Jonson, Lena. *Vladimir Putin and Central Asia: The Shaping of Russian Foreign Policy*. London: I. B. Tauris, 2004.

———. *Tajikistan in the New Central Asia: Geopolitics, Great Power Rivalry, and Radical Islam*. London: I. B. Tauris, 2006.

Saidov, Zafar. *Vneshnyaya politika prezidenta Rakhmonova* [President Rakhmonov's Foreign Policy]. Dushanbe: Avasto, 2000.
———. *Politika otkrytykh dverei* [The Open Door Policy]. Dushanbe: Sharqi Ozod, 2003.

SCIENCE AND TECHNOLOGY

Architecture and Planning

Fedorova, T. I. *Goroda Tadzhikistana i problemy rosta i razvitiya* [Cities of Tajikistan and Problems of Growth and Development]. Dushanbe: Irfon, 1981.
Veselovsky, V. G. *Arkhitektura i Gradostroitelstvo v Tadzhikistane* [Architecture and Urban Planning in Tajikistan]. Dushanbe: Tadzhikgosizdat, 1967.
Veselovsky, V. G., R. S. Mukimov, M. A. Mamadnazarov, and S. M. Mamadzhanova. *Architecture of the Soviet Tajikistan*. Moscow: Stroiizdat, 1987.
Voronina, V. L. *Izuchenie arkhitektury drevnego Pendzhikenta* [Study of the Architecture of the Ancient Panjakent]. Moscow-Leningrad: MIA SSSR, 1950.

Geography

Bartold, V. V. *An Historical Geography of Iran*. Ed. C. E. Bosworth. Trans. Svat Soucek. Princeton, N.J.: Princeton University Press, 1984.
Dienes, Leslie. "Economic Geographic Relations in the Post-Soviet Republics." *Post-Soviet Geography* 34 (October 1993).
Makievskiy, P., and Kh. Muhabbatov. "Tadzhikistan, Sarezskoye ozero: Geodinamicheskie, tekhnicheskie i sotsialnye aspecty problemy" [Tajikistan, Sarez Lake: The Geodynamic, Technical, and Social Aspects of the Problem]. *Central Asia and Caucasus* (Sweden) 2, no. 3 (1999).
Tadzhikistan: priroda i resursy [Tajikistan: Nature and Resources]. Dushanbe: Donish, 1982.

SOCIETY

Anthropology and Ethnography

Akbarzadeh, Shahram. "A Note on Shifting Identities in the Ferghana Valley." *Central Asian Survey* 16, no. 1 (1997).

Andreev, M. S. "Po etnografii tadzhikov: Nekotoryye svedeniya" (On the Ethnography of the Tajiks: Some Information). In *Tadzhikistan*. Tashkent: Obshchestvo dlya izucheniya Tadzhikistana i iranskikh narodnostey za yego predelami, 1925.

———. "Expeditsia v Yagnob v 1927 pod rukovodstvom M. S. Andreeva" [Expedition to Yaghnob in 1927 under the Leadership of M. S. Andreev]. *Bulleten SAGY* 17 (1928).

Andreev, M. S., E. M. Peshereva, and A. K. Pisarchik. *Yaghnobskiue texty: S prilozheniem Yagnobsko-Russkogo slovaria, sostavlennogo M. S. Andreeevym, V. A. Livshitsem, I. A. K. Pisarchik* [The Yaghnob Texts: Supplemented by Yaghnobi-Russian Dictionary, prepared by M. S. Andreev, V. A. Livshits, A. K. Pisarchik]. Moscow-Leningrad, 1957.

Andreev, M. S., and A. K. Pisarchik. *Tadzhiki doliny Khuf* [The Tajiks of the Khuf Valley]. Vols. 1–2. Stalinobad: Tadzhikgosizdat, 1953–1958.

Arkheologicheskie i Etnograficheskie Materialy po Istorii Kultury i Religii Srednei Azii [Archeological and Ethnographical Materials on the History and Religion of Central Asia]. Moscow: Nauka, 1977.

Evrei v Srednei Azii: Proshloye i Nastoyashchee [Jews in Central Asia: Past and Present]. St. Petersburg: Petersburg Jewish University, 1997.

Foltz, Richard. "The Tajiks of Uzbekistan." *Central Asian Survey* (June 1996).

Johnston, Charles. "Darwaz and Karategin." *Asiatic Quarterly Review* 3 (January–April 1892). Available at: www.angelfire.com/sd/tajikistanupdate/darkar.html).

Karklins, Rasma. *Ethnic Relations in the USSR*. Boston: Allen and Unwin, 1986.

Karmysheva, B. Kh. "On the History of Population Formation in the Southern Areas of Uzbekistan and Tadjikistan." In *7th International Congress of Anthropological and Ethnological Sciences*. Moscow: Nauka, 1964.

———. *Ocherki Etnicheskoy Istorii Iuzhykh Rayonov Tadzhikistana i Uzbekistana* [On the Ethnic History of the Southern Regions of Tajikistan and Uzbekistan]. Moscow: Nauka, 1976.

Kisliakov, Nikolay. "K voprosu ob etnogeneze tadzhikov" [On Ethnogenesis of the Tajiks]. *Sovetskaya Etnografiya* 6–7 (1947).

———. *Ocherki po Istorii Karategina: K Istorii Tadzhikistana* [Essays on the History of Qarategin: On the History of Tajikistan]. Stalinabad: Donish, 1954.

Kocaoglu, Timur. "The Existence of Bukharan Nationality in the Recent Past." In *The Nationality Question in Soviet Central Asia*, ed. Edward Allworth. New York: Praeger, 1973.

Komissarov, D. S. "Vydaiushchiisia Uchenyi, Organizator Vostochnogo Literaturovedeniia" [Prominent Scholar and Organizer of Studies of the History of Oriental Literature]. *Vostok* 4 (1995).

Kushkeki, Burhanuddin Khan. *Kattagan i Badakhshan* [Qataghan and Badakhshan]. Tashkent, 1926.

Madaminjanova, Zuhra. *Araby Iuzhnogo Tadzhikistana: Istoriko-Etnograficheskie Ocherki* [The Arabs of Southern Tajikistan: Historical and Ethnographical Essays]. Dushanbe: Donish, 1995.

Monogarova, L. *Tadzhiki* [The Tajiks]. Moscow: RAN, 1992.

Muhamadnazar, A., and R. Qodiri R., eds. *Darsi kheshtan-shinosi* [Lessons of Self-Perception]. Dushanbe: Irfon, 1991.

Naby, Eden. "Tajiks Reemphasize Iranian Heritage as Ethnic Pressures Mount in Central Asia." *Report of the USSR*, 16 February 1990.

Oranskii, I. M. *Tadzhikoiazychnye Etnograficheskie Gruppy Gissarskoi doliny, Sredniaia Aziia: etnolingvisticheskoe issledovanie* [Tajik-speaking Groups in the Hisor Valley, Central Asia: An Ethno-Linguistic Study]. Moscow: Nauka, 1983.

Rosen, Barry. "An Awareness of Traditional Tajik Identity in Central Asia." In *The Nationality Question in Soviet Central Asia*, ed. Edward Allworth. New York: Praeger, 1973.

Shishov, A. P. *Tadzhiki: Etnograficheskie i antropologichekie issledovania* [The Tajiks: Anthropological and Ethnographical Research]. Vols. 1–2. Tashkent, 1910.

Subtelny, M. E. "The Symbiosis of Turk and Tajik." In *Central Asia in Historical Perspective*, ed. B. F. Manz. Boulder, Colo.: Westview, 1994.

Tadzhikistan. Tashkent: Obshchestvo dlya izucheniya Tadzhikistana i iranskikh narodnostey za yego predelami, 1925.

Zarubin, I. I. *Naselenie Samarkandskoi oblasti* [Population of Samarqand Province]. Leningrad, 1926.

Education and Science

Abdullaev, Kamoludin. "Challenges to Tajikistan's Higher Education." *Central Asian Journal of Economic, Management, and Social Research* (January 2000).

Amsler, Sarah. *The Politics of Knowledge in Central Asia: Science between Marx and the Market*. London: Routledge, 2007.

Obidov I. O. *Istoria razvitia narodnogo obrazovania v Tadzhikskoi SSR, 1917–1967* [History of People's Education in Tajik SSR]. Dushanbe: Irfon, 1968.

Health

Davis, Christopher M. "Health Care Crisis: The Former Soviet Union," *RFE/RL Research Report* [Munich], 8 October 1993.

Gaibov, A. G., I. A. Gundarov, and N. B. Luk'ianov. *Tadzhikistan v zerkale mediko-demograficheskikh protsessov i obshchestvennogo zdorovoia na postsovetskom prostranstve* [Tajikistan in the Light of Ongoing Health and Demographic Processes in Public Health in Post-Soviet Countries]. Dushanbe: AzArt, 2007.

Strategia Respubliki Tadzhikistan po okhrare zdorovia naselenia do 2005 goda [The Strategy of the Republic of Tajikistan on the Health of Population Protection until 2005]. Dushanbe: Ministry of Health, 1996.

Religion

Akbarzadeh, Shahram. "Islamic Clerical Establishment in Central Asia." *South Asia: Journal of South Asian Studies* (December 1997).

Akcali, Pinar. "Islam as a 'Common Bond' in Central Asia: Islamic Renaissance Party and the Afghan Mujahidin." *Central Asian Survey* 17, no. 2 (1998).

Ashirov, Nugman. *Islam i Natsii* [Islam and Nations]. Moscow: Politizdat, 1975.

Atkin, Muriel. *The Subtlest Battle: Islam in Soviet Tajikistan*. Philadelphia, Pa.: Foreign Policy Research Institute, 1989.

Bennigsen, Alexandre, and Marie Broxup. *The Islamic Threat to the Soviet State*. London: Croon Helm, 1983.

Bennigsen, Alexandre, and Chantal Lemercier-Quelquejay. *Islam in the Soviet Union*. London: Pall Mall, 1967.

Bennigsen, Alexandre, and S. E. Wimbush. *Muslim National Communism in the Soviet Union*. Chicago: University of Chicago Press, 1979.

———. *Mystics and Commissars: Sufism in the Soviet Union*. Berkeley: University of California Press, 1985.

———. *Muslims of the Soviet Empire: A Guide*. London: Hurst, 1986.

Broxup, Marie. "Political Trends in Soviet Islam after the Afghanistan War." In *Muslim Communities Reemerge*, ed. Edward Allworth. Durham, N.C.: Duke University Press, 1994.

Carrere d'Encausse, Helene. *Islam and the Russian Empire: Reform and Revolution in Central Asia*. Berkeley: University of California Press, 1988.

Daftari, Farhad. *The Ismailis*. Cambridge: Cambridge University Press, 1990.

Emadi, Hafizullah. "The End of Taqiyya: Reaffirming the Religious Identity of Ismailis in Shughnan, Badakhshan: Political Implications for Afghanistan." *Middle Eastern Studies* 34, no. 3 (1998).

Gretsky, Sergei. "Profile: Qadi Akbar Turajonzoda." *Central Asian Monitor* 1 (1994).

Haghayeghi, Mehrdad. *Islam and Politics in Central Asia*. New York: St. Martin's, 1995.

Hetmanek, Allen. "Islamic Revolution and Jihad Come to the Former Soviet Central Asia: The Case of Tadjikistan." *Central Asian Survey* 12, no. 3 (1993).

Muminov, Ashirbek. "Traditsionnye i sovremennye religiozno-teologicheskie shkoly v Tsentral'noi Azii" [Traditional and Modern Religio-Theological Schools in Central Asia]. *Tsentralnaya Aziya i Kavkaz* 4–5 (1999).

Newman, Iver B., and Sergei Solodovnik. "The Case of Tajikistan." In *Peacekeeping and the Role of Russia in Eurasia*, ed. Lena Jonson and Clive Archer. Boulder, Colo.: Westview, 1996.

Niyazi, Aziz. "Vozrozhdenie islama v Tadzhikistane: Traditsia i politika" [Revival of Islam in Tajikistan: A Tradition and Politics]. *Central Asia and Caucasus* (Sweden) 5, no. 6 (1999).

Olcott, Martha Brill. "Islam and Fundamentalism in Independent Central Asia." In *Muslim Eurasia: Conflicting Legacies*, ed. R. Yaacov. London: Frank Cass, 1995.

Olimova, Saodat. "Politicheskiy islam i konflikt v Tadzhikistane" [Political Islam and the Conflict in Tajikistan]. *Central Asia and Caucasus* (Sweden) 4, no. 5 (1999).

Organization for Security and Cooperation in Europe (OSCE) Mission to Tajikistan. *Religioznyi ekstremizm v Tsentral'noy Azii: Problemy i perspektivy. Materialy konferentsii, Dushanbe, 25 aprelya 2002* [Religious Extremism in Central Asia: Problems and Perspectives. Proceedings of the Conference, Dushanbe, 25 April 2002]. Dushanbe: OSCE Mission to Tajikistan, 2002.

Rashid, Ahmed. *The Resurgence of Central Asia: Islam or Nationalism?* London: Zed, 1994.

———. *Jihad: The Rise of Militant Islam in Central Asia.* New Haven, Conn.: Yale University Press, 2002.

Stanishevskii, A. V. *Ismailism na Pamire: 1902–1931* [Ismailism in Pamir]. Tashkent: Tsentralnyi Arkhiv Uzbekskoi SSR, 1964.

Taheri, Amir. *Crescent in a Red Sky.* London: Hutchinson, 1989.

TAJIKS AND TAJIKISTAN'S NEIGHBORS

Russia

Chufrin, Gennady, ed. *Russia and Asia: The Emerging Security Agenda.* New York: Oxford University Press, 1999.

Dawisha, Karen, and Bruce Parrott. *Russia and the New States of Eurasia: The Politics of Upheaval.* Port Chester, N.Y.: Cambridge University Press, 1994.

Eickelman, Dale F., ed. *Russia's Muslim Frontiers: New Directions in Cross-Cultural Analysis.* Bloomington: Indiana University Press, 1993.

Evans, John L. *Russia and the Khanates of Central Asia to 1865*. New York: Associated Faculty Press, 1982.

Jonson, Lena. *Vladimir Putin and Central Asia: The Shaping of Russian Foreign Policy*. London: I. B. Tauris, 2004.

Karamshoev, D. Kharkavchuk. *Pogranichniki i zhiteli Pamira* [Frontier Guards and Pamir Inhabitants]. Dushanbe: Pamir, 1995.

Khalfin, N. A. *Politika Rossii v Srendei Azii (1857–1868)* [Russia's Central Asian Politics]. Moscow: Nauka, Izdatel'stvo vostochnoi literatury, 1960.

Khronika tadzhiksko-rossiskikh otnoshenii, 1992–1998 [The Chronicle of the Tajik-Russian Relationships, 1992–1998]. Moscow: Tajik Embassy, 1999.

Logofet, L. N. *Bukharskoye khanstvo pod russkim protektoratom* [The Bukharan Khanate under Russian Protectorate]. St. Petersburg: V. Berezovskii, 1911.

Makhonina, S. *Voenno-Politicheskoye Sortudnichestvo mezhdu Rossiei i Tadzhikistanom, 1992–1998* [Military-Political Cooperation between Russia and Tajikistan]. Dushanbe: Academy of Sciences, 1999.

Menon, R. "After Empire: Russia and the Southern 'Near Abroad.'" In *The New Russian Foreign Policy*. New York: Council on Foreign Relations, 1998.

Olimova, Saodat, and Igor Bosc. *Labour Migration from Tajikistan*. Dushanbe: Mission of the International Organization for Migration, 2003.

Pierce, Richard. *Russian Central Asia 1867–1917: A Study in Colonial Rule*. Berkeley: University of California Press, 1960.

Shlapentokh, V., M. Sendich, E. Payin, and M. Melvin. *The New Russian Diaspora: Russian Minorities in the Former Soviet Republics*. Armonk, N.Y.: M. E. Sharpe, 1994.

Starr, S. Frederick, ed. *The Legacy of History in Russia and the New States of Eurasia*. Armonk, N.Y.: M. E. Sharpe, 1994.

Zviagelskaia, Irina. *The Russian Policy Debate on Central Asia*. London: Royal Institute of International Affairs, 1995.

Uzbekistan

Biriukov, S. V. "Respublika Uzbekistan: Model Avtoritarnoy Modernizatsii" [The Republic of Uzbekistan: A Model of Authoritarian Modernization]. *Vostok* 1 (1997).

Foltz, Richard. "Uzbekistan's Tajiks: A Case of Repressed Identity." *Central Asia Monitor* 6 (1996).

Horsman, Stuart. "Uzbekistan's Involvement in the Tajik Civil War 1992–97: Domestic Considerations." *Central Asian Survey* 18, no. 1 (1999).

———. "The Tajik Minority in Contemporary Uzbekistani Politics." In *Ethnicity and Democratisation in the New Europe*, ed. K. Cordell. London: Routledge, 1999.

Karimov, Islam. *Uzbekistan na poroge XXI veka: Ugrozy bezopasnosti, usloviya i garantii progressa* [Uzbekistan at the Beginning of the Twenty-first Century: Challenges to Security and Guarantees of Progress]. Tashkent: Uzbekistan Publishing House, 1997.

Rakhimov, R. R. "K voprosu o sovremennykh tadzhiksko-uzbekskikh mezhnatsional'nykh otnosheniiakh" [The Question of Current Tajik-Uzbek Interethnic Relations]. *Sovetskaia Etnografiia* 1 (1991).

Schoeberlein-Engel, John S. "Perspektivy stanovlenia natsionalnogo samosoznaniya uzbekov" [Perspectives of the Formation of the National Self-awareness of Uzbeks]. *Vostok* 3 (1997).

Shepherd, Monika S. "The Effects of Russian and Uzbek Intervention in the Tajik Civil War." *Soviet and Post-Soviet Review* 23, no. 3 (1996).

Afghanistan

Abdullaev, Kamoludin. "Warlordism and Development in Afghanistan." In *Beyond Reconstruction in Afghanistan: Lessons from Development Experience*, ed. John D. Montgomery and Dennis A. Rondinelli. New York: Palgrave Macmillan, 2004.

Afghanistan: Voina i problemy mira [Afghanistan: War and Problems of Peace]. Moscow: Academy of Sciences, 1998.

Atkin, Muriel. "Tajikistan's Relations with Iran and Afghanistan." In *The New Geopolitics of Central Asia and Its Borderlands*, ed. Ali Banuazizi and Myron Weiner. Bloomington: Indiana University Press, 1994.

Dorronsoro, Gilles. "Les réfugiés tadjiks en Afghanistan." *La lettre d'Asie centrale* (Spring 1994).

Dupree, Louis. *Afghanistan*. Princeton, N.J.: Princeton University Press, 1980.

Iskandarov, Kosimsho. "Narkobiznes v Tadzhikistane: Sviaz s afganskim conflictom" [Narcobusiness in Tajikistan: Relations with the Afghan Conflict]. *Central Asia and Caucasus* (Sweden) 5, no. 6 (1999).

Kushkeki, Burhanuddin Khan. *Kattagan i Badakhshan* [Qataghan and Badakhshan]. Tashkent, 1926.

Mir Gulom, Muhammad Ghubor. *Afghanistan in the Course of History*. Trans. Sherief A. Fayez. Alexandria, Va.: Hashmat K. Gobar, 2001.

Naby, Eden. "The Concept of Jihad in Opposition to Communist Rule: Turkestan and Afghanistan." *Studies in Comparative Communism* (Autumn–Winter 1986).

Roy, Oliver. *Afghanistan: From Holy War to Civil War.* Princeton, N.J.: Darwin, 1994.

Rubin, Barnett. *The Fragmentation of Afghanistan: State Formation and Collapse in the International System.* New Haven, Conn.: Yale University Press, 1995.

Shahrani, M. Nazif Mohib. *The Kirghiz and Wakhi of Afghanistan: Adaptation to Closed Frontiers.* Seattle: University of Washington Press, 1979.

———. "Resisting the Taliban and Talibanism in Afghanistan." *Perceptions: Journal of International Affairs* 5, no 4 (December 2000–February 2001).

Shahrani, M. Nazif Mohib, and Robert L. Canfield, eds. *Revolution and Rebellions in Afghanistan: Anthropological Perspectives.* Berkeley: University of California Press, 1984.

Shalinsky, Audrey. *Long Years of Exile: Central Asian Refugees in Afghanistan and Pakistan.* Lanham, Md.: University Press of America, 1994.

Sokolov-Strakhov, K. I. *Grazhdanskaya Voina v Afganistane, 1928–1929* [The Civil War in Afghanistan]. Moscow: Gosizdat, 1931.

India and Pakistan

Bhatia, Vinod. *Jawaharlal Nehru and the Making of Indo-Soviet Relations, 1917–1947.* Moscow: Mysl, 1989.

India's Relations with Russia and China: A New Phase. New Delhi: International Institute for Asian-Pacific Studies, 1997.

Singh, Mahavir. *India and Tajikistan: Revitalising a Traditional Relationship.* New Delhi: Anamika, 2003.

Warikoo, K. *Central Asia and Kashmir: A Study in the Context of Anglo-Russian Rivalry.* New Delhi: Gian, 1989.

Iran

Atkin, Muriel. "Tajikistan's Relations with Iran and Afghanistan." In *The New Geopolitics of Central Asia and Its Borderlands,* ed. Ali Banuazizi and Myron Weiner. Bloomington: Indiana University Press, 1994.

Carlisle, Donald S. "Tajiks and the Persian World." In *Central Asia in Historical Perspective,* ed. Beatrice F. Manz. Boulder, Colo.: Westview, 1994.

Mesbahi, Mohiaddin. "Iran and Tajikistan." In *Regional Power Rivalries in the New Eurasia,* ed. Alvin Z. Rubinstein and Oles M. Smolansky. Armonk, N.Y.: M. E. Sharpe, 1995.

———. "Tajikistan, Iran, and the International Politics of the 'Islamic Factor.'" *Central Asian Survey* (June 1997).

China

Aksakalov, S. "A New Silk Road? Tajikistan-China Border Crossing Opens." *Central Asia-Caucasus Analyst*, 2 June 2004.

Arlund, Pam. "Research on Bilingual Phenomenon of Tajiks in Kashgar Prefecture." *Language and Translation* 1, no. 61 (2000).

Cristoffersen, G. "China's Intentions for Russia and Central Asian Oil and Gas." *NBR Analysis*, March 1998.

Dorian, J. P., B. Wigdortz, and D. Gladney. "Central Asia and Xinjiang: Emerging Energy, Economic, and Ethnic Relations." *Central Asian Survey* (December 1997).

Garver, J. W. "Development of China's Overland Transportation Links with Central, South-West, and South Asia," *China Quarterly* 185 (2006).

Paramonov, V., and A. Strokov. "Economic Involvement of Russia and China in Central Asia." *Central Asian Series* 7, no. 12 (2007).

Peyrouse, Sébastien. "Economic Aspects of the Chinese-Central Asia Rapprochement." *Silk Road Paper*, September 2007. Central Asia-Caucasus Institute and Silk Road Studies Program, 2007. Available at: www.silkroadstudies.org/new/docs/Silkroadpapers/2007/0709China-Central_Asia.pdf.

Swanstrom, N. "China and Central Asia: A New Great Game or Traditional Vassal Relations?" *Journal of Contemporary China* 14 (2005).

Swanstrom, N., N. Norling, and Li Zhang. "China." In *The New Silk Roads: Transport and Trade in Greater Central Asia*, ed. F. Starr. Central Asia-Caucasus Institute and Silk Road Studies Program, Johns Hopkins University-SAIS, 2007.

Umarov, A., and D. Pashkhun. "Tensions in Sino-Central-Asian Relations and Their Implications for Regional Security." *Central Asian Series* 6, no. 2 (2006).

Wu, Hsiu-Ling, and Chien-Hsun Chen. "The Prospects for Regional Economic Integration between China and the Five Central Asian Countries." *Europe-Asia Studies* 56, no. 7 (2004).

Zhao, Huasheng. "Central Asia in China's Diplomacy." In *Central Asia: Views from Washington, Moscow, and Beijing*, ed. E. Rumer, D. Trenin, and H. Zhao. Armonk, N.Y.: M. E. Sharpe, 2007.

INTERNET RESOURCES

Country Profile and Reference

www.cisstat.com/eng/mp-taj.html [Interstate Statistical Committee of the Commonwealth of Independent States on Tajikistan]

reference.allrefer.com/country-guide-study/tajikistan/ [Country guide]

www.state.gov/r/pa/ei/bgn/5775.htm [U.S. Department of State on Tajikistan]
www.world-gazetteer.com/wg.php?x=&men=gcis&lng=en&des=wg&srt=npa
n&col=abcdefghinoq&msz=1500&geo=-209 [World Gazetteer, Tajikistan]
www.nationmaster.com/country/ti-tajikistan [Nationmaster, Tajikistan]
www.cia.gov/library/publications/the-world-factbook/geos/ti.html [CIA World
Factbook, Tajikistan]
lcweb2.loc.gov/frd/cs/tjtoc.html [Library of Congress Country Studies:
Tajikistan]

General Information and Legislature

www.nyulawglobal.org/globalex/Tajikistan.htm [Law of the Republic of Tajikistan: A Guide to Web Based Resources. By Oleg Stalbovskiy and Maria
Stalbovskaya]
travel.state.gov/travel/cis_pa_tw/cis/cis_1037.html [Tajikistan Country Specific Information]
www.ilo.org/dyn/natlex/natlex_browse.country?p_lang=en&p_country=TJK
[International Labor Organization NATLEX, Tajikistan]
www.lexadin.nl/wlg/legis/nofr/oeur/lxwetaj.htm [Legislation Tajikistan]
www.doingbusiness.org/LawLibrary/?economyid=184 [Doing Business Law
Library, Tajikistan]
unpan1.un.org/intradoc/groups/public/documents/untc/unpan003670.htm
[Constitution of the Republic of Tajikistan, Dushanbe, 1994]

Intergovernmental and International Organizations

www.undp.tj [United Nations Development Program in Tajikistan]
www.untj.org [United Nations Tajikistan Information Platform]
osce.org/tajikistan [Organization for Security and Cooperation in Europe
(OSCE) Office in Tajikistan]
www.ecosecretariat.org/ [Economic Cooperation Organization (ECO)]
www.sectsco.org/EN/ [Shanghai Cooperation Organization (SCO)]
www.imf.org/external/country/tjk/rr/ [International Monetary Fund (IMF) in
Tajikistan]
www.worldbank.org/tj [World Bank in Tajikistan]
www.odkb.gov.ru/start/index_aengl.htm [Collective Security Treaty (CST)]
www.crisisgroup.org/home/index.cfm?id=1255&l=1 [International Crisis
Group, Tajikistan]
www.akdn.org/tajikistan [Aga Khan Development Network (AKDN)]
www.ebrd.com/country/country/taji/index.htm [European Bank for Reconstruction and Development (EBRD), Tajikistan homepage]

Tajik Government and Parliament

www.president.tj [President of Tajikistan]
www.majmilli.tj [Majlisi Melli (upper chamber)]
www.parlament.tj [Majlisi Namoyandagon (lower chamber)]
www.mid.tj [Ministry of Foreign Affairs]
www.met.tj [Ministry of Economy and Trade]
www.minfin.tj [Ministry of Finance]
www.medinfo.tojikiston.com [Ministry of Health Care]
www.stat.tj [State Statistics Agency]
www.tpp.tj [Chamber of Commerce and Industry]
www.mincom.tj [Ministry of Transport and Communication]
www.anticorruption.tj [Agency on Combating Corruption and Economic Crimes]
www.mop.tojikiston.com [Ministry of Environmental Protection]
www.education.tj [Ministry of Education]
www.apmp.tojikiston.com [Anti-Monopoly Committee]
www.minenergo.tj [Ministry of Energy]
www.tajinvest.tj [State Committee on Investments and State Property]
www.stat.tj [State Committee on Statistics]
www.akn.tj [Drug Control Agency]
www.dushanbe.tj [Dushanbe City Administration]

Tajik Banks

www.nbt.tj [National Bank of Tajikistan]
www.agroinvestbank.tj [Agroinvestbank]
www.orienbank.com [Orienbank]
www.sodirotbonk.com [Tajik Sodirot Bank]
www.eskhata.com [Bank Eskhata]

Diplomatic Missions

www.tjus.org [Tajikistan Embassy to the United States]
www.rusembassy.tajnet.com [Russian Embassy to Tajikistan]
www2.un.int/public/Tajikistan/0/English/ [Permanent Mission of the Republic of Tajikistan to the United Nations]

Libraries

www.aclib.tj [Central Scientific Library of the Academy of Sciences]

Education and Science

www.tgnu.tarena.tj [Tajik National University]
www.rtsu.tj [Russian-Tajik Slavonic University]
tut.freenet.tj [Technological University]

Information and Analysis on Tajikistan

www.lib.utexas.edu/maps/asia.html [Maps of Central Asia]
www.centralasianvoices.org [Central Asia Voices. Carnegie Endowment for International Peace]
www.indiana.edu/~iaunrc/caweb.html [Central Asia regional information, Indiana University]
www.usip.org/library/pa/tajikistan/pa_tajikistan.html [United States Institute of Peace. Peace Agreements Digital Collection, Tajikistan]
www.soros.org/about/foundations/tajikistan [Open Society Institute, Tajikistan]
eurasianet.org [Eurasianet]
www.fas.harvard.edu/~centasia/index.html [Harvard Forum for Central Asian Studies]
www.c-r.org/accord10/index.htm [Kamoludin Abdullaev and Catherine Barnes, *Politics of Compromise: The Tajikistan Peace Process*]
www.centralasianews.net [Central Asia News.net]
rferl.org [Radio Free Europe / Radio Liberty]
www.crisisweb.org/ [International Crisis Group]
iicas.org [International Eurasian Institute for Economic and Political Research]
www.angelfire.com/sd/tajikistanupdate/artj.html#cw [Tajikistan Update]
www.unccd.int/php/countryinfo.php?country=TJK [United Nations Convention to Combat Desertification: Tajikistan]
www.sarez.by.ru/index_en.shtml [Sarez Lake site]

News and Analysis Online International

news.bbc.co.uk/1/hi/world/asia-pacific/country_profiles/1296639.stm [BBC on Tajikistan]
www.rferl.org [Radio Free Europe]
www.tajik-gateway.org [Tajik Gateway]
www.tajikistannews.net [Tajikistan News.net, part of an international network]
www.eurasianet.org/resource/tajikistan/index.shtml [Eurasianet.org Tajikistan]
www.insidetajikistan.com [Inside Tajikistan]
www.cacianalyst.org [Central Asia-Caucasus Analyst, Johns Hopkins University, Paul H. Nitze School of Advanced International Studies, Washington, D.C.]

www.tol.cz/look/TOL/section.tpl?IdLanguage=1&IdPublication=4&tpid=14 [Transition online, Tajikistan]
www.iwpr.net/?apc_state=henprca [Institute on War and Peace Reporting]
www.einnews.com/tajikistan/ [EIN News: Tajikistan]
us.oneworld.net/places/tajikistan [One World News]
www.crisisgroup.org/home/index.cfm?id=1255&l=1 [International Crisis Group on Tajikistan]
www.reliefweb.int/rw/dbc.nsf/doc104?OpenForm&rc=3&cc=tjk [Relief Web: Tajikistan]
www.tajik-gateway.org [Tajikistan Development Gateway]
www.topix.net/world/tajikistan/ [Topix: Tajikistan]
www.ozodi.org [Ozodi Tajik Radio Free Europe / Radio Liberty, Tajik Service in Tajik]
www.times.kg/ [The Times of Central Asia]

Tajik Information and Analytical Agencies and Portals

www.asiaplus.tj/ [*Asia-Plus* Media Group. In Tajik, Russian, and English]
www.avesta.tj/ [*Avesta* independent news agency. In Tajik, Russian, and English]
www.gazeta.tj/ [*Charkhi Gardun* media group. In Tajik and Russian]
www.tajinfo.ru/ [*Tajinfo* Tajik Media Holding. Tajiks of Russia. In Russian]
www.ariana.su/ [*Ariana.* All about Tajikistan. In Russian]
www.nansmit.tj/ [National Association of Independent Mass-Media of Tajikistan NANSMIT. In Russian and English]
www.varorud.org/old/english/index.html [Khujand-based *Varorud* Informational-Analytical Agency. In Tajik, Russian, and English]
www.somoni.com [Tajik information portal]
www.tajnet.com/ [Tajnet Telecomm Technology. In Russian]
www.khovar.tj/ [*Khovar* National Information Agency of Tajikistan. In Tajik, Russian, and English]
tajmigrant.com/ [All-Russian Societal Movement: Tajik Labor Migrants. In Russian]
www.str-org.com/ [Union of Tajikistanis. In Russian]
www.millat.tj/ [*Millat* independent sociopolitical site. In Tajik]
www.tojikon.mpchat.com/ [Tajikistan Online Forum. In Russian]
www.centrasia.ru/person.php4 [*Who Is Who in Tajikistan.* In Russian]
www.history.tj/ [History of Tajiks. In Russian]
www.our-tajikistan.com/ [Our Tajikistan. In Russian]
tajikistan.neweurasia.net/ [Tajikistan Blogs. In English]
yaghnobi.wordpress.com/online-yaghnobi-lexicon/ [The Yaghnobi People: Their Language, History, and Culture. In English]

About the Authors

Kamoludin Abdullaev has studied and taught the modern history of Central Asia for more than 30 years. After graduating from the Tajik State University in 1972 and serving in the Soviet army in Trans-Baikal in 1972–1974, Abdullaev started his professional career in 1975 at the Institute of History of the Tajik Academy of Sciences. He wrote his dissertation, "The Newspapers of Soviet Turkestan as a Historical Source on the Elimination of Basmachism in Central Asia," at the Institute of the History of the USSR, Moscow, in 1983. In 1989, this research was published in Russian: "With the Weapon of the Printed Word." That same year, Abdullaev took an appointment at the Institute of History of the Communist Party under the Central Committee of the Communist Party of Tajikistan. In 1990, this institute was transformed into the Institute of Political Research, and he was appointed head of the department. Following the collapse of the Soviet Union and the closing of the institute, Abdullaev joined the Tajik State National University. In 1997–1999, he worked as project officer at the Aga Khan Humanities Project for Central Asia (Dushanbe).

Since 1992, Abdullaev has also been a policy analyst and independent consultant in international nongovernmental research organizations involved in civil society building, education, and conflict resolution in Central Asia. A two-time Fulbright Scholar (George Washington University in 1994 and Allegheny College, Pennsylvania, in 2005), Regional Exchange Scholar (Kennan Institute for Advanced Russian Studies, Woodrow Wilson International Center for Scholars in 1995), and a British Academy visiting fellow (SOAS, London University in 1996), Abdullaev is among the most active Central Asian participants in the U.S. government-sponsored research exchange programs in the field of history and political science. He was also a grant recipient of the Research Support Scheme of the Open Society Support Foundation

(1999–2001). From 2001 to 2009, as a visiting professor, he has taught modern Central Asian subjects from multidisciplinary perspectives at Yale University, Allegheny College, and the Ohio State University. He has written, co-written, or edited eight books in English and Russian and has published over 50 articles in English, Russian, and Tajik, and translated into French and Japanese. Abdullaev's last book, *Ot Sintsiana do Khorasana. Iz Istorii Sredneaziatskoi Emigratsii 20 veka* (From Xingjiang to Khurasan: From the History of the 20th Century Central Asia's Emigration), was published in Dushanbe in the end of 2009.

Shahram Akbarzadeh is associate professor and deputy director of the National Centre of Excellence for Islamic Studies at the University of Melbourne, Australia. His research interests include the politics of Islam in the Middle East and Australia, U.S. policy toward the Middle East, and Central Asian politics. He is a prolific author and has published in key refereed journals, including *Middle East Policy*, *Human Rights Quarterly*, and *Third World Quarterly*. Among his latest books are *Uzbekistan and the United States* (2005), *Islam and Globalization*, 4 volumes (2006), and *U.S. Foreign Policy in the Middle East* (2008).

CPSIA information can be obtained at www.ICGtesting.com
Printed in the USA
LVOW10*1755260615

444047LV00004B/6/P